FREEDOM OF SPEECH

FREEDOM OF SPEECH

Edited by

Ellen Frankel Paul, Fred D. Miller, Jr., and Jeffrey Paul

CAMBRIDGE
UNIVERSITY PRESS

32 Avenue of the Americas, New York NY 10013-2473, USA

Cambridge University Press is part of the University of Cambridge.

It furthers the University's mission by disseminating knowledge in the pursuit of education, learning and research at the highest international levels of excellence.

www.cambridge.org
Information on this title: www.cambridge.org/9780521603751

First published 2004

A catalogue record for this publication is available from the British Library

Library of Congress Cataloguing in Publication data
Freedom of Speech / edited by Ellen Frankel Paul,
Fred D. Miller, Jr., and Jeffrey Paul. p. cm.
Includes bibliographical references and index.
ISBN 0-521-60375-7
1. Freedom of Speech-United States.
I. Paul, Ellen Frankel. II. Miller, Fred Dycus, 1944- III. Paul, Jeffrey.
JC591.F776 2004
323.44′3′0973–dc22 2004045795
CIP

ISBN 978-0-521-60375-1 Paperback

The essays in this book have also been published, without introduction and index, in the semiannual journal *Social Philosophy & Policy*, Volume 21, Number 2, which is available by subscription.

CONTENTS

INTRODUCTION

Freedom of expression found perhaps its most eloquent advocate in John Stuart Mill, whose *On Liberty* (1859) encapsulated the case for the unfettered dissemination of ideas like no other work before or since. In words that would echo through debates over personal and press freedoms until our day, Mill declared: "If all mankind, minus one, were of one opinion, and only one person were of the contrary opinion, mankind would be no more justified in silencing that one person, than he, if he had the power, would be justified in silencing mankind."

While political philosophers and legal theorists have differed over the theoretical roots of free speech, and while it has sometimes foundered in confrontation with other values, few would deny the importance of expressive liberty to the feasibility and success of democratic societies. Whether free speech is defended as a fundamental right that inheres in each individual, or as a guarantee that all of society's members will have a voice in democratic decision-making, or as vital to a "marketplace of ideas" that facilitates the emergence of truth by allowing vigorous competition among diverse points of view, the central role of expressive freedom in liberating the human spirit is undeniable.

Freedom of expression is of fundamental concern for democracy generally, and nowhere has this freedom been subjected to such intense and searching debate as in the United States. Freedom of speech came to American law through the influence of the English common law and through eminent scholars of that law, particularly William Blackstone. Enshrined in the First Amendment to the United States Constitution with a brevity that would belie its subsequent history of intricate judicial parsing, freedom of expression was bequeathed to posterity by James Madison and the first Congress in a way that has since been emulated by nascent democracies throughout the world. The First Amendment proclaims that "Congress shall make no law respecting an establishment of religion, or prohibiting the free exercise thereof; or abridging the freedom of speech, or of the press; or of the right of the people to peaceably assemble, and to petition the Government for a redress of grievances." As interpreted by a Supreme Court increasingly zealous in the protection of expressive liberty as the twentieth century unfolded, this amendment became a bar not only to congressional and federal interference, but also, through the due process clause of the Fourteenth Amendment, to intrusion by state governments as well.

First Amendment absolutists notwithstanding, the constitutional rights of free speech and the press have undergone a frequently contorted history, as justices struggled over other, competing values ranging from national security to personal privacy and property rights. As many of our contributors observe, life's proclivity for spoiling clear and seemingly simple declarations was much in evidence as the courts confronted the great and controversial issues of the twentieth century. Loyalty oaths, political demonstrations, antiwar leafletting, flag burning, union picketing, convictions of Communist Party organizers, and state attempts to expose and subdue civil rights activists in the segregated South were all controversies that landed on the Supreme Court's docket and helped to forge First Amendment doctrine. Just as the origin and fate of the Sedition Act of 1798 influenced early Americans' concern to protect publications from prior restraint and subsequent criminalization, these more recent controversies have shaped conceptions of expressive freedom in our time.

As the essays in this volume illuminate, freedom of expression will be tested by new and continuing controversies as the twenty-first century unfolds. Advances in digital technology raise pressing questions regarding freedom of speech and, with it, intellectual property and privacy rights. The capacity to maintain large electronic databases has fueled fresh concerns about privacy and more fervent calls for restrictions on the exchange of information and ideas, a reaction that might prove as deleterious as the threat that inspires it. As growth of the Internet tests, and often confounds, laws and judicial decisions established in the era of the printing press, cyberspace looms as a relatively uncharted frontier for free speech and copyright law. Combating "hate speech" has spawned speech codes on American campuses, while campaign finance reform limits the formerly sacrosanct category of "political speech." Expressive liberties may face their greatest challenge from governmental efforts to thwart terrorism.

In recent years, the U.S. Supreme Court's free speech doctrines have been subjected to radical critiques. Our first three authors each examine these critiques and find them, for a variety of reasons, unpersuasive. In his essay, "Equality and Expression: The Radical Paradox," Andrew Altman observes that radical critics of liberalism attack the liberal state because it unjustifiably protects forms of speech that maintain racial and sexual oppression. He sketches the historical background of today's radicalism, finding it in the 1960s radicalism of Herbert Marcuse, who rejected any liberal system of expression as thinly disguised oppression. In contrast, proposals put forth by contemporary radicals to rectify liberal oppression are far more modest than Marcuse's. The very modesty that makes these proposals seem plausible, however, also makes them compatible with liberal principles. Altman describes some of the main elements of a liberal system of expression and defends them against the skeptics. He concludes by showing that the greater the role played by speech in maintaining the racial and sexual oppression that radicals allege to exist, the more weight that liberal arguments about free expression must carry in order for the current radical position on speech to be coherent.

Scott D. Gerber, in "The Politics of Free Speech," addresses both what freedom of speech means in American constitutional law and what it should mean. He examines how several prominent constitutional theorists have proposed various reasons for altering free speech law in order to further their preferred values and political objectives. Gerber surveys the free speech views of: the leading feminist legal theorist, who finds combating pornography sufficient reason to curtail the First Amendment; critical race theorists, who value the proscription of "hate speech" over unfettered liberty; legal republican theorists, who find "deliberative democracy" the more attractive value; and libertarian theorists, who critique the Court for devaluing commercial speech. Gerber assesses each position in light of the most trenchant criticisms that each view has garnered, whether the courts have been influenced by any of the radical views, and, in conclusion, whether it is possible to advance a nonpolitical, that is, a purely law-based or value-free, theory of free speech.

Two forms of free speech skepticism have been surprisingly influential in American academic circles, observes Daniel Jacobson in "The Academic Betrayal of Free Speech." First, progressives argue that the "silencing" of certain objectionable opinions can actually promote speech rights. Second, postmodern critics claim that free speech is conceptually impossible and that censorship is both ubiquitous and desirable. Jacobson finds that the classical liberal conception of freedom of speech has the resources necessary to answer both challenges. Moreover, although free speech skeptics claim to be especially sensitive to the social landscape, Jacobson responds that they actually distort the facts about the very social environment with which they are most familiar: academia. Despite their claims that they are concerned about promoting academic freedom, Jacobson finds these protestations merely opportunistic, leaving him unconvinced that the free speech skeptics have a sincere commitment to intellectual diversity.

The seven papers that follow each tackle a conflict or an alleged conflict between free speech and another important social or individual value. Judith Wagner DeCew, in "Free Speech and Offensive Expression," reviews philosophical arguments in defense of maximal free speech, consequentialist and other justifications for limiting free speech, and legal guidelines on offensive expression. She then examines how the United States Supreme Court has struggled to address sexually explicit expressive conduct that does not rise to the level of 'obscenity' under First Amendment jurisprudence. The Court has been sensitive to the competing values of communities that wish to preserve an environment conducive to family values and security. In DeCew's assessment, the Court appears to have implicitly recognized sexually explicit yet nonobscene expression as "lower value" speech, which is less fundamental and less worthy of First Amendment protection. DeCew argues that philosophical justifications for this position are inadequate, and that recent moves by the Court, especially in cases on city ordinances designed to curb nude dancing, undermine traditional First Amendment protection and point in the direction of an erosion of free speech in the United States.

In "Copyright, Trespass, and the First Amendment: An Institutional Perspective," Lillian R. BeVier addresses the supposed conflict between free speech and copyright law. She asks whether tangible property law could offer appropriate analogies to help resolve disputes over conflicting claims of access to the expressive content of copyrighted works, to content on the Internet (whether copyrighted or not), and to Web sites and proprietary e-mail networks. BeVier focuses on the institutional choices that are embedded in the question, and suggests that whether and how much to "propertize" digital content, and whether and how much to grant First Amendment rights of access to it, pose a fundamental choice about whether to lodge decision-making authority over access in private or public sector actors. BeVier defends the choice to lodge such authority in the hands of private owners. She concludes that tangible property law does indeed offer appropriate analogies because its principal instrumental justification—encouraging investment by rewarding owners with the profits of their investment decisions—applies equally well to intellectual property. In addition, she concludes that the First Amendment does not require owners of either tangible or intangible property to grant access to those who wish to use it without the owner's permission.

In his essay, "Restrictions on Judicial Election Campaign Speech: Silencing Criticism of Liberal Activism," Lino A. Graglia examines the oddity that had existed in twenty-seven states, where judges were elected by the people, but prevented from campaigning on their political or judicial views. In these states, judges had adopted codes of ethics that restricted the speech of judicial candidates. The practical effect of these codes, argues Graglia, was to silence any criticism of liberal judicial activism and to keep the electorate uninformed about opinions that deviated from liberal doctrine. In *Republican Party of Minnesota v. White* (2002), the Supreme Court, split 5 to 4, invalidated such a code as prohibited by the First Amendment. The First Amendment, oddly, thus permits states to not elect judges at all or to abolish judicial elections, but it does not permit the *restriction* of judicial election campaign speech if a state does select judges by election. The dissenting justices in *White* would have upheld the code of ethics by reiterating the central fiction of American constitutional law: that our judges, despite the power of judicial review, are not political actors, and that subjecting them to elections is therefore unnecessary, although not impermissible. Electing judges may not violate the First Amendment, but neither does it solve the problem of political rule by judges, which, Graglia laments, is an inevitable consequence of judicial review.

In "Property Rights and Free Speech: Allies or Enemies?" James W. Ely, Jr., notes that, historically, the rights of private property owners and the right to engage in expressive activity were linked; both were seen as essential to protecting personal freedom by restraining the power of government. Yet in recent decades, there has been controversy over the claimed right of nonowners to engage in expressive activity on privately owned property, such as shopping centers and residential communities. Ely points out that the right of owners to maintain exclusive possession of their premises has long been seen as an essential component of the concept of property. He contends that shopping centers and residential communities are not public forums for the purposes of the First Amendment. Moreover, he argues that owners have legitimate reasons to ban free speech activities from their property, and that they should not be compelled to furnish a forum for the views of others. Ely stresses that there is no artificial division between speech and property rights, and that both are essential to a free society.

David E. Bernstein observes that freedom of speech would be of little practical consequence if the government could suppress ideas by prohibiting individuals from gathering with others who share their views. Freedom of expression, Bernstein notes in "Expressive Association after *Dale*," must consist of more than the right to talk to oneself. The right of expressive association first garnered protection from the U.S. Supreme Court during the late 1950s and early 1960s, when the Court prevented states in the South from forcing the NAACP to disclose its membership lists. The right of expressive association then languished in obscurity for over two decades. When it reemerged, the Court was clearly not pleased that its creation, born to defend civil rights groups, was now being claimed by organizations that wanted to defend their discriminatory policies against women. Not until 2000, in *Boy Scouts of America v. Dale*, did the Court endorse a broad-based right of expressive association against the competing claims of an antidiscrimination law. While reaction to *Dale* by commentators has been predictably mixed, lower courts have given it a broad interpretation. As a result of *Dale*, Bernstein sees far-reaching implications for the free exercise of religion and for free speech on college campuses.

C. Edwin Baker's "Autonomy and Informational Privacy, or Gossip: The Central Meaning of the First Amendment" explores the tension between free speech and the desire for privacy. Baker notes that the right not to have others disseminate personal, private information about oneself has been considered one of the greatest innovations in the common law during the twentieth century. This innovation, however, is not an unalloyed benefit, since one person's right of informational privacy can conflict with another person's right to freedom of speech. To the extent that the two conflict, Baker maintains that speech freedom should prevail, since it is essential for individual autonomy. Nevertheless, recognizing this speech freedom leaves open a host of appropriate legal ways to protect informational privacy. Yet, he suggests that some of the impulse toward greater emphases on personal privacy may have a questionable pedigree. Often speech that violates privacy (gossip, for example), serves valuable social functions, including a more egalitarian distribution of power and the encouragement of social and political change.

The 2000 U.S. Presidential election witnessed a major effort to promote legislation restricting the marketing of violent and/or sexually explicit movies, music lyrics, and video games on the assumption that they are an underlying cause of violence by young people. In "Current Proposals for Media Accountability in Light of the First Amendment," Ronald D. Rotunda looks at the empirical evidence regarding a causal relationship between violence depicted in the entertainment media and violence in real life, and examines the theoretical bases of free speech law, in order to determine if government can or should restrict or regulate the marketing and distribution of entertainment products that depict violence, particularly when minors are in the audience. Rotunda concludes that such regulation is bad policy, in part because entertainment advertising is not deceptive: it is not misleading for Hollywood to advertise an R-rated movie as rated R or a PG-13 movie as PG-13. Moreover, Rotunda remains unconvinced of any causal relationship between, for example, watching a violent movie and then engaging in violence. Finally, as a constitutional matter, legal precedents likely forbid governmental efforts to limit advertising, a form of speech that has some First Amendment protection. This protection is heightened when advertising concerns entertainment, a form of speech that has complete First Amendment protection unless it is 'obscene', a legal term that does not apply to R-rated movies and similar fare. Free speech law increasingly suggests that government does not have the power to forbid truthful speech about lawful activities—particularly about activities that enjoy full First Amendment protection—simply because government wants to dampen interest in those activities. Nor may government prohibit advertising about a product that is lawful for adults simply because children are in the audience. As the Supreme Court held nearly a half century ago, such a sweeping effort would be "to burn the house to roast the pig."

The final two papers in this collection discuss modern free speech issues and doctrine through a historical lens. Thomas G. West explores the development and transformation of free speech from America's founding and early years to the articulation of modern free speech theories in the twentieth century. In "Free Speech in the American Founding and in Modern Liberalism," he casts grave doubt on the common conceit that there is more freedom of speech in America today than there was at the time of the founding. This thesis is correct, at least from the point of view of the political theory of modern liberalism, which sets minimal limits on obscenity and on speech promoting the overthrow of government. However, the thesis is not correct from the founders' point of view. Today's liberals, argues West, restrict speech where it ought to be free. With campaign finance reform acts, they ban some citizens from spending "too much" money publicizing their opinions on candidates for election or political issues. With antidiscrimination laws, they lay down rules forbidding certain kinds of speech in private schools and workplaces. With laws licensing and regulating broadcasting, they impose prior restraint on speech and, thereby, manipulate the content of broadcasting. From the founders' perspective, liberals have reversed the founders' understanding of free speech. Today's liberals protect licentiousness but not liberty; the founders protected liberty but not license.

In "Democratic Ideals and Media Realities: A Puzzling Free Press Paradox," Michael Kent Curtis notes that a central justification for the rights of free expression has been the role that freedom of speech, of the press, and of peaceful assembly play in maintaining representative government. The ideal suggests that freedom of expression provides citizens with information and opinion that are both sufficiently detailed and diverse to make it possible for voters to fulfill their democratic function. A danger to free speech that is rarely overlooked is governmental interference, but speech rights can be curtailed by private, concentrated power as well. Americans recognized these twin threats, and early commentators conducted vigorous debates over both dangers, even though there was little activity in the courts. Such events as the Sedition Act of 1798 and the controversy over the attempt to suppress abolitionists' anti-slavery arguments in the South, stimulated much thoughtful discussion. Some commentators addressed a concern that resonates with many people today, which is how to protect against abuse by the press of its power. A number of observers suggested that diversity of ownership and viewpoint in the mass media was both an existing fact in the young United States and a protection against the abuse of press power. Today, the ever more consolidated, corporate, mass media is a potential threat to democratic self-government. Curtis argues that the mass media—and particularly television—is failing in its democratic mission. Curiously, in spite of its shortcomings, he thinks that the press in the period between 1830 and 1868 in some ways made more substantial contributions to democratic dialogue than American media does today. Recognition of the danger posed by media monopolies is a crucial first step to thinking about reforms, Curtis concludes.

These essays contribute to the ongoing debate on the justification, limits, and conflicts of expressive liberty. William O. Douglas, one of the leading defenders of free speech absolutism on the Supreme Court, stated the importance of this liberty well, when he wrote:

> Full and free discussion even of ideas we hate encourages the testing of our own prejudices and preconceptions. Full and free discussion keeps a society from becoming stagnant and unprepared for the stresses and strains that work to tear all civilizations apart . . . . This has been the one single outstanding tenet that has made our institutions the symbol of freedom and equality. We have deemed it more costly to liberty to suppress a despised minority than to let them vent their spleen.

ACKNOWLEDGMENTS

The editors wish to acknowledge several individuals at the Social Philosophy and Policy Center, Bowling Green State University, who provided invaluable assistance in the production of this volume. They include Assistant Director Travis Cook, Mary Dilsaver, Terrie Weaver, and former Editorial Assistant Carrie-Ann Khan.

The editors extend special thanks to Publication Specialist Tamara Sharp for attending to the innumerable day-to-day details of the book's preparation, and to Managing Editor Teresa Donovan, for providing dedicated assistance throughout the editorial and production process.

CONTRIBUTORS

Andrew Altman is Professor of Philosophy at Georgia State University. He is the author of *Critical Legal Studies: A Liberal Critique* (1990) and *Arguing about Law: An Introduction to Legal Philosophy* (2d ed., 2001). He has published numerous articles in scholarly journals, such as *Ethics, Law and Philosophy, Legal Theory,* and *Philosophy & Public Affairs,* on topics including sexual harassment, hate speech, bias-crime legislation, racial bias in voting, and critical legal theory.

Scott D. Gerber is Assistant Professor of Law at the Claude W. Pettit College of Law, Ohio Northern University. He is also a Senior Research Scholar in law and politics at the Social Philosophy and Policy Center, Bowling Green State University. He clerked for Chief Judge Ernest C. Torres of the U.S. District Court of Rhode Island and practiced with the Boston-based law firm Bingham McCutchen (formerly Bingham, Dana & Gould). He has published dozens of scholarly articles, reviews, and editorials about constitutional law and history, and has made numerous radio and television appearances regarding these subjects. He is the author of *To Secure these Rights: The Declaration of Independence and Constitutional Interpretation* (1995) and *First Principles: The Jurisprudence of Clarence Thomas* (1999). He is the editor of *Seriatim: The Supreme Court before John Marshall* (1999) and *The Declaration of Independence: Origins and Impact* (2002).

Daniel Jacobson is Associate Professor of Philosophy at Bowling Green State University and a Resident Scholar at the Social Philosophy and Policy Center, Bowling Green State University. He works in moral philosophy, broadly construed, and has written on topics in ethical theory, history of ethics, moral psychology, and aesthetics, as well as political philosophy. He has published in *Ethics* and *Philosophy & Public Affairs,* among other journals, and his most recent work on John Stuart Mill can be found in the online journal *Philosophers' Imprint.* He is the author of *Rational Sentimentalism* (with Justin D'Arms, forthcoming).

Judith Wagner DeCew is Professor of Philosophy and former Associate Dean at Clark University. She served on the faculty at the Massachusetts Institute of Technology, was a Research Fellow at Harvard Law School and at the Bunting Institute at Harvard University, and received fellowships from the National Endowment for the Humanities, the American Council of Learned Societies, and the American Association of University Women. DeCew has published numerous scholarly articles on ethics, philosophy of law, and social and political theory. She is coeditor of

Theory and Practice (with Ian Shapiro, 1995) and is the author of *In Pursuit of Privacy: Law, Ethics, and the Rise of Technology* (1997) and *Unionization in the Academy: Visions and Realities* (2003).

Lillian R. BeVier is the John S. Shannon Distinguished Professor of Law and Class of 1963 Research Professor at the University of Virginia School of Law. She teaches property, copyright, and First Amendment law, and has written extensively on free speech, campaign finance regulation, and a variety of intellectual property issues. She is the author of *Campaign Finance "Reform" Proposals: A First Amendment Analysis* (1997) and *Is Free TV for Federal Candidates Constitutional?* (1998). She has also published articles in numerous scholarly journals including *The Supreme Court Review, Yale Law Journal, Stanford Law Review, Columbia Law Review, University of Chicago Legal Forum,* and *Harvard Journal of Law and Public Policy.*

Lino A. Graglia is the A. Dalton Cross Professor of Law at the University of Texas School of Law. He was an attorney with the U.S. Department of Justice and practiced law in Washington, DC, and New York City before joining the University of Texas law faculty in 1966, where he teaches courses in constitutional law and antitrust law. He is the author of *Disaster by Decree: The Supreme Court Decisions on Race and the Schools* (1976) and is a contributor to numerous anthologies, including *The Burger Court: Counterrevolution or Confirmation?* (1998) and *A Reader on Race, Civil Rights, and American Law* (2001). He has published widely on issues of constitutional law in both scholarly and popular journals.

James W. Ely, Jr., is Milton R. Underwood Professor of Law and Professor of History at Vanderbilt University. He is the author of numerous articles and books on American legal and constitutional history, including *The Chief Justiceship of Melville W. Fuller, 1888–1910* (1995), *The Guardian of Every Other Right: A Constitutional History of Property Rights* (2d ed., 1998), *Railroads and American Law* (2001), and *The Fuller Court: Justices, Rulings, and Legacy* (2003).

David E. Bernstein is Professor of Law at the George Mason University School of Law. He served as senior editor of the *Yale Law Journal* and was a John M. Olin Fellow in Law, Economics, and Public Policy at Yale Law School. After clerking for Judge David Nelson of the Sixth Circuit Court of Appeals, he served as a Mellon Foundation Research Fellow at Columbia University School of Law. He has published numerous articles in scholarly journals and is co-editor of *Phantom Risk: Scientific Inference and the Law* (with Kenneth R. Foster and Peter W. Huber, 1993). He is the author of *Only One Place of Redress: African-Americans, Labor Regulations, and the Courts from Reconstruction to the New Deal* (2001) and *You Can't Say That! The Growing Threat to Civil Liberties from Antidiscrimination Laws* (2003).

C. Edwin Baker is Nicholas F. Gallichio Professor of Law at the University of Pennsylvania School of Law. He has published widely in scholarly journals on the topics of free speech, equality, property, law and economics, jurisprudence, and the mass media. He has lectured on free speech issues throughout the United States and in Canada, the Czech Republic, England, Ethiopia, Hungary, Israel, and Scotland. He is the author of *Human Liberty and Freedom of Speech* (1989), *Advertising and a Democratic Press* (1994), and *Media, Markets, and Democracy* (2002), which earned the 2002 McGannon Communication Policy Research Award.

Ronald D. Rotunda is George Mason University Foundation Professor of Law at George Mason University School of Law. He is the author of the five-volume *Treatise on Constitutional Law: Substance and Procedure* (with John E. Nowak, 3d ed., 1999); the single-volume *Constitutional Law* (with John E. Nowak, 6th ed., 2000); *Legal Ethics: The Lawyer's Deskbook on Professional Responsibility* (2002); *Problems and Materials on Professional Responsibility* (with Thomas D. Morgan, 8th ed., 2003); and *Modern Constitutional Law: Cases and Notes* (7th ed., 2003). He has published more than two hundred articles in various law reviews, journals, newspapers, and other periodicals in the United States and throughout the world. In addition to serving as Constitutional Law Adviser to the Supreme National Council of Cambodia as that nation wrote its first democratic constitution, he has consulted for various new democracies in Eastern Europe and the former Soviet Union, including Moldova, Romania, and Ukraine.

Thomas G. West is Professor of Politics at the University of Dallas and a Senior Fellow of the Claremont Institute. His work has appeared in a variety of popular and scholarly journals, including *The American Enterprise, Claremont Review of Books, Texas Education Review,* and *Perspectives on Political Science.* He is the editor and translator of *Four Texts on Socrates: Plato's Euthyphro, Apology, Crito, and Aristophanes' Clouds* (with Grace Starry West, 1998); and is the author of *Vindicating the Founders: Race, Sex, Class, and Justice in the Origins of America* (1997).

Michael Kent Curtis is Judge Donald L. Smith Professor of Public and Constitutional Law at Wake Forest University School of Law. He has published numerous articles on free speech and civil liberties, and is the author of *No State Shall Abridge: The Fourteenth Amendment and the Bill of Rights* (1986) and *Free Speech, "The People's Darling Privilege": Struggles for Freedom of Expression in American History* (2000). He is the editor of *Constitutional Law in Context* (with J. Wilson Parker, Davison Douglas, and Paul Finkelman, 2003).

EQUALITY AND EXPRESSION: THE RADICAL PARADOX

By Andrew Altman

I. Introduction

The modern liberal state arose as part of a rebellion against the entrenched hierarchies of rank, power, and privilege that had characterized the feudal order of European society. Under that order, a person's prospects in life were determined almost entirely by his status at birth. The individual lacked the liberty to change his social and economic ranking and was rendered dependent on the will of those in higher-ranking positions. It was against this inclusive, closed, and ascriptive system of inequality and dependence that the proponents of the liberal state fought.

An important element of the new liberal state was strong legal protection for property rights and the economic liberty that accompanied such rights. Locke had argued that property rights were natural rights, which governments had an obligation to respect and protect. Property rights were grounded in the fact that "every man has a property in his own person" so that "the labor of his body and work of his own hands are . . . properly his."[1] Moreover, as Locke saw it, the invention and use of money meant that mankind had agreed to "an inequality of private possessions," which was bound to occur as "different degrees of industry were apt to give men possessions in different proportions."[2]

Kant contributed to the development of liberalism by formulating an account of citizenship within the liberal state. He argued that a citizen rightfully possesses three attributes: "lawful *freedom* to obey no law other than that to which he has given his consent . . . civil *equality* in recognising no-one among the people as superior to himself . . . and civil *independence* which allows him to owe his existence and sustenance not to the arbitrary will of anyone else among the people, but purely to his own rights and powers."[3] In fact, all three features involve different elements of the

* For valuable comments and suggestions on this essay, I am indebted to Ellen Frankel Paul, Jeffrey Paul, and Daniel Jacobson.

[1] John Locke, *The Second Treatise of Government* (1690; reprint, Indianapolis, IN: Bobbs-Merrill, 1952), 17.

[2] Ibid., 28–29.

[3] Immanuel Kant, *The Metaphysics of Morals*, 1797, in Hans Reiss, ed., *Kant: Political Writings* (New York: Cambridge University Press, 1991), 139. Kant goes on to distinguish *"active"* citizens, who have a right to vote and exercise political influence from *"passive"* citizens, who possess "the freedom and equality of all men as *human beings*" but lack political rights. The latter group includes women, minors, and wage laborers (139–40).

equality of liberal citizens: equal freedom under the law, equal political rights, and equal autonomy from the will of others.

However, radical critics of liberalism have long argued that there is an irresolvable conflict between the liberties protected by the liberal state and the equal citizenship it claims to provide, and that liberal thought and practice inevitably favor liberty over equality in the conflict. The locus classicus of this argument is Marx's "On the Jewish Question" (1843). Marx contended that the situation of the Jew, who was then still deprived of political rights in many liberal states, illustrated the dominance of economic power over the principles of political and civil equality: "The contradiction existing between the practical political power of the Jew and his political rights is the contradiction between politics and financial power generally." Politics had become the "serf" of financial power. [4] In other words, the liberal state allowed even Jews to turn economic advantage into political control. The supposedly "free, equal, and independent" Christian citizens were, in reality, dependent subjects of those who, in theory, were not even full citizens. Thus, the liberal revolution did not bring about "human emancipation." [5] For that, another turn of the revolutionary wheel of history would be necessary.

Marx's critique of the liberal state has survived in updated form among radical thinkers until the present day. Such thinkers contend that liberal economic freedoms create inequalities of power that make a mockery of the idea that citizens enjoy political and civil equality under the law. Moreover, in recent years there has surfaced a new and complementary form of the charge that the liberal state cannot redeem the promise of equality.

The new charge issued by radical critics is aimed at the liberal system of free expression, and the heart of the accusation is that the system unduly obstructs efforts to eliminate oppressive inequalities rooted in sex and race. Just as it has long been said that the market and liberal protections of private property generate concentrations of wealth that subvert political equality, it is now claimed that the liberal state's strong protection of expressive liberty creates indefensible obstacles to the pursuit of racial and sexual equality.

In this essay, my aim is to examine the radical critique of the liberal system of free expression. The essay proceeds as follows. In Sections II and III, I outline the principal elements of a liberal system of expression and defend the account against some skeptical arguments. Section IV then describes the position on free expression taken by one of the most influential radical thinkers of the 1960s, Herbert Marcuse. I show that Marcuse decisively rejected a liberal system of expression and that his rejection was entirely consistent with his underlying social theory, which

[4] Karl Marx, "On the Jewish Question," 1843, in Lawrence H. Simon, ed., *Karl Marx: Selected Writings* (Indianapolis, IN: Hackett, 1994), 23.

[5] Ibid., 21.

posited the existence of oppressive economic and social inequalities. In Sections V and VI, I discuss the views of contemporary radicals and show that, despite making theoretical claims similar to those of Marcuse, their treatment of expressive liberty is strikingly different from his. While Marcuse advocated drastic inroads on free expression, the proposals of contemporary radicals are far more modest and generally compatible with a liberal system of expression. In Section VII, I argue that, paradoxically, liberal arguments about free expression must carry considerable weight for the contemporary radical position on speech be coherent.[6]

II. Free Expression: Institutional Variations

It is imperative to recognize from the outset that the abstract ideal of a system of free expression can be translated into institutional practice in a variety of ways. It is "institutional fetishism," to borrow Roberto Unger's term, to think that there is just one natural, necessary, or correct way in which the abstract ideal can receive institutional embodiment.[7] Unger makes the case against institutional fetishism in connection with the ideals of the market and democracy. Yet, a parallel case can be convincingly made with respect to the liberal ideal of a system of free expression. Indeed, it makes sense to think of the different possible embodiments of such an ideal as tied to alternative institutional forms of democracy. Different systems of free expression constitute, in part, different forms of democracy.

It is true that there is much more to a particular form of democracy than its specific rules regarding expressive liberty. These rules do not dictate whether a democracy has a parliamentary system or a presidential one, a system of proportional representation or a district-based, "first-past-the-post" one. Nor do the rules dictate whether a democracy operates with judicial review of legislative and executive action or without such judicial power.

However, expressive activities occur within a framework that is broader than simply the rules that are explicitly and exclusively concerned with expression. The broader framework helps to shape the kind of system of expression a society has. This framework does not merely include the law of libel, the legal rules governing the production and distribution of pornography, the law concerning racist or anti-Semitic speech, and more

[6] I will use the terms 'expression' and 'speech' interchangeably. They refer to communicative activity in general, i.e., activity having the following features: its primary intent is to convey a certain semantic content; its secondary intent is to achieve the primary intent by getting others to recognize the primary intent; and the primary and secondary intent can be reliably achieved because there is a conventionally accepted set of rules linking certain sorts of verbal or nonverbal behavior to specific semantic contents. This account is a variation on Paul Grice, "Meaning," in Paul Grice, *Studies in the Way of Words* (Cambridge, MA: Harvard University Press, 1989), 220–21. Also see Peter Meijes Tiersma, "Nonverbal Communication and the Freedom of 'Speech'," *Wisconsin Law Review* (1993): 1525–89.

[7] Roberto Mangabeira Unger, *Democracy Realized: The Progressive Alternative* (London: Verso, 1998), 25.

generally, the abstract doctrinal principles concerning the authority of government to restrict expression on account of its propositional or emotive content. The framework also includes the nature of the political party and electoral systems, the power of courts, the rules regarding private property, the nature of the mass media, and much else that shapes the ways in which persons and groups engage in communicative activities.

Accordingly, liberal systems of free expression vary in their rules regarding expression and in the broader social, legal, and political framework in which they operate. That having been said, the abstract ideal of a liberal system is not wholly malleable. There are certain paradigmatic features, and when some system departs in significant measure from these features, there must be reasons that are not only strong but also of a characteristically liberal sort to justify the departures. Otherwise, the system's claims to be a liberal one will be weak or implausible.

United States Supreme Court Justice William J. Brennan described one of the central features of a liberal system: "debate on public issues should be uninhibited, robust, and wide-open."[8] In fact, this robust debate consists of a number of interconnected elements: there is a broad array of political views, which are voiced in a way that is readily accessible by a typical member of the public; disagreement and discussion over the validity of political programs, proposals, and policies take place in the open, without fear of suppression by government or illegitimate coercion by private parties; criticism of existing or alleged power structures can proceed without fear of rights-violating retaliation; and association for expressive purposes can occur without similar fears.

These aspects of robust public debate require certain institutional arrangements, or are at least fostered by such arrangements, under conditions of modern social and political life. For example, in the absence of a system of relatively strong property rights, liberals find it impossible to see how adequate public debate can exist. The assertion of an inextricable connection between property and political freedom was one of the main contentions of the major figures of modern liberalism.[9]

The twentieth century saw considerable debate within the liberal camp over the proper scope, strength, and grounds of rights to property. One of the key points of contention was whether liberal socialism was a viable institutional arrangement.[10] Notwithstanding these disputes, all current liberals would agree with Cass Sunstein's claim that liberal democracy

[8] *New York Times v. Sullivan*, 376 U.S. 254, 270 (1964).

[9] Accordingly, Benjamin Constant wrote, "Arbitrary power over property is soon followed by arbitrary power over people." Biancamaria Fontana, ed. and trans., *Benjamin Constant: Political Writings* (Cambridge: Cambridge University Press, 1988), 263.

[10] Among the major contributions to the debate were L. T. Hobhouse, *Liberalism*, 1911 (New York: Oxford University Press, 1964); John Rawls, *A Theory of Justice* (Cambridge, MA: Harvard University Press, 1971); Robert Nozick, *Anarchy, State, and Utopia* (New York: Basic Books, 1974); and Friedrich A. Hayek, *Law, Legislation, and Liberty*, vol 2: *The Mirage of Social Justice* (Chicago, IL: University of Chicago Press, 1978). Hobhouse and Rawls argued for the potential viability of liberal socialism, while Hayek and Nozick rejected such arguments.

"requires constitutional protections of many individual rights, including . . . the right to private property, for people cannot be independent citizens if their holdings are subject to unlimited government readjustment."[11] Moreover, it is clear that liberal principles require a market economy and flatly rule out any form of state socialism as unjust in principle and incompatible with free speech in practice.

Although robust debate on public issues is central to a liberal system of expression, the system must also protect forms of communicative activity that are neither political nor public. Much communication does not concern questions of law or policy, and even some expression that does implicate such questions occurs in settings reasonably regarded as private. Thus, much religious, scientific, and artistic expression is not intended or understood as contributing to debate on public issues, and communication among friends, family members, and fellow worshippers is typically outside the realm of public discussion. A liberal system will carve out a broad zone of communicative freedom for such private forms of expression.

Many thinkers take the principle of 'content neutrality' to capture one of the key guiding thoughts behind a liberal system of expression. In rough terms, the principle prohibits restrictions on speech based on its propositional or emotive content. However, the principle has been widely misunderstood. As legal scholar James Weinstein points out, the principle cannot be reasonably formulated as "a blanket rule against content discrimination."[12] There are too many kinds of noncontroversial content-based restrictions on expression, from libel laws and securities regulations to copyright and antitrust rules, for a general prohibition or even a strong presumption against content restriction to be plausible. Weinstein's more reasonable alternative is a principle against the content-based restriction of those forms of communication that help to constitute "the public discourse by which we govern ourselves and through which we build our culture."[13]

However, it is important to realize that even Weinstein's formulation of the principle of content neutrality cannot by itself capture all, or even most, of the key elements of a liberal system of expression. There is also a broad realm of private discourse that must be free from regulation, regardless of its content. Clearly, this realm does not include threats of violence or of other rights violations, but it must include the private expression of racist, sexist, or heterosexist attitudes. Moreover, even the principle of content neutrality must operate within the context of a regime of private property, multiparty politics, and the other institutions that make possible the robust public debate central to Justice Brennan's

[11] Cass Sunstein, *Designing Democracy: What Constitutions Do* (New York: Oxford University Press, 2001), 7.

[12] James Weinstein, *Hate Speech, Pornography, and the Radical Attack on Free Speech Doctrine* (Boulder, CO: Westview Press, 1999), 49.

[13] Ibid., 44.

understanding of free speech. In the absence of such institutions, a liberal system of expression could not exist.

III. Skeptical Challenges

Skeptics of the liberal view, including some radical critics, will argue that 'robustness', 'wide ranging', 'broad zone', and similar liberal terms are largely metaphorical and emotive in content. These skeptics will claim that the terms are little more than emotionally positive labels that liberals—or anyone else for that matter—affix to the systems of which they approve. If the skeptics are right, then I have not described a distinctively liberal system of expression but have simply constructed a set of empty conceptual boxes into which virtually any ideological position can pack its favored institutions.

Accordingly, Stanley Fish contends that "abstract concepts like free speech do not have a 'natural' content but are filled with whatever content and direction one can manage to put into them. 'Free speech' is just the name we give to verbal behavior that serves substantive agendas we wish to advance. . . . Free speech, in short, is not an independent value but a political prize."[14] Competing ideological factions struggle over the power to decide what verbal behavior "merits" this emotionally charged term, and "there's no such thing as free speech" because any conception of free speech will presuppose some particular set of political values.

Fish contradicts his claim that the concept of free speech has no natural content in the very next sentence of the passage from which I have cited: he asserts that the concept refers to verbal behavior. The reference to such behavior surely gives the concept some natural semantic content. In fact, a more sensible reading of the concept's content would explicate it much more broadly, in terms of communicative activity.[15] However, if we set this point aside and treat the claim about the absence of natural content as hyperbole, it is possible to make sense of Fish's understanding of the idea of free speech.

Fish is disaggregating the term 'free speech' into distinct descriptive and emotive elements. The descriptive element simply refers to verbal behavior or communicative activity more generally. The emotive element is the attitude of approval that the speaker, based on her political values, is expressing toward the protection of a certain sort of communicative activity from punishment by society.[16]

[14] Stanley Fish, *There's No Such Thing As Free Speech, and It's a Good Thing, Too* (New York: Oxford University Press, 1994), 102.

[15] See note 6 above.

[16] On an alternative reading, the noncognitive component in Fish's analysis is prescriptive rather than emotive, i.e., it involves some kind of imperative of the form "Let everyone do X," rather than the mere expression of the speaker's favorable attitude toward X. I am grateful to Daniel Jacobson for this suggestion. The criticisms I make of the emotivist version of Fish apply, mutatis mutandis, to the prescriptivist version.

On Fish's account, any set of rules regulating expression can count as a system of free speech: the speaker's own political values and preferences determine what rules count as such, and the political preferences of speakers run the gamut. Certainly, the range extends well beyond the particular preferences of liberals.

The kind of emotivist analysis that I am attributing to Fish has its precedents in twentieth century metaethics and has been subject to a wide range of criticisms.[17] The problem on which I intend to focus in criticizing Fish will show that there is much more descriptive content to the concept of free speech than Fish acknowledges. This criticism is not, by itself, inconsistent with an emotivist analysis that permits a fixed descriptive content. However, the criticism is inconsistent with Fish's analysis, because his account leaves the concept of free speech devoid of almost all fixed descriptive meaning.

My criticism stems from the idea that there is a kind of "folk political philosophy" whose propositions help to fix the meaning of the concept of free speech.[18] These propositions are platitudinous: "Totalitarian systems are incompatible with free speech," "Government suppression of dissenting political views typically violates free speech," "Whether a given instance of suppressing expression is compatible with free speech depends in part on the circumstances," "Banning works of art because the majority finds them offensive is a violation of free speech," "Private violence against nonviolent forms of religious worship violates free speech," "Multiparty political systems are essential to a system of free speech," "Tolerance of conflicting opinions is essential to a system of free speech," "Multiple, independent sources of news and information are essential to a system of free speech," and so on.

Philosopher Michael Smith has defended an account of conceptual analysis according to which "the aim of an analysis is to give us knowledge of all and only the platitudes surrounding our use of [a] concept."[19] I regard this account as presenting an oversimplified view of the connection between conceptual meanings and platitudes. It ignores the fact that concepts have an internal structure and a place within a wider network of concepts. Thus, some platitudes are more central to the meaning of a given concept than others, and the meaning of a concept is, in part, a function of its various links to other concepts that share its semantic field. Moreover, the platitudes surrounding our use of a given concept can to some extent change.[20] Nonetheless, it would be unclear how one could pick out any subject to talk about—free speech, water, tigers, or whatever—

[17] For an overview of twentieth century metaethics, including the debates over emotivism, see Stephen Darwall, Allan Gibbard, and Peter Railton, "Toward *Fin de siècle* Ethics: Some Trends," *Philosophical Review* 101, no. 1 (1992): 115–89.

[18] I am adapting the approach found in Frank Jackson, *From Metaphysics to Ethics: A Defence of Conceptual Analysis* (Oxford: Oxford University Press, 1998), 31–55.

[19] Michael Smith, *The Moral Problem* (Oxford: Blackwell, 1994), 44. Also see p. 33.

[20] Jackson seems to avoid some of the problems with Smith's account. See Jackson, *From Metaphysics to Ethics*, 38.

unless the platitudes surrounding the subject played a significant role in defining the meaning of the corresponding concept.

Fish would be quick to point out that the platitudes of the folk political philosophy of free speech are suspiciously liberal, and liberal they are indeed. We should not be surprised: the concept of free speech was, after all, constructed by modern liberal thinkers. Fish can contest the extent to which, or the way in which, a liberal system values free speech; he can argue for some alternative to a liberal system of free expression. However, if he rejects all or most of our liberal commonplaces, he is not talking about free speech from a different political viewpoint but is simply changing the subject.

Fish is unquestionably right in thinking that speakers use 'free speech' in a way that expresses an attitude of approval toward certain policies and conditions, such as constitutional protection for competing political parties or economic arrangements that will provide multiple and independent sources of news and information. However, the approval is linked in a specific way to the descriptive content of the concept: speakers think that there are justificatory reasons for favoring those policies. If someone rejects those policies, then he is not operating with a nonliberal conception of free speech but is, rather, opposing the policies implicit in the very idea of free speech.

I do not claim that Fish is himself such an opponent. In fact, I doubt that he is because there is no reason to think that he would reject the liberal commonplaces, despite his initial pejorative reference to some of them as "First Amendment pieties."[21] Rather, he is asserting one of the liberal platitudes as an unqualified generalization and elevating it to a privileged position above all of the others, namely, the platitude that whether a given instance of speech suppression violates free speech depends on the circumstances. Fish's formulation is this: "The question of whether or not to regulate will always be a local one, and we cannot rely either on abstractions that are empty of content or filled with the content of some partisan agenda to generate a 'principled' answer."[22] The sound approach is "to consider in every case what is at stake and what are the risks and gains of alternative courses of action."[23]

Fish's approach may seem to throw out all of the other liberal platitudes and to claim that particular circumstances are all that count in determining whether an instance of speech is an exercise of expressive freedom. However, in the end he winds up accepting the other liberal platitudes, even though he does not think that they can generate acontextual answers to questions about particular issues of speech regulation: "First Amendment formulas ... still serve a function that is not at all negligible: they slow down outcomes in an area in which fear of over-

[21] Fish, *There's No Such Thing*, 110.
[22] Ibid., 111.
[23] Ibid.

hasty outcomes is justified by a long record of abuses."[24] Fish's initially dismissive talk of "First Amendment pieties" has thus become a more respectful reference to "First Amendment formulas."

In any case, it seems dubious for Fish to elevate above all other free speech platitudes the one that concerns the circumstances of speech. The other platitudes are at least as important because no account of the circumstances of speech can ignore the considerations to which the other platitudes make reference, such as the existence of a multiparty system or a totalitarian one, the toleration of religious difference or private violence against dissenting creeds, the control by government of the media or multiple and independent sources of information, and so on. Nor is there any reason to think that the relevant particular circumstances are so variable that all presumptive generalizations about free speech are to be rejected in favor of the unqualified generalization that issues of free speech are "always local."

I do think that Fish is right to this extent: the free speech platitudes do not dictate in any simple way the answers to many of the free speech issues that confront liberal societies. I include among these issues the ones on which contemporary radicals focus: pornography regulation, sexual harassment rules, and restrictions on hate speech. Moreover, I agree with Fish that considerations of historical and social context ought to carry weight in dealing with these issues. None of these points is inconsistent with recognizing that the concept of free speech has a robust descriptive content or affirming that a liberal system of expression ought to be endorsed. Fish's efforts to show that the concept is inherently devoid of descriptive content fail. However, even if we can fix at least some of the content of the concept by reference to liberal platitudes, the question still remains whether a liberal system of expression ought to be endorsed.

IV. Marcuse and the Rejection of Liberalism

In the 1960s one of the most influential voices on the left was Herbert Marcuse (1898–1979), and he explicitly rejected a liberal system of expression in favor of what he regarded as an equality-promoting alternative. Marcuse did not defend his alternative as a permanent fixture. Rather, he believed that a liberal system could not be justified at this historical juncture because it tolerated forms of expression whose content blocked progress toward peace, equality, and effective freedom for all. The progress of history required the systematic suppression of certain ideas now so that a liberal system of free expression could be instituted at a later stage of social development.

For the advancement of freedom, peace, and equality, Marcuse advocated what he called a system of "liberating tolerance." In his writings, he describes what he has in mind in only the sketchiest of terms, but these

[24] Ibid., 113.

terms—together with the justification he offers for liberating tolerance—make it clear that he is advocating a radical alternative to a liberal system. Liberating tolerance would employ "apparently undemocratic means," including "the withdrawal of toleration of speech and assembly from groups and movements which promote aggressive policies, armament, chauvinism, discrimination on grounds of race and religion, or which oppose the extension of public services, social security, medical care, etc."[25]

In order to achieve a free and democratic society, "tolerance cannot be indiscriminate and equal with respect to the contents of expression."[26] The reason resides in the very framework of liberal capitalist society: "The antagonistic structure of society rigs the rules of the game. Those who stand against the system are a priori at a disadvantage, which is not removed by toleration of their ideas, speeches, and newspapers."[27] To achieve true equality requires "liberating tolerance [which] would mean intolerance against movements from the Right, and toleration of movements from the Left."[28] The result "would amount to an upheaval" and involve the "cancellation of the liberal creed of free and equal discussion."[29]

Marcuse is clear that liberating tolerance would involve sweeping restrictions on expressive liberty, and his account of the nature of post–World War II liberal society is meant to support such restrictions:

> The whole post-fascist period is one of clear and present danger. Consequently, true pacification requires the withdrawal of tolerance before the deed, at the stage of communication in word, print, and picture. Such extreme suspension of the right of free speech and free assembly is indeed justified only if the whole of society is in extreme danger. I maintain that our society is in such an emergency situation, and that it has become the normal state of affairs.[30]

In the foregoing passage, Marcuse is turning what had been a standard liberal rule of free expression into the basis for a repressive system. The rule was formulated by U.S. Supreme Court Justice Oliver Wendell Holmes, namely, the "clear and present danger" test. For much of the twentieth century, jurists saw this test as highly protective of expression. Holmes had written, in *Schenck v. United States* (1919), that government could restrict speech in a way that is consistent with the First Amendment only

[25] Herbert Marcuse, "Repressive Tolerance," in Robert Paul Wolff, Barrington Moore Jr., and Herbert Marcuse, *A Critique of Pure Tolerance* (Boston, MA: Beacon, 1965), 100.
[26] Ibid., 88.
[27] Ibid., 92n.
[28] Ibid., 109.
[29] Ibid., 101 and 106.
[30] Ibid., 109–10.

as long as the speech posed a "clear and present danger" of causing evils that government had the right to prevent.[31]

In his opinion for the Court, Holmes drew a distinction between wartime and peacetime, suggesting that expression receives less protection during the former. The context of war can make speech with a certain content a clear and present danger, when that same speech during peacetime would pose no such threat. The Court found that Schenck's antiwar pamphlets posed a clear and present danger, having been circulated during wartime and intended to obstruct the draft. Holmes employed his famous example of falsely shouting "Fire!" in a crowded theatre to illustrate the point that circumstances can make a difference in deciding whether an instance of speech ought to be protected as "free speech" or not.

Marcuse makes two moves to turn Holmes's clear and present danger test into a justification for "an extreme suspension of the right of free speech and free assembly." First, he goes beyond the Court's wartime exception to free speech by arguing that society is in an even more dire condition: a "state of emergency" in which it confronts "extreme danger." Second, he rejects the notion that this state of emergency is temporary: it is the "normal state of affairs" and has become entrenched in social life. Thus, he alludes again to Holmes and writes that the clear and present danger test "seems no longer adequate to a stage where the whole society is in the situation of the theater audience when somebody cries: 'fire.' "[32]

The emergency condition of society consists, in part, of the oppressive structural inequalities that characterize liberal capitalism. These inequalities are dehumanizing to those who suffer under their weight, but they also implant in the individual a false consciousness about his condition: his dehumanization appears perfectly normal to him. Marcuse then suggests the appropriate remedy:

> [E]fforts to counteract his dehumanization must begin at the place of entrance, there where the false consciousness takes form (or rather: is systematically formed)—it must begin with stopping the words and images which feed this consciousness. To be sure, this is censorship, even precensorship, but openly directed against the more or less hidden censorship that permeates the free media.[33]

Accordingly, Marcuse defends aggressive censorship in the service of dismantling the entrenched capitalist structures of inequality. However,

[31] *Schenck v. United States*, 249 U.S. 47, 52 (1919). A few years after Marcuse published his piece on tolerance, the Supreme Court further strengthened First Amendment protections by ruling that the advocacy of illegal action was protected speech unless it was intended to incite or produce "imminent lawless action" and was likely to do so. See *Brandenburg v. Ohio*, 395 U.S. 444 (1969).

[32] Marcuse, "Repressive Tolerance," 109.

[33] Ibid., 111.

he does not wish to abandon the idea that there is great value in a system of free speech, provided existing inequalities have been dismantled. Indeed, Marcuse explicitly endorses Mill's argument that freedom of speech is valuable because it fosters the discovery of truth, but then Marcuse claims that liberal capitalist societies are like the societies of "barbarians" who Mill said were not yet fit to rule themselves because they were not yet capable of rational deliberation and learning from their mistakes. "Radicalism now; liberalism later," is the essence of Marcuse's view on free speech.

Yet, the critical question that Marcuse fails adequately to address is, Who is to design and operate his system of censorship in the service of equality? Mill was certain of who should help the barbarians become civilized: Western powers such as Britain, which had achieved sufficient social maturity. Marcuse certainly did not think that the Soviet Union or Communist China was fit to play an analogous role in relation to liberal capitalist regimes. At times, he raises the possibility of a Leninist strategy of an intellectual revolutionary vanguard serving as the new ruling elite, and it seems that he was not prepared to rule out this strategy.[34]

Indeed, it is difficult to see how the Leninist strategy could be avoided given that "the people . . . are indoctrinated. . . . To enable them to become autonomous, to find by themselves what is true and what is false for man in the existing society, they would have to be freed from the prevailing indoctrination (which is no longer recognized as indoctrination)."[35] Marcuse contends that "the small and powerless minorities which struggle against the false consciousness and its beneficiaries must be helped" by the establishment of liberating tolerance.[36] However, the vast majority in society is surely not going to help, if Marcuse's social theory is accurate, thereby leaving an enlightened Leninist vanguard as the only real alternative. Perhaps the cunning of history can come up with some other trick to break the stranglehold of liberal false consciousness and the "totalitarian democracy" that the ideology supports, but Marcuse is at a loss to describe what that trick might be.[37]

V. Contemporary Radicals

In current debates over free speech issues, radical feminists and critical race theorists often echo Marcuse's approach, but with some important variations. Contemporary radicals tend to focus more on inequalities of race and sex than did Marcuse. In addition, they are more explicit than he

[34] Herbert Marcuse, *An Essay on Liberation* (Boston, MA: Beacon Press, 1969), 70. Also see Richard Lichtman, "Repressive Tolerance," in Robert Pippin et al., eds., *Marcuse: Critical Theory and the Promise of Utopia* (South Hadley, MA: Bergin and Garvey, 1988), 197.

[35] Marcuse, "Repressive Tolerance," 98–99.

[36] Ibid., 110.

[37] Ibid., 99.

was in asserting the power of communication and representation to create and sustain the oppressive hierarchies of power and privilege that they claim characterize liberal society. However, the contemporary radicals are in agreement with Marcuse in depicting society as a system of oppression and domination, and in appealing to such a depiction in order to criticize liberal institutions.

Charles Lawrence expresses a view characteristic of critical race theorists in claiming that we exist "in a society where racism is ubiquitous."[38] This racism typically goes unnoticed by whites, Lawrence contends, because it is "unconscious."[39] Moreover, speech plays a crucial role in creating the oppressive structures of our racist society: "all racist speech constructs the social reality that constrains the liberty of nonwhites because of their race. By limiting the life opportunities of others, this act of constructing meaning also makes racist speech conduct."[40] Lawrence proceeds to defend campus speech codes prohibiting racist forms of expression.

Another prominent critical race theorist, Mari Matsuda, affirms "the structural reality of racism," which consists of "the ideology of racial supremacy and the mechanisms for keeping selected victim groups in subordinated positions."[41] She claims that racist speech is among these mechanisms of subordination and argues that "a range of legal interventions, including the use of tort law and criminal law principles, is appropriate to combat racist hate propaganda."[42] Speech should be subject to criminalization when it conveys a message of racial inferiority against a historically oppressed group and the message is "hateful, persecutory, and degrading."[43]

For example, Matsuda would favor criminalizing anti-Semitic writings, including Holocaust denial literature. She would limit content-based restrictions on expression to racist speech because such speech "is best treated as a sui generis category, presenting an idea so historically untenable, so dangerous and so tied to the perpetuation of violence and degradation . . . that it is properly treated as outside the realm of protected discourse."[44]

Among other proposals made by critical race theorists are laws criminalizing incitement to racial hatred."[45] In criticizing constitutional doc-

[38] Charles R. Lawrence III, "If He Hollers Let Him Go: Regulating Racist Speech on Campus," in Mari J. Matsuda et al., *Words that Wound* (Boulder, CO: Westview Press, 1993), 69. Also see p. 77.

[39] Charles R. Lawrence III, "The Id, the Ego, and Equal Protection: Reckoning with Unconscious Racism," *Stanford Law Review* 39 (1987): 317–88.

[40] Lawrence, "If He Hollers," 62.

[41] Mari J. Matsuda, "Public Response to Racist Speech: Considering the Victim's Story," in Matsuda et al., *Words that Wound*, 23.

[42] Ibid., 35 and 38.

[43] Ibid., 36.

[44] Ibid., 35.

[45] Ibid., 30.

trine in the United States as formalistic and ahistorical, the theorists note that the United Kingdom and Canada, among other liberal democracies, already have such laws. These laws and the other proposals of the critical race theorists are seen as part of a defensible response to protect nonwhites from "racist assailants who employ words and symbols as part of an integrated arsenal of weapons of oppression and subordination."[46]

Radical feminist critics make parallel arguments when it comes to claims of sexual subordination and the alleged implications for the regulation of pornography. Thus, Catherine Itzin claims that "women are oppressed in every aspect of their public and private lives."[47] She goes on to contend that "the oppression of women is both institutionalized and internalized."[48] As with Marcuse's dehumanized and deluded masses, "Women are conditioned to conform to the stereotyped images of femininity and womanhood in such a way that they are often unaware that they are misrepresented and mistreated. They often, apparently willingly, agree to participate in misrepresentation and mistreatment."[49]

Itzin regards the depiction of women in pornography as playing a central role in the perpetuation of their oppression. On this basis, she defends "civil sex discrimination legislation against pornography [that] would enable women to take action on grounds of harm done to them by pornography."[50]

Itzin's position largely reflects the views of Catharine MacKinnon, who has been one of the principal architects of feminist antipornography legislation in the United States and whose legal arguments have played a crucial role in the creation of sexual harassment doctrine.[51] MacKinnon describes the condition of women's sexual oppression: "Rape, battery, sexual harassment, forced prostitution. . . . a woman is socially defined as a person who, whether or not she is or has been, can be treated in these ways by men at any time, and little, if anything, will be done about it."[52]

[46] Charles R. Lawrence III et al., introduction to Matsuda et al., *Words that Wound*, 7.

[47] Catherine Itzin, "Pornography and the Social Construction of Sexual Inequality," in Catherine Itzin, ed., *Pornography: Women, Violence, and Civil Liberties* (Oxford: Oxford University Press, 1992), 57.

[48] Ibid., 58.

[49] Ibid., 62. The false consciousness attributed to women by Itzin and other radical feminists (see the text accompanying notes 53 and 54 below) is one important point of contrast with critical race theorists. In the view of the latter, nonwhites are not deceived about their mistreatment. Rather, whites are the ones who deceive themselves about the oppressive racial order of society, while nonwhites are quite cognizant of that order.

[50] Catherine Itzin, "Legislating Against Pornography without Censorship," in Itzin, ed., *Pornography*, 424.

[51] MacKinnon's antipornography ordinances define pornography as "graphic sexually explicit materials that subordinate women through pictures or words." Catharine MacKinnon, *Only Words* (Cambridge, MA: Harvard University Press, 1993), 22. Indianapolis, Indiana, enacted a version of an ordinance drafted by MacKinnon and Andrea Dworkin, but it was struck down as unconstitutional on free speech grounds in *American Booksellers Association v. Hudnut*, 771 F.2d 323 (1985).

[52] Catharine MacKinnon, *Feminism Unmodified: Discourses on Life and Law* (Cambridge, MA: Harvard University Press, 1987), 169–70.

The result is that women are treated as "less than human, on the basis of sex," and Americans live under a system of "male supremacy" whose lynchpin is the sexual abuse of women by men.[53]

MacKinnon goes on to argue that this sexual oppression goes largely unrecognized: "[T]he force behind sexism, the subordination in gender inequality, is made invisible; dissent from it becomes inaudible as well as rare."[54] And so "there is a belief that in this society women and men are basically equals," and this belief is "an article of faith" even among "most women."[55]

In MacKinnon's view, any liberal remedy to women's subordination is misguided and futile from the start, especially if it depends on fighting sexist speech with the traditional liberal remedy of "more speech," famously articulated by Justice Louis Brandeis in 1927.[56] As she sees it, "To liberals, speech must never be sacrificed to other social goals. But liberalism has never understood that the free speech of men silences the free speech of women."[57] Liberal concepts "support power as currently organized."[58]

MacKinnon is especially critical of the liberal principle of content neutrality. She contends that the principle is invoked selectively to strike down antipornography ordinances, while it is ignored in the cases of other laws that are clearly content based, including traditional obscenity statutes. The result is that the "peculiar genius of liberalism has been to seem to accommodate fundamental challenges without fundamentally changing."[59] The absence of fundamental changes stems from the failure of liberalism "to grasp systematically the group-based determinants of inequality, and ... its relative blindness to organized power in diverse social forms, so that it often effectively sides with dominance."[60] Nonetheless, MacKinnon writes that liberalism "might work and its terms might mean what they are supposed to mean [under] conditions of sex equality."[61]

VI. Marcuse as the Model?

In their book, *The Shadow University*, historian Alan Charles Kors and attorney Charles Silverglate note the continuities in thinking between

[53] MacKinnon, *Only Words*, 23 and 60.

[54] MacKinnon, *Feminism Unmodified*, 166.

[55] Ibid., 168.

[56] Brandeis wrote that "the fitting remedy for evil counsels is good ones." *Whitney v. California*, 274 U.S. 357, 375 (1927) (Brandeis, J., concurring).

[57] MacKinnon, *Feminism Unmodified*, 156.

[58] Catharine MacKinnon, "'The Case' Responds," *American Political Science Review* 95: 3 (2001): 709.

[59] Ibid., 709–10.

[60] Ibid.., 709.

[61] Ibid.

Marcuse and contemporary radical critics of liberalism. For example, they write that "MacKinnon's rhetoric is unmistakably Marcusean, especially the notion that liberty is a zero-sum game, and that giving it simultaneously to 'dominant' and 'subordinated' groups inevitably reinforces the power of the dominant group."[62]

Kors and Silverglate are especially concerned with the way in which campus speech codes and related manifestations of political correctness have squelched speech on college campuses across the United States: "Marcuse's prescriptions are the model for the assaults on free speech in today's academic world."[63]

There are several key similarities between Marcuse and current radical thinkers. In particular, they share the idea that the liberal principle of content neutrality should be rejected under existing conditions because (1) there are serious systemic inequalities which ought to be eliminated; (2) various forms of speech play a critical role in sustaining these inequalities, in large measure by convincing most people that the inequalities are fully justified; (3) restrictions on speech are justifiable on the ground that they can play an important role in eliminating the inequalities; and (4) a liberal system of free expression can work as advertised by liberals only after the inequalities have been eliminated and safely relegated to the past.

Notwithstanding these important similarities, the differences between Marcuse and the current radicals are just as striking. In particular, none of the current radicals is prepared to endorse the "extreme suspension" of the right of free speech and the "cancellation of the liberal creed of free and equal discussion" involved in the implementation of Marcuse's scheme of liberating tolerance. Most of the radical proposals are modest and can in fact be found in the law of many liberal democracies. Even the most aggressive of the proposals cannot be fairly equated with the "upheaval" for which Marcuse called.

Consider MacKinnon's antipornography efforts. She is critical of legal doctrine in the United States for not taking women's equality seriously, but she does not endorse the generalized system of speech control that Marcuse had in mind. She writes, "When equality is recognized as a constitutional value and mandate, the idea that some people are inferior to others on the basis of group membership is authoritatively rejected as the basis for public policy. This does not mean that ideas to the contrary cannot be debated or expressed."[64] While Marcuse would be prepared to endorse general restrictions on the expression of anti-egalitarian ideas, MacKinnon's proposal is aimed at sexually explicit depictions of women's sexual subordination.

[62] Alan Charles Kors and Harvey A. Silverglate, *The Shadow University: The Betrayal of Liberty on America's Campuses* (New York: Free Press, 1998), 76.

[63] Ibid., 71.

[64] MacKinnon, *Only Words*, 106.

Moreover, MacKinnon regards Canadian law as taking women's equality seriously. Under the rulings of that nation's Supreme Court, antipornography laws have been upheld on grounds of sexual equality.[65] One can reasonably argue that Canadian constitutional doctrine rests on an inadequate understanding of liberal principles and that Canada's system of expression is not the most reasonable liberal system. However, it would be implausible to contend that Canada does not have a liberal system at all. Canada's laws and institutions form an institutional variant of a liberal system of expression. In her unrelenting criticism of liberalism, MacKinnon fails to recognize this important fact of institutional variation.

It is true that MacKinnon aims to put out of business the entire pornography industry, including the production and distribution of "soft core" pornography.[66] However, even if we agree that her favored ordinances violate any reasonable understanding of free speech principles, the slice of mass culture that the laws would affect would be quite narrow. In contrast, the "upheaval" in the treatment of speech for which Marcuse called would not leave the vast bulk of mass culture untouched. On his analysis, mass culture is what effectively indoctrinates people with the stultifying ideology of liberalism and what liberating tolerance is meant to combat. Although MacKinnon takes herself to be advocating principles deeply antagonistic to a liberal system of speech, her prescriptions are mild in comparison with those of Marcuse and, by her own admission, constitute part of the law in some existing liberal democracies.[67]

In contrast to MacKinnon's explicit hostility toward liberalism, several of the leading critical race theorists take pains to argue that their proposals are compatible with a liberal system of expression. Matsuda seeks "to recognize and accommodate the civil libertarian position" by recommending restrictions on hate speech that are "consistent with [F]irst [A]mendment values."[68] Lawrence agrees that "there are very strong reasons for protecting even racist speech" and believes that "good lawyers" can fashion speech codes capable of "limiting the harm of hate speech without opening the floodgates of censorship."[69] In a similar vein, Richard Delgado and Jean Stefancic write that "the experiences of Can-

[65] Ibid., 101.

[66] MacKinnon points out that her definition of pornography is "coterminous with the industry, from *Playboy*, in which women are objectified and presented dehumanized as sexual objects or things for use; through the torture of women . . . to snuff films." MacKinnon, *Only Words*, 22–23.

[67] Perhaps MacKinnon's most radical proposal is that it should be "actionable to force pornography on a person . . . in a home." MacKinnon, *Feminism Unmodified*, 183. The proposal appears to entail that a wife who objects to her husband's tacking a *Playboy* centerfold to the bedroom wall should be able to get an injunction ordering him to take it down. MacKinnon would certainly be right to think that such a legal intrusion could not be justified on liberal grounds. Yet, the intrusion is still far from the encompassing scheme of censorship favored by Marcuse.

[68] Matsuda, "Public Response," 35.

[69] Lawrence, "If He Hollers," 57 and 86.

ada, Denmark, France, Germany, and the Netherlands imply that limited regulation of hate speech does not invariably, or even frequently, weaken the respect accorded free speech."[70]

My point is not that the speech codes proposed by critical race theorists are the most reasonable responses to racist speech in universities or in society at large. Indeed, I regard Matsuda's suggestion that anti-Semitic literature should be criminalized as unreasonable, at least in liberal democracies outside of Germany. However, the key point to keep in mind is that Matsuda explicitly accepts the relevance of liberal principles of speech to her argument by seeking "to recognize and accommodate the civil libertarian position."

Such an argument contrasts with that of Marcuse, who explicitly rejected any accommodation with civil liberties. He believed that civil liberties would have to wait until the day when some form of radical equality was established and that accommodating such liberties now would block progress toward that day. Similar contrasts also can be drawn between Marcuse's view and that of the other critical race theorists.

On the feminist side, Itzin's argument also contrasts with that of Marcuse. She does not contend that the protection of civil liberties must wait until sexual equality is established. Rather, she holds that "[f]rom a civil liberties perspective, the greatest freedom would be achieved [by laws that] . . . would make incitement to sexual hatred and violence illegal and . . . would enable women who could prove that they were injured by pornography to sue and to seek compensation." In her view, "It is also possible to limit freedom of expression in the case of pornography on grounds of harm without any fundamental threat to freedom of speech."[71] Marcuse's position is that as long as oppressive inequalities exist—and both he and Itzin posit such inequalities—violations of freedom of speech are justifiable as necessary steps in the elimination of inequality. Itzin's argument only makes sense on the assumption that, just as liberals claim, free speech principles are important and cannot be justifiably ignored on the road to sexual equality.

Accordingly, contemporary radicals are prepared to argue within a framework that incorporates liberal principles of free speech and to operate politically within a liberal system of expression. The burden of their argument is that existing liberal systems of expression, especially in the United States, are insufficiently responsive to systemic and unjust inequalities based on race and sex. However, unlike Marcuse, they do not favor jettisoning the existing systems in favor of some antiliberal alternative. Marcuse's thinking may have been a model in some respects for current radicals, but it is a model whose radical elements they have refrained from endorsing. The question is, Why?

[70] Richard Delgado and Jean Stefancic, *Must We Defend Nazis? Hate Speech, Pornography, and the New First Amendment* (New York: New York University Press, 1997), 125.

[71] Catherine Itzin, "Pornography and Civil Liberties: Freedom, Harm, and Human Rights," in Itzin, ed., *Pornography*, 580.

VII. Wrong, Remedy, and Paradox

There is an apparent discrepancy in contemporary radical thought. On the one side is a diagnosis of the racial and sexual wrongs of existing society and of the role that expression plays in perpetuating these wrongs. These wrongs are severe, systemic, and entrenched, amounting to oppression based on race and sex. Expression is crucial in perpetuating the wrongs: the public media, among other modes of communication, create a cultural environment that makes it difficult for people to perceive the wrongs, even as such communication shapes the attitudes and beliefs that entrench the wrongs. On the other side is the remedy proposed by the radicals: campus speech codes, legal restrictions on pornography, laws against racial and sexual incitement. The remedy seems rather inadequate to the wrong.

Thus, the radical position involves a triad that, if not strictly an inconsistent one, does raise the question of whether the position is normatively coherent. The three key theses are as follows:

1. There is an oppressive racial and social order.
2. Speech plays a substantial role in maintaining the oppression, mainly by portraying oppression as normal and natural.
3. Restrictions on the speech that helps to maintain the oppressive order should be quite limited in scope.

The apparent normative incoherence derives from the discrepancy between the magnitude of the wrong presented by (1) and (2), on the one side, and the very limited nature of the remedy proposed by (3), on the other. There are several ways of trying to make sense of this discrepancy. One possibility is to argue that any remedy involving substantially greater incursions on speech would simply not create any marginal gains in the direction of greater racial and sexual equality. This pragmatic approach would not place any limits, in advance, on permissible speech restrictions, but simply endorses whatever restrictions would have the largest egalitarian impact. The judgment would be that only very limited restrictions have beneficial effects at the margin.

It is reasonable to regard Fish as taking this approach. On his analysis, there is no value in the protection of expressive liberty aside from the consequentialist benefits as measured in terms of values other than expressive liberty. However, his analysis purchases the coherence of the radical position at the price of normative implausibility. It entails that a Marcusean-style system of speech control would be justified if only it yields marginal gains in the direction of racial and sexual equality. Even if we were to agree that significant departures from content neutrality could be justified in a limited domain of expression when the departures produce substantial gains toward sexual or racial equality, we would still be a far cry from justifying the rejection of a liberal system of expression.

Indeed, MacKinnon makes precisely this kind of argument, and no contemporary radical has been prepared to go beyond it and to contend that a system of liberating tolerance would be justified if only it produces marginal egalitarian gains. The contention is not normatively plausible.

A second way of trying to render the radical position coherent is to argue that expressive liberty is inherently valuable and/or instrumentally valuable (apart from any equality-promoting consequences). Marcusean-style incursions on speech would not be justifiable on this view because they would violate the value of that liberty. On one line of argument, a liberal system of expression does a far better job of treating all persons with dignity than any alternative, including the Marcusean system. On another line of argument, a liberal system does a far better job of arriving at social, ethical, and scientific truths and of enabling persons to arrive at reasoned views and to better appreciate the significance of their own views.

Of course, the arguments that I have just sketched are quintessentially liberal ones.[72] Radicals may be hesitant to embrace them, but it is difficult to see what kinds of arguments other than liberal ones can be used to defend, on grounds other than purely pragmatic ones, a liberal system of speech in a society supposed to be riven by racial and sexual oppression. Indeed, the more the alleged oppression is said to be perpetuated by speech, the more weighty these liberal arguments must be in order to avoid the conclusion that a liberal system of expression ought to be jettisoned in favor of something akin to Marcuse's liberating tolerance. Aside from strictly practical considerations, there would be no good reason to withhold support from a Marcusean remedy unless one supposed that liberal considerations in favor of a system of free expression were quite weighty. If there is a great deal of public and private communication that serves to maintain oppression, then it would seem that strong reasons would be needed to defend the toleration of such communication. Liberal reasons are the only ones that could adequately play such a role.

In addition, support for a liberal system of expression in the face of an oppressive racial and sexual order sustained in substantial measure by speech would make little sense unless one also supposed that (a) the liberating power of speech could counteract its power to oppress and (b) false consciousness concerning the existence of oppression did not have a stranglehold over society. Without these suppositions, a system of free speech would be an unambiguous and unrelenting force for the maintenance of oppression. It is difficult to see why such a system should be tolerated. With the suppositions, however, we are back to Justice Brandeis's formula that the proper remedy for bad speech is good speech.

One might respond that, although the radicals' remedies are relatively modest and do not jettison the overall liberal system, the slice of speech

[72] On the argument from dignity, see Ronald Dworkin, *Freedom's Law: The Moral Reading of the American Constitution* (Cambridge, MA: Harvard University Press, 1996), 200. On the other arguments, see John Stuart Mill, *On Liberty*, 1859 (Indianapolis, IN: Hackett, 1978), chap. 2.

that they do target for legal restriction is especially important in maintaining racial and sexual oppression. For example, MacKinnon maintains that pornography is especially important in maintaining the subordination of women. Presumably, the elimination of pornography would be a major blow to the system of male supremacy, and so there is no need to buy into Justice Brandeis's liberal formula.

However, the MacKinnonite response is implausible for several reasons. First, even if her ordinance were enacted and enforced, it is reasonable to expect that a considerable amount of "underground" pornography would still circulate. To paraphrase what she has written about rape, pornography would not be banned so much as regulated.[73] More importantly, the subordination of women, assuming it exists, is clearly overdetermined. Women were subordinated well before there was a multibillion dollar pornography industry, and in light of how women are depicted in much of the mainstream media, there would be no reason for a radical feminist to think that a dramatic difference would be made in women's status by legal restrictions on pornography. Certainly the experience in Canada, whose antipornography laws are supported by MacKinnon, does not support the idea that a substantial improvement in women's status flows from legally restricting graphic depictions of women's sexual subordination.[74]

For critical race theorists, it is even more implausible to reject the potentially liberating power of speech than it would be for MacKinnon. She has a hypothesis, albeit an unsubstantiated and implausible one, concerning the essential role that pornography plays in maintaining sexual oppression. Critical race theorists favor campus speech codes and laws against the incitement of racial hatred, but none of the theorists hypothesizes that the speech that is targeted by such rules has a central role in perpetuating racial oppression. To the contrary, the theorists think that images and depictions throughout mass culture are largely responsible for the ubiquity of racism. Yet, critical race theorists reject a general ban on racist speech and, as we have seen, generally attempt to accommodate free speech concerns. This position is a coherent one if considerable weight is attached to at least some of the liberal arguments supporting free speech and to the idea that the liberating power of speech can counteract its oppressive force.

This, then, is the radical paradox: In order for the contemporary radical position on racist and sexist speech to be coherent, it must rely heavily on quintessential liberal arguments about free speech.[75] Marcuse avoided

[73] The exact quote is: "Rape is not illegal; it is regulated." MacKinnon, *Feminism Unmodified*, 26.

[74] The United States and Canada are in a virtual tie on the gender-related development index of the United Nations Development Programme, and Canada is only slightly ahead of the United States on the gender empowerment measure. See *Human Development Report 2002: Deepening Democracy in a Fragmented World* (New York: Oxford University Press, 2002), 224 and 226.

[75] I am using 'paradox' in the nontechnical sense to refer to something that is contrary to received opinion or expectation.

this paradox because his radicalism posited that the entire liberal system of expression was an insuperable obstacle in the way of dismantling an oppressive system. Modifying or qualifying one or another aspect of the system would be wholly insufficient. The whole system had to go if the oppression was to be undone. Accordingly, Marcuse's position on free speech was coherent with his social theory, even if the social theory was itself deeply flawed.

Current radicals want the radicalism of Marcuse's social theory without the radicalism of his political prescriptions. However, there is no plausible way to make this newer, truncated form of radicalism coherent, without conceding that liberals are right in according great weight to the value of speech.

VIII. Conclusion

On issues of racist and sexist speech, there is not much difference between radicals and liberals. The argument is over which institutional form for a liberal system of expression is the most reasonable. It is not an argument over whether to have a liberal system.

If my analysis is sound, then it leaves contemporary radicals in a bit of a bind. It has been central to my analysis that a liberal system of expression is not simply a matter of the rules explicitly concerned with speech, but also involves a set of institutional conditions: a multiparty political system, protections for private property, multiple and independent sources of information, and so forth. These institutional conditions are all characteristic of liberal democracy. Accordingly, it seems that radicals cannot buy into a liberal system of expression without also buying into a much larger set of liberal institutions. Perhaps there are nonliberal alternatives to the institutional conditions needed for free expression, but it certainly remains to be seen whether radical thought can formulate normatively plausible and workable forms of such alternatives.[76] On the matter of speech, however, the conclusion can be fairly drawn that there is no plausible and coherent alternative to a liberal system of expression. Even radicals themselves are committed to that conclusion.

Philosophy, Georgia State University

[76] The most systematic recent effort to develop a radical alternative that does not jettison free speech is in Unger, *Democracy Realized*.

THE POLITICS OF FREE SPEECH*

By Scott D. Gerber

I. Introduction

Freedom of speech long has been regarded as one of the "preferred freedoms"[1] in the United States: one of the freedoms the U.S. Supreme Court deems "implicit in the concept of ordered liberty."[2] However, what freedom of speech does—and should—mean is a highly charged question in American constitutional law. I will explore this question by examining how several prominent constitutional theorists have proposed particular approaches to free speech law in order to further their political objectives.[3] I will examine the free speech theories of the nation's leading feminist legal theorist (regarding pornography), critical race theorists (regarding hate speech), libertarian (regarding commercial speech), and legal republican (regarding deliberative democracy).[4] I also will discuss the principal criticisms of each of these theories, whether the courts have been influenced by any of them, and, in conclusion, whether it is possible to advance a nonpolitical (i.e., a purely law-based or value-free) theory of free speech.

Given that the constitutional theorists discussed in this essay are arguing for a reconceptualization of at least some aspects of existing free speech law, a brief word about the Supreme Court's free speech jurisprudence is in order. (I will have more to say about the Court in Section VII.)

* I thank John M. Jurco and LeAnna D. Smack for research assistance, and Mark A. Graber and Ellen Frankel Paul for helpful comments on a draft of this essay. I also thank William and Mary Law School for permitting me to use its library when I was in Virginia and Ohio Northern University College of Law for a summer research stipend.

[1] *Jones v. Opelika*, 316 U.S. 584, 608 (1942) (Stone, C.J., dissenting). See also *United States v. Carolene Products Company*, 304 U.S. 144, 152 n.4 (1938) (Stone, J.).

[2] *Palko v. Connecticut*, 302 U.S. 319 (1937) (Cardozo, J.).

[3] 'Politics' is, of course, an amorphous concept. *See, e.g.*, e-mail from Jack Balkin to a discussion list for constitutional law professors [ConLawProf@listserv.UCLA.edu, posted online September 10, 2002]: "I guess the big problem in answering your question is figuring out how you want to divide the 'political' from the 'purely law-based'.... It may be that you haven't found a nonpolitical principle of free speech because your conception of what makes something political is too capacious and your conception of what is 'purely law-based' is too demanding." I use the term 'politics' primarily as a synonym for moral and social objectives. I do not mean to imply that any of the theorists discussed in this essay are doing anything wrong in attempting to advance their particular objectives.

[4] I realize there are often differences of opinion among theorists within each jurisprudential perspective. For example, many feminists disagree with law professor Catharine A. MacKinnon's position on pornography. Space constraints require me to focus on the leading theorist or theorists (such as MacKinnon) within each category. My larger point about the politics of free speech should not be affected (see Section VII of this essay).

The Court's docket was largely devoid of free speech cases until after World War I,[5] but, as Daniel A. Farber colorfully puts it in his useful primer on the First Amendment to the U.S. Constitution, "[L]ike a late-talking toddler who is never quiet for an instant, once he finally gets started, the Supreme Court has more than made up for lost time."[6]

For approximately the first fifty years of the Court's involvement with the Free Speech Clause of the First Amendment ("Congress shall make no law . . . abridging the freedom of speech"), the most visible test of constitutionality was Justice Oliver Wendell Holmes Jr.'s "clear and present danger" test. It specified that in order to suppress speech the government had to prove that the speech in question posed an immediate danger to society.[7] (Revealingly, Justice Holmes quickly started disagreeing with how the Court applied his test in specific cases.)[8] The Court became even more protective of speech when Earl Warren assumed the chief justice's chair in 1953. Not only did the Court redefine "clear and present danger" in terms more protective of subversive speech, it also read the First Amendment as providing substantial protection for the press in libel suits brought by public officials, and some protection for the publishers of erotic literature and for civil rights and antiwar demonstrators. More recently, the Court under the more conservative chief justices Warren Burger (1969–86) and William H. Rehnquist (1986–present) generally has continued, to the surprise of many commentators, to expand free speech rights. For example, in *Texas v. Johnson* (1989), the Rehnquist Court struck down a Texas law that had made it a crime to burn the American flag. Justice William J. Brennan Jr. wrote for the Court that the state law in question violated the "bedrock principle" that "the government may not prohibit the expression of an idea simply because society finds the idea itself offensive or disagreeable."[9] Three years later, the Court, this time in an opinion by Justice Antonin Scalia in *R. A. V. v. City of St. Paul* (1992), held that it was also unconstitutional to prohibit cross burning in at least certain circumstances. Justice Scalia reiterated that the government may not regulate speech "based on hostility—or favoritism—towards the underlying message expressed."[10]

[5] *See, e.g.*, David M. Rabban, *Free Speech in Its Forgotten Years* (New York: Cambridge University Press, 1997).

[6] Daniel A. Farber, *The First Amendment* (New York: Foundation Press, 1998), 12.

[7] The landmark case is *Schenk v. United States*, 249 U.S. 47 (1919), in which a unanimous Court, per Justice Holmes, upheld the Conspiracy Act conviction of the general secretary of the Socialist Party for urging young men, in a passionately worded leaflet, to resist the draft during World War I.

[8] *See, e.g.*, *Abrams v. United States*, 250 U.S. 616 (1919) (Holmes, J., dissenting from the Court's upholding of convictions under the Sedition Act of 1918). Justice Louis D. Brandeis voted consistently with Justice Holmes in the "clear and present danger" cases.

[9] 491 U.S. 397, 414 (1989). Johnson had publicly burned an American flag as part of a political protest. He was convicted of flag "desecration," defined as damaging the flag "in a way that the actor knows will seriously offend one or more persons likely to observe . . . his action." The Court reversed Johnson's conviction by a 5–4 vote.

[10] *R. A. V. v. City of St. Paul*, 505 U.S. 377, 386 (1992). This case involved a teenager who had burned a cross on the lawn of a black family's home. He was subsequently convicted of violating a local ordinance that had prohibited the exhibition of symbols known by the

At the heart of much of the Supreme Court's free speech jurisprudence, then, is the notion that the government has no right to suppress unpopular, false, or even hateful ideas. Put directly, prevailing free speech law is, on matters of content, substantially libertarian in orientation—perhaps surprisingly so given the composition of the Court in recent decades. After all, Justice Brennan was an egalitarian liberal on most issues, and Justice Scalia is a Burkean conservative. Nevertheless, for the reasons that I will explain below, the Court is correct to take a libertarian approach to free speech. All that remains to be done to get this area of constitutional law "right" is some tinkering at the margins. First, though, it is necessary to explore the free speech theories of several constitutional theorists who would do more—*much* more—than tinker.

II. Smut Is Not "Only Words": Feminists and Pornography

Feminist legal theorists believe that gender significantly affects the manner in which the legal system functions.[11] One of the most prominent controversies in recent free speech jurisprudence is that surrounding the feminist critique of pornography, especially as articulated by University of Michigan law professor Catharine A. MacKinnon. What MacKinnon finds abhorrent about pornography is the harm it causes by perpetuating male power and gender inequality. In contrast, existing obscenity law concentrates on the moral offensiveness and prurience of pornographic material. (The Supreme Court's landmark 1973 decision *Miller v. California* specifies that obscenity is anything that appeals to the prurient interest, depicts or describes sexual activity in a patently offensive manner, and lacks any serious literary, artistic, political, or scientific value.)[12] MacKinnon maintains that pornography is a form of sex, not speech. She writes in *Only Words* (1993), her most concise discussion of the subject:

> Pornography consumers are not consuming an idea any more than eating a loaf of bread is consuming the ideas on its wrapper or the ideas in its recipe. . . . With pornography, men masturbate to women being exposed, humiliated, violated, degraded, mutilated, dismem-

---

exhibitor to arouse "anger, alarm or resentment in others on the basis of race, color, creed, religion, or gender. . . ." The Court struck down the ordinance by a 9–0 vote.

[11] *See generally* Judith A. Baer, *Our Lives Before the Law: Constructing a Feminist Jurisprudence* (Princeton, NJ: Princeton University Press, 1999).

[12] 413 U.S. 15 (1973). *Miller* involved a mass mailing campaign to advertise a line of sexually explicit books. A brochure sent through the mail presented in highly graphic detail pictures of people engaged in sexual activity. Miller was convicted of violating a California law that had made it illegal to knowingly distribute obscene material. The Court redefined obscenity, vacated the California Superior Court's decision upholding Miller's conviction, and remanded the case for further proceedings in light of the new definition. The Court's previous definition was more permissive. *See: Roth v. United States* and *Alberts v. California*, 354 U.S. 476 (1957) (obscene material has a "dominant theme"of prurience, is "patently offensive" to the prevailing community standards of sexual candor, and is "utterly without redeeming social value").

> bered, bound, gagged, tortured, and killed. In the visual materials, they experience this *being done*. What is real here is not that the materials are pictures, but that they are part of a sex act. The women are in two dimensions, but the men have sex with them in their own three-dimensional bodies, not in their minds alone. Men come doing this. This, too, is a behavior, not a thought or an argument. It is not ideas they are ejaculating over.[13]

MacKinnon had provided additional support for her claim that pornography is sex, not speech, when in one of her earlier writings she confronted head-on the classic free speech response to "speech" the listener does not like: remedy the disfavored "speech" with more "speech," not censorship. She countered that "the assumptions the law of the First Amendment makes about adults—that adults are autonomous, self-defining, freely acting, *equal* individuals—are exactly those qualities that pornography systematically denies and undermines for women. . . . Pornography makes women into objects. Objects do not speak."[14] The consequence of this for First Amendment law is that MacKinnon seeks to ban pornography, at least in the violent, extreme forms that she describes in the excerpt above, on gender discrimination grounds.

Unlike many legal theorists, MacKinnon has done more than simply announce her theory of free speech like Moses from Mount Sinai. For example, she and like-minded feminist Andrea Dworkin drafted a model antipornography, civil rights ordinance that they also helped get adopted in several localities. Importantly, the ordinance has been struck down on First Amendment grounds in seemingly every American jurisdiction that has adopted it. The most detailed judicial opinion about the ordinance is that of libertarian U.S. Court of Appeals Judge Frank Easterbrook in *American Booksellers Association v. Hudnut* (1985), a case involving Indianapolis, Indiana. Easterbrook, a former law professor at the University of Chicago, wrote for a Seventh Circuit panel that the ordinance in question (one limited to violent materials) amounted to unconstitutional viewpoint discrimination. He found particular fault with the ordinance's failure in its definition of pornography to address considerations mandated by the Supreme Court in *Miller v. California*: prurient interest, offensiveness, community standards, the work as a whole, and whether the work has literary, artistic, political, or scientific value. Judge Easterbrook wrote:

> We do not try to balance the arguments for and against an ordinance such as this. This ordinance discriminates on the ground of the content of the speech. Speech treating women in the approved way—in

[13] Catharine A. MacKinnon, *Only Words* (Cambridge, MA: Harvard University Press, 1993), 16–17 (emphasis in original).

[14] Catharine A. MacKinnon, *Feminism Unmodified: Discourses on Life and Law* (Cambridge, MA: Harvard University Press, 1987), 182 (emphasis in original).

> sexual encounters "premised on equality" . . . —is lawful no matter how sexually explicit. Speech treating women in the disapproved way—as submissive in matters sexual or as enjoying humiliation—is unlawful no matter how significant the literary, artistic, or political qualities of the work taken as a whole. The state may not ordain preferred viewpoints in this way. The Constitution forbids the state to declare one perspective right and silence opponents. . . . This is thought control.[15]

MacKinnon responded to the *Hudnut* decision by declaring that Judge Easterbrook, who had discussed her scholarship in his opinion, did not understand the point of the ordinance. She wrote: "[I]f a woman is subjected, why should it matter that the work has other value?"[16] MacKinnon maintains that pornography is the equivalent of hate speech (see Section III below) and that it is not entitled to constitutional protection. She further insists that the Supreme Court of Canada got it right in 1992 when it upheld Canada's criminal obscenity law. That court declared in a unanimous opinion that "if true equality between male and female persons is to be achieved, we cannot ignore the threat to equality resulting from exposure to audiences of certain types of violent and degrading material."[17]

MacKinnon's approach to pornography has been criticized by a number of legal scholars, including Nadine Strossen, a professor at New York Law School and the longtime president of the American Civil Liberties Union (ACLU). Strossen objects, like Judge Easterbrook did before her, on free speech grounds. She writes in *Defending Pornography: Free Speech, Sex, and the Fight for Women's Rights* (2000):

> If MacDworkinism [i.e., the position advanced by MacKinnon and Dworkin] should prevail in the courts, it would jeopardize all of the foregoing free speech precedents and principles. The government could outlaw flag burning and the teaching of Marxist doctrine because they might lead to the erosion of patriotism and our capitalist system; white supremacist and black nationalist speeches could be criminalized because they might lead to racial segregation; peaceful demonstrations for (or against) civil rights, women's rights, gay rights, and, indeed, any other potentially controversial causes could be banned because they might provoke violent counter-demonstrations; advertising for alcohol, tobacco, and innumerable other products

[15] *American Booksellers Association v. Hudnut*, 771 F.2d 323, 325, 328 (7th Cir. 1985), *summarily aff'd*, 475 U.S. 1001 (1986).

[16] Catharine A. MacKinnon, "Pornography, Civil Rights, and Speech," *Harvard Civil Rights-Civil Liberties Review* 20, no. 1 (1985): 21.

[17] *Regina v. Butler*, [1992] 1 S.C.R. 452, 497. The Canadian law provided: "[A]ny publication a dominant character of which is the undue exploitation of sex, or of sex and any one or more of the following subjects, namely, crime, horror, cruelty and violence, shall be deemed to be obscene."

> could be prohibited because it might cause adverse health effects; feminist expression could be stifled because it might threaten "traditional family values" and the attendant domestic order and tranquility; abortion clinic advertising and other pro-choice expression could be suppressed because it might lead to the termination of potential life; indeed, feminist anti-pornography advocacy could itself be suppressed because it could endanger cherished constitutional rights! The list is literally endless.[18]

In short, it is for lawyer/law professor Strossen, as it was for judge/former law professor Easterbrook, contrary to the Free Speech Clause of the First Amendment to suggest that speech of any kind, no matter how reprehensible, should be censored. To conclude otherwise is to forget that there is freedom of speech at all.[19]

III. The "N-Word" Hurts: Critical Race Theorists and Hate Speech

Critical race theorists—scholars of color such as law professors Richard Delgado, Charles R. Lawrence III, and Mari J. Matsuda, who seek to re-energize the fight for racial justice in the United States—advance arguments similar to those of MacKinnon. Indeed, they frequently cite her in their work. They also frequently disagree with the more cautious strategy of the traditional civil rights community (e.g., the NAACP). Critical race theorists are characterized most strongly by their belief that race consciousness is a necessary element in any analysis that seeks to explain how legal and cultural institutions operate in the United States.[20] With respect specifically to free speech,[21] critical race theorists wish to ban so-called racist hate speech (use of the "n-word," for example) on the grounds that (1) it has a direct psychic impact on the members of minority groups at whom it is directed; (2) it reinforces racist ideas in the minds of the majority, which further entrenches racism and leads to discriminatory acts; and (3) it violates the ban against racial discrimination embodied in the Thirteenth and Fourteenth Amendments and the Civil Rights Act of 1964.[22]

[18] Nadine Strossen, *Defending Pornography: Free Speech, Sex, and the Fight for Women's Rights*, new ed. (New York: New York University Press, 2000), 39–40.

[19] *But see* Scott Douglas Gerber, *The Law Clerk: A Novel* (currently under publication review) (suggesting that the impact of pornography on the performers has been underappreciated by existing free speech law).

[20] *See, e.g.*, Kimberlé Crenshaw et al., *Critical Race Theory: The Key Writings That Formed the Movement* (New York: New Press, 1995).

[21] For an examination of the critical race position on desegregation, voting rights, and affirmative action, *see* Scott Douglas Gerber, *First Principles: The Jurisprudence of Clarence Thomas*, exp. ed. (New York: New York University Press, 2002), chap. 3.

[22] The most convenient collection of writings on free speech by critical race theorists is Mari J. Matsuda et al., *Words That Wound: Critical Race Theory, Assaultive Speech, and the First Amendment* (Boulder, CO: Westview Press, 1993) (reprinting the groundbreaking law review articles of Richard Delgado, Charles R. Lawrence III, and Mari J. Matsuda).

Delgado, Lawrence, and Matsuda first try to work within the parameters of existing free speech law in their efforts to ban hate speech. For example, they insist that the Supreme Court's 1942 *Chaplinsky v. New Hampshire* decision, which held that "fighting words" are not entitled to First Amendment protection, can be invoked to outlaw racist speech. According to the Court in this case, there were certain types of words that "by their very utterance inflict injury or tend to incite an immediate breach of the peace." For the Court, these words included calling a city marshal a "God damned racketeer" and "a damned Fascist."[23] For Delgado, Lawrence, and Matsuda, "fighting words" include hateful comments directed at minorities. Such comments are, in Delgado's evocative phrase, "words that wound"[24]—words with profound *physical* consequences. Lawrence and Matsuda agree. In a line that could have been written by MacKinnon herself, Lawrence declares: "The racial invective is experienced as a blow, not a proffered idea."[25] Matsuda adds: "Victims of vicious hate propaganda experience physiological symptoms and emotional distress ranging from fear in the gut to rapid pulse rate and difficulty in breathing, nightmares, post-traumatic stress disorder, hypertension, psychosis, and suicide."[26]

Lawrence and Matsuda also appeal to the law of defamation[27] in their efforts to ban hate speech. (Delgado disagrees on technical grounds.) Just as calling an honest person a crook can slander (if spoken) or libel (if written) the person, so, too, the argument goes, can hate speech defame minorities. Matsuda, again sounding very much like MacKinnon, makes the point particularly well:

> When the legal mind understands that reputational interests . . . must be balanced against [F]irst [A]mendment interests, it recognizes the concrete reality of what happens to people who are defamed. Their lives are changed. Their standing in the community, their opportu-

[23] 315 U.S. 568, 569 (1942). *Chaplinsky* involved a state statute that had made it a crime for a person to address "any offensive, derisive or annoying word to any other person" in a public place. The Supreme Court, in a unanimous decision, upheld the defendant's conviction.

[24] Matsuda et al., *Words That Wound,* 89.

[25] Ibid., 68.

[26] Ibid., 24.

[27] I was going to write the "existing" law of defamation, but most legal scholars believe that the Supreme Court's group defamation decision *Beauharnais v. Illinois,* 343 U.S. 250 (1952) (unprotected libelous statements include defamations of groups as well as those of individuals), was overruled by *New York Times v. Sullivan,* 376 U.S. 254 (1964) (the free speech guarantee requires "a federal rule that prohibits a public official from recovering damages for a defamatory falsehood relating to his official conduct unless he proves that the statement was made with 'actual malice'"). Lawrence disagrees. He also insists that *Brown v. Board of Education,* 347 U.S. 483 (1954)—the Warren Court's landmark desegregation decision—is best interpreted as a group defamation case. Matsuda et al., *Words That Wound,* 75. Many legal scholars also question whether *Chaplinsky* remains good law. *See, e.g.,* John Hart Ely, *Democracy and Distrust: A Theory of Judicial Review* (Cambridge, MA: Harvard University Press, 1980), 114 (suggesting that subsequent Supreme Court decisions have limited the "fighting words" doctrine to, at most, "a quite unambiguous invitation to brawl").

> nities, their self-worth, their free enjoyment of life are limited. Their political capital—their ability to speak and be heard—is diminished. To see this, and yet to fail to see that the very same things happen to victims of racist speech, is selective vision.[28]

Critical race theorists do not limit their efforts to the application of First Amendment precedents. They also maintain that existing free speech law should be fundamentally rethought. To make the point more directly, they insist that the central tenet of the Supreme Court's free speech jurisprudence—content neutrality—should be abandoned. To reiterate, the Court long has held that it is unconstitutional for the government to prohibit speech because of its subject matter (with a few exceptions, such as obscenity) or because the "powers that be" do not like the point of view being expressed by the speaker. Importantly, it was the desire to jettison the existing law's commitment to content neutrality that was behind many of the anti-hate speech codes that popped up on college and university campuses during the past decade or so. Indeed, criticism of the critical race theorists' approach to hate speech is best addressed through a brief examination of the campus speech codes.

The University of Michigan instituted in 1988 one of the first and broadest of the campus anti-hate speech codes. The code prohibited behavior that "stigmatizes or victimizes an individual on the basis of race" (or other status) and that also involves a threat to, or foreseeably interferes with, an individual's academic pursuits. An interpretative guide that accompanied the code listed examples of violations of the policy, including the distribution in a residence hall of flyers containing racist threats or the transmission of racist computer messages.

The code was struck down on free speech grounds by a federal district court in Michigan. Judge Avern Cohn, who decided the case, opened his opinion by stating, "It is an unfortunate fact of our constitutional system that the ideals of freedom and equality are often in conflict." However, he noted that as a matter of constitutional law the case was an easy one for him to decide. Judge Cohn wrote:

> What the University could not do ... was establish an anti-discrimination policy which had the effect of prohibiting certain speech because it disagreed with ideas or messages sought to be conveyed.... Nor could the University proscribe speech simply because it was found to be offensive, even gravely so, by large numbers of people.[29]

[28] Matsuda et al., *Words That Wound*, 47.

[29] *Doe v. University of Michigan*, 721 F. Supp. 852, 853, 862, 863 (E.D. Mich., 1989). The Supreme Court's subsequent decision in *R. A. V. v. City of St. Paul* (1992) striking down a local ordinance against cross burning provides additional support for the district court's decision in the University of Michigan case. *See generally* Robert M. O'Neil, *Free Speech in the College Community* (Bloomington: Indiana University Press, 1999).

The federal court in the University of Michigan anti-hate speech case, like the federal court in the Indianapolis antipornography case, plainly took a libertarian approach to the free speech question before it.[30] So, too, does most of the academic commentary on the subject. For example, Harvard University's Laurence H. Tribe, almost certainly the United States' most celebrated law professor, criticizes those who advocate the proscription of racist speech for essentially wanting to have their cake and eat it too. According to Tribe, that is not how the First Amendment works. He writes in his classic treatise, *American Constitutional Law*: "If the Constitution forces government to allow people to march, speak, and write in favor of peace, brotherhood, and justice, then it must also require government to allow them to advocate hatred, racism, and even genocide."[31]

IV. Cool Kids Smoke Camels: Libertarians and Commercial Speech

The far Left is not alone in wishing to change at least some aspects of existing free speech law. Libertarian scholars—who maintain that each individual has the right and responsibility to make decisions that are important to his or her life[32]—disagree with the Supreme Court's practice of protecting so-called commercial speech (for example, an advertisement promoting the sale of goods or services) less vigorously than other types of speech, most notably "political" speech (for example, an election campaign stump speech). Alex Kozinski, a prominent libertarian U.S. Court of Appeals judge, sometimes jokes: "Nobody likes commercial speech. Liberals don't like it because it's commercial. Conservatives don't like it because it's speech."[33]

[30] Judge Cohn included an addendum to his opinion that referred to one of Matsuda's early articles on hate speech. That article was not brought to the court's attention until "after its Opinion was docketed.... An earlier awareness of Professor Matsuda's paper certainly would have sharpened the Court's view of the issues." *Doe v. University of Michigan*, 721 F. Supp. at 869.

[31] Laurence H. Tribe, *American Constitutional Law*, 2d ed. (Mineola, NY: Foundation Press, 1988), 838 n.17. Harvard Law School, "whose illustrious alumni have helped define the nation's free-speech rights," is the most prominent of the academic institutions recently said to be considering adopting an anti-hate speech code. Harvey Silverglate, a Harvard Law graduate and civil liberties litigator, was quoted as saying, "What I . . . find amazing is that it [i.e., an anti-hate speech code] should be considered at a law school, any law school, because one thing that law schools do is study the constitution, and these codes are clearly in violation of the First Amendment." As quoted in Jennifer Peter, "Harvard Law Considering Speech Code," *Tallahassee Democrat*, November 22, 2002, 5.

[32] *See, e.g.*, David Boaz, *Libertarianism: A Primer* (New York: Free Press, 1997), 291. I discuss the differences between "conservative" libertarianism and "civil" libertarianism in Section VII of this essay. *See generally* Mark A. Graber, *Transforming Free Speech: The Ambiguous Legacy of Civil Libertarianism* (Berkeley: University of California Press, 1991).

[33] I am grateful to Thomas W. Hazlett for this anecdote. *See generally* Alex Kozinski and Stuart Banner, "Who's Afraid of Commercial Speech?" *Virginia Law Review* 76, no. 4 (1990): 652. A former law clerk to Judge Kozinski, Banner is now a law professor at the University of California at Los Angeles.

Innumerable constitutional theorists have advanced a host of arguments over the years to try to explain why commercial speech deserves less protection than other types of speech (for example, it is not about literature, art, politics, or science). However, no one has convincingly explained why the *Supreme Court* came to view commercial speech as deserving less protection than other speech—and in 1942 (see below), *no* protection at all. In fact, one of the best known articles on the subject, Judge Kozinski's "The Anti-History and Pre-History of Commercial Speech," suggests that it just sort of happened.[34]

Doctrinally, *Valentine v. Chrestensen* (1942) was the watershed. In this case, a businessman claimed that a city ordinance that had made it illegal to distribute commercial and business ads in the streets violated his right to freedom of speech. In a two-and-a-half page opinion for a unanimous Court that amounted to little more than an assertion, Justice Owen J. Roberts disagreed. He wrote:

> This court has unequivocally held that streets are proper places for the exercise of the freedom of communicating information and disseminating opinion and that, though the states and municipalities may appropriately regulate the privilege in the public interest, they may not unduly burden or proscribe its employment in these public thoroughfares. We are equally clear that the Constitution imposes no such restraint on government as respects purely commercial advertising.[35]

Although the Court now affords *some* protection to commercial speech—the road to how the Court reached its current destination is a bumpy one littered with the justices' efforts both to articulate and to apply a series of virtually indecipherable multipart tests[36]—it suffices to say that commercial speech still receives *less* protection than most other types of speech and that libertarians such as Judge Kozinski are highly critical of this state of the law. In his first article on the subject, his influential 1990 *Virginia Law Review* piece with Stuart Banner, Judge Kozinski declared that the commercial/noncommercial speech distinction is meaningless. He pointed

[34] Alex Kozinski and Stuart Banner, "The Anti-History and Pre-History of Commercial Speech," *Texas Law Review* 71, no. 4 (1993): 747. *But see* C. Edwin Baker, "Commercial Speech: A Problem in the Theory of Freedom," *Iowa Law Review* 62, no. 1 (1976): 3 ("in our present historical setting, commercial speech is not a manifestation of individual freedom of choice"); and Thomas H. Jackson and John C. Jeffries Jr., "Commercial Speech: Economic Due Process and the First Amendment," *Virginia Law Review* 65, no. 1 (1979): 2 ("At bottom, the doctrine of commercial speech rests on a clean distinction between the market for ideas and the market for goods and services. In the realm of ideas, the [F]irst [A]mendment erects stringent safeguards against governmental restraint. In the economic sphere, by contrast, the majoritarian political process controls. Under the doctrine of commercial speech, ordinary business advertising is part and parcel of the economic marketplace and therefore is excluded from the protections of the [F]irst [A]mendment.").

[35] *Valentine v. Christensen*, 316 U.S. 52, 54 (1942).

[36] For more on this subject, *see* Gerber, *First Principles*, 154–61.

out that the text of the First Amendment draws no distinction between commercial speech and noncommercial speech, that commercial speech is no more or less objective than noncommercial speech, as well as no more or less durable, and that—the Court's oft-stated conclusion to the contrary notwithstanding—commercial speech does more than simply propose a commercial transaction. (For example, it often projects a lifestyle: drink Diet Pepsi [Budweiser, or whatever] and get the girl [or guy].)[37] Judge Kozinski also does not believe that, as proponents of the distinction maintain, affording the same level of protection to commercial speech as to noncommercial speech will result in the dilution of the protection afforded to noncommercial speech. He notes, by analogy, that heightening the level of protection afforded to inaccurate commentary about public officials, as was done in *New York Times v. Sullivan* (1964), did not result in an overabundance of libel.[38] In fact, he insists that greater protection of commercial speech would benefit communication, capitalism, and the free market.[39]

Judge Kozinski's call for the elimination of the distinction in the level of protection afforded to commercial and noncommercial speech has been cited in well over a hundred law review articles. Not surprisingly, some scholars agree with his position, and some do not. For example, the *Harvard Journal of Law and Public Policy*, arguably the nation's most libertarian law review, published a "recent development" commentary on the Supreme Court's 1997 commercial speech case *Glickman v. Wileman Brothers & Elliot, Inc.*, endorsing Judge Kozinski's position.[40] However, Ronald K. L. Collins and David M. Skover, two of the nation's most innovative commentators on the First Amendment,[41] are critical of it. They also come close to suggesting that commercial speech deserves *no* First Amendment protection at all (think *Valentine v. Chrestensen*). They write: "If Kozinski ... must divide the universe of First Amendment thinking, why must it be restricted to history-based or theory-based approaches alone? Why can't the '*real-life* First Amendment' ([his] words, our emphasis) be understood from the vantage point of the real-life experience of commercial discourse [which is ruining the country]?"[42]

[37] Kozinski and Banner, "Who's Afraid of Commercial Speech?" 628, 631, 634–38, 639.

[38] Ibid., 648, 651–52.

[39] Ibid., 652–53.

[40] Aaron A. Goach, "Recent Development: The Supreme Court of the United States, 1996 Term: Free Speech and Freer Speech: *Glickman v. Wileman Brothers & Elliot, Inc.*, 117 S. Ct. 2130 (1997)," *Harvard Journal of Law and Public Policy* 21, no. 2 (1998): 623. *Glickman* upheld compelled contributions to generic advertising expenses of fruit.

[41] *See, e.g.*, Ronald K. L. Collins and David M. Skover, *The Death of Discourse* (Boulder, CO: Westview Press, 1996); and Ronald K. L. Collins and David M. Skover, *The Trials of Lenny Bruce: The Fall and Rise of an American Icon* (Naperville, IL: Sourcebooks, 2002).

[42] Ronald K. L. Collins and David M. Skover, "The Psychology of First Amendment Scholarship: A Reply," *Texas Law Review* 71, no. 4 (1993): 829. In fairness to Collins and Skover, their work on commercial speech is less concerned with providing a particular "answer" to the commercial speech debate than it is with exploring the various consequences of the answers suggested by others, including Judge Kozinski. (The phrase "history-

Judge Kozinski's position also has been cited in more than a dozen cases. The most important of the cases is *44 Liquormart, Inc. v. State of Rhode Island* (1996).[43] This case involved two 1956 Rhode Island statutes that had forbidden sellers and the media from advertising the price of alcoholic beverages. The avowed purpose of the legislation was to promote temperance by increasing the price of alcohol. The statutes were upheld by the Rhode Island state courts in 1985, but subsequently invalidated on free speech grounds by the U.S. District Court for the District of Rhode Island. The U.S. Court of Appeals for the First Circuit reversed the District Court. However, the Supreme Court reinstated the District Court's ruling by a 9–0 vote. As is so often true in major cases decided during the modern era, the justices were divided in their reasoning—especially as to what test to apply (making *44 Liquormart* yet another bump in the Court's doctrinal road).[44] Chief Justice Rehnquist and Justices Sandra Day O'Connor, David H. Souter, and Stephen G. Breyer maintained that *Central Hudson Gas & Electric Corporation v. Public Service Commission of New York* (1980)[45] provided the relevant test. Justice Scalia agreed—for the moment (i.e., until counsel in a future case could persuade him that there is a better test to apply). Justices John Paul Stevens, Anthony M. Kennedy, and Ruth Bader Ginsburg argued that a blanket ban on a particular type of commercial speech must be viewed with "special care" and cannot be approved unless the speech is misleading or related to an illegal activity. Justice Clarence Thomas, citing Judge Kozinski's 1990 article, called for the abandonment of the distinction between commercial and noncommercial speech, at least when the objective of the government regulation in question is to manipulate consumer preferences about lawful products. Justice Thomas wrote: "Nor do I believe that the only explanations that the Court has ever advanced for treating 'commercial' speech differently from other speech can justify restricting 'commercial' speech in order to keep information from legal purchasers so as to thwart what would otherwise be their choices in the marketplace."[46]

Justice Thomas, like Judge Kozinski before him, is plainly a libertarian on at least some aspects of free speech law—including on the need to afford commercial speech the same level of protection as noncommercial

based or theory-based" in the quotation from Collins and Skover refers to Judge Kozinski's dualist approach to the origins of the modern commercial speech doctrine.)

[43] *44 Liquormart, Inc. v. Rhode Island,* 517 U.S. 484 (1996).

[44] *See* Scott D. Gerber and Keeok Park, "The Quixotic Search for Consensus on the U.S. Supreme Court: A Cross-Judicial Empirical Analysis of the Rehnquist Court Justices," *American Political Science Review* 91, no. 2 (1997): 390.

[45] *Central Hudson Gas & Electric Corporation v. Public Service Commission of New York,* 447 U.S. 557 (1980). The *Central Hudson* test consists of the following criteria: (1) the commercial speech must concern a lawful activity and not be misleading, (2) the asserted governmental interest must be substantial, (3) the regulation must directly advance the governmental interest, and (4) the regulation must not be more extensive than is necessary to serve that interest. A perusal of the Court's post-*Central Hudson* decisions reveals that these criteria are not easy to apply.

[46] *44 Liquormart,* 517 U.S. at 522–23 (Thomas, J., concurring in part and concurring in the judgment).

speech. Consequently, Judge Kozinski has one member of the Supreme Court in his corner.[47] For both of these provocative jurists, speech is speech, and free speech law should both value and vigorously protect it as such.

V. William Shakespeare, Yes; Danielle Steel, No: Legal Republicans and Deliberative Democracy

Some constitutional theorists have taken a strong interest in republicanism—the ideology, not the political party affiliation (academics are notoriously leftist in partisan orientation)[48]—in recent decades.[49] Cass R. Sunstein, a law professor at the University of Chicago, is the most prolific of the theorists who have done so. The cornerstones of what Sunstein alternatively terms a "deliberative democracy" and a "republic of reasons" are political deliberation, citizenship, agreement as a regulative ideal, and political equality. The four are interrelated, with political deliberation being the primary virtue and the other three elaborative of it. While it is difficult to summarize Sunstein's often open-ended argument, at bottom he seeks discussion among politically equal and active citizens about what choices should be made in the interest of the common good. And in typically republican fashion, he claims that such discussion will lead to "correct answers."[50]

In contrast to some of the other leading legal republicans who merely state their respective theories without offering suggestions for how their theories can be actualized, Sunstein supplements his theory with reform proposals. It is in these reform proposals where his theory of free speech takes center stage.

Sunstein advances what he claims is a Madisonian reading of the Free Speech Clause—an approach that he insists makes the protection of political speech the dominant purpose of the First Amendment.[51] (Robert H. Bork, arguably the nation's most influential legal conservative, makes a similar argument in his classic article on the subject, "Neutral Principles

[47] *See also*: *Lorillard Tobacco Company v. Reilly*, 533 U.S. 525, 575 (2001) (Thomas, J., concurring in part and concurring in the judgment) (citing Judge Kozinski's article).

[48] *See generally* Robert H. Bork, *Slouching Towards Gomorrah: Modern Liberalism and American Decline* (New York: Regan Books, 1996). *See also* Scott Douglas Gerber, *The Ivory Tower: A Novel* (New Orleans, LA: University Press of the South, 2002); and Scott D. Gerber, "Whose Judges Are They?" *Legal Times*, November 25, 2002, 38.

[49] *See generally* Scott D. Gerber, "The Republican Revival in American Constitutional Theory," *Political Research Quarterly* 47, no. 4 (1994): 985.

[50] Cass R. Sunstein, *The Partial Constitution* (Cambridge, MA: Harvard University Press, 1993), v, 9, 17, 137.

[51] Professor J. M. Balkin of Yale Law School quipped in a review of Sunstein's book *Democracy and the Problem of Free Speech* that "Sunstein's 'Madisonian' theory of the First Amendment is about as Madisonian as Madison, Wisconsin: It is a tribute to a great man and his achievements, but bears only a limited connection to his actual views." J. M. Balkin, "Populism and Progressivism as Constitutional Categories," *Yale Law Journal* 104, no. 7 (1995): 1955.

and Some First Amendment Problems.")[52] Sunstein maintains that the prevailing libertarian approach to free speech law protects too much speech in some areas (for example, pornography and racist speech) and too little speech in other areas (for example, access to government information and to the media during political campaigns). He therefore proposes that racial slurs be banned (but that other hate speech not be), that violent pornography be outlawed (but that erotic speech not be), and that the public be permitted to access government information (but that the government be allowed to decide which speech it will fund). He also supports limits on individual campaign expenditures (but argues for increased access by politicians to the media during political campaigns). He favors controls on advertisers (but maintains that corporations have First Amendment rights), and he calls for a dramatic improvement in the quality of television shows. (Mike Wallace and *60 Minutes* apparently are okay, but Mary Hart and *Entertainment Tonight* are not.)[53]

It is difficult to know quite what to make of Sunstein's proposals. Indeed, Burt Neuborne, a law professor at New York University and the former executive director of the ACLU, concludes in a review of Sunstein's book *Democracy and the Problem of Free Speech* (1993) that "many of Professor Sunstein's distinctions lack a principled basis, other than Cass Sunstein's own view of what should or should not be censored. . . . In the end, his argument comes down to allowing [his] social class to use the government to elevate its speech preferences over everyone else's."[54] In short, Neuborne maintains, Sunstein's book is merely the most prominent example of the impatience the "reformist left" has for certain types of "uncongenial" speech (for example, corporate speech) that previously had not enjoyed the impact on American society that it currently does.[55]

Neuborne appears to disagree with almost everything Sunstein says in his book. For example, he rejects the "prime value" that Sunstein chooses to "run his machine": political equality.[56] Neuborne invokes the work of the late Thomas I. Emerson of Yale Law School to suggest that "respect for individual autonomy is an integral part of any complete conception of the First Amendment."[57] Perhaps most importantly, Neuborne fears that "reformist censors"[58] such as Sunstein likely will rue the day they championed the suppression of *any* type of speech. He concludes his review with the following admonition:

[52] *See* Robert H. Bork, "Neutral Principles and Some First Amendment Problems," *Indiana Law Journal* 47, no. 1 (1971): 1.

[53] Cass R. Sunstein, *Democracy and the Problem of Free Speech* (New York: Free Press, 1993), 192–93, 214–16, 105–7, 114–18, 98–100, 104–5, 85–87, 82–85, 238–39.

[54] Burt Neuborne, "Review: Blues for the Left Hand: A Critique of Cass Sunstein's *Democracy and the Problem of Free Speech*," *University of Chicago Law Review* 62, no. 1 (1995): 423, 436, 440.

[55] Ibid., 425, 430.

[56] Ibid., 441.

[57] Ibid. (citing Thomas I. Emerson, *The System of Freedom of Expression* [New York: Random House, 1970]).

[58] Ibid., 432.

> My hope is that egalitarian reformers will stop trying to make things better by managing speech. It is only a matter of time until the left recharges its intellectual batteries and begins, once again, to produce serious political ideas calculated to change things for the better. When that happens, every inch of free speech protection is going to be needed to shield those ideas from censorship designed to block change. How sad it would be to have those ideas frustrated because impatient intellectuals couldn't wait.[59]

Neuborne would be pleased to know that Sunstein's theory of free speech has been fully embraced by only one judge of record. In *Painter v. Graley* (1994), a tort action by a former municipal chief deputy clerk who claimed he was wrongfully discharged for running for city council, Justice James A. Brogan of the Ohio Supreme Court wrote:

> Professor Cass Sunstein, the Karl Llewellyn Professor of Jurisprudence at the University of Chicago, embraces the notion that the First Amendment difficulties should be resolved with reference to Madisonian principles of free debate, political discourse, and civic participation. . . . I believe this court should embrace the Sunstein view and hold that our Ohio Constitution protects the rights of all citizens to seek political office, whether it be as a part-time village councilman or councilwoman or as a full-time state office holder, and that any restriction on that activity by the state must be justified by the demonstration of a compelling governmental interest.[60]

Unfortunately for legal republicans, Justice Brogan's opinion was a dissent. (It is also not clear from this dissent that Justice Brogan understands Sunstein's often open-ended argument.)

VI. Looking for Law in All the Wrong Places[61]

If the prior pages of this essay have demonstrated anything, they have demonstrated that politics is at the heart of the theories of free speech articulated by a number of the nation's most prominent constitutional theorists. Feminists such as MacKinnon and critical race theorists such as Delgado, Lawrence, and Matsuda are seeking to make the Free Speech Clause more egalitarian than the Supreme Court's existing free speech jurisprudence permits. (MacKinnon focuses on women's rights, while

[59] Ibid., 446.

[60] *Painter v. Graley*, 639 N.E.2d 51, 63 (Ohio 1994) (Brogan, J., dissenting). *See also*: *National Association of Social Workers v. Harwood*, 69 F.3d 622 (1st Cir. 1995) (Lynch, J., dissenting) (citing Sunstein's position that the Free Speech Clause is concerned primarily with political speech).

[61] *See* the classic country song "Looking for Love in All the Wrong Places" written by Wanda Mallette, Patti Ryan, and Bob Morrison.

Delgado, Lawrence, and Matsuda concentrate on the rights of minorities.) Judge Kozinski, as a libertarian, wants the Court to limit the government's power to curtail all forms of freedom, including the freedom to express the virtues or vices of particular commercial transactions. Finally, Sunstein, a legal republican, wishes to ensure that the American people are being exposed to the "right" kind of speech so that the community as a whole will be better off.

After examining these specific free speech theories, the question that quickly came to my mind was: Is it possible to articulate a theory of free speech that is not simply a vehicle for effectuating a given set of preconceived political value choices, whatever those value choices might be (e.g., the empowerment of women; the empowerment of blacks; the expansion of the sphere of individual liberty; making individuals and, hence, the community better)? My hunch, as someone who has written about the relationship of political values to constitutional law at a more generalized level than free speech—that of the Constitution as a whole—was that it is not.[62] However, in an effort to avoid the all too common trap of being overly comfortable with the conclusions of my prior research, I posted the following query to the "ConLawProf" discussion list:[63]

> I'm currently working on a paper ... on free speech. My paper, tentatively titled "The Politics of Free Speech," addresses how particular ... groups [of scholars] have advanced particular approaches to free speech in order to advance their particular political agendas. I anticipate examining the free speech theories of feminists (regarding pornography), critical race theorists (regarding hate speech), libertarians (regarding commercial speech), and [legal republicans] (regarding deliberative democracy). I also will address the criticisms of each of these approaches (I realize there are differences of opinion within each category), whether the courts have been influenced by any of the groups' arguments, and, in conclusion, whether it is possible to advance a non-political theory of free speech. It's this last point with which I'm having trouble. More specifically, I've yet to encounter a purely law-based theory of free speech. Perhaps the Crits are right. If not, I would be grateful for citations to any scholarship that attempts to articulate a purely-law based theory of free speech.[64]

[62] *See* Scott Douglas Gerber, *To Secure These Rights: The Declaration of Independence and Constitutional Interpretation* (New York: New York University Press, 1995).

[63] "ConLawProf" is a moderated Internet forum for law professors and others interested in constitutional law. Subscription and archival information may be found at www1.law.ucla.edu/~volokh/conlaw.htm [accessed June 13, 2003].

[64] E-mail from Scott D. Gerber to ConLawProf discussion list [posted online September 9, 2002].

Gregory C. Sisk, then a law professor at Drake University, replied that the "absolutist approach" of the late Supreme Court Justice Hugo L. Black might fit the bill. "[F]rom a textual and legalistic standpoint, one might argue that the seemingly mandatory and absolute prohibition of 'no law' creates a rather powerful presumption against limiting any expression for any reason, regardless of theory or politics or even (mostly) practical policy arguments."[65] Intriguingly, Sisk's post sparked a brief debate over whether Justice Black's approach was a "theory" at all. Craig N. Oren, a professor at Rutgers School of Law–Camden, insisted that it was not because Black's approach simply collapses into the question, "[S]o what does 'freedom of speech' mean?"[66] Sisk was resolute, though. He maintained:

> While "speech" may not be self-defining in all circumstances, it plainly covers political speech and presumably would cover most other types of expression on any topic. To read this language [of the First Amendment] as meaning that the government is barred from prohibiting, regulating, limiting expression in almost all situations—political speech, artistic expression, books, films, and even pornography—strikes me as theoretically coherent and textually faithful. The burden is then heavily upon anyone claiming exceptions.[67]

Oren, of course, remained committed to his view that the answer cannot be found in Justice Black's absolutism.[68] (Law professors, even more than most people, do not like to admit they might be wrong.)

I agree with Oren. However, before I explain why, I need to explore in more detail than Sisk was able to do in his post what Justice Black's "theory" of free speech was. Justice Black, who was appointed to the Supreme Court from the Senate by President Franklin Delano Roosevelt in 1937 and who served on the high bench until his death in 1971, insisted that the First Amendment declaration that the government[69] shall make "no law" abridging the freedom of speech means just that: the government shall make *no* law abridging the freedom of speech. Justice Black

[65] E-mail from Gregory C. Sisk to ConLawProf discussion list [posted online September 10, 2002].

[66] E-mail from Craig N. Oren to ConLawProf discussion list [posted online September 10, 2002].

[67] E-mail from Sisk to ConLawProf discussion list [posted online September 10, 2002].

[68] E-mail from Oren to ConLawProf discussion list [posted online September 10, 2002].

[69] The First Amendment speaks of "Congress," but Justice Black applied the amendment to the states as well. The purely law-based description of his theory of free speech arguably should fail on this point alone. In other words, although Justice Black's view that the Due Process Clause of the Fourteenth Amendment made the Bill of Rights applicable to the states is a widely shared one, this view is based on something other than a literal reading of the text. *See generally* Tinsley E. Yarbrough, *Mr. Justice Black and His Critics* (Durham, NC: Duke University Press, 1988).

made the point in dramatic fashion in a 1962 public interview with Professor Edmond N. Cahn of New York University School of Law:

> I learned a long time ago that there are affirmative and negative words. The beginning of the First Amendment is that "Congress shall make no law." I understand that it is rather old-fashioned and shows a slight naivete to say that "no law" means no law. It is one of the most amazing things about the ingeniousness of the times that strong arguments are made, which *almost* convince me, that it is very foolish of me to think "no law" means no law. But what it *says* is "Congress shall make no law respecting an establishment of religion," and so on. . . .
>
> Then I move on to the words "abridging the freedom of speech or of the press." It *says* Congress shall make no law doing that. . . . And being a rather backward country fellow, I understand it to mean what the words say. Gesticulations apart, I know of no way in the world to communicate ideas except by words. . . . It says "no law," and that is what I believe it means. . . .
>
> I am for the First Amendment from the first word to the last. I believe it means what it says, and it says to me, "Government shall keep its hands off religion. Government shall not attempt to control the ideas a man has. Government shall not attempt to establish a religion of any kind. Government shall not abridge freedom of the press or speech. It shall let anybody in this country talk.[70]

Justice Black's commitment to free speech absolutism was not limited to public conversations with law professors. He wrote numerous judicial opinions employing the approach, and in those opinions he purported to oppose *any* prior restraint of the press and *any* regulation of speech. For example, with respect to prior restraint of the press, in a concurring opinion in *New York Times v. United States* (1971), the so-called Pentagon Papers case in which the Court held by a 6–3 margin that a court order stopping publication of excerpts from a top-secret Defense Department history of the Vietnam War violated the First Amendment, Justice Black stated that, even when national security might be at stake, "the history and language of the First Amendment support the view that the press must be left to publish news, whatever the source, without censorship, injunctions, or prior restraints."[71] With respect to more general regulations on free speech, Justice Black dissented in a string of cases in which the Court upheld laws that penalized individuals for advocating the over-

[70] Edmond N. Cahn, "Justice Black and First Amendment 'Absolutes': A Public Interview," *New York University Law Review* 37, no. 4 (1962): 553–54, 563 (emphasis in original).

[71] *New York Times v. United States,* 403 U.S. 713, 717 (1971) (Black, J., concurring).

throw of the government.[72] In the most famous of these cases, *Dennis v. United States* (1951), wherein the Court affirmed the petitioner's conviction of conspiracy to organize a Communist party, Justice Black wrote:

> The opinions for affirmance [of the conviction] indicate that the chief reason for jettisoning the ["clear and present danger"] rule is the expressed fear that advocacy of Communist doctrine endangers the safety of the Republic. Undoubtedly, a governmental policy of unfettered communication of ideas does entail dangers. To the Founders of this Nation, however, the benefits derived from free expression were worth the risk. They embodied this philosophy in the First Amendment's command that "Congress shall make no law . . . abridging the freedom of speech, or of the press. . . ." I have always believed that the First Amendment is the keystone of our Government, that the freedoms it guarantees provide the best insurance against the destruction of all freedom.[73]

It is difficult not to be moved by Justice Black's evocative words. However, only one other member of the Supreme Court consistently shared his absolutist interpretation of the First Amendment: Justice William O. Douglas. Importantly, Justices Black and Douglas parted company on the so-called symbolic speech cases—a state of affairs that calls into serious question whether the absolutist approach to free speech is a purely law-based approach after all. Two cases decided a year apart illustrate the point: *Street v. New York* (1969)[74] and *Tinker v. Des Moines Independent Community School District* (1968).[75]

Street found the Court, in a 5–4 vote, reversing the conviction of appellant Sidney Street for violating a New York law that had made it a crime publicly to mutilate or "publicly [to] defy . . . or cast contempt upon [any American flag] either by words or act." Street, outraged that civil rights activist James Meredith had been shot and wounded, took an American flag he owned to a street corner near his Brooklyn home and ignited it. He shouted: "We don't need no damn flag. . . . If they let this happen to Meredith, we don't need an American flag."

[72] *See, e.g., Konigsberg v. State Bar of California*, 366 U.S. 36, 77–80 (1961) (Black, J., dissenting from the Court's holding that the California Supreme Court's refusal to admit the petitioner to the state bar because of his refusal to answer questions pertaining to his membership in the Communist Party did not violate the Free Speech Clause); *Barenblatt v. United States*, 360 U.S. 109, 145–46 (1959) (Black, J., dissenting from the Court's upholding of the conviction of an individual who refused to tell the House Un-American Activities Committee whether he was or ever had been a Communist); and *Dennis v. United States*, 341 U.S. 494, 579–80 (1951) (Black, J., dissenting from the Court's affirmation of the petitioner's conviction of conspiracy to organize a Communist party).

[73] *Dennis*, 341 U.S. at 580 (Black, J., dissenting).

[74] *Street v. New York*, 394 U.S. 576 (1969).

[75] *Tinker v. Des Moines Independent Community School District*, 393 U.S. 503 (1968).

Justice John Marshall Harlan II wrote for the Court that the New York law violated Street's right to freedom of speech because the record indicated that Street's conviction was either based solely upon his words or upon his words and his conduct. Justice Harlan explained:

> We have no doubt that the constitutionally guaranteed "freedom to be intellectually . . . diverse or even contrary," and the "right to differ as to things that touch the heart of the existing order," encompass the freedom to express publicly one's opinions about our flag, including those opinions which are defiant or contemptuous.[76]

Justice Douglas signed on to Justice Harlan's opinion for the Court. Justice Black, however, filed a dissenting opinion.[77] He stated: "If I could agree with the Court's interpretation of the record as to the possibility of the conviction's resting on [Street's] spoken words, I would firmly and automatically agree that the law is unconstitutional."[78] For him, though, Street's conviction was for "the burning of the flag and not the making of any statements about it."[79]

Tinker found the Court striking down, in a 7–2 vote, a public school regulation banning the wearing of armbands, as applied to the wearing of black armbands in protest of the Vietnam War. The Court, speaking through Justice Abe Fortas, treated this symbolic conduct as "pure speech" and concluded that the regulation discriminated on the basis of the speakers' viewpoint. The Court recognized that students' speech is not immune from regulation when it "materially and substantially interfere[s] with the requirements of appropriate discipline in the operation of the school," but concluded that such was not the case with the speech at issue because the three students in question had been quiet and passive when wearing the armbands. In Justice Fortas's memorable phrase, students do not leave their free speech rights "at the schoolhouse gate."[80]

Justice Douglas joined Justice Fortas's opinion for the Court. Justice Black filed another impassioned dissent. Importantly, he assumed for the sake of argument that the wearing of the armbands by the students in protest of the war *was* speech. This *type* of speech could be banned, however. He wrote: "[I]f the time has come when pupils of state-supported schools, kindergartens, grammar schools, or high schools, can defy and flout orders of school officials to keep their minds on their own school-

[76] *Street*, 394 U.S. at 593 (quoting *West Virginia State Board of Education v. Barnette*, 319 U.S. 624 [1943]).

[77] There were four separate dissents in the case: those of Justice Black, Chief Justice Earl Warren, Justice Byron R. White, and Justice Abe Fortas.

[78] *Street*, 394 U.S. at 609 (Black, J., dissenting).

[79] *Id.*

[80] *Tinker*, 393 U.S. at 505, 509, 506.

work, it is the beginning of a new revolutionary era of permissiveness in this country fostered by the judiciary."[81]

To borrow a line from the late singer Marvin Gaye, "What's going on?"[82] Why was Justice Black, the consummate absolutist, willing to regulate conduct that was clearly accompanied by speech (in the flag burning case) and conduct that he was willing to assume was speech (in the armband case)? The most plausible explanation seems to be that the speech in question ran contrary to certain values to which he was strongly committed: patriotism (in the flag burning case) and discipline in the schools (in the armband case). With respect to Justice Black's patriotism, the opinions he wrote on the Court during his three-plus decades of service and the books, articles, and speeches he authored as a private citizen are replete with references to his love of country. For example, he concluded his most well-known book, *A Constitutional Faith* (1968), as follows:

> My experiences with and for our government have filled my heart with gratitude and devotion to the Constitution which made my public life possible. . . . I have thoroughly enjoyed my small part in trying to preserve our Constitution with the earnest desire that it may meet the fondest hope of its creators, which was to keep this nation strong and great through countless ages.[83]

Justice Black's patriotism was not lost on his biographers. Indeed, Roger K. Newman describes the public outpouring of emotion at Justice Black's funeral as tears shed for a patriot:

> Part of the reason he was being so deeply mourned was his open and passionate love affair with the Constitution and with America. He cherished this "sweet land of liberty," silently bearing the mountains of calumny that came his way. He proudly called himself a patriot. For he had confidence in the good sense of a free people, the Blue and the Gray going forward together, under the Stars and Stripes, the children of the Flag advancing to the march of inevitable progress while retaining timeless human decencies.[84]

Apparently, for Justice Black, as for the members of the Court who dissented from *Texas v. Johnson* twenty years later, the flag was "different,"[85]

[81] *Id.* at 515, 518 (Black, J., dissenting). Justice John Marshall Harlan II also dissented. He viewed the wearing of the armbands as proscribable conduct. *Id.* at 526 (Harlan, J., dissenting).

[82] Marvin Gaye, "What's Going On" (Detroit, MI: Motown Records, 1971).

[83] Hugo L. Black, *A Constitutional Faith* (New York: Knopf, 1968), 65–66.

[84] Roger K. Newman, *Hugo Black: A Biography*, 2d ed. (New York: Fordham University Press, 1997), xv–xvi.

[85] *Texas v. Johnson*, 491 U.S. at 431 (Rehnquist, C.J., dissenting).

and, therefore, it was entitled to all the protection the law could afford—even if a consistent absolutist would recognize that an individual had a First Amendment right to burn it while *saying why* he was burning it.

Turning to the armband case—the case in which Justice Black was willing to assume that the wearing of a black armband in public school in protest of the Vietnam War was speech—Justice Black's belief in the importance of education, coupled with his obvious subscription to the adage that children should be "seen and not heard" in school, was apparently so strong that it trumped his absolutist reading of the First Amendment. His memoirs are replete with so many passages illuminating how highly he valued education[86] that it seems fair to conclude that it was *where* the speech occurred in *Tinker* that trumped his absolutist approach to the First Amendment in that case. Indeed, it is not unreasonable to suggest that Justice Black, himself an opponent of the Vietnam War, would have afforded *absolute* protection to the students in question had they been wearing the armbands outside of school—like, say, on the street corner near Sidney Street's Brooklyn home.

VII. Conclusion: The Supreme Court Has Had It (Almost) Right (Almost) All Along

Clearly, not even Justice Black subscribed to a purely law-based approach to free speech, which confirms my initial hunch that there is apparently no such thing.[87] The question that remains, then, is this: If political value judgments inevitably influence a person's approach to free speech, in light of which political theory should the First Amendment be interpreted? To make the point another way, one does not need to accept the argument advanced by the most enthusiastic proponents of the application of literary analysis to legal texts (Crits, primarily)—that meaning cannot be extracted from legal texts, but only can be put into them, in other words, that the Constitution means nothing and means anything—to appreciate the more modest claim that "texts can only be interpreted in some 'context.'"[88] And that context, I believe, should be classical liberal political theory.

[86] *See, e.g.*, Black, *A Constitutional Faith*, 65; and Hugo L. Black and Elizabeth Black, *Mr. Justice and Mrs. Black: The Memoirs of Hugo L. Black and Elizabeth Black* (New York: Random House, 1986), 8–10.

[87] Professor Michael A. Froomkin of the University of Miami School of Law mentions the work of Jurgen Habermas as a possibility. E-mail from Michael A. Froomkin to Scott D. Gerber, September 9, 2002. I disagree. As Professor Larry A. Alexander of the University of San Diego School of Law has demonstrated, Habermas's procedural conditions for his "ideal speech situation" are based on preexisting partisan substantive positions. Larry A. Alexander, "Trouble on Track Two: Incidental Regulations of Speech and Free Speech Theory," *Hastings Law Journal* 44, no. 4 (1993): 941–43.

[88] Sanford Levinson and Steven Mailloux, preface to *Interpreting Law and Literature: A Hermeneutic Reader*, ed. Sanford Levinson and Steven Mailloux (Evanston, IL: Northwestern University Press, 1988), xii.

Revealingly, critics of the feminist, critical race, and legal republican theories of free speech detailed above complain that those theories are inconsistent with a libertarian approach to the First Amendment. (I will explain below how a particular strand of libertarianism is synonymous with classical liberalism.) For example, Strossen and Judge Easterbrook object on libertarian grounds to MacKinnon's efforts to ban pornography, and Tribe and the federal district judge who struck down the University of Michigan's anti-hate speech code disapprove on libertarian grounds of critical race theorists' attempts to prohibit racist speech. Similarly, Neuborne is making a libertarian argument when he opposes Sunstein's legal republican efforts to establish a deliberative democracy in the United States. Whereas critics of the feminist, critical race, and legal republican theories invoke libertarian principles to refute these approaches to the First Amendment, Judge Kozinski relies on such principles to advance his claim that commercial speech deserves as much protection as noncommercial speech.

Perhaps most important of all, the Supreme Court itself, as Section I suggested, has taken a largely libertarian approach to the subject over the years (at least in theory, although not always in practice, as Justice Holmes's dissents from his own "clear and present danger" test make clear). My prior research on the general theory of American constitutional law is consistent with the idea that a libertarian approach to the First Amendment is the proper approach to take. In *To Secure These Rights: The Declaration of Independence and Constitutional Interpretation* (1995), I argued that the Constitution should be interpreted in light of the classical liberal principles of the Declaration of Independence.[89] My thesis was that the Declaration articulates the philosophical *ends* of the American regime and that the Constitution embodies the *means* to effectuate those ends. "To secure these rights," the Declaration proclaims, "governments are instituted among men." In my book, I did not spend much time on the Free Speech Clause, but I can think of no convincing reason why the same classical liberal approach should not be taken to interpreting this clause as well.

With respect to deciding specific questions of free speech law, a free speech theory that takes the Declaration of Independence seriously does *not* necessarily mean that free speech cases should be decided the way the Supreme Court has decided them over the years. Political scientist Mark A. Graber points out in his book *Transforming Free Speech: The Ambiguous Legacy of Civil Libertarianism* (1991)[90] that there has been more than one conception of libertarianism advanced throughout the course of American history. "Conservative libertarianism," which Graber maintains dominated the intellectual landscape between the Civil War and World War I,

[89] Gerber, *To Secure These Rights*.
[90] Graber, *Transforming Free Speech*.

stressed individual liberty and defended the right to speak freely on that basis. The more modern conception of libertarianism, which Graber terms "civil libertarianism" and which he associates most closely with the late Harvard Law School Professor Zechariah Chafee Jr. (1885–1957),[91] focuses on the benefits to society that free speech provides, particularly with regard to promoting the discovery of truth and to protecting the integrity of the democratic process. The civil libertarian approach is plainly less concerned with the individual liberty aspects of free speech than is the conservative libertarian approach, emphasizing as the civil libertarian model does the *societal* advantages that flow from protecting speech. Conservative libertarians, in contrast, focus on the benefits that free speech affords to the *individual*.

The conservative libertarian approach is more consistent with the classical liberal conception of the American regime in general and the U.S. Constitution in particular that I explored in *To Secure These Rights*, and it is the approach I endorse for interpreting the First Amendment. Both perspectives stress a commitment to individual freedom from government regulation and both do so on the basis of individual autonomy. Importantly, however, it is the civil libertarian approach that has most influenced the Court.[92] A conservative libertarian approach to the First Amendment would be even more protective of free speech than an already protective civil libertarian approach has been. In fact, it was the Court's *adoption* of the civil libertarian model following World War I that led it down the path that eventually would afford less protection to commercial speech than to other kinds of speech (especially political speech). After all, the heart of Chafee's theory of free speech was his belief that the Court should pay particular attention to policing legislation that threatens expression rights rather than any other kind of rights. This mindset led to the deferential stance toward economic legislation that currently exists. And since the "commercial" component of "commercial speech" is the one on which the Court has focused, commercial speech has been regarded as just another type of economic activity. It is more than that, though. Justice Thomas got it right when he observed in his concurring opinion in *44 Liquormart* that the Founders' "political philosophy equated liberty and property."[93] To mention but two leading statements of this view, James Madison wrote in *Federalist No. 10* that "the first object of government" is "the protection of different and unequal faculties of acquiring property,"[94] and John Adams maintained in *Discourses on*

[91] *See, e.g.*, Zechariah Chafee Jr., *Freedom of Speech* (New York: Harcourt, Brace, and Howe, 1920).

[92] *See* David M. Rabban, "The Emergence of Modern First Amendment Doctrine," *University of Chicago Law Review* 50, no. 4 (1983): 1215–16.

[93] *44 Liquormart*, 517 U.S. at 522 (Thomas, J., concurring in part and concurring in the judgment).

[94] *Federalist No. 10* (J. Madison), in Clinton Rossiter, ed., *The Federalist Papers* (New York: New American Library, 1961), 77–84, 78.

Davila that "property must be secured, or liberty cannot exist."[95] In short, the subordination of commercial speech to noncommercial speech in the hierarchy of judicial protection is a political decision by Supreme Court justices that should be abandoned. Other than that, the Court has gotten it about right. As anyone who has spent time reading legal scholarship can attest, that is an unusual statement for a law professor to make.

Law, Ohio Northern University

[95] In *The Works of John Adams*, ed. Charles Francis Adams, vol. 6 (Boston, MA: C. C. Little and J. Brown, 1850–56), 280.

THE ACADEMIC BETRAYAL OF FREE SPEECH*

By Daniel Jacobson

I. Skepticism about Free Speech

" 'Free speech' is just the name we give to verbal behavior that serves the substantive agendas we wish to advance"—or so literary theorist and professor of law Stanley Fish has claimed.[1] This cynical dictum is one of several skeptical challenges to freedom of speech that have been extremely influential in the American academy. I will follow the skeptics' lead by distinguishing between two broad styles of critique: the progressive and the postmodern. Fish's dictum, however, like many of the bluntest charges, belongs to neither class exclusively. As an initial characterization of the distinction between these critiques, progressive skepticism claims that freedom of speech is a bad thing, while postmodernist skepticism claims it to be conceptually impossible. Both forms of skepticism hold the classical liberal endorsement of free speech and condemnation of censorship to be both naive and reactionary. Skepticism about free speech flourishes at universities in the United States and is especially well represented among professors at the country's most prestigious law schools. As legal scholar Robert Post approvingly observes: "Liberated from traditional inhibitions against official suppression of speech, the left has mobilized to pursue a rich variety of political agendas."[2]

It is odd, but not inexplicable, that Post would refer to a "rich variety" of political agendas while simultaneously describing them all as leftist. The explanation of this remark, I will ultimately suggest, can be found in the ideological conformity of the American academy. However that may be, Post correctly observes that progressives (or leftists) have sought to advance several of their political aims by suppressing objectionable speech. According to this progressive critique, freedom of speech serves to maintain the status quo by bolstering a fundamentally oppressive and unjust society. Indeed, not merely objectionable opinions, but also those who seek to protect them from suppression, have come under attack by leftist

* I would like to thank my fellow contributors to this volume for their comments; Erin O'Connor for the invaluable resource of her Weblog, *Critical Mass* at http://www.erinoconnor.org/; and especially Ellen Frankel Paul for extremely helpful editorial suggestions.

[1] Stanley Fish, *There's No Such Thing As Free Speech, and It's a Good Thing, Too* (New York: Oxford University Press, 1994), 102.

[2] Robert C. Post, "Censorship and Silencing" in Robert C. Post, ed., *Censorship and Silencing: Practices of Cultural Regulation* (Los Angeles, CA: Getty Research Institute for the History of Art and the Humanities, 1998), 2.

academics who—as Post delicately puts it—have been "liberated from traditional inhibitions" against censorship. The architects of campus speech codes, and advocates of legislation against pornography and (so-called) hate speech, consider freedom of speech to be a tool of oppression and its advocates unwitting oppressors.[3]

Critical race theorists constitute one particularly strident group of progressive skeptics. In the introduction to their influential book, *Words That Wound: Critical Race Theory, Assaultive Speech, and the First Amendment*, legal scholars Mari J. Matsuda, Charles R. Lawrence III, Richard Delgado, and Kimberlè Williams Crenshaw write: "The first amendment arms conscious and unconscious racists—Nazis and liberals alike—with a constitutional right to be racist."[4] This rhetoric seems excessive, even if we do not infer from the claims that liberals are unconscious racists and that punishment is "an appropriate response to racist speech" the conclusion that liberal advocacy of freedom of speech should be suppressed.[5] It may be unclear why liberals, who as a matter of principle defend the speech rights of racists and critical race theorists alike, should be demonized as racists.

Consider the quintessential defender of the classical liberal conception of free speech, John Stuart Mill (1806–73). Although Mill's credentials as a feminist and antiracist are unimpeachable, he defended the "absolute freedom of opinion and sentiment on all subjects," which he understood to include not just thought but also its expression.[6] Even if such absolutism is untenable, this statement clearly belies Fish's cynical dictum. The opinions of Fish and the critical race theorists do not in any way advance the liberal cause, yet no liberal can place them beyond the pale of free speech protection. Hence, Fish's cynical claim founders, although he may prove to be giving an accurate gloss of his own usage.

A more challenging objection to the classical liberal conception of free speech, which we will consider presently, holds that since some limits to the protection of speech are unavoidable, there can be no real freedom of expression. But this conclusion, which I have termed 'postmodern', is too hasty, since even Mill did not take "absolute" freedom of speech to rule

[3] I am not denying, of course, that some opinions that fall under liberal free speech protection can aptly be termed hateful. However, arguments for the suppression of hate speech (or, for that matter, pornography) are seldom targeted precisely or consistently. For a notable exception, see Andrew Altman, "Liberalism and Campus Hate Speech: A Philosophical Examination," *Ethics* 103, no. 2 (1993): 302–17.

[4] Mari J. Matsuda, Charles R. Lawrence III, Richard Delgado, and Kimberlè Williams Crenshaw, introduction to *Words That Wound: Critical Race Theory, Assaultive Speech, and the First Amendment* (Boulder, CO: Westview Press, 1993), 15.

[5] Matsuda, "Public Response to Racist Speech: Considering the Victim's Story," in Matsuda et al., *Words That Wound*, 17. The implication drawn in the text is not flippant; the more broadly progressives level charges of racism, the more dangerous are their proposals to punish racist speech.

[6] J. S. Mill, *On Liberty* (1859), John Gray and G. W. Smith, eds. (London: Routledge, 1991), 33.

out any possible interference with verbal behavior. Rather, the first tenet of the liberal conception of free speech is the doctrine known as content (or viewpoint) neutrality. This is the view that, as Mill put it: "there ought to exist the fullest liberty of professing and discussing, as a matter of ethical conviction, any doctrine, however immoral it may be considered."[7] Not even the harmfulness of an opinion, per se, provides good (much less sufficient) reason to suppress it. Some commentators have obscured this point by attributing to Mill an overly strong 'harm principle', on which any harm to nonconsenting others provides reason to interfere with an agent's liberty.[8] Yet Mill expressly insists that the freedom to speak should be protected "[h]owever positive anyone's persuasion may be, not only of the falsity but of the pernicious consequences" of the opinion or sentiment expressed.[9]

According to the progressive critique, however, the liberal's toleration of even false, immoral, and harmful opinion is just the problem. Progressives see the overt suppression of objectionable views as aiding in the struggle against racism and sexism, and more generally against what they consider to be a grossly unjust American society. The problem with "free speech fundamentalism," as Fish pejoratively terms the liberal position, is that it "prevents you, as a matter of principle, from inquiring into the real world of consequences of allowing certain forms of so-called speech to flourish."[10] This looks like another crude exaggeration, since, in fact, Mill holds that one can and should inquire into the consequences of various opinions, specifically in order to combat harmful opinions with criticism and to mitigate their bad effects by noncoercive means. It is true, however, that for Mill no opinion or sentiment may be prohibited or punished, "whether the means used be physical force in the form of legal penalties, or the moral coercion of public opinion."[11] The second tenet of

[7] Ibid., 36n.

[8] In fact, Mill never uses the phrase 'harm principle'; rather, he advocates a principle of liberty, which is bounded by *certain kinds* of harm. Many commentators fall into error on this point, despite the fact that Mill's principle of liberty is stated conditionally (as a claim about the *only* legitimate grounds for interference) rather than biconditionally. The assumption of a biconditional reading is made explicit by Jonathan Riley, for instance, who claims that for Mill, "expression is legitimately subject to social control . . . since it is conduct which can harm others." See Jonathan Riley, *Mill on Liberty* (New York: Routledge, 1998), 49. Often this interpretation is buttressed by the claim that Mill understood "self-regarding" action as action that cannot affect (or harm) nonconsenting others. However, Mill's distinction between self-regarding and what he calls "social" action turns not on whether the act can harm nonconsenting others, even directly, but on whether the danger is of a sort against which people have the right to protection from the state. See esp. Mill, *On Liberty*, 96. But cf. Frederick Schauer, "The Phenomenology of Speech and Harm," *Ethics* 103, no. 4 (1993): 635–53. For development of the argument that Riley, Schauer, and others misread Mill on this point, see Daniel Jacobson, "Mill on Liberty, Speech, and the Free Society," *Philosophy and Public Affairs* 29, no. 3 (2000): 276–309.

[9] Mill, *On Liberty*, 43.

[10] Fish, *There's No Such Thing As Free Speech*, 125.

[11] Mill, *On Liberty*, 30.

the liberal conception of free speech thus focuses on this distinction between criticism (which is not merely permissible but encouraged) and coercion (which is proscribed).

Progressive critics reject this distinction on several grounds. First, it is possible that coercive measures might be more effective at limiting the bad consequences of some opinions, yet liberals rule out such measures on principle. (Hence, a more modest argument along the lines Fish suggests would be less easily refuted, but there is good reason to doubt the efficacy of legal suppression.)[12] Second, progressives commonly argue that legal guarantees of free speech inadequately protect the disempowered: those who lack the means to make their voices heard. Even some scholars who sincerely affirm the value of free speech claim that the principle can justify the censorship of certain opinions. For example, legal scholar Owen Fiss argues that the state "may even have to silence the voices of some in order to hear the voices of others."[13] Section II will examine in detail such 'silencing' arguments, which claim to promote freedom of expression by selectively suppressing opinion.

Yet the embrace of politically motivated censorship by academic leftists is already old news, according to Post, which has been made obsolete by more recent and radical scholarship. This postmodern critique claims that the liberal conceptions of free speech and censorship are not only politically retrograde but also philosophically incoherent. Whereas progressives defend censorship as a political tool and attack free speech as an ideology of oppression, postmodernists advance a thesis that would undermine liberal ideals even more profoundly. Post describes the current situation this way:

> [W]ithin the academy there has emerged a remarkably innovative new scholarship that has taken a more rigorous and uncompromising view of [censorship]. Focusing with a sharp Foucaultian lens on the constitutive micromechanisms of power, on the minute intersections of resistance and domination through which power is exercised, this new scholarship follows Foucaultian premises to their fundamental and radical implications.[14]

These implications are claimed to be radical indeed. The innovative new scholarship supposedly demonstrates that censorship is, in the words

[12] Laws against hate speech have not prevented the recent, dramatic rise in anti-Semitic speech and violence in Europe. Moreover, prosecution under hate speech laws has arguably been as capricious, and as dangerous to political speech, as it has been ineffective in combating racism. Consider for example the (fortunately unsuccessful) prosecutions of Oriana Fallaci and Michel Houellebecq in France.

[13] Owen M. Fiss, *The Irony of Free Speech* (Cambridge, MA: Harvard University Press, 1996), 4.

[14] Post, "Censorship and Silencing," 2.

of legal scholar and philosopher Frederick Schauer, "inevitable, necessary, and desirable." [15] Similarly, Post claims that this postmodern insight about the ubiquity of censorship undermines the liberal ideal of free speech, because to oppose censorship as such "is to assume a freedom no one has" or could ever have.[16] And Fish writes, "[the] truth is not that freedom of speech should be abridged but that freedom of speech is a conceptual impossibility because the condition of speech's being free in the first place is unrealizable." [17] Fish's scattershot arguments illustrate that the postmodern critique does not preclude a progressive political agenda. Yet, though many postmodernists embrace the progressives' claims, an obvious tension threatens this alliance. If the postmodern thesis is true, then the ubiquity of censorship jeopardizes the progressive assumption that the silencing of the disempowered can be remedied.

Post acknowledges this difficulty:

> The challenge is thus how to preserve the analytic force of the new scholarship without sacrificing the values and concerns of more traditional accounts. Recognizing always the pervasive, inescapable, and productive silencing of expression, can we say anything distinctive about the particular province of what used to define the study of censorship: the "direct control" of expression by the state? [18]

This question bears directly on an issue addressed in the conclusion of this paper. How can academics complain about violations of their intellectual freedom or their right to engage in political dissent, while also claiming that freedom of speech is both a faulty ideal and a conceptual impossibility? Fish proposes an answer that is, at any rate, admirably frank. "[A]s long as so-called free speech principles have been fashioned by your enemy," he councils, ". . . contest their relevance to the issue at hand; but if you manage to refashion them in line with your purposes, urge them with a vengeance." [19] This proposal should be kept in mind, as it will help explain what might otherwise be mysterious about the practical circumstances in academia that I will ultimately consider.

Although I will be concerned throughout this discussion with the concepts of free speech and censorship, I will not be doing First Amendment scholarship, which I can hardly dispute with the likes of Fiss, Post, and Schauer. But the innovative new scholarship that Post hails, even when

[15] Frederick Schauer, "The Ontology of Censorship," in Robert C. Post, ed., *Censorship and Silencing: Practices of Cultural Regulation*, 162.

[16] Post, "Censorship and Silencing," 2, quoting Michael Holquist, "Corrupt Originals: The Paradox of Censorship," *PMLA* 109 (1994), 16.

[17] Fish, *There's No Such Thing As Free Speech*, 115.

[18] Post, "Censorship and Silencing," 4.

[19] Fish, *There's No Such Thing As Free Speech*, 114.

practiced by law professors, is not primarily concerned with jurisprudence. Instead, this postmodern scholarship poses a theoretical challenge to the philosophical foundations of free speech; and, like the progressive critique, it sounds a political challenge to liberalism. I propose to take up the arguments on both the theoretical and political fronts, in defense of the putatively unsophisticated traditional position. I contend that the progressive arguments against free speech are not advocated consistently, and that they would have some surprising consequences if they were. Moreover, the innovative—or at any rate fashionable—new scholarship lauded by Post does not bear up under critical scrutiny. The postmodern critique of free speech is vulnerable to a reductio ad absurdum by its own examples, which have untenable results and elide fundamental moral distinctions.

In what follows, I will examine what I take to be the most philosophically interesting and challenging objections to freedom of speech as understood by Mill. Some of these skeptical challenges are compatible with liberalism, at least insofar as they are compelling, and those that are truly incompatible do not succeed. This new scholarship does not improve upon the Millian conception of free speech it claims to supersede. Finally, in conclusion, I want to briefly consider one sort of "real-world consequence" of the political agenda shared by the progressive and postmodern free speech skeptics. It is illuminating to examine the attitudes toward freedom of speech and inquiry prevalent on American colleges and universities, where the progressive political agenda has been most thoroughly implemented. My focus on American institutions is motivated by the unique tradition of nearly absolute deference to free speech principles in the United States, a fact agreed upon by all sides. "On almost every issue of free speech theory, doctrine, and practice," Schauer observes, "virtually every country on the face of the earth diverges from the United States, and diverges in the direction of lesser protection."[20] My focus on academia, and in particular on the humanities, is motivated by the common claim that universities are and ought to be bastions of intellectual and political freedom.

The radical critiques reveal that something worth calling 'silencing' does pervade American campuses. This term is most commonly used to refer to the social intolerance of divergent opinion, backed by an ideology and enforced by those who wield power in a given society. Silencing thus covers some of the middle ground between criticism and censorship. I will adopt something like Schauer's characterization of an ideology as "a prevailing idea existing within an environment in which adherence to the idea is more or less required, and challenge to the idea is more or less

[20] Frederick Schauer, "The First Amendment As Ideology," *William and Mary Law Review* 33 (1992): 857.

discouraged."[21] This gloss is a bit too narrow, since an ideology tends to be a *system* of ideas and norms, but with that small caveat Schauer's definition will serve our purposes well.

The irony of free speech skepticism is that the postmodern critique, which purports to focus "with a sharp Foucaultian lens" on the social facts of power and oppression, gets those facts wrong when it looks at itself. In fact, both the progressive and postmodern forms of skepticism obscure the abuse of official power by those whose self-conception puts them in solidarity with the powerless. Despite their insistence that neither power nor censorship is monopolized by the state, free speech skeptics conceive of *dissent* only in opposition to the state. Therefore, the ideology predominant on American campuses is blind to its own enforcement of orthodoxy, because it conceives of itself as "dissent" rather than "conformity," notwithstanding the social facts. This irony has deepened since the attacks of September 11, 2001, as academics who so fervently celebrated their liberation from free speech principles now claim to be silenced when their opinions are criticized as anti-American. Patriotism has long ceased to be considered a virtue in academic culture, where overt hostility to American values and interests is far too obvious now to be disguised. Indeed, there was little attempt to disguise the ideology of dissent that pervades the humanities, until it recently became expedient to do so.

II. Censorship, Ideology, and Diversity of Opinion

Fish poses the following dilemma for the liberal view, which he seems to find decisive. Either freedom of speech serves some instrumental purpose or it serves no purpose beyond itself. If free speech has no further purpose, then "there is no compelling—that is, serious—reason for adhering to it."[22] This conclusion is much too hasty, but I am more interested in the other horn of the dilemma. Suppose that free speech is just instrumentally valuable, whether as a means to individual autonomy, collective self-determination, the discovery of truth, or simply the flourishing of society. Fish thinks this concession is sufficiently damning. "[O]nce such a good has been specified," he contends, ". . . it becomes possible to argue that a particular form of speech, rather than contributing to its realization, will undermine and subvert it."[23] While Fish calls any argument that identifies an instrumental value of free speech 'consequentialist', this is vulgar consequentialism. It is equally true that once such a good has been specified, it becomes possible to argue that this good is

[21] Ibid., 855.

[22] Fish, *There's No Such Thing As Free Speech*, 123. A better question is whether any justification exists for a free speech principle as distinct from a more general principle of liberty, but that is beyond the scope of this paper.

[23] Ibid., 13–14.

more likely to be diminished than promoted by the suppression of opinions claimed to "undermine and subvert" it.[24]

For instance, it is possible to argue that skepticism about free speech—which aims to subvert freedom of expression by calling it unconsciously racist or conceptually impossible—threatens to undermine the liberal ideal. Yet for the liberal, this possibility does not justify the censorship of Fish and his school, for that would be a violation of their free speech. Three features specific to the free speech debate make cautionary arguments against unconstrained direct consequentialism particularly compelling. First, Fish makes no secret of his hostility to free speech, or his willingness to use even specious and intemperate arguments to undermine it; other skeptics are more circumspect but not always more sincere. Second, those with the power to censor speech have historically been prone to accept claims of harm based on ideological sympathy rather than evidence; and so it is with contemporary free speech skeptics, as we shall see. Third, when the confidence of diverse social groups in a political convention (such as punishment or freedom of speech) is tenuous, it is especially important to maintain strict procedural fairness, untainted by special pleading.

Yet Fish's argument, despite its crudeness, reveals an important point. It has become a common skeptical strategy to identify some value underlying free speech, and then to claim that other mechanisms have "silencing" effects comparable to censorship because they similarly diminish this value by in some way inhibiting speech. This silencing phenomenon demands further explication, since it cannot simply be inferred that speech rights conflict and, therefore, must be balanced against each other. To be sure, when both the intentions and the effects of some silencing acts resemble acts of censorship, the case for assimilating them as violations of free speech is strongest. When a speaker is "shouted down," and thus deliberately prevented from being heard, there is a compelling case that this should be treated as a violation of his speech rights. Hence, certain verbal behavior can conflict with freedom of speech, but this is not in itself very significant. Not all verbal behavior falls under the Millian defense of freedom of expression, which, of course, does not recognize any right to shout down another speaker.[25] A subtler point may prove more challenging, though, inasmuch as this example suggests that speech rights might extend, to some degree, to a right to be heard.[26] This conclusion would be more problematic. It opens up the possibility that the

[24] For an overview of one powerful form of indirect consequentialism, which focuses on the institution of punishment, see John Rawls, "Two Concepts of Rules," *The Philosophical Review* 64, no. 1 (1955): 3–32.

[25] This should be clear from even a casual reading of Mill's treatment of free speech and, in particular, his corn-dealer example (Mill, *On Liberty*, 72), where Mill acknowledges that the same statement can constitute different speech acts in different contexts. This point will be discussed in more detail below in the text.

[26] There are other ways of capturing the wrong involved in shouting down a speaker, which are less problematic for the liberal conception. For instance, the shouting down case

free speech of some might conflict with the speech rights of others, albeit not as straightforwardly as in the shouting down case. Another reason to doubt how broadly this case generalizes is that proscriptions against shouting down can easily be framed neutrally, without regard to the value of the speech being silenced—or, rather, drowned out. Nevertheless, perhaps there is something worth calling 'silencing' which, though short of censorship, should also be treated as a violation of speech rights.

Consider, for example, an argument made by Owen Fiss, a tempered defender of free speech who nevertheless claims that certain *opinions* (not just verbal behavior) have silencing effects. Fiss identifies his antagonists, in a memorable phrase, as "racists, pornographers, and the rich." [27] The challenge for Fiss lies in explicating this argument, since his targets do not deliberately suppress or literally drown out others' speech. Indeed, minorities, women, and the poor can and do voice their opinions without persecution. Yet, Fiss writes:

> It is asserted that hate speech tends to diminish the victims' sense of worth, thus impeding their full participation in many of the activities of civil society, including public debate. Even when these victims speak, their words lack authority; it is as though they said nothing. This silencing dynamic has also been attributed to pornography. In this view, pornography reduces women to sexual objects, subordinating and silencing them. It impairs their credibility and makes them feel as though they have nothing to contribute to public discussion.[28]

To be credible, though, these claims cannot simply be asserted; the "silencing dynamic" must be shown to exist and to be caused by the targeted speech rather than other social forces. It is curious that Fiss does not find it necessary to adduce evidence of this silencing, beyond citing the assertions and feelings of those who claim to be its victims. As previously noted, indirect consequentialist arguments that peremptorily rule out the suppression of speech, even for the purpose of promoting debate, are most compelling when censorial conclusions are prone to be accepted on inadequate evidence. Fiss's failure to subject these claims to any real scrutiny is telling. Further doubts are raised by the fact that the targeted speech is offensive to those who seek its suppression. Critical race theorists and antipornography feminists despise the speech they seek to censor, and, by their own admission, they do not share even Fiss's attenuated commitment to free speech principles. Many advocates of silencing ar-

might instead be taken to show that speech rights include a right not to be coercively *prevented from* being heard.

[27] Fiss, *The Irony of Free Speech*, 17.

[28] Ibid., 16.

guments would favor censoring hate speech and pornography whether they have any significant silencing effect or not.

Let us grant for the sake of argument that hate speech and pornography produce the silencing effects Fiss describes. It still must be argued that they constitute a violation of speech rights. Surely not everything that diminishes someone's sense of worth impedes her participation or authority in public debate, and not every such impediment is a rights violation. Furthermore, in order to advance a silencing *argument*—that is, an argument for using censorship to promote free speech—Fiss needs to show that censorship is the best remedy for silencing. This requires him both to identify the value of free speech and to explicate a conception of silencing on which it can further that value despite inhibiting speech. Fiss satisfies the first requirement, however contentiously, by identifying the primary value of free speech as its essential role in democratic governance. In his view, free speech principles primarily serve to advance social rather than individual freedom:

> The state is . . . trying to establish essential preconditions for collective self-governance by making certain that all sides are presented to the public. If this could be accomplished by simply empowering the disadvantaged groups, the state's aim would be achieved. But our experience with affirmative action programs and the like has taught us that the matter is not so simple. Sometimes we must lower the voices of some in order to hear the voices of others.[29]

Unfortunately, Fiss does not elaborate on this lesson taught by affirmative action, which he seems to assume will be obvious. But even if we accept Fiss's narrow and controversial view of the value of free speech, he offers little argument for his assertion that bad speech must be remedied not by more speech but less whenever "private parties are skewing debate and the [proposed] state regulation promotes free and open debate."[30] For now we can postpone the discussion of silencing arguments and focus on investigating claims of silencing.

One reason Fiss seems blithe about defending silencing claims is that he accepts an extremely capacious notion of them that is too broad to be identified with the violation of speech rights. For instance, he claims that in contexts of allocation, "a certain measure of silencing is inevitable" due to the scarcity of resources. Despite acknowledging that "the applicants who are denied the grant are still 'free' to pursue the project on their

[29] Ibid., 18. Fiss notes that "this view is predicated on a theory of the First Amendment and its guarantee of free speech that emphasizes social, rather than individualistic values." Ibid., 2.

[30] Ibid., 21. While I do not doubt that it is possible for private parties to "skew" debate, I am skeptical that any such regulation would be applied fairly and consistently. Certainly Fiss's politicized catalogue of targets for silencing provides no grounds for confidence.

own," Fiss characterizes this freedom as "largely formal," because some of those who are rejected will lack the necessary resources.[31] But this is dangerously misleading. Surely Fiss is right that some projects will never come to fruition due to lack of funding. Scores of unproduced screenplays attest to this fact and to the folly of trying to nurture every voice and idea. Yet such putative silencing-by-not-funding differs greatly from censorship in many other respects, including both its intentions and its secondary effects, even if the results (construed narrowly as the failure of some projects) are similar. Does someone whose grant proposal is not funded have a complaint that she has been silenced, her speech rights or academic freedom violated? This question seems to hang on the reasons for the negative decision, but Fiss's gloss of silencing makes no such distinction. It is one thing to compare censorship to the silencing caused by pressure to conform, backed by social rather than legal sanctions; it is quite another to compare censorship to the failure of one's projects to be funded. The problem with too capacious a notion of silencing is that it assimilates very different cases and thereby obscures crucial moral distinctions. Frustrated screenwriters waiting tables in Los Angeles have not been "silenced" in any significant sense, though screenwriters who were "blacklisted" for their political views in the 1950s were.

Although Fiss's allusion to affirmative action is terse, there are some obvious parallels to the affirmative action debate that might be used to sharpen his central claim. It is often argued that racial diversity furthers diversity of opinion. Another argument for traditional affirmative action is that there must be a "critical mass" of like-minded (or like-bodied) students and faculty in order for minority views to flourish and be heard. Yet, however that may be, Fiss's commitment to ensuring that all opinions are given a fair hearing in free and open debate seems to support a novel sort of affirmative action. If the goal is to ensure that all sides of an argument are heard, then an institution's responsibility must be to promote intellectual diversity: diversity of *opinion*. In circumstances where administrators have a commitment to fostering diversity of opinion or protecting intellectual freedom—either because of the pretensions of the institution or the nature of its funding—then the disappointed applicant *may* have grounds for complaint. In particular, when administrators do not merely fail to promote unorthodox opinion but suppress it for ideological reasons, claims of silencing are most plausible.

In an argument decrying the entrenchment of orthodoxy in academia, Schauer similarly concludes that universities should promote unorthodox views, without suggesting that this requires the suppression of popular opinions. Since "one earmark of intellectual honesty is confrontation of the best arguments for the opposing position," he plausibly contends that we have "an obligation either to find, or if necessary to create, the stron-

[31] Ibid., 35.

gest argument" for unorthodox views.[32] Schauer focuses on allocation rather than regulation, and he makes an overt comparison to a kind of affirmative action that aims directly at promoting diversity of opinion:

> First, those with the power to select, whether for journal articles, conference presentations, or projects to be funded, could engage in a form of affirmative action, taking the fact of a view's being currently underrepresented as a [nonconclusive] reason for selecting it.[33]

This is an extremely interesting suggestion, especially since it seems to apply equally well to hiring decisions in academia. While Schauer draws this conclusion in defense of free speech skepticism, his argument applies quite generally. Moreover, he contends that "the notion of an ideology presupposes some population within which the relevant idea is treated as ideology."[34] Schauer thus implies that intellectual honesty requires the promotion of views that are unorthodox *with respect to academia itself,* whenever an academic ideology exists. This conclusion should be kept in mind, as I will ultimately argue that there is a far broader and more pervasively entrenched ideology in American universities than Schauer imagines. Not only does the academic establishment fail to live up to the demands of intellectual honesty as he describes them, it deliberately and effectively inhibits debate of its dogmas. If this is true, then Schauer's argument supports the conclusion that scholars whose political views are grossly underrepresented in American universities should be favored in hiring and funding decisions.

These arguments concern the allocation of resources for speech—jobs, grants, publications, etc.—rather than the overt regulation of speech. Questions of allocation pose complex issues that I cannot pursue here, except to note that it is unclear what commitments liberalism has with regard to them. Mill, of course, was expressly committed to protecting even the most unpopular opinions from censorship. "If all mankind minus one, were of one opinion, and only one person were of the contrary opinion," he famously declared, "mankind would be no more justified in silencing that one person, than he, if he had the power, would be justified in silencing mankind."[35] But he did not mean to imply, as Fiss seems to, that the state must subsidize every unorthodox view in order to ensure that all opinions are presented to the public. Down that road lies the establishment of endowed chairs in creationist cosmology and Holocaust denial studies.[36] The real question is how to establish and administer the bound-

32 Schauer, "The First Amendment As Ideology," 867–68.
33 Ibid., 867.
34 Ibid., 855.
35 Mill, *On Liberty,* 37.
36 I am grateful to Andrew Altman for pressing this point.

aries of reasonable opinion and, perhaps most importantly, what constitutes corruption of this process?

Fiss offers an answer grounded in his view of the value of freedom of speech. "The choice among the unorthodox should not turn on the administrator's judgment about the goodness or badness of the ideas being advanced or whether the administrator thinks they have merit," he claims. "This would violate the democratic aspiration of the First Amendment, which is to leave judgments as to the merits of various ideas to the people."[37] Whether or not the First Amendment is motivated by democratic aspirations, Mill's rationale for protecting the expression of unpopular opinion and sentiment arises, rather, from liberal worries about the tyranny of the majority. Nevertheless, Fiss's appeal to democratic aspirations is more plausible with respect to allocation than regulation of speech, and a limited proposal focused on combating institutionally entrenched orthodoxy would be even more compelling. Schauer plausibly concludes that when it comes to questions of allocation, "we cannot avoid the most difficult questions of what functions the institutions are supposed to serve" and "whose choices we as a society wish to privilege and whose choices we wish to suspect."[38] This reference to the judgment of society suggests that, for Schauer too, these issues must be solved democratically—even if society ultimately decides to cede authority to experts. But insofar as society delegates these choices, this surely does not prevent it from scrutinizing the actions of those whom it has empowered, especially to ensure that they are not abusing their authority. When an institution that is ostensibly dedicated to free inquiry is administered by an ideological elite, buffered from external criticism, this constitutes a form of corruption. Choices that ought to belong to society at large have then been taken over in a manner that is antidemocratic and violates a basic canon of intellectual honesty. Or so Schauer's argument suggests, and I agree.[39]

These arguments for diversity of opinion and against the entrenchment of ideology can even be taken to vindicate, to a limited extent, Fish's most cynical suggestion. Recall his dictum that what one counts as free speech is whatever serves one's substantive agenda. This claim was belied by Mill's commitment to viewpoint neutrality, which protects even the arguments of free speech skeptics, despite the fact that they are intended to subvert freedom of speech. Nevertheless, Fish can be read as predicting that when experts abuse their authority by implementing ideologically driven criteria of value under the guise of merit, they will object to external criticism by declaring that their speech rights and intellectual free-

[37] Fiss, *The Irony of Free Speech*, 43.

[38] Schauer, "The Ontology of Censorship," 163. Schauer is much less circumspect in this article—which was published in Post, *Censorship and Silencing*, in 1998—than in his previous, and more compelling article, "The First Amendment As Ideology" (1992).

[39] I do not mean to suggest that Schauer would agree with this conclusion, just that his argument, if taken seriously and applied consistently, seems to entail it.

dom are under attack. In particular, academic ideologues faced with external criticism can be expected to defend themselves by invoking academic freedom and accusing their critics of censorship, regardless of how dubious and self-serving their claims might be. Were free speech skeptics content with the prosaic observation that popular *claims* of censorship are often so far-fetched as to be practically meaningless, they would be substantially correct. But they do not care much for this theoretically modest and politically uncongenial conclusion. The free speech skeptics have far more grandiose ambitions, and their commitment to intellectual diversity will prove tenuous.

Consider, for example, Post's commentary on complaints of censorship directed at attempts to remove books for ideological reasons from a library or course curriculum:

> This usage of the concept of censorship is odd, because no matter what speech the state does or does not fund, no matter what material it assigns or does not assign within a classroom, no matter what books it acquires or does not acquire for a library, the state will be acting for reasons that can properly be termed "ideological." This suggests the practical truth of the theoretical insight that all discursive practices establish themselves through the marginalization and suppression of competing practices. If we wish to condemn this as "censorship," then censorship is indeed everywhere and inescapable.[40]

Recall that I have suggested that the term 'censorship' be reserved for the suppression of speech, in accordance with the liberal conception; and that we use the term 'silencing' more broadly, for instance, to capture the abuse of authority that Fiss and Schauer identify. Putting aside the term 'censorship', then, what are we to make of Post's suggestion that *all* decisions about allocation are ideological and necessarily involve suppression? I contend that this is a gross exaggeration, which trades on an undifferentiated notion of ideology. Post's argument implies that if one library decides to acquire only books that it deems patriotic and bans all putatively anti-American works, while another library decides to select only the most powerful arguments for and against American political institutions, then both libraries act for reasons properly termed 'ideological'. This is the absurd result of accepting so capacious a notion of ideology that it cannot discriminate among any evaluative criteria.[41]

This seems a dubious theoretical insight, inadequate for supporting the claim that silencing, much less censorship, is inescapable. Since we have

[40] Post, "Censorship and Silencing," 6.

[41] In fact, Post's argument implies that a library that decides, ridiculously, to acquire all and only books written by authors whose names begin with some randomly chosen letter would also be making an ideological choice, which would count as censorship by his criterion.

two different terms available, it will be helpful not to use them synonymously. Therefore, in what follows I will let 'silencing' be a relatively capacious term for actions that discriminate among opinions on illegitimate grounds or that stifle expressive possibilities unjustifiably, but which may or may not violate speech rights. I will reserve the term 'censorship' for the overt suppression of opinion and sentiment. This is merely a terminological stipulation. It does not beg any important questions, because we can still ask whether the distinction marks an important moral difference: Should some or all silencing count as censorship?

III. Silencing for the Sake of Speech

My discussion of the more radical forms of free speech skepticism will focus primarily on Schauer's work, as he seems to have espoused almost every skeptical argument and typically gives them their most careful development. For instance, Schauer provides a clear overview of the terrain initially mapped by Post, on which there are three successively "deeper" levels of analysis of free speech and censorship: the liberal, progressive, and postmodern accounts. Like Post, he is sympathetic to the progressive cause while endorsing postmodern claims about the conceptual impossibility of free speech. Thus, while Post writes of "pervasive, inescapable, and productive silencing of expression," Schauer calls censorship "inevitable, necessary, and desirable."[42] And he, too, casts doubt on the utility of the liberal conceptions of free speech and censorship. "According to the ontology on which the traditional picture is founded," Schauer writes, "an act of censorship is an act of external interference with the internally generated communicative, expressive, artistic, or informational preferences of some agent."[43] Yet, he claims, "because this type of censorship is everywhere, it is . . . nowhere at all."[44]

But on what grounds do Schauer and Post, among others, attribute so expansive and useless a notion of censorship to liberalism? As usual, Schauer offers the clearest explanation. He notes, first, that the liberal conception focuses on external constraint and coercion: "agents interfering with what would otherwise be our expressive, communicative, artistic, and informational preferences."[45] Although it will prove overly broad, this characterization points in the right direction. Mill's defense of free speech denies that society or government can legitimately "determine what doctrines or what arguments [individuals] shall be allowed to hear."[46] According to Schauer, the trouble with this account is its commitment to an untenable theory of agency, on which our preferences, and in partic-

[42] Post, "Censorship and Silencing," 4; Schauer, "The Ontology of Censorship," 162.
[43] Schauer, "The Ontology of Censorship," 150.
[44] Ibid., 159. Schauer attributes this thesis, which he clearly endorses, to Richard Burt.
[45] Ibid., 148.
[46] Mill, *On Liberty*, 36.

ular our desires to speak or otherwise communicate, are "endogenous" and "antecedent." Our desires are supposed to be endogenous in that they are formed wholly by the agent, and antecedent in that they exist prior to the act of censorship. Yet this is misguided, he concludes, because "what we can say and how we can express ourselves is significantly a function of what others do."[47]

It would certainly be a mistake to insist that desires arise wholly from within an agent, without external influence. But why attribute this view to liberalism? Schauer tacitly assumes that because the liberal conception of censorship focuses on external coercion, it must hold that speech and thought are ordinarily—in the absence of external constraint—entirely "internally generated." Yet nothing about the liberal conception of censorship requires denying that there are various external influences shaping our desires; the liberal's rejection of coercion is, instead, a normative commitment that draws moral distinctions between different kinds of external influences. By contrast, Post acknowledges that the postmodern conception of censorship "seems to flatten distinctions among kinds of power, implicitly equating suppression of speech caused by state legal action with that caused by the market, or by the dominance of a particular discourse, or by the institution of criticism itself."[48] This is the fundamental disagreement. Although many limitations on our capacities, including our expressive capacities, are externally generated, liberalism holds that some such limitations are far more morally significant than others. While some influences destroy an agent's ability to make future decisions or change preferences, for instance, others do not. This can admittedly be a matter of degree, but there are several reasonably clear-cut distinctions to be drawn. At any rate, this normative claim—and not some patently false descriptive claim about the genesis of our desires—is the core commitment of the liberal conception.

Indeed, the postmodernists have no difficulty glossing the liberal concepts of free speech and censorship coherently and moderately, when it suits their purposes. Not every external influence on "communicative preferences" or "discursive practices" counts as censorship on the traditional liberal model. Thus, Post recognizes that the paradigm of censorship is "the 'direct control' of expression by the state"; he just doubts whether there is anything "distinctive" to be said about this class of action.[49] (While this is indeed the focus of First Amendment scholarship, Mill expressly denies the legitimacy of the power to coercively suppress speech, whether exercised by the people or by the state.) But the onus must be on the postmodernists to motivate conceptual reform or revision; they cannot simply conflate all external influences on communicative

[47] Schauer, "The Ontology of Censorship," 149.
[48] Post, "Censorship and Silencing," 4.
[49] Ibid., 4.

desires. When postmodernists do offer such an argument, it trades on the three-level analytical scheme. They first appeal to the progressive critique to motivate stretching the application of the concept of censorship, and then use this criticism as leverage to "unravel" the concept (as Schauer puts it), thereby rendering it "so expansive as to be empty."[50] Although conceptual reform is common enough as a philosophical strategy, a large argumentative burden must be put on any such argument that would reform a concept to death.

I will begin by considering the conceptual reforms motivated by the progressive level of analysis, which holds that the silencing of the disempowered should be seen as a form of censorship despite the absence of overt prohibition or punishment. Then I will consider the postmodern "insight" that censorship is not merely more prevalent than commonly thought, but that it is necessarily ubiquitous. In making this argument, Schauer introduces the crucial normative claim, common to the progressive and postmodern accounts, which the liberal must resist. He writes:

> When the discourse of others can silence us, it is argued, and when the actions of others create structures and institutions that stifle our expressive capabilities, *it is important to see such activities as censorious* in much the same way as we see the more overt restrictive actions of the state as censorious.[51]

This claim is stated far too broadly, and at too high a level of abstraction, to be acceptable. Perhaps some forms of silencing that fall short of the overt restriction of opinion should be seen in much the same way as censorship, but not all structures that influence, or even stifle, expressive capabilities are alike. There is a glaring difference between an upbringing that involves, say, the inculcation of religious beliefs, and one that involves sexual abuse, even if both can be said to shape one's desires. Moreover, although some of these desires will be desires to express opinions or sentiments, it obscures matters to consider these as free speech issues simply because they have something to do with expressive capacities and desires. This obfuscation threatens sound moral judgment. Arguments that some type of action should be seen in much the same way as censorship must be assessed on the merits of the particular case, not because we have swallowed a dubious theory and must stomach whatever conclusions it entails.

Some progressive skeptics of free speech marshal entirely different arguments for censorship, which do not rely on an expansive view of silencing. Most commonly, they argue that freedom of speech conflicts not with the speech rights of the disempowered but with other rights or com-

[50] Schauer, "The Ontology of Censorship," 160.
[51] Ibid., 149 (emphasis added).

pelling interests. Charles Lawrence claims that "the alternative to regulating racist speech is infringement of the claims of Blacks to liberty and equal protection. The best way to constitutionally protect these competing interests is to balance them directly."[52] I will not treat these broader balancing arguments here; instead, I want to consider the more philosophically ambitious argument made by the progressive analysis of what Schauer calls the "ontology" of censorship. This progressive critique focuses on the claim that because some speech silences other speech, peoples' speech rights directly conflict. Hence, it is argued, such forms of silencing are indeed comparable to censorship: both violate freedom of speech.

This claim is typically introduced by appeal to the "shouting down" scenario, but that case must be extended in two respects in order to support the idea that silencing constitutes a conflict of speech rights.[53] First, the verbal behavior that has this silencing effect must fall under the purview of the liberal conception of free speech. Second, the conflict of speech rights cannot be resolved with a content-neutral principle. These two features keep the shouting down case from threatening the liberal conception of freedom of speech. Of course, one need not drown out someone's speech in order to render it less effective. When a scientific theory is refuted by the evidence, for instance, its advocates' claims are undermined; yet we should not conclude that they have been silenced by the force of the better argument. To call this 'silencing' is to give up the aspiration to draw a moral comparison between silencing and censorship. In order for a silencing argument to make good on its pretensions, then, it needs to do two things. First, if its central claim is causal, it must present evidence of a specific silencing effect. Second, it needs to make a convincing normative claim that principles of free speech should prevent this form of silencing. This sets a difficult argumentative burden, which I do not think the progressive skeptics have seriously undertaken. As we saw in Section II, Fiss hardly attempted to do so before concluding that sometimes the state must silence for the sake of speech.

There is another form of silencing argument that is even more ambitious, since it seems to circumvent the need to provide empirical evidence. Catharine MacKinnon argues that pornography subordinates and silences women not as a matter of its causal effects, but because its very existence *constitutes* silencing. Even MacKinnon's allies admit that it is difficult to make literal sense of this claim, though some purport to do so.[54] Another way MacKinnon seeks to circumvent the burden on her

[52] Charles R. Lawrence III, "If He Hollers Let Him Go: Regulating Racist Speech on Campus," in Matsuda et al., *Words That Wound*, 64.

[53] See Jennifer Hornsby, "Speech Acts and Pornography," in Susan Dwyer, ed., *The Problem of Pornography* (Belmont, CA: Wadsworth, 1995): 220–32.

[54] See Rae Langton, "Speech Acts and Unspeakable Acts," *Philosophy and Public Affairs* 22, no. 4 (1993): 292–330. But compare Daniel Jacobson, "Freedom of Speech Acts? A Response to Langton," *Philosophy and Public Affairs* 24, no. 1 (1995): 64–79.

argument is by casting doubt on the distinction between speech and action, which is fundamental to the liberal conception of what is and is not within the purview of free speech protection. If certain actions like "shouting down" can be classed with mere speech, then it is much easier to show that speech rights can conflict. MacKinnon offers the following examples to call into question the liberal's basic distinction. Consider someone who gives the command "kill" to a trained guard dog; he only uses words, but his words are not protected by any principle of free speech. Similarly, a professor who offers his student an A for having sex with him is beyond the pale of such protection.[55] In both cases, regardless of the consequences of such speech, these acts of speaking constitute significant wrongs. (In the latter case, even if the student declines the proposition and gets an A nevertheless, she has been wronged.)

But such examples need not worry the liberal yet. Although Mill claims that "human beings should be free to form opinions, and to express their opinions without reserve," he adds this proviso: the freedom of opinion does not extend to acting on one's opinions, as opposed to merely expressing them.[56] Thus,

> No one pretends that actions should be as free as opinions. On the contrary, even opinions lose their immunity, when the circumstances in which they are expressed are such as to constitute their expression a positive instigation to some mischievous act. An opinion that corn-dealers are starvers of the poor, or that private property is robbery, ought to be unmolested when simply circulated through the press, but may justly incur punishment when delivered orally to an excited mob assembled before the house of a corn-dealer, or when handed about among the same mob in the form of a placard.[57]

Mill insists that even opinions, by which he means the assertion of opinions, "lose their immunity" when the context in which they are spoken makes their utterance a more deeply performative act of speech. This point has several important ramifications.

First, one cannot just look at the behavior—in particular, whether it is verbal—in order to determine what kind of action has been performed. Sometimes mere words constitute speech acts such as threats, contracts, or conspiracies, and these actions are not automatically immunized simply because they are performed by speech. However, a class of less deeply performative speech acts also exists, which we can call 'acts of expression', including assertion, discussion, and depiction, and this class con-

[55] See Catharine MacKinnon and Floyd Abrams, "Dialogue," *The New York Times Magazine*, March 13, 1994, 42.

[56] Mill, *On Liberty*, 72.

[57] Ibid., 72.

stitutes the proper objects of a free speech principle. As Mill observes, in certain contexts what would otherwise be just an assertion can become a positive incitement and thereby lose its immunity. Similarly, an action does not count as an act of expression just because it (in one sense) expressed an opinion. The assassination of President Abraham Lincoln by John Wilkes Booth expressed contempt for the Union, but that did not give immunity to the murder. Only purely symbolic nonverbal actions, such as flag burning, count as acts of expression; even then, symbolic acts are not immunized from fire codes and the like.

Stanley Fish scoffs at arguments founded on this distinction between speech and action. He writes,

> Basically the strategy is to declare that the forms of speech found unworthy or intolerable are not really speech and that therefore we do not compromise our free-speech principles by regulating them. Moreover, the strategy is reversible when a court comes upon a form of physical action whose consequences it is willing to tolerate; for then it can say that while the behavior in question appears to be action, it is really speech—expressive of some idea—and therefore outside the scope of judicial attention. It's a wonderful game, and those who play it are limited only by their own considerable ingenuity.[58]

This is powerful rhetoric, but Fish gives away the game with his hyperbole. In the first place, contrary to Fish's implication, there is no value judgment inherent in the identification of some speech acts as expressive and others as performative. Warnings and promises are not insignificant, much less unworthy, and many ordinary assertions are rubbish. Even so, their worthlessness does not make them something other than opinions, nor does it place them beyond the pale of free speech protection. Fish's own examples actually undermine his point: he describes a malicious "depiction" (in a parody of a public figure), degraded "portrayals" (of women), and a genocidal "message" (about Jews). Ugly, degrading, and immoral as these cases may be, his inability to describe them except in overtly representational terms—as depictions, portrayals, messages, and even ideas—undermines his cynical conclusion. There is, in fact, a commonsense pre-theoretic distinction at work here.

Nevertheless, if Fish were not so dogmatic, he might have chosen better examples. I do not deny that there are borderline cases, where it is problematic whether some behavior counts as speech or action. Nor am I claiming that this distinction will do all the work necessary to differentiate between what should and should not be assimilated with speech for

[58] Fish, *There's No Such Thing As Free Speech*, 125.

the purposes of formulating a free speech principle.[59] Owen Fiss thus gets something right and something wrong when he expresses his "doubts as to the usefulness of the speech/action distinction . . . because it masks all the hard judgments that the First Amendment requires."[60] The trouble with Fiss's complaint is not that it is false, but that many of the hard judgments he has in mind are hard *with respect to the distinction*; that is, what makes them difficult is that they are on the borderline between the categories of speech and action. The existence of borderline cases and hard judgments cannot justify wholesale conceptual revision, because hard cases are endemic to evaluative concepts. Some distinctions are more problematic than others, of course, but the costs of drawing any given distinction must be compared to those of doing without it. And we must be live to the possibility that some philosophers might have ulterior motives for attacking a distinction that may be not so much problematic as inconvenient.

It is, therefore, worth noting that MacKinnon's examples are not hard cases for the distinction between speech and action, but easy ones. Hence, her suggestion that pornography is a verbal action analogous to an order to kill is hard to take seriously. Perhaps philosopher Rae Langton comes closest to making good literal sense of the claim that pornography silences women constitutively. She does so by going more deeply into speech act theory and focusing specifically on 'illocutionary acts': what we do *in* saying something, as opposed to what we do *by* saying it. For instance, in saying the right words under the right conditions, we can do such things as marry, vote, command, threaten, promise, and so forth. Langton imagines a scenario in which women would count as being silenced in a specific and literal sense. They would be *illocutionarily disabled*, which is to be rendered unable to perform some illocutionary act.[61]

In Langton's scenario, a particular kind of violent pornography that depicts women saying "no," but really meaning yes, might make it literally impossible for women to decline sex. If so, then such pornography would constitute the silencing of women by rendering them illocutionarily disabled in this respect: everything that they can say to a sexual proposition constitutes consent to it. This is not really the case, of course, since it is quite possible for women to decline a sexual advance. Note that Langton cannot be claiming merely that refusals are not always honored, and women are sometimes raped. Rather, her claim is that, in the imagined scenario, the woman cannot (and hence does not) perform the illo-

[59] See Altman, "Liberalism and Campus Hate Speech," 302–17. Altman makes a careful and intellectually honest liberal argument for taking hate speech, narrowly defined, to constitute a specific type of performative speech act. While I do not accept his conclusion, I think I could do so consistently, and I grant that this is a harder case than either the Fish or MacKinnon cases discussed in the text.

[60] Fiss, *The Irony of Free Speech*, 13. Fiss's reference to the First Amendment can be replaced by "free speech principle" without significant change, in order for me to avoid committing First Amendment jurisprudence.

[61] Langton, "Speech Acts and Unspeakable Acts," 315–21.

cutionary act of declining sex. I have argued against this claim elsewhere and will not comment on it further here, except to note one especially pertinent problem with the argument.[62] The silencing that is illocutionary disablement, whereby someone is unable to perform certain illocutionary acts, is not wrong or even a harm, per se. For instance, children and people already married are illocutionarily disabled from marrying, but almost everyone will agree that this is a good thing. Illocutionary disablement goes on all the time, in a myriad of ways, and it can be good, bad, or indifferent. In other words, illocutionary disablement is pervasive, necessary, and productive—which is exactly the postmodern view of censorship, writ small.

IV. The Dubious Ubiquity of Censorship

Recall that, according to Schauer, the progressive conception of censorship is not the deepest level of analysis. The most sophisticated analysis, postmodernism, does not deny the phenomenon of silencing, but it criticizes the progressive view for implying that silencing can be overcome. Schauer complains that, "Langton presupposes the existence of the unsilenced or the uncensored and thus necessarily presupposes the existence of language whose meaning is uninhibited by the language of others."[63] One might worry that if the uncensored does not exist, then any complaint about the suppression of speech must be misguided. This seems like a bad result, but perhaps it is the price of following the postmodernists' premises to their radical conclusions. Once we understand that "*all* human behavior both constitutes and restricts our communicative possibilities," Schauer claims, we find that the very concept of censorship is problematic.[64] This is supposed to be the great postmodern insight about the ubiquity of censorship and the conceptual impossibility of free speech. Post summarizes the argument as follows:

> If censorship is a technique by which discursive practices are maintained, and if social life largely consists of such practices, it follows that censorship is the norm rather than the exception.[65]

[62] Jacobson, "Freedom of Speech Acts? A Response to Langton," 64–79. See also Jennifer Hornsby and Rae Langton, "Free Speech and Illocution," *Legal Theory* 4 (1998): 21–38; and Daniel Jacobson, "Speech and Action: Replies to Hornsby and Langton," *Legal Theory* 7, no. 2 (2001): 179–201. One further point: although the argument from illocutionary disablement is advertised as an argument against pornography, it only applies to a narrow genre. Moreover, if the argument worked, other material that is pornographic could actually mitigate the illocutionary disablement. In fact, if Langton were right, this would be a model instance of a case where the best remedy for speech is more speech—specifically, more pornography, but pornography that depicts women meaning no by "no" and yes by "yes."

[63] Schauer, "The Ontology of Censorship," 153.

[64] Ibid., 149 (emphasis added).

[65] Post, "Censorship and Silencing," 2.

However, this argument is logically invalid, and not just because it has a missing premise or requires some interpretive massaging. Not only is Post's argument fallacious, it exposes the fundamental error of postmodern skepticism about free speech. We can agree that censorship is *one* technique by which discursive practices are maintained, and if "discursive practices" just means activities like talking and writing, then surely social life does largely consist of such practices. *But there are other ways of maintaining discursive practices besides censorship.* Hence, it does not follow that censorship is the norm rather than the exception; indeed, nothing about the prevalence of censorship follows from Post's premises.[66] This error is not mere carelessness. It issues from the "unraveling" of concepts that are not especially problematic, and the consequent flattening of distinctions needed to avoid philosophical confusion and to differentiate between morally disparate cases.

The trouble with the vast postmodern assimilation is that it makes an enormous difference to all of us just how our discursive practices are maintained. Sometimes we influence people by persuasion and sometimes by coercion. Sometimes the line between these two methods is hard to draw, but that does not make persuasion just another form of coercion. Conflate the two and you can no longer tell the difference between inquisition and the Inquisition. Of course, Post could stipulate that he is using the word 'censorship' to refer to *any* technique for maintaining discursive practices, but this would not help his argument. To say this is merely to change the subject: Post would no longer be talking about censorship, he would merely be using the word. Schauer's argument suffers from the same peculiar malady. He claims that because our "communicative practices" are always affected by others, it makes no sense to identify as censorship only a subset of "something that is part and parcel of all human activity."[67]

The following discussion will illustrate why, *pace* Schauer and Post, we must not adopt so capacious and indiscriminate a conception of censorship. I propose letting the verdict rest on our assessment of Schauer's own examples, which are supposed to illustrate the ubiquity of censorship but instead lead us into absurdity. Consider the following example, which I have divided into three distinct claims:

> [1] Unlike the state of affairs a few years ago, to consume a bottle of French wine now is, possibly, and in some social circles, to make a

[66] Lest this be thought unfair, the argument can be tidied up without changing its meaning as follows. (1) Censorship is a technique of maintaining discursive practices. (2) Much of social life is the maintenance of discursive practices. (3) Hence, much of social life is censorship. Which is to say, "censorship is the norm [in social life] rather than the exception." Note that it does not help the argument to put the premises in the form of conditionals, as the 'ifs' superficially suggest. In any case, Post clearly means to be asserting (1) and (2), and deriving (3) from them—which is simply invalid.

[67] Schauer, "The Ontology of Censorship," 149.

> statement about nuclear testing. [2] Insofar as it was possible a few years ago to make a statement about French wine whose clarity was unencumbered by the "noise" . . . of a simultaneous statement about nuclear testing and the personality of the French people, it is now far less possible to make such a statement. [3] Those who would wish to do so, therefore, are deprived of the possibility of making a statement they previously could have made. In that sense, they have been silenced.[68]

Notice that Schauer expressly defines silencing so as to include any circumstance that deprives someone of an expressive possibility. He thus uses the terms 'silencing' and 'censorship' synonymously, and he gives them both the broadest possible scope.

The first claim presumably refers to the effort, now largely forgotten, to protest French nuclear testing in Polynesia by boycotting French wine. For the sake of argument, let us grant that Schauer's quasi-semantic claim was true in some social circles, which I will refer to as 'Cambridge': to consume French wine in Cambridge, Massachusetts, during the boycott was to "make a statement" about nuclear testing. The second claim states that an expressive possibility was temporarily foreclosed by this boycott. In order to explicate this claim, imagine that we are in Cambridge during the boycott. Of course, it is not merely possible but easy to consume French wine—albeit more difficult to find good value in a claret. Yet Schauer suggests that while it was once possible to express something *by* consuming French wine, this possibility has been foreclosed. Prior to the boycott, it was possible to make merely a statement of taste, perhaps, but now one inevitably makes a political statement as well. My wine purchase may express more than I want it to: it says that I am the kind of person who thinks it more important to buy a good bottle than to engage in the protest. I can imagine not wanting to make this statement, but, contrary to Schauer's third claim, it strains credulity to think of myself as thereby being silenced or censored. Yet this conclusion would be forced on us, were we to accept the capacious postmodern conception of censorship.

I will limit myself to two observations about this example. First, we need to be careful about such statements-in-action. While they may sometimes be more powerful than verbal expression, they are also inarticulate. It is not at all clear what, if anything, one expressed by buying French wine before the boycott. Was it something about one's taste, anxieties, budget, feelings for France as a nation, or something else entirely? One disanalogy with censorship is common to all (nonverbal) actions—or at least all those that are not wholly symbolic. It is an open question which acts should be said to "make a statement," and just what statements they make. Schauer may think that all actions qualify, but the more acts one

[68] Ibid., 159.

sees as expressive, the less contentful those expressions become. Moreover, even during the boycott one could still express disdain for France, or the Gaullist Chirac government and its unilateralist foreign policy, with words. Another disanalogy is that even if the boycotters intend to dissuade people from buying French wine, they do not intend to stifle anyone's expression; whereas that is precisely the aim of censorship (if not always of silencing). These are significant differences, which are surely relevant to any moral assessment. This brings us to my second observation: how little justification is given for the claim upon which Schauer's whole argument rests. He supposes that *anything* that can be said to restrict communicative possibilities, or even to affect expressive desires, should be seen as "censorious in much the same way as we see the more overt restrictive actions of the state."[69] This is a normative claim: a claim about how we *should* see these practices. But why should we think so?

Schauer postulates a purely descriptive sense of the word 'censorship', quite different from its use in ordinary language, in order to declare various distinctions unfounded. He thus asks, why does condemnation attach "to some acts and not others, if they are equally deserving of the label 'censorship' in a strictly descriptive sense?"[70] But this descriptive sense—on which anything that can be said somehow to restrict communicative possibilities counts as censorship—is all-inclusive. By his own admission, this is "part and parcel of all human activity."[71] However, the claim that all human activity equally deserves to be called censorship follows only if we accept his dubious conceptual analysis. Yet his example of the French wine illustrates why the capacious conception of censorship is misguided. It seems absurd, even decadent, to compare this case to, say, the Soviet suppression of dissidents. Even without Chateau Neuf in the faculty club, Cambridge is far from Siberia. If this seems like merely a rhetorical flourish, it will in due course prove bizarrely apt.

The problem is not only with one example, but with the whole argument for the inevitability of censorship and the conceptual impossibility of free speech. On its face, the claim that we are censored whenever someone does something that limits our expressive desires or capabilities seems far-fetched—to put it mildly. Worse, the postmodern approach threatens to conflate flippant cases with the gravest infringements of liberty. Consider another example, in which Schauer suggests that great art has some deep affinity with censorship, since "the best artists succeed in transforming artistic understanding, but in doing so they have not only made possible ways of seeing that were not possible before, they have also censored or silenced ways of seeing that used to be possible."[72] How

[69] Ibid., 149.
[70] Ibid., 160. The claim that the descriptive and evaluative content of a concept can be sharply separated is controversial, but I will grant it for the sake of argument.
[71] Ibid., 149.
[72] Ibid., 157.

so? Schauer reports that because of Marcel Duchamp's work *L.H.O.O.Q.*, he can no longer look at Leonardo Da Vinci's *Mona Lisa* without chuckling and wondering where her mustache is.[73] Insofar as Schauer's association of censorship with such postmodern darlings as Duchamp (and elsewhere Jenny Holzer) is supposed to lend the view panache, it is worth noting that many people cannot look at Rembrandt's *Syndics of the Textile Guild* without thinking of Dutch Masters cigars.

Even if Schauer's examples were convincing, they would not secure the most radical postmodern claim: that censorship is inevitable because it is stitched into the fabric of language. Whereas Fish is wont to toss off such claims without explanation or argument, Schauer, to his credit, tries to defend the idea. Here is his case:

> Moreover, the very possibility of language, the particular languages that exist within that possibility, and the particular meanings that exist within a language depend not only on the languages of others but also on the way in which the language of others creates rules that make language possible precisely by making some language impossible. When someone says, "fringulation begets commonly," and I say "Huh?," have I censored, or have I just done my part in reinforcing the rules that enable language to exist? Or have I done both, since what some would marginalize and condemn as censorship is part of the mechanism that allows communication to take place.[74]

This is a rhetorical question. Schauer claims that his act deserves to be called censorship—in the strictly descriptive sense—just as much as any other. But notice two things. First, unless the postmodern analysis is correct, it does not deserve to be called censorship in any sense, and this example suggests a reductio ad absurdum of that claim. Second, no one would seriously condemn Schauer's response, whether as censorship or anything else. The deep problem with the postmodern "insight" is that it leaves its theorists without the conceptual tools to draw fundamental moral and political distinctions. To be sure, his embrace of postmodernism does not *force* Schauer to condemn the correction of meaningless speech or to condone the execution of political dissidents. But by encouraging its advocates to conflate serious cases with frivolous ones, the postmodern analysis threatens to induce something worth calling 'decadence'.

[73] It is a bit strange that Schauer doesn't also have—or doesn't admit having—vulgar thoughts about the quality of the Mona Lisa's ass, but perhaps that innuendo from the title of Duchamp's work, pronounced in French, didn't take. Or maybe Schauer is "censoring" Duchamp by effacing the politically embarrassing aspect of *L.H.O.O.Q.*

[74] Schauer, "The Ontology of Censorship," 153.

Is it uncharitable to suggest that bad philosophy, under the guise of sophistication, might render the postmodern skeptic morally obtuse about censorship? Consider one final and most remarkable reflection that Schauer offers on the subject:

> All too often, what is at times characterized as censorship seems to be quite similar to what at other times is characterized as editing, or choice. At times it is "simply" speech, as when pundits blithely characterize the words of Salman Rushdie as the target of censorship and the words of the Ayatollah Khomeni in calling for a *fatwa* against Rushdie as censorship, even though, like Rushdie, words were the only things that the Ayatollah employed.[75]

Only blithe pundits, Schauer suggests—presumably in contrast to sophisticated intellectuals—claim that Rushdie was censored by the Ayatollah's death threat. Rushdie might see a difference between the two sorts of "words." He evidently took the threat and the bounty subsequently offered for his murder—both performative speech acts—rather more seriously, as they forced him into hiding for nearly a decade. What is more, Schauer here reiterates MacKinnon's categorization of all verbal behavior as "simply speech," deliberately ignoring the obvious fact that Khomeni's words constitute a murderous edict, whereas Rushdie's words compose a controversial novel.

According to Schauer, he is censored by the boycott of French wine and by Duchamp's mustached *Mona Lisa*; but it is blithe, not fully serious or sophisticated, to say that Rushdie was the target of censorship when he was threatened, terrorized, and forced into seclusion by murderous religious zealots. Rushdie could have edited himself, but instead the Ayatollah did it for him. Rushdie wrote a book; Khomeni wrote a *fatwa*. If these acts are indeed "quite similar" from the postmodern perspective, then I am content to leave it to the reader to decide whether this perspective should be considered sophisticated or decadent, innovative or retrograde.

V. Conclusion: On the Ideology of Academia

Contrary to the postmodern "insight," I have argued that not all human activity is indistinguishable from censorship. Rather, there is a reasonably specific class of speech—what Mill called the expression of opinion and sentiment—that is the proper object of free speech protection. And there is a limited sort of coercive suppression of such speech that constitutes censorship. This is not to deny the existence of hard cases on the border between speech and action, or between criticism and coercion. But borderline cases exist for every evaluative concept and distinction. Certainly the descriptive content of the concept 'racist' is by no means clear-cut, yet

[75] Ibid., 160.

postmodernists do not attempt to unravel or deconstruct this concept by attaching some extravagantly expansive gloss to it and then contending that it is useless as an analytic device—much less that racism is equally part and parcel of all human activity. I have also argued that progressive skeptics need to do much more to develop their silencing arguments, which advocate restricting speech for the sake of greater freedom of speech, in order to make these arguments seem more cogent than opportunistic.

But I have also noted that a more plausible argument can be made, along lines proposed by Fiss and Schauer, for the prevalence of a form of silencing that should *not* be assimilated to censorship or claimed to be inevitable. This is the silencing perpetrated by the corruption of institutions that are, or should be, dedicated to cultivating intellectual freedom and diversity of opinion. Schauer focuses on American colleges and universities in particular, and he argues that intellectual honesty requires that decisions about hiring, publication, and funding must not entrench an ideological orthodoxy. The silencing of the unorthodox is not tantamount to censorship, because no one's speech rights are being violated, but it nevertheless constitutes a form of corruption and a betrayal of academic freedom. Our academic institutions must not be allowed to preemptively answer questions of "whose choices we as a society wish to privilege" and "what functions the institutions are supposed to serve."[76] I contend that American society would surely reject the claim that U.S. colleges and universities should function as a political indoctrination program for students, or that the partisan choices of a self-perpetuating intellectual elite, in the grip of a radical ideology, should be "privileged" in academia.

Yet there is considerable evidence that this is exactly what has happened. According to surveys of voter registration and political self-identification, American college and university faculty are overwhelmingly leftist, especially in the arts, humanities, and social sciences.[77] This finding should come as no surprise to any informed observer. Indeed, when asked to comment on it, Stanley Fish responded, "I certainly agree that the large proportion of faculty members in [a] number of departments would be 90 percent liberal."[78] Recall Schauer's assertion that intellectual honesty requires diversity of opinion, and that it creates "an obligation

[76] Ibid., 163. Again, I do not mean to imply that Schauer accepts my conclusions, although I think they follow from a consistent application of his argument.

[77] See Karl Zinsmeister, "The Shame of America's One-Party Campuses," *The American Enterprise*, September 2002, 18-25. Zinsmeister's survey found that about 90 percent of the faculty, in liberal arts departments at twenty-one representative American colleges and universities were registered as Democrats or in other parties on the left.

[78] The quotes from Fish are from the official transcript of his September 24, 2002, appearance with Thor Havorseen, executive director of the Foundation for Individual Rights in Education, on the MSNBC television program *Hardball*. The transcript is no longer posted on the MSNBC Web site; a copy can be found on Erin O'Connor's Weblog, *Critical Mass*, at http://www.erinoconnor.org/archives/000476.html [accessed October 31, 2003]. I would replace the word 'liberal' with 'leftist' in the quotation, so as not to confuse the vernacular sense of 'liberal' with the traditional sense that I have been using throughout this paper.

either to find, or if necessary to create, the strongest argument" for opposing positions.[79] On the face of it, American academia seems to be failing dismally at this task. Yet Fish rejects this conclusion, despite granting the data supporting it. "The question," he asks, "is what does this mean for instruction in the schools or for the hiring practices that brought these people to the campus, and my answer would be nothing whatsoever."[80] Indeed, according to Fish, there "just aren't very many" free speech issues on campus.[81] If Fish is wrong, however, and the gross political bias of the academy does have serious implications for hiring practices and instruction, then it seems he would have to admit that there are large and troubling issues concerning freedom of inquiry on campus.

Ironically, Fish now seems to have no trouble glossing a narrow conception of censorship, postmodern claims notwithstanding. He recently wrote, "No one is silenced because a single outlet declines to publish him; silencing occurs when that outlet (or any other) is forbidden by the state to publish him on pain of legal action; and that is also what censorship is."[82] Of course, I have also quoted Fish's suggestion that whenever you can refashion free speech principles in line with your purposes, you should do so "with a vengeance."[83] This strategic advice might explain both the conveniently narrow conception of silencing Fish now claims to favor, and his inability to see many free speech issues on campus. Interestingly, Fish wrote a letter to the provost of Duke University in 1990 urging that forty-six professors who had formed a chapter of the (conservative) National Association of Scholars should not be allowed to serve on hiring committees because they were sexist, racist, and homophobic.[84]

What then should we make of Fish's claim that instruction is not affected by the grossly skewed political balance on campus? This, too, is hard to square with the overt dogma of the Left. Consider this statement of principle from prominent critical race theorists, which is hardly idiosyncratic:

> The struggle against institutional, structural, and culturally ingrained racism and the movement toward a fully multiculturalist, postcolonial university is central to the work of the liberationist teacher.[85]

[79] Schauer, "The First Amendment As Ideology," 868.

[80] Fish, debate on MSNBC *Hardball*, September 24, 2002. I have inserted a comma into this quotation for the sake of clarity, which is (I think mistakenly) absent from the transcript. This does not change Fish's meaning at all.

[81] Stanley Fish, "The Free Speech Follies," *The Chronicle of Higher Education*, June 13, 2003. Available online at: http://chronicle.com/jobs/2003/06/2003061301c.htm [accessed October 31, 2003].

[82] Ibid.

[83] Fish, *There's No Such Thing as Free Speech*, 114.

[84] See transcript of MSNBC *Hardball*, September 24, 2002 (details at note 78). Fish admitted that "I did say that," but defended himself by claiming that these faculty members should be barred from hiring decisions because of their bias.

[85] Matsuda et al., *Words That Wound*, 14.

The social facts about power in American academia, on which postmodern scholars are supposed to focus "with a sharp Foucaultian lens," are illuminating indeed.[86] I will mention only a few of the surfeit of recent cases that tell a disturbing and familiar story. The instructor of a composition course at the University of California, Berkeley, a graduate student, wrote in the official course description that "conservative thinkers are encouraged to seek other sections."[87] Further investigation revealed that this instructor had made similar statements in previous course descriptions, which could hardly have been missed by his department supervisors, but this was evidently ignored until it was exposed by external criticism. And this is not the first such controversy specific to composition courses in the University of California (UC) system. A mandatory composition course at UC, San Diego (UCSD) has generated complaints by parents, students, and even faculty for years, due to its transparent (and radical) politicization. A faculty-review committee convened to examine the program concluded: "If controversial issues are examined, multiple and contrasting points of view should be presented."[88] However, the provost, citing the academic freedom of the director of the writing program, claimed that he could do nothing about the situation. Apparently, even a required composition course that seems to focus more on political indoctrination than writing instruction is immune from effective criticism.

Yet the provost's indifference conflicts dramatically with the official statement on academic freedom that was current during this controversy, which declared:

> The function of the university is to seek and to transmit knowledge and to train students in the processes whereby truth is to be made known. To convert, or to make converts, is alien and hostile to this dispassionate duty. Where it becomes necessary, in performing this function of a university, to consider political, social, or sectarian movements, they are dissected and examined—not taught, and the conclusion left, with no tipping of the scales, to the logic of the facts.[89]

Perhaps this conflict was resolved by a recent revision to the University of California's statement on academic freedom, which was drafted by Robert Post himself. Post's revision effaces the passage quoted above and

[86] Post, "Censorship and Silencing," 2.

[87] See Tanya Schevitz, "Cramped Speech at UC Berkeley," *San Francisco Chronicle*, May 10, 2002. Article available online at http://www.sfgate.com/cgi-bin/article.cgi?f=/c/a/2002/05/10/BA122563.DTL [accessed October 31, 2003].

[88] Quoted in Stanley Kurtz, "Students Fight Back," *National Review Online*, December 2, 2002. Article available online at http://www.nationalreview.com/kurtz/kurtz120202.asp [accessed October 31, 2003].

[89] *University of California Regulations*, General University Policy Regarding Academic Appointees: Academic Freedom, APM-010, revised no. 5 (June 15, 1944).

similar passages: all condemnation of conversion, propaganda, and the domination by parties or sects has been dropped.[90]

University President Richard Atkinson offered this explanation of why he commissioned Post to revise the statement: "The statement [was] focused on the primacy of 'dispassionate' scholarship. Although appropriate for the time, it has become outdated and does not provide an adequate basis for understanding and defending academic freedom at the University of California in the 21st century."[91] Hence, Atkinson commissioned Post to draft a new version of the statement, which was ultimately passed with only minor revision. A footnote to the new statement, written by Post, echoes Atkinson's characterization of the old statement and justification of the new one:

> The original language . . . associated academic freedom with scholarship that gave "play to intellect rather than to passion." It conceived scholarship as "dispassionate" and as concerned only with "the logic of the facts." The revised version supercedes this standpoint. It holds that academic freedom depends upon the quality of scholarship, which is to be assessed by the content of scholarship, not by the motivations that led to its production. The revision . . . therefore does not distinguish between "interested" and "disinterested" scholarship; it differentiates instead between competent and incompetent scholarship.[92]

But close reading of the original statement reveals this characterization as tendentious at best. Whereas Post describes the former statement as conceiving *scholarship* as "dispassionate," what is claimed to be dispassionate is rather the *duty* to seek and transmit knowledge rather than to convert. And the original statement posits an obligation to see that *the conditions under which questions are examined* "give play to intellect rather than passion."[93] The invidious distinction between passion and reason is admittedly old-fashioned. But there seems to be a further and more questionable agenda underlying the primary justification for the revision. Post claims the old statement to imply that "faculty are unprofessional if they are urgently committed to a definite point of view."[94] Yet this conclusion follows only if the "urgency" of such commitments motivates attempts at

[90] Revision of the Academic Personnel Manual, Academic Freedom statement, APM-010 (rev. 6/18/03). See http://www.universityofcalifornia.edu/senate/ for documentation on the revision.

[91] Richard Atkinson, letter to Academic Council Chair Gayle Binion, March 21, 2003. Available online at http://www.universityofcalifornia.edu/senate/underreview/apm010prop.pdf [accessed October 31, 2003].

[92] Proposed Revision of Academic Personnel Manual, Academic Freedom statement, APM-010 fn 1. Post's draft (March 12, 2003) read that the new statement "repudiates" rather than "supercedes" the old standpoint.

[93] APM-010, revised no. 5.

[94] APM-010, rev. 6/18/03.

political indoctrination or compromises the conditions of inquiry. In fact, the distinction Post alludes to between "interested" and "disinterested" scholarship is simply not drawn in the original, *despite the use of quotation marks*. These must be taken as scare quotes—unlike all other quotation marks in the revised statement—for this not to be an outright distortion of the text. Even so, this might seem like quibbling. Why does it matter if it is the duty to teach rather than convert, and the conditions under which research is conducted—rather than scholarship itself or its underlying motivations—that was supposed to be dispassionate or driven only by the logic of the facts?.

The answer is that the official justification for the amendment focuses on a red herring. While it is true that, as Post writes, "[t]here is no academic norm that prohibits scholarship from communicating definite and politically salient viewpoints about important and controversial questions," the former statement did not claim otherwise.[95] It is thus quite significant that no distinction was originally drawn between interested and disinterested scholarship, and that the former statement repudiated not political commitment in scholarship but political indoctrination in teaching. For there *are* academic norms against using one's position of power to indoctrinate students, as well as professional norms against basing hiring decisions on those "politically salient" viewpoints. Indeed, the University of California's Faculty Code of Conduct (APM-015), which is not up for revision, suffices to illustrate that the social facts of the academy may constitute a form of corruption. According to this code, types of unacceptable professional conduct include both: "Use of the position or powers of a faculty member to coerce the judgment or conscience of a student" and "Discrimination, including harassment, against a student on political grounds."[96] What remains to be seen is whether the stated goals of the "liberationist teacher," which expressly include "the struggle ... toward a fully multiculturalist, postcolonial university"—and the manifestations of that struggle in the classroom—will ever be seen as conflicting with either the free inquiry or the antidiscrimination clauses of the Faculty Code of Conduct.

Moreover, Schauer's argument against ideological conformity turns on the basic norm of intellectual honesty, which requires the cultivation of diverse opinion in academia. Whether or not the distinction between interested and disinterested scholarship was part of the old conception of academic freedom, the distinction between competent and incompetent scholarship is expressly claimed to be at the core of the new standpoint. Yet worries about the effects of ideological conformity should raise serious doubts about how political orthodoxy affects not just hiring, promo-

[95] Post, letter to Atkinson, March 12, 2003. Available online at http://www.universityofcalifornia.edu/senate/underreview/apm010prop.pdf [accessed October 31, 2003].

[96] University of California Faculty Code of Conduct, APM-015, rev. 1/1/02, part 2, A, p. 5. Available online at http://www.ucop.edu/acadadv/acadpers/apm/apm-015.pdf [accessed October 31, 2003].

tion, and teaching practices, but scholarship as well. With this in mind, consider the July 2003 press release from the *UC Berkeley News* reporting that university researchers have now provided an "elegant and unifying explanation" of what makes for a political conservative.[97] "Some of the common psychological factors linked to political conservativism," according to this research, include the following: "Fear and aggression; dogmatism and intolerance of ambiguity; uncertainty avoidance; need for cognitive closure; terror management."[98]

Although the researchers consider the possibility that their analysis might be viewed as a partisan exercise, the press release notes their insistence that these findings "are not judgmental."[99] They also have a response to the objection that the intellectual traits they associate with political conservativism—resistance to change and acceptance of inequality—might not differentiate despots of the right from those of the left:

> The researchers conceded cases of left-wing ideologues, such as Stalin, Khrushchev or Castro, who, once in power, steadfastly resisted change, allegedly in the name of egalitarianism. Yet they noted that some of these figures might be considered politically conservative in the context of the systems that they defended. The researchers noted that Stalin, for example, was concerned about defending and preserving the existing Soviet system.[100]

Perhaps some will be convinced by this explanation, and think there is little danger that ideological conformity might undermine the competence of scholarly research. Others will continue to have their doubts.

Philosophy, Bowling Green State University

[97] Kathleen Maclay, "Researchers Help Define What Makes a Political Conservative," *UC Berkeley News*, July 22, 2003. See: http://www.berkeley.edu/news/media/releases/2003/07/22_politics.shtml [accessed October 31, 2003]. I am focusing on the press release rather than the article itself because my point is merely to illustrate the prima facie absurdity of the central claim—with its undifferentiated and alien (one might even say "Orientalist") notion of conservativism—backed ingenuously by the institution's vehicle of public relations. This is a symptom, not the disease.

[98] John T. Jost, Jack Glaser, Arie W. Kruglanski, and Frank J. Sulloway, "Political Conservativism As Motivated Social Cognition," *Psychological Bulletin* 129, no. 3 (2003).

[99] Maclay, "Researchers Help Define What Makes a Political Conservative."

[100] Ibid. Note that Stalin's resistance to change is here taken as (perhaps decisive) *evidence* of his political conservativism—his revolutionary Communism notwithstanding—thereby threatening to render the authors' central finding tantamount to the claim that those who resist change tend to be resistant to change.

FREE SPEECH AND OFFENSIVE EXPRESSION

By Judith Wagner DeCew

I. Introduction

Free speech has historically been viewed as a special and preferred democratic value in the United States, by the public as well as by the legislatures and courts. In 1937, Justice Benjamin Cardozo wrote in *Palko v. Connecticut* that protection of speech is a "fundamental" liberty due to America's history, political and legal, and he recognized its importance, saying, "[F]reedom of thought and speech" is "the matrix, the indispensable condition, of nearly every other form of freedom."[1] It is likely notable that in the Bill of Rights free speech is protected in the *First* Amendment rather than later.[2]

Although the terms 'free speech' and 'freedom of expression' may be used differently, I will use them synonymously in this essay. Thus, 'free speech' will be taken to cover not only the spoken word, but also the written word as well as conduct conveying a message and expression through symbols, demonstrations, and so on.

A difficult legal, moral, and public policy problem is determining how to protect freedom of speech vigorously while also recognizing a community's concern to maintain a type of environment that its members can tolerate. Speech or conduct that is offensive, and even outrageously so, is usually still worthy of protection under the First Amendment. There is no easy answer to the question about how to deal with expression that causes great pain and is possibly even dangerous because it is degrading, or racist, or anti-Semitic, or sexist, or homophobic, or pornographic, or in other ways offensive. A review of the major philosophical justifications for freedom of expression, and many of the arguments in U.S. Supreme Court cases on offensive expression over the past thirty years, can help assess ways to confront difficult decisions concerning offensive speech. In this essay, I shall narrow my focus: I shall not address racist, homophobic, or other expression called 'hate speech', but shall focus instead on material that is 'sexually offensive', that is, material that is erotic or sexually explicit but that does not meet the definition of obscene.

[1] 302 U.S. 319 (1937).

[2] See Archibald Cox, *Freedom of Expression* (Cambridge, MA: Harvard University Press, 1981), 1. Cox is one constitutional scholar who believes the numerical position is symbolic of the primacy of free speech rights.

II. Philosophical Arguments Defending Maximal Free Speech

Despite language about free speech as a right, and its articulation in the Bill of Rights, the most common defenses of free speech are consequentialist, citing the good effects of allowing it and the bad consequences of restricting it.[3] Most of these arguments were elucidated by John Stuart Mill in his famous 1859 treatise, *On Liberty,* although a few other justifications have become well known in the literature on free speech.[4]

One set of arguments focuses on the positive effects of allowing maximal freedom of expression. First, Mill outlined the benefits of *searching for and discovering the truth* to advance knowledge; open expression allows for the beneficial effects of acquiring justified beliefs and of identifying and correcting erroneous beliefs. Even if an opinion is false, Mill argued, the truth becomes better understood and justified by refuting the error. Beliefs are then founded on conviction. Moreover, since few opinions are either completely true or completely false, he pointed out, allowing free expression and the airing of competing views preserves the partial truth in various opinions.[5]

A second major justification for free speech given by Mill and others is a *political argument* that it is required by representative government to improve debate over public policy. Less accepting of majority rule than Locke, Mill was profoundly worried about the danger of suppressing minority opinions. This argument has led other commentators to focus on political speech as worthy of the highest protection, while other forms of speech may be less deserving. Legal scholar Alexander Meiklejohn first developed the distinction that "public" speech affecting civic issues and self-government must be wholly immune from infringement, while "private" or nonpolitical speech, including commercial, literary, and artistic expression, should be entitled to less complete protection.[6] One can reject Meiklejohn's extreme view on the primacy of political speech and nev-

[3] Some paragraphs from the early sections of this essay are drawn and adapted from Judith Wagner DeCew, "Free Speech on Campus," in Steven M. Cahn, ed., *Morality, Responsibility, and the University: Studies in Academic Ethics* (Philadelphia, PA: Temple University Press, 1990), 38–40, 48–50.

[4] John Stuart Mill, *On Liberty,* 1859, ed. Currin V. Shields (Indianapolis, IN: Bobbs-Merrill, 1985). Mill states he will forgo any advantage from an argument based on abstract right independent of utility. See Daniel Jacobson, "Mill on Liberty, Speech, and the Free Society," *Philosophy and Public Affairs* 29, no. 3 (2000): 276–309, for a novel interpretation of Mill's views.

[5] Mill, *On Liberty,* 43, 56, 64.

[6] Alexander Meiklejohn, *Free Speech and Its Relation to Self-Government* (New York: Harper, 1948). In response to criticism, however, Meiklejohn seemed to agree that literature, art, philosophy, and science ought to be granted First Amendment protection. See Alexander Meiklejohn, "The First Amendment Is an Absolute," *Supreme Court Review* (1961): 245. Others, such as legal theorist Robert Bork, maintain that Meiklejohn's original view on the primacy of political speech was correct. See Robert Bork, "Neutral Principles and Some First Amendment Problems," *Indiana Law Journal* 47 (1971): 1.

ertheless defend the political argument, which focuses on the beneficial value of free speech for a system of representative democracy where citizens serve a political function as electors who can bring about change and help limit governmental power.[7] The expression of more opinions and better access to as much information as possible enhance the development of public policy and generate a better informed citizenry and better educated voters. Electors also need the opportunity to question established values, and this avenue for dissent is provided by maximizing freedom of expression.

Third in the set of justifications focusing on the positive effects of free speech is an argument relating to individual integrity and autonomy. Freedom of expression provides many *benefits to individuals*. As Mill eloquently argued, liberty of expression allows personal growth and self-realization. Free speech serves as a vital way to guarantee one's ability to develop one's faculties and talents and to realize one's individual potential and creativity. Mill repeatedly urged that eccentricity is better than uniformity and stagnation. This defense is sometimes rephrased as a broader, nonconsequentialist argument that free speech enhances and protects individual autonomy, liberty, and self-development, and can also be justified in terms of fairness and respect for persons.[8] On this view, "an autonomous person cannot accept without independent consideration the judgment of others as to what he should believe or what he should do."[9]

In addition to these positive justifications of freedom of speech, another set of consequentialist arguments relies on articulating the negative effects of banning or restricting speech. First, as Mill pointed out, suppressing speech leads to *the possibility of banning the truth*. Unconventional or unpopular opinions may turn out to be correct; to assume otherwise is to assume one's infallibility. Restrictions on open and free discussion heighten the chance of losing true opinions.[10]

Second, a common argument given is that restriction of speech leads to a 'chilling effect', an effect that arises when banning some speech leads individuals to be more fearful, and thus more careful and conformist in what they dare to say. As restrictions on expression are added, individ-

[7] See Thomas Scanlon, "A Theory of Freedom of Expression," *Philosophy and Public Affairs* 1, no. 2 (1972): 204–26, reprinted in Ronald Dworkin, ed., *The Philosophy of Law* (Oxford: Oxford University Press, 1977), 153–71. See also John Hart Ely, *Democracy and Distrust: A Theory of Judicial Review* (Cambridge, MA: Harvard University Press, 1980).

[8] Mill, *On Liberty*, especially 71–79. Among those who insist on incorporating both consequentialist and nonconsequentialist arguments for free expression are Thomas Scanlon, "A Theory of Freedom of Expression," in Dworkin, ed., *The Philosophy of Law*, 157; Fred R. Berger, "The Right of Free Expression," *International Journal of Applied Philosophy* 3 (1986): 1–10; and Lawrence H. Tribe, *American Constitutional Law*, 2d ed. (Mineola, NY: Foundation Press, 1988), 787.

[9] Scanlon, "A Theory of Freedom of Expression," in Dworkin, ed., *The Philosophy of Law*, 163.

[10] Mill, *On Liberty*, 21, 64.

uals worry about whether what they are expressing is too close to the line between speech that is allowed and speech that is not. In this way they become more fearful of saying everything they believe—"chilled" from full expression—and the negative result is likely to be more restrained and homogeneous expression.

Third is the well-known 'slippery slope' argument. As speech is restricted, it becomes easier and easier for those in power to restrict or suppress even more expression. It becomes more difficult to find a clear way to draw the line between acceptable and unacceptable speech, with the consequence that more and more expression is restricted. Closely related to this is a fourth negative effect of restricting more expression, namely the *enhanced power it gives to the government* over the individual. When fewer views can be heard, the individual loses the ability to choose what to listen and pay attention to or what to read. Instead, government has the power to make more of these choices for the individual, concentrating additional power in centralized governmental hands.

These philosophical and largely consequentialist justifications support the general importance and priority of free speech. Yet additional, more specific considerations arise about protection of particular types of speech. Legal interpretations have helped to address questions about concepts such as "offensive" versus "obscene" speech and the "value" of speech.

III. Justifications for Limiting Free Speech

Although the U.S. Supreme Court's first major encounters with disputes over limitations on free speech did not arise until after World War I, such disputes are now common court business. As courts heard more of these cases, they differentiated certain standard justifications for limiting free speech. Generally, courts have taken the view that illegitimate justifications for restricting or suppressing speech are those based on the *content* of the material. This view has likely grown from the lessons of American history, given that the early settlers and citizens were particularly concerned to protect each individual's ability to express unpopular political and religious views. Thus, content that the government finds objectionable has not in general been deemed an adequate justification for banning the expression. Alternatively, courts have deemed justifications for restricting speech based on considerations other than content, such as *time, place, and manner* (excessive loudness, for example), to be adequate and legitimate reasons to limit expression.[11]

One serious difficulty, of course, is that the two types of justifications are not always easy to separate to determine when speech ought to be protected. Consider the classic case of a sound truck blaring messages in

[11] See Scanlon, "A Theory of Freedom of Expression," in Dworkin, ed., *The Philosophy of Law,* 157.

a quiet neighborhood at 2:00 A.M. On the one hand, if the message is about a politician's qualifications for office, bad timing and loud noise in an unacceptable place would presumably be legitimate justifications for banning the truck regardless of the political content of the message. If, on the other hand, the message is a warning about an impending tornado or imminent flood, content would override the otherwise inappropriate time, place, and manner. The truck might well be allowed precisely because of the content of the message. The reason this is a difficulty is that it highlights the malleability of the term "legitimate." Banning leaflets because of the litter they produce is likely legitimate. But if public officials ban leafleting on this ground when, in fact, they are trying to suppress the message on the leaflets—perhaps a political one—then they are concocting a "legitimate" reason to ban a message with a content they find objectionable, and this is an illegitimate reason for suppression.

Despite all the arguments in favor of maximal freedom of expression, both the positive effects of allowing maximal freedom of expression and the negative consequences of restriction and suppression, the First Amendment clearly does not guarantee protection of all expression. Justice Oliver Wendell Holmes's famous example of falsely crying "Fire!" in a crowded theater is one instance of speech that is not protected. Similarly, it has been uncontroversial that bribery, perjury, and counseling to murder are not protected under the First Amendment. As case decisions have carved out the guidelines further, it is clear that other speech is disallowed. In *Chaplinsky v. New Hampshire* (1942), the Supreme Court very clearly insisted that "obscenity" fell outside First Amendment protection, together with profanity, libelous speech, incitement to riot, and "fighting words" directed at someone close enough to the speaker that the words would "tend to incite an immediate breach of the peace" or convey "a quite unambiguous invitation to a brawl." All of these are categories of expression that are banned without hesitation.[12]

While most categories of unprotected speech are clearly unacceptable because of the danger or harm they cause, the Court's reasoning for banning obscenity stands out as distinctive. This is because the Court's decision to ban obscenity does not rely on an appeal to harm caused by such expression. The Court's discussions on obscenity are also problematic because it is not clear just what reasons the Court does find persuasive. As legal theorist John Hart Ely has pointed out, " 'Obscenity' or highly erotic material is . . . unprotected—for reasons it is difficult to make convincing."[13] Both the paternalistic argument that obscenity debases an individual's character and the claim that it is too offensive to others have been taken to be inadequate to justify complete suppression of obscene expression. Other justifications sometimes given for exclusion

[12] 315 U.S. 568 (1942); and Ely, *Democracy and Distrust*, 114.
[13] Ely, *Democracy and Distrust*, 114.

from First Amendment protection is the worry that obscene material leads to sex crimes and other criminal conduct, and that it is harmful because it erodes moral standards in society. Yet these are problematic as well, given the difficulty of establishing a causal relationship, not just a correlation, between obscene material and criminal behavior, and given concerns about permitting the government to enforce morals.[14] Certainly obscenity is not political speech, and some have argued that it is undeserving of protection because it is noncognitive as well.[15] Ultimately, the Court has relied on the reasoning that obscenity is "of such slight social value as a step to truth that any benefit that may be derived from [it] is outweighed by the social interest in order and morality."[16] The Court has continued to maintain that obscenity is unprotected and has added child pornography as an additional type of sexually explicit speech that is not covered by the First Amendment.[17]

A major difficulty facing the Court has been how to define or characterize material that is "obscene" and not merely "offensive." Commentators disagree on the extent to which the Court has been successful in excluding obscenity from First Amendment protection without curtailing or repressing important works of art and other properly protected speech. The Court struggled to develop standards for controlling obscenity over a period of about twenty years, beginning in 1957 in *Roth v. United States*.[18] Although throughout this period the Court continued to hold that the First Amendment did not protect obscenity, its justifications for excluding obscenity from protection varied. Justice William J. Brennan wrote for the Court in *Roth* that ideas having only the "slightest redeeming social importance" had guaranteed protection, whereas obscenity was "utterly without redeeming social importance." He stressed that sex and obscenity were not synonymous. Five members of the Court agreed that obscenity could be determined by asking "whether to the average person, applying contemporary community standards, the dominant theme of the material taken as a whole appeals to prurient interest," namely a "shameful or morbid interest in nudity, sex, or excretion."[19]

[14] Note that the 1986 U.S. Attorney General's Commission on Pornography did conclude that some forms of obscenity could cause violent crime and antisocial behavior, and that legally obscene material should remain unprotected by the First Amendment. There has been criticism of this report, however. On the enforcement of morals, see the debate between Lord Patrick Devlin, "Morals and the Criminal Law," and H. L. A. Hart, "Immorality and Treason," in Ronald Dworkin, ed., *The Philosophy of Law* (Oxford: Oxford University Press, 1977), 66–82 and 83–88. Note especially Hart's replies to Devlin that legislation relying solely on a majority view of moral standards is unacceptable.

[15] See Frederick Schauer, "Speech and 'Speech'—Obscenity and 'Obscenity': An Exercise in the Interpretation of Constitutional Language," *Georgetown Law Journal* 67 (1979): 899.

[16] *Chaplinsky*, 315 U.S. at 568.

[17] *Roth v. United States*, 354 U.S. 476 (1957); and *New York v. Ferber*, 458 U.S. 747 (1982), for example.

[18] 354 U.S. at 476.

[19] *Id.* at 484, 487, and 489 (citing the American Law Institute Model Penal Code section 207.10 [Tentative Draft No. 6, 1957] in defining "prurient interest").

Nevertheless, there seemed to be no clear majority view on obscenity. To the contrary, in the years following *Roth* there seemed to be hopeless confusion and a divergence of opinion among the justices over what Justice John Marshall Harlan called the "intractable obscenity problem." As the Court tried to come to terms with what is and is not obscene, different justices placed different emphases on three elements: an appeal to prurient interest, an affront to community standards, and a lack of redeeming social value. In his concurring opinion in 1964 in *Jacobellis v. Ohio,* Justice Potter Stewart made an observation that is now famous for capturing the Court's struggle to define obscenity. Stewart stated that he could not further define material that was obscene, adding, "But I know it when I see it."[20]

It was not until 1973, in the decisions in two cases decided together, *Miller v. California* and *Paris Adult Theatre I v. Slaton,* that the Court attempted a new definition of unprotected obscenity, abandoning its case-by-case review and shifting the burden of the determination to state and local courts.[21] The *Miller* case set the Court on its present course, and what is now called the '*Miller* test' is a three-pronged approach to defining obscenity. The basic guidelines are "(a) whether 'the average person, applying contemporary community standards' would find that the work, taken as a whole, appeals to the prurient interest [Roth] . . . ; (b) whether the work depicts or describes, in a patently offensive way, sexual conduct specifically defined by the applicable state law; and (c) whether the work, taken as a whole, lacks serious literary, artistic, political, or scientific value." In *Miller* the Court rejected the constitutional standard of "*utterly* without redeeming social value."[22] Justice Brennan wrote in his dissent in *Paris Adult Theatre* that the Court's efforts to implement the *Roth* approach in subsequent cases made clear the painful reality that there was as yet no workable definition of obscenity, and he argued, moreover, that the *Miller* test was still vague and offered no stability on the topic. Nevertheless, the test remains today as the standard for prohibiting obscenity without violating the First Amendment and without trampling on other protected areas of speech.

In terms of content, the Court continues to rely on the standard set in 1973 in *Miller*: obscene materials lack "serious literary, artistic, political, or scientific value" regardless of whether the government or a majority of the people approve of the ideas these works represent. Critics of *Miller* have rejected this justification, urging that it allows government to punish sexual dissent. Nevertheless, I shall take the view that obscene expression is legitimately excluded from protection under the First Amendment. Moreover, as constitutional scholars Gerald Gunther and Kathleen Sulli-

[20] 378 U.S. 184, 197 (1964) (Stewart, J., concurring).

[21] *Miller v. California,* 413 U.S. 15 (1973), and *Paris Adult Theatre I v. Slayton,* 413 U.S. 49 (1973).

[22] *Miller,* 413 U.S. at 24.

van have observed, "[I]f speech is sexually explicit but is not obscene and does not constitute child pornography, it is within the realm of First Amendment protection, but the Court has wrestled with the question whether it should occupy a subordinate position as 'lower value' speech."[23] Nudity alone is inadequate to make material obscene under the *Miller* test. Thus, there is the practical question of determining which materials are obscene under the Court's guidelines and which are not. There is, in addition, the more policy-oriented question of how to handle pornographic and sexually explicit material that is not obscene or child pornography. In the following sections of this essay, I shall discuss the arguments for protecting such expression. I shall also examine the arguments for and against designating it as "lower value" and less fundamental than other speech and, hence, less worthy of protection than, for example, political speech.

IV. Legal Guidelines on Offensive Expression

Following Justice Cardozo's articulate defense in 1937 of the importance of free speech, Justice Hugo Black, who served on the Supreme Court from 1937 to 1971, became an eloquent advocate of the strong view that First Amendment rights are "absolute," and that the charge to Congress to make "no law" abridging free speech means exactly that: make no such law. In contrast, Justices Felix Frankfurter and John Harlan, both of whom sat on the Court during Black's tenure, and Justice Lewis Powell, who was appointed as Black's replacement, are all associated with the rival view that absolute rules are too rigid and that First Amendment interpretation requires a candid weighing and balancing of competing interests. Black worried, in response to this position, that the approach would allow free speech rights to be balanced away whenever judges found conflicting state interests.[24] Although Frankfurter rejected the view that free speech was an "absolute" right and seemed to attack statements in Court opinions asserting the "preferred status" of First Amendment protection, legal theorists maintain that he nevertheless did not completely reject "a hierarchy of values with free speech high on the list. In short, he, too, found that First Amendment rights were specially protected ones."[25]

[23] Gerald Gunther and Kathleen M. Sullivan, *Constitutional Law*, 13th ed. (Westbury, NY: Foundation Press, 1997), 1125.

[24] Justice Frankfurter served on the Court from 1939 to 1962, and Justice Harlan from 1955 to 1971. *Konigsberg v. State Bar of California*, 366 U.S. 36 (1961) provides one classic confrontation between these two views as articulated by Justice Black and Justice Harlan. See Judith Wagner DeCew, "Moral Rights: Conflicts and Valid Claims," *Philosophical Studies* 54 (1988): 63–86, esp. sections 2 and 4, for an evaluation of alternative ways of understanding rights as "absolute."

[25] Gerald Gunther, *Individual Rights in Constitutional Law*, 4th ed. (Mineola, NY: Foundation Press, 1986), 646.

Even if there is agreement that the right to free speech is special in some sense, alternative methods of constitutional interpretation can affect the extent to which this preferred status is recognized. One type of interpretation, in the tradition of Harlan and Frankfurter, involves 'balancing' either the competing claims of the speaker and the protester or the right to express a message against the risk of harm. This is often viewed as the dominant constitutional theory, derived in large part from Justice Holmes's "clear and present danger" test.[26] The presumption is that a wide range of expression is protected by the First Amendment and can be repressed only when outweighed by a sufficiently strong governmental interest. Each case is evaluated individually based on the circumstances and the degree of the danger or other governmental interest at stake; thus, the special weight given to the value of free speech may vary. The balancing test avoids the extreme view that restriction of political speech is never justified, as well as the opposite extreme view that a speculative harm is sufficient to suppress speech. Yet balancing is often too flexible and vague to provide a very clear standard for judging which expression is allowable, and it may be too deferential to governmental interests in suppressing speech.[27]

Using a second type of interpretation, 'categorization', judges proceed by identifying and defining categories of speech that are not protected. Bribery, perjury, counsel to murder, lewd or obscene words, profanity, libel or slander, or "fighting words" that tend to incite an immediate breach of the peace fall outside of First Amendment protection. If the speech in question fits one of these excluded categories it is not protected; if it does not, it is protected.[28] The aim is to clarify standards for banning certain types of expression. Categorization precludes the balancing of interests in particular cases.

Balancing may give citizens insufficient notice of whether their speech will be allowed or not, because reasonable people can disagree in evaluating the weight of a governmental interest, such as danger or risk of danger. In other words, balancing appears to allow more judicial subjectivity. But it is worth noting that categorization is not always easy either. At what point do name calling and abusive language, or a pornographic image or film, cross the line from being merely offensive to being respectively fighting words or obscene?

Perhaps because of these difficulties, a third way of interpreting free speech cases has evolved. Using this newer way of distinguishing pro-

[26] *Schenck v. United States*, 249 U.S. 47 (1919).

[27] See Laurent Frantz, "The First Amendment in the Balance," *Yale Law Journal* 71 (1962): 1424 for a discussion of these criticisms of balancing. See also John Hart Ely, "Flag Desecration: A Case Study in the Roles of Categorization and Balancing in First Amendment Analysis," *Harvard Law Review* 88 (1975): 1482.

[28] See Kathleen M. Sullivan, "Post-Liberal Judging: The Roles of Categorization and Balancing," *University of Colorado Law Review* 63 (1992): 293.

tected from unprotected speech, the Supreme Court has sometimes struck down statutes as unconstitutional using 'overbreadth'. In such cases, the Court judged the statutes to be overly broad and hence likely, because of their vagueness, to repress too wide a swath of expression. This method of protecting free expression is beneficial because it avoids balancing, leaves the legislature the alternative of drafting narrower legislation, and takes seriously the chilling effect. But overbreadth is never well defined; accordingly, there is worry that it also is too manipulable a standard for consistent decision-making.[29]

In the 1971 decision in *Cohen v. California*, the U.S. Supreme Court majority opinion appears to illustrate the use of both balancing and categorization in its reasoning.[30] Young Mr. Cohen had worn a jacket emblazoned with the words "Fuck the Draft" through a California courthouse as a way of protesting the United States' involvement in the Vietnam War and the use of the draft to enlist those who would fight. The Supreme Court overturned Cohen's conviction or charges of violating a California state law that prohibited maliciously or willfully disturbing the peace by offensive conduct, thus defending his action as an exercise of free speech. Using the balancing method of constitutional interpretation, the Court felt that the words on Cohen's jacket did not pose a sufficient danger or threat to viewers to justify his conviction. The Court also argued, using categorization, that the words might be offensive but were not obscene, libelous, profane, or fighting words; offense was not deemed a sufficient condition for banning Cohen's expression.[31]

In *Cohen*, I find the categorization arguments to be the most compelling since they appear more likely to allow stronger protection of free speech than the balancing arguments. One way of interpreting the categorization arguments is to view the Court as holding that the list of categories of banned speech is settled, and the expression by Cohen did not fit in any of the categories on that list. In other words, the Court was clearly unwilling to expand the list by adding a new category of unacceptable speech, namely, offensive speech. This appears to be the stronger defense of free speech because it insists that the limited list of categories of unprotected speech is definitive; no new categories of expression can be suppressed. It seeks to provide clarity and guidance and to avoid exces-

[29] For an example of this type of reasoning, see *Gooding v. Wilson*, 405 U.S. 518 (1972).

[30] 403 U.S. 15 (1971). The earlier *Chaplinsky* case (*supra* note 12) can also be read as using both categorization and balancing.

[31] ". . . [T]his case cannot be said to fall within those relatively few categories of instances where prior decisions have established the power of government to deal more comprehensively with certain forms of expression. . . ." *Cohen*, 403 U.S. at 19–20 (Harlan, J.) (delivering the opinion of the Court). In paragraph 1 of his dissenting opinion, in which he was joined by Chief Justice Burger and Justice Black, Justice Blackmun claimed that Cohen's "immature antic" was conduct and not speech, and thus the case was not a First Amendment challenge at all. Since then, expressive conduct has been deemed to be speech under the First Amendment.

sive flexibility.[32] In contrast, when the Court uses a balancing argument, which depends on circumstances and context, many types of expression could presumably be banned if a sufficient number of justices find that the message or material carries a risk of harm and danger or conflicts with some other compelling governmental interest strong enough to merit its suppression.

In cases after *Cohen*, the Court has continued to grapple with issues surrounding offensive expression. In *Texas v. Johnson* (1989), a very divided Court issued a decision that upheld flag burning as expressive conduct worthy of protection under the First Amendment.[33] The majority argued that Texas failed to show an interest in regulating the conduct that was unrelated to the content of the message being delivered. Although the majority used several arguments to reject Texas's claim that it had a right to preserve the flag as a symbol of nationhood, it is notable that in one of these arguments the majority insisted that the Texas claim ultimately related to the regulation of ideas, because only another idea could challenge the idea of nationhood. In sum, the majority found that Texas did not have a legitimate content-neutral justification for suppressing the expression.

What we can learn from these and other related U.S. Supreme Court cases is that offensive speech and expression have been repeatedly protected. Disgusting or torrid as they may be, offensive speech and expressive conduct have been tolerated under free speech rights.[34] There are surely a number of reasons for this. One reason is the subjectivity of determining what expression is offensive and what is not.[35] While a "reasonable person" standard could be used, it is difficult to see how even that could provide an objective and consistent way to separate offensive from nonoffensive expression. What is offensive? Who is to decide? How revolting must an expression be to be deemed offensive enough to ban it? Moreover, in the case of offensive expression, especially pornography, nude dancing, or other erotic or sexually explicit speech or conduct, one must ask whether the content passes beyond the bounds of whatever

[32] See also Thomas Scanlon, "Freedom of Expression and Categories of Expression," *University of Pittsburgh Law Review* 40 (1979): 519. Scott D. Gerber has pointed out to me that there is a political danger in categorizing types of speech, yet I contend that there is a similar and perhaps more serious opportunity for decisions to be politicized using balancing. C. Edwin Baker has suggested that my preference for categorization over balancing may indicate that I favor a more deontological approach over a consequentialist one, and his suggestion may well be correct.

[33] 491 U.S. 397 (1989).

[34] See also Judith Wagner DeCew, "Violent Pornography: Censorship, Morality, and Social Alternatives," *Journal of Applied Philosophy* 1, no. 1 (1984): 79–94. Reprinted in *Right Conduct: Theories and Applications*, Michael D. Bayles and Kenneth Henley, eds., 2d ed. (New York: Random House, 1989), 246–56.

[35] As Justice Harlan noted in his majority opinion in *Cohen*, it is "often true that one man's vulgarity is another's lyric. Indeed, we think it is largely because governmental officials cannot make principled distinctions in this area that the Constitution leaves matters of taste and style [to] the individual." *Cohen*, 403 U.S. at 25.

might be tolerated, and thus may be banned on the grounds that it is correctly categorized as obscenity. Alternatively, one must repair to 'balancing' and consider whether the harm or potential harm, or some other governmental interest, is so great that it justifies suppression or regulation. Both sorts of determinations are extremely difficult to make, as the former (categorization) requires assessing the content of the material, which is normally an illegitimate justification for restriction or censorship, and the latter (balancing) requires establishing not merely a correlation but a causal relationship between expression and its effects that usually cannot be documented. Surely, in addition to the subjectivity of determining offensiveness, a second reason for allowing offensive expression continued protection is to hold the line on the types of speech excluded from First Amendment protection, and thus to avoid the slippery slope of adding more categories to the list of excluded speech.

Ultimately, determining guidelines for what should or should not be suppressed, especially when dealing with blatantly noxious material, is extremely difficult. Increasing governmental control over information always carries the cost of giving additional power to government officials and judges to decide what is or is not acceptable, what passes beyond the bounds of decency. Legal theorist Frederick Schauer, for example, has pointed out that free speech raises special reasons to distrust government's ability adequately to determine when material is obscene. On his view, history has shown a high proportion of governmental errors in suppression.[36] Thus, we are left with another sort of balancing problem: how to balance the harm of the offensive expression, such as a pornographic film or nude dancing, against the harm of giving power to government to decide for us what we can and cannot see and hear.

V. Supreme Court Struggles with Sexually Explicit yet Not Obscene Speech

The U.S. Supreme Court has been particularly divided in its consideration of cases concerning expression that is sexually explicit but is not child pornography or does not meet the definition of obscenity. It has repeatedly ruled that such material, including pornography and nude dancing, is not an unprotected category of speech. At least three cases prominently illustrate the protection of such expression.

First, in *Erznoznik v. Jacksonville* (1975), the Court upheld a challenge to an ordinance prohibiting drive-in movie theatres with screens visible from public highways from showing nonobscene films containing nudity.[37] Following *Cohen,* Justice Powell in his majority opinion reiterated that offense to political or moral sensibilities was insufficient reason to

[36] Frederick Schauer, *Free Speech: A Philosophical Enquiry* (Cambridge: Cambridge University Press, 1982).

[37] 422 U.S. 205 (1975).

allow government to decide that otherwise protected speech required suppression to protect unwilling viewers or listeners. Reiterating that not all nudity could be deemed obscene, he found the ordinance overbroad.

Second, in *Schad v. Mount Ephraim* (1981),[38] decided after the Court had in 1976 upheld a zoning ordinance aimed at adult theaters,[39] the Court struck down an ordinance that banned all "live entertainment," including nude dancing. Arguing again that nudity alone does not make expression obscene, and that a total ban on nudity is impermissible, the Court found that the ordinance prohibited a wide range of expression long held to be protected by the First Amendment. Third, similar reasoning led the Court, in *Sable Communications of California, Inc. v. FCC* (1989),[40] to refuse to ban "dial-a-porn" telephone services.

Commentators observe that in each of these three cases the Court indicated that "severe restrictions or total bans of such speech [sexual expression falling short of the definition of obscenity] will be strictly reviewed."[41] Moreover, in *Schad* the Court found that the ordinance did not further a sufficiently strong governmental interest, and found no evidence that live adult entertainment led to unusual problems.

Nevertheless, *restrictions* on sexually explicit but nonobscene expression have been defended. In *Young v. American Mini Theatres, Inc.* (1976), a zoning ordinance on adult entertainment establishments was upheld.[42] The impact was to move some establishments to particular areas of Detroit, not to ban such materials and displays entirely. Similarly, in *FCC v. Pacifica Foundation* (1978), regulation, though not censorship, of broadcasts deemed indecent but not obscene was upheld.[43]

An important question, then, is whether sexually explicit expression that is not child pornography or obscene, though not in an unprotected category, should occupy a subordinate position under the First Amendment. Is such expression less fundamental, less worthy of protection, and thus of "lower value" than other speech, especially political speech? Moreover, what are the implications of taking such a position? Early in his career, Justice John Paul Stevens appeared to be a major advocate of this view. As Gunther and Sullivan point out, "In several plurality opinions, Justice Stevens has supported content regulation of sexually offensive displays and speech under an approach that falls short of categorical exclusion of that type of communication from the First Amendment, but that treats such expression as less valuable than core, political speech and accordingly more readily restrainable."[44] In his plurality opinion in *American Mini Theatres*, for example, Stevens wrote:

[38] 452 U.S. 61 (1981).
[39] *Young v. American Mini Theatres, Inc.*, 427 U.S. 50 (1976).
[40] 492 U.S. 115 (1989).
[41] Gunther and Sullivan, *Constitutional Law*, 1155.
[42] *American Mini Theatres*, 427 U.S. at 50.
[43] 438 U.S. 726 (1978).
[44] Gunther and Sullivan, *Constitutional Law*, 1155.

> Moreover, even though we recognize that the First Amendment will not tolerate the total suppression of erotic materials that have some arguably artistic value, it is manifest that society's interest in protecting this type of expression is of a wholly different, and lesser, magnitude than the interest in untrammeled political debate that inspired Voltaire's immortal comment. Whether political oratory or philosophical discussion moves us to applaud or to despise what is said, every schoolchild can understand why our duty to defend the right to speak remains the same. But few of us would march our sons and daughters off to war to preserve the citizen's right to see "Specified Sexual Activities" exhibited in the theaters of our choice. Even though the First Amendment protects communication in this area from total suppression, we hold that the State may legitimately use the content of these materials as the basis for placing them in a different classification from other motion pictures.[45]

Furthermore, Stevens observed that "the city's interest in attempting to preserve the quality of urban life is one that must be accredited high respect," concluding "the city's interest in the present and future character of its neighborhoods adequately supports its classification of motion pictures."[46]

Stevens's view that sexually explicit but nonobscene expression is less fundamental and has lower value than other speech has not been explicitly embraced by a majority of the Court. Indeed, the dissenters in *American Mini Theatres* retorted that

> The kind of expression at issue here is no doubt objectionable to some, but that fact does not diminish its protected status any more than did the particular content of the "offensive" expression in [*Erznoznik, Cohen,* et al.].
>
> What this case does involve is the constitutional permissibility of selective interference with protected speech whose content is thought to produce distasteful effects. It is elementary that a prime function of the First Amendment is to guard against just such interference. By refusing to invalidate Detroit's ordinance the Court rides roughshod over cardinal principles of First Amendment law, which require that time, place, and manner regulations that affect protected expression be content neutral. . . .[47]

[45] *American Mini Theatres,* 427 U.S. at 70–71 (Stevens, J., plurality opinion). The "immortal comment" attributed to Voltaire is: "I may disagree with what you have to say, but I shall defend, to the death, your right to say it."

[46] *Id.* at 72 and 73.

[47] *Id.* at 85–86 (Stewart, J. dissenting). Justice Stewart was joined in the dissent by Justices Brennan, Marshall, and Blackmun. Justice Blackmun wrote separately "to identify an independent ground" for holding unconstitutional the challenged ordinance: vagueness.

They continued,

> The fact that the "offensive" speech here may not address "important" topics—"ideas of social and political significance," in the Court's terminology . . .—does not mean that it is less worthy of constitutional protection.[48]

Thus, it is interesting to wonder whether the regulations and restrictions upheld on such sexually explicit and nonobscene expression ultimately do implicitly categorize such speech as less valuable and less worthy of protection on the grounds that political speech would not be so regulated. If so, is this justifiable?

A decade later the Court still did not endorse Stevens's "lower value" speech approach, but, rather, reverted to Powell's balancing approach and treated the zoning-type ordinance in *City of Renton v. Playtime Theatres, Inc.* (1986) as "aimed not at the *content* of the films shown at the 'adult motion picture theatres,' but rather at the *secondary effects* of such theatres on the surrounding community."[49] These secondary effects were found to be a governmental interest important enough to justify the zoning.[50]

Then a 1991 challenge to Indiana's ban on public nudity as applied to nude dancing, in *Barnes v. Glen Theatre, Inc.*, evoked sharp disagreement on the Court and a 5–4 decision upholding the state's public indecency law.[51] The plurality opinion agreed that "nude dancing of the kind sought to be performed here is expressive conduct within the outer perimeters of the First Amendment, though we view it as only marginally so."[52] The majority vote depended on three different opinions, however. The Court held that "the Indiana statutory requirement that the dancers in the establishments involved in this case must wear pasties and G-strings does not violate the First Amendment."[53]

In *Barnes,* Chief Justice Rehnquist and Justices O'Connor and Kennedy defended the ordinance as based on concerns of public health, safety, and morals, government interests unrelated to suppression of expression. Justice Scalia, concurring only in the judgment, urged that the regulation was about conduct and, thus, that this was not a First Amendment case at all. Justice Souter, also concurring, disagreed that the state interest in

[48] *Id.* at 87.

[49] 475 U.S. 41 (1986). See also Gunther and Sullivan, *Constitutional Law,* 1163.

[50] Interestingly, Ellen Frankel Paul has noted that the Court said it was a "substantial government interest" rather than a "compelling government interest," suggesting an intermediate test, perhaps because zoning was involved. The best reply is Justice Souter's, that the secondary effects were not justified empirically. Regarding the principle of secondary effects see Sections V and VI of this essay.

[51] 501 U.S. 560 (1991).

[52] *Id.* at 566 (Rehnquist, C.J., plurality opinion).

[53] *Id.* at 565.

order and morality was adequate to defend the ordinance, but justified the decision, following *Renton,* based on preventing the secondary effects correlated with nude dancing, including prostitution, sexual assaults, and other criminal activity unrelated to the suppression of free expression.

The four dissenters in *Barnes*—Justice Byron White joined by Justices Thurgood Marshall, Harry Blackmun, and John Paul Stevens—scoffed in response that the law was aimed at the communicative impact of nude dancing, arguing that "it is precisely because of the distinctive, expressive content of the nude dancing performances at issue in this case that the State seeks to apply the statutory prohibition." [54] This dispute over whether or not the ordinance is directed at the suppression of expression is key, since it affects the level of scrutiny that the Court will apply. If the governmental purpose in enacting the ordinance is unrelated to such suppression, the ordinance need only satisfy a so-called intermediate standard as set out in *United States v. O'Brien* (1968). The '*O'Brien* test' requires content-neutral laws to "further an important or substantial governmental interest" and involve an "incidental restriction on alleged First Amendment freedoms" not greater than what is necessary to further that interest.[55] The dissenters claimed, in contrast, that the *Barnes* case deserved a more exacting standard called 'strict scrutiny', as used in *Texas v. Johnson,* the flag-burning case, rather than the weaker *O'Brien* test, because the governmental interest was related to the expression's content.[56] They argued, in addition, that the interest cited by the state was not compelling.

It is clear in this sequence of cases, including *American Mini Theatres* and *Barnes,* that the justices struggled over the First Amendment threat and the weightiness of the secondary effects that they considered. There are multiple split decisions: plurality decisions, decisions cobbled together from three sets of opinions, and so on. The Court's confusion emphasizes the deep problems associated with dealing with sexually explicit but not obscene expression, and the need for clearer standards and tests.[57]

Nearly a decade after *Barnes,* the Supreme Court was confronted with another free speech case involving nude dancing. In 2000, in *City of Erie v. Pap's A.M.,*[58] the Court again grappled with the questions of how to

[54] *Id.* at 592 (White, J., dissenting opinion).

[55] *United States v. O'Brien,* 391 U.S. 367 (1968).

[56] The issue of level of scrutiny resurfaced in *City of Erie v. Pap's A.M.* (*see infra* note 58), but my focus is on arguments of a different nature.

[57] I am grateful to Ellen Frankel Paul for emphasizing this point.

[58] 529 U.S. 277 (2000). Justice O'Connor wrote the opinion for the Court with respect to Parts 1 and 2, in which Chief Justice Rehnquist and Justices Kennedy, Souter, and Breyer joined, and an opinion with respect to Parts 3 and 4, in which Rehnquist, Kennedy, and Breyer joined. Justices Scalia and Thomas issued a separate opinion concurring in the judgment. Justice Souter filed an opinion concurring in part and dissenting in part. Justice Stevens filed a dissenting opinion in which Justice Ginsburg joined. David Bernstein has posed an interesting question concerning why the cases on nude dancing have become a focus of the Court's struggles with nonobscene but sexually explicit expression: Does it being "live" make it more of a worry?

deal with sexually explicit expression that is not obscene or child pornography, and how offensive expression must be to no longer be protected by the First Amendment. While the 7–2 vote seems to show a Court less divided, both the history of the case and the multiple opinions demonstrate deep divisions on how to handle sexually explicit material and the concerns of communities to protect their social values. The City of Erie in Pennsylvania had enacted a public indecency ordinance prohibiting knowingly or intentionally appearing in public in a "state of nudity." As in *Barnes*, to comply with the ordinance, female nude dancers had to wear, at a minimum, pasties and a G-string. A corporation that owned a nude dancing establishment filed a complaint against enforcement of the ordinance. The Erie County Court of Common Pleas struck down the statute as unconstitutional, and the Commonwealth Court reversed the decision of the trial court. The Pennsylvania Supreme Court reversed again, holding in part that nude dancing was expressive conduct entitled to some protection under the First Amendment, and that the ordinance was content based and thus unconstitutional. The U.S. Supreme Court reversed the Pennsylvania Supreme Court decision, and ultimately held that the ordinance banning nude dancing was constitutional. But nuances in the arguments of the justices (beyond the issue of mootness) show the difficulty of assessing cases concerning laws limiting sexually explicit offensive material and the implications for free speech.

Six of the justices in *Pap's A.M.*, four joining the plurality opinion and two dissenters, agreed that nude dancing performed as entertainment was expressive conduct entitled to some First Amendment protection. But the plurality judged the ordinance to be content neutral because it banned all nudity and did not target nudity that contained an erotic message. Moreover, they found the primary purpose of the ordinance to be the city's interest in combating the harmful secondary effects associated with establishments featuring nude dancing, including "violence, sexual harassment, public intoxication, prostitution, and the spread of sexually transmitted diseases." They considered this to be a legitimate governmental interest in deterring crime and promoting public health, safety, and welfare, and unrelated to the suppression of free expression, ultimately viewing the regulation as constitutional. The plurality also found that the ordinance imposed minimal restrictions on the dancers' ability to convey their erotic message. In contrast, Justices Antonin Scalia and Clarence Thomas concurred in the judgment, but argued that the ordinance was not subject to First Amendment scrutiny at all.

The dissenting justices, notably Justice Stevens joined by Justice Ruth Bader Ginsburg, argued that the secondary effects justification was just one rationale for the ordinance, and they contended that the ordinance was clearly intended to restrict erotic expression. More generally they argued:

> Far more important than the question whether nude dancing is entitled to the protection of the First Amendment are the dramatic changes in legal doctrine that the Court endorses today. Until now, the 'secondary effects' of commercial enterprises featuring indecent entertainment have justified only the regulation of their location. For the first time, the Court has now held that such effects may justify the total suppression of protected speech. Indeed, the plurality opinion concludes that admittedly trivial advancements of a State's interests may provide the basis for censorship.[59]

The dissenters worried that relying on the secondary effects test to defend the ordinance was not supported by any precedents. Also, they again defended past practice by the Court in limiting the secondary effects rationale to permitting zoning, declining to extend the rationale to justify total bans, on the grounds that zoning is a minimal imposition while a total ban is far more drastic.

In sum, the dissenters urged that "[t]he Court's use of the secondary effects rationale to permit a total ban has grave implications for basic free speech principles. . . . Under today's opinion, a State may totally ban speech based on its secondary effects. . . ."[60] Noting that the plurality had conceded that restricting dancers to wearing pasties and G-strings might not greatly reduce the harmful secondary effects, the dissenters insisted that it was likely that the restrictions would have no impact at all on the tendency for a nude dancing establishment to attract crime, prostitution, and other ills.[61] Banning expressive conduct "by the mere possibility of *de minimis* effects on the neighborhood," they said, is unjustifiable and goes far beyond previous precedents.[62]

VI. Implicit Recognition of "Lower Value" Expression

On one hand, if the ordinance prohibiting nudity in *City of Erie v. Pap's A.M.* is taken to be a ban on nude dancing, as the dissenters claimed and as the explicit wording in the ordinance supports, then the use of secondary effects arguments is now a new way, mirroring balancing, to repress expression long held to be protected by the First Amendment. On this interpretation, this type of sexually explicit expression is, in effect, a new category of unprotected speech.[63] On the other hand, if the ordi-

[59] *Id.* at 317–18 (Stevens, J., dissenting).

[60] *Id.* at 322–23.

[61] Justice Souter had agreed that the secondary effects were unrelated to suppression of expression, but found insufficient evidence or showing of the seriousness of the threatened harm. This echoes the argument in *Schad*, *supra* note 38, that there was no evidence adult entertainment led to unusual problems.

[62] *Pap's A.M.* 529 U.S. 277, at 324 (Stevens, J., dissenting).

[63] As noted, the ordinance prohibited "knowingly or intentionally" appearing in public in a "state of nudity" and the wording thus supports the dissenters and their interpretation.

nance is viewed as a mere regulation, like zoning, and not a new way to suppress expression, the Court is nevertheless implicitly declaring that, in an important sense, sexually explicit and nonobscene speech is "lower value" expression. Indeed, the plurality in *Barnes v. Glen Theatre, Inc.*, called nude dancing expressive conduct "marginally" and placed it "on the outer perimeters" of First Amendment protection, and in *Pap's A.M.* the justices who agreed it was expressive conduct described it as entitled only to "some" protection under the First Amendment. In essence, on either interpretation, the Court appears to be slipping down a slope, either adding a new category of unprotected speech or differentiating levels of importance within speech traditionally protected by the First Amendment. Can this be justified?

It might be tempting to avoid the above conclusion about the erosion of free speech protection by agreeing with those justices who have argued that the ordinances in question in *Pap's A.M.* and similar cases are not really subject to First Amendment protection at all. In other words, one could argue that sexually explicit material that is not obscene or child pornography really is not expressive "speech" that communicates ideas. On this view, one could claim that such material is merely aimed at sexual arousal with no message of substance to convey. This account, however, directly conflicts with the views of the majority of the justices as well as the history of cases reviewed here, repeatedly reiterating that sexually explicit material that is neither obscene nor child pornography is not in one of the excluded categories and, thus, is protected as expressive conduct under the First Amendment.

Alternatively, one might argue that such expression is properly of lower value and less deserving of protection by the First Amendment. In support of this view, one could point to the major philosophical justifications for free speech, which focus on the benefits of maximal free expression. One could argue that not all of these justifications—(1) truth-seeking, (2) political advantages, and (3) individual benefit—and perhaps only the latter, apply as defenses for this type of sexually explicit expression. That is, as Justice Stevens argued in *American Mini Theatres*, it is difficult to see how pornographic material in general and nude dancing in particular can be defended by the political argument in favor of maximal free speech. The argument that free speech enhances representative government and democratic participation by citizens does not appear to apply to distasteful or indecent sexually explicit expressive conduct, whereas it clearly supports unpopular political speech.

While Mill's arguments for free speech based on the search for the truth apply more broadly than the political advantages argument to protect expression beyond political speech, including scientific and philosophical debate and perhaps even literary expression, it is far less clear that Mill's defense supports expression such as nude dancing. One could argue, however, that the third justification based on individual integrity and autonomy best defends artistic expression, including sexually explicit and nonobscene expression. On this view, the best rationale for protecting such speech may be that it maximizes opportunities for self-realization and for individuals to express their identities. One could conclude, therefore, that if only one or two of these philosophical justifications applies to a type of expression, then it has a lower value than speech that can be justified by all three arguments. This clearly places political speech on the top tier as most valuable and most worthy of protection.[64] Nevertheless, this differentiation is clearly unacceptable, for then the slippery slope begins anew. This is because almost *any* nonpolitical speech will be supported by less than all three of the philosophical arguments, and thus all nonpolitical speech will end up as lower value speech, leading back to Meiklejohn's extreme view (discussed in Section II).

Are there better ways to justify restraining sexually explicit and nonobscene expression and treating it as lower value expression?[65] Here I shall explore five possible responses. First, as with obscenity, one might argue that such materials corrupt an individual's character and morals. This is a paternalistic argument, not generally found persuasive for banning obscenity and, thus, for the same reasons, unlikely to be deemed dispositive for a less obnoxious type of speech. Basically, the paternalistic argument grants far too much power to the state to decide what an individual may hear or see, leading to a slippery slope of its own by which the government could claim the power to restrict any expression it deemed damaging to an individual's character or moral development.[66]

Second, one might try to appeal to an offense justification, arguing that sexually explicit and nonobscene material is precisely the sort of material that offends the sensibilities of most audiences and thus ought to be curtailed.[67] But this is exactly the sort of argument that the Court rejected in the earlier categorization cases; no matter how offensive, such expression has not been deemed subject to suppression due to the subjectivity

[64] Lillian Reimer BeVier pointed out to me that there is a reverse argument, namely, that if the Court protects borderline sexually explicit speech, this can ultimately devalue political speech. Given the history of free speech protection in the United States, however, I see no danger of political speech being jeopardized under the First Amendment.

[65] See also DeCew, "Violent Pornography: Censorship, Morality, and Social Alternatives," in *Right Conduct*, Bayles and Henley, eds., 246–56.

[66] Philosopher Joel Feinberg writes, "The liberty-limiting principle called legal paternalism justifies state coercion to protect individuals from self-inflicted harm, or, in its extreme version, to guide them, whether they like it or not, toward their own good.... Put this bluntly, paternalism seems a preposterous doctrine. If adults are treated as children they will come in time to be like children. Deprived of the right to choose for themselves, they will soon lose the power of rational judgment and decision." Joel Feinberg, *Social Philosophy* (Englewood Cliffs, NJ: Prentice-Hall, 1973), 45–46, with further discussion at 46–52. See also Gerald Dworkin, "Paternalism," in Richard A. Wasserstrom, ed., *Morality and the Law* (Belmont, CA: Wadsworth Pub. Co., 1971), reprinted in Joel Feinberg and Jules Coleman, eds., *Philosophy of Law*, 6th ed. (Belmont, CA: Wadsworth/Thomson Learning, 2000), 271–80, for a discussion of paternalism and an argument about the types of cases for which it can be justified.

[67] See Joel Feinberg, *Offense to Others: The Moral Limits of the Criminal Law* (Oxford: Oxford University Press, 1985); and Feinberg, *Social Philosophy*, 41–45.

of determining what is offensive and the chilling effect such an inquiry would cause.

Third, one could appeal to a moralism justification to argue that restriction of such material is needed to protect children against exposure and to protect society's moral standards from erosion.[68] Criticizing such justifications, legal scholar H. L. A. Hart persuasively asked, "[W]hy should we not summon all the resources of our reason, sympathetic understanding, as well as critical intelligence, and insist that before general moral feeling is turned into criminal law it is submitted to scrutiny. . . ? Surely, the legislator should ask whether the general morality is based on ignorance, superstition, or misunderstanding. . . ."[69] Given the difficulty of determining the appropriate moral standards for society, it is clear that justifications based on the enforcement of morals can at most support regulations such as zoning, but not outright bans.

Fourth, one might urge that sexually explicit though nonobscene material should be restricted to safeguard against violent and antisocial behavior and to improve the tone and quality of a city, community, or neighborhood. Both of these considerations fall in the category of secondary effects addressed by the Court in the recent cases that I previously discussed. Both provide more serious and persuasive arguments than the first three for treating such expression as lower level speech.[70] It seems that one has to acknowledge the value of a governmental interest in reducing crime, and one has to sympathize with the interests of a community in maintaining an atmosphere where residents can stand to live. Nevertheless, there is substantial controversy over whether sexually explicit but nonobscene material and nude dancing do cause sex crimes, prostitution, drug use, and violence. Thus, it is again difficult to see how such concerns can justify anything beyond regulations such as zoning, which allows communities to protect their neighborhoods.[71]

Fifth, and finally, one might argue that sexually explicit and nonobscene materials should be restricted to promote equality, that is, to minimize discrimination by curbing materials that contribute to the subordination of women and sexual harassment. This may well be the strongest argument against such expression. Nevertheless, it is difficult to see how this concern can justify bans and censorship on a category

[68] Feinberg, *Social Philosophy*, 36–41.

[69] H. L. A. Hart, "Immorality and Treason," in Dworkin, ed., *The Philosophy of Law*, 87.

[70] I thank Andrew Altman for pointing out that this also highlights the interesting and complex connections between the "secondary effects" arguments and "low value" speech arguments used by various members of the Court.

[71] In comments to me, Thomas G. West worried that zoning simply pushes problems associated with sexually oriented businesses onto others, especially the poor who cannot afford to move, and he suggested that neighborhood concerns could support a total ban. Adopting West's suggestion, however, gives rise to the danger of pushing such businesses underground, where they would be far more difficult to monitor than when regulated through zoning.

of expression traditionally held to be protected by the First Amendment. Moreover, it fails to justify ordinances that ban nude dancing based on secondary effects. An ordinance such as that challenged in *Pap's A.M.*, requiring slight covering to avoid total nudity, is surely unlikely to minimize subordination and discrimination against women.

Disgusting or distasteful as some speech may be, settled First Amendment law fails to justify a total ban on sexually explicit yet nonobscene expression. Nor do any of the arguments considered here justify treating this type of expression as lower level speech, although many justices on the Court appear to be at least implicitly making such a distinction. Moreover, cases show there is continuing lack of evidence that ordinances requiring nude dancers to wear pasties and G-strings will in any way reduce the alleged secondary effects of criminality and blighted neighborhoods. Indeed, there is good reason to doubt that such ordinances will have any effect at all on the level of criminal activity, on the quality of a neighborhood, or on the treatment of women. If my arguments are correct, then regulations such as those requiring zoning in *American Mini Theatres* and *Renton* do differ from the requirements of the ordinances in *Barnes* and *Pap's A.M.* There is good reason for viewing the former as legitimate, non-content regulation of location that does not suppress the expression but can help communities preserve neighborhoods in which residents feel comfortable. At the same time, one can understand ordinances against nudity—defended by some on the Court using secondary effects analysis, but probably aimed at suppressing erotic expression—as content-based regulation. Since the latter are unlikely in any event to minimize secondary effects, they constitute unacceptable and dangerous tampering with the traditions of First Amendment protection of expression.

VII. Conclusion

In sum, despite some difficulties, categorization is the interpretive method that provides the strongest way to protect free speech. It is also likely to be the most appropriate method to pursue in order to make difficult decisions about sexually explicit and nonobscene speech. By maintaining the principle that the categories of restricted speech remain the same, and that offensive expression will not be added as a category of banned speech, there is less likelihood of generating an increased chilling effect, less likelihood of traveling down the slippery slope to more and more suppression, and less likelihood of granting more power to government, including the judicial branch, to remove individual choice about what each of us may see and hear. What undeniably remains, however, is case-by-case decision-making about whether expression that some consider merely offensive, actually crosses the boundary into obscenity, an unprotected category.

Ultimately, the Supreme Court's most recent cases focusing on nude dancing as sexually explicit material that is neither obscene nor child pornography, *Barnes* and *Pap's A.M.*, show a return to balancing and an almost chaotic disagreement and lack of consensus. Neither case generated a majority opinion, yet these cases point in an ominous direction of eroding free speech protection. The Court's decisions undermine categorization, arguably the strongest way of protecting free speech; undermine the traditional doctrine that sexually explicit but nonobscene expression or conduct is protected by the First Amendment; and undermine the established view that offensive and objectionable material and expression may be regulated, but not prohibited. Whether intended or not, the Court's moves support the view that political speech is special and because it is a higher level of speech warrants more protection. Sexually explicit and nonobscene expression is left on the fringes as lower level, despite a lack of adequate justification for such a view. While this type of sexually explicit expression may seem unimportant, how it is treated under the First Amendment has ramifications for free speech in general. In splitting levels of speech, even implicitly, the Court starts us down the slippery slope leading to other forms of nonpolitical speech being treated as lower level speech, thus jeopardizing the strong defense of free speech that has been the hallmark of First Amendment jurisprudence in the United States.

Philosophy, Clark University

COPYRIGHT, TRESPASS, AND THE FIRST AMENDMENT: AN INSTITUTIONAL PERSPECTIVE*

By Lillian R. BeVier

I. Introduction

In this paper I discuss one facet of the multifaceted question of whether strong protection for intellectual property rights—in particular, rights in expressive works and in information in digital form—is, in principle, at odds with the First Amendment guarantee of freedom of speech. The question has assumed particular urgency in recent years because the Internet and digital technology seem to have rendered formerly serviceable legal boundaries obsolete, and doctrines that sufficed in a print-on-paper world no longer seem adequate. Vigorous debate rages about what has come to be referred to as 'propertization'. Commentators ask whether, and how, and based upon what empirical assumptions, old boundaries ought to be redrawn and doctrines modified. The academic literature tilts heavily away from endorsing strong property rights in digitized content, and toward expanded user rights and intensified First Amendment review in copyright cases. This paper tilts in a different direction. It swims against the academic tide not only in the direction of its analysis but, more importantly, in the kinds of questions it considers relevant and in its analytical focus. Readers should understand that the analysis is deliberately provisional and suggestive rather than completely developed, and the conclusions are tentative. The paper does not purport to be a definitive study that draws confident conclusions. It is offered as speculation and in the hope that readers will approach it in that spirit.

The facet of the larger question that the paper addresses is whether the principles that undergird the common law of trespass can provide useful guidance for the resolution of disputes over conflicting claims of access either to the expressive content of copyrighted works or to content on the Internet, whether copyrighted or not. At first blush, this question may not seem particularly relevant to freedom of expression. I hope to show, however, that it is completely germane. In brief summary, First Amendment rights serve a number of instrumental goals, as do the private property rights in tangible things that the action of trespass vindicates.

* For helpful comments, thanks go to Brad Handler, Mitchell Kane, Ed Kitch, Clarisa Long, Tom Nachbar, and Rip Verkerke, as well as my fellow contributors to this volume and participants in a faculty workshop at the University of Virginia. The errors that remain are mine alone.

The United States Supreme Court has squarely held that, despite the important instrumental goals that the First Amendment serves, there is no First Amendment right to trespass on privately owned real property, whether to engage in expressive activity there, or to acquire information, or to communicate with the property owner. Thus, if one were to conclude that the trespass analogy is helpful in resolving disputes over access to digital content, it would imply the corollary conclusion that there should be no First Amendment right of access to digital content. Hence the paper's relevance to freedom of expression.

The issue of the conflict between intellectual property and freedom of speech is far from hypothetical, and the academic literature addressing it is abundant. In 2003, the Supreme Court rejected a First Amendment challenge to the Copyright Term Extension Act (CTEA) that Congress passed in 1998.[1] In doing so, however, the Court left a number of arguments unexamined. In addition, in 1998, Congress passed the Digital Millennium Copyright Act (DMCA),[2] which made it unlawful both to circumvent technological measures installed by copyright owners to control access to their works and to traffic in devices designed to circumvent technological control measures.[3] These provisions, generally referred to as the anticircumvention and antitrafficking provisions, confer on copyright owners rights that are functionally similar—though they are not, of course, doctrinally identical—to the protection that a trespass law offers to owners of tangible property. Though Congress directed the Librarian of Congress to exempt particular classes of works from the DMCA's anticircumvention provisions if the Register of Copyrights determines that technological protection measures are diminishing the ability of individuals to use copyrighted works in ways that are otherwise lawful,[4] in its first rulemaking proceeding the Copyright Office declined to adopt significant exemptions from the DMCA's provisions.[5] The courts have applied the act with a surprisingly vigorous embrace of its goals,[6] and as of

[1] *Eldred v. Ashcroft*, 537 U.S. 186 (2003). The Copyright Term Extension Act (CTEA), Pub. L. 105-298, §§ 102 (b) and (d), 112 Stat. 2827-2828 (1998) (amending 17 U.S.C. §§ 302, 304), extended the duration of copyrights by 20 years. The extension applied not only to future works but also to those already in existence. The act's challengers contended that the act's application to already created works exceeded Congress's power, under art. 1, § 8, cl. 8 of the Constitution, to secure authors' exclusive rights "for limited times." The Court disagreed, relying principally on the general ground that "it is . . . for Congress, not the courts, to decide how best to pursue the Copyright Clause's objectives." *Eldred*, 537 U.S. at ___, 123 S. Ct. 769, 785.

[2] Pub. L. 105-304, 112 Stat. 2860 (1998).

[3] 17 U.S.C. § 1201(a)(2)(A) (anticircumvention), §§ 1201(a)(2)(A), (B), (C) (antitrafficking).

[4] 17 U.S.C. § 1201(a)(1)(C).

[5] 37 C.F.R. pt. 201. Library of Congress, Copyright Office, "Exemption to Prohibition on Circumvention of Copyright Protection Systems for Access Control Technologies," Part V, 65 FR 64556 (2000).

[6] See, e.g., *Universal City Studios, Inc. v. Reimerdes*, 111 F. Supp. 2d 294 (S.D.N.Y. 2000), *affirmed*, *Universal City Studios, Inc. v. Corley*, 273 F.3d. 429 (2d Cir. 2001); and *RealNetworks, Inc. v. Streambox, Inc.*, 2000 Wash. Laws 127311 (W.D. Wash. 2000).

mid-2003 the anticircumvention provisions had withstood First Amendment challenge.[7] In addition, and to the dismay of many in the academy,[8] courts have sustained trespass causes of action brought by Web-site operators[9] and Internet service providers.[10] Although in the 2003 case of *Intel Corp. v. Hamidi*[11] the California Supreme Court, by a vote of 4–3, reversed the grant of relief in a trespass to chattels cause of action brought by the owner of a proprietary e-mail system against the sender of unwanted messages, the majority acknowledged that the defendant in fact had "no *right to use* [plaintiff's] personal property."[12] In the *Intel* case, the intermediate Court of Appeals had explicitly addressed, and rejected, the defendant's First Amendment claim,[13] but the California Supreme Court did not reach the First Amendment issue.

This paper's most significant departure from the perspective of most academic commentators is its focus on the institutional choices that are embedded in Congress's and the courts' decisions. The paper will suggest that answering the questions of whether and how much to propertize—that is, to recognize and enforce private property rights in—digital content and whether and how much to grant First Amendment rights of access to it requires a fundamental collective choice about whether to lodge decision-making authority, over access to digital content and to information, in private or public sector actors. Because it speculates about the allocation of decision-making authority, the paper is primarily about "who decides"—private parties or government officials—and only secondarily about "what is decided." The institutional choice perspective stems from the conviction that incentives motivate human behavior, that the design of institutions and the allocation of decision-making authority within them powerfully affect the incentives of individual actors, and, accordingly, that an adequate evaluation of constitutional doctrines, congressional statutes, and common law rules must include an effort to account for the incentives they create and for the way in which they allocate decision-making authority.

Section II outlines the institutional conception of the regime of private property that will drive the ensuing analysis. It describes private property

[7] *Corley*, 273 F.3d 429.

[8] Professor Mark A. Lemley's comment is typical of many academic commentators in tone and substance: "[R]eliance on the *cyberspace as place* metaphor [upon which courts sustaining trespass actions in cyberspace have supposedly relied] is leading courts to results that are *nothing short of disastrous as a matter of public policy*." Mark A. Lemley, "Place and Cyberspace," *California Law Review* 91 (1980): 522 (emphasis added).

[9] *eBay, Inc. v. Bidder's Edge, Inc.*, 100 F. Supp. 2d 1058 (N.D. Cal. 2000).

[10] See, e.g., *America Online, Inc. v. National Health Care Discount, Inc.*, 174 F. Supp. 2d 890 (N.D. Iowa 2001); *Oyster Software, Inc. v. Forms Processing, Inc.*, No. C-00-0724, 2001 WL 1736382 (N.D. Cal. Dec. 6, 2001); and *Register.Com, Inc. v. Verio, Inc.*, 126 F. Supp. 2d 238 (S.D.N.Y. 2000).

[11] 2003 Cal. LEXIS 4205.

[12] *Id.* at *29 (Werdegar, J.) (emphasis added).

[13] *Intel Corp. v. Hamidi*, 114 Cal. Rptr. 2d 244 (Cal. Ct. App. 2001), *review granted*, 43 P.3d 587 (Cal. 2002), *reversed*, 2003 Cal. LEXIS 4205.

rights as reflecting a collective choice to allocate authority to make decisions about the use, possession, and disposition of tangible resources to actors in the private sector. It specifies some of the reasons why one might endorse such a choice in preference to a regime in which such decisions are made by public sector actors, whether legislatures, bureaucrats, or courts. The reasons are principally instrumental and, of course, they reflect assumptions about how incentives work and about the differences between the incentives confronting governmental and individual—public and private—decision-makers. Specifying these reasons and their underlying assumptions will seem to some to be stating the obvious. But, though they do not couch their arguments explicitly in institutional terms, the many commentators who take a dim view of propertization in the digital world seem, in fact, also to take a dim view of the function of and instrumental justification for property rights in tangible things. Accordingly, by restating some of the reasons and assumptions that might be offered in support of a private property regime in tangible things, and by casting a property rights regime as a collective decision to delegate decision-making authority to the private sector, the paper represents an explicit, though tentative, attempt to recast the propertization debate as a debate about institutional choice, and to invite argument about the implications of taking such an approach.

Section III focuses the institutional lens on the question of propertization in the digital world. It argues that it is also useful to think of propertization in the digital world as reflecting a collective decision to allocate to the private sector rather than to government actors the authority to make decisions about who should have access to information and expressive works in digital form and on what terms. Building on Section II's perspective on how property rights function and why we have them in the tangible world, Section III both defends propertization of intangible works in digital form and offers rebuttals to some of the most frequently propounded objections to it.

Section IV summarizes current First Amendment doctrine as it applies to questions of judicially mandated access to privately owned property. This doctrine is to the effect that there is "no First Amendment right to trespass." Section IV analyzes this doctrine, too, as an allocation of decision-making authority, and suggests that the doctrine enhances liberty despite its failure to privilege access for First Amendment activity. Section V applies a similar analysis to what some regard as a conflict in principle between intellectual property rights and the First Amendment.

II. Private Property in Tangible Things

The way legal institutions assign the power to make decisions profoundly affects the incentives of decision-making actors. The most fundamental aspect of the institution of private property is that, as a baseline proposition, it represents a collective decision to assign to private individuals and not to government actors the authority to make enforceable decisions about how property is to be used, by whom and for what purpose it is to be possessed, and to whom and on what terms it ought to be transferred.[14] This does not mean, even as a baseline proposition, that the state has no role to play with respect to decisions about resource production and use. The state's principal role, however—its function as a "state actor"—is not to *make* decisions but to *enforce* the decisions that private actors make, and to supply rules—of property, tort, contract, and criminal law—that both render owners' rights secure and facilitate the market transactions that tend to move assets from lower- to higher-valued users.[15] Rules of trespass, for example, enforce owners' decisions to exclude, while rules of contract and conveyancing enforce their decisions to transfer.

Tangible property is intrinsically scarce, which means that its consumption is necessarily rivalrous. "It is the nature of wheat or land or any other tangible property that possession by one person precludes possession by anyone else."[16] Property rights both respond to and exploit the fact of scarcity. Legally enforceable physical boundaries serve significant economizing and internalizing functions.[17] By conjoining in one owner the exclusive right to make decisions about use, possession, and alienation of scarce goods, property rights create a link between decisions and rewards. This link encourages owners of real property, for example, to make decisions that will enhance its value, and it encourages producers of tangible things to decide to produce them to the point where the marginal revenues from an extra unit are equal to the marginal cost.

There exists widespread agreement that a system of exclusive private rights in tangible things has at least two utilitarian or consequentialist arguments to support it. Both build on strong intuitions about how individual incentives work. The first argument is that private rights prevent

[14] The qualification that the institution of private property assigns to private actors decision-making authority *as a baseline proposition* is an important one in practice, though it does not go to the heart of this paper's analysis. Since the revolution in constitutional doctrine that took place in the 1930s, when the Supreme Court interpreted the Constitution so as to remove it as a significant impediment to regulation of economic matters, the *baseline* assignment of decision-making authority has been subjected to a significant degree of legislative reassignment. Indeed, since the 1926 decision in *Euclid v. Ambler Realty Co.*, 272 U.S. 365 (1926), private decisions about how to use privately owned real property have been subjected to ever-increasing collective oversight. The point of this paper, however, remains valid: as a *baseline* proposition, the distinguishing feature of a system of private property is that it assigns decision-making authority about the use, possession, and transfer of resources to actors in the private sector.

[15] For further development of the view of the state's role in the enforcement of private decisions, and of the implications of the fact that it clearly "acts" for constitutional purposes when it enforces private choices, see John Harrison and Lillian BeVier, "State Action and Its Critics" (forthcoming, 2004).

[16] Douglas G. Baird, "Common Law Intellectual Property and the Legacy of *International News Service v. Associated Press*," *University of Chicago Law Review* 50 (1983): 413.

[17] See generally Robert C. Ellickson, "Property in Land," *Yale Law Journal* 102 (1993): 1315.

wasteful overuse of resources and stave off the tragedy of the commons. The second is that they encourage optimal investment since gains and losses "come back to the owner."[18] Both of these arguments reflect the conviction that when individual decision-makers may internalize the benefits and must internalize the costs of the decisions they make, they are systematically likely to make better, more socially optimal decisions than would individual decision-makers who are either unable to appropriate the gains or able to externalize the losses. The utilitarian case for internalization of costs and benefits reflects the belief that when decision-makers can internalize the gains from their decisions, they are more likely to make decisions that produce gains than when the gains will be enjoyed by others; and when they must internalize the losses they are more likely to avoid making decisions that decrease value. The case reflects the reasonable assumptions that people are rationally self-interested and that they generally prefer to be richer rather than poorer, to have more value rather than less.

An important reason why decision-makers who will internalize the effects of their decisions tend to make better ones than those who will not is that good decision-making requires good information, and when both the gains and losses of a decision will be internalized, the decision-maker has powerful incentives to acquire good information about what the gains and losses of alternative courses of action are likely to be. The ability to appropriate the gains from value-enhancing decisions encourages owners to gather, and continually to evaluate and act upon, relevant information. The market prices of various inputs, plus the market's predictions about the expected value of outputs or the expected return on investment, provide information about costs and benefits that is clear, transparent, and relatively responsive to changing circumstances.

The utilitarian advantages of a property rights regime of decentralized decision-making about the production, use, and disposition of resources tend to make societies that recognize strong property rights wealthier and bless their citizens with more liberty than those where the decisions are made collectively by centralized government institutions, such as legislatures, courts, and administrative agencies. These particular utilitarian advantages of assigning decision-making authority to private individuals cannot, of course, be achieved when the presence of externalities or other market failures renders market prices an unreliable signal of relative value, and hence policymakers often turn their attention to devising legal fixes to perceived market failures. Regardless of whether market failures might be thought to justify collectively modifying the decision-making authority of private actors, however, it is certain that the particular advantages of internalization of costs and benefits are inevitably sacrificed when government actors become the decision-makers. This is because a

[18] Carol M. Rose, "Romans, Roads, and Romantic Creators: Traditions of Public Property in the Information Age," *Law and Contemporary Problems* 66 (2001): 90.

most important, indeed a definitional, fact about government actors—legislators, judges, or administrators—is that they are *required not* to internalize the economic benefits and costs of their decisions. To the extent that the market value of resources affected by their decisions is a reliable indicator that the decisions were value enhancing, the inability of government actors to appropriate the gains from increased value, and their ability to escape from internalizing the losses, results in a significant attenuation of their incentives to make socially value-enhancing decisions, and to gather good information upon which to base those decisions. The problem that this fact about the incentives of government actors poses for institutional design is not met by asserting that, precisely because they are required to forgo private gain, government actors are likely to be able and motivated to make decisions in the "public interest." In the first place, it is not certain that there is a real-world analogue of the "public interest" that is different from or better than the outcome of the sum of private preferences.[19] Secondly, and more to the point, public choice theory has seriously undermined the claim that government actors are uniquely non-self-interested or public regarding. Indeed, its basic insight is that government actors act from rationally self-interested motives just as do actors in the private sector, though the self-interest that government actors pursue must be something other than their own financial gain. Because it is impossible to generalize about the nature of the self-interest that individual government actors pursue, it is rash to speculate about the nature and source of their incentives to make socially value-enhancing decisions. We may know in a very general way, for example, that the incentives of legislators are somehow "political," but this tells us almost nothing, because we know so little about "the causal relationship between social costs and benefits, financial inflows and outflows from the treasury, and the [self-interested] political incentives of government actors."[20] And we know almost nothing about the incentives of judges except that they get no personal financial reward if they craft good rules and, at least if they are federal judges, they will not be fired if they devise bad ones.[21]

III. Private Property in Intangible Things

This section considers whether the principal instrumental justification that supports assigning decision-making authority over production and

[19] Frank H. Easterbrook, "The State of Madison's Vision of the State: A Public Choice Perspective," *Harvard Law Review* 107 (1994): 1328 ("We are doomed by the logic of majority voting to aggregate private preferences rather than find a common public good.").

[20] Daryl Levinson, "Making Government Pay: Markets, Politics, and the Allocation of Constitutional Costs," *University of Chicago Law Review* 67 (2000): 415.

[21] See, e.g., Frederick Schauer, "Incentives, Reputation, and the Inglorious Determinants of Judicial Behavior," *University of Cincinnati Law Review* 68 (2000): 615; Richard A. Posner, "What Do Judges and Justices Maximize? (The Same Thing Everybody Else Does)," *Supreme Court Economic Review* 3 (1994): 1.

use of tangible things to private actors also supports a similar assignment of authority over expressive works in digital form. If it does, it would supply a powerful argument in support of a regime that, as a baseline proposition, (1) grants strong property rights, such as copyright, in expressive works in digital form, and (2) permits producers of both expressive works and information to use tangible property doctrines such as actions in trespass and their anticircumvention analogue to control and thus to profit from selling access. Also, this section considers whether, functionally, the assignment of decision-making authority over expressive works and information in digital form to the private sector is consistent in principle with the legal rules similarly assigning decision-making authority in the physical world.

The view taken here stands in sharp contrast to the perspective of many academic commentators.[22] Those who have concluded that less propertization of digital content would be better than more place great emphasis on the fact that, unlike consumption of tangible things, which are inherently scarce, consumption of both expressive works and of information is nonrivalrous. In other words, *once an expressive work or a piece of information has been produced,* it is not inherently scarce: consumption by one person does not reduce the amount available to others. In this sense, information and expressive works are public goods, though it is important to recognize that they do not necessarily have the feature of inherent nonexcludability of nonpayers that is commonly thought to be part of the definition of a public good. Expressive works and information come "fixed" in tangible objects, from which it is possible to exclude nonpayers. Of course, the easier it is to copy and distribute such works—to reproduce the work without reproducing the tangible object in which it is fixed and then to distribute the reproduced work to others—the more difficult it is in practice to exclude nonpayers.[23] With expressive works and informa-

[22] The literature that these commentators have produced is so extensive that to attempt to cite any but a representative sample would swamp the available space. See, e.g., Lemley, "Place and Cyberspace," *supra* note 8; Yochai Benkler, "Through the Looking Glass: Alice and the Constitutional Foundations of the Public Domain," *Law and Contemporary Problems* 66 (2003): 173; Dan Hunter, "Cyberspace as Place and the Tragedy of the Digital Anticommons," *California Law Review* (2003): 441; Edward W. Chang, "Bidding on Trespass: *eBay, Inc. v. Bidder's Edge, Inc.*, and the Abuse of Trespass Theory in Cyperspace Law," *American Intellectual Property Association Quarterly Journal* 29 (2001): 445; Dan L. Burk, "The Trouble with Trespass," *Journal of Small and Emerging Business Law* (2000): 27; Seth F. Kreimer, "Technologies of Protest: Insurgent Social Movements and the First Amendment in the Era of the Internet," *University of Pennsylvania Law Review* 150 (2001): 145–47; Maureen A. O'Rourke, "Shaping Competition on the Internet: Who Owns Product and Pricing Information?" *Vanderbilt Law Review* 53 (2000): 1965; and Maureen A. O'Rourke, "Property Rights and Competition on the Internet: In Search of an Appropriate Analogy," *Berkeley Technology Law Journal* 16 (2001): 561. For additional references, see Lemley, "Place and Cyberspace," *supra* note 8, at 521, n.2 and 527, n.24.

[23] This, of course, is why control over access is so important in the digital environment.

> If one believes that the market for hard copies is likely to recede as works become ubiquitously available through audio and video streaming and downloading, then digital networks will supply the principal markets for copyrighted works. This means

tion, however, it is possible to create excludability of nonpayers—to create scarcity, if you will—by legal rules. Indeed, this is precisely what property rights in such works do, as do rules that give their creators the right to control access to them.

The nonrivalrous aspect of consumption of expressive works and information implies that increasing access to them, whether for productive or for consumptive use, is certain to be socially beneficial. That more access by definition is better inclines some commentators to the conclusion that weaker rather than stronger property rights for their producers are, in general, to be preferred. Mark A. Lemley, for example, claims that "[t]he economic rationale underlying much privatization of land, the tragedy of the commons"[24] does not apply to expressive works and data because, since their consumption is nonrivalrous, they cannot by definition be overconsumed. Therefore, he concludes, trespass analogies are inapt in the digital world, and weaker forms of protection should be offered. As Lemley and other commentators who share his view are surely aware, however, avoiding the tragedy of the commons is not the only rationale for privatization of land. The other most commonly invoked rationale for privatization—that it encourages optimal production and investment—applies with equal force to the production of expressive works and information. Moreover, contrary to Lemley's implicit suggestion, encouraging investment would be a powerful enough rationale to justify privatization of tangible things even if there were no tragedy of the commons. Each rationale for privatization alone provides sufficient support. Thus, that intellectual property rights are supported only by the desire to encourage investment in the production of new works and not by the need to prevent the tragedy of the commons does not mean they are only half as justified as property rights in tangible things. That it is socially value-enhancing to increase access to digital content that has already been produced represents only part of the story, for it remains a fact that it is only possible to obtain access to information and expressive works *that have been produced*. The trick is to get private actors to decide to produce them, and doing this is the essential function—the reason for being—of intellectual property rights. In deciding whether to grant strong property rights to expressive and informational works in digital form, a crucial fact to remember is that, in general, it is private parties and not government actors who decide whether and how much to invest in producing such works, just as private producers of tangible goods decide whether and how much to invest in producing them and private owners of tangible property decide whether and how much to invest in putting

> that control over access to digitally distributed works will become the principal way in which exclusive rights are exercised.

Jane C. Ginsburg, "Copyright and Control over New Technologies of Dissemination," *Columbia Law Review* 101 (2001): 1634.

[24] See, e.g., Lemley, "Place and Cyberspace," *supra* note 8, at 536.

it to a permissible use. Giving producers of expressive works and information property-like protections—in the form of copyright and anticircumvention protections—reflects the same strong intuition that the decision to propertize tangible things reflects. Permitting producers to internalize the benefits of the expressive works and information that they decide to produce, by giving them the enforceable right to decide to make and sell copies and to grant access in exchange for a price, creates incentives for them to decide to invest in creating these products in the first place.

Commentators often point to the costs of propertization, in particular to the costs of allowing producers to decide to charge for access or to deny access altogether to nonpayers. In particular, commentators often cite the cost that is inherent in permitting producers to sell their works at more than the marginal cost of copying it. It is a fair bet that commentators overstate the former cost, however. As Edmund W. Kitch has observed, the focus on the marginal cost of copying tends to obscure the reality that "the marginal cost of making copies is not the relevant marginal cost for the pricing of goods; the marginal cost should include all of the costs necessary to bring the good to market, and there are many other costs than the costs of making a single copy."[25]

Commentators who disfavor propertization also imply that allowing producers to deny access altogether to nonpayers is problematic, if only because "not all people will have the coins to make the turnstiles turn."[26] The general claim seems to be that intellectual property rights *reduce* overall access to expressive works and information. These commentators usually acknowledge the need for law to create incentives for producers to produce such work, but they assert that the task of courts and legislatures confronting intellectual property questions is to "balance" the need for incentives and the benefits of (presumably free) access. They think that the needs of "the public" for access to completed works are different from and in inevitable tension with the "intertwined interests of creators, improvers, [and] competitors."[27] These commentators imply that legal rules or decisions whose *ex ante* effect is to enhance incentives by strengthening property rights have the necessary effect of reducing access precisely on account of the fact that they permit producers to price some potential users out of the market and to deny access to others altogether. In the short run, and as to expressive works and information already produced, this implication appears correct. It is worth noting, however, that the implicit baseline from which access is "reduced" is one that never existed, where access is available on demand to payers and nonpayers alike. In other words, in a world of free ac-

[25] Edmund W. Kitch, "Elementary and Persistent Errors in the Economic Analysis of Intellectual Property," *Vanderbilt Law Review* 53 (2000): 1734.

[26] L. Ray Patterson, "The DMCA: A Modern Version of the Licensing Act of 1662," *Journal of Intellectual Property Law* 10 (2002): 41.

[27] Mark A. Lemley, "Romantic Authorship and the Rhetoric of Property," reviewing James Boyle, *Shamans, Software, and Spleens: Law and the Construction of the Information Society*, in *Texas Law Review* 75 (1997): 888.

cess to all works in digital form, any decision by anyone to restrict or deny access for any reason—that is, anything that limits access in any way—would constitute a "reduction in access" to such works.

On a dynamic or systemic view, and considering that we never have lived in a world in which completely free access was the baseline, and considering further that the effect of incentives is to induce the production of new works, it is difficult to discern the basis for the prediction that stronger intellectual property rights will lead to an overall reduction in access. This is because, since it is private parties who will decide whether and what quantity of new works to produce, granting them property rights is the only way we know to induce them to decide to produce them, and only if they decide to produce them can access to them be had, by anyone on any terms. With regard to copyright, for example, the point worth emphasizing is that the argument for using property rights to create incentives is not that copyright owners are likely to *deny* access but rather that they are induced by the prospect of gain to *grant* it, albeit at prices that consumers are willing to pay. In other words, if the assumptions about incentives that supply the principal rationale for intellectual property have any basis in fact, it is because producers are motivated to create by the prospect of granting—not the prospect of denying—access to those who are willing to pay the price. Thus, there is an important sense in which incentives and increased access do not need to be "balanced," for they are not in genuine tension. They go hand in hand.[28] It turns out that when commentators and courts refer to the need to "balance" incentives and access, the "access" to which they refer is only access for *non*payers, and what they have in mind are rights of "end users to open and free access to consume works of authorship."[29] It is important to realize, however, that when commentators call for "balancing" nonpayers' claims against incentives, they implicitly concede that to require objecting owners to grant access to nonpayers, either with general rules or in the application of particular doctrines to particular facts, is almost certain to reduce the incentives of future producers.[30]

[28] Indeed, in the 2000 study, mandated by Congress, of whether particular classes of works ought to be exempted from the DMCA's anticircumvention provisions, the Copyright Office concluded that control over access increased rather than decreased the availability to the public of works of authorship because protection of technological measures removed what had been a disincentive for copyright owners to disclose or distribute otherwise vulnerable works. Library of Congress, Copyright Office, "Exemption to Prohibition on Circumvention of Copyright Protection Systems for Access Control Technologies," *supra* note 5, at 64561, 64567. For an interesting argument that property rights in information are likely to increase rather than diminish the quality of open information, *see* R. Polk Wagner, "Information Wants to Be Free: Intellectual Property and the Mythologies of Control," *Columbia Law Review* 103 (2003): 995.

[29] Jane C. Ginsburg, "Authors and Users in Copyright," *Journal of the Copyright Society of the U.S.A.* 45 (1997): 3.

[30] Note, too, that any decision, by a court or a legislature, to compel owners to grant access—either for free or at a collectively determined price—is in effect a decision to replace private decision-making about how much access should be granted and on what terms with that of public sector actors.

In making their arguments for reduced copyright protection, commentators frequently refer pejoratively to the copyright "monopoly." They thus imply that there is systematic failure in the market for copyrighted works, and, therefore, that there is reason to decide collectively to replace copyright owners' access and pricing decisions with decisions made by government actors. The rhetorical momentum gained by invocation of the monopoly bugaboo is, however, analytically unhelpful, if not positively misleading. In fact, as Kitch points out, "it seems likely that ... almost all copyrights ... are *not* monopolies."[31] Casual empiricism—admittedly not particularly reliable, though perhaps more trustworthy than unverified claims of impending disaster[32]—reveals that expressive works of all kinds compete intensely with one another for the favor of consumers. Indeed, the range of choice from competing works in the multiplicity of intellectual property markets—among works of fiction, non-fiction, and poetry, as well as among cookbooks, gardening books, self-help books, movies, "films," documentaries, pop music, country music, classical music, dramatic plays, musicals, modern dance, classical dance, painting, sculpture, computer software, and computer games, not to mention the hundreds of offerings available simultaneously every minute of the day and night on cable television—seems to this observer, at least, to put the lie to the claim that copyrights as a rule confer monopoly power. The fact that they confer exclusive rights in original works of expression on their owners does make it appropriate to call copyrights 'property rights', and it is true that these property rights may have value because consumers will pay more to obtain copies than the marginal cost of making them, even when the marginal cost is accurately calculated. But this fact does not mean that all copyrights are monopolies.[33] Thus, to invoke the pejorative "monopoly," even rhetorically, as a reason for conferring weaker rather than stronger property rights—that is, as a reason to displace private with public decision-making—is to wield a red herring. Moreover, if monopoly is or becomes a problem with regard to any particular copyright owner's market power, antitrust law ought to be adequate to fix it. If antitrust law is not adequate, then it is antitrust law that should be tweaked, not copyright law.

I turn now to the question of control over access to works in digital form, and to the anticircumvention provisions of the DMCA, as well as the use of trespass analogies in the digital context. Because digital tech-

[31] Kitch, "Elementary and Persistent Errors," *supra* note 25, at 1737. See also Mark A. Lemley, "The Economics of Improvement in Intellectual Property Law," *Texas Law Review* 75 (1997): 996 n.26 (emphasis added); and William M. Landes and Richard A. Posner, "An Economic Analysis of Copyright Law," *Journal of Legal Studies* 18, no. 2 (1989): 325, 361.

[32] *See, e.g.*, Hunter, "Cyberspace as Place," *supra* note 22, at 442 ("Down one road lies a future of completely propertized and privatized ownership of intellectual activity. Down the other road is a future where the interests of society at large are fostered, which at times leads to private ownership ... and at other times demands that some public intellectual space be kept as commons for all.").

[33] Kitch, "Elementary and Persistent Errors," *supra* note 25, at 1735.

nology has made it so easy and so cheap to produce perfect copies, and because in a networked environment distribution of copies is the mere matter of the click of a mouse, those who wish to profit from the expressive works they create and the information they produce must be able to control access. This they have attempted to do by both technological and legal devices. The DMCA's anticircumvention provisions provide legal backing for technological access controls with respect to copyrighted works. Think of a technological access control, such as a password requirement or encryption, as the cyber-equivalent of a doorbell or a lock, which in physical space would function to permit a property owner to identify and exclude unwelcome visitors. Think of technological circumvention of an access control as entering without ringing the doorbell or by forcing the lock. Understand, then, that the anticircumvention provisions are to copyrighted content in digital form as trespass laws are to physical space: both enforce the owner's decision regarding the terms on which and the persons to whom access should be granted.[34] Similarly, trespass doctrines enforce occasional decisions to exclude by private Web-site proprietors and operators of proprietary e-mail networks. Thus, in virtual space these doctrines perform the same function that they do in real space; namely, they delegate to private actors decision-making authority regarding access, with the state's role being limited to enforcing the private decision.[35]

One aspect of both the anticircumvention provisions and the use of trespass claims to protect virtual space that has particularly troubled critics is the fact that they permit private control over work that could not be protected by copyright. Anticircumvention devices foreclose even 'fair users'[36] from obtaining unauthorized access, and Web-site operators can use trespass laws to control access to uncopyrightable facts, as eBay was able to do when it successfully pursued a trespass claim against Bidder's

[34] The Second Circuit made this point in *Universal City Studios, Inc. v. Corley*, 273 F.3d 429, 452–53 (2d Cir. 2001), in which it sustained the anticircumvention provisions of the DMCA:

> [W]e must recognize that the essential purpose of encryption code is to prevent unauthorized access. Owners of all property rights are entitled to prohibit access to their property by unauthorized persons. Homeowners can install locks on the doors of their houses. Custodians of valuables can place them in safes. Stores can attach to products security devices that will activate alarms if the products are taken away without purchase.

[35] Note that the claim in the text is not a claim about doctrine. It is not a claim, in other words, that the DMCA's anticircumvention provisions are doctrinally identical to trespass laws. Nor is it a claim that the cyberspatial metaphor is an apt one or that cyberspace is "really" a place. Rather, the claim that drives the analysis is the claim that both the DMCA and trespass laws represent collective decisions to allocate decisions with respect to access—to virtual and to physical things respectively—to private producers and owners rather than to make such decisions collectively.

[36] 'Fair users' are those who would be able successfully to defend a copyright infringement action not on the ground that their conduct was not otherwise infringing but, rather, on the ground that it was excused under § 107 of the Copyright Act, which is to the effect that "fair use of a copyrighted work . . . is not an infringement of copyright." 17 U.S.C. § 107.

Edge for the latter's access to, and robotic collection of, electronic auction price data on eBay's Web site.[37] The fair-users problem worried Congress, and it delayed implementation of the anticircumvention provisions of the DMCA for two years while directing the Librarian of Congress to determine classes of works that should be exempt because the implementation of the anticircumvention provisions would diminish "the ability of individuals to use copyrighted works in ways that are otherwise lawful."[38] Concluding, however, that "in most cases thus far the use of access control measures has sometimes enhanced the availability of copyrighted works and has rarely impeded the ability of users of particular classes of works to make noninfringing uses,"[39] the Librarian, acting upon the recommendations of the Register of Copyrights, exempted only two relatively trivial classes of works.[40]

Regarding the use of trespass laws to control access to uncopyrightable facts, critics repeatedly point approvingly to the holding in *Feist Publications, Inc. v. Rural Telephone Service*.[41] In *Feist*, the Court held that facts are both constitutionally and by statute uncopyrightable, the reason being that they lack originality. In so holding, the Court explicitly rejected the possibility that a producer's "sweat of the brow" might support copyright in facts even in the absence of originality. *Feist* raises a number of complex and interesting issues that are beyond the scope of this paper. Contrary to what many critics of the DMCA imply, however, the case neither holds nor suggests that facts once discovered and information once produced fall automatically into the public domain. Nor did the Court suggest that the Constitution prohibits information producers from invoking legal doctrines other than copyright to control access. In this connection, it becomes relevant that private producers of information have always had the enforceable power to decide whether, on what terms, to whom, and under what circumstances to disclose it. Trade secret law, for example, enforces promises to keep information confidential, thus protecting the trade secret owner's ability to control access to the information without regard to whether it is copyrightable or not. Contract law enforces agreements not to disclose information, as well as agreements to pay for disclosure. Moreover, by enforcing their rights to control access to the physical location of information, trespass law has always provided ancillary protection to information producers who want to control access

[37] *eBay, Inc. v. Bidder's Edge, Inc.*, 100 F. Supp. 2d 1058 (N.D. Calif. 2000).

[38] Report of the House Committee on Commerce on the Digital Millennium Copyright Act of 1998, H.R. Rep. No. 1-5-551, pt. 2, at 37 (1998).

[39] Library of Congress, Copyright Office, "Exemption to Prohibition on Circumvention of Copyright Protection Systems for Access Control Technologies," *supra* note 5, at 64563.

[40] The Librarian determined exemptions for "[c]ompilations consisting of lists of websites blocked by filtering software applications," and for "[l]iterary works, including computer programs and data bases, protected by access control mechanisms that fail to permit access because of malfunction, damage, or obsoleteness." *Id.* at 64561.

[41] 499 U.S. 340 (1991).

to it. Thus, with regard to access to facts, providing a functional equivalent to the action of trespass to real or personal property in the virtual world neither departs in principle from, nor significantly expands, the kind and scope of protection that has always been available to information producers.

What remains to be addressed is the most vexing aspect of the question of whether to continue to authorize private parties to make decisions about the production and terms of access to expressive works and information in digital form or to collectivize such decisions: there exists no reliable empirical data about any of the factors that might usefully guide the analysis. We do not know, for example, what incentives are "enough" to prod producers to create the socially optimal number, quality, and diversity of works. While it may be the case, for example, that "many works would be created and disseminated even without copyright protection,"[42] it is no doubt also true that many works, and in particular those whose production requires a substantial up-front investment of resources—works that Jane C. Ginsburg calls "sustained works of authorship"[43]—would not be created without such protection. It is impossible to calculate either the costs, in terms of works not created, of collectivizing the access decision or the benefits, in terms of works that would not otherwise have been produced, of privatization.

Even more fundamentally, we do not know nor could we know what the "socially optimal" amount of works would be. We do not know whether producers will be systematically inclined to abuse their private power, either by denying access altogether or by charging exorbitant prices. We do not have anything like a reliable estimate of what the social costs are of denying access to nonpayers, nor do we know what the incentive effects of mandating access would be. We have no idea what mix, both in quantity and quality, of expressive works and information private producers would produce were decision-making authority over access to be assumed by government actors. "[T]here is no factual study that shows how much incentive is enough to further creative activity, or what kinds of incentives work: money, control, or time."[44] What George Priest observed about the literature on the scope of the patent right is

[42] Neil Weinstock Netanel, "Locating Copyright within the First Amendment Skein," *Stanford Law Review* 54 (2001): 28. For the classic argument that the basic case for copyright protection is weak, *see* Stephen Breyer, "The Uneasy Case for Copyright: A Study of Copyright in Books, Photocopies, and Computer Programs," *Harvard Law Review* 84 (1970): 322–23; *but cf.* Barry Tyerman, "The Economic Rationale for Copyright Protection for Published Books: A Reply to Professor Breyer, *U.C.L.A. Law Review* 18 (1971): 1100.

[43] Jane C. Ginsburg, "Putting Cars on the 'Information Superhighway': Authors, Exploiters, and Copyright in Cyberspace," *Columbia Law Review* 95 (1995): 1499.

[44] Marci A. Hamilton, "An Evaluation of the Copyright Term Extension Act of 1995: Copyright Duration Extension and the Dark Heart of Copyright," *Cardozo Arts and Entertainment Law Journal* 14 (1996): 656.

equally true of the literature on propertization of digital works: "The ratio of empirical demonstration to assumption in [the] literature must be very close to zero."[45] We "know almost nothing about the effect on social welfare of . . . systems of intellectual property."[46] Thus, when commentators make assertions such as "[w]ith the enactment of the DMCA . . . copyright, in the sense of protection intended primarily to serve the public interest, will surely have died,"[47] their conclusions are grounded not on facts but on assumptions—and on remarkably dire assumptions at that. Similarly, when advocates express fear that recognizing a trespass theory with regard to Web-site access will cause "many of [the] benefits of e-commerce" to disappear,[48] or when they claim that "[if] mere 'unauthorized use' of a web site is actionable, then millions of Americans are turned into lawbreakers for doing what they do every day—namely, surfing the Internet for information,"[49] their fears and claims are based not on fact but on dire assumptions. Sometimes, though not often, commentators articulate the assumptions upon which their predictions are based, in which case it becomes possible to evaluate a particular assumption's plausibility. Glynn S. Lunney, for example, has predicted that allowing free private copying will not "threaten copyright's public purpose." He bases the prediction on the explicit assumption that private copying increases as a work's popularity increases and thus will reduce revenue most substantially for the most popular works, which "typically receive an economic return far in excess of that *necessary to ensure their creation*."[50] The assertion that I have italicized here renders Lunney's prediction—that free private copying will not threaten copyright's public purpose—implausible, for the straightforward reason that producers simply cannot know *ex ante* what the economic return for any particular work will be.[51] And, of course, contrary assertions—to the effect that property-like rules that leave decisions regarding access to private producers are more likely to be socially value-enhancing than rules that collectivize such decisions—are similarly grounded on assumption and not on fact. All we know with any certainty is that we do not know, and cannot know, what the actual effects of various legal regimes are going to turn out to be.

[45] George L. Priest, "What Economists Can Tell Lawyers about Intellectual Property: Comment on Cheung," *Research in Law and Economics* 8 (1986): 19.

[46] Ibid., 21.

[47] Glynn S. Lunney, Jr., "The Death of Copyright: Digital Technology, Private Copying, and the Digital Millennium Copyright Act," *Virginia Law Review* 87 (2001): 814–15.

[48] Brief of Mark A. Lemley et al. as *Amici Curiae* in Support of Bidder's Edge, *eBay, Inc. v. Bidder's Edge, Inc.*, 9th Cir. No 00-15995 (2000), at 6–7.

[49] Appellant's Reply Brief, *Intel Corp. v. Hamidi*, California No. S103781 at 8-9.

[50] Lunney, "Death of Copyright," *supra* note 47, at 825 (emphasis added).

[51] *Cf.* Tad Friend, "Letter from California: Remake Man," *The New Yorker*, June 2, 2003, 41. (The movie industry's "besetting inefficiency, of course, is that studios never know what moviegoers will want to buy.")

This brings us to perhaps the hardest and most unrelentingly difficult question of all: Which way does our intractable ignorance about the consequences of private versus government control cut? Does it cut in favor of private or government control over access to digital works? Intractable ignorance being what it is—intractable—the answer one is inclined to give to this question doubtless is a function of one's more general views about the relative merits of private versus public decision-making. Many academic commentators, for example, view markets as relatively coercive compared to collective decision-making[52] and entertain deep suspicions about the way private actors tend to behave.[53] Not surprisingly, they argue against lodging substantial control over access in private hands.[54] In arguing in favor of more government-mandated access, they display a touching faith in the ability of legislatures and courts to gather sufficient information about the likely effects of their decisions to make it appropriate for them to substitute their judgment about whether access should be granted and on what terms for that of Web-site operators, copyright owners, or information producers.[55] They suggest, for example, that nuisance rather than trespass principles would permit judges to set the "optimal regulatory standard" for each case, by allowing "computer owners on the Net to exclude unreasonably costly uses of their servers, while allowing access for socially beneficial uses,"[56] implying, of course, that judges in fact possess the capacity to discern the "optimal regulatory standard."

For reasons having to do principally with my assessment of the incentives that are in play, I do not share the commentators' relatively greater distrust of actors in the private sector as compared to actors in the public

[52] *See, e.g.*, C. Edwin Baker, "First Amendment Limits on Copyright," *Vanderbilt Law Review* 55 (2002): 902–3 ("[M]arket transactions are exercises of power over other people. . . . These transactions are presumptively subject to legislative control [which by implied contrast is not an exercise of power over other people], which properly determines the socially desirable forms of private instrumental power.").

[53] *See, e.g.*, Hunter, "Cyberspace as Place," *supra* note 22, at 446 ("Private interests are reducing the public ownership of, and public access to, ideas and information in the online world . . . . [and will] move us towards a digital anticommons where no one will be allowed to access others' cyberspace 'assets' without using some form of licensing or some other form of transactionally expensive permission mechanism.").

[54] Lemley, "Place and Cyberspace," *supra* note 8, at 533–35 (suggesting that on the Internet, there are good reasons to think that the balance should be tilted in favor of public space in many contexts, and we should be more worried about the consequences of privatization in online space than we are in real space.)

[55] *See, e.g.*, Netanel, "Locating Copyright," *supra* note 42, at 69 (arguing in behalf of rigorous judicial scrutiny of copyright in order to "ensure that the copyright law is narrowly tailored to burden no more speech than is essential to furthering the legitimate objectives and purposes of the Copyright Act [and] make certain that copyright enforcement leaves 'open ample alternative channels' for communication of the burdened speech," and seeming to assume that it is within the judicial capacity both to gather the information and to make the evaluative judgments entailed by the obligation to engage in such rigorous scrutiny).

[56] Burk, "The Trouble with Trespass," *supra* note 22, at 30-31.

sector. Among other things, I worry that the incentives confronting public sector decision-makers make it quite unlikely that they will be moved to gather and accurately to assess the kind of information about the relative values of various alternatives that will enable them reliably to discern the socially optimal course. I am inclined to believe that our ignorance about the incentive effects of collectivizing access decisions cuts in favor of continuing to allocate authority over access to the private actors who produce the content. The principal reason is that I assume—though I acknowledge that I cannot prove it—that collectivizing access decisions will have negative incentive effects, and I fear that in the long run these will swamp the potentially negative effects of individual decisions either to deny access or to charge "too much" for it. Putting the decisions both about production and about access in private hands, and enforcing those decisions by legal rules such as copyright, trespass, and anticircumvention provisions, is, of course, no guarantee that the effects of the substantive decisions that private actors make will be socially optimal. Some of the naysayers' predictions of doom and gloom may in fact come to pass, in which case it would then be appropriate to consider increasing collective control over access. It is important to recognize, however, that putting the access decision in the hands of government actors carries no guarantee of optimality either. In addition, if the government actors get it wrong and require "too much" free access, so that the flow of new works and the rate of information production decrease significantly, it will be difficult to reverse course. As Judge Frank H. Easterbrook observed,

> [w]hen free distribution is socially optimal, people will not enforce their property rights in such a way that they try to hold up other people for money. If you start from property rights, you can negotiate for distribution at zero cost. If you start from a world of no property rights, it is extremely difficult, if indeed it is possible at all, to work to a world of compensation for intellectual property.[57]

Finally, I believe that producers of expressive works and information respond positively to the incentives generated by their control over access to the works they decide to produce. So long as the decision to produce expressive works and information is left to the private sector, and so long as we are not certain that the present configuration of incentives induces producers to create "too many" such works and "too much" information, and so long as we remain ignorant about how precisely to reconfigure the legal rules so that we maintain a level of incentives that is "just right," we reduce incentives at our peril.

[57] Frank H. Easterbrook, "Comment on Property Rights in the 21st Century," *Intellectual Property News* 3, no. 1 (E. L. Wiegand Practice Groups, 1999): 4.

IV. The First Amendment and Private Property in Tangible Things

Sections II and III described and defended an institutional conception of tangible and intangible property rights that regards a private property rights regime as reflecting a collective decision to allocate the authority to make decisions about investment, production, and access to actors in the private sector rather than to government officials. With regard to access, actions in trespass, either to real property or to chattels, and the DMCA have been the principal vehicles for collective enforcement of individual decisions to exclude. This section begins to address the constitutional aspects of the institutional choice to enforce private owners' decisions to deny access. In particular, it asks whether the First Amendment requires a reversal of that institutional choice. Subsection *A* summarizes current First Amendment doctrine on the issue of whether individuals have a constitutional right of access to private property contrary to the wishes of the property owner for the purpose of engaging in expressive activity. Subsection *B* describes First Amendment doctrine as it concerns the rights of persons who wish to communicate with a property owner who does not wish to receive their message.

A. Access for expressive activity

The first time the Court addressed the question of the First Amendment rights of those who wish to engage in expressive activity against the wishes of a private property owner was in the 1946 case of *Marsh v. Alabama*.[58] *Marsh* suggested that the Court was inclined to be receptive to the First Amendment claim, for it reversed the trespass conviction of a Jehovah's Witness who had attempted to distribute religious literature on the streets of a privately owned company town. Defending the conviction, the state argued that the owner corporation's "right to control the inhabitants of Chickasaw is coextensive with the right of a homeowner to regulate the conduct of his guests."[59] Though it implicitly acknowledged that a guest in a private home would have no First Amendment right to stay and speak if the owner wished to exclude him, the Court nonetheless held that

> the circumstance that the property rights to the premises where the deprivation of liberty ... took place, were held by others than the public, is not sufficient to justify the State's permitting a corporation to govern a community of citizens so as to restrict their fundamental

[58] 326 U.S. 501 (1946).
[59] *Id.* at 506.

> liberties and the enforcement of such restraint by the application of a state statute.[60]

In other words, in *Marsh* the Court attributed the private owner's decision to exclude to the state, and held that the state was not free to make such a decision consistent with the First Amendment.

Marsh has never been overruled, but it has had virtually no impact as a First Amendment precedent. During the Civil Rights movement of the 1960s, for example, the Court was frequently asked—and just as frequently refused—to hold that the First Amendment protects protestors and demonstrators on private property that the owner has opened to the public for purposes of commerce.[61] *Marsh* seemed to have suggested an affirmative answer to the question, but the Court's refusal to rely on it in the sit-in cases—indeed, its positive disinclination even to confront the issue that the cases presented—strongly implies that the Court intended to confine *Marsh* strictly to its own particular facts. The inference that this continues to be the Court's intention is supported by the fact that the Court first backtracked from and then explicitly overruled the only case in which it had relied on *Marsh*, namely its 1968 holding in *Amalgamated Food Employees Union Local 590 v. Logan Valley Plaza*.[62] The Court in *Logan Valley* held that, in a shopping center that was "the functional equivalent of the business district of Chickasaw involved in *Marsh*," the state could not enforce its trespass laws to support the decision of the owner to exclude "members of the public wishing to exercise their First Amendment rights."[63] However, just four years later, in *Lloyd Corporation v. Tanner*[64] the Court sustained a private shopping center's ban on the distribution of handbills. The center had invoked its ban to exclude antiwar leafleteers. Though purporting to distinguish *Logan Valley* on the ground that it involved First Amendment activity that was related to the shopping center's operations, Justice Lewis Powell's opinion in *Lloyd* expressed a view quite at odds both with *Logan Valley* and with the impulses that had led the Court to decide as it had in *Marsh*:

> Although accommodations between [speech and property values] are sometimes necessary, and the courts properly have shown a special solicitude for the First Amendment, this Court has never held

[60] *Id.* at 509.

[61] See Monrad G. Paulsen, "The Sit-In Cases of 1964: 'But Answer Came There None,'" *Supreme Court Review* (1964): 137 (describing the Court's refusal to reach the central question of the extent to which the Fourteenth Amendment forbids states to support private choices that could not constitutionally be made by the judiciary, the executive, or the legislature).

[62] 391 U.S. 308 (1968), *overruled by Hudgens v. NLRB*, 424 U.S. 507 (1976).

[63] 391 U.S. at 318–20.

[64] 407 U.S. 551 (1972).

that a trespasser or an uninvited guest may exercise general rights of free speech on property privately owned.[65]

And four years after *Lloyd*, in *Hudgens v. NLRB* (1976),[66] the Court expressly overruled *Logan Valley* (though it left *Marsh* at least formally intact). As had *Logan Valley, Hudgens* involved labor picketers. But, wrote Justice Potter Stewart unequivocally, "the constitutional guarantee of free expression has no part to play in a case such as this."[67] He noted, "if the respondents in the *Lloyd* case did not have a First Amendment right to enter that shopping center to distribute handbills concerning Vietnam, then the pickets in the present case did not have a First Amendment right to enter this shopping center for the purpose of advertising their strike."[68]

The upshot of these cases, and in particular of *Hudgens* since it is both the most recent and the most unequivocal, is that the enforcement of trespass laws at the behest of private property owners who wish to exclude persons who want to engage in expressive activity on the owner's property does not violate the First Amendment. Even if the access seekers could not constitutionally be excluded from otherwise similar but publicly owned property, state law may permit a private property owner to enlist the aid of a court to exclude them.

Notice what this means in institutional terms. It means that the First Amendment permits the decision whether to exclude or not to rest with the property owner. It means that courts may enforce that decision without regard either to the message the access seekers wish to convey or to the property owner's reasons for wishing to exclude. It means, in other words, that insofar as the content of the speech is concerned—its ideas or the message it conveys—the courts (i.e., the government) will not take sides.

In several cases the Court has analyzed claims of compelled access to private property for speech by asking whether being required to grant access violated the property owner's *First Amendment* rights as opposed to the owner's *property rights*. In most of these cases the access seekers did not claim that the First Amendment of its own force guaranteed them a right of access. Instead, they invoked one or another statutory or regulatory scheme that purported to grant them access to the property of others. The results of these cases are somewhat evenly divided between those sustaining the compelled access claim and those sustaining the First Amendment challenge to it. However, the facts, as well as the rhetoric and tone, of two of the most significant opinions sustaining compelled access suggest that the Court regarded them as exceptional cases that

[65] *Id.* at 567–68 .
[66] 424 U.S. 507.
[67] *Id.* at 521.
[68] *Id.* at 520–21.

required departures from the mainstream of First Amendment doctrine. The 1969 case of *Red Lion Broadcasting Co. v. FCC*,[69] for example, sustained the FCC's 'fairness doctrine', which required licensed broadcast stations to present discussions of both sides of public issues and to provide free reply time to those seeking to respond to personal attacks and political editorials. The holding followed from the Court's belief that "differences in the characteristics of new media justify differences in the First Amendment standards applied to them."[70] In particular, the opinion stressed the "scarcity of broadcast frequencies, the Government's role in allocating those frequencies, and the legitimate claims of those unable without government assistance to acquire access to those frequencies for expression of their views."[71] Commentators have long challenged both the conceptual and the empirical validity of the 'spectrum scarcity' rationale that provided the underpinning for *Red Lion*;[72] and the Supreme Court, acknowledging the criticism, has hinted that it might be prepared to reconsider the rationale if it were directly challenged in a relevant case.[73] Perhaps more interesting still is that the FCC itself repealed the fairness doctrine in 1987 because it found that compelled access in practice worked not to enhance diversity but to inhibit the presentation of controversial issues of public importance.[74]

The other case in which the Court departed from the mainstream of First Amendment doctrine to sustain a compelled access claim was the 1980 case of *PruneYard Shopping Center v. Robins*,[75] in which high school students sought access to a private shopping center for the purpose of protesting a UN resolution against Zionism. The California Supreme Court interpreted the California state constitution to guarantee access for speech to privately owned shopping centers. The U.S. Supreme Court concluded that "state constitutional provisions, which permit individuals to exercise free speech and expression rights on the property of a privately owned

[69] 395 U.S. 367 (1969).

[70] *Id.* at 386.

[71] *Id.* at 400.

[72] *See, e.g.*, Thomas G. Krattenmaker and Lucas A. Powe, Jr., *Regulating Broadcast Programming* (Boston, MA: MIT Press and Washington, DC: AEI Press, 1994), 204–19 ("Because the [scarcity] rationale is so untenable, its continued existence demonstrates that there is *something* about broadcasting that leads people to know that it may be regulated without regard to the First Amendment. That 'something' is the reason for continued regulation. We await its revelation. We only know it is not scarcity."); see also David Lange, "The Role of Access Doctrine in the Regulation of the Mass Media: A Critical Review and Assessment," *North Carolina Law Review* 52 (1973): 1.

[73] *Turner Broadcasting System v. FCC*, 512 U.S. 622, 637–39 (1994) (*Turner I*) ("Although courts and commentators have criticized the scarcity rationale since its inception, we have declined to question its continuing validity as support for our broadcast jurisprudence . . . and see no reason to do so" in a case in which "*the broadcast cases are inapposite.*") (emphasis added).

[74] Syracuse Peace Council, 2 FCC Rec. 5043 (1987); FCC Fairness Doctrine Obligations of Broadcast Licensees, 102 FCC 2d 143 (1985).

[75] 447 U.S. 74 (1980).

shopping center to which the public is invited" do not violate the center owner's "First Amendment right not to be forced by the state to use his property as a forum for the speech of others."[76] As the Court described its view, three key facts saved the access requirement from constitutional invalidity: because of the public availability of the center the views expressed would not be identified with the owner; the state did not dictate a specific message; and the owner could expressly disavow any connection with the petitioners.

The only case in which the Court has sustained compelled access using its customary First Amendment analytical tools is *Turner Broadcasting System v. FCC* (1994) (*Turner I*).[77] *Turner I* involved the "must-carry" provisions of the Cable TV Consumer Protection and Competition Act of 1992, which require cable operators to carry the signals of a certain number of local broadcast stations. Cable operators challenged the provisions on First Amendment grounds, claiming that they were content-based regulations that could not survive strict scrutiny. Justice Anthony Kennedy's opinion for the Court acknowledged that at the First Amendment's core "lies the principle that each person should decide for him or herself the ideas and beliefs deserving of expression, consideration, and adherence."[78] In addition, he conceded that "[g]overnment action ... that requires the utterance of a particular message favored by the [g]overnment, contravenes this essential right."[79] Nevertheless, the Court concluded that the must-carry provisions were "content-neutral," not "content-based," and thus they were subject to only intermediate scrutiny.[80] On rehearing the case in 1997, the Court ultimately concluded that the provisions passed constitutional muster because they furthered important governmental interests in competition and diversity.[81]

Two cases squarely rejected the government's effort to compel access for speech purposes. In *Miami Herald Publishing Co. v. Tornillo*,[82] decided in 1974, the Court invalidated Florida's right of reply law, which required newspapers to give political candidates a right to equal space to reply to editorial criticism. The opinion vividly illustrates the difference between the First Amendment rights of broadcasters, who lost their challenge to right of reply requirements in *Red Lion*, and print publishers, who re-

[76] *Id.* at 76, 85.

[77] 512 U.S. 622 (1994)(*Turner I*).

[78] *Id.* at 641.

[79] *Id.*

[80] On one hand, when a government regulation is aimed directly at the content of speech, the Court will subject it to 'strict scrutiny', and will generally invalidate it unless it serves a compelling state interest by the least restrictive means. On the other hand, when a regulation restricts speech but is not aimed directly at its content—when, in other words, it is 'content neutral'—the Court will subject it to 'intermediate scrutiny', and will generally sustain it if it is narrowly tailored to serve a significant government interest and leaves open ample alternative channels for communication of the speech.

[81] *Turner Broadcasting System v. FCC*, 520 U.S. 180 (1997) (*Turner II*).

[82] 418 U.S. 241 (1974).

soundingly won theirs. It also illustrates how the First Amendment, like private property rights, functions to allocate to private property owners and not to government officials decision-making authority about what resources shall be used to communicate what messages. Whereas the upshot of *Red Lion, PruneYard,* and the *Turner* rulings was to lodge decision-making authority in government actors—courts, legislatures, the FCC—the upshot of *Tornillo* was to lodge it in private owners and editors.

The 1986 case of *Pacific Gas & Electric Co. v. Public Utilities Commission of California*[83] is to the same effect, though the context was different. The California Public Utilities Commission adopted a requirement that PG&E allow a private advocacy group to use the "extra space"[84] in its billing envelopes four times a year. Relying heavily on *Tornillo,* and distinguishing *PruneYard,* the Court sustained PG&E's challenge to the requirement on the ground that being compelled to include in its billing envelope speech of a third party with which it disagreed violated its First Amendment rights. Again, the institutional upshot of the holding is that decision-making authority regarding access to private property for speech purposes resides in the hands of private owners.

B. Access for communication with the property owner

The Supreme Court has been steadfast if occasionally somewhat oblique in recognizing property owners' right to decline to grant access to those who wish to communicate with them. The flagship case, decided in 1970, is *Rowan v. United States Post Office Dept.,*[85] in which the Court upheld a federal statute that permitted a person who "in his sole discretion" has determined that certain advertisements are "erotically arousing or sexually provocative" to insulate himself from such advertisements by requesting the Postmaster General to order the sender to refrain from further mailings. The Court interpreted the relevant statutory provision to remove "'the right of the Government to involve itself in any determination of the content and nature of these objectionable materials.' "[86] It then addressed the plaintiff mail order businesses' argument that the statute violated their constitutional right to communicate. The plaintiffs' brief had broadly asserted that "'[t]he freedom to communicate orally and by written word and, indeed, in every manner whatsoever is imperative to a free and sane society."[87] The Court conceded that "[t]o make the householder the exclusive and final judge of what will cross his threshold undoubtedly has the effect of impeding the flow of ideas, in-

[83] 475 U.S. 1 (1986).

[84] The "extra space" was the difference between the maximum weight mailable with a postage stamp and the weight of the monthly bill.

[85] 397 U.S. 728 (1970).

[86] *Id.* at 733 (citation omitted).

[87] *Id.* at 735.

formation, and argument that, ideally, he should receive and consider."[88] It concluded, nevertheless, that "[n]othing in the Constitution compels us to listen to or view any unwanted communication, whatever its merit."[89]

Rowan relied on *Martin v. City of Struthers*,[90] a 1943 case that invalidated an ordinance prohibiting door-to-door solicitation, drawing a distinction between the city government's right to protect homeowners from unwanted solicitations and the enforceable right of an individual homeowner to protect himself. This distinction explains the results in a number of cases in which legislatively enacted bans on or permit requirements for certain types of communication have been invalidated even though a majority of the jurisdiction's homeowners probably would not have wanted to receive or be bothered by the material.[91] The distinction warrants emphasis. It helps to bring the "who decides" aspect of the First Amendment access issue into focus. In *Rowan* the Court sustained the statute because it put the decision whether to reject mail in the hands of the individual citizen. The Postmaster General's job was merely to enforce the private decision. In *Martin*, by contrast, the town did more than simply enforce individual owners' decisions to exclude. The ordinance that town officials passed attempted "to make this decision for all [the town's] inhabitants,"[92] but the Constitution does not generally allocate decision-making authority regarding access for purposes of communication with private property owners to local legislators or other government officials. Instead it allocates it to the private property owner.

It remains to justify these outcomes, a task made more difficult by the fact that the Court itself has done little to explain them. In addition, at first glance the decisions seem to run counter to the frequently invoked rhetorical commitment to the "principle that debate on public issues should be uninhibited, robust and wide-open."[93] Those who seek access to *any* place, public or privately owned, for the purpose of engaging in First Amendment activity invoke this principle as a sword to compel the property's unwilling proprietor either to let them in or to require him to satisfy a court that his reasons for not doing so have merit. The access seekers in

[88] *Id.* at 736.

[89] *Id.* at 737.

[90] 319 U.S. 141 (1943).

[91] *See, e.g.*: *Consolidated Edison Co. v. Public Service Comm'n.*, 447 U.S. 530 (1980)(invalidating an order prohibiting the inclusion in monthly electric bills of inserts that discussed controversial issues of public policy); *Bolger v. Youngs Drug Products Corp.*, 463 U.S. 60 (1983)(invalidating a federal law barring the mailing of unsolicited advertisements for contraceptive products); *Staub v. City of Baxley*, 355 U.S. 313 (1958)(invalidating an ordinance prohibiting the solicitation of membership in dues-paying organizations without a permit from city officials); *Hynes v. Mayor of Oradell*, 425 U.S. 610 (1976)(invalidating an ordinance requiring advance notice to police in writing by persons desiring to canvass, solicit, or call from house to house for a recognized charitable or political campaign or cause).

[92] 319 U.S. at 141.

[93] *New York Times v. Sullivan*, 376 U.S. 254, 270 (1964).

effect make the claim that mandating property owners to grant them access will result in more speech, and more speech is presumptively better. They assert that compelled access achieves the purpose of the Free Speech Clause, which they imply is to *assure* the widest possible debate about matters of concern to the community.[94] But this view, as Charles Fried has pointed out, "mistakes an effect of the principle for the principle itself. The First Amendment protects a liberty—liberty of expression—and it is an effect of this liberty that there is wide and uninhibited discussion of political matters."[95] In other words, the fact that wide and uninhibited discussion occurs when private citizens have liberty to speak should not be taken to imply that the Constitution directly guarantees that the widest possible debate must occur. It would be impossible for the Court to administer such a guarantee, if for no other reason than that the Court would have to make factual determinations in particular cases that it would be impossible for it honestly or confidently to make. The Court could not possibly hope to discern how much access for what kinds of speech activity on what kinds of property would provide the "widest possible debate," and it is certain that the Constitution contains no criteria in terms of which the Court could evaluate when granting a particular claim of access would be required in order for there to be "enough" speech.[96]

There are at least two additional explanations for the Court's refusal to grant First Amendment rights of access to private property in addition to the fact that the Constitution does not actually purport to assure that debate will be uninhibited, robust and wide open. One is that the refusal to grant access rights is grounded in the Court's understanding that the Constitution itself has very little—indeed, almost nothing—to say about either the substance of laws that resolve disputes between private individuals or about the reasons why private actors invoke the aid of courts. The Constitution takes as given that states supply certain generally applicable background rules—the rules of property, contract, and tort, for example—for the resolution of private disputes. The extent to which legislatures or courts are constitutionally free to change those rules, and, in particular, to modify them so as to transfer decision-making authority

[94] See, e.g., Owen Fiss, "State Activism and State Censorship, *Yale Law Journal* 100 (1991): 2100–01.

[95] Charles Fried, "The New First Amendment Jurisprudence: A Threat to Liberty," in Geoffrey R. Stone, Richard A. Epstein, and Cass R. Sunstein, eds., *The Bill of Rights in the Modern State* (Chicago, IL: University of Chicago Press, 1992): 226–27.

[96] *Cf.* Lillian R. BeVier, "Rehabilitating Public Forum Doctrine: In Defense of Categories," *Supreme Court Review* (1992): 115–21 (noting the difficult fact-finding and evaluative issues lurking in case-by-case determinations of whether in particular instances a " 'fair accommodation of the individual's interest in effective expression . . . , the public's interest in receiving the communication, and legitimate countervailing interests of the state' " has been achieved) (quoting Geoffrey R. Stone, "Fora Americana: Speech in Public Places," *Supreme Court Review* [1974]: 253–54).

from private to public actors, is the subject of intense debate both on the Court[97] and off.[98] With regard to access, for example, the Supreme Court has squarely held that legislatures may not authorize an unwanted "permanent physical occupation" of private property without paying just compensation.[99] On other occasions, the Court has sustained collective modifications of the property owner's right to exclude in certain circumstances: the public accommodations title of the Civil Rights Act of 1964,[100] for one example, and *PruneYard* for another. And, though the decision has not gone unchallenged by commentators,[101] the New Jersey Supreme Court has interpreted its state common law and the "public trust doctrine" to grant to the general public a right to use privately owned land for recreational purposes.[102] But so long as the background rule is that the property owner has the right to exclude, and the state merely enforces the property owner's decision to exercise that right, the Constitution is indifferent either to the reason access is desired or to the reason it is denied.

A second justification for the refusal to read the First Amendment as a guarantee of access to private property is that enforcing the right to exclude does not entail any risk of deliberate government discrimination among viewpoints. That trespass laws may, in particular cases and from time to time, fall more heavily on particular viewpoints does not signal deliberate viewpoint discrimination. Trespass laws are neutral as to the points of view of both the access seeker and the property owner. Enforcing trespass laws does not put judges in a position to censor or punish particular speakers, or to manipulate public debate by selectively denying speech opportunities to disfavored views or granting them to favored ones. As the Court itself noted in *Rowan*, vesting decision-making authority in individuals with regard to what communications come onto their private property is a way to avoid "vesting the power to make any discretionary evaluation of the material in a government official,"[103] including in a judge.

[97] *See, e.g.*: *Tahoe-Sierra Preservation Council, Inc.* v. *Tahoe Regional Planning Agency*, 535 U.S. 302 (2002) (mere enactment of temporary moratoria against all viable economic use of property does not constitute a per se taking of property); *Lucas.* v. *South Carolina Coastal Council*, 505 U.S. 1003 (1992) (where the state seeks to sustain regulation that deprives land of all economically beneficial use, it may resist paying compensation only if the right to make the proscribed use was not part of the title to begin with.)

[98] The literature is far too voluminous to cite. Examples of two prominent opposing views are Richard A. Epstein, *Takings: Private Property and the Power of Eminent Domain* (Boston, MA: Harvard University Press, 1985); and Cass R. Sunstein, *The Partial Constitution* (Boston, MA: Harvard University Press, 1994).

[99] *Loretto v. Teleprompter Manhattan CATV Corp.*, 458 U.S. 419 (1982).

[100] 42 U.S.C. §§ 2000a-a-6 (2000).

[101] *See* Barton H. Thompson, Jr., "Judicial Takings," *Virginia Law Review* 76 (1990): 1541 (arguing that "there is no justification for exempting the judiciary from those property protections that are necessary where other branches of the government are concerned.").

[102] *Matthews v. Bay Head Improvement Ass'n.*, 95 N.J. 306, 471 A.2d 355, *cert. denied*, 469 U.S. 821 (1984).

[103] *Rowan v. United States Post Office Dept.*, 397 U.S. 728, at 737.

V. The First Amendment and Private Property in the Digital World

Continuing to deploy an institutional conception of property rights in tangible and intangible things, this section addresses the First Amendment implications of the choice to enforce private decisions to deny access by copyright owners, digital information producers, and Web-site and proprietary e-mail system operators.

A. Copyright and the First Amendment

This subsection considers whether, as several academic commentators have recently argued, copyright law in principle is in significant tension with the First Amendment. For example, Mark Lemley and Eugene Volokh regard copyright as facially problematic because "[c]opyright law restricts speech: it restricts you from writing, painting, publicly performing or otherwise communicating what you please. If your speech copies ours, and if the copying uses our 'expression,' not merely our ideas or facts that we have uncovered, your speech can be enjoined and punished . . . ."[104] For another example, Jed Rubenfeld claims that copyright ignores three basic principles of free speech jurisprudence, namely, the principles that content-based restrictions of speech command strict scrutiny, that prior restraints on speech (which are routinely granted in copyright infringement cases) are deeply disfavored, and that speech restrictions that are based on the speaker's viewpoint are practically unconstitutional per se.[105] For a third example, Yochai Benkler maintains that, because they prevent some people from using or communicating information, "*all* property rights in information conflict with the 'make no law' injunction of the First Amendment."[106]

The Supreme Court has directly confronted the question of copyright's compatibility with the First Amendment on two occasions in the last two decades. In neither case was the Court receptive to the idea that copyright infringers have serious claims to First Amendment sympathy. In both cases, the Court focused almost exclusively on copyright's incentive effects and seemingly regarded the restrictions it places on the speech of infringers as for all practical purposes irrelevant to the First Amendment

[104] Mark A. Lemley and Eugene Volokh, "Freedom of Speech and Injunctions in Intellectual Property Cases," *Duke Law Journal* 48 (1998): 147. See also Eugene Volokh and Brett McDonnell, "Freedom of Speech and Independent Judgment Review in Copyright Cases," *Yale Law Journal* 107 (1998): 2431 ("Copyright law restricts speech.").

[105] Jed Rubenfeld, "The Freedom of Imagination: Copyright's Constitutionality," *Yale Law Journal* 112 (2002): 1.

[106] Yochai Benkler, "Free as the Air to Common Use: First Amendment Constraints on Enclosure of the Public Domain," *New York University Law Review* 74 (1999): 393 (emphasis added).

analysis. In 1985, in *Harper & Row Publishers v. Nation Enterprises,*[107] the magazine *The Nation* sought to excuse on First Amendment grounds its use of verbatim excerpts from President Gerald Ford's copyrighted but not-yet-published memoirs. *The Nation* argued that the ordinary rule, which is to the effect that "the author's right to control the first public appearance of his undisseminated expression will outweigh a claim of fair use,"[108] should be relaxed in view of "the substantial public import of the subject matter of the Ford memoirs."[109] Deploying what Melville B. Nimmer had described in an influential law review article fifteen years earlier[110] as a "definitional balancing" methodology, the Court firmly rejected the magazine's claim. The methodology relied for the accommodation of First Amendment values on doctrines internal to the Copyright Act, namely, the "Act's distinction between copyrightable expression and uncopyrightable facts and ideas, and the latitude for scholarship and comment traditionally afforded by fair use."[111] More importantly, the Court did not regard the Copyright Act as in any way fundamentally inconsistent with the First Amendment. To the contrary, the Court said, by "supplying the economic incentive to create and disseminate" works, "the Framers intended copyright itself to be the engine of free expression."[112]

More recently, in the 2003 decision of *Eldred v. Ashcroft,*[113] the Court rejected a facial First Amendment challenge to the Copyright Term Extension Act (CTEA).[114] Despite the recent outpouring of academic commentary and several amicus briefs urging the Court to reconsider, the Court showed no hesitation in continuing to embrace *Harper & Row*'s analytical underpinnings. "Copyright's purpose is to *promote* the creation and publication of free expression,"[115] the Court said. The *Eldred* challengers had argued that, because it "bars unauthorized use or dissemination of copyrighted works, copyright law restricts speech."[116] They claimed that congressionally enacted copyright law "must be justified under intermediate review."[117] The Court disagreed, affirming that "uncommonly strict scrutiny" is not necessary for "a copyright scheme that incorporates its own speech-protective purposes and safeguards."[118] Distinguishing CTEA from the Telecommunications Act's must-carry provisions, to which the challengers had analogized it and to which the Court

[107] 471 U.S. 539 (1985).

[108] *Id.* at 555.

[109] *Id.* at 556.

[110] Melville B. Nimmer, "Does Copyright Abridge the First Amendment Guarantees of Free Speech and Press?" *UCLA Law Review* 17 (1970): 1180.

[111] *Harper & Row,* 471 U.S. at 560.

[112] *Id.* at 558.

[113] 537 U.S. 186 (2003).

[114] Pub. L. 105–298, § 102(b) and (d), 112 Stat. 2827–2828 (amending 17 USC §§ 302, 304).

[115] *Eldred,* 537 U.S. at ___, 123 S. Ct. 769, 788.

[116] Brief for Petitioners Eric Eldred, et al., No. 01–618, at 37.

[117] *Id.*

[118] *Eldred,* 537 U.S. at ___, 123 S. Ct. at 788.

did give intermediate scrutiny in *Turner I* (1994),[119] Justice Ruth Bader Ginsburg's opinion concluded that restricting the speech of copyright infringers is generally not to be regarded as an "abridgement" for First Amendment purposes:

> CTEA ... does not oblige anyone to reproduce another's speech against the carrier's will. Instead, it protects authors' original expression from unrestricted exploitation. Protection of that order does not raise the free speech concerns present when the government compels or burdens the communication of particular facts or ideas. The First Amendment securely protects the freedom to make—or decline to make—one's own speech; it bears less heavily when speakers assert the right to make other people's speeches.... [W]hen ... Congress has not altered the traditional contours of copyright protection, further First Amendment scrutiny is unnecessary.[120]

Eldred is striking in several respects. Most significant was the Court's affirmation of *Harper & Row*'s focus on copyright's incentive effects on producers of original works of authorship in the face of the increasing scholarly attention to the fact that the law restricts the speech of infringers. The Court was brusque in dismissing the CTEA challengers' First Amendment arguments, and it paid the academic literature virtually no heed whatsoever. While its decision to regard copyright as generally not problematic for First Amendment purposes, and its determination to focus almost exclusively on copyright's incentive effects is clear, its failure seriously to engage the arguments that emphasize copyright's speech restrictive effects is unfortunate.

From the point of view of preserving its institutional capital, the Court's indifference to the commentators' arguments is understandable. Had the arguments been found persuasive, the Court would have had not only to redraw a long-standing First Amendment boundary, but also to adumbrate its parameters in completely uncharted territory. The latter task might well have seemed particularly daunting. It is difficult to envision how heightened First Amendment scrutiny in copyright cases would or should or could actually work in practice, and equally hard to imagine how it would be possible to keep the doctrine from becoming just one more multifactored but essentially rootless, unprincipled pocket of First Amendment jurisprudence.[121] Still, the arguments in favor of heightened

[119] 512 U.S. 622 (1994)(*Turner I*).

[120] *Eldred*, 537 U.S. at ___, 123 S. Ct. at 774.

[121] *Cf.* Robert Post, "Reconciling Theory and Doctrine in First Amendment Jurisprudence," in Lee Bollinger and Geoffrey R. Stone, eds., *Eternally Vigilant: Free Speech in the Modern Era* (Chicago, IL: University of Chicago Press, 2002): 153 ("Doctrine becomes confused when the requirements of theory make little sense in the actual circumstances of concrete cases, or when doctrine is required to articulate the implications of inconsistent theories. First Amendment doctrine has unfortunately suffered from both these difficulties.").

scrutiny have sufficient prima facie appeal to merit a more considered rebuttal than the cold shoulder they received from the Court. In what follows, I shall try to put the case that the result in *Eldred* stands on firmer ground than the Court's rather offhand analysis might imply.

The first strand in the argument points to the awkward fact that copyright and the First Amendment have coexisted practically since the United States' founding,[122] and until fairly recently the alleged First Amendment anomaly of copyright law struck few people as problematic. Before the recent avalanche of scholarly interest, there was little important scholarly literature that even raised the issue. The literature that did exist neither discerned profound conflict between copyright and First Amendment values nor regarded the speech of copyright infringers as having significant First Amendment worth.[123] Ironically, the conclusion of one of the few early commentators, Melville B. Nimmer, that copyright law itself contained the appropriate "definitional balance" between copyright owners and First Amendment values, provided the touchstone for the Court's analysis in *Harper & Row* and was reaffirmed in *Eldred*, though without reference to the fact that Nimmer himself had thought that the "reasons ... justifying first amendment subordination to copyright [do not] justify [an] extension of an existing copyright term." [124] And there exist few cases in which First Amendment claims have been seriously considered.[125]

The historical pedigree and stubborn persistence of copyright's immunity to a successful First Amendment assault seems something of a puzzle today. Many scholars argue that the immunity is anomalous. They do not seem to think there exists a satisfactory explanation for it, and they cer-

[122] Congress proposed the Bill of Rights in 1789. It passed the first Copyright Act in 1790 (Act of May 31, 1790, ch. 15, 1 Stat. 124). The Bill of Rights was ratified in 1791.

[123] The principal literature essentially consisted of four articles: Robert C. Denicola, "Constitutional Limitations on the Protection of Expression," *California Law Review* 67 (1979): 283 (concluding that internal rules of copyright doctrine generally operate to avoid conflict with the First Amendment, but recommending narrow First Amendment privilege when necessary to enable users to contribute their ideas effectively to the public dialogue); Paul Goldstein, "Copyright and the First Amendment," *Columbia Law Review* 70 (1970): 983 (concluding that copyright law itself advances First Amendment values, but recommending that it should be subject to two accommodative principles in order to protect infringing uses that "independently advance the public interest" [at 988] and to require plaintiffs to demonstrate actual damages); Nimmer, "Does Copyright Abridge the First Amendment?" *supra* note 110 (concluding that in the idea-expression dichotomy, copyright law contains its own definitional balance that, for the most part, comports adequately with the underlying rationale for freedom of expression); and Lionel S. Sobel, "Copyright and the First Amendment: A Gathering Storm?" *Copyright Law Symposium* 19 (American Society of Composers, Authors and Publishers, 1971): 43 (since the First Amendment was designed to encourage and protect the communication of diverse ideas, and since copyright law protects only particular expressions, copyright does not conflict with any of the First Amendment's purposes). An exception to the statement in the text is Diane Leenheer Zimmerman's "Information As Speech, Information As Goods: Some Thoughts on Marketplaces and the First Amendment," *William and Mary Law Review* 33 (1992): 665 (arguing that intellectual property claims are unlikely to take adequate account of speech values).

[124] Nimmer, *supra* note 110, at 1194–95.

[125] For a summary of the case law since 1970, see Netanel, "Locating Copyright," *supra* note 42, at 10–12.

tainly do not regard its longevity as posing a legitimate impediment to change.

Some commentators contend that developments in copyright law and the profound technological innovations of recent years have brought about a copyright regime that differs in kind and not just in degree of protection from that which obtained earlier. At the time of the founding, only literal copying was prohibited and printing and copying were in their infancy. During the mid-twentieth century, the decades in which First Amendment doctrine as we know it today was being forged, technological change had not yet become transformative.[126] The claim appears to be that copyright has become a fundamentally different legal animal, with fundamentally different consequences, from what it was at the time of the founding. Those who make this claim regard the seemingly endless outward thrust of copyright protection—which has come to include derivative works, "substantially similar" as well as literal copies, and anticircumvention rights—as significant because it has expanded the extent of the copyright owner's control and thus put in private hands power over more speech than formerly. They also regard technological innovations as significant because digital technology makes it so easy and so cheap for individuals to make perfect copies of works. Anyone with a computer can do it, and just about everyone does. Computers make more copying possible than ever before, critics claim, and, therefore, enforcing copyright restricts more speech than ever before.

Commentators are correct to point out that Congress has responded to technological innovations—in particular to the ever-advancing technology of copying—and to changes in the market for copyrighted works by continually adjusting, indeed by steadily expanding, copyright owners' exclusive rights. Commentators are also correct to note that the anticircumvention provisions of the DMCA enhanced copyright owners' legal control over easily copied works in digital form. Refuting the inferences they draw from these facts will bring us to the second strand in the argument to demonstrate that the result in *Eldred* stands on firm ground, at least insofar as it denies heightened First Amendment scrutiny in run of the mill copyright cases: the continual adjustments of copyright owners' rights do not alter a previously immutable copyright balance, for there never was such a thing. In fact, as Jane Ginsburg has demonstrated, the history of copyright's evolution has been one in which each significant development of technology—the printing press, movable type, photography, motion pictures, audio recording, Xerography, digitization and digital networks—has willy-nilly altered the balance of control between

[126] *See, e.g.*, L. Ray Patterson and Judge Stanley F. Birch, "Copyright and Free Speech Rights," *Journal of Intellectual Property Law* 4 (1996): 3 ("New technology provides new means of mass communication that . . . enables the copyright owner to control access."); L. Ray Patterson, "Free Speech, Copyright, and Fair Use," *Vanderbilt Law Review* 40 (1987): 48 (The "copyright owner's right to control access to the work far exceeds what could have been imagined in 1841.").

authors and users, and each has eventually prompted "a new legal calibration" of the proper balance.[127] Moreover,

> [a]lthough the DMCA's regulation of technological measures may endeavor to ensure greater control for copyright owners over new markets created by new technology than in the past, the logic underlying this legislation is consistent with earlier approaches to copyright/technology conflicts.[128]

More to the point from this paper's perspective, the expansions of copyright owners' rights do not so alter the nature of copyright as a restriction on speech as to render the founders' understanding of the First Amendment implications of copyright no longer pertinent. The reason is that the Copyright Clause of the Constitution authorizes Congress "to secur[e] to authors . . . the *exclusive right* to their . . . writings.[129] Since the very definition of a property right is that it is an "exclusive right," the Copyright Clause explicitly contemplates propertization. Beginning with the first copyright statute, and continuing to the present day, Congress has granted what are and always have been the functional equivalent of property rights (regardless of what they were called) to authors of original works. Though their scope has been altered and expanded from time to time, and the degree of protection they afford has been adjusted to reflect both significant developments in intellectual property markets and revolutionary changes in the technology of copying, these property rights have since the founding given copyright owners the power to call upon the courts for enforcement by restricting expression that infringes. Since Congress passed the first copyright statute granting property rights in 1790, and the Bill of Rights was proposed by Congress in 1789 and ratified in 1791, and since the fundamental legal nature of copyright has remained unchanged, it seems that Justice Ginsburg was correct in *Eldred* when she concluded that the Bill of Rights' proximity in time to the first copyright statute "'indicates that, in the Framers' view, copyright's limited monopolies [i.e., property rights] are compatible with free speech principles."[130]

Some scholars who support expanded First Amendment review in copyright cases seem to suggest that, whatever the historical reality, expanded review would correct what has become an obvious and unjustified doctrinal error.[131] They maintain that copyright as it is presently enforced is simply not compatible with First Amendment doctrine as it is currently

[127] Jane C. Ginsburg, "Copyright and Control over New Technologies of Dissemination," *Columbia Law Review* 101 (2001): 1614.

[128] Ibid., 1617.

[129] U.S. CONST., art. I, § 8, cl. 8 (emphasis added).

[130] *Eldred v. Ashcroft*, 537 U.S. at ___,123 S. Ct. at 788.

[131] *See, e.g.*, Volokh and McDonnell, "Independent Judgment Review in Copyright Cases," *supra* note 104, at 2446 (copyright laws must be seen as a speech restriction because they ban people from "saying a particular thing," and are thus speech restricting by definition).

enunciated.[132] Their analysis implies (and sometimes it explicitly avers) that the success of a copyright plaintiff involves a *government* decision to restrict speech. They do not specify whether the reason they characterize it as the government's decision is because Congress passed the Copyright Act or because copyright owners invoke the aid of courts for the enforcement of their rights. Viewing the matter as a "who decides" question, however, the point is of no particular importance. We can assume *arguendo* that Congress acted when it passed successive versions of the Copyright Act, and that when courts rule in plaintiffs' favor in copyright cases they do so in their capacity as state actors. The assumption does not compel the conclusion that a judgment for a plaintiff in a copyright case represents the *government's* decision to restrict speech. Just as property rights in tangible things reflect a collective decision to allocate enforceable decision-making authority regarding use, possession, and disposition to private owners, property rights in original works of authorship reflect a collective decision to allocate decision-making authority regarding reproduction, derivative works, distribution, and the like, to private owners. In other words, when Congress decided to grant property rights in authors' original works, and from time to time revised the boundaries of and expanded the available enforcement mechanisms for such rights, Congress in effect allocated to *copyright owners* the decision whether to "restrict speech." As we have seen, in making this allocation, Congress acted consistently with the First Amendment and pursuant to the Copyright Clause of the Constitution. When a judge enjoins or awards damages for an infringement of copyright, though she is a government actor acting in her official capacity, she is not "deciding to restrict speech." Rather, pursuant to Congress's direction to put the decision whether to restrict speech in the hands of the private copyright owner, she is merely ascertaining the boundaries of the plaintiff's property right, determining that the defendant has trespassed upon it, and, enforcing the *copyright owner's* "decision to restrict speech."[133]

From an institutional perspective, there is a close analogy between what a court does in a copyright case and what a judge does who enforces a trespass law at the behest of an owner of real property who

[132] *See, e.g.*, Netanel, "Locating Copyright," *supra* note 42, at 4 ("As copyright law has evolved over recent decades, copyright owner prerogatives have steadily become more bloated. . . . In parallel, even if free speech law might have presented little ground for subjecting copyright to First Amendment scrutiny in the past, the evolving precepts and analytic framework of First Amendment doctrine now fully support, if not demand, such scrutiny.")

[133] The use of the word 'merely' in the text ought not to be taken to imply that the decisions that a judge makes in a copyright infringement suit are easy, or that they are uncontroversial, or that they raise no questions of policy regarding where the boundary of the plaintiff's property right ought to be located, for such is very far from being the case. The point being made in the text is, rather, that however difficult the decision about where the boundary should be located in a particular case, what the judge is attempting to do in institutional terms is to determine where the copyright owner's decision-making authority ends and the judge's authority begins.

seeks to exclude someone who would use the owner's property for First Amendment—speech—purposes. In the trespass case, of course the government is "acting," but for constitutional purposes its action is reflected in its anterior decision to enforce private owners' decisions to exclude. Having decided to enforce such decisions via the law of trespass, the government cannot meaningfully be said to have endorsed the particular (speech-restrictive) consequences of any particular owner's decision. By a parity of reasoning, the government "acts" in a copyright case too, but the constitutional significance of its action is contained in its anterior decision to enforce private copyright owners' decisions to exclude infringers who wish to use any particular owner's property—his "original work of authorship"—for speech purposes. True, the trespass cause of action will lie regardless of whether the trespasser was speaking and without regard to what he wanted to say, whereas deciding that there has been a copyright infringement will require the fact-finder to look at the content of both the plaintiff's and the defendant's speech. Because the inquiry into content is limited to determining the boundaries of the plaintiff's property right and whether the defendant's speech infringes, it raises none of the risks that the prohibition on restricting speech "because of its content" is designed to forestall. The judge in the copyright case will not inquire, for example, into either the infringer's or the copyright owner's point of view, nor will she ask about the effects their substantive messages are likely to have on the audience. I develop these points in the analysis that follows.

Jed Rubenfeld is among the commentators who reject the copyright-trespass to real property analogy, and his argument provides a good platform from which to assess more thoroughly the analogy's soundness. Rubenfeld presents three main objections. First, he observes, the law of trespass to real property does not make speaking an element of the offense. Copyright law, in contrast, makes people liable not only because they are speaking but also because of what they say. Second, he claims that the relevant comparison is not between copyright and the First Amendment-trespass case of *Hudgens v. NLRB*, but between copyright and the First Amendment-libel case of *New York Times v. Sullivan*.[134] Third, he claims that the reasons why state enforcement of trespass laws do not violate the First Amendment "disappear when we turn to copyright."[135]

Consider the first objection, which is based on Rubenfeld's observation that copyright law makes people liable not only because they are speaking but also because of what they say, whereas trespass does not make speaking an element of the offense. The observation seems to imply that copyright law necessarily conflicts with the canonical doctrine, enunci-

[134] 376 U.S. 254 (1964).

[135] Rubenfeld, "Copyright's Constitutionality, *supra* note 105, at 29.

ated *in dictum* in the 1972 case of *Police Department of Chicago v. Mosley*,[136] that "above all else, the First Amendment means that government has no power to restrict expression because of its message, its ideas, its subject matter, or its content."[137] In response, it is important to emphasize that, because it aims at speech *that infringes*, and restricts a defendant's expression only if it reproduces the plaintiff's, copyright liability does not represent a genuine threat to the implementation of the First Amendment strategies embodied in the *Mosley* dictum.

In fact, it is plausible to argue that copyright infringement liability neither punishes nor deters *speech* on account of its content. Instead it aims at *conduct* that infringes: unauthorized reproduction, preparation of derivative works, distribution, public performance, and the like. Viewing copyright infringement as behavior that combines speech and nonspeech elements would require the Court to subject copyright law to First Amendment review, but it would be the lenient scrutiny prescribed by the Court in the draft-card burning case of *United States v. O'Brien*.[138] In *O'Brien* the Court held that a regulation of behavior that combines speech and nonspeech elements will be sustained if it is

> within the constitutional power of the Government; if it furthers an important or substantial governmental interest; if the governmental interest is unrelated to the suppression of free expression, and if the incidental restriction on alleged First Amendment freedoms is no greater than is essential to the furtherance of that interest.[139]

The most significant part of the *O'Brien* test is the determination whether the government's interest in the regulation is "unrelated to the suppression of freedom of expression," because the answer is likely to be outcome determinative. If the Court determines that the government's interest is unrelated to the suppression of freedom of expression, then it is likely in practice to subject the regulation, both on its face (as discerned from the terms of the regulation itself) and as applied (as evidenced from the particular application at issue), to extremely lenient review, which means that the regulation is very unlikely to be found to violate the First Amendment. Though the cases applying the test for whether a regulation is "unrelated to suppression of free expression" are not entirely uniform, it is possible to discern a consistent theme: where the harm that the statute (or its application) is seeking to avert is one that is independent of the message being regulated—that is, the harm arises from something other than a fear of how people will react to what the speaker is saying—the

[136] 408 U.S. 92 (1972).
[137] *Id.* at 95.
[138] 391 U.S. 367 (1968).
[139] *Id.* at 377 (Warren, C.J.).

government's interest is "unrelated to suppression."[140] Application of this test to copyright law on its face, or as it is applied in an infringement judgment in any particular case, yields the conclusion that copyright is regulation unrelated to suppression of freedom of expression. The reason is that the harm the copyright statute (or its application in a particular case) seeks to avert—the harm to the copyright owner's property that unauthorized reproduction, preparation of derivative works, distribution, and the like create—is independent of the infringer's message that is being regulated and arises from something quite other than a fear of how people will react to the ideas the infringing speaker is attempting to convey.

Rubenfeld's implication that copyright law is at odds with the First Amendment's aversion to content regulation takes no account of a very important fact: even if the question of whether the defendant has infringed turns in every case on the "content" of both the plaintiff's and the defendant's work, the nature of the inquiry into content will not bring into play any of the reasons for the aversion to content regulation. The Court's express distrust of content-based regulations is more than a convenient knee-jerk doctrinal guideline. It reflects a number of concerns that emerge from consideration of the First Amendment's animating values.[141] For example, it reflects a concern for equality—that particular categories of speech be treated equally so as to deflect the government from attempting to manipulate public discourse. Second, it reflects a concern to prevent government from regulating speech based on its communicative impact, thus forestalling restrictions of speech that surreptitiously rely on constitutionally disfavored justifications. It reflects a concern to foreclose the possibility that government will deliberately distort debate by preventing the communication of particular disfavored ideas, viewpoints, or items of information. Finally, it reflects a concern with improper legislative motivation. But a judgment that a copyright defendant's work reproduces the plaintiff's, or is based upon it, or distributes or publicly performs it, though it will of course be based on the content of both the plaintiff's and the defendant's speech, simply raises none of these concerns. It does not jeopardize the equality of treatment of particular categories of speech so as to enable government to manipulate discussion. It does not turn on the speech's communicative impact. And it does not raise the risk of an improper government motivation to prevent the dissemination of particular ideas, viewpoints, or items of information that the government disfavors. In fact, the predicate for copyright liability is not the communicativeness of an infringer's speech at all. It is, rather, its similarity to the plaintiff's—

[140] See generally John Hart Ely, "Flag Desecration: A Case Study in the Roles of Categorization and Balancing in First Amendment Analysis," *Harvard Law Review* 88 (1975): 1482.

[141] See generally Geoffrey R. Stone, "Content Regulation and the First Amendment," *William and Mary Law Review* 25 (1983): 217.

and even then it is only its similarity to the plaintiff's expression, not to the ideas or facts therein.

Rubenfeld analogizes the Copyright Act to the flag-burning statute that prohibited "defacing or destroying an American flag in a fashion that intentionally communicates disrespect" and that the Court declared unconstitutional in 1989 in *Texas v. Johnson*.[142] In fact, the two statutes are very unalike. The flag-burning statute was held unconstitutional, to be sure, but not as Rubenfeld claims "because it [made] the *communicativeness* of the defendant's actions an element of the offense."[143] Instead, the problem with the statute was that defendant's liability "depended on the likely *communicative impact* of his conduct.[144] More particularly, liability depended on the fact that the message he communicated "would cause serious offense to others."[145] A copyright defendant's liability does not turn on the communicative impact of his conduct, nor on the fact that his message might cause offense to his audience. It turns only on the form his expression takes and on whether it copies the plaintiff's.[146]

Next consider Rubenfeld's second objection to the copyright-trespass analogy, which is based on the claim that the appropriate comparison is not between copyright and *Hudgens v. NLRB* but between copyright and *New York Times v. Sullivan*,[147] the 1964 case in which the Supreme Court for the first time subjected libel law to First Amendment scrutiny. Ruben-

[142] 491 U.S. 397 (1989).

[143] Rubenfeld, "Copyright's Constitutionality," *supra* note 105, at 26 (emphasis added).

[144] *Texas v. Johnson*, 491 U.S. at 411–12 (emphasis added).

[145] *Id.* at 411.

[146] This observation is also relevant to another of Rubenfeld's claims, namely, that copyright law is in significant tension with the line of First Amendment cases that he says "systematically rejects the notion that a regulation of speech is constitutional if it 'merely' prohibits particular forms of expressing ideas, rather than the ideas themselves." Rubenfeld, "Copyright's Constitutionality," *supra* note 105, at 14. In *Cohen v. California*, 403 U.S. 15 (1971), the Court overturned the disturbing the peace conviction of a man whose jacket bore the inscription "Fuck the Draft" on the back. In Rubenfeld's view, "if the First Amendment protected only ideas, and not particular expressions thereof, Cohen should have gone to jail." Rubenfeld, "Copyright's Constitutionality," *supra* note 105, at 15. A careful reading of *Cohen*, however, suggests that the reason the Court protected the expression in that case was, in fact, that the Court perceived that "excising as offensive conduct one particular scurrilous epithet" from the language carried too great a risk of permitting censorship of *ideas*. Indeed, the Court was explicit about this: "[W]e cannot indulge in the facile assumption that one can forbid particular words without also running a substantial risk of suppressing ideas in the process." 403 U.S. at 26. In other words, in *Cohen*, the Court was convinced that the idea and the expression effectively merged, so that to suppress the particular expression amounted to suppression of the particular idea. Copyright law's idea-expression dichotomy, however, assumes that most ideas can be adequately expressed in a wide variety of ways; when courts are convinced that there are but one or a few ways of expressing an idea, they will apply the copyright merger doctrine and leave the expression unprotected. See *Morrissey v. Procter & Gamble Co.*, 379 F.2d 675 (1st Cir. 1967) (holding that when the subject matter is very narrow, so that the topic necessarily requires only a limited number of forms of expression, the merger doctrine will apply so as to deny copyright to the subject matter at all). In any case, copyright law does not proscribe particular expressions, as the state argued that the California statute did in *Cohen*. Rather, copyright law proscribes copying of particular expressions.

[147] *New York Times v. Sullivan*, 376 U.S. 254 (1964).

feld is not alone in regarding *Sullivan* as analogous,[148] but he puts the argument most succinctly: "Copyright stands to property law as libel stands to tort law; copyright makes speech property, as libel makes speech a tort."[149] The conclusion that since libel must conform to First Amendment constraints, so must copyright, is said to follow. The conclusion does not, however, necessarily follow, though the reasons are complicated and thoroughly to explore them is beyond the scope of this paper, as they raise surprisingly profound issues of First Amendment theory. I shall attempt, however, to give the reasons in broad outline.

My reasons begin with a restatement of the First Amendment implications of the fact that "copyright makes speech property." As I have demonstrated, the argument is straightforward (though, as I hope I have made clear, I do not claim it is uncontroversial): the Copyright Act confers the functional equivalent of property rights on authors, and infringement of copyright is thus the functional equivalent of trespass. According to *Hudgens*, there is no First Amendment right to trespass on tangible property, and by a parity of reasoning there is no First Amendment right to "trespass" on intangible property, that is, there is no First Amendment right to infringe copyright. This, in a nutshell, is why the copyright-trespass analogy is apt. Rubenfeld rejects this analogy in favor of the copyright-libel analogy, but he does so not because copyrights are not property rights. Rather, he thinks that what matters is that copyrights differ from "ordinary" property rights in the crucial respect that copyrights, like libel laws, render "speaking an element of the offense."[150] And he asserts that it was "precisely because libel . . . makes speech as such illegal [that] courts were eventually obliged to address and redress its First Amendment consequences."[151] This assertion, in my view, mischaracterizes the reason why courts—in particular, the Supreme Court—undertook to constitutionalize the law of libel, and it is this mischaracterization that renders Rubenfeld's equation of copyright and libel problematic. It was not a concern with "speech as such" that moved the Court in *Sullivan*. It was, instead, the concern to prevent the punishment of seditious libel, to protect those who criticize government and the conduct of government officials. On account of this focus, and not on account of the supposed importance of "speech as such", the *Sullivan* case was hailed for having discerned the "central meaning" of the First Amendment.[152] True enough, defamation juris-

[148] *See, e.g.*, Benkler, "Free as the Air to Common Use," *supra* note 106, at 393–94 (arguing that copyright doctrine is "no different" from libel law); and James Boyle, "The First Amendment and Cyberspace: The Clinton Years," *Law and Contemporary Problems* 63 (2000): 340–48 (arguing that *New York Times v. Sullivan* provides an apt analogy for resolving copyright/First Amendment conflicts).

[149] Rubenfeld, "Copyright's Constitutionality," *supra* note 105, at 26–27.

[150] Ibid., 25.

[151] Ibid., 26.

[152] Cf. Harry Kalven, "The *New York Times* Case: A Note on 'The Central Meaning of the First Amendment,'" *Supreme Court Review* 1964 (1964): 191.

prudence in the Supreme Court soon detached itself from its seditious libel roots,[153] and by now the First Amendment has been held to apply to false statements of fact about private figures whether or not the speech is even about matters of public concern.[154] In addition, recent case law provides some support for the claim that the Court may have become persuaded that "speech as such" is worth protecting,[155] but there is case law that points in quite the opposite direction.[156] Thus, the fact that copyright, like libel, "renders speaking an element of the offense" does not provide unequivocal support for the conclusion that the First Amendment constrains copyright, as it constrains libel. Nor is it reason enough to reject the conclusion that, as the First Amendment does not constrain the law of trespass, so it does not constrain the law of copyright.

Consider next Rubenfeld's third objection to the copyright-trespass analogy, which he discusses under the heading "Private Power over Public Speech." He claims that the reasons why state enforcement of trespass laws do not violate the First Amendment "disappear when we turn to copyright."[157] One of those reasons, he says, is that property owners lack general power to block the speech of the public at large, whereas a "copyright owner's power applies to the public at large, anywhere and everywhere."[158] The argument fails to account for the fact that a copyright owner's power over the speech of the public at large exists only with regard to particular expression and not with regard to ideas. Thus, the important implication of this aspect of copyright law, which is known as the 'idea-expression dichotomy', is that, though it is notoriously difficult to apply in practice, *in principle* it embodies a significant limitation on a copyright owner's power to "block the speech of the public at large." Just

[153] *See, e.g.*: *Curtis Publishing Co. v. Butts*, decided together with *Associated Press v. Walker*, 388 U.S. 130 (1967) (holding the *New York Times* standard of liability for defamation applicable to libel actions brought by "public figures" as well as by "public officials.")

[154] *Gertz v. Robert Welch, Inc.*, 418 U.S. 323 (1974) (holding that strict liability for defamation is not compatible with the First Amendment, but that so long as they do not impose liability without fault, the states may define the appropriate standard of liability for false statements of fact about private individuals).

[155] *See, e.g.*, Robert Post, "Recuperating First Amendment Doctrine," *Stanford Law Review* 47 (1995): 1249 (arguing that contemporary First Amendment jurisprudence seeks to protect the abstract fact of communication, but that in doing so it has become deeply incoherent). See, e.g., *Bartnicki v. Vopper*, 532 U.S. 514 (2001) (holding that the application of a federal statute prohibiting the disclosure of material that the disclosing party had reason to know had been illegally and intentionally intercepted violated the First Amendment); and *Hustler Magazine v. Falwell*, 485 U.S. 46 (1988) (holding that public figures and public officials may not recover for intentional infliction of emotional distress by publication without showing that the publication contained a false statement of fact that was made with "actual malice," that is, with knowledge of its falsity or with reckless disregard of its truth).

[156] *Cohen v. Cowles Media Co.*, 501 U.S. 663 (1991) (holding that the First Amendment does not protect a publisher from damages for revealing confidential sources); and *Zacchini v. Scripps-Howard Broadcasting Co.*, 433 U.S. 562 (1977) (holding that the First Amendment does not protect a broadcaster from damages for broadcasting a performer's entire act without his consent).

[157] Rubenfeld, "Copyright's Constitutionality," *supra* note 105, at 29.

[158] Ibid.

as trespassers who are denied access to a particular parcel of real property may communicate their ideas or messages in an almost infinite variety of alternative forums, so, too, may infringers who are denied the right to copy particular expressions communicate the same ideas or messages in an almost infinite variety of alternative formulations. The continual outpouring of new expressive works—books, movies, songs, and plays—that do not infringe existing works would seem to testify to the narrowness of a copyright owner's rights to control the speech of the public at large, not to its breadth.

Rubenfeld thinks it matters that when ordinary property owners invoke their right to exclude, we "tend to" regard them as "exercising First Amendment rights of their own,"[159] but when copyright owners exercise their statutory rights to prevent infringement, we do not so regard them. To be sure, there are cases where compelled access to property for the purposes of speech has been held to have violated the property owners' First Amendment rights,[160] but these holdings have not applied in the cases in which First Amendment claims of access to private property have failed on property rights grounds, and the soundness of the copyright-trespass analogy therefore does not depend on them. *Hudgens v. NLRB*[161] is, of course, the principal case in which the Court held that there is no First Amendment right to trespass on real property. Its holding rests unequivocally on the owner's property right to exclude. The opinion makes no mention of the owner's First Amendment rights. Rubenfeld points out that "no one has a First Amendment right to be the only speaker of certain words,"[162] but the relevance of this fact to the copyright-trespass analogy is not as obvious as he thinks. Copyright does not grant authors exclusive rights in "certain words." Rather, it grants them rights in their expressions, that is, in words arranged in particular sequence, conveying ideas in particular ways. Moreover, and more importantly, copyright ownership does not purport to give copyright owners *First Amendment* rights to prevent infringement; instead, it gives them property rights in their original expressions, rights that are purely creatures of statute—products of Congress's collective judgment to lodge decision-making power regarding the exploitation of original works of authorship in the hands of those who create them.

B. Trespass in virtual space and the First Amendment

This subsection considers the conformity to the First Amendment of the anticircumvention provisions of the DMCA, such as those that were litigated in *Universal City Studios, Inc. v. Corley*,[163] as well as the trespass

[159] Ibid., 28.
[160] See, e.g., *Miami Herald Publishing Co. v. Tornillo*, 418 U.S. 241 (1974).
[161] 424 U.S. 507 (1976).
[162] Rubenfeld, "Copyright's Constitutionality," *supra* note 105, at 29.
[163] 273 F.3d 429 (2d Cir. 2001).

claim that was sustained by the California district court of appeal decision in *Intel Corp. v. Hamidi*.[164] In institutional, "who decides," terms, the effect of the anticircumvention provisions is to lodge control over access to copyrighted works in the hands of copyright owners and the effect of the court decision sustaining the trespass claim is to lodge control over communication with persons on proprietary networks in the hands of their private proprietors. Thus, the way to frame the inquiry pursued in this section, consistent with this paper's institutional perspective, is to ask whether the Constitution forbids Congress or state common law rules to vest in private hands substantively unreviewable authority to control access. The more conventional way to frame the inquiry, and to make it more specific, is to ask whether access seekers have First Amendment rights to compel private owners to let them in, either for purposes of using, copying, or disseminating content on a Web site or for the purpose of communicating content to those on an e-mail network. If the question is framed in this conventional way, and the conclusion is that access seekers do have First Amendment rights, this means that the Constitution lodges in government decision-makers—namely judges—the ultimate power to make substantive judgments about when, and on what terms, and for what purposes access shall be granted to privately owned Web sites or e-mail networks. The anticircumvention provisions present the question whether compelled access for the purpose of digitally gathering content is constitutionally required, while *Intel* raises the question whether the Constitution mandates access for the purpose of communicating.

Given the First Amendment results canvassed in Section IV, if the trespass to tangible property analogy developed in Section III is sound, then the answer to the question posed in this section is virtually a foregone conclusion: the First Amendment neither requires that access be granted to digital content nor commands that proprietary networks receive communications they do not welcome. It is worthwhile, nevertheless, to summarize the cases that have addressed the issues.

Take first *Universal City Studios, Inc. v. Corley*,[165] in which the U.S. Court of Appeals for the Second Circuit dismissed a First Amendment challenge to the anticircumvention provisions of the DMCA. The defendant had posted a decryption computer program on his Web site. The program circumvented encryption technology that motion picture studios use to prevent unauthorized viewing and copying of their movies. Eight studios sought injunctive relief against the defendant, relief that the district court granted and the Second Circuit affirmed. The defendant argued that, because computer code is "speech," and the DMCA regulates it, the DMCA must be subjected to strict scrutiny. Judge Jon O. Newman's opinion for the Second Circuit first concluded that, because of what computer code is

[164] 114 Cal. Rptr. 2d 244 (Cal. Ct. App. 2001), *review granted*, 43 P.3d 587 (Cal. 2002), *reversed*, 2003 Cal. LEXIS 4205.

[165] 273 F.3d 429.

and what its normal functions are, it should be treated as combining nonspeech and speech elements, and that "the causal link between the dissemination of circumvention computer programs and their improper use is more than sufficiently close to warrant selection of a level of constitutional scrutiny based on the programs' functionality."[166] The court analogized the decryption code to "a skeleton key that can open a locked door, a combination that can open a safe, or a device that can neutralize the security device attached to a store's products,"[167] but because computer code is a form of communication and thus has a claim to being "speech," the court declined to hold that "Congress has as much authority to regulate the distribution of computer code . . . as it has to regulate distribution of skeleton keys."[168] Therefore, the court applied the intermediate scrutiny that the *Turner I* case prescribes for content-neutral regulation, and concluded that the DMCA and the provisions of the injunction that prohibited the defendant from posting the decryption code on the Internet or from linking to other sites that contained it were targeted at the nonspeech element of computer code, namely, at the code's capacity to instruct a computer to decrypt the studios' encryption code and at the capacity of linking "instantly to enable anyone anywhere to gain unauthorized access to copyrighted movies."[169] Accordingly, the court held that these provisions of the injunction survived scrutiny.

In *Intel Corp. v. Hamidi*,[170] the defendant, a former employee whom Intel had fired, flooded Intel's internal e-mail system on a number of occasions with grievances about the company. He sent thousands of copies of the same message on six occasions over a period of twenty-one months, ignored Intel's requests to stop, and was able to evade its efforts to block his messages. Intel brought a trespass to chattel claim, the California trial court granted an injunction, and the intermediate appellate court affirmed. After canvassing treatises and cases regarding the necessity of showing actual damage in order to recover damages for trespass to chattels, the court determined that the availability of damages was irrelevant: "Intel seeks no damages."[171] The important fact was that "Hamidi's conduct was trespassory,"[172] and "[j]udicial enforcement of neutral trespass laws has been held *not* to constitute state action."[173] Though the court addressed the issue principally as though the result were a function of the formal absence of "state action," it relied equally on the more substantively realistic claim that it was not the absence of state action that justified the result, but, rather, the fact that the Supreme Court "has never

[166] *Id.* at 452.
[167] *Id.* at 453.
[168] *Id.*
[169] *Id.* at 457.
[170] 114 Cal. Rptr. 2d 244 (Cal. Ct. App. 2001), *review granted*, 43 P.3d 587 (Cal. 2002), *reversed*, 2003 Cal. LEXIS 4205.
[171] *Id.* at 249.
[172] *Id.*
[173] *Id.* at 253–54.

held that a trespasser or an uninvited guest may exercise general rights of free speech on property privately owned and used nondiscriminatorily for private purposes only."[174]

Thus, both the U.S. Court of Appeal for the Second Circuit and the California Court of Appeal for the Third Appellate District implicitly embraced the trespass rationale for resolving access claims in the digital world. The courts did not reason in terms of the institutional analysis offered here, and they did not frame their conclusions as having been driven by "who decides" considerations. Nevertheless, it is possible to understand both cases as applications of the principle that the Constitution permits the government to allocate enforceable decision-making authority about production and use of resources, including intangibles and including the resources' use for speech purposes, to private actors.

VI. Conclusion

This essay addressed the question of whether the institutional choices that are reflected in the common law of trespass can provide useful guidance for resolving conflicting claims of access either to the expressive content of copyrighted works or to Internet content and proprietary e-mail systems. It described the principal instrumental justification for adopting a system of private property rights to control access to tangible things, and suggested that the justification applies with equal force to intellectual property. It analyzed the First Amendment dimensions of the access question and concluded that there is no First Amendment right to compel a private owner to grant access either to tangible or to intangible property.

Law, University of Virginia

[174] *Id.* at 254, quoting *Lloyd v. Tanner*, 407 U.S. 551, 568 (1972).

RESTRICTIONS ON JUDICIAL ELECTION CAMPAIGN SPEECH: SILENCING CRITICISM OF LIBERAL ACTIVISM

By Lino A. Graglia

I. Introduction

Constitutional law in the United States is, for most practical purposes, the product of 'judicial review', the power of judges to disallow policy choices made by other officials or institutions of government, ostensibly because those choices are prohibited by the Constitution. This extraordinary and unprecedented power, America's dubious contribution to the science of government, has made American judges the most powerful in the world, not only legislators but super-legislators, legislators with virtually the last word. Because lawmaking power divorced from popular will is tyranny, most states have attempted to reconcile the lawmaking power of judges with representative self-government by subjecting all or some judges to some form of popular election.[1] In all but four such states, judges, encouraged and supported by their fellow lawyers in the organized bar—would-be judges and beneficiaries of judicial power—have responded by adopting codes of judicial ethics that limit what candidates for election to judicial office are permitted to say.[2] The effect is to undermine elections as a control on judicial power by limiting criticism of judicial activism, the misuse of judicial power.

'Judicial activism' may be defined most simply as judges making rather than applying the law. 'Constitutional judicial activism', which is its most serious form because the decisions made are hardest to change, may be defined as judges holding policy choices unconstitutional that the Constitution does not, in fact, clearly prohibit. I say "clearly" because in a democracy the judgment of elected legislators should prevail in cases of doubt.[3] Although activism can and has in the past served conservative

[1] Thirty-one states select all or some of their judges by regular popular election, and fifteen, following some type of "merit" or "Missouri" plan, subject them after appointment to uncontested retention elections. American Judicature Society, *Judicial Selection in the States: Appellate and General Jurisdiction Courts* (Dec. 2002), available on-line at http://ajs.org/js/JudicialSelectionCharts.pdf [accessed July 7, 2003].

[2] *Republican Party of Minnesota v. White,* 122 S. Ct. 2528, 2541 (2002).

[3] The reverse situation, that is, judges upholding as constitutional a policy choice the Constitution clearly prohibits, very rarely occurs, because the Constitution wisely precludes few policy choices—and even fewer that American legislators, who are at least as committed to constitutional principles as judges, have occasion or inclination to make. The clearest example of this happening in American history is probably *Home Building & Loan Ass'n v.*

causes—by, for example, disallowing restrictions on economic freedom or property rights—in today's cultural milieu it operates overwhelmingly, on both the state and the federal levels, to move policy choices to the left. It is left-liberals today, therefore, far more than conservatives, who seek to obtain through the courts policy changes not obtainable through the ordinary political process because they are opposed by a majority of the American people. And it is liberal, far more than conservative, activism that is likely to present important issues in judicial election campaigns. The result is that it is criticism of liberal judicial activism that restrictions on judicial campaign speech serve overwhelmingly to repress.[4]

II. Origin and Meaning of Judicial Review

Although the Constitution does not explicitly provide for judicial review, as one would expect for so obviously dangerous an innovation, that it would result was assumed and objected to by populist opponents of ratification[5] and defended by the more aristocratic Alexander Hamilton.[6] The great defect of democracy, Hamilton thought, along with James Madison,[7] was that debtors, always much more numerous than creditors, would soon realize that majority rule puts the means of escaping their financial obligations in their own hands. The most significant limitation on state power in the original Constitution, the Contracts Clause,[8] was the founders' attempt to correct this defect by prohibiting the enactment of debtor-relief laws. Hamilton saw judges, presumably lawyers grown prosperous primarily through protection of property interests, as natural

Blaisdell, 290 U.S. 398 (1934) (upholding clearly unconstitutional debtor-relief legislation). In any event, a refusal to intervene in the ordinary political process demonstrates not activism, but restraint.

4 *See infra* notes 48–55.

5 The Antifederalist "Brutus" foresaw that the Supreme Court "would be exalted over all other powers in the government, and subject to no control." "I question," he said, "whether the world ever saw, in any period of it, a court of justice invested with such immense powers, and yet placed in a situation so little responsible." The *Letters of Brutus* (1787–88) are the Antifederalist counterpart of the essays of "Publius," which were written by Alexander Hamilton, James Madison, and John Jay and later published as *The Federalist*. It is generally assumed that "Brutus" was Robert Yates, a New York lawyer and judge who, like Hamilton, had been a delegate to the Constitutional Convention. See Lino A. Graglia, "The Antifederalists and the Federal Judiciary," *Arizona State Law Journal* 28 (1996): 21, 22.

6 *Federalist No. 78* (A. Hamilton), in Clinton Rossiter, ed., *The Federalist Papers* (New York: New American Library, Mentor Books, 1961), 464.

7 *Federalist No. 10* (J. Madison), in Rossiter, ed., *The Federalist Papers*, 79 (noting that "the most common and durable source of factions has been the various and unequal distribution of property"). Aristotle similarly criticized democracy as rule by "men of low birth and no property," which is true enough, but fails to take into account that the alternatives, as Churchill famously pointed out—life being a series of bad choices—are even worse.

8 U.S. Const. art. I, § 10, prohibiting the states from, among other things, passing any "Law impairing the Obligation of Contracts." In placing restrictions on state powers, the framers, it appears, were indeed concerned to protect minority rights, as is commonly thought, but primarily the rights of bankers.

bulwarks against dangerous egalitarian-redistributionist democratic tendencies. He therefore insisted that judges should be appointed, rather than elected, and given lifetime tenure.[9] More important, he rationalized and defended giving them the power of constitutional judicial review by denying that it would make them superior to legislators.[10] Hamilton's equally property-protective acolyte, Chief Justice John Marshall, created an opportunity to exercise, and thereby securely establish, this power in the famous case of *Marbury v. Madison* in 1803.[11]

The plaintiffs in *Marbury* brought suit directly in the Supreme Court, supposedly to have the Court order the Jefferson Administration to issue their "commissions" entitling them to positions of justice of the peace in Washington, DC. Although Marshall, as Secretary of State in the Adams Administration, had been directly responsible for the nondelivery of the commissions, he did not recuse himself from hearing the case. Instead, he took the opportunity gratuitously to chastise his political enemy, President Jefferson, as a violator of plaintiffs' rights, only to conclude that the Court lacked jurisdiction in the matter. He reached this conclusion, first, by imaginatively interpreting a statute as adding to the original jurisdiction granted the Court in the Constitution, and then by holding, also imaginatively, that the grant implied a prohibition of Congress's adding to the Court's original jurisdiction. The result was a victory for Jefferson, which precluded any challenge to the decision and spared the Court the embarrassment of issuing an order that he surely would have ignored. Judicial review was thus established in a made-up ruling, on the basis of a made-up statutory interpretation and made-up constitutional prohibition, and based on reasoning no one has found persuasive.[12] Judicial review, born in sin, has rarely risen above the circumstances of its birth.

Through most of U.S. history, judicial review served, as Hamilton and Marshall expected, as a conservative force, protecting property rights and economic freedom and putting a brake on social change. Among the Court's most important uses of the power were decisions invalidating a prohibition on the spread of slavery,[13] a federal statute that prohibited race discrimination in places of public accommodation,[14] statutes that

[9] *Federalist No. 78* (A. Hamilton), *supra* note 6.

[10] Ibid., 465. Lacking "influence over either the sword or the purse," and having "neither FORCE nor WILL," the judiciary, he argued, will be the "weakest" (i.e., the least dangerous) branch of government. Judges would disallow, in accordance with "the intention of the people," only laws found to be in "irreconcilable variance" with the Constitution (ibid., 467), and would have no "arbitrary discretion," because they would be "bound down by strict rules and precedents, which serve to define and point out their duty in every particular case. . . ." (ibid., 471).

[11] *Marbury v. Madison*, 5 U.S. (1 Cranch) 137 (1803).

[12] *See, e.g.*, William W. Van Alstyne, "A Critical Guide to *Marbury v. Madison*," *Duke Law Review* 18, no. 1 (1969); and Morris R. Cohen, *The Faith of a Liberal* (Freeport, NY: Books for Libraries Press, 1946), 178–80.

[13] *Dred Scott v. Sandford*, 60 U.S. 393 (1856).

[14] *Civil Rights Cases*, 109 U.S. 3 (1883).

sought to restrict the employment of child labor,[15] and various elements of President Franklin Roosevelt's New Deal.[16] The Court's invalidation of state laws served primarily to protect creditors[17] and, during the "*Lochner* era," to combat price and wage controls, labor laws, and other "socialistic" legislation.[18]

The policymaking role assumed by the Supreme Court changed drastically with its 1954 decision in *Brown v. Board of Education* (holding school segregation unconstitutional),[19] which was quickly followed by decisions striking down all official racial discrimination.[20] The decision in *Brown v. Board of Education* convinced many people of the superiority of policymaking by unelected judges on the basis of "principle" over policymaking by elected officials. If the Court could decree racial oppression impermissible, what other advances in morality could it not require, and if it could, why should it not do so? The result was to change judicial review from a brake upon to, instead, the nation's primary initiator and accelerator of social change. The result, incredible as it may seem in a nation supposedly based on representative self-government, federalism, and separation of powers, is that almost every important change in domestic social policy over the past half-century on a vast array of issues has come not from elected legislators, state or federal, but from the justices of the United States Supreme Court, in the guise of constitutional interpretation. Issues that the Court removed from the ordinary political process and assigned for decision to itself include abortion, capital punishment, criminal procedure, legislative reapportionment, prayer in the schools, government aid to religious schools, public display of religious symbols, religious exemption from ordinary legal requirements, busing for school racial balance, restriction of pornography, limits on street demonstrations, vagrancy control, libel law, and classifications on the basis of sex, illegitimacy, or alienage.[21]

[15] *Hammer v. Dagenhart*, 247 U.S. 251 (1918); and *Bailey v. Drexel Furniture Co.*, 259 U.S. 20 (1922).

[16] *See, e.g.*: *A. L. A. Schecter Poultry Corp. v. United States*, 295 U.S. 495 (1935); *Carter v. Carter Coal Co.*, 298 U.S. 238 (1936); and *United States v. Butler*, 297 U.S. 1 (1936).

[17] *See, e.g.*: *Sturges v. Crowninshield*, 17 U.S. 122 (1819).

[18] *Lochner v. New York*, 198 U.S. 45 (1905); *see* Kathleen M. Sullivan and Gerald Gunther, *Constitutional Law*, 14th ed. (New York: Foundation Press, 2001), 466–69.

[19] *Brown v. Board of Education*, 347 U.S. 483 (1954).

[20] *See, e.g.*: *Baltimore City v. Dawson*, 350 U.S. 877 (1955); and *Holmes v. Atlanta*, 350 U.S. 879 (1955).

[21] *See, e.g.*: *Roe v. Wade*, 410 U.S. 113 (1973) (abortion); *Furman v. Georgia*, 408 U.S. 238 (1972) (capital punishment); *Miranda v. Arizona*, 384 U.S. 436 (1966) (criminal procedure); *Baker v. Carr*, 369 U.S. 186 (1962) (reapportionment); *Engel v. Vitale*, 370 U.S. 421 (1962) (prayer in schools); *Everson v. Board of Education*, 330 U.S. 1 (1947) (aid to religion); *County of Allegheny v. American Civil Liberties Union*, 492 U.S. 573 (1989) (public display of religious symbols); *Sherbert v. Verner*, 374 U.S. 398 (1963) (religious exemption); *Swann v. Charlotte-Mecklenberg Bd. of Educ.*, 402 U.S. 1 (1971) (busing); *Memoirs v. Massachusetts*, 383 U.S. 413 (1966) (pornography); *Cox v. Louisiana*, 379 U.S. 536 (1965) (demonstrations); *Papachristou v. City of*

Two things characterize the resulting constitutional law. The first is that it has very little to do with the Constitution, as should be clear enough from the fact that so little of the Constitution is usually even purportedly involved. The great majority of rulings of unconstitutionality invalidate state, not federal, law, and nearly all of these rulings purport to turn on a single sentence, ultimately four words, from the Fourteenth Amendment: "due process" and "equal protection". By detaching these phrases from their historical context and meaning—as guarantees of basic civil rights to blacks—the Court has made them empty vessels into which any meaning may be poured. The result has been the creation of a "living" Constitution, changeable as new conditions are seen by judges to require, and, therefore, no constitution of fixed limits at all, but, instead, a warrant for judges to assign to themselves final policymaking authority on any subject they might choose.

No jurisprudential sophistication is required to understand that the states did not lose the right to restrict abortions in 1973[22] because the Court discovered in the Due Process Clause of the then 105-year-old Fourteenth Amendment something that had not been noticed before. Another example of the Constitution's irrelevance to constitutional law is the fact that there has been a time when it permitted, a time when it prohibited, and a time (the present) when it sometimes requires the assignment of students to public schools on the basis of race,[23] without the Constitution being changed in any relevant respect. All that changed or had to change was the judges making the decisions; a natural scientist would have no difficulty concluding that the Constitution is not the operative variable. Scholarly debates on methods of constitutional interpretation are, therefore, of no real relevance to the Court's controversial rulings of unconstitutionality, because in none of them has any question of interpretation in fact been involved.

The second distinguishing characteristic of the Court's controversial rulings of unconstitutionality is that they have not been random in their political impact, sometimes favoring the Right and sometimes the Left. They have almost always—for example, on every one of the issues noted above—invalidated a policy choice reached in the ordinary political process, only to substitute a choice more to the left on the American political spectrum, the choice advocated by, for example, the American Civil Liberties Union (ACLU), America's paradigmatic constitutional litigator. Although it does not always win, it would be only a small exaggeration to

Jacksonville, 405 U.S. 156 (1972) (vagrancy); *Gertz v. Robert Welch, Inc.*, 418 U.S. 323 (1974) (libel); *Craig v. Boren*, 429 U.S. 190 (1976) (sex discrimination); *Levy v. Louisiana*, 391 U.S. 68 (1968) (illegitimacy); and *Graham v. Richardson*, 403 U.S. 365 (1971) (alienage).

[22] *Roe v. Wade*, 410 U.S. 113.

[23] *Plessy v. Ferguson*, 163 U.S. 537 (1896) (permitted); *Brown v. Board of Education*, 347 U.S. 483 (1954) (prohibited); and *Swann v. Charlotte-Mecklenberg Bd. of Educ.*, 402 U.S. 1 (1971) (required).

say that the ACLU never loses in the Supreme Court. The ACLU usually either obtains a policy decision it could not obtain through the ordinary political process, such as a prohibition on state-sponsored prayer in the schools, or it is left where it was to try again on another day.[24] This, of course, is not a fortuity. Virtually by definition, it is liberals, not conservatives, who seek to overturn traditional American morality, practices, and institutions, and, therefore, it is liberals who are most in need of judicial power to defeat the popular will.

The salient fact of contemporary American political life is the wide gap in views on social policy issues that exists between, on the left, a cultural elite made up of academics and their progeny in the media and other verbal professions and, on the right, a large majority of the American people. Judges, state as well as federal, are all or almost all educationally, economically, and socially themselves members of the elite, solicitous of its approval, and irresistibly tempted to use their power to advance its policy preferences.[25] The result is that constitutional law in the past half-century has been little more than a ruse by means of which judges enact liberal policies that would not and could not be enacted by elected legislators. Despite anguished cries by liberal constitutional scholars that we now have a "conservative" Court,[26] the activism of the Rehnquist Court continues to be predominantly activism of the Left.

For a court to be "conservative," according to liberal constitutional scholars, it is not necessary that it give conservatives positive victories comparable to major liberal victories. Thus, to be labeled "conservative," the Court does not have to hold that permitting, rather than restricting, abortion is unconstitutional, or that failing to provide rather than providing for prayer in public schools is unconstitutional. Nor is it even necessary that the Court rescind prior liberal victories by, for example, overruling decisions creating abortion rights or prohibiting provision for

[24] It was only on the third try, for example, that the Court was persuaded to invalidate Connecticut's anti-contraception law in *Griswold v. Connecticut*, 381 U.S. 479 (1965), which became the basis for *Roe*, 410 U.S. 113. Connecticut, it might be said, is not big enough for such a law and for Yale University, some of whose law professors led the attack. The opinion in *Griswold* was by Justice William O. Douglas, a former Yale law professor.

[25] William F. Buckley, Jr., famously and wisely said that he "would sooner be governed by the first 2,000 names in the Boston telephone book than by the 2,000 members of the Harvard faculty." See William F. Buckley, Jr., "Au Pair Case No Reason to Condemn Courts," *Houston Chronicle*, November 8, 1997, 36 (quoting his earlier statement). The result of constitutional law is that the American people are being indirectly ruled by the Harvard faculty, especially the law faculty, and its counterparts in other elite institutions, through their intellectual progeny: Supreme Court justices serving as mirrors and mouthpieces of liberal academic opinion.

[26] *See, e.g.*, Larry D. Kramer, "No Surprise. It's an Activist Court," *New York Times*, December 12, 2000, late edition-final, sec. A, p. 33, col. 2 ("[C]onservative judicial activism is the order of the day. . . . The Warren Court was retiring compared to the present one."); and Cass R. Sunstein, "Tilting the Scales Rightward," *New York Times*, April 26, 2001, late edition-final, sec. A, p. 23, col. 1 ("We are now in the midst of a remarkable period of right-wing judicial activism. The Supreme Court has moderates but no liberals.").

prayer in public schools and returning the issues to the ordinary political process. For the Court to be "conservative" according to liberals, it is quite enough that liberal victories come less surely or quickly.

The Rehnquist Court has not only failed to positively protect the unborn child by holding laws permitting abortion unconstitutional or even to return the issue to the states by simply overruling *Roe v. Wade*, but, instead, it has extended *Roe* even to so-called partial birth abortions.[27] Instead of moving from a prohibition to a requirement of state-sponsored school prayer or even merely rescinding the prohibition, the Rehnquist Court has extended the prohibition even to a nonsectarian invocation of the deity at a middle school graduation ceremony.[28] Instead of overruling or merely relaxing the Burger Court's disallowance of distinctions on the basis of sex, the Rehnquist Court has extended it even to military schools.[29] Instead of overruling *Miranda*[30] and its exclusionary rule, the Rehnquist Court invalidated a congressional attempt to limit its application.[31] Instead of overruling *Mapp v. Ohio*[32] and its exclusionary rule, the Court continues to expand the notion of unconstitutional searches and seizures to include, for example, pointing a heat-sensing device at the exterior of a building[33] and having a drug-sniffing dog walk around an automobile.[34] The Court has held that the people of Colorado may not by referendum amend their state constitution to preclude the grant of special rights to homosexuals,[35] has invalidated federal attempts to restrict child pornography,[36] and has overturned state laws imposing term limits on their congressional representatives.[37] The Court continues its march toward the total abolition of capital punishment, and, most recently, the Court has upheld race preferences in admissions to a state law school and invalidated state sodomy laws.[38] In quantity as well as importance, a large majority of the Rehnquist Court's rulings of unconstitutionality continues to favor liberal causes.[39]

If a Court that continues to produce such an impressive string of important liberal victories can be characterized as "conservative," one must wonder what a liberal Court might do. The Rehnquist Court can be

[27] *Stenberg v. Carhart*, 530 U.S. 914 (2000).
[28] *Lee v. Weisman*, 505 U.S. 577 (1992).
[29] *United States v. Virginia*, 518 U.S. 515 (1996).
[30] *Miranda v. Arizona*, 384 U.S. 436 (1966).
[31] *Dickerson v. United States*, 530 U.S. 428 (2000).
[32] *Mapp v. Ohio*, 367 U.S. 643 (1961).
[33] *Kyllo v. United States*, 533 U.S. 27 (2001).
[34] *City of Indianapolis v. Edmond*, 531 U.S. 32 (2000).
[35] *Romer v. Evans*, 517 U.S. 620 (1996).
[36] *Denver Area Education Telecommunications Consortium, Inc. v. FCC*, 518 U.S. 727 (1996).
[37] *U.S. Term Limits, Inc. v. Thornton*, 514 U.S. 779 (1995).
[38] *See, e.g.*: *Atkins v. Virginia*, 122 S. Ct. 2242 (2002) (regarding capital punishment). See *Grutter v. Bollinger* 123 S. Ct. 2325 (2003) (race preferences); *Lawrence v. Texas* 123 S. Ct. 2472 (2003) (sodomy).
[39] *See* Lino A. Graglia, "The Myth of a Conservative Supreme Court: The October 2000 Term," *Harvard Journal of Law and Public Policy* 26 (2003): 281.

denounced as conservative by liberals only because liberal victories are seen as the norm, virtually the entire point of judicial review and constitutional law, while an occasional conservative victory—such as a few rulings of unconstitutionality in federalism,[40] just compensation,[41] and race preference cases[42]—is seen as an aberration, a disruption of the natural order.

III. Selecting Judges

State constitutional law usually follows and often expands on federal rulings of unconstitutionality, and this is why it remains of crucial importance to liberals that state judges, like federal judges, not be subject to elections, or if they are, that the elections be made ineffective. Following the federal model, the states originally selected judges by appointment with lifetime tenure.[43] In every state, the judges, also following the federal model, asserted the power of constitutional judicial review, despite the fact that no state constitution, any more than the federal Constitution, explicitly made provision for it.[44] As the policymaking power of judges became more clear, a movement arose, especially in the more populist Jacksonian era (1828–37), for the codification of laws to limit judicial discretion and, more importantly, for the selection of judges by popular election.[45] Because the power of constitutional judicial review inevitably makes judges the ultimate legislators, this result can be avoided only by abolishing the power. An unreasoning tendency to emulate federal practice, however, apparently has been too strong to permit such an obvious conclusion. Instead, most states have in effect decided to accept the fact that their judges are legislators and to subject them, like other legislators, to some form of popular election.

Today, thirty-one states choose all or some of their judges by election, and fifteen, including California, have adopted some form of the so-called merit or Missouri plan, in effect subjecting appointed judges to popular

[40] *See, e.g.*: *United States v. Lopez*, 514 U.S. 549 (1995). For a skeptical view of the likely effect of these decisions as a limit on federal power, see Lino A. Graglia, "*United States v. Lopez*: Judicial Review Under the Commerce Clause," *Texas Law Review* 74 (1996): 719.

[41] *See, e.g.*: *Lucas v. South Carolina Coastal Council*, 505 U.S. 1003 (1992); *but see*: *Tahoe-Sierra Preservation Council, Inc. v. Tahoe Regional Planning Agency*, 122 S. Ct. 1465 (2002).

[42] *See, e.g.*: *Adarand Constructors v. Pena*, 515 U.S. 200 (1955). *But see*: *Grutter v. Bollinger*, 123 S. Ct. 2325 (2003) (upholding race preferences).

[43] Anthony Champagne and Judith Haydel, *Judicial Reform in the States* (Lanham, MD: University Press of America, 1993), 2.

[44] Some state constitutions now do make provision for general or limited constitutional judicial review. *See* Robert F. Williams, *State Constitutional Law: Cases and Materials*, 3d ed. (Charlottesville, VA: Lexis Law Publishing, 1999), 700.

[45] *See* Steven P. Croley, "The Majoritarian Difficulty: Elected Judiciaries and the Rule of Law," *University of Chicago Law Review* 62 (1995): 716. "Jefferson (who prior to becoming President supported life tenure of judges subject only to good behavior) argued after *Marbury* that judicial terms should be limited to six years and suggested that judges should be elected by the people." Ibid., at 715.

recall by requiring them to stand for an uncontested "retention" election after a period of service.[46] Each state that has judicial elections has them by reason of the state constitution or a statute, and all but four also have codes of judicial conduct, imposed by the judges themselves and enforced by penalties up to and including disbarment.[47] Put forth in the name of protecting judicial independence, impartiality, and the appearance of impartiality, the actual purpose and effect of the codes is to protect judicial policymaking power, which almost always means in practice the power to enact liberal social policies by rulings of unconstitutionality. The codes do this by restricting the speech of judicial candidates, the principal effect of which is to preclude conservative candidates from taking advantage of the unpopularity of those rulings by criticizing them in election campaigns.

Judicial candidates have been censured or threatened with censure most often, apparently, for seeking to announce "pro-life" views on the abortion issue;[48] for wanting to speak on "capital punishment, . . . the state's budget, and public school education";[49] for accusing an opponent of seeking to "require the State to license same-sex marriages," criticizing "traditional moral standards," and calling "the electric chair 'silly'";[50] for using voter guides published by the Christian Coalition of Alabama;[51] for stating that "the state simply doesn't get a fair trial in [opponent's] court," and opponent "would have lowered indigent standards";[52] for claiming to be "tough" while accusing an opponent of being "soft" on crime;[53] for stating that as a judge he "would not accept plea bargaining";[54] and for wanting to state his belief as to "the limits on the conduct and discretion of a sitting judge."[55]

[46] *See supra* note 1.

[47] *Republican Party of Minnesota v. White*, 122 S. Ct. 2528, 2531 (2002).

[48] *See, e.g.*: *Republican Party of Minnesota v. White*, 247 F.3d 854 (8th Cir. 2001); *In Re Disciplinary Proceeding against Sanders*, 955 P.2d 369 (Wash. 1998); *Deters v. Judicial Retirement & Removal Comm'n*, 873 S.W.2d 200 (Ky. 1994); and *Buckley v. Illinois Judicial Inquiry Bd.*, 997 F.2d 224 (7th Cir. 1993).

[49] *Buckley, supra*, note 48.

[50] *Weaver v. Bonner*, 114 F. Supp. 2d 1337, 1340 (N.D. Ga. 2000).

[51] *Pittman v. Cole*, 117 F. Supp. 2d 1285 (S.D. Ala. 2000).

[52] *In re Riley*, 691 P.2d 695, 704–5 (Ariz. 1984).

[53] *In re Chmura*, 608 N.W.2d 31, 33–34 (Mich. 2000); *In re Disciplinary Proceeding against Kaiser*, 759 P.2d 392, 394–95 (candidate claimed to be a "tough no-nonsense judge" and "toughest on drunk driving"). *See also*: *Butler v. Alabama Judicial Inquiry Comm'n*, 111 F. Supp. 2d 1224 (M.D. Ala. 2000) (candidate in Republican primary criticized opponent's "record of sentencing in drug cases").

[54] *Beshear v. Butt*, 863 F. Supp. 913, 915 (E.D. Ark. 1994).

[55] *American Civil Liberties Union, Inc. v. The Florida Bar*, 744 F. Supp. 1094, 1098 (N.D. Fla. 1990).

See also: *Ackerson v. Kentucky Judicial Retirement & Removal Comm'n*, 776 F. Supp. 309, 311 (W.D. Ky. 1991) (candidate wanted to discuss "alleged backlog of cases, methods of assignment of cases, numbers of pending cases, hiring and firing of employees, and administrative expenses relating to travel"); *J.C.J.D. v. R.J.C.R.*, 803 S.W.2d 953, 954 (Ky. 1991) (candidate criticized "the 'fireman's rule,' laws against carrying handguns by felons, and the standard

Restrictions on judicial campaign speech have recently come under attack in several states, however, and have generally fared badly in the lower courts.[56] *Republican Party of Minnesota v. White* was the exception.[57] Restrictions were upheld in the lower courts, only to be disallowed by a 5–4 decision of the U.S. Supreme Court.

IV. *Republican Party of Minnesota v. White*

The Minnesota Constitution has provided for the election of state judges from the time the state entered the union in 1858. In 1974, the Minnesota Supreme Court promulgated a Code of Judicial Conduct based on the Model Code of Judicial Conduct adopted by the American Bar Association (ABA) two years earlier. One provision, known as the "announce clause," prohibited a candidate for judicial office, including an incumbent, from "announc[ing] his or her views on disputed legal or political issues."[58] In 1996, when Gregory Wersal campaigned for the position of associate justice of the Minnesota Supreme Court, a complaint was filed with the agency charged with enforcing the code. The complaint objected to statements in his literature that were critical of some Minnesota Supreme Court decisions. Although the complaint was dismissed by the agency, at least in part because of doubts as to the code's constitutionality, Wersal withdrew his candidacy, "fearing that further ethical complaints would jeopardize his ability to practice law."[59]

As usual, the speech to be suppressed was critical of liberal rulings of unconstitutionality. Candidate Wersal did not want to criticize the Minnesota Supreme Court for being insufficiently protective of the interests of women seeking abortions, of criminal defendants, or of the poor. There is usually no electoral advantage in that, because those are the "politically correct" views of the elite, not of most people. On the contrary, he wanted to criticize the court as being activist, pro-abortion, soft on criminals, and

for court review of workers' compensation cases"); and *Berger v. Supreme Court of Ohio*, 598 F. Supp. 69, 72 (S.D. Ohio 1984) (candidate wanted to state that as a judge he would "first attempt to have the parties who appear before him mediate their disputes, without the presence of their attorneys").

But see: *Stretton v. Disciplinary Board of S. Ct. of Pa.*, 944 F.2d 137, 139 (3d Cir. 1991) (candidate said, at an NAACP meeting, that there were too many Republican judges, and a "need for the election of judges with an 'activist' view," who recognized the "obligation of judges at every level of the judicial system to look at societal changes when ruling on challenges to existing law"); and *In re Discipline of Hopewell*, 507 N.W.2d 911, 912–13 (S.D. 1993) (candidate, a "friend, compatriot and advocate" of "distressed elements of society," accused opponent of giving "the most severe of punishments," under the "cruel and deceptive guise of deterrence of crime").

[56] *See* Robert M. O'Neil, "The Canons in the Courts: Recent First Amendment Rulings," *Indiana Law Journal* 35 (2002): 701.

[57] 122 S. Ct. 2528 (2002).

[58] *Id.* at 2531.

[59] *Id.*

overly protective of welfare benefits,[60] that is, for being on the elite side of the cultural divide. These issues involved, of course, major liberal causes and standard conservative complaints. The practical purpose and effect of the announce clause was to protect the power of Minnesota's judges to advance such causes by prohibiting politically effective conservative criticism of their decisions.

Although Wersal might have been sanctioned for criticizing the Minnesota Supreme Court's liberal decisions, the enforcement agency, as if to add insult to injury, provided him with a list of topics that he would be permitted to discuss. These included "how he proposes to ensure that minorities and women are treated more fairly by the court system"[61] and possible "remedies for race and gender bias."[62] That is, he was told that he was free, indeed encouraged, to promote precisely the politically correct liberal causes he had sought to publicly criticize. The part of the political spectrum occupied by the people who created and enforced this arrangement was not, one may be sure, the part occupied by Wersal, yet they would have forced him to act as if it were and to espouse the very policies to which he objected. Perhaps nothing better illustrates the tendency of liberals to see their own political choices as incontrovertible, making it seem appropriate to them that objectors be silenced or, still better, coerced into advocating liberal views.

In 1998 Wersal campaigned for the office again, and sought but was unable to obtain an advisory opinion from the enforcement agency as to whether the "announce clause" would be enforced. He then brought suit in federal district court against the agency, referred to as the Lawyers Board, seeking a declaration of the clause's invalidity under the federal Constitution and an injunction against the clause's enforcement. The Minnesota Republican Party joined the suit as plaintiff, claiming that Wersal's inability to state his views on legal issues left the party unable to decide whether to support his candidacy. The district court granted summary judgment for the defendants, and a divided Court of Appeals for the Eighth Circuit affirmed.[63]

The U.S. Supreme Court granted certiori and reversed. The solid liberal bloc made up of Justices John Paul Stevens, David Souter, Ruth Bader Ginsburg, and Stephen Breyer predictably voted to protect judicial power

[60] One piece of Wersal's campaign literature stated that "[t]he Minnesota Supreme court has issued decisions which are marked by their disregard for the Legislature and a lack of common sense." It went on to criticize a decision excluding from evidence confessions by criminal defendants that were not tape recorded, asking "[s]hould we conclude that because the Supreme Court does not trust police, it allows confessed criminals to go free?" It also criticized a decision striking down a state law restricting welfare benefits, asserting that "it's the Legislature which should set our spending policies." And it criticized a decision requiring public financing of abortions for poor women as "unprecedented" and a "pro-abortion stance." *White*, 122 S. Ct. at 2532–33.

[61] *Id.* at 2534.

[62] *Id.* at 2553.

[63] *Id.* at 2531–32.

by upholding the restrictions, and Justices Sandra Day O'Connor and Anthony Kennedy separately joined Chief Justice William Rehnquist and Justices Antonin Scalia and Clarence Thomas in voting to invalidate. Scalia wrote the majority opinion; O'Connor and Kennedy wrote concurring opinions; Ginsburg wrote the principal dissent, and Stevens a shorter one, each dissenter joined by the other as well as by Souter and Breyer.

A. Justice Scalia's opinion for the Court

The Court's first task, Justice Scalia began, was to determine the scope of the announce clause, which proved not to be easy. On its face, it disallowed any statement by a judicial candidate on any "disputed legal or political issues," which would seem to cover most of what a candidate would want to discuss. In addition, it must have been intended to go beyond a candidate's promising to decide a particular issue in a particular way, as that was prohibited by a separate "pledges or promises" clause. However, according to the Lawyers Board, the Court of Appeals for the Eighth Circuit, and finally the Minnesota Supreme Court in an opinion in another case, the announce clause did not prohibit statements critical of appellate court decisions, even though such statements clearly indicated the candidate's view on disputed legal or political issues. Further complicating the Supreme Court's task, the district court had interpreted the clause to apply only to issues likely to come before the candidate if he should be elected, and the court of appeals and Minnesota Supreme Court endorsed this interpretation as well.[64]

These apparently severe limitations on the literal broad scope of the announce clause turned out, Justice Scalia found, to mean less than they seemed to mean. Limiting the scope of the clause to issues likely to come before a court is really not a limitation, he pointed out, because it is only such issues that are likely to be subjects of a judicial election campaign. On the much more important issue of whether a candidate could criticize specific appellate court decisions, as respondents claimed, Scalia found, on the basis of a concession supposedly made by counsel for respondents at oral argument, that a candidate could do so only if he simultaneously stated that he believed in *stare decisis* and, therefore, would not overrule the decisions he criticized. The result, Scalia concluded, is that "the announce clause prohibits a judicial candidate from stating his views on any specific nonfanciful legal question within the province of the court for which he is running, except in the context of discussing past decisions—and in the latter context as well, if he expresses the view that he is not bound by *stare decisis*."[65]

[64] *Id.* at 2532–33.
[65] *Id.* at 2534.

In her dissenting opinion, Justice Ginsburg insisted that this conclusion was incorrect in two respects. First, the announce clause did not bar a candidate from generally "stating [her] views" on legal issues, but only "from 'publicly making known how [she] would *decide*' disputed issues."[66] It is difficult to see, however, how a candidate can state "her" views on an issue without "making known" how "she" would be likely to decide them, especially since "making known" means less than making a commitment, which is separately prohibited by the pledges or promises clause.

Justice Ginsburg's second and stronger objection was that both the Lawyers Board and the court of appeals "stated without qualification that the Clause does not prohibit candidates from discussing appellate court decisions."[67] Neither body indicated that a candidate could do so only if he affirmed his belief in *stare decisis*. Justice Scalia based his contrary conclusion on a confused and confusing exchange at oral argument in which respondents' counsel hopelessly tried to defend the distinction between a candidate permissibly stating his views on an issue and impermissibly indicating how he would vote on the issue.[68] There was no need for Scalia to bolster his argument by this implausible reading of the

[66] *Id.* at 2553. Bracketed material in the original. Losing no opportunity to demonstrate her commitment to radical feminist ideology, Justice Ginsburg substituted feminine for generic masculine pronouns not only in her own statements but even when quoting Justice Scalia and others.

[67] *Id.*

[68] MR. GILBERT [counsel for respondents]: . . . [T]he candidate can, as Mr. Wersal did, criticize a prior decision of the Court. And that's very clear from what has happened in the Wersal case. What the candidate cannot do is say that, "If I'm elected, I'm going to overturn that decision."

QUESTION: Does that dichotomy make any sense at all?

MR. GILBERT: Well, it does in the sense, Your Honor, that there's different dynamics involved once a judge is elected and has to overturn a decision that's already precedent in the State of Minnesota.

. . .

QUESTION: May he also, at the same time as they criticized the decision, say, "I do not believe in stare decisis"?

MR. GILBERT: Yes. He can't, because that is—

QUESTION: Well, then isn't he saying how he's going to rule on the case then?

MR. GILBERT: Well, Your Honor—it might be, Your Honor. People might be able to imply from it, but it's still—the distinction is—

QUESTION: Might be able to imply that I don't believe in stare decisis and I think this case is wrong.

(Laughter)

QUESTION: Pretty clear, I think.

MR. GILBERT: No, and I understand what you're saying, Your Honor. The distinction that's made, if you look at all the cases that have dealt with this issue, is a distinction between past cases on one hand and then pending and future cases on another.

QUESTION: As long as you're silent on your views on stare decisis, that's a fine distinction. But if you do reveal your views on stare decisis, that distinction is meaningless.

MR. GILBERT: Perhaps. There could be other issues that come up in terms of a case that would be a vehicle to overturn particular decisions—standing, things of that kind.

QUESTION: So now you're saying there's a distinction between issues and cases. And I'm saying you're categorically stating your view about a particular issue, as the Chief Justice's

announce clause; it should have been enough that, as interpreted by the court of appeals and the Minnesota Supreme Court, the clause had no definite meaning. It was essentially a vague and uncertain threat that judicial candidates who criticized appellate court decisions risked punishment. Its only real purpose, Scalia later pointed out, was to undermine the effectiveness of judicial elections as a means of limiting judicial power.[69]

Because the announce clause not only limited speech "on the basis of its content," but also limited speech that "is 'at the core of our First Amendment freedoms'—speech about the qualifications of candidates for public office," it must be subject, Justice Scalia said, to "strict scrutiny." This highest level of scrutiny means that the ordinary presumption of constitutionality is reversed and unconstitutionality will be found unless the defendant shows that the measure serves a "compelling" state interest and is "narrowly tailored" to do so in the least restrictive way. In practice, when the Court invokes strict scrutiny it identifies an area in which it is willing to substitute its policy preference for the policy preference under review, and its strong inclination to disallow that policy choice.[70] But this "test" does not preclude a court from upholding a challenged measure if it chooses to do so, as is illustrated by the fact that the announce clause survived "strict scrutiny" in the court of appeals. The clause served the compelling interests, respondents contended and the court of appeals found, of preserving the impartiality and the appearance of impartiality

---

example states, and you also categorically state, "I think stare decisis has no place in constitutional adjudication." Can he do that?

MR. GILBERT: Your Honor, again, the—no, under the State's interpretation of the rule. And I understand your point. It is a fine distinction. But what the State is trying to do is protect the integrity of the judiciary at that point.

Republican Party of Minn. v. Kelly, No. 01-521, U.S. S. Ct. Official Transcript, pp. 21-23, March 22, 2002, 2002 WL 492692 (U.S. Oral Arg.).

[69] *White*, 122 S. Ct. at 2538 ("[T]he purpose of the announce clause is . . . the undermining of judicial elections.").

[70] *Id.* at 2534. The Court has for some time been unable to decide a constitutional challenge, it would seem, without first deciding on the appropriate intensity or "level" of "scrutiny." The more intense the scrutiny, the more likely a violation will be found. The "rational basis" level, the lowest, which is used mostly for challenges to business or economic regulation, indicates that the Court has very little (usually, no) interest in overturning the policy choice involved. The "strict" level indicates, as noted, a very high interest. In addition, there is supposedly an "intermediate" level, used, for example, for sex discrimination cases and usually also resulting in invalidation.

How or why this elaborate construction aids in the resolution of disputes is far from clear, but it is apparently seen as adding an element of objectivity, a law-like quality, to the Court's decisions. Once the appropriate level is decided upon, supposedly on the basis of some general principle, the decision in most cases seemingly becomes almost automatic. How little objectivity or predictability the technique adds in operation is indicated by the fact that judges can disagree as to a test's applicability (as in this case), as well as to its effect, if applicable (as in the court of appeals). One apparent perversity produced by this approach, if taken seriously, is that discrimination in favor of women (intermediate scrutiny) would be easier to justify than discrimination in favor of blacks (strict scrutiny). What the Court really decides before making a ruling of unconstitutionality in a new area of law is whether to remove decision-making from the political process on yet another issue and assign it to itself; the appropriate level of scrutiny "test" is just window dressing.

of the state judiciary. The first interest was said to be compelling because it "protects the due process rights of litigants" and the second because it "preserves public confidence in the judiciary."[71]

Justice Scalia, however, reached a different, more typical result when strict scrutiny is invoked. He agreed with the appeals court that judicial impartiality in the sense of lack of bias in favor of either party is undoubtedly a compelling state interest, but the announce clause, he found, was not narrowly tailored to serve it. Indeed, it hardly served judicial impartiality (or its appearance) in this sense at all, he said, because it prohibited speech as to issues, not as to the parties. Moreover, if judicial impartiality meant the absence of preconceptions as to the law, it could not be a compelling interest "since avoiding judicial preconceptions on legal issues is neither possible nor desirable." Judges are expected to and even required to have views on the law.[72]

Finally, "impartiality" might mean open-mindedness, a willingness to consider both sides of an issue. The announce clause could not have been intended to serve impartiality in this sense, Justice Scalia said, because campaign statements are "an infinitesimal portion of the public commitments to legal positions that judges (or judges-to-be) undertake."[73] Judges often express commitment to one side of an issue in books, articles, lectures, non-campaign speeches, and most importantly, in their judicial opinions. Justice Scalia disagreed with Justice Stevens's claim that a successful judicial candidate is likely to consider campaign statements as particularly binding. The statements at issue are, after all, only statements of views, not pledges or promises, which are separately prohibited, and even campaign promises, Scalia added in his signature sardonic style, "are—by long democratic tradition—the least binding form of human commitment."[74]

The notion that speech otherwise protected may be restricted *because* it was uttered in an election campaign, Justice Scalia argued, "sets our First Amendment jurisprudence on its head": " 'Debate on the qualifications of

[71] *Id.* at 2535.

[72] *Id.* at 2536.

[73] *Id.* at 2537.

[74] *Id.* Justice Stevens had also asserted that to the extent a candidate's statements on legal issues "seek to enhance the popularity of the candidate by indicating how he would rule in specific cases if elected, they evidence a lack of fitness for the office." *Id.* at 2547. If such statements show unfitness, Justice Scalia responded, so do statements on legal issues made to enhance one's chances of confirmation by the United States Senate: "Since such statements are made, we think, in every confirmation hearing, Justice Stevens must contemplate a federal bench filled with the unfit." *Id.* at 2538 n.8.

Justice Ginsburg responded that each member of the Court during his or her confirmation hearings refused to furnish senators with information as to his or her views on particular legal issues, indicating a belief that to do so would be inconsistent with proper performance of the judicial function. Justice Scalia's answer that there is a difference between voluntarily refusing to speak and being required to refuse, Ginsburg correctly pointed out, missed the point. *Id.* at 2552 n.1. A better answer would be that these refusals to disclose relevant information are in fact unjustifiable even though they have the sanction of long practice.

candidates' is 'at the core of our electoral process and of the First Amendment freedoms.' "[75] This, in effect, begged the question in dispute, which was whether judicial election campaigns are to be treated as essentially the same as other election campaigns. The state's alleged compelling interest in preserving public confidence in the judiciary clearly could not justify the clause, because the state cannot have an interest in preserving a higher degree of public confidence than the judiciary in fact merits. The state's interest, on the contrary, should be to see that the public has an accurate perception of the performance of the judiciary, even if the result is, as it should be, to shake public confidence.

Having found the stated justifications for the announce clause singularly unpersuasive, Justice Scalia bluntly stated the fact of the matter: "The purpose behind the announce clause is not open-mindedness in the judiciary, but the undermining of judicial elections,"[76] and Justice Ginsburg's dissent "confirms rather than refutes" this conclusion.[77] The Court had often held, Justice Ginsburg pointed out, that the due process rights of litigants are violated when a judge has a "direct, personal, substantial, and pecuniary interest" in the outcome of a case. A judge who as a judicial candidate had announced "her" views on an issue would have such an interest, Justice Ginsburg argued, if she were to hear a case that raised the issue, because if she deviated from her announced view she would risk being "voted off the bench and thereby lose her salary and emoluments."[78] But, Justice Scalia pointed out, all "elected judges—regardless of whether they have announced any views beforehand—*always* face the pressure of an electorate whose members might disagree with their rulings and therefore vote them off the bench."[79] Justice Ginsburg's argument is therefore less a defense of the announce clause than an argument against the election of judges; by its logic, "the practice of electing judges is itself a violation of due process."[80]

Except for this invalid argument, Justice Scalia concluded, Justice Ginsburg's dissent consisted of "attacking arguments we do not make," namely, "that the First Amendment requires campaigns for judicial office to sound the same as those for legislative office."[81] It is indeed the basis of Justice Ginsburg's dissent that the majority failed sufficiently to recognize the difference between the two types of campaign. If Justice Scalia's opinion does not, as he says, "assert or imply"[82] that the First Amendment requirements for judicial and legislative campaigns are essentially the same,

[75] *Id.* at 2538, citing *Eu v. San Francisco Cty. Dem. Central Comm.*, 489 U.S. 214, 222-23 (1989).
[76] *Id.* at 2538.
[77] *Id.*
[78] *Id.* (quoting Justice Ginsburg at 2556).
[79] *Id.*
[80] *Id.* at 2539.
[81] *Id.*
[82] *Id.*

it certainly seems to assume that they are very similar (otherwise, limiting judicial campaign speech would not be setting the Court's prior First Amendment jurisprudence, which was concerned only with political campaigns, on its head). Justice Scalia seems less than candid in denying Justice Ginsburg's charge.[83]

"There is an obvious tension," Justice Scalia observed, "between the article of Minnesota's popularly approved Constitution which provides that judges shall be elected" and the announce clause which, like all such restrictions on speech by judicial candidates, is "the product of judicial fiat." The ABA, "which originated the announce clause, has long been an opponent of judicial elections." This opposition may be well taken, Justice Scalia conceded, and judicial elections could simply be abolished. Thus, judicial campaign speech can be totally eliminated, but it cannot merely be restricted, because the First Amendment prohibits "leaving the principle of elections in place while preventing candidates from discussing what the elections are about."[84] The announce clause is therefore unconstitutional.

B. Justices O'Connor and Kennedy concur

Though Justices O'Connor and Kennedy both joined Justice Scalia's opinion, they found it necessary, as they often do, also to announce their views separately, and Justice O'Connor's view of judicial elections turned out to be much closer to Justice Ginsburg's than to Justice Scalia's. While he saw these elections as products and instruments of a healthy democracy (a "popularly approved Constitution") that were being undermined

[83] The only possible difference that his opinion seems to recognize is that a state might prohibit judicial, though not legislative, candidates from explicitly promising to vote in certain ways on certain issues. But even this is not clear, because instead of approving of the pledges or promises clause, as Justice Ginsburg did, Justice Scalia merely noted that it was not before the Court. The more candid answer would have been that the lawmaking power of American judges is such that First Amendment requirements for judicial and legislative elections *should* be essentially the same, and that Justice Ginsburg's argument to the contrary rests entirely on reiteration of the conventional fiction that judges do not exercise such lawmaking power. It would seem to follow, of course, that under the constitutional guarantee of a republican form of government (U.S. Const., art. IV, § 4), a state *must* provide for the election of judges as long as it permits them to perform a legislative function.

[84] *Id.* at 2541. He continued, quoting *Renne v. Geary*, 501 U.S. 312, 349 (1991) (Marshall, J., dissenting):

> The greater power to dispense with elections altogether does not include the lesser power to conduct elections under conditions of state-imposed voter ignorance. If the State chooses to tap the energy and the legitimizing power of the democratic process, it must accord the participants in that process ... the First Amendment rights that attach to their roles.

Nor could the announce clause be supported, as the court of appeals had suggested, Justice Scalia said, on the ground that it reflected a long and well-established practice. Restrictions on statements by candidates for judicial office did not appear until after the first quarter of the twentieth century, and even today four states that use judicial elections have no candidate speech restrictions, and one state has no restriction comparable to the announce clause. *White*, 122 S. Ct. at 2540–41.

by "judicial fiat," Justice O'Connor believed they should be abolished and, unlike Justice Ginsburg, was not reluctant to state this view openly. Elected judges are almost inevitably biased or seen as biased, Justice O'Connor believed, because of their need to seek popular favor and campaign contributions.[85]

Justice O'Connor differed from Justice Ginsburg only in that O'Connor was unwilling to permit Minnesota to deal with the problem by restricting judicial candidate speech. If Minnesota "has a problem with judicial impartiality," she said, "it is largely one the State brought upon itself by continuing the practice of popularly electing judges." Minnesota apparently deserved to be punished for making so serious and foolish a mistake, and could not be permitted to escape its full consequences by adopting half-measures. The First Amendment, according to Justice O'Connor, prohibits the announce clause not, as Justice Scalia thought, to preserve meaningful judicial elections, though elections could be abolished, but for exactly the opposite and even more surprising reason: to give the states an inducement to abolish them.

Apparently, Justice Kennedy concurred separately simply to reiterate his view, similar to that of the late Justice Black, that there are First Amendment absolutes that condemn restrictions on speech, regardless of their justifications or consequences. "I adhere to my view," he said, "that content-based speech restrictions that do not fall within any traditional exception should be invalidated without inquiry into narrow tailoring or compelling government interests." The "traditional exceptions" are that the state may suppress speech that is "obscene" or "defamatory," or "tantamount to an act otherwise criminal," or "an impairment of some other constitutional right," or "an incitement to lawless action," or "calculated or likely to bring about imminent harm [that] the State has the substantive power to prevent."[86] Why one more exception may not be added to so long a list—long enough to make the absoluteness of the rule seem doubtful—Kennedy did not undertake to explain. He also neglected to consider that the only reason an exception for judicial candidate speech is not "traditional" may be that the Court had never considered it before.

Justice Kennedy emphatically agreed with respondents that the state interest in protecting judicial integrity is of "vital importance," and believed that "explicit standards of judicial conduct provide essential guidance for judges in the proper discharge of their duties and the honorable conduct of their office." Those who promulgate such standards, therefore, "perform a vital public service." Even essential guidelines may not be used, however, to regulate candidate speech in judicial election campaigns, "simply because content-based restrictions on political speech are 'expressly and positively forbidden by' the First Amendment."[87] A du-

[85] *Id.* at 2542-44 (O'Connor, J., concurring).
[86] *Id.* at 2544 (Kennedy, J., concurring).
[87] *Id.* at 2545, quoting *New York Times v. Sullivan*, 376 U.S. 254, 274 (1964).

tiful justice must, of course, follow express and positive constitutional prohibitions no matter how bad the consequences, but Justice Kennedy's ability to find content-based restrictions on political speech "expressly and positively" prohibited by a First Amendment in which neither content-based restrictions nor political speech is mentioned demonstrates only that the level of accuracy understood to be permissible in constitutional argument is even lower than that of legal argument generally.[88] Justice Kennedy's rule would make unconstitutional, it seems, not only the announce clause, but the pledges or promises clause as well. It would, therefore, answer the question the Court purported to leave open and make clear that there is no First Amendment difference between judicial and other elections.[89]

C. *Justices Ginsburg's and Stevens's dissents*

How little law and how much ideology has to do with the Court's constitutional decisions is perhaps nowhere more clearly illustrated than in the consistency of voting patterns, especially by the four most liberal justices, over a very wide range of issues. The Court's membership has not changed in more than nine years, since the appointment of Justice Breyer in 1994, an exceptionally long time. During this time, Justices Stevens, Souter, Ginsburg, and Breyer have voted so consistently and reliably as a group for the liberal position on any disputed issue as almost to constitute a single judicial unit with four votes. Chief Justice Rehnquist and Justices Scalia and Thomas vote nearly, though not quite, as consistently together on the conservative side.

The Court's decision on any issue involving a liberal-conservative split usually depends, therefore, on the votes of Justices O'Connor and Kennedy. The conservatives have the advantage that O'Connor and Kennedy tend to support them on many issues—though often, as in *White*, with

[88] Justice Kennedy continued in his usual high moral tone with a series of statements, nearly every one of which is subject to question. "Courts, in our system," he said, "elaborate principles of law in the course of resolving disputes. The power and the prerogative of a court to perform this function rest, in the end, upon the respect accorded to its judgments. The citizen's respect for judgments depends in turn upon the issuing court's absolute probity." *Id.* at 2544. Yet, in almost every area of constitutional law, scholars report great difficulty in discerning the "principles of law" that determine and explain the Court's decisions. The Court's power to make effective its controversial decisions—on, say, prayer in the schools or the *Miranda* rule—probably rests less on the average citizen's respect for the Court than on the fact that he can do very little about those decisions. If the Court's power depended on the informed citizen's belief in its "absolute probity," its power would undoubtedly be considerably less.

[89] Justice Kennedy took Justice O'Connor to task for criticizing states that have chosen "to use open elections to select those persons most likely to achieve judicial excellence." *Id.* at 2545. (The use of elections is probably better explained, however, by a concern with uncontrolled judicial power rather than with judicial excellence.) To criticize judicial elections, Justice Kennedy remonstrated, is implicitly and undeservedly to criticize elected judges, many of whom "have discovered in the law the enlightenment, instruction, and inspiration that make them independent-minded and faithful jurists of real integrity." *Id.* at 2546.

reservations, qualifications, or differences—but the disadvantage that they must have both, while the liberals need only one, and at least one is frequently available. The result, as already noted, is that despite the myth of a conservative Supreme Court, rulings of unconstitutionality by the Rehnquist Court, like the Warren and Burger Courts, continue overwhelmingly to advance liberal rather than conservative causes.[90] Restrictions on judicial campaign speech are now unconstitutional only because both Justices O'Connor and Kennedy, for their own separate reasons—and O'Connor's position, as noted, is actually closer to the dissents' than the majority's—decided in this instance not to give the more committed and consistent liberals the crucial fifth vote.

Justices Ginsburg's and Stevens's dissenting opinions rest on nothing more than their iteration of the patently fallacious proposition that judicial elections are different from other elections in that judges do not play an important policymaking role in the American political system. Judges perform, Justice Ginsburg declared, "a function fundamentally different from the people's elected representatives," for their "mission is to decide 'individual cases and controversies' on individual records" by "neutrally applying legal principles."[91] She has apparently failed to notice or has forgotten that, at least in their rulings of unconstitutionality on controversial social policy issues, such as abortion or prayer in the schools, judges, herself very much included, function indistinguishably from elected representatives in voting their personal policy preferences.

The only difference between legislators and activist judges is that judges are freer from external constraint, except that they must suffer the embarrassment—which, as Justices Ginsburg's and Stevens's opinions show, troubles them very little—of having to claim, as convention requires, to be interpreting the Constitution. For the author of an opinion declaring that it is the U.S. Constitution that requires even military schools to enroll women[92]—in accordance with the feminist principles to which she has devoted her legal career—to claim that judges decide only individual cases on individual records by neutrally applying legal principles is to carry cynicism to new heights. In the very opinion in which Justice Ginsburg assures us that judges "are not political actors,"[93] she demonstrates her commitment to liberal "political correctness" and radical feminism by substituting feminine for generic masculine pronouns, not only in her own statements, but even when quoting Justice Scalia and others.[94] It has often been noted that those willing to abuse the language in furtherance of their causes are likely willing to abuse much else.

[90] *See* text at *supra* notes 27-39.
[91] *White*, 122 S. Ct. at 2550.
[92] *United States v. Virginia*, 518 U.S. 515 (1996).
[93] *White*, 122 S. Ct. at 2551.
[94] *See* text at *supra* note 66.

All the parties to the case agreed, Justice Ginsburg argued, that the pledges or promises clause is constitutional,[95] because an elected judge who made a promise as to an issue would have a pecuniary interest in keeping it for fear of otherwise losing "her" position and emoluments at the next election, and litigants, therefore, would be denied due process. This reasoning establishes the constitutionality of the announce clause as well, she said, because judicial candidates could otherwise evade the pledges or promises clause simply by putting their statements in a non-promissory form, even though "the 'nonpromissory' statement averts none of the dangers posed by the 'promissory' one." Therefore, a candidate, must be prohibited not only from saying, for example, "If elected, I will vote to uphold the legislature's power to prohibit same-sex marriages," but also from saying, "I think it is constitutional for the legislature to prohibit same-sex marriages."[96] Ginsburg is correct that the announce clause must have been meant to do more than the pledges or promises clause, or it would not have been worth defending,[97] but the result is to confirm the majority's conclusion that the announce clause virtually negates the point of judicial elections by "plac[ing] most subjects of interest to the voters off limits."[98]

Although he joined Justice Ginsburg's dissenting opinion "without reservation," Justice Stevens added his own in order "to emphasize the force of her arguments" and the danger he saw in the Court's underestimation, in his view, of the importance of judicial independence and impartiality.[99] Justice Stevens is certainly correct that judicial independence (that is, freedom from pressures to decide other than on the basis of the law) is an essential component of the rule of law, but it has little to do with the issue in *White*. The need and the reason for judicial elections is that American judges are independent not only of extralegal pressures, but also of the law itself.[100]

[95] *White*, 122 S. Ct. at 2554. In fact, because the pledges or promises clause was not challenged, the issue was not before the Court. If it had been, Justice Kennedy, as noted, apparently would have held it unconstitutional.

[96] *Id*. at 2558.

[97] Responding to constitutional concerns, in 1990 the ABA weakened its related canon to a provision prohibiting only judicial candidates' "statements that commit or appear to commit the candidate with respect to cases, controversies, or issues that are likely to come before the Court." The Minnesota Supreme Court, however, unlike other jurisdictions, explicitly refused to adopt this language in place of the announce clause. *Id*. at 2534 n.5.

[98] *Id*. at 2541.

[99] *Id*. at 2546.

[100] The Constitution, "Brutus" noted, makes

> the judges *independent*, in the fullest sense of the word. There is no power above them, to control any of their decisions. There is no authority that can remove them, and they cannot be controlled by the laws of the legislature. In short, they are independent of the people, of the legislature, and of every power under heaven. Men placed in this situation will generally soon feel themselves independent of heaven itself.

Essays of Brutus, No. XV, N.Y. J. (Mar. 20, 1788), reprinted in *The Complete Anti-Federalist*, Herbert J. Storing, ed. (Chicago, IL: University of Chicago Press, 1981), 2:437, 442.

It is good, as Special Prosecutor Leon Jaworski assured Americans when President Nixon was forced to abide by a Supreme Court decision, that even the president is subject to law,[101] but to whom is the Court subject? As the self-declared "supreme" expositor of the law of the U.S. Constitution,[102] the Court has an independence that, rather than being essential, is antithetical to the rule of law.[103] It is judicial policymaking power, not judicial independence, that elections seek to limit and the liberal dissenters in *White* sought to protect. In doing so, they simply voted their self-interested preference for rule by judges over rule by democratically enacted laws to which they are so often strongly opposed.

The majority also failed to recognize, Justice Stevens echoed Justice Ginsburg, the "critical differences between the work of a judge and the work of other public officials. In a democracy issues of policy are properly decided by majority vote."[104] This is indeed how policy decisions are made in a democracy, but how can Justice Stevens have failed to note, after a quarter of a century as one of the Court's most activist justices, that it is not how many of the most important policy decisions are made in the United States? In the United States, he must know, they are made by majority vote of the people only to the extent that a majority of the justices is willing to refrain—and Justice Stevens is one of the justices least willing to refrain—from removing the issue from the ordinary political process.[105]

V. Judicial Integrity and Impartiality

Much more obvious and serious than any failure by the majority of the Court to recognize the difference between judges and legislators is the willingness of the dissenters to pretend not to know that in the United States judges, and the dissenters themselves above all, act not only as legislators, but as super-legislators. Their unembarrassed assertion of the

[101] "From Watergate we learned what generations before us have known: our Constitution works. And during the Watergate years it was interpreted again so as to reaffirm that no one—absolutely no one—is above the law." Leon Jaworski, *The Right and the Power: The Prosecution of Watergate* (New York: Reader's Digest Press, 1976), 279. *See*: *United States v. Nixon*, 418 U.S. 683 (1974). Jaworski's statement is reassuring, but unfortunately incorrect: Supreme Court justices are not subject to, but are the creators of, "the law." As chief justice to-be Charles Evans Hughes pointed out long before the Court reached its present peak of power, "We are under a Constitution, but the Constitution is what the judges say it is." Speech, 1907, quoted in Jesse H. Choper et al., *The American Constitution*, 9th ed. (St. Paul, MN: West Group, 2001), 8.

[102] *See, e.g.*: *Cooper v. Aaron*, 358 U.S. 1 (1958).

[103] "Whoever hath an absolute authority to interpret any written or spoken laws, it is he who is truly the lawgiver, to all intents and purposes, and not the person who first spoke or wrote them." Bishop Hoadly's Sermon, preached before the King, 1717, quoted in Choper et al., *The American Constitution*, 1.

[104] *White*, 122 S. Ct. at 2547.

[105] For the past half-century, the Supreme Court has played in the American system of government a role similar to that once played in some Latin American nations by the junta: results reached in the ordinary political process were permitted to stand only so long as the junta did not disapprove.

patently false—the "noble lie" of constitutional law—demonstrates how little there is of the judicial integrity they claim to be concerned to protect. They are able to make such an assertion only because of a general understanding and acceptance by commentators on constitutional law, and by no one more clearly than the judges themselves, that the ordinary standards of accuracy and candor applicable in serious argument are not applicable to constitutional law. Constitutional law exists in a world of "let's pretend," entirely dependent on the willingness of defenders of judicial review to assert the falsehood that the justices' rulings of unconstitutionality derive from something other than their personal policy preferences. Except for this convention, the entire structure of constitutional law would crash to the ground, seen as the elaborate ruse that it is for the substitution of the elite's policy preferences for those of the majority. The nightmare of the cultural elite would follow: public policymaking in the hands of the American people, with such consequences as a freer use of capital punishment, prayer in schools, and restrictions on pornography and abortion. Who, the elite may ask, would want to live in a world like that?

Nor is the dissenters' performance likely to inspire public belief in judicial impartiality. Involved in *White* was a dispute in which one side was seeking the right to criticize pro-abortion judicial decisions, while the other was seeking to suppress such criticism and to encourage instead discussions of "race and gender bias" and how to ensure better treatment of women and minorities. Suppose now that a disinterested observer familiar with Justice Ginsburg's lifelong advocacy of feminist causes had been asked to predict how she would likely vote. How likely would he have been to consider it necessary to acquire a deep understanding of her views on the First Amendment? If the disinterested observer was also familiar with the fact that Justices Stevens, Souter, and Breyer almost always vote with Ginsburg on the liberal-elite side of issues that reflect the cultural divide, perhaps most certainly where what is seen as a feminist issue is somehow involved, he would have had little difficulty in predicting Ginsburg's vote and at least three others, again with no need to consider the First Amendment. The predictable and near-perfect alignment of the dissenters' votes with the dictates of a particular political ideology tells us more about judicial impartiality than their claim to be concerned to protect it.[106]

[106] The votes of Chief Justice Rehnquist and Justices Scalia and Thomas are also highly predictable on many issues, but on the whole probably less so than those of the liberals. The conservatives will, for example, sometimes supply the deciding vote or votes for overturning a criminal conviction; it is much less likely that Justice Ginsburg, for example, will supply the deciding vote in a decision to affirm. The predictability of the conservatives' votes is also explicable, in part, by their generally greater willingness to let stand the results of the ordinary political process. The votes of Justices O'Connor and Kennedy are much less predictable, as is illustrated, in part, by the distinct positions they took in *White*.

Far from being necessary to protect judicial integrity or to preserve public faith in judicial impartiality, as the dissenters claimed, silencing criticism of liberal judicial policymaking is likely to have the opposite effect. It is likely to encourage judges to engage wrongfully in even more such policymaking, which will make their lack of impartiality even more obvious, if possible. In any event, where, as in *White*, judicial rulings of unconstitutionality on basic social policy issues, such as abortion, are implicated, there is ordinarily very little judicial impartiality or public belief in judicial impartiality to protect. If judges did in fact what they invariably claim to do—enforce constitutional prohibitions—rulings of unconstitutionality would be so rare as to be of little consequence,[107] and there would be little demand for judicial elections. An activist judge, one who makes rulings of unconstitutionality not clearly required by the constitution he is purporting to enforce, is by definition not a person of integrity even if he has convinced himself that his robe has made him a superior person entitled to coercively instruct elected legislators and his other fellow citizens.

As for a state's interest in protecting the public's belief in judicial impartiality, it is unlikely that many concerned persons, at least those on the losing side of rulings of unconstitutionality, have such a belief. To the extent that any do, the state's interest, as already noted, should be to see that they are better informed. It is unlikely that such a belief can be found, for example, among the people of Colorado who had their decision to preclude special rights for homosexuals overturned by the Supreme Court on the ground that it could only be based on irrational "animus."[108] Nor is a belief in judicial impartiality likely to be found among the citizens of Hialeah, Florida, who were told that their attempt to ban animal sacrifice could only be a product of religious prejudice.[109] It is not likely to be found among the millions of persons who consider abortion, or at least so-called partial birth abortion, akin to murder but are told that a fundamental right to abort miraculously appeared in the Constitution in 1973.[110]

Belief in judicial impartiality is also not likely to be found among parents across the United States who have been subjected to court orders requiring that their children, because of their race, be excluded from their neighborhood schools and transported to more distant schools in a futile attempt, destructive of public school systems, to compel integration under the guise of "desegregation."[111] The fact that courts could and did in the busing cases impose on school districts a requirement of racial dis-

[107] *See supra* note 3.

[108] *Romer v. Evans*, 517 U.S. 620, 634 (1996). *See* Lino A. Graglia, "*Romer v. Evans*: The People Foiled Again by the Constitution," *University of Colorado Law Review* 68 (1997): 409.

[109] *Church of the Lukumi Babalu Aye, Inc. v. City of Hialeah*, 508 U.S. 520 (1993). *See* Lino A. Graglia, "*Church of the Lukumi Babalu Aye*: Of Animal Sacrifice and Religious Persecution," *Georgetown Law Journal* 85 (1996): 1.

[110] *Roe v. Wade*, 410 U.S. 113 (1973); *Stenberg v. Carhart*, 530 U.S. 914 (2000).

[111] *Swann v. Charlotte-Mecklenberg Bd. of Educ.*, 402 U.S. 1 (1971).

crimination in the name of enforcing a prohibition of such discrimination and in blatant defiance of the 1964 Civil Rights Act, America's greatest civil rights statute, gives reason to believe that judges may be the least impartial or trustworthy of government officials.[112] This should hardly be surprising given that America's judges are all lawyers, skilled only in the manipulation of language to reach predetermined ends and, more important, the public officials least subject to electoral accountability.

Judges of the highest state courts may, of course, be even more willing to engage in liberal activism than federal judges, as the California Supreme Court demonstrated by holding capital punishment, unequal school district funding, and racially unbalanced schools unconstitutional.[113] Other illustrations include the recent spate of state supreme court opinions finding constitutional violations in the failure of state legislatures to recognize "same-sex marriage"[114] and the war many state courts are conducting against tort reform. Tort reform is not only strongly opposed by the trial bar because it would mean less litigation and less remuneration for trial lawyers, it is also equally strongly opposed by activist judges because it would somewhat lessen their policymaking opportunities. Some element of tort reform legislation has already been invalidated in no fewer than twenty-six states, a further demonstration of judicial review operating against the public good.[115]

The great bulk of state court rulings of unconstitutionality, no less than the Supreme Court decisions that created a "right of privacy" on the basis of "penumbras, formed by emanations"[116] from the Constitution or that abolished traditional legal distinctions based on illegitimacy by invoking the authority of Edgar the Bastard in *King Lear*,[117] demonstrate not integrity or impartiality, but judicial contempt for both law and public opinion. Reciprocating this contempt, most concerned people understand or should be brought to understand, is the only appropriate reaction. Permitting candidates for judicial office to criticize liberal activism is not likely to increase that justified contempt, but might provide citizens an occasion and incentive to act on it.

[112] See Lino A. Graglia, *Disaster by Decree: The Supreme Court Decisions on Race and the Schools* (New York: Cornell University Press, 1976); and Lino A. Graglia, "When Honesty Is 'Simply ... Impractical' for the Supreme Court: How the Constitution Came to Require Busing for School Racial Balance," *Michigan Law Review* 85 (1987): 1153.

[113] *People v. Anderson*, 493 P.2d 880 (1972) (capital punishment); *Serrano v. Priest*, 487 P.2d 1241 (1971) (equal funding); and *Crawford v. Board of Education*, 551 P.2d 28 (1976) (school racial balance).

[114] *See*: *Tanner v. Oregon Health Services Univ.*, 971 P.2d 435 (Or. Ct. App. 1998); and *Baker v. State*, 744 A.2d 864 (Vt. 1999). *See also*: *Baehr v. Lewin*, 852 P.2d 44 (Haw. 1993) (an arguably correct interpretation of the state's "equal rights" amendment).

[115] *See* Samuel Jan Brakel, " 'Besting' Tort Reform in Illinois (and Other Misnomers): A Reform Supporter's Lament," *Capital University Law Review* 28 (2000): 823.

[116] *Griswold v. Connecticut*, 381 U.S. 479, 484 (1965).

[117] *Levy v. Louisiana*, 391 U.S. 68, 72 n.6 (1968).

VI. Does the First Amendment Permit Abolishing Judicial Election Campaigns but Forbid Restricting Judicial Election Campaign Speech?

That the purpose and effect of the announce clause was to protect the power of Minnesota judges to continue to enact liberal policies over popular opposition does not mean, however, that it is unconstitutional. If a state may constitutionally abolish judicial elections, as Justice Scalia conceded, totally eliminating the possibility of judicial campaign speech, it is not clear why it may not constitutionally hold elections in which campaign speech is restricted. Even accepting the incorporation fiction that makes the First Amendment applicable to the states as well as to the federal government[118] and assuming, contrary to fact, that "freedom of speech" has sufficiently ascertainable meaning to be considered a provision of law,[119] how can the First Amendment be understood to prohibit restricting speech in elections that could simply be abolished, with the result that there would be less rather than more speech?

Justice Scalia's bald assertion that a state may not leave "the principle of elections in place while preventing candidates from discussing what the elections are about," seems to have less to do with protecting speech than with preventing the state from engaging in some kind of chicanery. The state, he seems to be saying, can have no judicial elections, but not watered-down or restricted judicial elections. Perhaps some such prohibition can be derived from a statute like the Federal Trade Commission Act that prohibits certain "deceptive acts or practices,"[120] but it is hard to see how it can be derived from the First Amendment. Subjecting judges to even severely restricted elections would seem to be at least marginally better in terms of facilitating speech and limiting judicial power than, as in many states, granting judges lifetime

[118] The "Bill of Rights" (the first ten amendments to the Constitution), adopted in 1791, two years after ratification of the Constitution, was intended to apply to and restrain only the federal government. *See*: *Barron v. Mayor and City of Baltimore*, 32 U.S. 243 (1833). In 1947, however, Justice Hugo Black announced his view that it was also made applicable to the states by reason of "incorporation" in section one of the Fourteenth Amendment. *Adamson v. California*, 332 U.S. 46, 68 (1947) (Black, J., dissenting). Though never accepted by the Court, Black's position has essentially prevailed by means of an even less historically justified process of "selective incorporation." *See*: *Duncan v. Louisiana*, 391 U.S. 145 (1968). That Black's position lacks historical warrant was persuasively established by constitutional historian Charles Fairman in "Does the Fourteenth Amendment Incorporate the Bill of Rights? The Original Understanding," *Stanford Law Review* 2 (1949): 437: *but see, e.g.*, Michael K. Curtis, *No State Shall Abridge: The Fourteenth Amendment and the Bill of Rights* (Durham, NC: Duke University Press, 1986).

[119] See *Federalist No. 84* (A. Hamilton), in Rossiter, ed., *The Federalist Papers*, 514: "What is the liberty of the press? Who can give it any definition which would not leave the widest latitude for evasion?" "[T]hose aphorisms which make the principal figure in several of our State bills of rights," Hamilton pointed out, "would sound much better in a treatise of ethics than in a constitution of government." Ibid., 513.

[120] Federal Trade Commission Act, 15 U.S.C. § 41.

tenure with no elections at all. As an originalist, Justice Scalia cannot conclude that the Constitution prohibits deception simply because it ought to be prohibited. How, then, can he have the Court in the name of the First Amendment set itself up as a kind of Federal Trade Commission for judicial election campaigns?

Nor can it really be claimed, as Justice Scalia did, that the *White* result was logically compelled by precedent.[121] Lawyerly skill in making distinctions is usually quite adequate to escape the requirements of precedent. The Court had never before considered the precise question of restricting judicial candidate speech, and one more vote for the dissenters would have shown that the precedents were for that reason easily distinguishable, as the court of appeals had found.

Perhaps, however, *White* is the rare case where judicial activism—a ruling of unconstitutionality not clearly required by the Constitution—can be defended, following John Hart Ely, on the ground that it actually furthers democracy[122] or, appeasing Alexander Bickel, that it is actually pro- rather than anti-majoritarian.[123] The Minnesota Supreme Court judges promulgated the announce clause to vitiate the effect of elections required by the "popularly approved" Minnesota Constitution and to protect their power to frustrate democracy. If judicial activism is ever justified, surely it is most easily so, as some have argued in defense of *Bush v. Gore*,[124] when used to defeat judicial activism.[125] But could not the Minnesota legislature defend the Minnesota Constitution and reject the self-serving antidemocratic act of the Minnesota Supreme Court? Or does the legislature have too many lawyers with a professional interest in enhanced judicial power for that to be a realistic possibility?

The answer, if we in fact believe in popular government and federalism, has to be that resolution of the problem should have been left for the people of Minnesota, not five U.S. Supreme Court justices. It just happens to be the case that nothing in the U.S. Constitution prohibits Minnesota's method of selecting its judges. The lawyers in the Minnesota legislature may have been self-interested in letting the announce clause stand, but to accept that the U.S. Supreme Court has a roving commission to see that all laws are in the public interest, whatever that may be, is to give up on self-government.

[121] *White*, 122 S. Ct. at 2538 (this Court's decisions do not allow "the government to prohibit candidates from communicating relevant information to voters during an election").

[122] John Hart Ely, *Democracy and Distrust: A Theory of Judicial Review* (Cambridge, MA: Harvard University Press, 1980).

[123] Alexander Bickel, *The Least Dangerous Branch: The Supreme Court at the Bar of Politics* (Indianapolis, IN: Bobbs-Merrill, 1962).

[124] 531 U.S. 98 (2000).

[125] *See* Richard A. Posner, *Breaking the Deadlock: The 2000 Election, The Constitution, and The Courts* (Princeton, NJ: Princeton University Press, 2001).

VII. Conclusion

White is correct in concluding that the purpose of restrictions on judicial campaign speech is to undermine the effectiveness of subjecting judges to electoral accountability. The principal effect of such restrictions is to insulate liberal judicial activism from criticism by conservative opponents in election campaigns. It does not follow that such restrictions can realistically be said to be prohibited by the Constitution or even by the Court's prior First Amendment decisions regarding nonjudicial elections. To prohibit speech-restricted elections where the likely alternative, strongly favored by the organized bar and legal academia, is no elections at all, does not seem to advance the cause of freedom of speech or of democratic government that freedom of speech is meant to serve.

Like virtually all rulings of unconstitutionality, the decision in *White* is the result not of a clear constitutional command or prohibition, but simply of the policy preference of a majority of the justices. The only unusual thing about the ruling in *White* is that it is a conservative rather than a liberal judicial preference that is being imposed, which can occasionally happen on the present Court, although usually, as here, by only a 5–4 vote and often, as also here, with a separate concurrence that puts the result in doubt. Any conservative satisfaction in the result should be tempered by the realization that it represents still another example, in fact an expansion, of dominant judicial power, and that accepting expansion of judicial policymaking power is not in today's world a move in the direction of limited or sound government. In today's America, substituting government by judges for government by the people operates and will continue to operate for the foreseeable future overwhelmingly in favor of liberal causes.

The people of Minnesota have it within their means to solve the problem of judicial usurpation of legislative power by the Minnesota Supreme Court. Eventually, perhaps, the people might even come to realize that, although effective judicial elections might restrain or correct some of the court's worst abuses, the problem can really be solved only by abolishing judicial review itself. They could hardly do themselves as well as the nation a greater service than by doing so, thereby providing their countrymen with an example that the people of at least one state believe that they can be trusted to govern themselves without the supervision and correction of judges. The people of Minnesota would be better advised, in any event, to suffer the usurpations of the Minnesota Supreme Court than to accept "rescue" from the U.S. Supreme Court, thereby validating a much more serious usurpation. Those who support the federalist system of representative self-government contemplated by the framers of the Constitution should see it as their civic duty to oppose the Court's interventions on policy issues not clearly required by the Constitution, even when the interventions produce results they favor.

Of course, devotees of *realpolitik* might argue that as long as it remains unlikely that judicial activism will end, there is no reason why it should exclusively serve liberal causes.[126] The result, however, is to preclude the possibility of principled objection to judicial activism and to abandon any hope for change. Change, admittedly, appears extremely unlikely, but to the extent the American people can be reawakened to the founding belief that democracy and federalism are the best, if not the only, protections against government tyranny, they will come to see—as even some liberals are coming to see as a result of *Bush v. Gore*—that it is intolerable that the most basic issues of social policy should be decided nationally by majority vote of a committee of nine lawyers, unelected and holding office for life.

Law, University of Texas

[126] *See, e.g.*: *Dolan v. City of Tigard*, 512 U.S. 374, 392 (1994) (Rehnquist, C.J., arguing that there is no reason why the just compensation clause of the Fifth Amendment should not be interpreted as broadly as the First Amendment).

PROPERTY RIGHTS AND FREE SPEECH: ALLIES OR ENEMIES?*

By James W. Ely, Jr.

I. Introduction

Free speech has been treated as a preeminent constitutional right in the United States for more than half a century. The rights of property owners, on the other hand, have received little constitutional protection since the New Deal period of the 1930s. This modern dichotomy is particularly striking because it obscures an older constitutional tradition that equated economic liberty and freedom of expression. This tradition saw both property rights and speech rights as essential to the protection of personal freedom by restraining the power of government.

The framers of the U.S. Constitution and the Bill of Rights, drawing upon Whig political theory,[1] did not differentiate between the rights of property owners and other individual rights.[2] Indeed, in his famous 1792 essay, "Property," James Madison treated speech as a property right of individuals. He explained that "a man has a property in his opinions and the free communication of them."[3]

Following in Madison's path, leading jurists sometimes equated free speech and property rights. Thomas M. Cooley was a member of the Michigan Supreme Court and the author of *A Treatise on the Constitutional Limitations Which Rest Upon the Legislative Power of the States* (1868), the most important analysis of constitutional law in the late nineteenth century. In this seminal work he argued that freedom of speech entailed more than just the absence of prior restraints. Dissenting in an 1881 libel law

* I wish to acknowledge the helpful research assistance of Catheryne E. Pully.

[1] Whig political theory refers to a set of beliefs associated with the Whig Party in Great Britain during the eighteenth century. Drawing on the philosophy of John Locke, Whigs favored limits on monarchical power and stressed the rule of law and the right to personal freedom. They regarded the right to enjoy property as a natural right and fashioned doctrines to defend the rights of property owners. Whiggism, with its emphasis on limited government and property rights, exerted a profound influence on constitutional thought in Revolutionary America. H. T. Dickinson, "Whiggism in the Eighteenth Century," in John Cannon, ed., *The Whig Ascendancy: Colloquies on Hanoverian England* (New York: St. Martin's Press, 1981), 28–43; Gordon S. Wood, *The Creation of the American Republic, 1776–1787* (Chapel Hill: University of North Carolina Press, 1969), 16–28.

[2] James W. Ely, Jr., *The Guardian of Every Other Right: A Constitutional History of Property Rights*, 2d ed. (New York: Oxford University Press, 1998), 43.

[3] James Madison, "Property," *National Gazette*, March 27, 1792, reprinted in Robert A. Rutland et al., eds., *The Papers of James Madison*, vol. 14 (Charlottesville, VA: University Press of Virginia, 1983), 266.

case, which involved allegations of professional misconduct directed against an attorney, Cooley stressed that everyone must exercise rights with due regard for the rights of others. "This is as true of the right to free speech," he observed, "as it is of the right to the free enjoyment of one's property." [4]

Justice George Sutherland, the intellectual leader of the conservative bloc on the U.S. Supreme Court during the 1930s, also stressed the link between economic liberty and freedom of expression. In *New State Ice Company v. Liebmann* (1932), Sutherland, writing for the Court, found that an Oklahoma statute conferring de facto monopoly on established ice businesses infringed the due process right of others to engage in a lawful endeavor. Regulatory schemes in the 1930s were often justified as experiments in economic planning. Sutherland, however, insisted that government could not dispense with the essentials of liberty in the name of experiments. Revealingly, he ended his opinion in *New State Ice* with the following assertion:

> [T]he theory of experimentation in censorship was not permitted to interfere with the fundamental doctrine of the freedom of the press. The opportunity to apply one's labor and skill in an ordinary occupation with proper regard for all reasonable regulations is no less entitled to protection.[5]

As this indicates, Sutherland was disinclined to distinguish between economic controls and regulations impacting First Amendment rights. In his mind, the sanctity of speech and the sanctity of economic liberty were equally deserving of constitutional protection.[6]

The support accorded free speech by Cooley and Sutherland points toward the now largely forgotten conservative libertarian tradition of the nineteenth and early twentieth centuries that urged constitutional protection for both expressive and property rights. The conservative libertarians believed that respect for free speech and regard for private property were equally necessary to demarcate a sphere of individual autonomy. Thus, the prominent political scientist John W. Burgess asserted in 1896 that individual liberty encompassed security of private property as well as freedom of expression and conscience.[7] As Mark A. Graber pointed

[4] *Atkinson v. Detroit Free Press Company*, 46 Mich. 341, 376; 9 N.W. 501, 520 (1881) (Cooley, J., dissenting).

[5] *New State Ice Company v. Liebmann*, 285 U.S. 262, 280 (1932). For a cogent analysis of Justice Sutherland's opinion in *New State Ice*, see Hadley Arkes, *The Return of George Sutherland: Restoring A Jurisprudence of Natural Rights* (Princeton, NJ: Princeton University Press, 1994), 53–60.

[6] For a helpful discussion of Justice Sutherland's First Amendment views, see Samuel R. Olken, "The Business of Expression: Economic Liberty, Political Factions, and the Forgotten First Amendment Legacy of Justice George Sutherland," *William and Mary Bill of Rights Journal* 10 (2002): 242–357.

[7] John W. Burgess, *Political Science and Comparative Constitutional Law*, vol. 1 (Boston, MA: Ginn and Company, 1896), 178.

out, conservative libertarians "claimed that the liberty of speech was the same sort of right as the liberty of contract and, indeed, that the system of freedom of expression could only function if the government also protected private property."[8]

This affinity between property rights and free speech was torn asunder during the New Deal era. In the early twentieth century, Progressive thinkers launched a sustained attack on the constitutional protection of property and contractual rights. Assuming the desirability of state intervention in economic matters, they saw constitutionalized economic rights as barriers to legislation advancing their conception of the public good.[9] Their criticism eventually bore fruit in the late 1930s, when the Supreme Court began to uphold the validity of New Deal legislation and retreated from meaningful judicial review of economic regulations. After this dramatic shift, known as the constitutional revolution of 1937, the Court in short order sustained state minimum wage laws[10] similar to those it had earlier condemned and approved a dramatic enlargement of federal governmental controls over the economy. For example, the justices upheld the National Labor Relations Act, which was designed to encourage trade unions,[11] as well as sweeping federal regulation of agricultural production.[12] The Court also strengthened state rate-making authority over public utilities.[13] The cornerstone of New Deal constitutionalism was Footnote 4 of *United States v. Carolene Products Co.* (1938), which placed the rights of property owners in a subordinate category entitled to only a lesser degree of due process protection than other personal liberties.[14] *Carolene Products* was the source of bifurcated judicial review and led to the elevation of free speech to the status of a fundamental or preferred right and the nearly total uninterest in even hearing property right cases. However, as the New Deal Court empowered the federal government by largely abandoning the constraints of federalism and property rights, a new problem arose: How to restrain the power of the state? The justices turned to an expansive reading of free speech in order to check potential governmental abuses by means of the free expression of opinions and reliance on the political process.[15]

[8] Mark A. Graber, *Transforming Free Speech: The Ambiguous Legacy of Civil Libertarianism* (Berkeley: University of California Press, 1991), 21. The conservative libertarian defense of free speech saw expression as one aspect of personal freedom. Modern civil libertarians, in contrast, separate free speech from property rights and justify the former in terms of promoting democratic governance rather than as an individual right. For the communitarian vision of the First Amendment, see Cass R. Sunstein, *Democracy and the Problem of Free Speech* (New York: The Free Press, 1993).

[9] See generally Barbara H. Fried, *The Progressive Assault on Laissez-Faire: Robert Hale and the First Law and Economics Movement* (Cambridge, MA: Harvard University Press, 1998).

[10] *West Coast Hotel Co. v. Parrish*, 300 U.S. 379 (1937).

[11] *National Labor Relations Board v. Jones & Laughlin Steel Corp.*, 301 U.S. 1 (1937).

[12] *Wickard v. Filburn*, 317 U.S. 111 (1942).

[13] *Federal Power Commission v. Hope Natural Gas Co.*, 320 U.S. 591 (1944).

[14] 304 U.S. 144, 152–153 n.4 (1938).

[15] See John O. McGinnis, "The Once and Future Property-Based Vision of the First Amendment," *University of Chicago Law Review* 63 (1996): 49.

Not surprisingly, in some situations the newly enlarged concept of free speech was held to trump the rights of property owners. For example, in *Marsh v. Alabama* (1946), the Supreme Court ruled, by a 5-3 margin, that streets in a privately owned company town were to be treated as a public forum for purposes of expressive activity.[16] A plurality of the Court reasoned: "Ownership does not always mean absolute dominion. The more an owner, for his advantage, opens up his property for use by the public in general, the more his rights become circumscribed by the statutory and constitutional rights of those who use it."[17] For a time, some observers saw *Marsh* as heralding a broad expansion of constitutional protection of First Amendment activities carried out on private property open to the public. Indeed, the Court in *Amalgamated Food Employees Union Local 590 v. Logan Valley Plaza* (1968) ruled that a privately owned shopping mall was the equivalent of a company town and, therefore, was subject to the mandate of the First Amendment.[18] It followed that union picketers could not be excluded from a private shopping center. This line of cases underscored the secondary constitutional status of private property. But the story does not end here. A harbinger of change was Justice Hugo Black's dissenting opinion in *Logan Valley*. Black, the author of the majority opinion in *Marsh*, insisted that there was no resemblance between a shopping center and a company town. He added that "whether this Court likes it or not, the Constitution recognizes and supports the concept of private ownership of property."[19]

II. Right to Exclude

Despite its diminished constitutional position, private property remains central to the American economic system. Thus, it is important to understand the nature of ownership.

The right to maintain exclusive possession has long been seen as an essential component of the concept of property. William Blackstone, commenting in the late eighteenth century, provided a classic expression of this principle:

> There is nothing which so generally strikes the imagination, and engages the affections of mankind, as the right of property; or that sole and despotic dominion which one man claims and exercises

[16] 326 U.S. 501 (1946) (Justice Jackson took no part in the case). The case involved a Jehovah's Witness who tried to distribute religious literature. The Court specifically invoked the First Amendment freedoms of religion and of the press, but in today's parlance it is seen as a free speech case.

[17] *Id.* at 506.

[18] 391 U.S. 308 (1968).

[19] *Id.* at 330.

> over the external things of the world, in total exclusion of the right of any other individual in the universe.[20]

Blackstone's articulation of a right of "despotic dominion" seems somewhat excessive to modern ears.[21] It is hard to accept that an individual has total economic control over his or her land. Even in Blackstone's day the authority of landowners was limited by the law of nuisance.[22] Yet Blackstone's comment, however hyperbolic, is also insightful. In many respects the right of an owner to exclude others is vital to the enjoyment of property. Exclusive possession is necessary so that an owner can use or alienate property and thus derive economic gain. As a prominent modern scholar has aptly pointed out, "to the extent one has the right to exclude, then one has property; conversely, to the extent one does not have exclusion rights, one does not have property."[23]

During the nineteenth and early twentieth centuries, courts gave relatively little attention to defining property. Still, prominent jurists recognized the importance of the right to exclude others as an essential quality of property ownership. Justice Oliver Wendell Holmes, for example, explained in 1908: "The notion of property starts, I suppose, from confirmed possession of a tangible object and consists in the right to exclude others from interference with the more or less free doing with it as one wills."[24] In 1913, Justice Joseph McKenna similarly declared:

> The conception of property is exclusiveness, the rights of exclusive possession, enjoyment and disposition. Take away these rights and you take all that there is of property. Take away any of them, force a participation in any of them and you take property to that extent.[25]

Five years later Justice Louis D. Brandeis followed suit: "An essential element of individual property is the legal right to exclude others from enjoying it."[26]

In recent years, since the high Court began showing a renewed interest in reviewing property rights cases in the 1970s, both federal and state

[20] William Blackstone, *Commentaries on the Laws of England*, vol. 2 (Oxford: Clarendon Press, 1766; reprint, Chicago, IL: University of Chicago Press, 1979), 2.

[21] A. W. B. Simpson, "Land Ownership and Economic Freedom," in Harry N. Scheiber, ed., *The State and Freedom of Contract* (Stanford, CA: Stanford University Press, 1998), 13–43.

[22] *Id.* at 25 ("Both regulatory law and the law of nuisance imposed curbs on the despotic dominion of the landowner.").

[23] Thomas W. Merrill, "Property and the Right to Exclude," *Nebraska Law Review* 77 (1998): 753.

[24] *White-Smith Music Publishing Company v. Apollo Company*, 209 U.S. 1, 19 (1908) (Holmes, J., concurring).

[25] *Pipe Line Cases*, 234 U.S. 548, 571 (1913) (McKenna, J., dissenting).

[26] *International News Service v. Associated Press*, 248 U.S. 215, 250 (1918) (Brandeis, J., dissenting).

courts have repeatedly emphasized the fundamental nature of the right to exclude in a variety of situations.[27] A few examples will suffice. In the leading case of *Kaiser Aetna v. United States* (1979), the Supreme Court, in an opinion by then-Justice William H. Rehnquist, declared "that the 'right to exclude,' so universally held to be a fundamental element of the property right," could not be taken by the government without the payment of just compensation.[28] Likewise, in *Loretto v. Teleprompter Manhattan CATV Corp.* (1982), the Court insisted: "The power to exclude has traditionally been considered one of the most treasured strands in an owner's bundle of property rights."[29] Similar sentiments have been expressed by numerous state courts. The Supreme Courts of Ohio[30] and Nevada[31] were especially forceful in articulating this view.

III. Public Forum Doctrine

In the late nineteenth century there was controversy over the rights of persons to engage in expressive activity on public property, such as streets and parks. The prevailing view was that individuals had no protected right to speak on public property. As Holmes maintained in 1895 while serving on the Supreme Judicial Court of Massachusetts: "For the Legislature absolutely or conditionally to forbid public speaking in a highway or public park is no more an infringement of the rights of a member of the public than for the owner of a private home to forbid it in his house."[32] Holmes analyzed the case entirely in property terms, treating public facilities the same as private property for the purpose of excluding certain uses. In his view, the government as a proprietor had the same authority as a private landowner. Holmes concluded that municipal authorities could forbid speech in the Boston Common by a lay preacher without a permit. The Supreme Court affirmed this decision in 1897.

This restrictive attitude, of course, was overthrown in the late 1930s when the Supreme Court ruled that government could not ban speech-related activities in streets and parks that served as public forums.[33] Such a conclusion, however, flew in the face of the prevailing line of authority from the nineteenth century. Ignoring historical practice, the Court rather

[27] See David L. Callies and J. David Breemer, "The Right to Exclude Others From Private Property: A Fundamental Constitutional Right," *Washington University Journal of Law and Policy* 3 (2000): 39–59.

[28] 444 U.S. 164, 179–180 (1979).

[29] 458 U.S. 419, 435 (1982).

[30] *Bresnik v. Beulah Park Limited Partnership, Inc.*, 67 Ohio St. 3d 302; 617 N.E.2d 1096 (1993).

[31] *S.O.C., Inc. v. Mirage Casino-Hotel*, 117 Nev. 403, 23 P.3d 243 (2001).

[32] *Commonwealth v. Davis*, 162 Mass. 510, 511, 39 N.E. 113 (1895), *aff'd.* 167 U.S. 43 (1897).

[33] *Hague v. Committee for Industrial Organization*, 307 U.S. 496 (1939). Not all types of public property, however, are necessarily available for speaking or other First Amendment activities. There is no constitutional right, for example, to conduct protest demonstrations on the grounds of a jail, an area not traditionally open to the public. *Adderley v. Florida*, 385 U.S. 39, 47 (1966) ("The State, no less than a private owner of property, has power to preserve the property under its control for the use to which it is lawfully dedicated").

fancifully asserted that streets and parks had long been used for speech and assembly, and unconvincingly sought to distinguish prior authority.[34] It was the extension of the public forum doctrine to privately owned land, as in *Marsh v. Alabama* (discussed above), that set the stage for our contemporary disputes over speech in shopping malls.

IV. Free Speech in Shopping Malls

Over the past forty years the retail shopping pattern of most Americans has shifted away from downtown business districts. People today tend to shop and congregate in privately owned suburban malls.[35] With the decline of city streets as primary places for the dissemination of views, people desirous of exercising expressive rights have sought to gain access to malls. They have argued, in effect, that shopping centers are comparable to yesterday's town square and should be open to speech-related activity. This has given rise to a prolonged controversy over whether the common areas of such centers should be treated as public forums for First Amendment purposes. Not surprisingly, the owners of malls have stoutly resisted the notion that their property is a public forum.

A somewhat checkered line of Supreme Court decisions has established that there is no right under the U.S. Constitution to engage in expressive activity on the grounds of privately owned shopping centers. Only a few years after *Logan Valley* was decided, the Supreme Court began to back away from its ruling that a privately owned shopping mall was the equivalent of a company town and, thus, subject to the mandate of the First Amendment. In *Lloyd Corporation v. Tanner* (1972), a mall was allowed to ban the distribution of antiwar handbills. The Supreme Court ruled that a shopping center does not "lose its private character merely because the public is generally invited to use it for designated purposes."[36] Moreover, the Court stressed that the First Amendment only restrains *governmental* limitations on free speech and does not reach private actions. The Court revealingly concluded by noting the importance of both property and free speech rights:

> We do say that the Fifth and Fourteenth Amendment rights of private property owners, as well as the First Amendment rights of all citizens, must be respected and protected. The Framers of the Constitution certainly did not think these fundamental rights of a free society are incompatible with each other. There may be situations

[34] Justice Pierce Butler, dissenting in *Hague*, accurately observed that the majority's position was contrary to the holding in *Davis v. Massachusetts*, 167 U.S. 43 (1897), discussed in the text at note 32. See 307 U.S. at 533. See generally David M. Rabban, *Free Speech in Its Forgotten Years* (Cambridge: Cambridge University Press, 1997), 165–69, 372–74.

[35] See generally William Severini Kowinski, *The Malling of America: An Inside Look at the Great Consumer Paradise* (New York: William Morrow, 1985).

[36] *Lloyd Corporation v. Tanner*, 407 U.S. 551, 569 (1972).

where accommodations between them, and the drawing of lines to assure due protection of both, are not easy.[37]

If nothing else, *Lloyd* signaled that the rights of property owners would not be mechanically downplayed in favor of asserted speech rights.

Four years later, the Supreme Court in *Hudgens v. NLRB* (1976) overruled *Logan Valley* and found that shopping centers were not the functional equivalent of company towns.[38] Thus, a mall could ban labor picketing directed against an individual business located in the center. The *Hudgens* decision made clear that the First Amendment conferred no protection on expressive activities in shopping centers when the owners objected. The Supreme Court has not revisited this issue. Lower federal courts have consistently ruled that private shopping malls are not subject to the First Amendment.[39]

Application of the public forum doctrine to private property in the federal courts has been steadily shrinking since the 1970s. *Marsh* has become an isolated precedent, limited to the largely obsolete company town. One leading scholar, William Van Alstyne, saw this development as reinvigorating the historical connection between rights of property ownership and other basic civil liberties.[40]

The decisions upholding the right to exclude in the shopping center context also portended a series of Supreme Court decisions strengthening the Takings Clause of the Fifth Amendment. The Fifth Amendment provides in part, "nor shall private property be taken for public use, without just compensation." This clause clearly prevents outright confiscation of property by the government. In *Loretto v. Teleprompter Manhattan CATV Corp.* (1982), the Supreme Court ruled that any governmentally authorized permanent physical occupation of property constituted a taking for which compensation must be paid.[41] The Court also began to put some teeth into the regulatory takings doctrine, which recognizes that a land use regulation might be so severe as to effectuate a taking of property. In *Lucas v. South Carolina Coastal Council* (1992), for example, the Court held that land use controls that deprive a landowner of all economically viable use of his property amount to a taking.[42]

Denied First Amendment protection as a result of cases such as *Lloyd* and *Hudgens*, those seeking to exercise free speech rights in privately owned shopping centers turned to the state courts. They hoped to secure rulings that state constitutions secured broader speech rights of visitors

[37] *Id.* at 570.

[38] *Hudgens v. NLRB*, 424 U.S. 507 (1976).

[39] *Southwest Community Resources, Inc. v. Simon Property Group, L.P*, 108 F. Supp. 2d 1239 (D. New Mexico 2000)

[40] William W. Van Alstyne, "The Recrudescence of Property Rights As the Foremost Principle of Civil Liberties: The First Decade of the Burger Court," *Law and Contemporary Problems* 43 (1980): 66–82.

[41] 458 U.S. 419 (1982).

[42] 505 U.S. 1003 (1992).

on private property than those afforded by the federal Constitution. This strategy paid a handsome dividend in 1979 when the California Supreme Court, by a 4–3 vote, held that the state constitution safeguarded speech and petitioning in privately owned malls.[43] The majority stressed the growing importance of shopping centers in American life. The dissenters correctly pointed out that the majority "relegates the private property rights of the shopping center owner to a secondary, disfavored, and subservient position vis-a-vis" free speech claims.[44] The dissenters maintained that the Court's ruling in effect constituted a taking of a valuable property right in violation of the federal Constitution.

In *PruneYard Shopping Center v. Robins* (1980), the U.S. Supreme Court, in an opinion by then-Justice Rehnquist, affirmed the California decision, declaring that state courts were free to give more expansive protection to free speech rights than that afforded by the federal Constitution.[45] Although recognizing that the California Supreme Court's interpretation of the state constitution destroyed the right to exclude others, the U.S. Supreme Court nonetheless concluded that this did not amount to a taking of the center owner's property. The Court stressed that the exercise of expressive rights in the shopping center did not impair the commercial use of the property.

Rehnquist's opinion in *PruneYard* is problematic on two points.[46] First, since the decision converted the shopping center into a kind of commons, it is difficult to square with Rehnquist's stress on the essential character of the right to exclude in other contexts. Second, the decision is inconsistent with the language in *Lloyd* describing private property as one of the "fundamental rights of a free society." If California courts felt that robust protection of free speech necessitated public entry into malls, the logic of *Lloyd* would indicate that a taking of a property right had occurred. Rehnquist endeavored to escape this dilemma by invoking the notion of property-owner consent, but this argument ultimately falls flat. The owners of shopping centers could invite the public for a specific purpose—that is, retail shopping—without extending a blanket invitation to all to enter for any purpose. Consent, moreover, as in *PruneYard* itself, can be expressly revoked.[47] Rehnquist's puzzling *PruneYard* opinion can best be explained as an expression of his deep concern for state autonomy in the federal system. Political scientist Sue Davis has observed that the

[43] *Robins v. PruneYard Shopping Center*, 23 Cal. 3d 899, 592 P.2d 341 (1979).

[44] *Id.*, 23 Cal. 3d at 911, 592 P.2d at 348.

[45] 447 U.S. 74 (1980).

[46] For a thoughtful critique of the *PruneYard* decision, see Richard A. Epstein, "Takings, Exclusivity, and Speech: The Legacy of *PruneYard v. Robins*," *University of Chicago Law Review* 64 (1997): 21–69.

[47] It is a hornbook rule that a license to enter the property of another is revocable for any reason. See *State v. Wicklund*, 589 N.W.2d 793, 802 (Minn. 1999) ("While the public is invited to many privately-owned places to shop, dine, or be entertained, the invitation creates only a license which may be revoked"); *Mosher v. Cook United, Inc.*, 62 Ohio St. 2d 316, 405 N.E.2d 720 (1980) (license of customer to enter grocery store revoked).

opinion "provides perhaps the clearest illustration of the value he [Rehnquist] places on federalism over property rights."[48]

Whatever the shortcomings of *PruneYard*, it opened the door for a new round of litigation in state courts over expressive rights in shopping centers.[49] These cases focused on the protection given free speech under state constitutions. Such provisions in state constitutions vary widely. Some emulate the wording of the First Amendment, but others contain broader language that could be read to confer an affirmative right to speech. Two examples are instructive:

1. New Hampshire Constitution, Part 1, Article 22:
   Free speech and liberty of the press are essential to the security of freedom in a state: They ought, therefore, to be inviolably preserved.
2. Ohio Constitution, Article 1, Section 11:
   Every citizen may freely speak, write, and publish his sentiments on all subjects, being responsible for the abuse of the right; and no law shall be passed to restrain or abridge the liberty of speech, or of the press.

Such language is ambiguous as to whether the state free speech clause protects the exercise of speech rights against interference by private parties as well as by government.

Litigation in the state courts about access to privately owned malls has produced decidedly mixed results. A few jurisdictions, including Colorado,[50] Massachusetts,[51] and New Jersey, have followed the lead of California. The decision of the Supreme Court of New Jersey, in *New Jersey Coalition Against War in the Middle East v. J.M.B. Realty Corp.* (1994), rendered by a 4–3 vote, is particularly noteworthy for its dismissive attitude toward the rights of property owners.[52] The majority opinion took "judicial notice of the fact" that downtown business districts have declined since 1950, and that such decline has been accompanied by the emergence

[48] Sue Davis, *Justice Rehnquist and the Constitution* (Princeton, NJ: Princeton University Press, 1989), 121.

[49] Kevin Francis O'Neill, "The Regulation of Public Protest: Picketing, Parades, and Demonstrations," in Daniel R. Mandelker and Rebecca L. Rubin, eds., *Protecting Free Speech and Expression: The First Amendment and Land Use Law* (Chicago, IL: American Bar Association, 2001), 253–55.

[50] *Bock v. Westminster Mall Co.*, 819 P.2d 55 (Colo. 1991).

[51] *Batchelder v. Allied Stores International, Inc.*, 388 Mass. 83, 445 N.E.2d 590 (1983) (holding only that persons had constitutional right to solicit signatures for a candidate's ballot application in the common areas of a mall, and declining to consider broader question of free speech rights in shopping centers).

[52] *New Jersey Coalition Against War in the Middle East v. J.M.B. Realty Corp.*, 138 N.J. 326, 650 A.2d 757 (1994). For a critical analysis of *New Jersey Coalition*, see Stanley H. Friedelbaum, "Private Property, Public Property: Shopping Centers and Expressive Freedom in the States," *Albany Law Review* 62 (1999): 1252–62 ("That private property rights in the historic sense have been substantially impaired in the surge of a few activist state courts to expand the role of shopping centers is difficult to refute.").

of regional malls.[53] The majority concluded that the New Jersey Constitution's guarantee of free speech was broader than the First Amendment's, and protected speech from both governmental abridgement and restrictive conduct by private entities.[54] It characterized the mall's invitation to the public as one embracing a variety of activities, and not limited to retail shopping.[55] In a strongly worded dissent, three judges accused the majority of disregarding the private property provisions of the state constitution and insisted that the primary purpose of shopping centers was retail trade, not communication.

The overwhelming majority of state courts, however, have declined to adopt free speech rights more extensive than the First Amendment's in cases involving malls. Most state courts have concluded that their constitutional free speech provisions, like the First Amendment, reach only state action and do not control the conduct of private parties who curtail expressive activity on their own land. Courts in New York[56] and Michigan,[57] for example, have held that state free speech guarantees are limited to state action, and that shopping centers are not functionally equivalent to municipalities. Nor have most state courts been persuaded to construe state constitutional language as creating an affirmative right to exercise free speech upon private property.[58] Instead, despite different phraseology, they have found that state free speech protection is coextensive with that of the First Amendment.

Even those state courts that initially upheld the exercise of expressive activity on private property have begun whittling back the breadth of this right. In 1999, a California court refused to extend the public forum doctrine to a freestanding retail store with an abutting parking lot. The court reasoned that even a large single store is not the equivalent of a shopping center and that, therefore, the store's "interest in maintaining exclusive control over its private property is stronger than the interest of a shopping mall owner."[59] More recently, another California court ruled that a large supermarket did not invite the public for noncommercial purposes and could prevent the solicitation of signatures for initiative petitions on its premises.[60] Similarly, the Supreme Court of Washington curtailed the reach of free speech rights in shopping centers: reversing an earlier decision, the court declared that the state constitution does not

[53] *New Jersey Coalition*, 138 N.J. at 344–47, 650 A.2d at 767–68.

[54] 138 N.J. at 352–54, 650 A.2d at 770–71.

[55] 138 N.J. at 357–59, 650 A.2d at 772–73.

[56] *SHAD Alliance v. Smith Haven Mall*, 66 N.Y.2d 496, 488 N.E.2d 1211 (1985) (declaring that the decision of the California Supreme Court in *PruneYard* "is hardly persuasive authority").

[57] *Woodland v. Michigan Citizens Lobby*, 423 Mich. 188, 378 N.W.2d 337 (1985).

[58] See, e.g., *Cologne v. Westfarms Associates*, 192 Conn. 48, 469 A. 2d 1201 (1984); *State v. Wicklund*, 589 N.W.2d 793 (Minn. 1999).

[59] *Trader Joe's Company v. Progressive Campaigns, Inc.*, 73 Cal. App. 4th 425, 433; 86 Cal. Rptr. 2d 442 (1999).

[60] *Waremart, Inc. v. Progressive Campaigns, Inc.*, 85 Cal. App. 4th 679, 102 Cal. Rptr. 2d 392 (2000), *rev'd dismissed*, 119 Cal. Rptr. 2d 697, 45 P.3d 1161 (Cal. 2002).

afford a right to demonstrate or distribute literature at a mall.[61] Equally striking was the decision of the Supreme Court of Oregon in *Stranahan v. Fred Meyer, Inc.* (2000), holding that the state constitution did not confer a right to solicit signatures in a shopping center for a ballot initiative.[62] In reaching this result, the Oregon court reversed an earlier, contrary decision. The upshot of these developments is that, at the present, only California, Colorado, and New Jersey apparently recognize broad expressive rights in privately owned malls (and even California, as noted above, has begun paring back these rights).

V. Concerns of Mall Owners

Since most legal commentators have endorsed the view that courts should recognize free speech rights in shopping centers,[63] it is useful to consider the objections raised by mall owners to such activity. The owners present several practical and jurisprudential arguments: opening of shopping centers to groups advocating controversial political and social views creates burdens that private owners are ill equipped to handle; enforcement of time, place, and manner restrictions on free speech poses difficult questions and will likely involve owners in litigation; advocacy groups may well offend employees and shoppers, thereby directly hampering commercial activity; distribution of leaflets commonly results in litter that the owners must remove; increased security will be expensive, and the costs will ultimately be passed along to consumers; and in the present litigious climate, mall owners may be subject to tort claims if the exercise of free speech by advocacy groups results in altercations or personal injuries to patrons.

In addition, mall owners contend that their First Amendment rights are violated when they are compelled to furnish a forum for the views of others. There are two prongs to this argument. First, despite any disclaimers, shopping centers may be identified with the contested views of advocacy groups. Second, mall owners are, in effect, being forced to subsidize the expression of opinions with which they may disagree.[64]

There is support for the proposition that compelling a corporation to provide a forum for the views of others impairs the company's free speech rights. At issue in *Pacific Gas & Electric Company v. Public Utilities Com-*

[61] *Southcenter Joint Venture v. National Democratic Policy Committee,* 113 Wash. 2d 413, 780 P.2d 1282 (1989) (distinguishing and limiting *Alderwood Associates v. Washington Environmental Council,* 96 Wash. 2d 230, 635 P.2d 108 [1981]).

[62] 331 Or. 38, 11 P.3d 228 (2000).

[63] See, e.g., Curtis J. Berger, "*PruneYard* Revisited: Political Activity on Private Lands," *New York University Law Review* 66 (1991): 651–52 (declaring that "a state's interest in promoting political expression in . . . public places may . . . override the values associated with private ownership"); Jennifer Niles Coffin, "The United Mall of America: Free Speech, State Constitutions, and the Growing Fortress of Private Property," *University of Michigan Journal of Law Reform* 33 (2000): 615–49.

[64] Epstein, "Takings, Exclusivity, and Speech," *supra* note 46, at 50–52.

mission of California (1986) was a state commission's order directing a utility company to include messages in its billing envelopes from a consumer group that differed with the utility's attitude toward regulatory policy.[65] Justice Lewis Powell, writing for a plurality of the Supreme Court, determined that the order abridged the utility's rights under the First Amendment. He insisted that a private party cannot be forced to spread a message with which it disagrees. "That kind of forced response," Powell wrote, "is antithetical to the free discussion that the First Amendment seeks to foster."[66] Not only was there a danger that compelled access might cause the company to change its own message, but also, he pointed out, the company was being required to use its property to spread someone else's views. Hence, the order impermissibly burdened the expression of the utility's views. Although Powell sought to distinguish *PruneYard*,[67] mall owners might well object to the content of speeches and pamphlets on their land.[68] It would seem that the same rules should apply. Indeed, legal scholar Richard Epstein has asserted: "Covert subsidies, such as those involved in *PruneYard*, are an enemy to freedom of speech every bit as much as explicit taxes or oppressive regulations."[69] It is as offensive to commandeer my property as to compel a financial contribution from me to advance opinions that I do not share.

An allied issue is presented by recent litigation over the constitutionality of Interest on Lawyers' Trust Account (IOLTA) programs adopted by most state supreme courts. Lawyers' trust accounts are used for the temporary deposit of clients' funds, and state courts have appropriated the interest on these accounts to pay for legal services for indigents, a practice that has been challenged. Much of the debate has centered on whether the clients of attorneys have a property interest in IOLTA income, and whether such schemes amount to a taking of this property in violation of the Fifth Amendment.[70] But it has also been argued that the use of IOLTA revenue

[65] 475 U.S. 1 (1986).

[66] *Id.* at 16. See also *Wooley v. Maynard*, 430 U.S. 705 (1977) (state cannot compel individual to disseminate a message on automobile license he finds objectionable); *Keller v. State Bar of California*, 496 U.S. 1 (1990) (use of compulsory dues by state bar association to finance political activities with which some members disagree violated their First Amendment rights); *Michigan Park Producers Ass'n v. Veneman*, 348 F.3d 157 (6th Cir. 2003) (mandatory assessment on pork producers to fund promotion of pork violates First Amendment guarantee against compelled speech).

[67] *Pacific Gas*, 475 U.S. at 12. Dissenting, Justice Rehnquist maintained that the right of access in this case was indistinguishable from *PruneYard*. *Id.* at 26.

[68] See generally *Waremart, Inc. v. Progressive Campaigns, Inc.*, 139 Wash. 2d 623, 641, 989 P.2d 524, 533 (1999) (noting but not addressing store's "contentions that forcing it to allow Progressive to solicit signatures for an initiative on its private property would violate its First Amendment rights").

[69] Epstein, "Takings, Exclusivity and Speech," *supra* note 46, at 52.

[70] *Phillips v. Washington Legal Foundation*, 524 U.S. 156 (1998) (holding that the interest generated by funds in IOLTA accounts is the property of the owner of the principal on deposit); *Brown v. Legal Foundation of Washington*, 123 S. Ct. 1406 (2003) (assuming that interest on IOLTA accounts represented private property ultimately taken for public use, but concluding that owners suffered no pecuniary loss and were therefore not entitled to compensation under the Fifth Amendment).

to fund controversial advocacy by legal aid attorneys violates the First Amendment rights of IOLTA clients. Complainants allege that they are being forced to support speech that they find objectionable.[71]

VI. Accommodation of Rights

Compelling policy considerations as well as the decided weight of judicial authority make clear that, under most circumstances, shopping center owners should retain the right to prevent the exercise of expressive activity by visitors on their premises. Such a conclusion, of course, is simply a reaffirmation of the traditional doctrine that the right to exclude is a fundamental aspect of the constitutional right to own and enjoy private property.

The Constitution and Bill of Rights, however, seek to safeguard a number of fundamental values. Neither the rights of property owners nor any other constitutional rights can be enjoyed without any restraint. Competing interests must sometimes be reconciled. Therefore, despite the importance of the right to exclude, I would contend that in a few situations the societal interest in fostering free speech outweighs the right of private property owners to maintain control of their premises. As discussed below, these exceptions are unlikely to apply to shopping centers.

A. *Viewpoint discrimination*

Property owners who invite the public to enter their premises must have and enforce a consistent policy. They should not be able to differentiate between persons seeking access to speak or distribute literature based on their political or social views. In this connection, it is noteworthy that courts upholding a mall owner's right to exclude have frequently emphasized that the owner was applying an evenhanded policy.[72] Viewpoint discrimination would raise the specter of private censorship, and courts might well be less willing to vindicate the right to exclude under these circumstances.[73] For example, an owner should not be able to per-

[71] *Washington Legal Foundation v. Texas Equal Access to Justice Foundation*, 94 F.3d 996, 999 (5th Cir. 1996).

[72] *Woodland v. Michigan Citizens Lobby*, 423 Mich. 188, 194; 378 N.W.2d 337, 339 (1985) (observing that mall "maintains a strict written trespass policy prohibiting any activity in the shopping center that is not directly related to the enhancement of commercial retail sales"); *SHAD Alliance v. Smith Haven Mall*, 66 N.Y.2d 496, 498; 488 N.E.2d 1211, 1212 (1985) (mall "has consistently and nondiscriminatorily prohibited all leafletting, and all types of political activities or gatherings"); *Charleston Joint Venture v. McPherson*, 308 S.C. 145, 151; 417 S.E.2d 544, 548 (1992) (mall policy was "to exclude any type of overtly political or religious activity, and all forms of solicitation and handbilling").

[73] See *Laguna Publishing Company v. Golden Rain Foundation*, 131 Cal. App. 3d 816, 182 Cal. Rptr. 813 (1982) (private residential community required "to act fairly and without discrimination toward others in the exercise of their state constitutional rights of free speech and free press"). See also *Guttenberg Taxpayers and Rentpayers Association v. Galaxy Towers Condominium Association*, 297 N.J. Super. 404, 688 A.2d 156 (1996) (condominium association that

mit pro-life groups to exercise expressive rights while excluding pro-choice groups. As a practical matter, shopping center owners would almost surely decide to exclude all speech-related activity by visitors.

A mall owner, however, does not forfeit his or her own right of free speech. People are entitled to use their own resources to advance their views. The exercise of this right by mall owners (for example, by posting a sign) should not impair the ability of owners to exclude others who wish to engage in expressive activities so long as this is done on a non-discriminatory basis. In contrast, the owner of a private home would be under no such limitation. Homes are not typically open to the general public. Not only can homeowners express their personal views on any topic, but they are free to encourage the expression of some opinions while excluding persons who seek to express contrary views. In other words, homeowners should be under no obligation to be evenhanded in allowing others to engage in expressive activity on their premises.

B. *Isolated groups*

Where a group is isolated, on someone else's property, from the larger community and from the usual means of communication, it may be appropriate for courts to breach the owner's dominion. Thus, the New Jersey Supreme Court ruled that representatives of governmental and welfare agencies had a limited right to enter a farm in order to offer services to migrant farmers.[74] This result could be analogized to the common law doctrine of necessity, which justified entries onto an owner's land to deal with unusual circumstances, such as stopping the spread of fire, preventing crime, or saving lives. Public officials are also entitled to enter private land to perform their duties.[75] But such narrow privileges to intrude upon private land would seem inapplicable to shopping centers. The middle class patrons of malls are neither isolated from their communities nor cut off from other means of communication.

C. *Adequate alternative forums*

Courts should be especially reluctant to override an owner's right to exclude where there are adequate alternative avenues of communication. Often, of course, public streets and parks are available for expressive activity. Moreover, in the age of the telephone and the Internet, other

---

endorsed local political candidates became "in essence a political 'company town'" and could not bar distribution of campaign literature by other candidates).

[74] *State v. Shack*, 58 N.J. 297, 277 A.2d 369 (1971) (decided on the basis of state property law and not addressing a First Amendment claim).

[75] A. James Casner, ed., *American Law of Property: A Treatise on the Law of Property in the United States*, vol. 6A, § 28.10 (Boston, MA: Little, Brown and Company, 1954), 31–34; and David A. Thomas, ed., *Thompson on Real Property* (Charlottesville, VA: Michie Company, 1994), 205.

means of disseminating a message are widely available. The mere fact that it might be convenient for groups to engage in speech-related activity on private property does not justify ignoring the constitutional rights of owners.[76]

VII. Other Access Issues

Although most of the litigation and commentary has focused on free speech in shopping centers, similar issues have been presented with respect to other privately owned facilities. Even state courts that have upheld expressive activities in malls have confined application of the public forum doctrine to property open to the general public. Absent such a public character, courts have allowed landowners to ban the exercise of speech rights. For example, in *Golden Gateway Center v. Golden Gateway Tenants Association* (2001), a divided Supreme Court of California ruled that an apartment complex was not the functional equivalent of a traditional public forum.[77] It followed that the apartment complex could halt the distribution of leaflets within the building by a tenants' association without a specific tenant request. Moreover, in another California case, a medical center was deemed private in character rather than a public forum.[78]

A new challenge to the exercise of free speech rights was posed by the growth of private residential communities during the late twentieth century.[79] Such communities commonly collect fees and provide a variety of services, including road maintenance, landscaping, garbage collection, and recreational facilities. Access to these communities is typically restricted to residents and guests, and this policy is sometimes policed by private guards. Residential community associations also enforce comprehensive land use regulations in the form of 'real covenants', which are contractual arrangements that attach to the land and bind future owners' land. Indeed, these associations have assumed many of the functions traditionally associated with local government. A primary motivation to

[76] An instructive case in this regard is *Lechmere, Inc. v. National Labor Relations Board*, 502 U.S. 527 (1992), which held that an employer did not commit an unfair labor practice by barring nonemployee union organizers from its property. The Supreme Court reasoned that the employees were accessible to union contact by signs, mailings, phone calls, and picketing. It concluded that an employer need not accommodate nonemployee union organizers on its property unless the employees are isolated from the ordinary flow of information.

[77] 26 Cal. 4th 1013, 29 P.3d 797 (2001) (the majority opinion also noted considerable criticism of the *PruneYard* decision and indicated some doubt whether the same result would be reached if the issue were being presented for the first time).

[78] See, e.g., *Allred v. Harris*, 14 Cal. App. 4th 1386, 18 Cal. Rptr. 2d 530 (1993).

[79] See generally Sheryll D. Cashin, "Privatized Communities and the 'Secession of the Successful': Democracy and Fairness Beyond the Gate," *Fordham Urban Law Journal* 28 (2001): 1675–92; and Paula A. Franzese, "Does It Take A Village? Privatization, Patterns of Restrictiveness and the Demise of Community," *Villanova Law Review* 47 (2002): 553–93.

join a residential community is the desire for enhanced privacy and security.

The covenant regimes of these privatized communities regulate a wide range of behavior by residents, and many of the restrictions implicate First Amendment freedoms. For example, these communities may regulate the posting of signs, curtail public assembly on community streets, and ban the unsolicited distribution of newspapers.[80] Homeowners have objected to covenants that prohibit them from displaying American flags, and as a result, a number of states have enacted legislation that bans such prohibitions.[81] In addition, dominion over the streets allows residential communities to prevent their use for speech-related activities by nonresidents.[82]

At first glance, residential community associations seem close to the type of company town treated as a public forum in *Marsh*. Yet there are significant differences. Unlike the company town in *Marsh*, residential communities do not contain a business district and their streets are not open to public use. Company towns typically contained employees highly dependent on the company for jobs, while modern residential communities cater to affluent individuals who have ready access to numerous expressive venues. Moreover, community residents are generally deemed to have consented to the covenant restrictions when they purchased a home in the community.[83] Nonetheless, one commentator has argued that privatization of local government threatens constitutional liberties and that residential associations should be viewed as state actors.[84] There is as yet little litigation testing the regulatory schemes in private resident communities. It seems likely, however, that the stage is set for another round of adjustments between the rights of property owners and the enjoyment of expressive rights.[85]

VIII. Conclusion

America's traditional constitutional strictures were designed to protect liberty by restricting the power of government. To this end, the rights of

[80] Steven Siegel, "The Constitution and Private Government: Toward the Recognition of Constitutional Rights in Private Residential Communities Fifty Years After *Marsh v. Alabama*," *William and Mary Bill of Rights Journal* 6 (1998): 469–71.

[81] See, e.g., Ariz. Rev. Stat. §§ 33-1261, 32-1804 (Supp. 2002); 2002 Fla. Laws ch. 2002-50; S.C. Code Ann. § 27-1-60 (Supp. 2002).

[82] Note, "Residential Associations As State Actors: Regulating the Impact of Gated Communities on Nonmembers," *Yale Law Journal* 105 (1995): 771–73.

[83] *Laguna Publishing Company v. Golden Rain Foundation*, 131 Cal. App. 3d 816, 836; 182 Cal. Rptr. 813, 824–25, (1982) (rejecting argument that private residential community should be likened to company town).

[84] Siegel, "The Constitution and Private Government," *supra* note 80, at 461–563; Note, "Residential Associations As State Actors," *supra* note 82, at 778–93.

[85] *Laguna Publishing Company*, 131 Cal. App. 3d at 839, 182 Cal. Rptr. at 826 (1982) (observing that "the gated and walled community is a new phenomenon on the social scene"). See also David L. Callies, Paula A. Franzese, Heidi Kai Guth, "*Ramapo* Looking Forward: Gated Communities, Covenants, and Concerns," *The Urban Lawyer* 35, no. 1 (2003): 192–94.

property owners and the right of free speech usually work in tandem. Clearly, the framers of the Constitution and Bill of Rights did not perceive a fundamental conflict between them. There is no artificial divide between speech and property, and both are essential to a free society. Moreover, as a practical matter, secure property rights make possible the meaningful communication of ideas. Some private resources are essential for robust political dialogue.

Admittedly, the existence of private property may in some situations influence and even curtail the exercise of expressive rights. The courts must necessarily police the tension that arises at the border between property and speech. But there is no constitutional warrant for mechanically preferring one set of rights over the other as the New Deal consensus preferred speech to property. Indeed, at a time when some on the political Left seem as disenchanted with free speech as the Old Left was with property rights,[86] it may be a propitious moment to rediscover the conservative libertarian tradition.

Law and History, Vanderbilt University

[86] McGinnis, "The Once and Future Property-Based Vision of the First Amendment," *supra* note 15, at 55–56; and Steven Shiffrin, "The Politics of the Mass Media and the Free Speech Principle," *Indiana Law Journal* 69 (1994): 689–92 (discussing criticism by liberal scholars of free speech as a bulwark for the powerful).

EXPRESSIVE ASSOCIATION AFTER *DALE*

By David E. Bernstein

I. Introduction

The right to join with other people to promote a particular outlook, known as the right of expressive association, is a necessary adjunct to the right of freedom of speech, which is protected by the First Amendment of the United States Constitution. Freedom of speech would be of little practical consequence if the government could suppress ideas by bluntly prohibiting individuals from gathering with others who share their perspective. Freedom of expression must consist of more than the right to talk to oneself.

Freedom of speech could also be more subtly eroded if the government could force organizations dedicated to promoting a particular perspective to accept as members individuals who have a conflicting perspective. Such members would immediately dilute an organization's message because their membership would confuse public perceptions of the organization. In the longer term, dissenting members forced upon an organization by the government could achieve sufficient power to change the organization's values. For example, if a gay rights organization in Mississippi could not control its membership, conservative Christian activists could join and ultimately take over the organization. Conversely, if a conservative Christian organization in San Francisco, California, were banned from discriminating in selecting members, the organization would be at risk of a takeover by gay rights activists.

Concerns about the autonomy of private, nonprofit organizations recently led the U.S. Supreme Court to issue a rousing endorsement of the right of expressive association. In *Boy Scouts of America v. Dale* (2000),[1] the high Court found that because the Boy Scouts of America (BSA) as an organization promotes a belief in chastity outside of marriage, the BSA had a First Amendment expressive association right to exclude an openly homosexual adult volunteer. *Dale* is likely to prove to be one of the most important First Amendment cases of recent years because the Court enforced a broad right of expressive association against the competing claims of antidiscrimination laws.

The Supreme Court first articulated the right of expressive association in the course of protecting civil rights activists from racist state governments in the South in the late 1950s and early 1960s. For the next two

[1] 530 U.S. 640 (2000).

decades, the right to expressive association languished in relative obscurity as few relevant cases were decided. Renewed controversy over constitutional protection of expressive association arose in the 1980s, when private associations claimed the right to discriminate in membership when such discrimination would aid the associations in pursuing their goals.

The Supreme Court seemed aghast that the expressive association right, with its origins in the civil rights struggle, had been embraced by those who sought to use it as a shield against antidiscrimination laws. In a series of opinions during the mid to late 1980s, the Court both narrowly defined the circumstances in which expressive association rights are impinged and suggested that antidiscrimination laws are always "compelling government interests" sufficient to override these rights. Expressive association rights had become a virtual nullity, at least in cases involving competing antidiscrimination claims.

The tide began to turn in 1995 with a significant, if somewhat ambiguous, ruling in *Hurley v. Irish-American Gay, Lesbian and Bisexual Group of Boston*, and in 2000 *Dale* dramatically revived the right of expressive association. The Court found that the Boy Scouts had an expressive association right to exclude gay scoutmasters even though the Scouts' anti-homosexual activity policy was neither well publicized nor central to its mission. Moreover, the Court rejected New Jersey's claim that its law, which prohibited sexual-orientation discrimination in places of public accommodation, justifiably applied to the Boy Scouts because of the state's compelling interest in eradicating discrimination against homosexuals.

This essay examines the right of expressive association and the consequences of its reinvigoration by the Supreme Court in *Dale*. Section II recounts the ups and downs of the right, from its inception in civil rights cases almost fifty years ago, to its low ebb following the Court's 1984 decision in *Roberts v. United States Jaycees*,[2] to its reinvigoration in *Dale*. Section III discusses reactions to *Dale* and concludes that after *Dale* expressive association rights will receive vigorous, but not unlimited, protection. Section IV examines post-*Dale* lower court decisions that implicitly interpret *Dale* as adopting a broad-based expressive association right fully applicable to a variety of situations. Finally, Section V looks at some of the untapped potential uses of the right of expressive association.

II. The Rise and (Temporary) Fall of the Right of Expressive Association

The significance of *Dale's* broad protection of the right of expressive association is apparent when one considers the earlier trend established by the Court's previous decisions in this area. Pre-*Dale* decisions reflected an ebb and flow that saw the right develop from a powerful

[2] 468 U.S. 609 (1984).

shield for civil rights organizations to a neglected weak sibling of the First Amendment.

A. Origins of the right to expressive association

The first explicit recognition of the right of expressive association by the Supreme Court came in the 1950s, when the civil rights movement in the South was gathering steam. In *NAACP v. Alabama* ex rel. *Patterson,*[3] the question before the Court was whether the State of Alabama—a state that rigorously enforced discriminatory laws against African Americans—could compel the Alabama branch of the National Association for the Advancement of Colored People (NAACP), the leading civil rights organization in the state, to reveal to the state attorney general the names and addresses of its members. The state planned to turn these names over to local "White Citizens' Councils." The state expected that the councils would use the information to help squelch the growing civil rights movement by harassing NAACP members. Here we see an example of how expressive association rights are necessary for the exercise of free speech rights: African Americans in the South never could have succeeded in promoting their pro-civil rights message to the American public if the Southern states had been permitted to use law to intimidate civil rights organizations like the NAACP.

The Court found that requiring the NAACP to turn over its membership lists illicitly infringed on NAACP members' right to expressive association. In discussing the right of expressive association, the Court stated that "[i]t is beyond debate that freedom to engage in association for the advancement of beliefs and ideas is an inseparable aspect of the 'liberty' assured by the Due Process Clause of the Fourteenth Amendment, which embraces freedom of speech."[4] The Court added that it was "immaterial whether the beliefs sought to be advanced by association pertain to political, economic, religious or cultural matters"; rather, regulation that might have the effect of burdening freedom of expressive association would receive "the closest scrutiny."[5] Given the relatively minor benefit of disclosure to the state's asserted interest of determining whether the NAACP was engaged in technical violations of state law, the Court determined that Alabama had failed to show a compelling interest sufficient to overcome the "deterrent effect on the free enjoyment of the right to associate" that compelled disclosure was likely to have.[6]

Following *Patterson,* the Court decided several other expressive association cases pitting the associational rights of the NAACP and its mem-

[3] 357 U.S. 449 (1958).
[4] *Id.* at 460.
[5] *Id.* at 460-61.
[6] *Id.* at 462-66.

bers against the obstructionist policies of state governments in the South.[7] In each of these cases, the Court applied strict scrutiny to the asserted state interest involved and resolved the cases in favor of associational rights.[8] Strict scrutiny, also known as the 'compelling interest test', is the highest level of scrutiny the Court gives to regulations, requiring that to pass constitutional muster a regulation must be narrowly tailored to achieve a compelling governmental interest.

While the Court strictly protected expressive association rights in cases involving racial discrimination, similar assertions of expressive association rights by the Communist Party were less well received. In two cases during the late 1950s and early 1960s, the Court found that national security concerns overrode the Communist Party's freedom of association rights and, thus, upheld legislation requiring the party to relinquish its membership lists.[9] The only case involving Communism from this era in which the Court sided with expressive association also involved racial discrimination: in *Gibson v. Florida Legislative Investigation Committee* (1963),[10] a committee of the Florida Legislature attempted to gain access to the membership list of the Miami branch of the NAACP for the stated purpose of investigating whether its members were involved with the Communist Party. The Court found that there was no evidence of any substantial relationship between the NAACP and Communist activities and, therefore, there was no compelling state interest in acquiring the NAACP's membership records.[11]

B. *A shift in focus brings a shift in application*

Expressive association cases largely died out for a time after the civil rights movement achieved its major legislative goals in the 1960s, rendering moot attempts by state governments to stifle the movement, and with the end of the "Red Scare" of the 1950s. Ironically, the civil rights movement's legislative triumphs also sowed the seeds for new litigation over expressive association. Following the federal government's lead, states began either to pass new laws or to enforce old laws guaranteeing African Americans and other beneficiaries of the civil rights movement equal access to "places of public accommodation." When these laws were passed, legislatures had in mind restaurants, hotels, theaters, and other public spaces. Some state courts gradually expanded their interpretations

[7] *See*: *Bates v. City of Little Rock*, 361 U.S. 516, 523–27 (1960)(requirement forcing NAACP to disclose membership lists violated freedom of expressive association); *NAACP v. Alabama* ex rel. *Flowers*, 377 U.S. 288, 307–10 (1964)(order enjoining NAACP from conducting business violated freedom of expressive association); see generally *NAACP v. Button*, 371 U.S. 415 (1963).

[8] *See*: *Bates*, 361 U.S. at 527; *Flowers*, 377 U.S. at 308–10; *Button*, 371 U.S. at 428–29.

[9] *Uphaus v. Wyman*, 360 U.S. 72, 77–81 (1959); *Communist Party of the United States v. Subversive Activities Control Bd.*, 367 U.S. 1, 90–104 (1961).

[10] 372 U.S. 539 (1963).

[11] *Id.* at 555–57.

of public accommodations laws so that they covered private membership organizations, even those with no permanent meeting places. The phrase "places of public accommodation" was stretched to include the membership policies of these organizations, despite the obvious semantic problem with fitting that particular square peg into that particular round hole. State courts that applied public accommodations laws to membership organizations held that their membership policies could not discriminate against protected groups. Thus, a new class of expressive association litigants was born: membership organizations raising the right of expressive association as a defense against antidiscrimination laws.

Roberts v. United States Jaycees (1984)[12] involved the assertion of the right to expressive association by a membership organization that sought exemption from a state public accommodations law prohibiting discrimination on the basis of sex. At the time, the United States Jaycees admitted only men between the ages of eighteen and thirty-five as full members, although it allowed women to be associate members with no voting or office-holding rights.[13] In 1974 and 1975, two Minnesota chapters of the organization began admitting women as full members. The Jaycees' national organization imposed sanctions against the chapters for this violation of membership rules and began proceedings to revoke their charters.[14]

The chapters then filed a complaint with the Minnesota Department of Human Rights, contending that the Jaycees' membership rules violated Minnesota's law banning discrimination in public accommodations.[15] The national Jaycees sought relief from the enforcement of the law in federal court, arguing that "application of the [law] would violate the male members' constitutional rights of free speech and association."[16] The Jaycees noted that their charter called for the organization to "promote the interests of young men," a presumptively easier task for an organization with an all-male membership than for a mixed-sex organization.

The national Jaycees lost at the district court level, but won on appeal before the Eighth Circuit Court of Appeals.[17] The Eighth Circuit held that the national Jaycees had a right to associate as the means to achieve their expressive ends, including the advancement of the interests of young men, and that allowing women as full members would directly burden that right.[18] The Eighth Circuit also found that Minnesota's asserted com-

[12] 468 U.S. 609 (1984).

[13] *Id.* at 612-13.

[14] *Id.* at 614.

[15] *Id.* at 614-15. The law in question prohibited the denial to "any person the full and equal enjoyment of the goods, services, facilities, privileges, advantages, and accommodations of a place of public accommodation because of race, color, creed, religion, disability, national origin or sex." Minn. Stat. § 363.03(3) (1982).

[16] 468 U.S. at 615.

[17] *See*: *United States Jaycees v. McClure*, 534 F. Supp. 766 (D. Minn. 1982); *United States Jaycees v. McClure*, 709 F.2d 1560 (8th Cir. 1983).

[18] *United States Jaycees v. McClure*, 709 F.2d at 1566-72.

pelling interest, the prevention of discrimination in places of public accommodation on the basis of sex, was not sufficiently compelling to overcome the national Jaycees' right to expressive association.[19]

Minnesota appealed, and in its *Roberts* decision the U.S. Supreme Court reversed the Eighth Circuit's ruling. Justice William Brennan wrote the opinion for the Court, joined by four of his colleagues. Justice Sandra Day O'Connor and Justice William Rehnquist concurred in the judgment, while Chief Justice Warren Burger and Justice Harry Blackmun did not participate. Justice Brennan's opinion, while acknowledging a broad right to expressive association and recognizing that the central purpose of the national Jaycees was the promotion of the interests of young men, held that forcing the organization to admit women as full members would not infringe the national Jaycees' right to expressive association.[20] He stated that there was no evidence that the admission of women would substantially impair the organization's promotion of the interests of young men, and that without further evidence he would "decline to indulge in the sexual stereotyping that underlies appellee's contention that, by allowing women to vote, application of the Minnesota Act will change the content or impact of the organization's speech."[21]

Justice Brennan added that even if Minnesota's public accommodations law did impinge on expressive association, and the Court therefore had to apply strict scrutiny, the law served Minnesota's compelling interest in eliminating discrimination and ensuring its citizens equal access to publicly available goods and services. Moreover, the law was narrowly tailored because it abridged the national Jaycees' expressive association rights only incidentally and insofar as it was necessary to accomplish the act's purpose.[22] Brennan also suggested that discriminatory practices were analogous to "violence or other types of potentially expressive activities that produce special harms distinct from their communicative impact" and that such activities were "entitled to no constitutional protection."[23]

Justice Brennan's opinion in *Roberts* is significant in two respects. First, he tendentiously interpreted the facts to find that expressive association rights were not impinged. His assertion that it is merely stereotypical thinking to assume that women as a group are less inclined than young men as a group to desire to promote the interests of young men seems almost risible.[24] Second, and even more significant, Brennan characterized the Jaycees' discriminatory practices as akin to violence and not

[19] *Id.* at 1572-76.

[20] *Roberts v. United States Jaycees*, 468 U.S. at 622-28.

[21] *Id.* at 627-28.

[22] *Id.* at 623-26, 628-29.

[23] *Id.* at 628.

[24] For criticisms of this part of the *Roberts* opinion, see David E. Bernstein, "Antidiscrimination Laws and the First Amendment," *Missouri Law Review* 66 (2001): 97-98 (hereinafter, Bernstein, "Antidiscrimination"); Neal E. Devins, "The Trouble with *Jaycees*," *Catholic University Law Review* 34 (1985): 913-14; Douglas O. Linder, "Freedom of Association After *Roberts v. United States Jaycees*," *Michigan Law Review* 82 (1984): 1892.

worthy of constitutional protection, and therefore gave the right of expressive association short shrift in his compelling interest analysis. In adopting this argument, the Court sent the message that expressive association was far less important than other First Amendment rights.[25]

Justice O'Connor's concurring opinion in *Roberts* was far narrower. She recognized that an association's right to define its membership is an important part of the right of expressive association. She nevertheless concluded that the Jaycees were not entitled to claim the right because they were primarily a "commercial" association—providing networking contacts to young businesspeople—rather than a primarily expressive one.[26]

After the *Roberts* opinion, the Court rejected two other expressive association challenges to public accommodations laws and, in doing so, reinforced the idea that the right to expressive association was a weak constitutional right at best.[27] In *Board of Directors of Rotary International v. Rotary Club of Duarte* (1987), the Court held that Rotary International, a membership organization, could not revoke the membership of a local Rotary Club that admitted two female members in violation of Rotary International's policy. As in *Roberts*, in *Duarte* the Court argued that requiring the admission of female members would not hinder the advancement of the club's purposes.[28] The Court also applied the same lax version of strict scrutiny it had adverted to in *Roberts*, finding that any infringement on the right to expressive association was justified by the State's compelling interest in eliminating discrimination against women.[29]

Similarly, in *New York State Club Association v. City of New York* (1988), the Court brushed aside a challenge by a consortium of New York private clubs and associations to the application of the antidiscrimination provision of the New York City Human Rights Law. While acknowledging the existence of a right to expressive association, the Court stated that the New York law at issue did not on its face "affect 'in any significant way' the ability of individuals to form associations that will advocate public or private viewpoints."[30]

[25] *See* David E. Bernstein, "The Right of Expressive Association and Private Universities Racial Preferences and Speech Codes," *William and Mary Bill of Rights Journal* 9 (2001): 623 (arguing that the *Roberts* decision sent a message that expressive association rights were not to be taken seriously).

[26] *Roberts*, 468 U.S. at 633–40 (O'Connor, J., concurring).

[27] *See*: *Bd. of Dirs. of Rotary Int'l v. Rotary Club of Duarte*, 481 U.S. 537 (1987); *New York State Club Ass'n v. City of New York*, 487 U.S. 1 (1988).

[28] *Duarte*, 481 U.S. at 548. In fact, the Court stated that the admission of women would promote Rotary International's goals of providing humanitarian service, encouraging high ethical standards, and ensuring that Rotary clubs represented a cross section of their communities. *Id.* at 548–49.

[29] *Id.* at 549. In all, the Court's entire discussion of both the effect of the admission of women on the ability of the organization to promote its goals and the compelling interest test consists of only three paragraphs. *See id.* at 548–49.

[30] *New York State Club Ass'n*, 487 U.S. at 13 (quoting *Duarte*, 481 U.S. at 548). In rejecting the plaintiffs' challenge, the Court did note that "if a club seeks to exclude individuals who do not share the views that the club members wish to promote," then different issues would arise, perhaps leading to a different result. *Id.* at 13.

The Court's apparent disdain for expressive association claims had a marked effect on lower courts. Following Justice Brennan's opinion in *Roberts*, lower federal courts and state supreme courts routinely held that the right of expressive association had to yield to antidiscrimination statutes.[31]

C. The tide begins to turn

From the mid 1980s to 1995, protection of the right of expressive association was at a low ebb, with courts generally refusing to enforce it in the face of conflicting antidiscrimination legislation. However, the tide began to turn in favor of expressive association beginning with the 1995 Supreme Court opinion in *Hurley v. Irish-American Gay, Lesbian and Bisexual Group of Boston*.[32]

In *Hurley*, the Boston Irish-American Gay, Lesbian and Bisexual Group (GLIB) sought to require the organizers of Boston's annual St. Patrick's Day Parade to allow the organization to march under its own banner. GLIB argued that the privately sponsored parade was subject to Massachusetts' public accommodations law, which banned discrimination against homosexuals.[33] The organizers of the parade countered that the admission of GLIB to the parade under its own banner would violate the organizers' right to expressive association by forcing them to convey a sexual message.[34]

The trial court, following the *Roberts* methodology, found that any burden on the organizers' right to expressive association caused by allowing GLIB to march in the parade was merely "incidental."[35] Further, the trial court held that this incidental burden was justified by Massachusetts' interest in "eradicating discrimination."[36] The Massachusetts Supreme Court affirmed.[37]

[31] *See, e.g., Isbister v. Boys' Club of Santa Cruz, Inc.*, 707 P.2d 212 (Cal. 1985); *Quinnipiac Council, Boy Scouts of Am., Inc. v. Comm'n on Human Rights & Opportunities*, 528 A.2d 352 (Conn. 1987).

[32] 515 U.S. 557 (1995).

[33] See *id.* at 560–61. The public accommodations law prohibited, in pertinent part, "any distinction, discrimination or restriction on account of . . . sexual orientation . . . relative to the admission of any person to, or treatment in any place of public accommodation, resort or amusement." Mass. Gen. Laws § 272:98 (1992).

[34] *See*: *Hurley*, 515 U.S. at 563.

[35] *Id.* at 563.

[36] *Id.*

[37] *Irish-American Gay, Lesbian and Bisexual Group of Boston v. City of Boston*, 636 N.E. 2d 1293 (1994). Interestingly, in the interim between the decision of the Massachusetts Supreme Court and the United States Supreme Court's decision, a Massachusetts federal district court issued a declaratory judgment holding that the organizers of the parade had a right to exclude GLIB. *South Boston Allied War Veterans Council v. City of Boston*, 875 F. Supp. 891 (D. Mass. 1995). The federal district court distinguished *Roberts* and *Duarte*, finding that the Massachusetts public accommodations statute significantly burdened the organizers' right to expressive association, and that even if Massachusetts had a compelling interest in eradicating discrimination, this could not overcome that right. *Id.* at 915–17.

However, the U.S. Supreme Court reversed in a unanimous opinion written by Justice David Souter. The Court noted that the organizers of the parade disclaimed any interest in excluding homosexuals generally from the parade, but, rather, were seeking to bar GLIB from marching as its own parade unit under its own banner. The Court stated that "[s]ince every participating unit affects the message conveyed by the private organizers, the state courts' application of the statute produced an order essentially requiring petitioners to alter the expressive content of their parade."[38] Thus, according to the Court, the Massachusetts courts' application of the public accommodations statute had the effect of "declaring the sponsor's speech itself to be the public accommodation," which was contrary to the fundamental rule of the First Amendment that "a speaker has the autonomy to choose the content of his own message."[39]

The Court distinguished *Roberts*, as well as *New York State Club Association*, by noting that in those cases "compelled access to the benefit [provided by the organization] . . . did not trespass on the organization's message itself."[40] Here, according to the Court, even if the parade could be called a public accommodation, "GLIB could nonetheless be refused admission as [its own parade unit in the same manner that] a private club could exclude an applicant whose manifest views were at odds with a position taken by the club's existing members."[41] Interestingly, there was no mention of the compelling interest test.

The Court's decision in *Hurley* seemed to halt the trend away from protection of the right to expressive association, but its implications were somewhat ambiguous. The *Hurley* opinion was unclear as to whether its holding relied on the right to expressive association or on the right to free speech, and whether there was a meaningful distinction between these two rights. However, the Court's decision in *Dale* soon initiated a dramatic change in the legal status of the right to expressive association.

D. *Dale*: The right reinvigorated

The issue in *Dale* was whether the Boy Scouts of America could revoke the membership of an assistant scoutmaster due to his acknowledged (and publicly known) homosexuality. James Dale had become active in scouting at the age of eight and had continued his involvement through age eighteen, ultimately achieving the rank of Eagle Scout.[42] He applied for adult membership in the Boy Scouts and was approved for the position of assistant scoutmaster for a Boy Scout troop. In 1989, Dale left home to attend college, and there first acknowledged his homosexuality. While at college, he attained a leadership position in a campus group advocat-

[38] *Hurley*, 515 U.S. at 572–73.
[39] *Id.* at 573.
[40] *Id.* at 580.
[41] *Id.* at 580–81.
[42] *Dale*, 530 U.S. at 644.

ing homosexual interests.[43] In July 1990, a newspaper published an interview that it had conducted with Dale at a seminar addressing the psychological and health needs of homosexual teenagers. In the article, which was accompanied by Dale's photograph and identified his leadership position with the campus advocacy group, Dale spoke about his efforts to help meet "homosexual teenagers' need for gay role models."[44]

Following the publication of the article, Dale received a letter from the local scouting council revoking his membership on the basis that the "the Boy Scouts 'specifically forbid membership to homosexuals.'"[45] Dale filed a complaint against the BSA in state court, alleging that the revocation of his membership had violated New Jersey's public accommodations statute.[46]

The trial court granted summary judgment in favor of the BSA. The court held, among other things, that the BSA's position with regard to homosexuality was clear and that forcing the BSA to allow Dale to be an adult member and scout leader would violate the BSA's right to expressive association.[47] The New Jersey Superior Court of Appeals, however, reversed.[48] With regard to the right to expressive association, the Court of Appeals, in a very *Roberts*-like opinion, first determined that forcing the BSA to allow Dale as a member would not significantly affect the BSA's ability to express its views or carry out its interests.[49] The court then distinguished *Hurley*, determining that it had involved "pure forms of speech" rather than expressive association, and that *Hurley's* reference to expressive association was dicta.[50] The court also followed *Roberts's* lead by applying a weak version of strict scrutiny and concluding that any infringement was justified by New Jersey's compelling interest in eradicating discrimination.[51]

The New Jersey Supreme Court affirmed.[52] The court found that the forced inclusion of Dale as a member would not significantly affect the

[43] *Id.* at 644–45.

[44] *Id.* at 645.

[45] *Id.*

[46] *Id.* The New Jersey public accommodations law prohibited, inter alia, discrimination in privileges of any place of public accommodation due to sexual orientation. N.J. Stat. Ann. § 10:5-4 (West Supp. 2000).

[47] *Dale*, 530 U.S. at 645–46.

[48] *Dale v. Boy Scouts of Am.*, 706 A.2d 270 (N.J. Super. Ct. App. Div. 1998).

[49] *Id.* at 288. As a part of this analysis, the court expressed skepticism regarding whether the BSA's policy against homosexual members was, in fact, a public position taken by the organization. The court noted that, according to BSA rules and bylaws, the only membership requirements were age, gender, and willingness to adhere to the Scout Law and Scout Oath. The court also noted that, although the BSA had contended that its policy was that the requirements in the Scout Law and Oath that a scout be "morally straight" and "clean" prohibited homosexuality, the policy was of fairly recent vintage and had not been widely disseminated. *Id.* at 288–89.

[50] *Id.* at 291–92.

[51] *See id.* at 293.

[52] *Dale v. Boy Scouts of Am.*, 734 A.2d 1196 (N.J. 1999).

ability of the BSA to disseminate its message, because the BSA did not associate to promote the message that homosexuality is immoral.[53] The court invoked *Roberts* for the proposition that "[s]tate laws against discrimination may take precedence over the right of expressive association because 'acts of invidious discrimination in the distribution of publicly available goods, services, and other advantages cause unique evils that the government has a compelling interest to prevent.'"[54] Finally, the court determined that any infringement on the BSA's right to expressive association was justified by New Jersey's compelling interest in preventing discrimination.[55]

The opinions of the New Jersey Superior Court of Appeals and the New Jersey Supreme Court were consistent with the expressive association doctrine that the U.S. Supreme Court had developed in *Roberts* and its progeny. However, in *Dale,* the U.S. Supreme Court reversed the lower courts' holdings in a 5–4 opinion written by Chief Justice William Rehnquist, who had succeeded Chief Justice Burger in 1986.

In *Dale,* the Court started off by noting that in *Roberts, Duarte,* and *New York State Club Association* it had applied the compelling interest test to public accommodations laws that allegedly infringed on associational rights. The Court, however, then emphasized that "forced inclusion of an unwanted person in a group infringes on the group's freedom of expressive association if the presence of that person affects in a significant way the group's ability to advocate public or private viewpoints."[56] Then, in contrast to its rulings in the *Roberts* line of cases, in which the Court had independently evaluated whether the antidiscrimination laws in question truly infringed on the respective organizations' expressive activities, the majority opinion in *Dale* stated that "it is not the role of the courts to reject a group's expressed values because they disagree with those values or find them internally inconsistent."[57] The Court noted that the record contained evidence of the BSA's belief that homosexual conduct is not "morally straight," and declined further inquiry into the sincerity of that belief.[58]

In further contrast to the dismissive manner in which the Court in *Roberts* and its progeny had determined whether expressive association rights were impaired, the majority in *Dale* stated that deference should be given to an organization's view of what would impair its expression.[59] The Court concluded by analogizing the case to *Hurley*: "[T]he presence of Dale as an assistant scoutmaster would just as surely interfere with the

[53] *Id.* at 1225.
[54] *Id.* at 1223 (citing *Roberts,* 468 U.S. at 628).
[55] *Id.* at 1228.
[56] *Dale,* 530 U.S. at 647–48.
[57] *Id.* at 651.
[58] *Id.* at 651–52.
[59] *Id.* at 653.

Boy Scouts' choice not to propound a point of view contrary to its beliefs."[60] In determining that Dale's inclusion would significantly affect the BSA's right of expressive association, the Court rejected the New Jersey Supreme Court's finding that there was no significant impairment because the purpose of the BSA's association was not to disseminate the belief that homosexuality is immoral. The U.S. Supreme Court found that (1) associations do not have to associate for the purpose of disseminating a specific message to be entitled to First Amendment protection; (2) even if the BSA discourages leaders from disseminating views on sexual issues, this does not negate the sincerity of its belief that homosexuality is immoral; and (3) the First Amendment simply does not require that every member of a group agree on every issue in order for the group's policy to be "expressive association."[61]

The Court proceeded to apply the compelling interest test. The *Roberts* line of cases had suggested that the compelling interest test generally justified antidiscrimination laws challenged on expressive association grounds. In *Dale*, the Court gave the test short shrift, stating simply that "[t]he state interests embodied in New Jersey's public accommodations law do not justify such a severe intrusion on the Boy Scouts' rights to freedom of expressive association."[62] *Dale* left no doubt that the compelling interest test as used in *Roberts* and its progeny, through which a state's interest in eradicating discrimination trumped expressive association rights, had been repudiated. Even though *Dale* was a 5–4 decision, not even the dissenters argued for the use of the *Roberts*-style compelling interest test.[63] Rather, the dissenters argued that the BSA's anti-homosexual activity message was too vague, unpublicized, and irrelevant to the organization's core mission to warrant protection under the expressive association doctrine.

The majority opinion in *Dale* marks a substantial step toward the reinvigoration of expressive association and its recognition as a full-fledged First Amendment right. The right to expressive association had been treated by *Roberts* and its progeny as a second-class right, which could be infringed upon in most instances due to the narrow definition of an association's expressive interests and the lax nature of the compelling interest test that the Court used. *Dale*, in contrast, held that the expressive association right could be asserted by an organization even though the organization did not associate for the purpose of expressing the particular message in question, propounded that message only implicitly, and tolerated dissenting views. Moreover, under *Dale* the courts will no longer defer to a government's claim that its invasion of expressive association rights serves interests sufficiently compelling to justify its invasion, but will instead skeptically review such claims. This is quite a reversal from

[60] *Id.* at 654.
[61] *Id.* at 655–56.
[62] *Id.* at 659.
[63] *See id.* at 663–700 (Stevens, J., dissenting); *id.* at 700–2 (Souter, J., dissenting).

the *Roberts* legacy of deference toward government and skepticism toward groups asserting their right to expressive association.

III. Reaction to *Dale*

Reaction to *Dale* and its possible implications has been mixed, and ranges across a wide spectrum of constitutional philosophy. On one extreme is legal scholar Richard Epstein, who applauds the Court for its reinvigorated enforcement of the right to expressive association, yet argues that the Court's opinion did not go far enough, and that the Court should have recognized that the state has no interest in counteracting discrimination by private groups that lack monopoly power.[64] According to Epstein, *Dale's* reasoning should be extended to nonexpressive organizations, including for-profit businesses not organized for expressive purposes: if the First Amendment applies, as the *Dale* opinion suggests, to all situations where the organization merely engages in expressive activity that could be impaired, then "every organization engages in expressive activity when it projects itself to its own members and to the rest of the world."[65]

Epstein argues for a broad associational freedom, rather than a narrow test that attempts to apply the government's interest in antidiscrimination legislation "to the literally thousands of organizations that engage in business, charitable, religious, or recreational endeavors, or some mixture thereof." Courts should recognize the unity between the common law rules that treat private property, freedom of contract, and freedom of speech as equals, and associational freedom should be seen as derivative from these rights. State regulation should only be exercised under traditional police power grounds, such as the prevention of monopolies.[66] Today, by contrast, property and contract rights are neglected by the courts relative to freedom of speech.

While Epstein argues that *Dale* did not go far enough, law professor Andrew Koppelman argues that the *Dale* opinion is "sheer lunacy."[67] Like Epstein, Koppelman agrees that under the Court's opinion in *Dale*, "[a]lmost any organization is eligible for the protection from antidiscrimination laws that the Court provides."[68] Koppelman contends that the Court's statement that an association need only engage in expressive

[64] See Richard A. Epstein, "The Constitutional Perils of Moderation: The Case of the Boy Scouts," *Southern California Law Review* 74 (2000): 120.

[65] *Id.* at 140.

[66] *Id.* at 139–42. Epstein recognizes that this approach would invalidate much of the Civil Rights Act, including Title VII, which bans certain categories of employment discrimination. However, he believes that his position would assist voluntary affirmative action, as well as other sex- and race-conscious decisions. *Id.* at 142

[67] Andrew Koppelman, "Signs of the Times: *Dale v. Boy Scouts of America* and the Changing Meaning of Nondiscrimination," *Cardozo Law Review* 23 (2002): 1819.

[68] *Id.* at 1821.

activity that could be impaired in order to receive protection, coupled with its statement that it will not question the association's statement of its expressive purpose and will defer to the association's view of what would impair that purpose, means that "an expressive association claim is available to any entity that wants to discriminate at any time for any purpose."[69]

Others scholars contend that *Dale's* impact will not be so dramatic. Law professor Dale Carpenter argues that *Dale* will not have "the revolutionary consequences" that either its "harshest critics," such as Koppelman, or "most libertarian cheerleaders," such as Epstein, predict.[70] He asserts that the crucial distinction the Court will make after *Dale* in the area of expressive association will be akin to the approach suggested by Justice O'Connor's concurrence in *Roberts*. The Court will provide *Dale's* heightened protection to organizations whose activities are primarily expressive, while other groups whose activities are primarily commercial will receive a minimal level of protection.[71] Carpenter contends that this distinction is also somewhat analogous to the Court's treatment of core political and commercial speech.[72] He also argues that this distinction is consistent with the results in both *Roberts* and *Dale* because the Jaycees is primarily a commercial organization, while the BSA is primarily expressive. Carpenter concludes that "there is little doubt that a majority of the Court is now following Justice O'Connor's approach in delineating associational freedom," even though *Dale* did not articulate this explicitly.[73]

Other scholars have suggested that *Dale* does not signal a complete repudiation of the *Roberts* standard, but is, rather, an anomaly generated by the parties involved: the venerable institution of the BSA on the one hand, and the homosexual minority with its tenuous social and legal status on the other.[74] In particular, commentators who hold this view argue that the Court's ruling would have been different in a case concerning race or sex discrimination.[75] Some attribute this difference to the Court's majority and its lack of sympathy for gay rights, suggesting that

[69] *Id.* at 1822.

[70] Dale Carpenter, "Expressive Association and Anti-Discrimination Law After *Dale*: A Tripartite Approach," *Minnesota Law Review* 85 (2001): 1516–17.

[71] *Id.* at 1571.

[72] *Id.* at 1568. Carpenter notes that content-based restrictions on core political speech are subject to strict scrutiny, while restrictions on commercial speech receive only intermediate scrutiny. *Id.*

[73] *Id.* at 1570. Carpenter advocates the addition of a category for "quasi-expressive" associations, which mix a significant degree of expressive and commercial activity, and would be granted protection consistent with the nature of the internal operation sought to be brought into compliance with the antidiscrimination law. *Id.* at 1576–77.

[74] *See* Erwin Chemerinsky and Catherine Fisk, "Perspectives on Constitutional Exemptions to Civil Rights Law: *Boys Scouts of America v. Dale*," *William and Mary Bill of Rights Journal* 9 (2001): 616–17; Darren Lenard Hutchinson, " 'Closet Case': *Boy Scouts of America v. Dale* and the Reinforcement of Gay, Lesbian, Bisexual, and Transgender Invisibility," *Tulane Law Review* 76 (2001): 106–20; Arthur S. Leonard, "*Boy Scouts of America v. Dale*: The 'Gay Rights Activist' as Constitutional Pariah," *Stanford Law and Policy Review* 12 (2001): 32.

[75] Chemerinsky & Fisk, *supra* note 74, at 617.

the Court believes that eradicating discrimination against African Americans or women, but not gays, is a compelling government interest.

Others have suggested that the source of the distinction in expressive association cases between those that involved gays and those that did not is the Court's Fourteenth Amendment equal protection jurisprudence. For equal protection purposes, the Court engages in strict scrutiny of laws that classify by race (requiring that the classification at issue be narrowly tailored to achieve a compelling government interest), intermediate scrutiny of laws that classify by sex (requiring that the classification serve important government interests and be substantially related to the achievement of that goal), and rational basis scrutiny of laws that classify by sexual orientation (requiring merely that a classification be rationally related to a legitimate state interest and rest on grounds not wholly irrelevant to the achievement of the state's objective). Antidiscrimination laws will be protected from expressive association claims under the compelling interest test based on the degree of protection that the group facing discrimination receives under equal protection doctrine. It should be noted that scholars who hold such views are speculating, and nothing in *Dale* suggests that race discrimination cases would get treated differently than sexual orientation discrimination cases. Quite the contrary, the Court wrote that "public or judicial disapproval of a tenet of an organization's expression does not justify the State's effort to compel the organization to accept members where such acceptance would derogate from the organization's expressive message."[76]

It seems likely that *Dale* does mark a turning point in the judicial treatment of the right of expressive association, regardless of which group is harmed by the discrimination at issue. In contrast to the limited and toothless right given lip service by the Court in *Roberts, Dale* establishes expressive association as a robust First Amendment right. I agree with Dale Carpenter that the right to expressive association is likely limited by the primarily expressive/primarily commercial dichotomy that Justice O'Connor enunciated in her concurrence in *Roberts*. Justice O'Connor's vote was necessary to secure the 5–4 majority in *Dale*, and *Dale*'s result is consistent with the application of the dichotomy in her *Roberts* concurrence, thus suggesting that *Dale* does not represent a change in her views. The defense of the right of expressive association is probably limited solely to nonprofit organizations, as it would be difficult to argue that a profit-making enterprise exists *primarily* for noncommercial purposes.

IV. Case Law Following *Dale*

The Supreme Court has not addressed the right of expressive association since *Dale*. However, the limited cases in the lower courts since *Dale* generally support the theory that *Dale* has ushered in a new era of broad

[76] *Dale,* 530 U.S. at 661.

protection of the right to expressive association. In *White v. Lee* (2000), for example, the Ninth Circuit Court of Appeals relied in part on *Dale* in holding that the Department of Housing and Urban Development could not launch a civil rights investigation against homeowners who, for allegedly discriminatory reasons, organized opposition to a plan to turn a motel into a group home. The court cited *Dale* for the proposition that "[t]he right to expressive association includes the right to pursue, as a group, discriminatory policies that are antithetical to the concept of equality for all persons."[77]

In *Donaldson v. Farrakhan* (2002)[78] the Supreme Court of Massachusetts found that forcing a Nation of Islam mosque to admit a woman to a men-only religious meeting would significantly burden the organization's right of expressive association and was not justified by a compelling government interest. This decision belies the notion that *Dale*'s holding is applicable only to cases involving discrimination against homosexuals and that *Roberts*'s "forgiving" compelling interest test would otherwise apply. Had the Massachusetts Supreme Court relied on *Roberts* rather than *Dale*, the public accommodations statute would have prevailed as serving the compelling interest of eradicating discrimination against women.

Further evidence that the states'-style of inquiry is no longer viable after *Dale* was provided by the District of Columbia Court of Appeals in *Boy Scouts of America v. District of Columbia Commission on Human Rights* (2002).[79] This case, like *Dale*, involved the question of whether the BSA could deny membership to homosexuals. The D.C. Commission on Human Rights had found that the BSA could not claim an expressive association right to exclude homosexuals. The commission had tried to distinguish *Dale* by arguing that it had conducted its own detailed examination of the BSA's views with regard to homosexuality and concluded that the BSA did not truly express a position on the morality of homosexual relations.[80] On appeal by the BSA, the D.C. Court of Appeals rejected the commission's attempt to rely upon a *Roberts*-style detailed examination of the expressive position of the organization.[81] Instead, the court found *Dale* to be controlling and ruled in favor of the BSA.

There is, however, one case decided by the Third Circuit Court of Appeals that has some restrictive implications for the right of expressive association. In *Pi Lambda Phi Fraternity, Inc. v. University of Pittsburgh* (2000),[82] a fraternity that had been stripped of its status as a recognized student organization following a drug raid raised the right of expressive association in a lawsuit against the university. The Third Circuit Court of

[77] *White v. Lee*, 227 F.3d 1214, 1227 (9th Cir. 2000).

[78] 762 N.E.2d 835 (Mass. 2002).

[79] 809 A.2d 1192 (App. D.C. 2002).

[80] *Id.* at 1200.

[81] *Id.* at 1200–1. The court similarly refused to credit an attempt by the commission to show that, unlike the plaintiff in *Dale*, the two complainants in its case were not "gay activists." *Id.* at 1201–3.

[82] 229 F.3d 435 (3d Cir. 2000).

Appeals, not surprisingly, rejected the fraternity's claim.[83] However, as part of its analysis, the court determined that the fraternity was not engaged in expressive activity sufficient to qualify for First Amendment protection.[84] In reaching this conclusion, the court engaged in an extensive analysis of the fraternity chapter's activities, finding that it did nothing to perpetuate the purported associational ideals of the national fraternity.[85] Therefore, the court held that the chapter was not engaged in expressive activity.[86] The court added that even if the fraternity had been engaged in expressive activity, the university's conduct would not have significantly infringed upon it.[87]

Although the Third Circuit's ultimate conclusion that the university's actions did not infringe on the fraternity's right of expressive association is correct, the court's determination that the fraternity was not engaged in expressive activity is belied by *Dale*. First, like *Roberts* but unlike *Dale*, the court analyzed the validity of the organization's expressive beliefs while ignoring its stated expressive purpose. Second, the court employed a highly restrictive definition of expressive behavior, which equated the fraternal organization at issue with a for-profit dance club. Such a restrictive definition seems inconsistent with *Dale's* broad-based definition of expressive activity.[88] While ultimately unnecessary to its conclusion, the Third Circuit's analysis in *Pi Lambda Phi* serves notice that the specter of *Roberts* still haunts the area of expressive association.

V. The Future of Expressive Association

Although the newly reinvigorated right of expressive association has seen only limited use in the short time since the Supreme Court's decision in *Dale*, it has enormous potential to affect the law in a variety of areas. One of these areas concerns the expressive association of religious organizations. Prior to *Dale*, religious associations burdened by antidiscrimination laws that conflicted with their religious beliefs were forced to rely on the First Amendment's Free Exercise Clause.[89] These claims were rarely successful, and with the Supreme Court's ruling in *Employment Division v. Smith* (1990)[90]—that religious organizations had no right to be exempted from neutral, generally applicable laws that burden their free exercise of religion—even this small chance of success faded.

After *Dale*, however, a religious association confronted with an antidiscrimination law that requires it to act in a way that inhibits its ability to

[83] *Id.* at 447.
[84] *Id.* at 443–45.
[85] *Id.* at 444.
[86] *Id.*
[87] *Id.* at 445–47.
[88] See *Dale*, 530 U.S. at 649–50.
[89] *See, e.g.*, *Bob Jones Univ. v. United States*, 461 U.S. 574, 602 (1983).
[90] 494 U.S. 872 (1990).

promote its beliefs should be able to raise expressive association rights as a defense. For example, contrary to pre-*Dale* precedent, church-run schools have a right to fire unmarried teachers who become pregnant if sex outside of marriage is frowned on by their sponsoring church.[91] Justice Scalia's concurring opinion in *Good News Club v. Milford Central School* (2001),[92] arguing that a public school's exclusion of a Christian student club from the use of school facilities impinges on the right of expressive association, is an indication that religious organizations will be among the beneficiaries of *Dale*.

Universities will also be a primary beneficiary of the newly reinvigorated right of expressive association. The right of expressive association may be used to protect a private university's speech code against state statutes such as California's "Leonard Law," which requires private schools to follow First Amendment requirements in regulating speech. A private university could conceivably win an expressive association case if it can show that it is committed to creating a campus environment that is inclusive and welcoming to minority students, even at the expense of free speech on campus.[93] The First Amendment, which only restricts governmental activity, exists to protect pluralism from government attempts to impose orthodoxy, not to impose a free speech orthodoxy on private institutions. Protecting the expressive association rights of universities may decrease free speech on particular campuses, but increase social and ideological pluralism overall by allowing universities to choose their identities and to attract like-minded faculty and students based on those identities.

If forced to make an explicit choice, many universities would undoubtedly choose to promote themselves as free speech havens, as many already have. Yale University, for example, has volunteered that it will not punish any speech on campus if that speech would be protected against government action by the First Amendment. Other universities would establish themselves as institutions devoted to particular religious and social ideologies, as many implicitly or explicitly already have. As law professor Randall Kennedy suggests, the proper response to private sector experimentation with speech rules is to "let a thousand flowers bloom."[94] Freedom of speech and expressive association must include the right of private institutions to determine what speech they will and will not countenance.

[91] *Cf. Ganzy v. Allen Christian Sch.*, 995 F. Supp. 340, 348 (E.D.N.Y. 1998); *Vigars v. Valley Christian Ctr.*, 805 F. Supp. 802, 808 (N.D. Cal. 1992); *Dolter v. Wahlert High Sch.*, 483 F. Supp. 266, 271 (N.D. Iowa 1980).

[92] 533 U.S. 98 (2001).

[93] *See* Bernstein, "The Right of Expressive Association," *supra* note 25, at 640–41.

[94] Transcript of discussion in Gara LaMarche, ed., *Speech and Equality: Do We Really Have to Choose?* (New York: New York University Press, 1996), 75; see also Michael S. Greve, "The Libertarian Case for Speech Codes," *Reason*, July 1995; available online at http://reason.com/9507/GREVEcol.jul.shtml [accessed September 12, 2003].

The expressive association right to enact speech codes is only pertinent in the few jurisdictions, such as California, where speech codes at private universities are illegal. A broader potential use for the right of expressive association by universities nationwide would be to protect affirmative action—that is, racial preferences in admission—from laws banning discrimination in educational institutions. The U.S. Supreme Court recently held that such preferences are generally allowed,[95] but the decision was 5-4, with one of the justices in the majority, Sandra Day O'Connor, rumored to be ready to retire soon. Moreover, while the Court's opinion permitted preferences, it did ban some commonly practiced admissions tactics, including giving all African American applicants a blanket edge in admissions, regardless of individual circumstances.

The right of expressive association, however, may provide a defense to private universities that seek to avoid any present or future restrictions on affirmative action. Under *Dale,* universities could assert that they have a commitment to the promotion of racial diversity and assistance to disadvantaged minorities, and that the prohibition of racial preferences would significantly burden their expressive association right.[96]

This approach is not perfect. Asserting a First Amendment defense against Title VI of the 1964 Civil Rights Act, which prohibits any institution that receives federal assistance from discriminating on the basis of race, color, or national origin, may be unavailing in the face of the Court's decision in *Grove City College v. Bell* (1984).[97] This case involved Title IX of the Education Amendments of 1972, which prohibit educational institutions that receive federal funds from discriminating on the basis of sex, thus remedying the omission of sex in Title VI. In *Grove City,* the Court held that since the college's financial aid office received federal funds through student loans, the college could not claim a First Amendment right to refuse to comply with Title IX regulations promulgated by the Department of Education. The Court determined that the First Amendment rights of the college were not infringed because the college could avoid the impact of Title IX at any time by simply refusing the federal student loans.[98] In theory, a court might similarly hold that statutory restrictions on affirmative action do not violate the First Amendment for the same reason. However, as I have argued elsewhere, *Grove City* may not in fact be applicable, especially because the negative consequences for universities that disobey federal guidelines have grown dramatically since the Court decided that case.[99]

[95] *Grutter v. Bollinger,* 123 S. Ct. 2325 (2003).

[96] *See* Bernstein, "The Right of Expressive Association," *supra* note 25, at 634.

[97] 465 U.S. 555 (1984).

[98] *Id.* at 575–76.

[99] *See* David E. Bernstein, *You Can't Say That! The Growing Threat to Civil Liberties from Antidiscrimination Laws* (Washington, DC: Cato Institute Press, 2003). David E. Bernstein, "Sex Discrimination Laws Versus Civil Liberties," *University of Chicago Legal Forum* (1999): 152.

VI. Conclusion

The full magnitude of the change in the jurisprudence of the right of expressive association wrought by the Supreme Court's 2000 decision in *Dale* is still not clear. What is apparent, however, is that *Dale* failed to follow the *Roberts* line of cases and, instead, rejuvenated the right of expressive association. The right emerged from the decision in *Dale* as a robust shield for expressive associations against government attempts to directly or indirectly influence their ability to independently form and promote their messages. Further, while the lower court decisions are sparse and sometimes inconsistent, it appears that the Supreme Court's expansive definition of the right has application beyond the facts and circumstances in *Dale,* although the scope of that right is not as broad as some commentators have argued. Expressive association rights will limit the encroachment of antidiscrimination laws on the membership and employment policies of nonprofit associations, but will not provide a means for American businesses to evade these laws.

Much of the potential of the right of expressive association remains untapped. In particular, as interpreted by *Dale,* the right of expressive association has great possibilities for use by religious organizations and private universities faced with antidiscrimination laws that would interfere with their ability to promote their respective ideologies. Expressive association may also ultimately protect the affirmative action policies of private universities from government intrusion.

Law, George Mason University

AUTONOMY AND INFORMATIONAL PRIVACY, OR GOSSIP: THE CENTRAL MEANING OF THE FIRST AMENDMENT*

By C. Edwin Baker

"Gossip is no longer the resource of the idle and of the vicious, but has become a trade. . . ." [1]

Book dedication: "To Vito Russo, in gratitude for much good conversation and great gossip. . . ." [2]

"I find that when I am gossiping about my friends as well as my enemies I am deeply conscious of performing a social duty; but that when I hear they gossip viciously about me, I am rightfully filled with righteous indignation." [3]

I. Introduction

My thesis is simple. The right of informational privacy, the great modern achievement often attributed to the classic Samuel Warren and Louis Brandeis article, "The Right to Privacy" (1890),[4] asserts an individual's right not to have private personal information circulated. Warren and Brandeis claimed that individual dignity in a modern society requires that people be able to keep their private lives to themselves and proposed that the common law should be understood to protect this dignity by making dissemination of private information a tort. As broadly stated, this right not to have private information distributed directly conflicts with a broadly conceived freedom of speech and of the press. My claim is that, in cases of conflict, the law should reject the Warren and Brandeis innovation. Speech and press freedom should prevail; the privacy tort

* An earlier version of this essay was presented to Martha Nussbaum and David Strauss's Law and Philosophy Workshop at the University of Chicago Law School in 2000. I thank the participants in that workshop, fellow contributors to this volume, Michael Madow, Diane Zimmerman, and the editors of *Social Philosophy & Policy* for helpful comments, questions, and encouragement.

[1] Samuel Warren and Louis Brandeis, "The Right to Privacy," *Harvard Law Review* 4 (1890): 193–220.

[2] Larry Gross, *Contested Closets* (Minneapolis: University of Minnesota Press, 1993), dedication page.

[3] Max Gluckman, "Gossip and Scandal," *Current Anthropology* 4, no. 3 (1963): 307–16, at 315.

[4] Warren and Brandeis, *supra* note 1. This article has been described as "perhaps the most famous and certainly the most influential law review article ever written." Melville B. Nimmer, "The Right of Publicity," *Law and Contemporary Problems* 19 (1954): 202, 203.

should be ignored. This conclusion requires a normative argument concerning the appropriate basis and status of speech freedom that this essay will not really provide but for which I have argued elsewhere.[5] Here, instead, I will describe that theory of speech freedom, explore its implications for informational privacy, and finally suggest some reasons to think that rejection of the privacy tort should not be so troubling and is, in fact, pragmatically desirable.

The essay proceeds in the following way. Section II describes different possible informational privacy rights, identifying the one at stake in this essay. Section III describes two conceptions of autonomy, showing that both speech freedom and informational privacy serve the ultimately most important substantive conception, which is characterized as "meaningful" autonomy. Section III argues, however, that the right of free speech is better seen as based on the other, "formal" conception of autonomy, and that this grounding implies overriding the legal protection of informational privacy recommended by Warren and Brandeis. Thus, Section IV describes various ways that the law could treat informational privacy, but recommends treatment consistent with the formal right of free speech. Section V argues that protection of speech freedom leaves many ways of serving informational privacy fully available. Speech freedom turns out to be fully compatible with prohibiting possibly the most common and important ways in which informational privacy is invaded. This discussion should relieve some of the anticipated resistance to my thesis. Finally, Sections VI and VII offer two pragmatic reasons to find the thesis acceptable. Section VI argues that the popular appeal of privacy may be to some significant degree misguided. Section VII argues that speech that invades privacy—speech that I illustrate with gossip but that also includes other forms of individual expression as well as media invasions of privacy—serves valuable functions that help make the constitutional status of free speech appealing and explicable. Thus, Sections V, VI, and VII together should make more plausible both the thesis of this essay and the formal conception of autonomy on which I claim the right of free speech is based.

II. Informational Privacy

Informational privacy involves (some) limitation on inspection, observation, and knowledge by others. The appropriate legal response to claims for informational privacy depends, of course, on the more specific content of the claims. Among other possibilities, informational privacy could re-

[5] C. Edwin Baker, *Human Liberty and Freedom of Speech* (Oxford: Oxford University Press, 1989); C. Edwin Baker, "Harm, Liberty, and Free Speech," *Southern California Law Review* 70 (1997): 979.

fer to one, or some combination, of the following: (1) *inalienable private information,* that is, categories of information that are not permissibly exposed to or held by anyone other than the original holder or, in the case of joint holders, possibly resulting from joint participation in a private activity, by any nonintimate; (2) *control over initial disclosure* of information; as an almost necessary corollary, this right implies the availability of a range of meaningful contexts in which private information can be created, discovered, or used in ways that do not necessarily result in any disclosure; or (3) *control over further uses and dissemination* of (private) information after an initial disclosure, that is, a virtual property right in private information quite analogous to various intellectual property rights.[6] Thus, informational privacy could refer at least to the following: *information inalienability, disclosure control,* and *dissemination control.* Of course, none of these three conceptions need be absolute. Sympathy for, or legal recognition of, dissemination control, for example, could vary depending on the circumstances of the initial disclosure. Different conclusions might follow if the disclosure occurred only after an agreement of no further disclosure (e.g., after a private request and an agreement among friends not to repeat what was said, or after a journalist's promise to a confidential source),[7] or only as a result of legal compulsion (e.g., information found through trial discovery).[8] Likewise, conclusions might vary if the initial disclosure occurred as a result of violation of the law (e.g., information initially obtained by trespass or illegal electronic eavesdropping),[9] or only after an accidental betrayal of information (e.g., being unknowingly overheard), or as a result of practical necessity (e.g., having to traverse public space to get to work or to the hospital). In any event, it is possible that legal rules can recognize and address each of these varying circumstances under which a person might claim a right to control further dissemination.

The first of the three conceptions of informational privacy that I enumerated above—information inalienability—seems overtly contrary to the individual agency of the person required to keep information private. For example, the U.S. military's "Don't ask, don't tell" policy prevents a gay male or lesbian from disclosing his or her homosexuality, thereby coercively creating a degree of information inalienability. Still, information inalienability might be thought in some contexts to serve (a certain conception of) personhood, a decent society, or other values. If so, this service

[6] Julie Cohen, "Examined Lives: Informational Privacy and the Subject As Object," *Stanford Law Review* 52 (2000): 1373–1438

[7] *Cohen v. Cowles Media Co.,* 501 U.S. 663 (1991) (promissory estoppel can apply to newspaper that promised confidentiality).

[8] *Seattle Times Co. v. Rhinehart,* 467 U.S. 20 (1984) (newspaper can be ordered not to publish information obtained through discovery).

[9] *Bartnicki v. Vopper,* 532 U.S. 514 (2001).

could provide a rationale for this interpretation of informational privacy. Privacy would be, to some limited extent, inalienable. This approach to privacy comes close to the premise behind child pornography laws, although that premise may be crucially affected by the added paternalistic assumption that children are not capable of giving appropriate consent to disclosure and that any parent or guardian who gives consent is not acting properly in the child's interest.[10] More obviously, a prohibition of *public* nudity that applies even where all people exposed to the nudity are consenting adults mandates a degree of inalienable privacy.[11]

If, as claimed here, a person has a right to disseminate private information about another person, surely she should have the same right to disseminate information about herself. An obviously essential individual power is the capacity to reveal or expose oneself, be it to one's lover or to the world, at least to the extent that the person can find effective means to disseminate her verbal or pictorial self-portrait. If taken to its extreme, a regime of inalienable privacy would mandate

[10] The Court relied upon concerns about a child's participation in the making of child porn and with the availability of the permanent record of the child's participation to justify the law in *New York v. Ferber*, 458 U.S. 747 (1982), harms that distinguish this case from *Ashcroft v. Free Speech Coalition*, 535 U.S. 234 (2002) (striking down prohibition of computer-created child porn in which no actual child was used).

[11] *Barnes v. Glenn Theatre, Inc.*, 501 U.S. 560 (1991); *City of Erie v. Pap's A.M*, 529 U.S. 277 (2000) (upholding bans on public nudity as applied to dancers in dance halls or adult establishments). Both cases generated strong dissents. The dissenters distinguished public nudity before unconsenting adults, who might be considered to be viscerally assaulted by the nudity, and before exclusively consenting parties such as in a theater, where the state interest seems directed specifically at stopping expressive communication. (Elsewhere, I have suggested that in an advocacy as opposed to an entertainment context, nudity should sometimes be protected even in relation to those who are offended: Baker, *Human Liberty*, *supra* note 5, at 135, 173–78, 306 n.27, 318 n.29; and C. Edwin Baker, "The Evening Hours During *Pacifica* Standard Time," *Villanova Sports and Entertainment Law Journal* 3 [1996]: 45.) The plurality in *Pap's A.M.* attempted to meet the objection that the law aimed at suppressing communication by arguing that, instead, the state interest was related to preventing "secondary effects," that is, effects not dependent on whether anyone received the message and not involving any condemnation of the communicative exposure. The purported secondary effect would occur if people who may not even have received the communication come to the area and engage in activities that the state properly restricts, such as prostitution. Previously, purported secondary effects have only justified "zoning" the expression in a manner hoped to reduce these bad effects, which makes sense of the fact that secondary effects cases are analyzed much like "time, place, or manner" cases. No case prior to *Pap's A.M.* used secondary effects analysis to entirely bar the expression, a point emphasized by the dissent. Arguably, the plurality in *Pap's A.M.* only makes doctrinal sense if the complete ban on intentionally appearing in public in a "state of nudity" was not a complete ban on the particular expression. The plurality argues this is so. The dancer could make the same communication, the plurality implied, because she could be almost nude, a view ridiculed by the dissent, which claimed audiences distinguish dancing nude from dancing with "pasties and G-strings." The plurality seems overtly inconsistent with *Cohen v. California*, 403 U.S. 15 (1971), which emphasized not only that "the Constitution leaves matters of taste and style . . . largely to the individual" but also that the First Amendment protects the important emotive function of using a particular word, "fuck." *Cohen* also noted that any bar on the word's use runs the danger of suppressing ideas.

invisibility, a social erasure practiced in some totalitarian countries and possibly the experience of many subordinated peoples.[12] *Any* general policy of inalienability of private information is inconsistent with respect for autonomy or agency.[13] However, this point plays little role in most theoretical discussions of informational privacy and will not be my concern here.

Largely because of its obvious potential to conflict directly with speech freedom, but also because it is often seen as the most important innovation of the Warren and Brandeis article and possibly the major development of the common law in the twentieth century, the third sense of informational privacy will be the focus of this essay; that is, this essay will focus on control over further dissemination once someone else holds one's personal information. More specifically, my question is whether an adequate and appropriate legal response to informational privacy claims should be limited mostly to maintaining or strengthening privacy in the second sense—control over initial disclosure and the maintenance of private spaces—and, in any event, should not extend to a more general, property-like claim to control others' dissemination of private information about oneself. My thesis is that a person's control over other people's dissemination of private information about the person, purportedly recognized under the rubric of protecting privacy, should be rejected in any case where it would restrict freedom of speech or of the press as properly understood. But the complete story will be more complex, including caveats on when limitations on further dissemination are not contrary to First Amendment requirements.

To jump ahead, the direction of the argument for these caveats will be twofold. First, as opposed to the strong sense of information inalienability rejected above—for example, a person cannot appear nude, even in an enclosed public space—there is also a more limited notion of *market inalienability.*[14] Some (not all) people who consider an absolute bar on sodomy or on all sex outside of marriage as an outrageous affront to autonomy, consider a bar on prostitution (sex overtly for sale in the market) not to be so obviously impermissible. Likewise, laws that restrict one from selling certain information about oneself—market inalienability—may be desirable in some situations and are contrary neither to free speech nor to individual autonomy. For example, privacy may be properly served by barring Internet transactions in which, in exchange for access, payment, or other benefit, the Internet provider collects private information about the other party for largely unregu-

[12] Cf. Ralph Ellison, *The Invisible Man* (New York: Random House, 1952).

[13] But cf. Anita L. Allen, "Coercing Privacy," *William and Mary Law Review* 40 (1999): 723–57, 740, 752–53.

[14] Margaret Jane Radin, *Contested Commodities* (Cambridge, MA: Harvard University Press, 1996), 18–20.

lated later uses. In contrast, these policy reasons would not apply if the computer user consciously and voluntarily exposed the information about herself with the intent that it be available for general use. Second, as for property-like control of private information, this control will sometimes be acceptable in specific contexts. Specifically, it may be proper to give a person the right to control collection, use, or dissemination of certain private information by commercial, nonmedia enterprises or government agencies. Crucial to such an argument will be the claim that in these contexts the parties regulated do not have an autonomy or other constitutional, speech-based claim at stake.

III. Two Conceptions of Autonomy

A. Meaningful autonomy

'Effective' or 'meaningful' individual agency or autonomy might be described, loosely, as a capacity (including the necessary opportunities) to lead a meaningfully self-authored life without unnecessary or inappropriate frustration by others. The precise formulation or definition of the term 'meaningful autonomy' is not a major concern here. Rather, my point is that any such notion is not an on/off variable but a matter of degree. A key function of social policy and of the legal order ought to be to create the conditions that enhance meaningful autonomy. Meaningful autonomy is also concrete; the concern is not with having maximum abstract freedom of choice but with having opportunities to make those choices one actually wants to make. Enhancing effective autonomy for one person will often impair it for another. Conflicts are inevitable. A legal order that provides one person with great wealth, for example, will normally advance her effective autonomy, though this often means someone else will have less wealth, with the consequence that the latter's effective autonomy will be restricted. Recognizing that one of two claimants has a right to a plot of land (or a bank account) will typically advance the winner's capacity to lead a self-authored life while having the opposite effect on the losing claimant.

Many, many things—education, John Rawls's primary goods, sensible environmental policies—including informational privacy, can serve effective individual agency. Elimination of "informational" privacy was a major evil imagined in George Orwell's *1984*, a fictional horror not unlike what technology is rapidly making possible today. However, informational privacy is only one of many resources that can serve meaningful autonomy. To pick the key category of this essay, consider, for example, speech and information. Some have invoked as a central rationale for freedom of speech the premise that (effective) individual autonomy requires *information* and access to varying viewpoints.[15] For example, one person's meaningful autonomy might be enhanced by knowledge about her spouse, whom she thought loved her but who does not and who is actually having an affair, or is spending all of his time watching video porn, or is suffering in silence. The knowledge that potentially supports her self-authorship or effective autonomy potentially interferes with his informational privacy and his effective autonomy. In a world where the goal is to maximize, or fairly distribute, or provide appropriately conceived sorts of effective autonomy, the correct policy toward informational privacy would seldom be clear. Feminists, for instance, are among those who advocate more privacy in which appropriate forms of intimacy can flourish and yet also call for more exposure of people engaged in various forms of private abuse.[16]

The claim that meaningful autonomy requires privacy often involves assertions that for development, experimentation, and repose, individuals need the capacity to shield themselves, at various times and places and to varying degrees, from exposure to the critical eyes of the world. A common assertion is that the public sphere depends on and is, in this sense, parasitic on the private sphere (and, many commentators go on to add, vice versa).[17] Most public persons will need, and certainly will have needed while developing into adulthood, to be able to withdraw occasionally into a private realm.[18] Lack of opportunities to be private or anonymous is injurious to individuality and allows for extreme social control.[19] Interestingly, these assertions in behalf of informational privacy

[15] Thomas Scanlon, "A Theory of Freedom of Expression," *Philosophy & Public Affairs* 1, no. 2 (1972): 204-26; David A. Strauss, "Persuasion, Autonomy, and Freedom of Expression," *Columbia Law Review* 91 (1991): 334-71; and Richard H. Fallon, Jr., "Two Senses of Autonomy," *Stanford Law Review* 46 (1994): 875-905.

[16] Anita L. Allen, *supra* note 13; Julie Cohen, *supra* note 6.

[17] This is similar to Habermas's claim that private autonomy and public autonomy are co-original. Jürgen Habermas, *Between Facts and Norms: Contributions to a Discourse Theory of Law and Democracy*, trans. William Regh (Cambridge, MA: MIT Press, 1996), 104, 121-22, 263, 314, and 454. Individual rights are created by the exercise of public autonomy (the liberty of the ancients), but the exercise of public autonomy requires autonomous individual rights holders. See *infra* note 145.

[18] Long a subject of science fiction, this need for privacy in order to develop as a full person was the theme of two recent popular Hollywood movies, *The Truman Show* (1998) and *Ed TV* (1999).

[19] First Amendment doctrine recognizes this need for privacy, emphasizing the role that anonymity played in revolutionary pamphleteering and, more generally, its role in creating a willingness to engage in political activities. See *NAACP v. Alabama ex rel Patterson*, 357 U.S. 449 (1958) (First Amendment protects against state demand for disclosure of membership lists); *Talley v. California*, 362 U.S. 60 (1960) (ban on anonymous leafletting is unconstitutionally overbroad); *Brown v. Socialist Workers '74 Campaign Committee*, 459 U.S. 87 (1982) (Socialist Workers Party has right not to report the identity of campaign contributors); *McIntyre v. Ohio Elections Commission*, 514 U.S. 334 (1995) (person has right to distribute anonymous campaign literature). See generally Seth F. Kreimer, "Sunlight, Secrets, and Scarlet Letters: The Tension between Privacy and Disclosure in Constitutional Law," *University of Pennsylvania Law Review* 140 (1991): 1-147. Fifth Amendment limits on compelled disclosure might also be seen, in part, as protecting these interests.

seem to emphasize (and maybe only require) the second interpretation of privacy: individual control over whether and when to make publicly available information about oneself. Nothing about providing considerable scope for a private sphere, sometimes understood as itself required by the First Amendment,[20] necessarily implies any direct or overt restriction on freedom of speech.

Even this second sense of privacy, disclosure control, would be potentially problematic if there is a constitutional, presumably a First Amendment, right of access to information—a right said to serve individuals' autonomy interests.[21] This conflict with the First Amendment is avoided, however, by those theorists who see the point of the First Amendment differently, that is, as more a matter of freedom to say what one chooses than to have access to information. In this alternative view, which I subscribe to, access to both privately held and governmentally held information is not a free speech matter but, rather, a policy issue usefully served by devices such as legislatively sculpted freedom of information acts combined with a constitutionally protected free press.[22] Often, but not always, compelled private disclosure could be required when the disclosure serves some plausible informational policy goal.[23] In this view, when to compel, as well as when to forbid, government disclosure is properly decided on the basis of legislative or executive policy judgments rather than on the basis of a constitutional right of access to information. In any event, policy measures to protect informational privacy by securing rights to a shielded private sphere and to refuse to disclose information can contribute to meaningful autonomy. These rights do not conflict with speech freedom as conceived of in this essay.

Even if *meaningful* autonomy requires both access to some sorts of information about others and some capacity to limit disclosure, surely autonomy or agency is not robbed of value simply because a person does not possess *all* possible information or complete control over access to information about herself. Maximizing both access to information and the capacity to limit disclosure would be contradictory. Adding to one person's privacy decreases another person's information. The same informational privacy that contributes to one person's meaningful autonomy can undermine that of another. It is equally undesirable to try to *maximize* either access to information or privacy. Not only does a person not need either in maximal amounts, but meaningful autonomy probably does not require that a person always have any specifiable type of information about others available or about herself hidden.

[20] See cases cited in note 19.

[21] See Scanlon, Strauss, and Fallon articles, *supra* note 15.

[22] Justice Potter Stewart, "Or of the Press," *Hastings Law Journal* 26 (1975): 631–37; Baker, *Human Liberty*, *supra* note 5, chap. 10.

[23] See, e.g., *Buckley v. Valeo*, 424 U.S. 1 (1976) (upholding disclosure requirements).

Still, both cloaking and making available particular categories of information may be valuable. Whether meaningful autonomy will be increased more by one or the other will characteristically vary not only among cultures and between various subgroups of a society, but also among different people within any subgroup or for the same person over time. These variations reflect the fact that both information availability and informational privacy relate to autonomy more as instrumental supports than as defining elements. Neither information nor privacy is, itself, a self-authored activity (though the activity of disclosure or hiding can be). Rather, both information and privacy are resources that make people more capable of various meaningful or valuable self-authored choices. Typically a person has more power of self-authorship when she has more of both the privacy and the information that *she* values. In contrast, for this person, gaining more of the wrong sort of privacy or information is at best a diversion, and sometimes can be a burden that reduces her capacity for meaningful self-authorship. Given that obtaining more of privacy or information imposes costs of various sorts, both on the person gaining the resource and on others, and given that obtaining either resource will vary in significance, the socially ideal amount and type of informational privacy or information availability will be controversial and contested.

B. Formal autonomy

The claim in the previous section is that both information (including privacy-invading information) and informational privacy instrumentally support meaningful autonomy. However, a potentially controversial distinction can be made between 'abstract autonomy', or what I will often call 'formal autonomy', and 'meaningful autonomy', a distinction roughly equivalent to what Rawls called "liberty" and the value or "worth of liberty."[24] The law affirms the formal conception of autonomy to the extent that the law recognizes an agent's legal right to choose what to do with herself (and her property—more on this later). The law recognizes her dominion over her own mind and body, given the inherent constraints of the environment and given her lack of any right to interfere directly with another's decisions about himself (and his property). This formal autonomy implies nothing about actual capacity, opportunity, or the availability of needed resources.

Although I will not defend them here,[25] three claims about formal autonomy need to be noted. First, the legitimacy of the legal order may depend on the law respecting individuals' (formal) autonomy. Second,

[24] John Rawls, *A Theory of Justice* (Cambridge, MA: Harvard University Press, 1971), 204.
[25] See Baker, *Human Liberty, supra* note 5; Baker, "Harm," *supra* note 5.

unlike meaningful autonomy, which is always a goal that could be even better realized, the possibility exists for rather uncompromising recognition of or respect for—that is, legal embodiment of—formal autonomy. Third, respect for formal autonomy provides the best basis for the constitutional (and absolute) status of free speech.[26]

Different theoretical accounts could be given for the status of formal autonomy. The account that I have found persuasive sees the legitimacy of the legal order as dependent on respecting people as equal and autonomous agents.[27] Only such respect can sustain the claim that people have an obligation to obey the law. And such respect both requires democracy as the basis for collective, legal authority and constrains democracy so that it does not deny people's autonomy or equality, requirements that can be fleshed out in consequent theories of equality and liberty.

In many respects, this view of two conceptions of autonomy repeats approaches that are relatively common in legal and political theory. The theory of criminal punishment that views legitimate punishment as limited by a principle of proportionality, but as extending no further than is beneficial for the collective welfare, embodies a formal conception of autonomy as a restraint and a more utilitarian element that controls within the bounds allowed by the constraint.[28] Likewise, a common conception of morality is that it makes universal claims, while ethics is a comprehensive doctrine concerning the good for a group or an individual. The view, which I have elsewhere called a two-level theory,[29] that ethics should

[26] In free speech literature, my distinction between meaningful and formal autonomy parallels Richard Fallon's distinction between "descriptive" and "ascriptive" autonomy. See Fallon, *supra* note 15. According to Fallon, in the past, First Amendment autonomy theorists have mostly ignored ascriptive autonomy in favor of descriptive autonomy, but that free speech doctrine ought to respond to both. Fallon observes that the two conceptions place sometimes conflicting demands on the legal order—and descriptive autonomy can lie on both sides of an issue. He then concludes that the proper approach balances all the autonomy claims (although when he does the balancing, it seems he usually favors the strongest claims made on behalf of descriptive autonomy). In my view, many scholars (including myself) whom Fallon characterizes as advancing *negative liberty, descriptive autonomy* claims were in fact offering *ascriptive autonomy* theories. See C. Edwin Baker, "Realizing Self-Realization: Corporate Political Expenditures and Redish's 'The Value of Free Speech'", *University of Pennsylvania Law Review* 130 (1982): 646–77 (criticizing Martin H. Redish for adopting a descriptive conception of autonomy). Although Fallon is right that both types of autonomy are important for law and policy, I provide a different account of their proper relationship. Namely, I propose that, rather than balance what are in effect apples and oranges, the law ought consistently to respect ascriptive (or formal) autonomy as a trump or side constraint in developing ways to promote descriptive (or meaningful) autonomy. I suggest that this approach is both more consistent with First Amendment law and more normatively defensible, although both points are disputed.

[27] C. Edwin Baker, "Foundations of the Possibility of Legitimate Law" (unpublished essay, 2003).

[28] See H. L. A. Hart, *Punishment and Responsibility: Essays in the Philosophy of Law* (New York: Oxford University Press, 1968), 1–27; and Kent Greenawalt, "Punishment," in Joshua Dressler, *Encyclopedia of Crime and Justice*, 2d ed. (New York: Macmillan, 2002), 1282–94, at 1289.

[29] C. Edwin Baker, "Sandel on Rawls," *University of Pennsylvania Law Review* 133 (1985): 895–928.

be determinative but only within the constraint of morality,[30] describes the relation that I claim here should apply between the two conceptions of autonomy. Basically, in each example, formal autonomy responds to what might be described as deontological claims, while descriptive or meaningful autonomy is more empirical or teleological.

The law respects formal autonomy to the extent that it meets two conditions. First, it must allocate ultimate control over a person's mind, body, and property to that person, except when that person would use her body or property to interfere with another's legitimate realm of decision-making control. Second, the law must not aim at eliminating or suppressing people's freedom to make decisions about behavior or values. These requirements have clear implications for speech, namely, that a person should be able to decide for herself what to say. These requirements, however, imply nothing about whether she will have the capability to say something, which would require, for example, knowledge on her part and which is more a matter of meaningful autonomy.

Obviously, legal recognition of formal autonomy (or liberty) is not necessarily absolute. A person could have autonomy in respect to some choices, could be free to say some things, and not others. Thus, as with meaningful autonomy, a person could have more or less formal autonomy. Nevertheless, formal autonomy is unlike meaningful autonomy, which conceptually could not be provided in any complete sense, and it is unlike either information availability or privacy, which may justifiably *not* be maximized (not only for cost reasons but also because of their diverse relation to meaningful autonomy). Decisions to impose direct legal limits on formal autonomy are not a necessary part of a legal order and should be especially troublesome. Such restrictions appear aimed at serving collective purposes by means of *unnecessarily* disrespecting or forbidding self-authorship rather than, for example, by *necessarily* distributing inherently limited resources. Thus, laws aimed at restricting choice are unlike laws selecting among different distributions, which inevitably affect different people's meaningful autonomy differently but do not themselves restrict formal autonomy, that is, individuals' choices about themselves and their property.

Legal rules that limit liberty (or formal autonomy, as described here) are not a logically necessary part of a legal order, while legal rules that limit the value or "meaningfulness" of a person's liberty—and that limit it differently for different people—are inherent to any legal order.[31] Roughly, the claim is that most laws distribute the right to make particular choices (e.g., property law) or protect (i.e., most criminal and much tort law) or help rearrange (e.g., contract law) the distribution. These laws do not

[30] See, e.g., Rainer Forst, *Contexts of Justice: Political Philosophy beyond Liberalism and Communitarianism*, trans. John M. M. Farrell (Berkeley: University of California Press, 2002).

[31] The points merely asserted here and in the next two paragraphs are developed in Baker, "Harm," *supra* note 5.

themselves increase or decrease the choices that can be made about the use of resources (although they may make it more likely that people will engage in productive activities that will increase possible choices). These laws do determine who gets to make a particular choice, but they do not prohibit the possibility of making the choice. If the distribution does not give a person the right to make a particular choice, there is someone else who could give it to her. Of course, laws allocating choices have huge consequences for the worth of liberty. They do not, however, themselves restrict liberty. Formal liberty or autonomy is a person's right to make either choices that the law has allocated to that person or choices that the person can make once securing the consent of another person to whom the choice was previously allocated.

In contrast to these *allocative* or distributive laws are a second sort, which I label 'general prohibitions'. These laws prohibit certain choices on the part of everyone: for example, no one can engage in sodomy, say bad things about the president or the country, eat pork, drink bourbon, or charge a higher price. These general prohibitions are directed at making some choices unavailable, which usually means they are directed at limiting formal autonomy. Moreover, unlike allocative rules, general prohibitions are not an inherent or logically required aspect of a legal order. Thus, a commitment to respect formal autonomy suggests the following possible general principle: do not allow general prohibitions even when a general prohibition predictably increases the worth of liberty to many people more than it decreases the worth of liberty to others. I have defended such a principle in those contexts where formal liberty seemed to be actually at stake, that is, where the general prohibition was properly seen as blocking valued exercises of autonomy as opposed to merely making certain choices instrumentally more difficult, which distributional rules regularly do. Thus, my reformulated general principle is: a state acts improperly when its aim is to suppress individual choice as a means of carrying out even the state's good aims. This principle of liberty must be contrasted with the propriety of (sometimes) protecting a person's chosen actions from interference by another, which recalls the distributive or allocative issue.

One additional characteristic of this description of respect for formal autonomy merits attention. This view centrally identifies the person with agency, with action, and with the possibility of choice. In a sense, this is an activity view of personhood: it favors a person's activity of speech over the status of being unknown. This perspective accords, I think, with the view of Justice William J. Brennan, who, after asserting that "freedom of speech is itself an end," went on to say that "freedom of speech is . . . intrinsic to individual dignity," and who characterized "a democracy like [the United States]" as one "in which the autonomy of each individual is accorded equal and incommensurate respect."[32] This would explain why

[32] *Herbert v. Lando*, 441 U.S. 153, 184 n.1 (1979) (Brennan, J., dissenting in part).

he concluded elsewhere that "freedom of expression is made inviolate by the First Amendment."[33] This identification of the person with activity is not the only one possible. Warren and Brandeis characterized the privacy that they defended as based on the principle of "an inviolate personality."[34] Both Brennan's and the conflicting Warren/Brandeis view characterize something as fundamental about the person that the law must respect, but they differ as to what that core aspect is.

Though in this essay my concern is primarily to explore the significance for informational privacy of a commitment to speech freedom, some comment on these (at least partially) conflicting views about what should be legally "inviolate" is warranted. Essentially, favoring "choice" over "personality" privileges a view of the fundamental aspect of personhood as activity rather than something static. To assert as basic a person's right to have a characterization of her personality unchallenged by others' expression is an assertion of power over others—in practice over their speech choices but in ambition over even their mental views. Though recognizing a person's legitimate interest in others' choices, the claim that a person should have this type of power over others seems very problematic. It is difficult to see why the legitimacy of a legal order would depend on its recognition of power over others. Certainly, it is not a power that a person would have in the absence of a legal grant. Thus, my premise will remain that formal autonomy of the sort described, which includes a person's choices about her own speech, is plausibly something that the legal order should treat as inviolate. In contrast, any notion of personality that includes control over others' speech is not a plausible candidate for treatment as inviolate. However, the latter view of personality still implicates often supremely important interests that merit various forms of incomplete legal as well as informal, customary support.

Whether or not formal autonomy as a conception of autonomy is appealing in general, if we narrow our gaze just to speech freedom it is clear that this kind of autonomy has the virtue that it could be, whether or not it should be, fully guaranteed. A person, whenever she is in a place where she has an unrestricted right to be, could be free to say whatever she wants. Of course, allocation rules will affect where (or when) a person can say particular things. Still, there is no category of "content" that a person necessarily must be prohibited from saying in order to authorize another person to make choices for herself, for example, whether or not to say the

[33] *Richmond Newspapers, Inc. v. Virginia*, 448 U.S. 555, 585 (1980) (Brennan, J., concurring in the judgment).

[34] Warren and Brandeis, *supra* note 1, at 205. Lillian BeVier suggests that privacy is the equivalent of speech as a constitutive element of liberty. I find this to be a strange conception of liberty. It implies that liberty is not merely a power of choice about one's own action. Rather, it identifies liberty either with a state of affairs (i.e., the information is not known) or with power over other people's acts (i.e., they cannot speak what they know). This notion of liberty, however, may explain why, in her contribution to this volume, BeVier does not find copyright's restriction on people's speech choices in conflict with the First Amendment, a view that I find equally strange.

same thing, to say something else, or to say nothing. Censorship—i.e., prohibitions on people's choices to communicate particular content—amounts to general prohibitions. (I put aside a preliminary theoretical inquiry, presumably informed by why speech should be protected, of identifying particular behavior as "speech" in a normatively or constitutionally relevant sense. Critics of free speech absolutism almost always mischaracterize the absolutists' position by assuming that absolutists believe that the First Amendment protects every verbal or vocal act, a view clearly repudiated by every prominent First Amendment absolutist. For example, no prominent First Amendment absolutist of whom I am aware ever defended First Amendment protection for perjury or commercial speech. Rather, absolutists claim that properly protected speech choices should not be suppressed on the basis of an instrumental balancing analysis of the sort that enamors the current Supreme Court majority.)

Of course, a formal autonomy speech right may not lead to much meaningful autonomy if a speaker never has access to the resources (e.g., educational, informational, conceptual, experiential) that are needed to have anything meaningful to say or the material resources that are necessary to communicate with her intended audience. Still, many civil libertarians (including me) incline toward absolutely protecting this type of formal autonomy against abridgement. Opponents of this position typically argue that such a principle should at best be a rule of thumb or a rebuttable presumption. That is, they argue that the claim of formal autonomy (or liberty) should be rejected when its recognition detracts seriously enough, as it sometimes does, from other people's meaningful autonomy, or when it seriously interferes with a more egalitarian provision for meaningful autonomy. In the context of privacy concerns, the opponents of absolutism might claim that speech freedom can detract from meaningful autonomy by allowing one person to expose personal information about another, and that this intrusion may justify limiting speech freedom.

In contrast to formal autonomy-based speech rights, meaningful autonomy-based, speech-related "interests" cannot be fully or absolutely protected or served. This conclusion should be obvious from our discussion, since provision of the same information that invades one person's privacy (and undermines her meaningful autonomy) can affirmatively serve someone else's meaningful autonomy. Both having information and having privacy are autonomy-based interests, but full provision of one necessarily limits the other: privacy limits information, sometimes access to information limits privacy. The conflict can be resolved only by a decision, presumably a policy decision, that tries best to balance or accommodate the competing interests.

As noted, my premise here is that the central justification for the *constitutional* status of freedom of speech relates to a need for the law to respect individual autonomy in the formal sense of protecting a person's choice of what to say (or her choice to listen to a willing speaker).[35] An implication of this premise is that the constitutional status of speech is not centrally based on its instrumental contributions to meaningful autonomy.[36] Of course, this premise does not deny that speech freedom sometimes makes extraordinarily valuable and in some ways unique instrumental contributions to meaningful autonomy. However, like many resources that make instrumental contributions, speech freedom's instrumental contribution varies. Often, less emphasis on particular speech freedoms and more on other goods (e.g., privacy or equality) would arguably further a society's instrumental or policy concerns better than does protecting speech. Almost always, however, there is the necessarily speculative empirical possibility that an *instrumentally even better* policy would pursue meaningful autonomy only by means that did not limit formal autonomy's speech freedoms.[37] While instrumental contributions provide important reasons to value speech, they are a doubtful basis for giving it rule-like or constitutional protection. The instrumental contributions of speech are more like the contribution that many other factors make to meaningful autonomy. Certainly, anyone who reads the constitutional protection of speech as valuable for instrumental reasons must be constantly ready (except when convinced by rule-utilitarian arguments) to balance the interests served by speech freedom against other interests, including speech-related interests, served by particular restrictions of speech freedom.

IV. Privacy and Autonomy in Law

I have argued that informational privacy can contribute to meaningful autonomy, and so can information that exposes private matters. Some degree of privacy may be an essential aspect of human dignity, although there is no reason to believe that privacy about any particular fact is essential. Cultures and individuals will vary in respect to the information that they find most important to keep private. Policy analysis should evaluate the significance of both informational privacy and information exposure in particular contexts. Policymakers can often choose which to favor, as illustrated by the trade-offs that generated the Privacy Act of 1974[38] as a statutory part of, and a limitation on, the Freedom of Information Act of 1966.[39] Although these policy choices will be contested, their content should mostly reflect judgments about distribution, effi-

[35] See Baker, *Human Liberty, supra* note 5.

[36] For a differing view, see articles listed in note 15. Also Martin H. Redish, "The Value of Free Speech," *University of Pennsylvania Law Review* 130 (1982): 591–645.

[37] Cf. Carlin Meyer, "Sex, Sin, and Women's Liberation: Against Porn-Suppression," *Texas Law Review* 72 (1994): 1097–1201.

[38] 5 U.S.C. 552(a).

[39] 5 U.S.C. 552. The Freedom of Information Act provides a right of access to much of the information maintained in federal agency records. The Privacy Act exempts from disclosure much information that would intrusively and arguably unnecessarily expose private information about individuals.

ciency, and matters of cultural or collective self-definition.[40] In any event, given the conflicting requirements of and generally instrumental importance of both information availability and informational privacy, *most* legal rules favoring or disfavoring one or the other should presumably be a matter of social policy and not constitutional principle.

Nevertheless, sometimes favoring or disfavoring a particular version of informational privacy can be a constitutional matter. Consider, first, two provisions of the U.S. Constitution that provide important protections of informational privacy. Protecting informational privacy is probably part of the explanation for, and certainly one consequence of, the Fourth and Fifth Amendments.[41] Specifically, the second conception of informational privacy described at the beginning of Section II—disclosure control—is advanced when the Constitution limits searches and seizures (Fourth Amendment) or allows a person to refuse to be a witness against himself (Fifth Amendment). These amendments help protect initial disclosure against demands from a prying government, thereby helping to assure a person the seclusion needed for self-development.

Second, control over disclosure may be a significant aspect of First Amendment holdings protecting a person's right of anonymity, although whether the First Amendment justification for protecting anonymity really involves a general concern with a person's autonomous control over exposure of private information is doubtful. Often the justification involves anonymity's instrumental effect of making speech acts less costly to the speaker and, hence, of preventing the loss of publicly available speech due to the "chilling effect" of exposure. The goal may not be informational privacy itself but, rather, having more speech and, as a result, more information within a marketplace of ideas.[42] Alternatively, maybe anonymity involves merely a formal speech right not to say things, like one's name, that one does not want to say.[43] Again, such a right would have nothing to do with any constitutional concern with informational privacy. Either explanation might explain why the First Amendment sometimes protects a person's choice not to identify herself while it

[40] C. Edwin Baker, "Posner's Privacy Mystery and the Failure of Economic Analysis of Law," *Georgia Law Review* 12 (1978): 475–95.

[41] But compare Lessig's observation concerning the need to determine whether the point of these amendments is to prevent intrusions, or to prevent insults to a dignity-based informational privacy, or substantively to limit government power, or, presumably, some combination of these goals. Lawrence Lessig, *Code and Other Laws of Cyberspace* (New York: Basic Books, 1999), 146–50.

[42] *NAACP v. Alabama* ex rel *Patterson*, 357 U.S. 449 (1958); *Brown v. Socialist Party*, 459 U.S. 87 (1982); *McIntyre v. Ohio Elections Commission*, 514 U.S. 334 (1995).

[43] Cf. *Bowen v. Roy*, 476 U.S. 693 (1986) (rejecting claim that a child receiving AFDC benefits had a religious free exercise claim to stop the federal government from requiring an identification number for receipt of benefits, but suggesting that the child might have a right not to use the number herself). In a demonstration at Stanford University in 1969, participants decided to give the movement's name in response to requests by the authorities that the demonstrators identify themselves. This tactic was neither an attempt to deceive nor a maneuver to hide (taking pictures was not discouraged) but a political statement of solidarity.

also protects other people's right to expose the person who wishes anonymity. That is, an anonymity right might be less about informational privacy and more about speech freedom. In fact, sometimes, anonymity can itself be part of a person's message, in which case any guarantee of speech freedom would require that the person be able to refrain from self-identification.

Sometimes a right not to disclose one's identity or other personal information obviously serves a person's instrumental need for a secluded expressive space in which to develop and to define herself. Consider recognition of an especially strong copyright in unpublished letters.[44] At least when a person plans never to publish, the right is not easily justified by American copyright theory, in which the constitutionally permissible ground for copyright is to encourage the creation and public availability of useful writings.[45] In contrast, the impulse to protect the contents of unpublished letters is quite understandable from the perspective of a person's interests in informational privacy. In any event, the conception of privacy as disclosure control is not the subject of this essay's critique of the third conception of informational privacy—control over dissemination. In fact, the possibility of strengthening control over initial disclosure provides a reason to reduce objections to not recognizing control over further dissemination.

Alternatively, First Amendment rights might disfavor informational privacy by trumping some privacy-affirming policies. Consider two possible types of First Amendment claims. First are claims made in behalf of a right to know or to have access to information, even when this information might be considered private. Imagine, for example, a claim that the public and/or the media have a right to enter a prison in a manner that a prisoner views as infringing upon her already-infringed-upon privacy. Although in closely divided decisions the Supreme Court basically rejected this claim, certainly there is plausibility to the idea that there is a constitutional right to access some information that someone else considers private.[46] Despite a legislative policy decision to protect minor victims of sex offenses against public exposure, a constitutionally based access claim prevailed when the press demanded the right to be present for a

[44] Cf. *Salinger v. Random House, Inc.*, 811 F.2d 90 (2d Cir. 1987) (recognizing strong rights in respect to unpublished letters, relying on *Harper & Row, Publishers, Inc. v. Nation Enterprises*, 471 U.S. 539 [1985]), with 17 U.S.C. § 107 (as amended in 1992 to make fair use of unpublished materials more acceptable).

[45] U.S. Const., art. I, § 8 (Congress has power "to promote the progress of science and useful arts by securing for limited times to authors . . . the exclusive right to their respective writings . . ."). This "limited grant . . . is intended to motivate the creative activity of authors. . . . The monopoly . . . thus rewards the individual author in order to benefit the public." *Harper & Row Publishers, Inc. v Nation Enterprises*, 471 U.S. at 546 (1985) (quoting *Sony Corporation of America v. Universal City Studios, Inc.*, 464 U.S. 417, 429, 477 [1984] [dissenting opinion]).

[46] *Pell v. Procunier*, 417 U.S. 817 (1974); *Saxbe v. Washington Post Co.*, 417 U.S. 843 (1974); *Houchins v. KQED, Inc.*, 438 U.S. 1 (1978).

child-witness's testimony in a 1982 sexual misconduct case.[47] So far the Supreme Court has recognized access claims only in cases involving the judicial process—essentially, access to the courtroom. Possibly the rationale is based less on the instrumentally valuable right to information than on a traditional liberty right to be present in the courtroom in order to observe the administration of public justice.[48]

The second type of First Amendment claim is the limit on privacy policies that is central to this essay. Formal autonomy—or, more specifically, speech freedom—allows a person to say what she wants. This right, I claim, exists even when her speech causes harm, for example, even if the speech exposes information about another that the other wants to keep private.

Constitutional rights are often usefully viewed as trumps or side constraints. A privacy trump, such as a Fourth or Fifth Amendment right, requires the legal order to protect or favor privacy over certain forced information exposures. The claim here is the opposite: that a First Amendment trump limits the ways that the law can protect privacy. The formal conception of autonomy centers on the agent being the final authority over decisions about herself or, in the case of speech, about her speech. This corresponds to the common conception that people should be free to say what they want and to listen to what someone else with a right to speak wants to disclose. The right exists even if, as is often the case (sometimes intentionally), her speech is instrumentally harmful to another. Moreover, respect for a person's expressive autonomy should mean that the person is free to listen and observe in places where she has a right to be and among people with whom she has a right to interact in order to learn more and then speak about it. If recognized as an aspect of freedom of speech, this autonomy-based speech right would mean that the law cannot protect privacy by limiting people's speech.

The argument for speech rights of media entities differs somewhat from the argument for individual speech rights. The arguments differ because institutional entities like press enterprises have no intrinsic autonomy claims.[49] The constitutional status of media entities is better conceptualized as based on how their freedom instrumentally serves people's

[47] *Globe Newspaper Co. v. Superior Court*, 457 U.S. 596 (1982).

[48] *Richmond Newspapers, Inc. v. Virginia*, 448 U.S. 555 (1980).

[49] See Frank I. Michelman, *Brennan and Democracy* (Princeton, NJ: Princeton University Press, 1999), 12–14. There is generally no reason to think that the typical market-oriented, corporate media entity composed of numerous persons expresses or represents the unified, autonomous views of individuals involved in the enterprise, individuals who lose no individual expressive rights merely because of some regulation of the collective entity. Still, this claim may be less true in the case of voluntary expressive associations organized around the participants' solidaristic aims, which is why the Supreme Court has treated their First Amendment claims more generously than those of commercial or market-oriented corporations. Cf. *Austin v. Michigan State Chamber of Commerce*, 494 U.S. 652 (1990) with *Federal Election Commission v. Massachusetts Citizens for Life, Inc.*, 479 U.S. 238 (1986).

interest in gaining information and vision and how it advances various other goods, especially democratic values such as those described in the Fourth Estate role or checking function of the press.[50] Still, there is normally no reason to expect, nor has the Court ever suggested,[51] that the speech rights of individuals and the media will differ in scope, at least in respect to the factual or visionary content that the press can disclose.[52] Thus, for present purposes, I will equate the *speech* rights of individuals and media entities.[53]

I put aside whether the First Amendment restricts the state's power to limit information-gathering activities. For example, does the First Amendment prevent the state from forbidding all information-gathering trespasses or, more interestingly, forbidding an inquirer from asking specific people, maybe jurors, for information about their deliberations? Likewise, I put aside whether the First Amendment limits the government's ability to impose damages or punishment on people for the dissemination of information that was initially acquired illegally, either by the speaker or by others.[54] Nor do I doubt that a person can often bargain away or give up these rights to speak, although sometimes such a bargain will be void as either an "unconstitutional condition" or an agreement contrary to public

[50] See Stewart, *supra* note 22; Vince Blasi, "The Checking Value in First Amendment Theory," *American Bar Foundation Research Journal* (1977): 521; and Baker, *Human Liberty, supra* note 5, chap. 10.

[51] But see note 52. Justice Stewart's view that the press has greater speech rights (Stewart, *supra* note 22), a view never accepted by the Court, creates the absurd image of a person being liable for reading aloud to her breakfast companion a newspaper story that the newspaper had a right to print.

[52] I can think of one exception. Although copyright restricts the freedom of both individuals and the press to say or print what they want, the press's constitutional role as a provider of information and vision may be adequately protected by a combination of an expansive fair use privilege and the idea/expression distinction. In combination, these guarantee a right to copy the idea or facts but not the actual words of a copyrighted item. In contrast, copyright should be unconstitutional under the First Amendment to the extent that it prevents an individual from expressing herself by repeating or distributing specific copyrighted expression. C. Edwin Baker, "First Amendment Limits on Copyright," *Vanderbilt Law Review* 55 (2002): 891–951.

[53] Rights other than speech rights may differ. The government may have power to legislate regarding media structure or ownership in order to make the media better serve its public functions without having an analogous power over individuals. C. Edwin Baker, "Turner Broadcasting: Content-Based Regulation of Persons and Presses," *Supreme Court Review* (1994): 57–128. And the First Amendment may be a source of *defensive rights* that protect the institutional integrity of press entities, such as a "reporter's privilege" not to disclose a secret source, again without analogy to any individual rights. Baker, *Human Liberty, supra* note 5, chap. 10.

[54] For skeptical conclusions, see *Bartnicki v. Vopper*, 532 U.S. 514 (2001) (invalidating restriction on publication of information of public importance that was obtained through illegal wiretap); *Nebraska Press Ass'n v. Stuart*, 427 U.S. 539 (1976) (Brennan, J., et al, concurring) (indicating injunction against publication of information about the accused was improper no matter how shabbily the information was obtained); *Food Lion v. Capital Cities/ABC, Inc.*, 194 F.3d 505 (4th Cir. 1999) (rejecting publication damages for communicative content obtained through illegal means).

policy.[55] The "default position," however, is the right to observe, listen, and learn, and then to speak.[56] The autonomy claim, which largely corresponds to Court decisions, is that law should not prevent a person or a media entity from disclosing at least lawfully obtained information, for example, the name of a juvenile defendant or of a rape victim.[57] If this conclusion is accepted, then the gossiping against which Warren and Brandeis inveighed would be a matter of protected First Amendment right.

V. Protection of Privacy

Unrestricted speech freedom does not leave informational privacy without protection. It only requires that the law not use a particular means—that is, abridging speech freedom—to protect privacy. The structure of this requirement is quite conventional in First Amendment contexts. The Court routinely holds that the government can pursue various goals, even the goal of effectively restricting what people or the press are *able to communicate* in order to preserve secrecy, confidentiality, or privacy, *as long as the means do not involve restricting speech.* Most obviously, the law may leave a person free to communicate whatever she knows but leave her unable to communicate certain information by denying her access to it. One permissible reason to deny her access is precisely to prevent her from being able to communicate certain information.

Thus, the Court would undoubtedly and unanimously hold that the state's interest in the confidentiality of preliminary investigations of judicial fitness justifies the *state's* nondisclosure (i.e., its preservation of the secrecy or privacy) of complaints about fitness, of the existence of an investigation, or of the information gathered therein. The state could reject requests by the public or the press for this information. The purpose of nondisclosure is to achieve state aims of informational privacy by disabling people from engaging in speech with particular content: what the press does not know, it cannot report. Nevertheless, in *Landmark Communications v. Virginia* (1978),[58] the Court unanimously held that this kind of legitimate state interest in restricting this kind of speech does not justify a bar on publication of such information once acquired. If "strangers to the inquiry" obtain this information, the state interest in preventing speech on this subject, which justified nondisclosure rules, does not justify restricting the speech of those who now have knowledge. The same

[55] *Cohen v. Cowles Media Co.*, 501 U.S. 663 (1991). Generally, confidentiality—a restriction on speech—can be required of an employee or a person with an agency relationship to another.

[56] But cf. Jerry Kang, "Information Privacy in Cyberspace Transactions," *Stanford Law Review* 50 (1998): 1193–1294.

[57] Cf. *Smith v. Daily Mail Publishing Co.*, 443 U.S. 97 (1979) (juvenile); *Florida Star v. B. J. F.*, 491 U.S. 524 (1989) (rape victim).

[58] 435 U.S. 829 (1978).

is true in many contexts. The Court, for example, is clear that a state can choose not to disclose the name of a rape victim or a juvenile defendant in order to protect privacy. Still, in *Smith v. Daily Mail Publishing Co.* (1979)[59] and *Florida Star v. B. J. F.* (1989),[60] the Court rejected restrictions on the publication of information that the press had legally acquired.

Both the rules that the Court would presumably uphold (government nondisclosure) and the rules that it struck down in *Landmark, Florida Star,* and *Daily Mail* (prohibitions on communications) aim at restricting dissemination of the same information. Both sets of rules, if allowed and effective, would accomplish the same end: preventing communication. The most salient difference is that the permissible restrictions directly limit only access to a resource, namely information, that is instrumentally useful to speakers and arguably to listeners (i.e., to their effective autonomy), while the impermissible restrictions explicitly limit a speaker's *choice* to speak or publish (i.e., limit her formal autonomy). The state acts properly in basing its information policies on instrumentalist, policy judgments about the value of privacy as compared to the value of information accessibility. The Court, however, blocks the execution of the state policy if the policy is carried out by means that violate formal autonomy. (Note that because both sets of rules serve the same state interest and thwart the exposure of the same information, the distinction between the rules is difficult—although maybe on rule-utilitarian grounds, possible—to explain on a marketplace-of-ideas theory of the First Amendment, which values speech instrumentally in terms of its contribution to the information available to people. In contrast, the difference is easily explained on grounds of respecting speakers' autonomy.)

This example makes clear that privacy is not without statutory protection. Privacy may also gain a degree of constitutional status due to people's episodic opportunities to be in nonpublic spaces. Consider, as I previously pointed out, the Fourth Amendment's protection of the home and of private papers, and the Fifth Amendment's protection in one special context of the right not to self-disclose. Other means exist to promote a world in which privacy is treated with greater regard. I share to some degree Warren's and Brandeis's tastes for more serious content in newspapers, although at dinner among colleagues, it is easy to see that even educated people (whether or not they are as aristocratic as Warren and Brandeis were) gossip, especially about academics who are not present. Possibly the government should try to structure media industries so that they would favor more "serious" content.[61] However, the legal order's

[59] 443 U.S. 97 (1979).

[60] 491 U.S. 524 (1989).

[61] Although the Court in *Turner Broadcasting System v. FCC*, 512 U.S. 622 (1964) appeared to rule this purpose constitutionally impermissible, all the Supreme Court's prior cases involving structural regulation of the media suggest the opposite. Baker, "Turner Broadcasting," *supra* note 53.

respect for formal autonomy or, as more commonly stated, for freedom of speech as manifest in much existing constitutional doctrine, requires that protection of privacy not take the form of directly limiting gossip.[62]

The law can intervene to protect informational privacy at distinct junctures and in different ways. Most generally, the legal order can (1) restrict or regulate the initial alienation of private information; (2) restrict or regulate the gathering of information, most obviously by aiding a person in keeping information from originally being nonconsensually exposed; (3) prohibit further dissemination of information to which the subject objects; and (4) restrict or regulate particular uses (other than dissemination) of information that has been gathered. That is, the law can protect informational privacy by restricting the alienation, gathering, dissemination, and use of information. The first of these means, at least if applied to an individual's speech about herself, violates her speech rights, although I will suggest a different conclusion in the context of market alienations. The third of these means, at least as applied to individual speakers or to the media, violates the free speech principles assumed here. Subsections A and B below explore the second and fourth means of protecting informational privacy.

A. Restrictions on gathering private information

Many restrictions on gathering information are uncontroversial. As noted previously, the Fourth and Fifth Amendments impose gathering restrictions at least on government actors. (Conversely, the Sixth Amendment grants the accused a right to compulsory process for obtaining witnesses in his favor; this information-gathering right potentially intrudes into informational privacy and has been extended by other discovery rules and provisions for compulsory process.) One function of private property may be to protect a physical zone of privacy.[63] Generally, protection of physical and mental "zones" of privacy is either constitutionally compelled or a permissible policy choice.

Protection of "private zones" does not mean that the government should have unrestricted authority to limit gathering information. Prohibitions on journalists or presumably on anyone else observing, "monitoring," or even photographing a person when she appears in public realms should be (and probably are) impermissible, even though the observations necessarily expose information.[64] In public places, people generally have a

[62] For the best development of this claim, see Diane L. Zimmerman, "Requiem for a Heavyweight: A Farewell to Warren and Brandeis's Privacy Tort," *Cornell Law Review* 68 (1983): 291–367.

[63] C. Edwin Baker, "Disaggregating the Concept of Property in Constitutional Law," in Nicholas Mercuro and Warren J. Samuels, *The Economics of Legal Relationships*, vol. 4, *The Fundamental Interrelationships between Government and Property* (Stamford, CT: JAI Press, 1999).

[64] Cf. *Galella v. Onassis*, 487 F.2d 986 (2d Cir. 1973).

First Amendment autonomy right not only to speak but also to listen and look, that is, to gather information. When engaged in advocacy, people generally have a right to try to obtain new audiences by leafletting or even approaching people in order to try to engage them in discussion,[65] although continued pursuit of a targeted person who rejects such an approach eventually turns into legally proscribable harassment. The right to speak, however, presumably includes not just the right to advocate but also the right to question; that is, two slightly different premises protect information gathering. In public spaces, not only is gathering information by observation and passive listening generally permissible, but also gathering information can itself be a matter of speaking and then listening. Still, there may be circumstances that justify legal limits on information gathering even in public places or from willing information suppliers.

As noted, the Court has struck down applications of laws against publishing the name of juvenile defendants or rape victims, at least it has when the name has been "lawfully obtained."[66] It would seem illogical for the state to be able to change the result simply by making receipt of the information unlawful. For example, could the state make it unlawful for a private person to obtain information by reading a newspaper even if the newspaper itself had no right to possess or publish the information? Likewise, for the newspaper, as long as it receives the information from a voluntary source or obtains it by interviewing people, a law making the receipt illegal would violate the First Amendment guarantee of freedom to listen.

Nevertheless, the Court has written its opinions in this area very narrowly. In troubling dicta, the Court in *Florida Star,* while protecting publication of the rape victim's name, left open the question of whether "the Constitution permitted a State to proscribe *receipt* of [this] information," and, if it did, whether it could then prohibit publication.[67] Certainly, the government can forbid breaking and entering to get information. The Court's suggestion in *Florida Star* that the government can sometimes forbid "nonconsensual acquisition" of certain sensitive information leaves some ambiguity about the person whose consent is relevant. The most appropriate understanding surely is that the actual party from whom a person acquires the information must consent, for example, by speaking, or by handing over papers, or perhaps by the implied consent of appearing in a public place where observation will suffice to acquire the information. Alternatively, however, some read the Court's comment to mean that the acquisition is nonconsensual if obtained without consent from the person *about whom* the information refers. Still, it is difficult to believe that the government can restrict knowledge by requiring people to keep

[65] But cf. *Hill v. Colorado*, 530 U.S. 703 (2000).

[66] *Smith v. Daily Mail Publishing Co.*, 443 U.S. 97 (1979); *Florida Star v. B. J. F.*, 491 U.S. 524 (1989).

[67] *Florida Star*, 491 U.S. at 536.

their eyes shut, and their questioning mouths closed, and their ears clogged. At dinner in the evening, a person should be able to report to her companion what she has seen or heard during the day, at least unless she is bound to confidentiality due to a special relation of trust with the party from whom she obtained the information. The same should be true for journalists (or gossip columnists). Possibly the best analysis is that information-gathering acts are themselves expressive or autonomy liberties, or press rights, protected by the First Amendment whenever they would not be illegal except for the content of the information obtained.

Two additional problematic questions concern illegally obtained information. First, no one doubts that a person is liable for any tort or crime committed while gathering information, but can she also be punished or have damages increased for communicating the information that she obtained illegally?[68] Second, if a person obtains information knowing or having reason to know that someone else originally obtained it illegally, can she be prohibited from further dissemination?[69] There are clear reasons to resist uniform yes or no answers. Liability directly punishes speech. Liability aims at cloaking potentially valuable information. The press regularly receives significant information from almost institutionalized systems of leaks or from disgruntled persons acting as whistle-blowers. Often, the press will have every reason to suspect that a source acted illegally in obtaining or passing on information. This certainly was the situation in the 1971 "Pentagon Papers" case,[70] in which the Supreme Court dramatically rejected the government's request for an injunction against publication of excerpts from a classified report that verified many of the antiwar movement's criticisms of U.S. military activities in Vietnam. As this case also illustrates, society often benefits from and presumably the First Amendment protects such speech. In contrast to this example, most people would find it quite horrifying if the First Amendment protected continued dissemination of sexually explicit or nude photos or personal diary entries obtained by illegal, nonconsensual entry into or spying on their bedrooms. It seems insufficient for minimal punishment or liability for trespass to be the only penalties for a person who invades another's privacy, takes explicit pictures or copies personal diary entries, and then either publishes the illegally obtained material or gives it to others to publish, just to fulfill a voyeuristic public's salacious interests in celebrities or even in random private individuals. However, when journalists were found to have trespassed on the premises of a grocery

[68] Cf. *Food Lion v. Capital Cities/ABC Inc.*, 194 F.3d 505 (4th Cir. 1999) (rejecting, on First Amendment grounds, publication damages resulting from dissemination of illegally obtained information), with *Dietemann v. Time, Inc.*, 449 F.2d 245 (9th Cir. 1971) (allowing damages for tort to be enhanced due to publication).

[69] *Pearson v. Dodd*, 410 F.2d 701 (D.C. Cir. 1969) (rejecting damages for publication where publisher did not commit the illegal intrusion).

[70] *New York Times v. United States*, 403 U.S. 713 (1971).

chain in 1992 and to have obtained pictures that, when broadcast on television, led to millions of dollars of damage to the chain, the Court of Appeals allowed only $2 damages for the trespass and the breach of a duty of loyalty, but nothing for the publication, even though surely the real harm of the intrusion was the loss due to exposure.[71]

Lower courts have struggled without arriving at a uniform answer to either question raised in the previous paragraph. Recently, in *Bartnicki v. Vopper* (2001),[72] the Supreme Court found First Amendment protection for a newspaper that published information of "public concern," distinguishing such information from other private information, even though the paper knew or should have known that the information was illegally obtained in violation of the wiretap law by a third party unconnected with the newspaper. This resolution at first seems appealing: it protects dissemination in contexts like the "Pentagon Papers" case while generating no incentive (or mercy) for dissemination of illegally obtained information that is trivial for public discourse but central to an individual's privacy. However, my claim has been that the First Amendment should protect speech about anything, including "private" information that judges are unlikely to characterize as being about matters of public concern. When a person has information she wants to communicate, certainly when she has committed no crime, her speech should be protected.[73]

Drawing on distinctions possibly important for copyright, a different analysis is possible. Arguably, copyright should be understood to violate the First Amendment if it prevents a person in a noncommercial context from saying whatever she likes, including the entire content of a copyrighted item. Such a restriction directly infringes the speaker's liberty, in particular, her freedom of speech, on the basis of content. (Note, although closer to existing law than might be at first imagined, the analysis here does not purport to track existing case law but represents my attempt to show the constitutionally legitimate scope of copyright law.)[74] Very few of the privacy fears expressed in the spying-on-their-bedrooms scenario described above would be seriously raised in relation to this speech. Few noncommercial speakers will engage in breaking and entering designed to obtain salacious content appealing to voyeuristic interests; moreover, the fear of such an invasion primarily concerns the public (usually commercial) dissemination of whatever scandalous material is produced.

In contrast, copyright's goal of providing an incentive for valuable creative behavior properly protects people's expressive works from *commercial* appropriation without consent, while appropriately broad interpretations of two doctrines—'fair use' and the noncopyrightability of

[71] *Food Lion*, 194 F.3d 505.

[72] 532 U.S. 514 (2001).

[73] Long the doctrinal norm, this principle has been rejected in the arguably unique circumstances of child porn. *New York v. Ferber*, 458 U.S. 747 (1982).

[74] Baker, *supra* note 52.

'facts and ideas', only of expression—prevents any real limitation on the instrumentally justified constitutional role of the press. Since the media has no autonomy interests and often no constitutional interest in the precise expressive formulation of its product, but only a constitutional interest in being able to provide the public with information or vision, copyright as limited by a broad interpretation of these two doctrines does not abridge the press's constitutionally protected role. The Court's distinction in *Bartnicki* relating to material of public concern is roughly analogous. Explicit photographic images and private diary language can provide the public with valuable perspectives on human alternatives, but it is unclear that for this the media needs illegally obtained content. Either fictionalized or consensually obtained material would arguably suffice. Thus, prohibiting media reproduction of illegally obtained content that lacks "public concern" may be appropriate.[75] The prohibition does not interfere with the constitutional role of the media but merely limits some commercial exploitation of its position. In fact, almost the same analysis may be implicit in lower court decisions concerning the application of 'right of publicity' laws, which protect a person's interest in commercial use of his or her image, but which virtually always—and probably constitutionally must—exempt use for journalistic purposes. Although the press is free to increase its appeal by offering gossipy stories about celebrities, including revealing pictures, lower courts find that if a media report is knowingly false, then the account can be treated not as journalism but as commercial exploitation.[76] In constitutional terms, this distinction permits liability when a media entity is no longer performing its constitutionally protected role.

Additional questions arise about which both the law and normative theory seem unclear. Even if it is granted that people have an autonomy-based First Amendment right to gather information by either observing or listening to another person in public, does this right restrict the extent to which the state (1) can limit when space is considered "public" or (2) restrict use of technologically enhanced means of gathering information? My tentative answer to both questions is that existing law rightfully assumes that the state has such policymaking authority and that there is no persuasive First Amendment basis for objection.

[75] The argument in the text would not seem confined to illegally obtained information. For instance, the state could argue that the name of a rape victim or the name of person who in the distant past engaged in some disreputable behavior is or is no longer a matter of public interest. So far, courts have, in my view properly, mostly rejected these arguments. *Cox Broadcasting Corp. v. Cohn*, 420 U.S. 469 (1975); *Hayes v. Alfred A. Knopf, Inc.*, 8 F.3d 1222 (7th Cir. 1993). The information may add to the journalistic or scholarly integrity of the reports as well as provide truthful information about individuals that other persons may want.

[76] See *Eastwood v. Superior Court*, 149 Cal. App. 3d 409 (1983); *Hoffman v. Capital Cities/ABC, Inc.*, 33 F. Supp. 2d 867 (C.D. Cal. 1999). This point does not suggest that a right to protect one's image from unwanted use is wise policy even in these contexts. See Michael Madow, "Private Ownership of Public Image: Popular Culture and Publicity Rights," *California Law Review* 81 (1993): 125–240.

Note that the two questions are parallel. The normative premise behind the idea of a public space is not that all information should necessarily be public but that, when in a public space, people should have an anarchic right to provide, gather, and receive information. There does not seem to be, however, any logical or natural way to determine in particular instances the borders of the public sphere in which this right of a flesh and blood person obtains. The informational-privacy-related reason to protect private property is to provide places beyond the peering eyes and listening ears to which a person is exposed in public. The law, though, could reduce protection of privacy by eliminating or limiting trespass laws to certain types of private property.[77] Likewise, the law could increase protection even on public property by protecting people from eavesdroppers when in a relatively secluded spot that provides a reasonable basis for assuming privacy.

Information that is only available to listeners or observers through technologically enhanced means should not be understood as inherently "in" a public space. Rather, allowing nonconsensual use of technology amounts to saying that the information it generates is effectively in a public space, while limiting the technology's use amounts to the opposite, treating the information as in a private sphere and the technology's use as trespassing. Both property rules and rules about technology use construct realms where people either are or are not protected from nonconsensual exposure. Both property and technologically enhanced observation could be regulated to protect privacy so that access only comes with permission, or could be left unrestricted so people are exposed. Just as the legal creation of both public space and private property is sociologically important, it seems likely that the law ought not automatically treat all the different technologies or different contexts of their use in the same way. Certainly, the value of privacy justifies treating some uses of technology as the equivalent of an invasion of a legally protected private sphere.

Telephone conversations are typically carried on cable or fiber optic lines that cross public space or on electromagnetic radio waves. Technology may allow a nonparticipant to hear (and record) conversations, although these eavesdroppers are as uninvited as if the conversation occurred in one's private home. Existing wiretap laws sensibly treat conversations floating across public spaces as private, even if an intruding listener is traveling on a public road and the participants in the conversation are in a public park using cell phones.

[77] Cf. *Florida Publishing v. Fletcher*, 340 So. 2d 914 (1976); *Prahl v. Brosamle*, Case No. 152-062, Circuit Court, Dane County, August 28, 1982, cited in Marc A. Franklin, David A. Anderson, and Fred H. Cate, *Mass Media Law*, 6th ed. (New York, Foundation Press: 2000), 570. Neither the notion of private property nor the Constitution requires a trespass doctrine like that common in most American jurisdictions. A court developing an implied consent for reporters' presence on private property, such as developed in *Fletcher* or *Prahl*, obviously does not assume that the owner would have actually consented in these circumstances, but, rather, assumes a public policy justification for treating reporters' presence as "custom."

Available technology allows a person receiving a call to identify the caller or, under readily available current technology, at least to identify the listed owner of the caller's phone. To protect the caller's privacy, could the government restrict the use of this "caller ID" technology, leaving it to the initiator of the call to voluntarily disclose her identity? The general assumption emphasized above is that people cannot be restricted from using their eyes and ears to identify a person. Putting aside the policy merits of this assumption, the question now is, does this freedom apply when the observation only occurs through use of technology? My claim has been that neither the interest in privacy nor the right to gather information automatically determines the best answer. A person should not automatically be assumed to have appeared in public for observation because she uses a telephone. Rather, whether she has so appeared should depend on society's policy choices about borders.

Even before the recent commercialization of "caller ID" technology, the architecture of the existing phone system allowed telephone companies to identify the phone initiating a call in order to route the recipient's reply to the right phone and to direct the phone bill to the responsible party. That is, the technology required a caller to identify herself (or at least her phone) to the phone company and its record keepers. Any law that limits a phone company's freedom to further utilize or communicate these records amounts to declaring the phone call private, which would be like treating it as having occurred on visually or aurally secluded private property controlled by the speakers, despite the caller having in a sense "voluntarily" exposed herself to the phone company. The law protects privacy in the call by restricting the phone company's speech. At first glance, the restraint might seem analogous to, but even less permissible than, restraints on further communications of illegally obtained information. The cases are distinguishable for two reasons, however. First, the telephone company should not be treated as having First Amendment speech rights. Second, the law can be treated as, in effect, creating a mandatory confidentiality term to the contract between the phone user and the company.

Likewise, the government should be able to protect privacy by declaring that disclosures functionally necessary for computer interactions are not to be treated as in a public space or as having been, in a constitutionally relevant sense, voluntarily exposed. Law professor Jerry Kang persuasively argues that the government should make the default rule be that the observer (the other computer or its owner) or the owner of the transmission system cannot permissibly "know" (make use of) the information *except* as needed to engage in the particular communicative interaction then occurring.[78] How this conclusion is understood is important. This default rule could follow from a notion of property in personal information (for example, property maintained until purposefully aban-

[78] Kang, *supra* note 56.

doned in a specific transaction).[79] This property premise, however, strikes too hard at the concept of a First Amendment 'commons' where people generally are free to observe and hear what they can and then to talk about it. The better premise is to understand Kang's default position as having treated technology's capacity to expand this experiential commons or public sphere as subject to policy-based restrictions. The default rule simply rejects treating disclosures that are technologically necessary for a transaction-facilitating purpose as placing the technologically generated information into a public space.

Technology, of course, changes many things. Not only does technology enhance the power to hear or observe, it also allows making a permanent record of what is currently available to a person to see, hear, and repeat or publish verbatim. Some states outlaw taping without the consent of all speakers. Since my only point here is that protection of a broad speech freedom, which includes the right to disseminate "private information" about another, does not prevent appropriate legal regulation of the information-gathering process, I leave aside the issue of whether this regulation of technology should be permissible. Journalists have argued to no avail that these laws make their reporting less accurate because they must rely on memory and notes, and, even when their stories are accurate, the laws leave the media much more vulnerable to defamation suits because it is more difficult to prove the accuracy of their reports.[80] Even if regulating technologically enhanced means of invading privacy sometimes may be both desirable and not contrary to any notion of speaker/observer autonomy, restrictions on taping seem much more problematic.[81] Still, a person may want to control when, or how, or even if *she* makes particular information public. Maybe the rule is more legitimate if directed against those who would force a person to be the unwilling or unknowing instrument (through recording) of communication.

B. *Uses and users of information*

Even though a party *properly* gathers or observes personal information about another, the use of such information presents an additional issue. An employer might freely observe another's race or sex but be forbidden to use that information in her hiring decisions. Free speech issues arise when the government regulates further communication of the information. Still, although the contexts are variable and sometimes raise contro-

[79] See Ann Bartow, "Our Data, Ourselves: Privacy, Propertization, and Gender," *University of San Francisco Law Review* 34 (2000): 633–704.

[80] *Dietemann v. Time, Inc.* 449 F.2d 245 (9th Cir. 1971); *Shevin v Sunbeam Television Corp.*, 351 So. 2d 723 (Fla. 1977).

[81] Diane Leenheer Zimmerman, "I Spy: The Newsgatherer under Cover," *University of Richmond Law Review* 33 (2000): 1185–1231 (review and tentative First Amendment critique of these restraints).

versial constitutional issues, restrictions on other uses usually are and should be permitted.

Consider cases where information initially was legally obtained but by means that were not themselves constitutionally protected, for example, it was not gathered within constitutionally protected conversation or through constitutionally protected observation in a public sphere. Under such circumstances, the source—the government or private party—may have imposed as a condition of access that the information only be used for particular purposes or that it not be used in particular ways. Often the government restricts the use of personnel files, sometimes just to the uses that justified gathering the information in the first place. It regularly provides certain government employees with personal or private information about other employees or about members of the public, but limits any further disclosure of the records apart from the purpose for which they were provided.[82] In *Seattle Times v Rhinehart* (1984),[83] the Court upheld a protective order, arguably a "prior restraint", prohibiting publication of private information that the press obtained through use of the governmentally granted discovery power. On the other hand, sometimes a restriction on publication of or conversation about information obtained with government help or permission is held to be unconstitutional. Such restrictions are always potentially subject to attack as 'unconstitutional conditions'.[84]

In the late 1990s, lower courts invalidated a law that, though it made available names and addresses of arrestees to private parties for many purposes, including media exposure, denied the information to recipients who intended to use the information directly or indirectly to sell a product or service. In *Los Angeles Police Department v. United Reporting Publishing Corp.* (1999), the Supreme Court reversed.[85] Chief Justice William Rehnquist (never known to worry much about unconstitutional conditions) simply treated the law as a facially permissible restriction on access to information. He distinguished this limit on access from what would be an overtly objectionable prohibition on speaking. Although he reached the right result, his reasoning should be very troubling. The permissibility of conditioning access should depend on both the context of the original receipt and the content of the restrictions.

[82] *Cf. Snepp v. United States*, 444 U.S. 507 (1980) (federal government can require former CIA employee not to disclose information obtained during employment without approval of agency).

[83] 467 U.S. 20 (1984).

[84] See *Seattle Times*, 467 U.S. at 37 (Brennan, J., and Marshall, J., concurring). Analogous to the unconstitutional condition doctrine, restrictions imposed by employers on further use by employees or restrictions imposed by contract could be unenforceable because contrary to public policy. A court could have easily decided to protect publication of the source's name in *Cohen v. Cowles Media Co.*, 501 U.S. 663 (1991), or information provided by whistleblowers on this nonconstitutional ground.

[85] 528 U.S. 32 (1999).

Such restraints should always be potentially vulnerable to an unconstitutional condition attack, which was precisely the point of Justices John Paul Stevens and Anthony Kennedy in their dissent. They would find the law unconstitutional for denying access to certain parties because of those parties' use of the information for particular (commercial) speech purposes. (If such restrictions were imposed by a private party, a reasonable argument could be made that courts should deny enforcement of the agreement as "state action" that would violate the First Amendment or as unenforceable because "contrary to public policy.")[86] However, if commercial speech as well as other commercial practices either should not be constitutionally protected[87] or, as under the current doctrinal regime,[88] are more easily subject to limitation, then the dissent's final conclusion should be rejected at least to the extent that the restricted uses of the information were all commercial.

In addition to regulating certain uses of "private" information (for example, for hiring decisions) and imposing appropriate conditions on governmentally supplied information, another basis for restricting use may be especially important: the government's general authority to regulate businesses and commercial practices, including those of professionals. Securities laws illustrate that this power extends to regulating speech involved in this business. Disclosures are required—and sometimes prohibited. Insider use of information is forbidden. In the legal world, also, government regularly restricts speech and the use of information. Although sometimes cast as a disagreement over the propriety of regulating speech that is inconsistent with a defense attorney's role, arguably the disagreement that ensued among the justices over the standard for regulating a defense attorney's out-of-court speech was primarily over their differing visions of a defense attorney's role.[89] Lawyers, doctors, psychologists, and other professionals are often prohibited by malpractice rules or rules of professional ethics from engaging in role-inconsistent speech. Usually these rules restrict the dissemination of private information gathered from clients. The premise in these examples is that it is constitutionally permissible in commercial or professional interactions to legally restrict the use of personal information to the functions for which it was given, unless the person specifically and voluntarily grants per-

[86] See *supra* note 84.

[87] Baker, *Human Liberty*, *supra* note 5, chap. 9.

[88] *Central Hudson Gas & Electric Corp. v. Public Service Commission of New York*, 447 U.S. 557 (1980).

[89] *Gentile v. State Bar of Nevada*, 501 U.S. 1030 (1991) (5–4 decision upholding particular restriction on defense attorney's out-of-court speech). The case involved a lawyer's public statements at a news conference that he called to defend his client and to attack the veracity of the police. The Nevada Supreme Court had issued rules preventing defense attorneys from making public statements that might taint the jury pool. The attorney's case against the state disciplinary board's recommendation that he be reprimanded eventually reached the U.S. Supreme Court.

mission for broader use. More generally, I have argued elsewhere that a commitment to an autonomy or liberty-based theory of freedom of speech would not justify any protection for the speech of commercial entities (except the press).[90] Though controversial, I will assume this conclusion here without repeating my arguments. Most advocates of speech rights for corporations do not reject my claim about the implications of an autonomy-based theory but instead base their claims on an alternative, usually a marketplace-of-ideas theory of speech, and emphasize the instrumental contribution of corporate speech in supplying people with information.[91]

If commercial entities can be limited in ways that would be impermissible to restrict noncommercial or media entities, determining what constitutes a media entity will sometimes be crucial in determining the permissibility of privacy regulations. One possibility is that First Amendment protection extends to any *information provider,* any entity that sells or has information (or opinion or art or music) as its product. This, however, seems too broad. Lawyers and doctors and accountants are largely information providers but are not likely candidates to be characterized as "the press." Alternatively, the protected entity could be one that offers *nonindividualized* communications as its product and makes this expression widely available to an interested public. The Investment Act of 1940 restricts who can engage in the investment-advice business, but exempts those who give advice by means of a bona fide publication of general and regular circulation. The Court majority in *Lowe v. Securities and Exchange Commission* (1985),[92] found that this exemption covered a publisher of an investment-advice newsletter. Rejecting this statutory interpretation, Justice Byron White's concurrence found the defendant nonexempt under the act but protected by the First Amendment. Both opinions are plausible on the facts. The interesting question is whether White's *constitutional* analysis could distinguish this newsletter publisher from nonmedia commercial actors, for example those selling more individualized investment advice. Justice White said that he did not "suggest that it would be unconstitutional to [apply the act's restrictions to] persons who, for compensation, offer personal investment advice to individual clients." He thereby implicitly accepted the distinction that I offered above: the permissibility of restricting dissemination by commercial entities but the impermissibility of restricting dissemination of the same information by the press (or, presumably, individuals acting noncommercially). Moreover, arguably even the press can be regulated when delivering advertising—speech that is paid for—

[90] See, e.g., Baker, *Human Liberty, supra* note 5, chap. 9.

[91] *Virginia State Board of Pharmacy v. Virginia Citizens Consumer Council, Inc.,* 425 U.S. 748 (1976); *First National Bank of Boston v. Bellotti,* 435 U.S. 765 (1978); Burt Neuborne, "The First Amendment and Government Regulation of Capital Markets," *Brooklyn Law Review* 55 (1989): 5–63.

[92] 472 U.S. 181 (1985).

rather than providing its own information and opinion.[93] In *SEC v. Wall Street Publishing Institute* (1988),[94] the D.C. Circuit Court of Appeals suggested that the government could require a paper to disclose the consideration (other than provision of free text) paid by the issuer of a security in exchange for the paper's publication of information about the security. Since the disclosure "carries an inherently pejorative connotation," the requirement should be seen as restricting the paper's freedom in disseminating paid-for speech, that is, advertising.[95]

The difficulty of deciding what counts as media may apply to (commercially accessible) databases. They are part of an information-supplying or communications industry. Should they either always or sometimes be treated as constitutionally protected media? Maybe not. In *Dun & Bradstreet v. Greenmoss Builders, Inc.* (1985),[96] the majority allowed punitive damages when a credit reporting business inaccurately (defamatorily) reported to a client that a major business in the community had filed for bankruptcy. The Court based its ruling on the speech not being a matter of public concern, thereby presumably taking personal information that is not a matter of public concern outside the constitutional protection of *Gertz v. Robert Welch, Inc.* (1974).[97] (*Gertz* had held that, as for defamatory information of public concern, the law could not provide punitive damages unless the speaker knew the information was false or recklessly disregarded the question of its truthfulness.) Although the dissent in *Greenmoss* persuasively argued that speech about "economic matters ... is an important part of our public discourse," the claim in this essay is that the majority's reasoning should be troubling even if the majority were right that a major local employer's bankruptcy was not a matter of public concern. Still, the outcome of the case may be right. The business of credit reporting is in many respects more like professions that are regulated than like the press. Just as an accountant sells tax advice, a credit reporting agency sells specific, individualized financial information to clients who seek the information to guide their commercial transactions.[98] These features distinguish credit reporting from both individuals' noncommercial speech and media communications.[99] If, but only if, my

[93] *Lewis Publishing Co. v. Morgan*, 229 U.S. 288 (1913). See generally, C. Edwin Baker, *Advertising and a Democratic Press* (Princeton, NJ: Princeton University Press, 1994), 118–37.

[94] 851 F.2d 365 (D.C. Cir. 1988).

[95] Despite this "commercial speech" explanation for the court's conclusion, the court's actual analysis was based on "government's broad power to regulate the securities industry." Clearly, however, the court was misguided to imply any broad, general governmental authority to regulate individuals' noncommercial speech or media speech about the securities industry.

[96] 472 U.S. 749 (1985).

[97] *Gertz v. Robert Welch, Inc.*, 418 U.S. 323 (1974).

[98] *Hadden View Investment Co. v. Coopers & Lybrand*, 70 Ohio St. 2d 154, 436 N.E.2d 212 (1982) (accountant malpractice).

[99] *Gutter v. Dow Jones Inc.*, 22 Ohio St. 3d 286, 490 N.E.2d 898 (1989) (liability for error in stock table denied in contrast to liability for accountant error).

proposed ground for the decision were accepted, it would be permissible for a law to require a credit reporting agency to allow a person to review her file, to maintain a procedure for challenging inaccuracies, or to include in its report an indication that the person reported on disputes certain information contained therein[100]—requirements that would mostly be unconstitutional if applied to newspapers.

Though *Greenmoss* could be understood to be about regulating a nonmedia business, a general power to regulate databases raises a somewhat different issue. Modern computer-based technology makes databases increasingly cheap to construct and easy to use. In finding a "personal privacy" interest in information that had previously been made public and was now stored on an FBI database containing rap sheets maintained on 24 million persons, the Court properly observed that "there is a vast difference between the public records that might be found after a diligent search of courthouse files, county archives, and local police stations throughout the country and a computerized summary located in a single clearinghouse of information."[101] But what follows for regulatory power? Consider, for example, four possible contexts: (1) laws generally restricting the conversion of certain types of properly obtained information into data collections; (2) laws regulating the maintenance of databases; (3) laws restricting creation of databases for certain (commercial) uses; and (4) laws restricting certain (commercial) uses of database information.[102]

As to the first context, using computer technology in processing and organizing information about a person is in many respects parallel to using technology to gather information on her that would not otherwise be available to our eyes and ears. Arguably, both uses of technology should be equally subject to regulation. Or maybe an even closer analogy is tape recording. Even when a person has a constitutional right to hear and publish verbatim the contents of a speech, current doctrine permits a legal prohibition on recording it without the consent of the speaker, thereby preventing the listener from making the most accurate use of information that she rightfully possesses. In each of these cases, information about a person has been exposed, but the law would restrict technology that makes the information more usable. Nevertheless, it might be wise to resist these pro-regulatory conclusions. Not having a general right to process, comprehend, or access information that one rightfully has (and then to communicate it) seems to contradict the freedom of the intellect that surely is part of the meaning of free speech. Could a newspaper be barred from keeping and using files of its past stories? If not, could it be prohibited from using computers to do so at a lower cost than before?

[100] Cf. Fair Credit Reporting Act (1970) and Consumer Credit Reporting Act of 1996, 15 U.S.C. § 1681–1681t.

[101] *United States Dep't of Justice v. Reporters Committee for Freedom of the Press*, 489 U.S. 749 (1989).

[102] My thinking here was prompted by Cohen, *supra* note 6.

Can individuals, for example, sociologists or historians, be prohibited from engaging in such activities? If the answer to these questions is "no," although the issue is not beyond doubt, then general restrictions—for example, restrictions that apply not just to certain businesses or to certain uses but to all individuals and the press—on entering information into databases seem very questionable. Moreover, as to the second context, the same arguments apply to regulation of the maintenance of databases.

Regarding the third and fourth contexts—laws restricting creation or uses of databases for certain commercial purposes—the permissibility of such laws may well be the same as the permissibility of regulating other commercial practices. All commercial practices, including the creation and use of databases, are generally subject to regulation while noncommercial and media uses of information are properly protected unless a particular use (e.g., for criminal purposes) is independently outlawed.[103] Certainly, commercial uses of information about a person's race or sex are subject to prohibition. Some versions of a right of publicity restrict unconsented use of a person's image even when the image is itself the product. This use of a person's image is equivalent to the media providing the public with an expressive product that contains information or vision. Despite the questionable constitutionality of the right of publicity in this context, forbidding unconsented use of a person's image for advertising is more clearly constitutional.[104] Restrictions on collecting information or using information in databases designed for commercial uses may be more like, and as permissible as, the second category of right of publicity claims: those restricting unconsented use of the person's image in advertising. The law cannot give a person a general property right in her *persona,* that is, in personal information, but it can give her such a right assertable against nonmedia commercial uses.

If the restrictions described in the above paragraph are acceptable, then the implications are huge for greater protection of privacy. Those espousing privacy values often state them in sweeping, general terms as a purported right of a person to control (usually personal or private) information about herself. However, the issue is mostly inflamed by people's sense of being ever more subject to manipulation, harassment, or targeting (e.g., unwanted phone solicitations) by market entities (or by government). If gathering, assembling, and using private information for commercial purposes were limited, the major concerns of privacy advocates would be met. These rules could also dramatically reduce the incentives for construction of offending databases, thereby further reducing the threat to privacy.

[103] But cf. the government's questionable concession in *United Reporting, supra* note 85, that if the commercial user "independently acquires the data, the First Amendment protects its right to communicate it to others." 528 U.S. at 45 (Stevens, J., dissenting).

[104] All scope for a right of publicity is critiqued in Michael Madow, *supra* note 76. My claim here is that the constitutional critique should only apply to nonadvertising appropriations of another person's image.

Regulation of market activities might even go a step further. General rules forbidding alienation of private information impermissibly restrict a person's speech about herself. I suggested, however, that the law could establish a default position that information exposed by engaging in digital communications could only be used for functionally necessary aspects of the particular interaction involved. Still, commercial entities may be in a powerful strategic position to obtain consent to unrestricted use of the information in exchange for something they offer, such as access to their Web site, individualized service, a lower price or free use, or whatever. Standard reasons to regulate market transactions—for example, unequal information, structures that create inappropriate amounts of power of one party over the other, negative impact on third parties—could possibly justify prohibitions on market alienation of private information. A person would be left free, though, to publish personal information or even to give it to a particular commercial entity, except not in exchange for some benefit.

Many privacy advocates will not be satisfied with the protections defended here. Nevertheless, much of the rise in popular concern about disappearing privacy apparently, and quite reasonably, relates to fears about the collection and manipulative use of information by corporate and governmental bodies. Basically, my claim is that most privacy-protection policies that relate to *these* threats, although possibly difficult to secure politically, do not conflict with First Amendment principles. The area of real conflict between free speech and privacy is much more limited. The abstract principle that requires respect for people as autonomous agents in control of their own speech choices dictates that, in this discrete context, privacy claims should lose. Sections VI and VII will argue that this result is pragmatically justified on the basis of plausible, though inevitably inconclusive, consequentialist considerations. However, before taking up that issue, a final means of protecting privacy, which turns out to be fully consistent with the First Amendment, merits comment.

C. Strongest protector: Nonlegal norms

Probably the greatest protection of informational privacy comes through voluntary decisions not to disclose "private" information about another person or, possibly more often, to monitor closely when and to whom to make disclosures. These decisions are often quite rigidly determined by nonlegal social norms, such as the injunction not to "snitch." All communities value privacy, although to varying degrees and in relation to different information. Communities predictably develop different privacy-protecting social norms or practices that embody their judgments about privacy. Robert Post is surely correct about the necessity of "civility rules" for the maintenance of communities, communities that are themselves necessary for autonomous individuals to develop.[105]

The mistake would be to assume that these civility rules require legal or other formal enforcement mechanisms. As an empirical matter, I expect that reliance on social practice will maintain sufficient civility rules to fully meet Post's concern with having an environment in which people can develop as (autonomous) individuals. In contrast, legal enforcement of civility rules that protect privacy against offending communications, as well as enforcement of most other civility rules relating to expression, may make communities more rigid, oppressive, and slow to adopt useful change.

Contrary to frequent communitarian characterizations of liberal theory, my claims on behalf of the First Amendment never assume that individuals are factually "unencumbered" or that effective or meaningful autonomy can be a context-free conception. Both legal and societal respect for formal autonomy and practical realization of meaningful autonomy are historical achievements, not abstract realities that provide an ahistorical basis for some mythical social contract.[106] Rather, liberal theory's more modest claim is that appropriate respect for people's autonomy requires that individuals be left with the right to accept or at least to attempt to reject actual "encumbrances," that is, that they be left formally free to help to create or change their context by their choices. In this view, civility rules, though valuable as a category, in any particular case may be misguided or, at least, appropriately contestable. When these rules ought to be maintained, normally people's voluntary allegiance and informal enforcement will suffice. Change occurs when more and more individuals decide that the rules are wrong and act on their rebellious views. Behavioral votes are in a sense much more democratic and engaged than are the government's official decisions. Each person's behavioral vote contributes to the creation of the culture, the social rules. In many respects, this approach to civility rules is analogous to language. Both the existence of grammar and shared word meanings are necessary for social life. However, both are maintained—and changed—by a behavioral summing of people's speech choices.

The voluntariness of language rules does not mean that grammar and shared word meanings are not of major significance or a proper subject of government policy. Public education and, in a curiously different way, public support for the arts both, at times, exemplify such policies. (This

[105] Robert C. Post, "The Social Foundations of Defamation Law: Reputation and the Constitution," *California Law Review* 74 (1986): 691; Robert Post, *Constitutional Domains: Democracy, Community, Management* (Cambridge, MA: Harvard University Press, 1995). For a liberal account of the necessity of community for development of individual autonomy and its implications for political theory, see also Will Kymlicka, *Liberalism, Community, and Culture* (Oxford: Oxford University Press, 1989).

[106] See Baker, "Sandel on Rawls," *supra* note 29.

fact is roughly analogous to the point of the two preceding subsections.) Information privacy can be a matter of policy embodied in legal rules even if not protected directly by law that prohibits offending speech choices. Civility rules—group choices—about what information should be private and private in what ways or to what extent, operate within a legal structure that protects against certain information-collection devices (e.g., secretly taping what happens in the bedroom) and that regulates various commercial uses of information.

These nonlegal norms protecting privacy can be both extraordinarily important and quite effective. They often protect secretive individuals, adding to their freedom. They both maintain and are maintained by group solidarity. Legal scholar Randall Kennedy describes how most African Americans know of other blacks who "pass." Despite African Americans' general disapproval of passing and despite their capacity to prevent it by exposure, social norms effectively prohibit exposure, especially exposure to whites.[107] Even in a world in which "passers" could hardly expect the law to protect them against exposure, these social norms have provided considerable protection. Interestingly, speech freedom provided not only *unused* power that blacks could have used over other "passing" blacks, but also power to enforce the informal civility rule of nonexposure. In the 1930s when an exclusive, "whites-only" restaurant hired blacks to identify passers who were attempting entry, presumably on the theory that it takes one to know one, Kennedy reports that "a Negro-owned newspaper published the names of the lookouts." [108] In a sense, the newspaper revealed personal information about some people in order to enforce, and to punish them for violating, the civility rule against revealing certain personal information about others.

The account offered by communications professor Larry Gross of the history and debates over "outing" of gays makes the point even more powerfully.[109] The rule against exposing another person's homosexuality has incredible strength, especially among gay men and lesbians. "Outing" had long been considered as a possible political strategy. It was debated by what Gross described as the first homosexual emancipation movement, but the Scientific Humanitarian Committee, founded in Germany in 1897, quickly rejected the "frequently suggested 'path over corpses.' " [110]

[107] Randall Kennedy, "Racial Passing," *Ohio State Law Journal* 62 (2001): 1145–93, 1171–73. Even if African Americans mostly condemn passing, many also view it as a method to flout and subvert silly but oppressive racist laws and norms. *Id.* at 1169–70. Kennedy observes that "Langston Hughes repeatedly defended passing as a joke on racism." *Id.*

[108] *Id.* at 1171 (citing Shirlee Taylor Haizlip's account). Cf. *NAACP v. Claiborne Hardware Co.*, 458 U.S. 886 (1982) (among constitutionally protected methods of exercising power, boycotters of white businesses applied pressure on black "violators" by reading aloud their names in church and by publishing their names in a local black newspaper).

[109] This paragraph is based entirely on Gross, *supra* note 2.

[110] *Id.* at 9. Corpses may lie with both alternatives. Gross notes the suggestion that lack of positive role models contributes to the severely disproportionate number of suicides among gay youth. *Id.* at 126.

The history of outing and especially the debate over outing in the 1980s and 1990s shows the extreme continuing power of the rule forbidding disclosure. Most mainstream gay and lesbian groups and leaders claim to reject outing in any circumstances, although some evidence indicates that most individual gay men and lesbians viewed "outing" as appropriate in specific circumstances, most commonly in cases where the outed person exercised considerable power and publicly and effectively used that power to harm gays and their causes. Some thought the social good that could be expected to result from outing justified its use in somewhat broader contexts, for example, in identifying major sports, entertainment, or business figures who were potential role models. Interestingly, these supporters of outing typically argued their case within the homosexual community and, even though legally free to speak and thereby advance the good as they saw it, they seldom violated the community consensus not to out. That is, although the rule was nonlegal and unwritten, the possibility to propose "amendments" or repeal existed within the large gay public sphere, and yet when unamended, the rule remained generally effective—with occasional and usually very limited occasions of "civil disobedience" by "radicals."

The lesson of this history of outing, as well as the history of passing, might be threefold. First, informational privacy can be extraordinarily important and valuable even when, as the example of passing illustrates, the legal order would happily condone disclosure. Second, especially among those who have the information and, thus, often the power[111] to violate informational privacy, social norms protecting privacy can be extraordinarily effective.[112] Third, the existence of speech freedom allows for both participatory debate and practice that can challenge and change, or defend and maintain, these rules.

VI. Overvaluation of Privacy

My abstract thesis is that formal autonomy, or free speech rights, should operate as a side constraint on policy formulation, that is, it should act as a "trump." Speech rights should prevail even when they run roughshod

[111] The capacity of someone with information to "out" another should not be assumed too quickly. A common mainstream view has been that homosexuality is not *so* bad as long as kept secret. The "Don't ask, don't tell" policy had not yet been invented by the U.S. military when Gross wrote his book, but he fully explained the appeal of such a policy. Gross, *supra* note 2, at 144–52. The mainstream press reflected this view by engaging in "inning," that is, by refusing to indicate a person's homosexuality in contexts where it would indicate a person's heterosexuality. Similarly, the press often refused to report as "news" that a major figure who assumed a public heterosexual image was actually gay, while routinely reporting other personal "news" about the figure.

[112] This point should not obscure the fact that "outing" in neighborhoods, employment, and social contexts of gays, usually by nongays, also occurs and often has tremendously harmful consequences. At the end of my discussion of gossip below in the text, I note that gossip has overtly negative as well as useful consequences.

over people's desire to keep information private. This thesis rejects giving people any property right in information about themselves that can be used to control the communicative choices of other individuals or the media.

Nevertheless, informational privacy is extraordinarily important to individuals and to communities. The information that should be kept private and the appropriate methods of guarding this privacy, however, are matters on which people and communities will differ. Societal self-definition involves creating particular types of communities, encouraging certain values and practices, and even supporting certain images of persons. In formulating privacy policies, all of these considerations, as well as concerns about efficiency and distribution, should have a role. Of course, the proper content and weight of these efficiency, justice, and self-definitional concerns, even as goals, are contestable. Nevertheless, elsewhere I have argued that their appropriate elaboration would lead to considerable legal protection for the privacy of persons and much less protection for the privacy of instrumentally valued, institutional creations such as corporations (or governments).[113] Informational privacy is a valuable resource. Control over information can be a major form of power. Since each person would be a beneficiary, a personal right of informational privacy would be, distributionally, relatively egalitarian as compared to rights to material wealth that are often held very unequally. This egalitarian quality is a major plus in favor of a personal informational privacy right. But possibly most important is the contribution that privacy makes to meaningful autonomy, the capacity to lead a self-authored life. In contrast, these same concerns point the opposite way in respect to powerful institutions. An egalitarian or democratic social policy should be hesitant about unnecessarily increasing the power of already powerful institutions, including their ability to protect their own privacy and their capacity to invade the privacy of individuals. Thus, Section V drew from the work of many privacy scholars, as well as constitutional precedent, to suggest a wide variety of ways in which the law should be able to protect personal informational privacy.

Now, I want to take a different tack. This section suggests that privacy, no matter how essential for people's flourishing, currently is in danger of being seriously overrated, at least in many contexts. Thus, my claim here begins an inevitably incomplete pragmatic defense of the thesis that, when at stake, formal autonomy should "trump" privacy or, if the trumping conception is resisted, that formal autonomy justifies great caution before being compromised by pro-privacy policies.

Warren and Brandeis's encomiums for a right of informational privacy have resounded more in the court of public opinion than in the courts of

[113] Baker, "Posner's Privacy Mystery," *supra* note 40. This argument responds to the opposite conclusion offered in Richard Posner, "The Right of Privacy," *Georgia Law Review* 12 (1978): 393–422.

law. Currently, great popular support exists for a right to privacy from the snooping eyes of government, of the media, and of corporate marketers. Also, people commonly disapprove of, for somewhat different reasons, neighborhood or office "gossip." Although I certainly cannot prove it, I am inclined to believe that there has been a recent surge in the popular appeal of informational privacy.[114] Not only is the informational privacy tort a twentieth century invention, but my impression is that in the twenty-some years since legal scholar Diane Zimmerman's "requiem" for the tort,[115] it has found greater judicial backing.

Greater popularity may reflect the plausible view that the increase in commercial use of newly cheapened, individualized marketing strategies and mounting encroachments by government have put privacy in greater danger today than ever before. Resistance to the "disciplinary agencies" of government and the market is surely progressive and justified. Possibly the central factor in their greater power, as well as a prime generator of increased fears, is the incredible advances in computer and related digital technologies that dramatically reduce the cost of collecting information and, possibly more ominously, lower the cost of indexing, storing, and retrieving it.[116] If this power is driving the public's concern with informational privacy, the concern embodies a value orientation very similar to that implicit in my emphasis on autonomy. To be the author of their own lives, people want to evade the intrusive eyes of those who can exercise power over them. Of course, as contrasted to the claims of formal autonomy for speech rights and for locating final authority for choice in the individual, this concern refers more to the practical level of making autonomy effective or meaningful. From this perspective, society should resist any retreat from the defense of informational privacy and reject, for example, the advice of right-wing demagogues who recommend giving up civil liberties, including rights of privacy, in an irrational reaction to the criminal acts of September 11, 2001. Protection of privacy can be a sign of a self-assured society. Sound arguments justify many policy responses to popular demands for privacy, except, in my view, those aimed at limiting individuals' speech freedom or at censoring (as opposed to restructuring) the media.

Nevertheless, another possible basis for the growing popularity of privacy rights may be a sign of cultural sickness. Troublingly, the high valuation of privacy may reflect increasing desires to withdraw from civil society and especially from the public sphere. This increasingly common preference for virtually complete withdrawal stands in dramatic contrast to the classic vision of a private realm as a necessary base to which a person periodically repairs, but always with the hope and expectation of returning to the public world. My fear is that the current positive valu-

114 Zimmerman, "I Spy," *supra* note 81.

115 Zimmerman, "Requiem for a Heavyweight," *supra* note 62.

116 Oscar H. Gandy, Jr., *The Panoptic Sort: A Political Economy of Personal Information* (Boulder, CO: Westview Press, 1993).

ation of privacy reflects a society in which all value is increasingly seen as located in private life. To an increasing extent, people seem to find all meaning in private interactions of family and other personal associations or, even more disconcertingly, in a more purely commodity-oriented world of private consumption with value largely based on wealth and material goods.[117] According to this account, the value-orientation of commercial advertisers has virtually won. My concern is not with people recognizing that privacy and private life have true worth, but with their loss of a sense of value in public life. The public sphere is increasingly devalued and disinhabited. Though this point requires more development, my claim is that as a normative matter, the classical vision of society and of public life is more appealing, and the newer vision of "withdrawal" represents a dangerous decline.

Withdrawal represents a direct threat to the First Amendment values of dissent and challenge to the status quo.[118] Often people will not merely withdraw themselves, but will also seek to enforce withdrawal. They fear that an active public sphere would disrupt conventional norms and private life. Not everyone loves a parade if, for example, it is a civil rights, antiwar, or neo-Nazi march. In his useful study of gay politics, Larry Gross noted how protection of privacy has been central to the gay agenda. In the years immediately after the "liberal" British *Wolfenden Report* in 1957,[119] which recommended decriminalizing private homosexual behavior, and the British adoption of this policy, what resulted was an increase in prosecutions for arguably public homosexual behavior as the govern-

[117] I am not in a position to prove this characterization to those who do not see it. Still, declining levels of voting, the media's reduced emphasis on policy-oriented or political news, the view that society's problems are more a matter of charity or private action than public policy, a cynical view of politicians and public servants, the so-called "bowling alone" phenomenon, as well as interpretations of popular culture, are among the features of social life that I would examine for evidence. Battles over taxes (or the size of government) can be seen as disagreements about whether *marginal* value lies more in public or private expenditures of resources and energies. A retreat to private life, if it exists, may be a uniformly global phenomenon or it may be that the United States is alone or at least in the vanguard, in which case comparative evidence would be informative. For example, the only reports that appeared in the mainstream American media on the 2003 Finnish parliamentary elections emphasized the lack of policy differences or issues, other than how to respond to increased unemployment, between the two dominant parties, which produced a voter turnout of only 70 percent. Lizette Alvarez, "Finnish Center Party Edges Past Social Democrats in Election," *New York Times*, March 17, 2003, late edition–final, sec. A, p. 2, col. 3. Only by going beyond U.S. media, say, by viewing BBC online, could one discover that another prominent issue was the losing Social Democrats' inadequate opposition to President Bush's military policy toward Iraq. A Finnish academic told me, however, that the real story was the dramatic loss of seats by the conservative party, which apparently fell from favor because of the unpopularity of its promise of a tax cut, while both leading leftist parties picked up seats.

[118] Steven H. Shiffrin, *Dissent, Injustice, and the Meanings of America* (Princeton, NJ: Princeton University Press, 1999).

[119] *Report of The Committee on Homosexual Offenses and Prostitution, The Wolfenden Report*, authorized American ed. (New York: Stein and Day, 1963). The report stimulated a famous debate between Patrick Devlin and H. L. A. Hart. See Patrick Devlin, *The Enforcement of Morals* (Oxford: Oxford University Press, 1965); and H. L. A. Hart, *Law, Liberty, and Morality* (Stanford, CA: Stanford University Press, 1963).

ment tried to enforce closeting. Gross explained that mainstream opinion was often most adamant about preserving the *public* prevalence of heterosexual norms. Conservative policy could tolerate the private practice of homosexuality, while focusing its attention on the suppression of any public expression of homosexuality.[120] In an American example of the same phenomenon, the *Houston Post*, which apparently accepted the *private* homosexuality of its star minority columnist, nevertheless fired him when it became known that the paper had forced him to delete from his column a *public* disclosure of his homosexuality. Eventually, the paper rehired him, but only after public protests by Houston's Hispanic community and the local chapter of Queer Nation.[121]

As I previously noted, during the late 1980s and 1990s when "outing" was a central topic within the gay community, the matter of informational privacy almost inevitably came to the fore. Describing it as a right/left split, Gross noted two views of outing. First, many gay advocates argued that "the primary issue for the gay movement (perhaps the only issue) was the protection of the right of privacy." [122] Opposition to "outers" was shrill even among some very thoughtful, important gay advocates. Randy Shilts, for one, characterized outers as "lavender fascists who would force their ideology on everyone." [123] Others described outing as immoral, as McCarthyism, terrorism, cannibalism, or as equivalent to a "bunch of Jews lining up other Jews to go to a concentration camp." [124] On the second view, which Gross characterized as the more leftist of the two, the issue was seen as one of gays' "right to create communities and their right to publicity" and its advocates argued that "[i]t is primarily our *public* existence, and not our right to privacy, which is under assault by the right." [125]

Gross observed that publicity played a key role in the process of societal change in attitudes toward heterosexual cohabitation. He concluded that there is "no way to move beyond [antigay] attitudes without accepting and acting on the presumption that homosexuality must be seen and treated the same as heterosexuality. . . . [I]t behooves . . . us . . . to act accordingly, and outing—or [as journalist and activist Gabriel Aotello calls it], equalizing—is a means to this end." [126] Basically, this claim is that "[e]mphasizing [the right of privacy] plays right into our enemies' hands. Private is . . . exactly what they want us to be. . . . [W]e are . . . fighting less for the right to privacy than for the right not to have to be private." [127]

[120] Gross, *supra* note 2, at 144–50. See also Larry Cata Becker, "Exposing the Perversions of Toleration: The Decriminalization of Private Sexual Conduct, the Model Penal Code, and the Oxymoron of Liberal Toleration," *Florida Law Review* 45 (1993): 755–802.

[121] Gross, *supra* note 2, at 149–50.

[122] *Id.* at 146.

[123] *Id.* at 152.

[124] *Id.* at 127.

[125] *Id.* at 146.

[126] *Id.* at 169–70.

[127] *Id.* at 172 (quoting Benjamin Schatz, "Should We Rethink the Right to Privacy?" *Advocate*, February 1991).

Another illustration of the devaluing of public life can be found in a rarely commented upon aspect of libel law. A society that highly valued public life and civic participation would presumably reward and encourage, not penalize and burden, participation in public life. Although such a society would maintain and respect a private sphere to which all people could repair for relief, provisions, contemplation, and amusement, it would hardly encourage a total retreat to a "purely" private life. People in public life share with people who shun public roles a legitimate interest in maintaining their reputations and in conducting their private lives free from prying eyes. Actually, the parallel is not exact. For a person in public life, the consequences of injury to her reputation among people whom she does not know, with whom she does not work, and whom she will probably never meet, are normally much more severe than is a similar injury for those who do not enter public life. Reputation among strangers is often a major asset, a virtual currency, for people in public life, but it is of little instrumental significance for a purely private person. To oversimplify, reputation is truly valuable for a private person only among her close compatriots, while for the public person it is also extraordinarily valuable among strangers. Media libels carry a greater risk of influencing the perceptions of a public figure in the minds of strangers than of friends. Strangers will have fewer or no firsthand alternative bases on which to evaluate the libel, fewer opportunities to hear the libeled person's defense, and often less incentive to inquire further. Thus, as compared to libels communicated to friends or even acquaintances, libels communicated to strangers are more likely to be determinative of their views. In other words, the legitimate interest in protection from media libels seems to be much greater in the case of people in public life.

Yet, existing defamation law reverses both my normative premises and my descriptive hypotheses. Rather than reward a person for becoming a public official or public figure by specially honoring her legitimate interests (e.g., in being spoken about truthfully), defamation law burdens such a person with greater legal vulnerability to libelous falsehoods.[128] To recover, she must prove that the libel was made with knowledge of its falsity or reckless disregard of its falsity, while the private person must only prove fault (i.e., negligence). (For public figures, increased vulnerability, apparently, also applies in the context of intentional infliction of emotional distress through public ridicule.)[129]

This result does not reflect merely the judgment that (hopefully truthful) information about public issues is especially important, and, thus, the First Amendment should be especially protective in this context. Private figures receive more legal protection than public figures from injurious

[128] *Gertz v. Robert Welch, Inc.*, 418 U.S. 323 (1974).

[129] The Court has not ruled on the application of this tort to private persons. However, in *Hustler Magazine v. Falwell*, 485 U.S. 46 (1988), while applying the *Sullivan* standard of "actual malice" to inflictions of emotional distress, the Court emphasized that the case involved public figures.

speech even if the speech involves reporting on vitally important public issues. In *Gertz*, the Court reversed the normative principles that I suggested above and said "private individuals are . . . more *deserving of recovery*," (emphasis added) apparently because private persons have made no attempt to assume "an 'influential role in ordering society.' " To this lack of involvement, the Court contrasted "[a]n individual who decides to seek governmental office," who, the Court says, "must accept certain necessary consequences."[130] The fallacies in this argument are twofold. First, the consequence at issue, nonprotection from damaging falsehoods, is not "necessary"; rather, it results specifically from the Court's own doctrine that denies protection. The Court decided to impose the greater danger on, by denying protection to, the person who chose to participate actively in the public sphere. Second, desert should have cut the opposite way. Public participation should be valued and could have been rewarded. Instead, the Court implicitly concluded that the state appropriately burdens this choice to become a public figure (believing that virtually all people who acquire this status do so voluntarily) by requiring that public figures give up much of their legal claim not to be subjected to reputational and emotional injuries. Essentially, the Court said that the state acts properly in rewarding people for avoiding the public sphere.

In discussions of informational privacy, 'private' refers to a characteristic of the information. In contrast, defamation law introduces a somewhat different, dual conception of 'private'. First, it raises a question about whether the information at issue involved "matters of public importance," a characteristic similar to that which fuels informational privacy analyses. However, courts usually wish to avoid the appearance of ideological regulation of the marketplace of ideas. Courts should be, and often have been, loath to say that any content that a newspaper decided to publish was not about a matter of public importance.[131] Defamation law utilizes a second conception of privacy, and here courts are more active in interjecting their own judgments. Defamation law asks whether the person allegedly defamed is a public figure or a private person.

These two usages, privacy of the information and of the person, are connected in at least two ways. First, a person might want not to be a public figure precisely because she values control over her personal or private information, and she reasonably expects that it will be more difficult (even putting the law aside) to have this control if she becomes a public figure. A public figure loses her privacy both because the law protects it less and because people have a greater interest in knowing personal facts about her. Second, treatment of informational privacy as especially valuable may make for a culture that is more inclined to praise and reward private life, while the society that values and rewards active

[130] *Gertz*, 418 U.S. at 344–45.

[131] *Dun & Bradstreet v. Greenmoss Builders, Inc.*, 472 US 749 (1985), is a rare exception where the Court, despite the dissent's devastating critique, characterized the content as private.

participation in the public sphere, although not ignoring the value of informational privacy, is likely to rank fame higher and informational privacy lower in its list of values. In any event, a positive valuation of civic participation and public excellence provides a reason for caution about maintaining too great an emphasis on informational privacy, except, as noted in Section V, when that emphasis relates specifically to preventing manipulation and control by governmental or corporate entities.

VII. The Value of Gossip

The common practice most at war with informational privacy is gossip, though the notion of gossip may understate the area of my concern. Warren and Brandeis may be right about gossip being the activity of the idle,[132] in that at least some researchers make idleness part of its definition.[133] Other characteristics are relevant here. 'Gossip' is generally about a person and conducted behind that person's back. Personal information that a person would not want known is its usual content, which suggests why gossip and informational privacy clash.[134] However, my focus in this essay is broader than the conventional understanding of the term 'gossip' indicates. The essay covers speech involving personal information even when it is used more overtly and more purposefully than is usually the case when we refer to 'gossip'. As noted earlier, the conception of formal autonomy as a trump—or a requirement of full protection for speech—would protect gossip. My claim here is that this protection is not an unfortunate aspect of our initial commitment to formal autonomy, so unfortunate as to plausibly justify a reconsideration of our original normative impulse favoring speech freedom. Quite the contrary, gossip is a valuable aspect of free speech.[135]

Even if gossip occurs most often when people are idle, so does the preponderance of most people's *other* conversation, including political discussions. Though Warren and Brandeis did have some legitimate complaints, their association of gossip with idleness probably represented an attempt to belittle the activity. Nevertheless, the productive work done by gossip is multifarious, important, and often political in significant ways. Gossip provides a major mechanism for teaching social norms, often helping to show the norms' real, as opposed to perceived, weight. Psycholo-

[132] Warren and Brandeis, *supra* note 1, at 196.

[133] John Sabini and Maury Silver, *Moralities of Everyday Life* (Oxford: Oxford University Press, 1982), 92–94.

[134] Nothing here turns on a more precise definition of gossip; Sabini and Silver devote most of a chapter to describing the concept. *Id.* at 89–106. I should emphasize that nothing about gossip implies anything about whether it is or is not accurate, but the gossip that I defend here is only gossip that is not subject to the critique of being knowingly or recklessly false.

[135] This section draws heavily on Sabini and Silver, *supra* note 133; Gluckman, *supra* note 3.

gists John Sabini and Maury Silver observe that gossip is almost surely the way by which most people would unpack the ambiguities implicit in an abstract ethical injunction such as "Sex must be part of a meaningful relationship." [136] Gossip is also a major device for enforcing group norms. It is a central means of social control. Max Gluckman, one of the leading anthropologists of the twentieth century, emphasized how gossip, which is virtually a duty of membership in small groups, plays a crucial role in maintaining the unity of a group and its norms, as well as in establishing and policing the borders of the group.[137] English professor Patricia Meyer Spacks adds that gossip not only is "a crucial means of self-expression, a crucial form of solidarity," but also "provides a resource for the subordinated." [138] This is a theme she frequently reasserts.[139] Using fiction as her primary data on humanity, she finds that gossip not only "exemplifies the communal," it performs a "reparative function for the socially deprived." [140] Larry Gross, observing the use of gossip about celebrities in the "crafting of gay subcultural identity," [141] indirectly relies on Spacks' "analysis of gossip as an alternative discourse through which 'those who are otherwise powerless can assign meanings and assume the power of representation . . . reinterpreting . . . materials from the dominant culture into shared private meanings.' " [142] Relatedly, gossip is often a way of exercising power over dominant figures in one's community, and sometimes a method of partially removing oneself from their power.

Formulating, debating, teaching, and changing the norms of social life may be the most important social function of gossip. Certainly, there is more to be said for gossip, even more than noting its apparently universal appeal, an appeal almost as universal as that of sex, which is often its subject. Gossip is an essential means of communication. "[S]ex and gossip alike comprise modes of intimate communication," both of which are widely available to the dispossessed and marginalized as well as the powerful, are self-expressive, and are thereby "unpredictable and uncontrollable." [143] Additionally, gossip's democratic qualities should not be ignored. The ubiquity of the capacity to gossip and roughly equal distri-

[136] Sabini and Silver, *supra* note 133, at 100–101.

[137] Gluckman, *supra* note 3.

[138] Patricia Meyer Spacks, *Gossip* (New York: Alfred A. Knopf, 1985), 5. See also James C. Scott, *Domination and the Arts of Resistance* (New Haven, CT: Yale University Press, 1990), 142–43.

[139] See, e.g., Spacks, *supra* note 138, at 46. She claims that "gossip gives voices to the dominated as well as the dominant." *Id.* at 263.

[140] *Id.* at 256.

[141] Gross, *supra* note 2, at 125.

[142] *Id.* at 124 (quoting Andrea Weiss, "'A Queer Feeling When I Look at You': Hollywood Stars and Lesbian Spectatorship in the 1930s," in Christine Gledhill, ed., *Stardom: Industry of Desire* [London: Routledge, 1991], 283–99).

[143] Spacks, *supra* note 138, at 40. The role of sex as a form of communication is the reason that I have given for providing First Amendment protection to consensual sex. See, e.g., C. Edwin Baker, "Op-Ed: First Amendment Protection for Gays," *New York Times*, July 27, 1991, late-edition final, p. 23.

bution of this capacity make gossip an especially significant democratic tool of societal self-constitution. That is, not only is gossip possibly the most widely practiced method of participation in collective life, but it is also a relatively democratically distributed form of power to participate, and it is often used against people in positions of authority, sometimes bringing down or at least humbling them.

This essay places on center stage a conception of formal autonomy or liberty of choice that is often criticized as too individualistic.[144] In contrast, democratic participation is praised as a form of liberty that is appropriately and overtly oriented toward the public. Some scholars who advance this critique contrast liberty of choice, "the liberty of the moderns," unfavorably with democratic participation, "the liberty of the ancients."[145] The two are connected, however, in that both are about self-determination, which necessarily involves individual choices *and* participation in inherently collective choices. Gossip, like political speech, brings together the individual and the collective in another way. The capacity to gossip is an individual power, usually practiced outside the limelight of any official public sphere. It functions, however, to substantially involve the individual in the collective enterprise of norm creation, evaluation, and enforcement. These activities are fundamentally political. Arguably, much norm-evaluative, norm-exploratory, or norm-enforcement gossip merits the label "political speech" even more directly than the campaign speech that is merely instrumental to the selection of office holders.[146]

First Amendment scholar Thomas Emerson listed four functions or values of speech that justified constitutional protection. His third function emphasized political participation in decision-making by all members of society. But this significant aspect of speech freedom, Emerson argued, "carries beyond the political realm. It embraces the right to participate in the building of the whole culture. . . ."[147] This extension is surely right. People make their individual decisions within and are greatly influenced by their social context. This context includes legal rules, formal structures, and official enforcement mechanisms. However, a larger part of the social framework is created and maintained informally. People's expressive choices can directly change this informal social realm; they can create new

[144] I have replied to this criticism when leveled against John Rawls in Baker, "Sandel on Rawls," *supra* note 29.

[145] Benjamin Constant, "The Liberty of the Ancients Compared with That of the Moderns," (1819), in Biancamaria Fontana, ed. and trans., *Political Writings* (Cambridge: Cambridge University Press, 1988), 309–28. The "liberty of the ancients" consisted in "active and constant participation in collective power." *Id.* at 316. My claim is that gossip has important similarities.

[146] C. Edwin Baker, "Campaign Expenditures and Free Speech," *Harvard Civil Rights–Civil Liberties Law Review* 33 (1998): 1–55.

[147] Thomas I. Emerson, *The System of Freedom of Expression* (New York: Random House, 1970), 7.

behavioral standards and possibilities for action. Thus, the potential democratic contributions of both individuals' informal, apparently private speech and their behavioral choices provide an important reason, beyond respect for individuals' formal autonomy, for broad protection of expressive autonomy. New ideas and new norms frequently seem, especially to dominant groups, to be the height of irrationality when first expressed.[148] Often these ideas and norms can only develop and gain appeal and plausibility when actually embedded in new practices, usually of some dissenting subgroup or avant-garde.[149]

Beyond the observation that individual behavioral choices, including speech choices, create the social realm that in turn influences further individual choices, is the more "dialogic" question: How do people discuss and evaluate these choices? Possibly the most common and central means is gossip: "Sally did *x*; that's pretty bad! Or is it? She was faced with *y*. What do you think?" A negative verdict on the behavior may well sway (or punish) Sally and lead others to avoid (or hide) doing *x*. Alternatively, frequent gossip about *y* may result in the rejection or relaxation of the established social prohibition on *x*.

Thus, any proponent of protecting only or primarily political speech *should* have a hard time ruling out protection of gossip or other presentations of private information. In *New York Times v. Sullivan* (1964),[150] the Court gave constitutional protection both to a newspaper and to various individuals whose advertisement purportedly defamed a public official. *Sullivan* might be limited to defamation of *public officials* if the decision were based solely on a right to criticize the government. There is a history that ties First Amendment freedom to the rejection of seditious libel, that is, libel of the government and its leaders. Legal scholar Harry Kalven, Jr., treated rejection of this offense as definitive of a free society. And rejection of seditious libel, he said, represents "the central meaning of the First Amendment."[151] In contrast, the theory assumed in this essay suggests a broader scope to speech rights based on respect for individual autonomy. But a broader scope should also follow even within a narrow political-speech conception of free speech. A progression at least from public officials to public figures to matters of public concern as subjects of protected speech was clearly predictable even in a theory that emphasized only the democratic role of speech.[152] No major modern First Amendment justification of speech freedom distinguishes speech about public officials

[148] See Kenneth Karst, "Boundaries and Reasons: Freedom of Expression and the Subordination of Groups," *Illinois Law Review* 1990 (1990): 95–149.

[149] Baker, *Human Liberty*, *supra* note 5, chap. 4.

[150] 376 U.S. 254 (1964).

[151] Harry Kalven, Jr., *A Worthy Tradition: Freedom of Speech in America* (New York: Harper & Row, 1988), 63.

[152] See Harry Kalven, Jr., "The *New York Times* Case: A Note on 'The Central Meaning of the First Amendment,'" *Supreme Court Review* (1964): 191–221, at 221.

from speech about other prominent or powerful people.[153] Thus, Justice Brennan quickly led the Court to apply the *Sullivan* standard to public figures. Even more obviously, the valuable public discourse that is essential to democracy could hardly have been limited to occasions when it concerned important people. Public discourse needs to consider all important matters. Thus, Justice Brennan, first bringing the Court with him in 1971 and then in dissent in 1974, extended the application of *Sullivan's* "actual malice" standard to matters of public importance.[154] This extension might be the end of the formal progression. Under this regime, state law imposing stricter liability for all defamatory falsehoods about *private* matters would not be problematic. (Even the First Amendment absolutists, who only concurred in *Sullivan* and claimed that they would absolutely protect speech about public matters, seemed willing to allow defamation judgments if the challenged speech was about matters sufficiently private.)[155] In fact, this is one of two doctrinal areas (the other being government employment) that routinely distinguishes speech content that is or is not about matters of public concern. The argument here, however, is that gossip's discussion of so-called private persons and private matters is political in creating, maintaining, enforcing, critiquing, or changing the societal norms that regulate and guide people's behavior. As such, even under a political theory of the First Amendment, *Sullivan* ought to apply here, too. Of course, the formal autonomy theory does not concede that only political speech should receive full protection. For it, merely the enjoyment of and desire to engage in "great gossip," that is, to reveal private facts, suffices to justify protection.

Another way to get to protection of gossip is to ask: Who is to decide what matters are of public importance? For the government, of which the courts are one branch, to define public importance detracts from the potential public sphere—a point Robert Post fondly makes.[156]

[153] This may be a slight overstatement. Vince Blasi suggests that the checking function of the First Amendment argues for the propriety of giving challengers in electoral contests a right-to-reply such as the one struck down in *Miami Herald Publishing Co. v. Tornillo*, 418 U.S. 241 (1974), although he thought the checking function was not served by giving such a right to incumbents. Blasi, *supra* note 50. However, Kalven, who might have implied this view by suggesting that rejection of seditious libel is definitive of democracy, in fact saw the key to *New York Times v. Sullivan* in its adoption of Alexander Meiklejohn's political speech theory of the First Amendment. See Kalven, *supra* note 152.

[154] *Rosenbloom v. Metromedia*, 403 U.S. 29 (1971); *Gertz v. Robert Welch, Inc.*, 418 U.S. 323 (1974) (Brennan, J., dissenting).

[155] A possible explanation is that absolutists do not credit "lies" as speech under the First Amendment. Absolutists never suggest, for example, that perjury or fraud constitute protected speech. If so, then they still might protect lies about political matters for prophylactic reasons. For example, they might distrust either state officials' or jurors' evaluation of the intentionality of falsehoods made during partisan debate. Falsehoods usually are knowing lies when made by the opposition but, when "we" make them, the falsity is always accidental and made in good faith! For this reason, absolutists might protect these, but only these, purportedly "knowing" falsehoods.

[156] Post, *Constitutional Domains*, *supra* note 105, 119–78.

In the media context, the predictable and arguably only acceptable answer is that if a newspaper thinks a matter worth presenting to the public, and if the public willingly buys the newspaper, the matter must be treated, at least constitutionally, as a matter of public importance. Editors should be free to challenge existing orthodoxy within the community about what matters are properly exposed and discussed. Thus, in rejecting the tort of public disclosure of private facts, Justice Hans Linde argued that the "editorial judgment of what is 'newsworthy' . . . is not properly a community standard. . . . [Some editors] may believe that the community should see or hear facts or ideas that the majority finds uninteresting or offensive."[157]

Justice Linde's point illustrates not only how judgments about newsworthiness are controversial and ideological, but also how the capacity to contradict those judgments is central to the capacity to use speech to challenge the status quo, a point made more concretely in my earlier discussions of "outing." In Linde's opinion, editors make the decision about "public importance" when they decide whether to include a story. Of course, their occasional dissent from established conventions[158] will likely be condemned as at best pandering and at worst evil,[159] but the fact of their choice has the potential to change the social world. A debate about the propriety but not the suppression or legal punishment of their choice to challenge conventional norms is always appropriate.

Both informational privacy and the right to gossip can support meaningful autonomy. Both privacy and the ability to expose are resources or forms of power. Unlike material wealth, lawmaking power, or instruments of violence, the direct or "natural" connection to the person of both privacy and the ability to expose it necessarily results in their comparatively equal distribution. Thus, those who are committed to a democratic or egalitarian distribution of power and capabilities would have reason to value legal recognition of both. This point, however, does not explain why, in cases of conflict, the speech claim—the right to gossip—should trump the interest in privacy. Note, however, that absent (illegal) coercion, people usually can choose, initially, not to disclose information about themselves. The priority of speech freedom does not deprive people of this right. They and others can continue to avoid (or limit) disclosure or, alternatively, can choose to speak. Re-

[157] *Anderson v. Fisher Broadcasting Companies*, 300 Ore. 452 (1986).

[158] Gross noted that in the debates on outing at the first convention of the National Lesbian and Gay Journalists Association in 1992, "it was easy to tell who was on which team by the uniforms: those in favor are most often clad in multiple earrings and sassy T-shirts. Those opposed wear suits and ties." Gross, *supra* note 2, at 151. Still, one wonders which side was most committed to "official" journalistic norms that emphasize truth-telling and the public's right to know. In 1990, Michelangelo Signorile observed that to print a story "about a closeted gay man's woman friend as his lover . . . is applauded," but "if you print the truth you are deemed 'frightening and offensive.' " *Id.* at 60 (quoting Signorile).

[159] Karst, *supra* note 148; Shiffrin, *supra* note 118.

spect for autonomy should be seen as requiring that the choice between these alternatives be left to the individual, which is a voluntarist method of determining what information will be made available to a public. Similarly, the political as well as the autonomy-based claim on behalf of speech is that speech is a power that people should have and be able to use to try to change the world. The debates and practices about "outing" illustrate not that people will necessarily make the right choices—for what is "right" is inherently contestable—but that they will take their responsibilities in the exercise of this speech power seriously.

I would be remiss if I did not note the underside of gossip, although neither my comments here nor my earlier defense of gossip does either side justice. Gossip is often unfair in two ways and undesirable in a third. First, gossip is frequently inaccurate. Moreover, in contrast to falsehoods published in the media, these inaccuracies can be particularly hard for the unfairly treated person to discover and, thus, to refute. Nevertheless, the argument here only defends "true" gossip. Inaccurate gossip does not so much violate informational privacy as create a defamation type of injury. Application of *Sullivan's* actual malice standard to the inaccuracies in reports about a family's response to being taken hostage (a so-called "false light" privacy case) follows easily from either an autonomy notion of individual speech freedom or a standard conception of the media's speech rights.[160]

Second, even when true, gossip can be unfair. It can treat as important something about a person that should not, at least not now, be relevant for the person's public *persona* or for most other evaluative purposes. Gossip can be a true report, but out of context. Most unfairly, even true gossip can provide a hard-to-challenge opportunity for prejudice to operate, or can stimulate or reinforce prejudices, often to the distinct disadvantage of members of vulnerable groups.

Third, gossip can unfairly divert attention from what should be important about a person or divert attention from society's real problems. Is gossip the opiate of the masses? Personally, I find sensationalism, a part of the news at least since Roman times,[161] hard to justify. A plausible characterization of most contemporary news content is that its focus on individuals and dramatic events detracts from vital and more complicated, but less "sexy," structural issues. Still, limiting individual or media speech on these grounds seems paternalistic. For reasons noted above, maybe people become clearer about what they consider important by being able to explore issues in ways made possible by gossip or by gossip's media equivalent. Providing a more vivid impression of actual pri-

[160] *Time, Inc. v. Hill*, 385 U.S. 374 (1967).

[161] John D. Stevens, *Sensationalism and the New York Press* (New York: Columbia University Press, 1991), 6–7.

vate practices may itself be valuable and do more for increasing toleration (and the perspicacity of critiques) than would the "closeting" of gossip. In the best of all worlds, maybe politics should be more about issues and less about personalities. But that is not our world, where most officeholders try to hew toward whatever the latest public opinion poll indicates. If they exercise little independent judgment, then political candidates' personalities, integrity, competence, and honesty, which are the usual focus of sensationalist news and gossip, may be the most significant matters about them for electoral purposes. The point is, there is room for multiple views of relevance and relevance for different purposes. Even people's guilty consumption of gossip and sensationalist news might make valuable social contributions.

Although much can be said—and too much was said—about the Bill Clinton/Monica Lewinsky affair, a common observation was that the drawn-out exposé fascinated and engaged even many people who reported that the affair and the cover-up did not determine, possibly was not even relevant to, their view of whether President Clinton should have remained in office. I am hesitant about the observation that I shall next make, partly because I did not follow either scandal too closely. Still, I wonder about differences between the impact of revelations about Clinton's sexual activities and the earlier sexual harassment allegations leveled against Clarence Thomas at the time of his nomination to the Supreme Court. Arguably, discussion of allegations against Thomas helped put sexual harassment on the cultural map, a desirable result. Arguably, too, discussion of Clinton's escapades constituted an implicit debate about how society ought to react when a public official's personal life intersects with his public role, possibly a debate moving us closer to toleration. If there were these positive effects, then privacy-invading gossip and media sensationalism may have led to a useful discursive evaluation of norms. Admittedly, I continue to believe that both educational practice and social norms should encourage more interest in substantive public policy issues, which elites like me consider central. And I think governmental media policy should encourage the development of media institutions with less sensationalist, more serious (as well as more interesting and culturally playful) foci. Still, the affirmative reasons favoring gossip suggest that these choices are appropriately both contextual and contestable. This contextual inconclusiveness provides further pragmatic grounds, despite gossip's underside, to reject *legal* restriction of so-called non-newsworthy, utterly offensive disclosures of private information.

VIII. Conclusion

Keeping all or some of the power to expose or to use private information out of the hands of the "disciplinary agencies" of government and profit-oriented enterprises is often desirable. The press, however, must be exempted from this conclusion since it constitutes a crucial part of the public sphere. The propriety of legislative limitations on the power of government and market enterprises is similar to keeping from these institutions the power to be secretive. Limits on market entities' use of private information and Privacy Acts limiting government have the same legitimacy as the Freedom of Information Act, open meeting laws, and modern demands for transparency. Government's capacity to have easy, cheap, and not really consensual access to database information containing detailed personal profiles is leading us down a slippery slope at the end of which lies government decrees ordering people to wear an identifying star. Before reaching that dire end, government intrusiveness contributes to the creation of a timorous, docile population that tries to avoid any behavior that might, say, fit the profile of a terrorist. Surely individual autonomy must receive some protection from both governmental and corporate infringements of informational privacy.

In contrast, sometimes privacy may need to be breached if social progress is to be achieved. As Randall Kennedy's stories of "passing" and Larry Gross's account of "outing" illustrate, both privacy and exposure are forms of power that can be used by members of marginalized groups to pursue their cultural, political, and personal goals. (Of course, both privacy and exposure are also used by dominant groups to help maintain their favored norms.) Gossip teaches and maintains, but also helps to change norms of social relations, as it serves to reinforce the identity and cohesion of the oppressed.

My normative claim has been that speech freedom, including freedom to expose any private information that a person knows, is an aspect of formal autonomy that government must respect if it is to remain legitimate in its pursuit of conditions that make meaningful autonomy possible. My pragmatic claim has been that society and, especially, its oppressed segments benefit by leaving speech choices—whether to choose privacy or exposure—largely free of legal limitation. Speech freedom is a relatively egalitarian power that people can and will claim and use.

Law, University of Pennsylvania

CURRENT PROPOSALS FOR MEDIA ACCOUNTABILITY IN LIGHT OF THE FIRST AMENDMENT*

By Ronald D. Rotunda

I. Introduction

The year 1999 witnessed the horrific shootings at Columbine High School in Littleton, Colorado, where two teenage boys killed twelve of their classmates, a teacher, and then themselves.[1] What lessons are to be learned from this tragedy? Certainly, it tells us that in a nation with approximately one third of a billion people, even an infinitesimal percentage of mentally unstable persons can create mayhem. Are there other lessons?

The Columbine incident sparked a renewed interest in looking for underlying causes of violent behavior in American society. President Bill Clinton ordered the Federal Trade Commission (FTC) to study whether the entertainment industry in general, and Hollywood in particular, were in some manner responsible. The entertainment industry often depicts violence in movies, video and computer games, and music lyrics. Is Hollywood the culprit behind violence, especially among youths? And, if so, what if anything can we do about it?

The FTC investigated these questions and issued a report in September 2000 that became an important issue in the presidential election.[2] The Democratic candidate urged legislation to regulate advertising of movies and other advertising deemed not suitable for children, while the Republican candidate argued that families should decide what their children should see.[3]

Since September 11, 2001, the focus of political leaders in the United States has changed to terrorism and ways to combat it, and the issue of media accountability has, in a sense, moved off the front burner. But it is not in the deep freeze. After 9/11, one would think that acts of terrorism by extremist Muslims, most of whom grew up in a country that bans all alcohol and most videos, might teach us that violence can flourish even

* I thank Professors William W. Van Alstyne and Eugene Volokh for their helpful comments. Unfortunately, I must assume responsibility for any errors that remain.

[1] *See, e.g.*, discussion in Federal Trade Commission, *Marketing Violent Entertainment to Children: A Review of Self-Regulation and Industry Practices in the Motion Picture, Music Recording & Electronic Game Industries* (Washington, DC: Federal Trade Commission, 2000), at p. 1 of "Executive Summary."

[2] *Id.*

[3] *E.g.*, Yochi J. Dreazen, "Democrats May Be Goring Their Own Ox As Lieberman, Hollings Target Hollywood," *Wall Street Journal*, June 20, 2001, A 20.

where entertainment and other media are tightly controlled. But that is not the lesson learned by those who seek to regulate the marketing of certain types of entertainment in the United States. On the local, state, and national levels, there are continuing efforts to restrict media advertising of certain types of entertainment. This paper looks at the empirical evidence regarding a causal relationship between violence depicted in the entertainment industry and violence in real life, and examines the theoretical bases of free speech case law to determine if government can or should restrict or regulate the marketing and distribution, particularly to minors, of entertainment depicting violence.

II. Recent Developments

A. The FTC report

Let us start with the FTC report, *Marketing Violent Entertainment to Children: A Review of Self-Regulation and Industry Practices in the Motion Picture, Music Recording & Electronic Game Industries*. The executive summary of this report noted that "parents, social scientists," and others "have struggled to understand how and why some children turn to violence. The dialogues took on new urgency with the horrifying school shooting on April 20, 1999, in Littleton, Colorado."[4] However, not until we turn to an appendix do we find the FTC's conclusion on causality, written in the complex style so common to bureaucrats. The FTC advises us that the researchers are in "general agreement" that media violence "likely explains a relatively small amount of the total variation in youthful violent behavior."[5]

Ultimately, the FTC report found an insignificant causal connection between the entertainment industry and violence in America. Yet the FTC did not focus on this point, but instead criticized the entertainment industry for marketing products that are often not suitable for the young. Perhaps many reporters never read the relevant appendix, for the typical media story was that the FTC report "expos[ed] with impressive particularity the devastating impact that Hollywood entertainment is having upon America's children."[6]

More than a few public officials and lawyers reacted to the FTC report by recommending that the states sue the Hollywood entertainment industry for the allegedly misleading way it promotes its products, just as states earlier sued the tobacco industry for its advertisements.[7] The at-

[4] FTC report, *supra* note 1, at p. 1 of "Executive Summary."

[5] FTC report, *supra* note 1, Appendix A, "A Review of Research on the Impact of Violence in Entertainment Media," at p. 9.

[6] Charlie Condon, "Should States Sue the Entertainment Industry As They Did Big Tobacco? Yes," *Insight On the News*, October 30, 2000, 40. Available online at www.insightmag.com/main.cfm?include=detail&storyid=213359 [accessed October 28, 2003].

[7] Ibid.

torneys general of most states had instituted litigation against the tobacco companies that marketed in the United States, claiming that their marketing was misleading, induced smokers to think that smoking is not dangerous, and did not disclose internal tobacco company studies that showed the connection between smoking and ill health. The states wanted reimbursement for the medical payments they made on behalf of sick smokers. The parties eventually settled, with the tobacco companies agreeing to pay billions of dollars to the states: over a twenty-five year period the money goes to the states, not to the smokers.[8]

Whatever one thinks of the nationwide tobacco settlements involving the states and the tobacco companies, the settlements were based on four arguments that do not apply to Hollywood advertising.[9]

1. It is against the law to sell cigarettes to children. In contrast, it is not illegal for children under age seventeen to attend R-rated movies or for twelve-year-olds to watch PG-13 movies. The ratings are voluntary guidelines and impose no legal duties on children, parents, or the movie industry.
2. The underlying activity of smoking is not a constitutionally protected activity. The government could ban the sale of tobacco just like some jurisdictions ban the sale of alcohol. In contrast, watching movies, listening to CDs, and playing video games are, unlike smoking, a matter of free speech protected by the Constitution's First Amendment.
3. The Surgeon General has determined that smoking causes cancer and other illnesses. We know from the FTC report that the agency found no causal relationship between entertainment and violence: R-rated movies do not cause tragedies like the Columbine shootings.
4. Plaintiffs in the tobacco cases argued that the tobacco industry's advertisements were misleading because they pictured smoking as fun and de-emphasized the cancer risks, even though the advertisements also carried the Surgeon General's health warning. In contrast, it is hard to argue that advertising is misleading when Hollywood advertises an R-rated movie as "R-rated."

[8] Ronald D. Rotunda, *Legal Ethics: The Lawyer's Deskbook on Professional Responsibility*, 2d ed. (St. Paul, MN: West Group, 2002), §6-3.33, at pp. 118–21. The lawyers representing the states also earned billions from the settlements. For example, the Florida attorneys received $3.43 billion, the largest attorneys' fee in history as of that point. Ann Davis, "Arbitration for $8.2 Billion in Fees in Tobacco Suit Reflects Lobbying," *Wall Street Journal*, December 14, 1998, B7.

[9] Ronald D. Rotunda, "Should States Sue the Entertainment Industry As They Did Big Tobacco? No," *Insight On the News*, October 30, 2000, 41 (debate with Charles Condon, the Attorney General of South Carolina who was advocating such lawsuits). Available online at www.insightmag.com/main.cfm?/include=detail&storyid=213338 [accessed October 28, 2003].

While few legal commentators expect that the states' attorneys general will be successful it they join forces and file a lawsuit against Hollywood, this does not mean that the issue is dormant. Instead of litigation, there are proposals for legislation. Let us turn to this legislative approach.

B. Proposals for reform

The FTC's report accused the entertainment industry of being deceptive and warned of government action. That action may eventually come to pass. In April 2001, various U.S. senators introduced S. 792, the proposed *Media Marketing Accountability Act of 2001*, a bill designed to prohibit what it called "the targeted marketing to minors of adult-rated media as an unfair or deceptive practice, and for other purposes." [10] Yet this formulation ignored what should be obvious: that it is not "deceptive" to advertise an adult-rated film as "adult-rated."

This bill is hardly a legislative orphan; it was merely the most prominent of the recent proposals on the federal level.[11] Similar legislation has been introduced in more recent sessions of Congress.[12] We should expect these efforts to mandate media accountability to continue on the national level. In addition, since the beginning of 2003, legislators in various states and cities have introduced sixteen anti-video game bills.

These proposals raise three key issues of law and policy. First, however well-intentioned these proposals are, all of them are subject to the iron law of unintended consequences. Banning or restricting minors' access to certain forms of entertainment may increase the desire of America's youth to view R-rated movies, or listen to taboo musical lyrics, or play mature or M-rated computer games, because regulation may give such entertainment the air and smell of forbidden fruit. It is sometimes said that the

[10] Introductory section to S. 792, 107th Cong. (2001). The original sponsors of the bill were Senators Joseph Lieberman (D-CT), Herb Kohl (D-WI), Hillary Clinton (D-NY), and Robert Byrd (D-IL). Senator Lieberman is a presidential contender in the 2004 election, so we should expect him to raise the media accountability issue in the course of his campaign.

[11] A year before S. 792 was introduced, on May 2, 2000, Senators John McCain (R-AZ) and Joseph Lieberman introduced the *Media Violence Labeling Act of 2000*, S. 2497. This bill proposed that the manufacturers and producers of audio and audiovisual products, such as motion pictures, video games, and music, suggest a system to label "violent content [an undefined term] in audio and visual media products and services (including labeling of such products and services in the advertisements for such products and services)...." S. 2497, § 2(a), adding new §(b), *Policy Regarding Violence in Audio and Visual Media Products and Services*.

[12] Joseph Pereira, "Just How Far Does First Amendment Protection Go?" *Wall Street Journal*, January 10, 2003, B1. See also Vanessa O'Connell, "Marketers to Attack Bills Restricting Ads," *Wall Street Journal*, July 25, 2001, B5; and Adam Thierer, "Regulating Video Games: Must Government Mind Our Children?" *TechKnowledge*, no. 52 (Washington, DC: Cato Institute, June 24, 2003). In 2003, Representative Joe Back (D-CA) introduced the "Protect Children from Video Game Sex and Violence Act of 2003," H. R. 669, 108th Cong. (2003).

"stolen watermelon tastes sweeter."[13] When the government seeks to restrict some expression, it supplies that expression with free publicity, which may encourage individuals to view or hear or experience that expression, so that they can discover for themselves what the fuss is all about. If you want a great turnout, put a "banned in Boston" sign on the movie marquee.

Second, whenever the United States seeks to limit free speech for ostensibly good reasons—whether that speech relates to movies, music lyrics, electronic games, or the wide-open new frontier of the Internet—it gives unintended support to foreign dictators who endeavor to restrict speech for less noble reasons.[14] These dictators would like to argue, by way of example, that even the United States concedes that there is a need to restrict certain types of speech, or limit access to the Internet, or dampen people's interest in certain products by prohibiting truthful speech about those products. Supreme Court decisions that protect the First Amendment undermine this argument.[15]

Third, and the primary focus of this paper, is the issue of the constitutionality under the First Amendment of restrictive proposals such as S. 792. While the professed goal to "save our children" is one to which we all subscribe, free speech doctrine, as we shall see, does not accept this shibboleth as a cloak for limiting the free speech of adults.[16] The case law teaches that if the government wants to make Hollywood more account-

[13] For example, one video game maker aimed for a rating of "teenager and up" instead of a rating suitable for preteens. The higher rating is thought to *increase* sales. *See* Rebecca Buckman et al., "A Whole Lot of Shakin'," *Wall Street Journal,* May 18, 2000, B6. Some young people, desirous of tasting forbidden fruit, find it more alluring to buy or rent videos or other audio or audiovisual entertainment that is rated higher than their age bracket.

[14] Peter Maggs and Ronald D. Rotunda, "Meanwhile, Back in Mother Russia," *Legal Times,* October 2, 1989, 35.

[15] Ronald D. Rotunda, "Exporting the American Bill of Rights: The Lesson from Romania," *University of Illinois Law Review* (1991): 1065.

[16] Thus, the Court, in *Ashcroft v. Free Speech Coalition,* 535 U.S. 234 (2002), invalidated the Child Pornography Prevention Act of 1996 (CPPA) because it expanded the federal prohibition of child pornography to include "virtual pornography," that is, sexually explicit images that appear to depict minors but are produced without using any real children. The images could be created by using adults who look like minors or by using computer imaging. The new technology makes it possible to create realistic images of children who do not exist. The CPPA was not directed at obscene speech, which a different statute prohibits. The issue before the Court was whether the CPPA was constitutional although (a) it did not prohibit the exploitation of real children, and (2) it prohibited speech that is not "obscene"in the constitutional sense, as the Supreme Court defined that term in *Miller v. California,* 413 U.S. 15 (1973). Justice Anthony Kennedy, speaking for the Court, affirmed the Ninth Circuit and invalidated the law. [*Miller* had held that work is "obscene," and a state may prohibit it, when the work: (a) taken as a whole, appeals to the prurient interest in sex; (b) portrays sexual conduct in a patently offensive way, specifically defined by the applicable state law; and (c) taken as a whole, does not have serious literary, artistic, political, or scientific value. The Court rejected an earlier test requiring that the "obscene" work must be "utterly without redeeming social value."] *Ashcroft v. Free Speech Coalition* rejected other arguments—such as the claim that the CPPA is necessary inasmuch as pedophiles may use virtual child pornography to seduce children—because "speech within the rights of adults to hear may not be silenced completely in an attempt to shield children from it." 122 S.Ct. 1389, 1402.

able, the preferred remedy is more speech, not less. Government officials certainly may use their bully pulpits to persuade people not to choose certain types of entertainment, but can they reach that goal by restricting the marketing of entertainment when the underlying product is fully protected by the First Amendment, simply because that marketing reaches children? Federal and state governments cannot ban PG-13 films; can they ban truthful advertising about such films so that fewer ten-year-olds will nag their parents to see PG-13 movies?

III. Noncommercial Speech, Strict Scrutiny, and Commercial Speech

A. The dichotomy between commercial and noncommercial speech

Under modern American constitutional law, 'commercial speech' receives less protection under the First Amendment than other speech, such as political campaign speech.[17] (I shall discuss the distinction in greater detail in subsection C, but 'commercial speech' is often defined as speech that proposes no more than a commercial transaction, such as an offer to sell a good or service at a particular price.) As a general matter, the First Amendment prevents the government from restricting expression because of its message, its ideas, its subject matter, or its content.[18] However, if the speech is 'commercial', the government has greater power to restrict content.[19]

The reasons for Court's bipolar position are not self-evident. As William Van Alstyne has noted, the Constitution places very few roadblocks in the way of the government banning or taxing products directly, so there is less need for regulators to turn to restricting speech in order to dampen demand for a product or service. Far from commercial speech warranting a more relaxed standard, one

> might well argue . . . that there is far less reason in this area ("commerce") than in others (e.g., "politics" ?) to depart from strict scrutiny review, given the extent to which Congress and the states are otherwise granted such a wide sweep of legislative powers they are conceded to possess in determining what may be lawfully provided, and on what terms, to whom, when, and where.[20]

[17] See discussion in Ronald D. Rotunda, "Judicial Elections, Campaign Financing, and Free Speech," *Election Law Journal* 2, no. 1 (2003): 79.

[18] *Police Department of Chicago v. Mosley*, 408 U.S. 92, 95 (1972).

[19] Ronald D. Rotunda, "Lawyer Advertising and the Philosophical Origins of the Commercial Speech Doctrine," *University of Richmond Law Review* 36 (2002): 91.

[20] William W. Van Alstyne, "To What Extent Does the Power of Government to Determine the Boundaries and Conditions of Lawful Commerce Permit Government to Declare Who May Advertise and Who May Not?" *Emory Law Journal* 51 (2002): 1554.

If the government seeks to dampen demand for a particular sort of product, such as high-energy consuming air conditioners, it has many tools at its disposal, and there is no compelling reason to restrict the advertising that promotes energy-inefficient air conditioners. The government can simply ban air conditioners that do not meet certain minimum standards, or the government can impose a heavy tax on inefficient air conditioners. If the government really believes that consumers are at the mercy of advertisers, it can use the money that it raises from taxes to pay for counteradvertising to educate people about the need to conserve energy.

Given all the powers that the government already has because of the deference that the Court has given to economic regulation of business, it is not necessary for the government to limit truthful speech in order to achieve its objective of reducing the number of inefficient air conditioners.[21] In contrast, the Court's more active review of political speech gives the government significantly fewer choices, for free speech cases impose severe limits on the government's power to regulate "who may lawfully form a political party, solicit memberships, field candidates, make extravagant appeals" and "seek to (mis)lead voters as to their own best interests, vote for their 'product,' and take over the reins of government itself."[22]

Perhaps someday the Court will reevaluate its position on its comparatively weaker protection for commercial speech, but for now it seems settled that government has broader powers to regulate commercial speech than it has to regulate political speech. Thus, the government could ban misleading *commercial* speech but not misleading *political* speech.[23] Hence, we must first turn to the basic principles of free speech to determine if the marketing of movies, music, and electronic games should be judged as 'commercial speech'.

B. The marketing of products that are constitutionally protected

Normally, we think of 'advertising' as obviously 'commercial speech', but the advertising of entertainment is different than advertising other products such as prescription drugs or bananas because advertising of entertainment promotes underlying products (e.g., movies, electronic games, or music) that receive the full protection of the First Amendment.

As discussed below, if a movie were "obscene" in a First Amendment sense, a state or the federal government could make it a crime to show the movie. A state could prohibit advertising that markets this obscene movie

[21] Ronald D. Rotunda, "The Commercial Speech Doctrine in the Supreme Court," *University of Illinois Law Forum* (1976): 1080.

[22] William Van Alstyne, *supra* note 20, at 1554 n.102.

[23] The Court believes that there is a greater potential for deception or confusion in the context of certain advertising messages, and thus allows reasonable regulations to preclude misleading commercial speech. *In re R. M. J.*, 455 U.S. 191, 200 (1982); *Friedman v. Rogers*, 440 U.S. 1 (1979) (upholding prohibition on use of trade names by optometrists).

for the same reason it could prohibit advertising for any illegal act, such as a want ad for a hit man or an advertisement for a position limited to white males when the law bans racial and sexual discrimination in hiring.[24] But the cases hold that if a movie is not obscene, then it enjoys full First Amendment protection.

Consider the example of the New York Times Company, a publicly traded company that publishes the *New York Times*, a daily newspaper. The Times Company makes money selling its news and commentary. In the case of marketing of commercial speech, such as an advertisement that promotes diet pills, the government could prohibit "misleading" speech. Yet, the case law does not hold that the government could prohibit, as misleading, an advertisement for the *New York Times* that markets the newspaper as giving readers "objective news" or "all the news that is fit to print." The Times Company may print either slogan in its newspaper or on its Web page. Some people may regard the *New York Times* as objective and others may disagree, but this is a not a dispute that the First Amendment allows the government to resolve.

When commercial speech is at issue, often the underlying product is not constitutionally protected in the sense that the *New York Times*, or other newspapers, or movies, art, and political speech are protected. Compare advertising the *Times* to advertising a prescription drug price. In the latter case, the underlying product is not constitutionally protected because the state can regulate the purchase of the drug; in fact the state does regulate who may buy the drug by requiring the purchaser to obtain a prescription. Even further, the federal government can ban the drug and allow no one to buy it if the Food and Drug Administration (FDA) finds the drug to be unsafe or ineffective. Yet the Supreme Court has held that states cannot forbid truthful price advertising that markets prescription drugs even though that advertising reaches children and other people who cannot lawfully purchase the product because they do not have a prescription.[25]

Advertising movies, music recordings, and video and computer games serves to market underlying products that are not only legally available but also constitutionally protected. Hence, whatever the First Amendment protections are for marketing prescription drugs, the protection for advertising entertainment-related products should be at least as great or even greater. Marketing restrictions against entertainment-related products have only one purpose: to dampen demand for a prod-

[24] *Pittsburgh Press Co. v. Pittsburgh Commission on Human Relations*, 413 U.S. 376 (1973) (holding that the state may constitutionally prohibit a newspaper from publishing sex-related help-wanted advertising when the employer could not legally make the hiring decision on the basis of sex).

[25] *Bolger v. Youngs Drug Products Corp.*, 463 U.S. 60 (1983). See Martin H. Redish, "Product Health Claims and the First Amendment: Scientific Expression and the Twilight Zone of Commercial Speech," *Vanderbilt Law Review* 43 (1990): 1433.

uct that the government cannot ban because the First Amendment fully protects it.[26]

The avowed purpose of federal and state proposals to restrict the marketing of entertainment is to reduce demand for the underlying product by restricting truthful advertising about it even though the underlying product is constitutionally protected, since the government cannot directly reduce demand by banning the product or heavily taxing it. The *Media Marketing Accountability Act of 2001* (S. 792), a typical proposal, candidly states that the purpose of its marketing constraints are to "restrict, to the extent feasible, the sale, rental, or viewing to or by minors of such products."[27]

The proposed laws would not directly ban a video game or R-rated movie or explicit music recording because they cannot constitutionally do that,[28] but they aim to ban advertising about such products in the hope that children, if kept in the dark, will be less likely to play the video game, or see the movie, or buy the music. If children are likely to be in an audience exposed to such advertising, the proposals typically seek to ban

[26] Prior to 1975, the U.S. Supreme Court held that commercial speech had *no* First Amendment protection. *Bigelow v. Virginia*, 421 U.S. 809 (1975), was the first case to grant First Amendment protection to commercial speech.

Pre–1975 cases created or appeared to create distinctions that are unlikely to survive the post-*Bigelow* world. Compare *Breard v. Alexandria*, 341 U.S. 622 (1951), with *Martin v. Struthers*, 319 U.S. 141 (1943). *Breard* upheld a city ordinance (called a "Green River Ordinance") requiring peddlers and solicitors, before approaching a residence for the purpose of soliciting orders, to obtain the prior permission of the owners of the residences. The majority noted that "[u]nwanted knocks on the door by day or night are a nuisance or worse to peace and quiet. The local retail merchant, too, has not been unmindful of the effective competition furnished by house-to-house selling in many lines." (341 U.S. at 626–27.) The particular vendor in this case solicited subscriptions for *magazines*. Yet earlier, *Struthers* invalidated, on First Amendment grounds, a city ordinance when applied to a person distributing free leaflets advertising a *religious* meeting and hawking the *WatchTower*, a Jehovah's Witnesses magazine. The Court, in short, invalidated an ordinance that limited marketing a religious magazine but upheld an ordinance that limited marketing a secular magazine.

Since *Breard* and *Struthers*, the Court has rejected this commercial/noncommercial distinction. Thus, it invalidated laws that restricted the marketing and solicitation of *professional* fundraisers. *Riley v. National Federation for the Blind of North Carolina, Inc.*, 487 U.S. 781 (1988). Five years later, it invalidated a law that limited the distribution of commercial publications that advertised real estate in freestanding news racks on the public streets when the state allowed the distribution of newspapers on the public streets; the ordinance in question defined "newspapers" as publications published daily or weekly and *primarily* covering or commenting on public events. *City of Cincinnati v. Discovery Network, Inc.*, 507 U.S. 410 (1993). Although the real estate magazines (the ordinance called them "commercial handbills") were commercial and the newspapers covered "public events," the Court refused to grant less protection to the commercial handbills.

[27] S. 792 § 102 (b)(2)(B).

[28] R-rated movies simply do not meet the test of what is constitutionally "obscene." *Miller v. California*, 413 U.S. 15 (1973). In *Jenkins v. Georgia*, 418 U.S. 153 (1974), Justice William Rehnquist, for the Court, held that Georgia could not ban *Carnal Knowledge*, a film that depicted nudity and sexual conduct, but in a way that was not obscene. The movie included scenes where sexual conduct, including "ultimate sexual acts," was to be understood to be taking place, and also included occasional scenes of nudity, but it did not depict sexual conduct in a "patently offensive" way. This movie was on many "Ten Best" lists for 1971, the year of its release.

the advertising. However, parents have the legal right to take their children to see R-rated movies simply because the law does not forbid it.[29] The theory of the proposed laws appears to be that if fewer children see the advertisements for R-rated movies or violent video games, et cetera, then they are less likely to nag their parents about them. We know that adults buy 90 percent of all video games, which means that parents are buying many of the violent or mature-rated games for their own children.[30]

C. *The Central Hudson test*

The normal test in evaluating laws governing the *content* of entertainment is that the courts will evaluate the law with 'strict scrutiny'.[31] To survive strict scrutiny, the law must be "narrowly tailored" to promote a "compelling" government interest, and if a "less restrictive alternative" would serve the government's purpose, the legislature must use that alternative.[32]

'Strict scrutiny' is the highest test that the Court employs to assess the validity of government regulations. Very few laws survive the strict scrutiny test, which represents very active judicial review. In contrast, the weakest or least active test is the 'rational basis test'. Under the rational basis test, the Court will ask only whether it is conceivable that a regulation or classification bears a rational relationship to an end of government that is not prohibited by the Constitution. So long as it is arguable, or "rational," that the legislative branch of government had such a basis for creating the classification, a court will not invalidate the law.[33] For example, in 1979 the Court held that it is "rational" for the government to require foreign service workers to retire at age sixty, even though many workers are still quite capable at age sixty-one or beyond and even though

[29] The movie ratings are voluntary guidelines and impose no legal duties on parents, their children, or the movie industry.

[30] Joseph Pereira, "Just How Far Does First Amendment Protection Go?" *supra* note 12, at B1, B3.

[31] *E.g., United States v. Playboy Entertainment Group, Inc.*, 529 U.S. 803 (2000), invalidated § 505 of the Telecommunications Act of 1996, which stipulated that cable television operators providing channels "primarily dedicated to sexually-oriented programming" must "fully scramble or otherwise fully block" those channels, or they must limit their transmissions to hours when children are unlikely to be viewing (set by administrative regulation as between 10 p.m. and 6 a.m.). The Court advised that, because § 505 is a content-based regulation (even though it did not impose a complete prohibition), it must satisfy "strict scrutiny" to meet constitutional requirements.

[32] *Id.* Sponsors of federal statutes to regulate marketing of movies and other entertainment protected by the First Amendment have recognized the constitutional problems posed by 'strict scrutiny', typically by adding a severability clause to proposed legislation, providing that if part of an act is held to be unconstitutional, then the remainder of the act should be severed from its unconstitutional part, e.g., S. 792 § 202.

[33] See comparison of the strict scrutiny and rational basis tests in Ronald D. Rotunda and John E. Nowak, *Treatise on Constitutional Law: Substance and Procedure*, 3d ed. (St. Paul, MN: West Group, 1999), vol. 3, at §18.3.

the federal Civil Service Retirement System at the time did not mandate retirement until age seventy.[34]

The Court, many years ago, announced that the strict scrutiny test does not apply to commercial speech. Before 1975, speech that was viewed as commercial received *no* First Amendment protection.[35] Since then, the Court has ruled that the First Amendment offers greater protection to commercial speech, but it still receives less protection than noncommercial speech.[36] The Court applies to commercial speech a standard that is somewhere between strict scrutiny and rational basis.

The leading case articulating this intermediate standard is *Central Hudson Gas & Electric Corp. v. Public Service Commission of New York* (1980).[37] The Court held that commercial speech deserves some First Amendment protection, but the state could regulate such speech if it satisfies a four-prong test:

> At the outset, we must determine whether the expression is protected by the First Amendment. For commercial speech to come within that provision, [1] it at least must concern lawful activity and not be misleading. Next, [2] we ask whether the asserted governmental interest is substantial. If both inquiries yield positive answers, we must determine [3] whether the regulation directly advances the governmental interest asserted, and [4] whether it is not more extensive than is necessary to serve that interest.[38]

The reference to "whether the asserted governmental interest is substantial" is the Court's way of indicating that it is applying an intermediate test, somewhere between the "compelling government interest" standard of strict scrutiny and the "rational relationship" standard of the most deferential test.

Because *Central Hudson* gives commercial speech less protection than the First Amendment gives to other speech (such as movies, art, or newspapers), it becomes important to determine if the marketing of entertainment is 'commercial' or 'noncommercial' speech; that is, does the marketing

[34] *Vance v. Bradley*, 440 U.S. 93 (1979).

[35] *Bigelow v. Virginia*, 421 U.S. 809 (1975), rejecting *Valentine v. Chrestensen*, 316 U.S. 52, 54 (1942), which treated "commercial speech" as not "speech" and thus completely outside the protection of the First Amendment. *Compare: Miller v. California*, 413 U.S. 15 (1973) (obscenity is not "speech" for First Amendment purposes). See William Van Alstyne, "Some Cautionary Notes on Commercial Speech," *UCLA Law Review* 43 (1996): 1635.

[36] *Virginia State Board of Pharmacy v. Virginia Citizens Consumer Council, Inc.*, 425 U.S. 748, 771–72, n.24 (1976); *Central Hudson Gas & Electric Corp. v. Public Service Commission of New York*, 447 U.S. 557, 562–63 (1980).

[37] 447 U.S. 557.

[38] *Id.* at 566. *See also* 447 U.S. at 575 (Blackmun, J., joined by Brennan, J., concurring in the judgment), citing Ronald D. Rotunda, "The Commercial Speech Doctrine in the Supreme Court," *University of Illinois Law Forum* (1976): 1080–83.

of entertainment receive the limited protection of the commercial speech doctrine or the full protection of the First Amendment?

As noted above, 'commercial speech' is often defined as speech that proposes no more than a commercial transaction, such as an offer to sell a particular good or service for a specified price. The Court has referred to what it calls a "'commonsense' distinction" between commercial speech, which "occurs in an area traditionally subject to government regulation, and other varieties of speech."[39] Sometimes this definition is not as commonsensical as one would think. Could the state ban or severely limit the advertising of a newspaper, such as the *New York Times* or *Chicago Tribune*, because the advertising merely is an offer to sell a newspaper? We know that the contents of the newspaper itself are fully protected by the First Amendment. Should the free speech analysis change because the movie section of the newspaper advertises R-rated movies and children can read the newspaper?

A few examples will illustrate the lesser protection given to commercial speech compared to noncommercial speech. First, there is the issue of regulating speech based on its content. The First Amendment seldom allows the government the power to restrict noncommercial expression because of its message, its ideas, its subject matter, or its content.[40] In contrast, the Court is less troubled by regulation of commercial speech based on content because commercial speech has a "greater potential for deception or confusion in the context of certain advertising messages."[41] Hence, the federal courts allow some content-based restrictions on commercial speech in order to prevent misleading speech, such as making illusory or delusive health claims for a product.[42]

While the Court will allow important restrictions on misleading commercial speech, it will not allow similar restrictions on noncommercial speech. Thus, the Court will not allow a defamation action that serves to punish speech, for example, a suit against a newspaper for printing an advertisement criticizing a government official, even though the government official claims that the advertisement is misleading. In *New York Times v. Sullivan* (1964), a defamation action, the Court held that the plaintiff, a government official, would have to demonstrate not merely that the defamatory speech was misleading but also that it was false, that

[39] *Ohralik v. Ohio State Bar Association*, 436 U.S. 447, 455–56 (1978).

[40] *Police Department of Chicago v. Mosley*, 408 U.S. 92, 95 (1972).

In a limited class of situations, the Court has allowed content-based restrictions. The Court summarized the basis principles in *Bolger v. Youngs Drug Products Corp.*, 463 U.S. at 65 n.7: "Our decisions have displayed a greater willingness to permit content-based restrictions when the expression at issue fell within certain special and limited categories. *See, e.g., Gertz v. Robert Welch, Inc.*, 418 U.S. 323, 340 (1974) (libel); *Miller v. California*, 413 U.S. 15 (1973) (obscenity); *Chaplinsky v. New Hampshire*, 315 U.S. 568, 572–73 (1942) (fighting words)."

[41] *Bolger*, 463 U.S. at 65. *See also: In re R. M. J.*, 455 U.S. 191, 200 (1982).

[42] *National Commission on Egg Nutrition v. FTC*, 570 F.2d 157 (7th Cir. 1977) (enforcing, in part, an FTC order prohibiting false and misleading advertising by an egg industry trade association concerning the relationship between cholesterol, eggs, and heart disease).

it was *materially* false, and that it was *knowingly* false.[43] One can understand this standard better by looking at the facts of *New York Times v. Sullivan.*

Sullivan, a police commissioner, sued the *New York Times*, claiming that he had been libeled by statements in a full-page advertisement that the *Times* published on March 29, 1960, titled "Heed Their Rising Voices." The advertisement began by stating: "As the whole world knows by now, thousands of Southern Negro students are engaged in widespread non-violent demonstrations in positive affirmation of the right to live in human dignity as guaranteed by the U.S. Constitution and the Bill of Rights." Of the ten paragraphs in the advertisement, the third and a portion of the sixth were the basis of Sullivan's claim of libel. The third paragraph said:

> In Montgomery, Alabama, after students sang "My Country, 'Tis of Thee" on the State Capitol steps, their leaders were expelled from school, and truckloads of police armed with shotguns and tear-gas ringed the Alabama State College Campus. When the entire student body protested to state authorities by refusing to re-register, their dining hall was padlocked in an attempt to starve them into submission.[44]

The sixth paragraph said, in part:

> Again and again the Southern violators have answered Dr. King's peaceful protests with intimidation and violence. They have bombed his home almost killing his wife and child. They have assaulted his person. They have arrested him seven times—for "speeding," "loitering" and similar "offenses." And now they have charged him with "perjury"—a felony under which they could imprison him for *ten years*. . . .[45]

It was, in the words of the Supreme Court, "uncontroverted" that some of the statements were inaccurate or false, but they were not "materially false." For example, although

> Negro students staged a demonstration on the State Capitol steps, they sang the National Anthem and not "My Country, 'Tis of Thee." Although nine students were expelled by the State Board of Education, this was not for leading the demonstration at the Capitol, but

[43] 376 U.S. 254, 265–66 (1964) (in libel action brought by a public official, the plaintiff must prove that the speech was defamatory and that defendant acted with *scienter*, that is, either that the speech was knowingly false or that the defamer acted with reckless disregard of whether the speech was true or false).
[44] *Id.* at 257.
[45] *Id.* at 257–58.

> for demanding service at a lunch counter in the Montgomery County Courthouse on another day. Not the entire student body, but most of it, had protested the expulsion, not by refusing to register, but by boycotting classes on a single day.[46]

Furthermore, the *Times* did not make any "knowingly" false statements. Although the *Times* could have checked its old newspaper files to determine what songs the students really sang, the "mere presence of the stories in the files does not, of course, establish that the *Times* 'knew' the advertisement was false, since the state of mind required for actual malice would have to be brought home to the persons in the *Times'* organization having responsibility for the publication of the advertisement."[47]

The *Times* sold the advertisement, but the *content* of an advertisement is not something that the newspaper would necessarily embrace. Still, the Court did not consider the advertisement as "commercial" speech. Instead it treated the advertisement as fully within the protections of the First Amendment. Sullivan argued that "the constitutional guarantees of freedom of speech and of the press are inapplicable here, at least so far as the *Times* is concerned, because the allegedly libelous statements were published as part of a paid, 'commercial' advertisement."[48] However, the Court simply rejected this view: "The publication here was not a 'commercial' advertisement" because it "communicated information, expressed opinion, recited grievances, protested claimed abuses, and sought financial support on behalf of a movement whose existence and objectives are matters of the highest public interest and concern."[49]

A second example of the differing degrees of protection given to commercial and noncommercial speech is found in cases involving the advocacy of various sorts of illegal acts. The government may not normally punish noncommercial speech that "advocates" or urges the listeners to engage in "violence." While the government may punish the actual violence if any ensues, it may not punish the speaker who advocated it unless the government can also demonstrate that the speaker was objectively and subjectively intending to "incite" lawless action and that this action was "imminent." Thus, the Court has made clear, in a case where the speaker was charged with urging violence, that, "the constitutional guarantees of free speech and free press do not permit a State to forbid or proscribe advocacy of the use of force or of law violation except where such advocacy is directed to inciting or producing imminent lawless action and is likely to incite or produce

[46] *Id.* at 258–59.
[47] *Id.* at 287.
[48] *Id.* at 265.
[49] *Id.* at 266.

such action."[50] In other words, the state could punish the instigator of a lynch mob if the speaker was objectively and subjectively intending to "incite" a lynching and this action was "imminent." The connection between the advocacy and the illegal conduct must be almost knee-jerk, leaving no time for thought or reflection.

In contrast, the Court allows the government to prohibit commercial speech that merely proposes an illegal activity. For example, the government can forbid a newspaper from publishing help-wanted advertising that offers a job based on sex, when the law bans sex-based criteria for employment.[51] In that case, the help-wanted advertisement would be proposing an illegal act: hiring on the basis of sex. While the commercial speech doctrine allows a state to forbid advertisements soliciting a Mafia hit man, the First Amendment does not allow a state to forbid a racist speaker from ineffectually urging violence.[52]

IV. When the Underlying Activities Being Advertised Are Themselves Fully Protected by the First Amendment

Because the Supreme Court grants commercial speech less First Amendment protection than other speech, it often becomes important to determine whether speech is 'commercial', subject to only limited First Amendment protection within the parameters set by *Central Hudson*, or 'noncommercial', and thus subject to the full panoply of First Amendment protection.

The underlying activity that is the focus of the entertainment industry's marketing efforts—the actual movie, or music, or video game, et cetera—is, of course, subject to full First Amendment protection.[53] Movies, music, video games, and other entertainment generally are treated as 'speech' deserving of the full protection of the First Amendment, just as any work of art is fully protected under the First Amendment. As Justice William O. Douglas advised over a half-century ago:

> Under our system of government there is an accommodation for the widest varieties of tastes and ideas. What is good literature, what has educational value, what is refined public information, what is good art, varies with individuals as it does from one generation to another.

[50] *Brandenburg v. Ohio*, 395 U.S. 444, 447 (1969) (per curiam). The Court invalidated, under the First and Fourteenth Amendments, the Ohio Criminal Syndicalism Act, because, by its own words and as applied, it punished "mere advocacy," criminalized assembly with others merely to advocate the described type of action, and failed to distinguish mere advocacy from incitement to imminent lawless action.

[51] *Pittsburgh Press Co. v. Pittsburgh Commission on Human Relations*, 413 U.S. 376 (1973).

[52] *Hess v. Indiana*, 414 U.S. 105 (1973) (per curiam).

[53] *E.g., Hannegan v. Esquire*, 327 U.S. 146, 157–58 (1946).

> There doubtless would be a contrariety of views concerning Cervantes' *Don Quixote*, Shakespeare's *Venus and Adonis*, or Zola's *Nana*. But a requirement that literature or art conform to some norm prescribed by an official smacks of an ideology foreign to our system.[54]

The government may not ban entertainment unless the speech is constitutionally 'obscene', a term that the Court narrowly defines with relative precision.[55] This term is substantially more narrow than the speech that would be regulated by present-day proposals.[56] These proposals do not pertain to 'prurient sex', rather, they impose restrictions on the marketing of 'violence'.[57] Indeed, the proposals go well beyond existing regulations because they would restrict G-rated advertisements or G-rated movie trailers about PG-13 or R-rated movies. (Trailers advertise upcoming movies and they play in theaters and on TV.) Both the trailers and the underlying movies that these trailers advertise are fully protected by the First Amendment because none of them are 'obscene' in the constitutional sense: the movies are only rated PG-13 or R, and the marketing tools, the trailers, are G-rated. If an advertised movie were 'obscene', the government could simply ban it as well as all advertising promoting it.

However, recent proposals that deal with media marketing do not purport to ban the underlying entertainment. Rather, they seek to govern the

[54] *Id.*

[55] *Miller v. California*, 413 U.S. 15, 24 (1973), defined "obscenity" and set forth a three-part test:

> The basic guidelines for the trier of fact must be: (a) whether "the average person, applying contemporary community standards" would find that the work, taken as a whole, appeals to the prurient interest . . . (b) whether the work depicts or describes, in a *patently offensive way, sexual conduct* specifically defined by the applicable state law; and (c) whether the work, taken as a whole, *lacks serious literary, artistic, political, or scientific value.* (emphasis added)

The touchstone in obscenity cases is, of course, "sex." In contrast, S. 792 is based on a different touchstone: "violence." Thus, it does not fit under the standards that *Miller* authorized. Because S. 792, like the *Communications Decency Act of 1996*, regulates speech that does not fit the definition of "obscenity" articulated in *Miller*, the Court would most likely invalidate it, as it invalidated a similar regulatory effort in *Reno v. American Civil Liberties Union*, 521 U.S. 844 (1997).

[56] *E.g., Reno v. American Civil Liberties Union*, 521 U.S. 844 (1997), holding, inter alia, that the *Communications Decency Act of 1996* was unconstitutional because its provisions criminalized legitimate protected speech (including sexually explicit indecent speech) as well as unprotected obscene speech, and thus the law was overinclusive, and hence unconstitutional.

[57] As Justice Stevens explained in *Reno v. American Civil Liberties Union*, the *Communications Decency Act of 1996* (which the Court invalidated) was not limited to prurient sexual conduct: "the *Miller* definition is limited to 'sexual conduct,' whereas the CDA extends also to include (1) 'excretory activities' as well as (2) 'organs' of both a sexual and excretory nature." 521 U.S. at 873. He added, quoting *Sable Communications of California, Inc. v. FCC*, 492 U.S. 115, 126 (1989): "[W]e have made it *perfectly clear* that 'sexual expression which is indecent but not obscene is protected by the First Amendment.'" 521 U.S. at 874 (emphasis added).

marketing or *advertising* of movies, video games, and music, *not* the content.[58] If the government cannot constitutionally ban an R-rated movie, may it constitutionally restrict the marketing of that movie by, for example, banning the showing of a G-rated trailer promoting the R-rated movie when children are likely to see the trailer? Is the advertising or marketing of speech that is fully protected by the First Amendment to be treated like commercial speech? This latter question is one that the Court raised, but did not decide, in *Bolger v. Youngs Drug Products Corp.* (1983).[59]

In *Bolger,* a manufacturer and distributor of contraceptives challenged a federal statute prohibiting the unsolicited mailing of contraceptive advertisements. The Court treated the advertisements as commercial speech, but added, in a footnote, an intriguing statement that invited more protection for the marketing of First Amendment activities: "Of course, a different conclusion may be appropriate in a case where the pamphlet advertises an activity itself protected by the First Amendment."[60]

Bolger suggested that advertising about protected speech might not be treated as mere "commercial speech," and thus laws regulating such advertising would be subject to greater First Amendment scrutiny. The *Bolger* Court, in this dictum, then cited *Murdock v. Pennsylvania* (1943),[61] which it described as holding that "advertisement for religious book[s] cannot be regulated as commercial speech."[62]

Bolger also referred to *Jamison v. Texas* (1943).[63] In this case, a city ordinance prohibited the distribution on city streets of handbills disseminating information. *Jamison* declared this law unconstitutional as applied to the distribution of handbills inviting the public to attend a meeting of a religious sect at which no admission was to be charged, even though the handbills also contained an advertisement promoting a religious book that the sect distributed.

In both the *Murdock* and *Jamison* cases, which were decided before the Supreme Court gave any protection to commercial speech,[64] the underlying speech was religious speech, fully protected by the First Amendment. The Court treated advertising about this type of speech as fully protected speech. The underlying speech of newspapers, movies, video games, and music is also fully protected under the First Amendment. Does this mean that the Court will treat advertising about this speech as fully protected, or will the Court consider this type of advertising as mere 'commercial speech'?

[58] S. 792 § 106(5).
[59] 463 U.S. 60 (1983).
[60] *Id.* at 68 n.14.
[61] 319 U.S. 105 (1943).
[62] 463 U.S. 60, 68 n.14.
[63] 318 U.S. 413 (1943).
[64] *Valentine v. Chrestensen,* 316 U.S. 52, 54 (1942) treated "commercial speech" as outside the protection of the First Amendment. The Court did not reject this doctrine until *Bigelow v. Virginia,* 421 U.S. 809 (1975).

Consider an advertisement for a newspaper. The editorial and news content of a newspaper are not commercial speech, and the newspaper is fully protected by the First Amendment. One would think that the government could regulate an advertisement for a newspaper if it were truly inaccurate. For example, the government could prohibit a newspaper from advertising that a subscription costs "only 25¢ per day, and *save even more* by purchasing a yearly subscription at only $100," when, in fact, it would only cost $91.25 if one paid the 25¢ for 365 days. In this case, the government would be regulating the marketing of a product (an offer to buy a newspaper for a certain amount) only to the extent that it ensures that the advertisement is not false.

Alternatively, if the newspaper proclaims that it is "the voice of the common citizen," the government should not be able to require the newspaper to publish a disclaimer that states: "The attorney general has determined that this newspaper publishes un-American views and is not the voice of the common citizen." (We can assume that the newspaper refuses to say that it is not really the "voice of the common citizen" or that it publishes "un-American views.") In this case, the government's purpose in making the newspaper publish the attorney general's disclaimer would be to restrict demand for the newspaper.[65] "[T]he First Amendment guarantees 'freedom of speech,' a term necessarily comprising the decision of both what to say and what not to say."[66]

It does not matter if the attorney general's determination is considered an opinion (the newspaper is "un-American in the view of the attorney

[65] *E.g., Riley v. National Federation of the Blind of North Carolina, Inc.*, 487 U.S. 781 (1988). The North Carolina law at issue regulated the fee schedule of professional charitable solicitors. Justice Brennan, for the Court, invalidated this provision of the law. The Court also invalidated the portion of the law that required professional fundraisers to disclose to potential donors the percentage of charitable funds collected during the previous twelve months that were actually turned over to the charity. The Court found this provision defective, because the freedom to speak encompasses the freedom not to speak. The majority rejected the dissent's claim that the state's "regulation is merely economic, having only an indirect effect on protected speech." 487 U.S. at 790 n.5.

Contrast *Meese v. Keene*, 481 U.S. 465 (1987). In this case the Court did allow the attorney general to require agents of foreign countries to label any communication "reasonably adapted to, or intended to influence, the recipient within the United States." The Court ruled that Congress may require labeling information to disclose the foreign origin of a communication. The law in question used the term "political propaganda," but the term (which some regard as pejorative) did *not* appear in the disclosure form that had to be filed. The Court upheld this modest disclosure of foreign origin by a divided vote of 6 to 3. Justice Scalia did not participate and Justice Blackmun dissented in part and filed an opinion in which Justices Brennan and Marshall joined. The majority, in approving this foreign-origin disclosure rule, noted that there was no evidence that public misunderstanding of the term "political propaganda," or fear thereof, had actually interfered with the exhibition of significant numbers of foreign-made films. The term "political propaganda," in the law, was neutral because it not only includes "slanted, misleading advocacy in the popular, pejorative sense, but also encompasses materials that are completely accurate and merit the highest respect." 481 U.S. at 477.

[66] *Riley*, 487 U.S. at 782.

general") or a fact ("it is a fact that the attorney general has this view, this belief, about this newspaper"). In either case, for First Amendment purposes, there is no distinction between compelling the newspaper to publish the attorney general's opinion or compelling the newspaper to publicize the fact that the attorney general has this opinion, "because either form of compulsion burdens protected speech."[67]

This type of forced disclosure is different than the laws mandating tobacco companies to disclose on their packages that cigarettes have been shown to cause cancer and other diseases. Smoking cigarettes is not a First Amendment right; publishing newspapers is, just like the First Amendment right exercised by the religious sect in *Jamison* when it advertised its book. This is why the Court has previously invalidated efforts to force newspapers to publish material that they simply do not wish to publish.[68] In contrast, because the underlying activity is not constitutionally protected, state governments could simply ban smoking, just as some states allow counties to ban or severely limit the sale of liquor. In fact, federal, state, and local governments have already banned smoking by minors, by anyone in commercial airplanes, or by anyone in various public places.

We would not expect a court to treat as 'commercial speech' advertising that urged people to watch a network's news program or attempted to persuade people to read the *New York Times*. The Supreme Court has held that speech is not necessarily commercial simply because "it relates to [a] person's financial motivation for speaking."[69] Hence, the Court may, if ever called upon, decide to evaluate under the strict scrutiny doctrine instead of the less demanding commercial speech doctrine any legislation that restricts and regulates the entertainment industry's advertising and marketing. This is likely because the underlying activity (movies, music, and video games) is fully protected under the First Amendment.

In addition, when the law regulates advertisements for movies with the very purpose of affecting who attends these movies, the marketing of entertainment is intertwined with the entertainment itself. Commercial speech, the Court has held, does not retain "its commercial character when it is inextricably intertwined with otherwise fully protected speech."[70] Without advertising for movies, music, and video games, "the flow of

[67] *Id.* On the issue whether the speech is commercial or not, the Court said: "But even assuming, without deciding, that such speech in the abstract is indeed merely 'commercial,' we do not believe that the speech retains its commercial character when it is inextricably intertwined with otherwise fully protected speech." 487 U.S. at 796.

[68] *Miami Herald Publishing Co. v. Tornillo*, 418 U.S. 241 (1974) (invalidating a state statute granting a political candidate a right to reply to a newspaper's criticism and attacks on his record by requiring the newspaper to publish the candidate's response).

[69] *Riley*, 487 U.S. at 795–96. *Accord: Bolger v. Youngs Drug Products Corp.*, 463 U.S. 60, 66 (1983): "The mere fact that these pamphlets are conceded to be advertisements clearly does not compel the conclusion that they are commercial speech."

[70] 487 U.S. at 796.

such information and advocacy would likely cease,"[71] because the advertising and the underlying speech are intertwined. When the "component parts of a single speech are inextricably intertwined, we cannot parcel out the speech, applying one test to one phrase and another test to another phrase. Such an endeavor would be both artificial and impractical. Therefore, we apply our test for fully protected expression."[72]

When a professional fundraiser requests money for charity, the solicitation is merely an economic activity, but the underlying speech by the charity is fully protected under the First Amendment. While the solicitors are working for hire, they are also distributing information about the charity as well as collecting money. Thus, in *Village of Schaumburg v. Citizens for a Better Environment*, the Court invalidated laws restricting charitable solicitation by professional solicitors because the solicitation (even when professional fundraisers engage in this activity) "must be undertaken with due regard for the reality that solicitation is characteristically intertwined with informative and perhaps persuasive speech . . . , and for the reality that without solicitation the flow of such information and advocacy would likely cease."[73] Advertisements about movies are likewise intertwined with informative speech: that a movie is R-rated, or that it is based on a historical incident, or that it speculates about what the world might be like in the distant future, or that it illustrates how human beings should cope with adversity, or that it shows who heroes truly are, or that it exhibits an actress in the best performance of her life.

Given that the underlying activity is fully protected by the First Amendment, that entertainment advertising is not necessarily commercial simply because it relates to the industry's financial motivation *for* advertising, and that such advertising is intertwined with informative speech, courts are likely to evaluate under a strict scrutiny test legislation that restricts the *marketing* of entertainment. Few laws survive strict scrutiny. Conversely, the Court may once again dodge the question it raised in *Bolger* (i.e., whether the marketing of speech that is fully protected by the First Amendment should be regarded as commercial speech),[74] if it determines that the more limited commercial speech protections of *Central Hudson* prohibit constraints on entertainment advertising. To analyze this prospect, let us first briefly look at the metes and bounds of S. 792, because it is typical of the proposals to regulate the entertainment industry on the grounds that its marketing is deceptive.

[71] *Village of Schaumburg v. Citizens for a Better Environment*, 444 U.S. 620, 632 (1980). *See also: Secretary of State of Maryland v. Joseph H. Munson Co.*, 467 U.S. 947, 959–60 (1984); *Meyer v. Grant*, 486 U.S. 414, 422, n.5 (1988); *Thomas v. Collins*, 323 U.S. 516, 540–41 (1945).

[72] 487 U.S. at 796.

[73] 444 U.S. at 632.

[74] 463 U.S. at 68 n.14.

V. A Typical Proposal: The Basic Parameters of S. 792

S. 792 was an effort to regulate what is sometimes called "politically incorrect" speech.[75] In the past, such proposals that became law did not survive legal challenge, although they were justified as an attempt to protect children. Consider, for example, the *Communications Decency Act of 1996*. The Supreme Court held that this law, which sought to place various restrictions on the Internet, violated the First Amendment.[76] In response to this ruling, Congress passed the *Child Online Protection Act*, which President Clinton signed into law on October 21, 1998, and which made it unlawful to use the World Wide Web to disseminate any "material that is harmful to minors."[77] On February 1, 1999, just two months and two days after this law was to take effect, a federal district court enjoined its enforcement, the Third Circuit eventually affirmed, and the U.S. Supreme Court remanded for further proceedings to consider constitutional problems with the law.[78] On remand, the Third Circuit again invalidated the law.[79]

That the courts have invalidated prior laws designed to protect children does not doom new attempts if they are really distinguishable. Hence, one should look to proposals such as S. 792, which is a paradigm bill, to see if they overcome the problems associated with prior attempts. S. 792 would prohibit the "targeted advertising or other marketing to minors of an adult-rated motion picture, music recording, or electronic game"[80] by defining such advertising (for example, truthful advertising of an R-rated movie as R-rated) as a "deceptive" act.[81] Recall that *Central Hudson* made

[75] *E.g.*, Ronald D. Rotunda, "A Brief Comment on Politically Incorrect Speech in the Wake of *R. A. V.*," *Southern Methodist University Law Review* 47 (1993): 9; Eugene Volokh, "Freedom of Speech, Cyberspace, Harassment Law, and the Clinton Administration," *Law and Contemporary Problems* 63 (2000): 299.

[76] *Reno v. American Civil Liberties Union*, 521 U.S. 844 (1997). See discussion in Eugene Volokh, "Freedom of Speech, Shielding Children, and Transcending Balancing," *Supreme Court Review* (1997): 141.

[77] 47 U.S.C. § 231 (1998).

[78] *ACLU v. Reno*, 31 F. Supp. 2d 473 (E. D. Penn. 1999), *affirmed*, *ACLU v. Reno*, 217 F.3d 162 (3d Cir. 2000), *vacated sub nom*, *Ashcroft v. American Civil Liberties Union*, 535 U.S. 564 (2002).

[79] *ACLU v. Ashcroft*, 322 F.3d 240 (2003). Judge Garth, speaking for the Third Circuit, upheld the preliminary injunction against, because: (1) plaintiffs established a substantial likelihood of prevailing on the claim that the Child Online Protection Act was not narrowly tailored to achieve the government's compelling interest and therefore failed the strict scrutiny test under First Amendment, and (2) the plaintiffs also established a substantial likelihood of prevailing on the claim that the Child Online Protection Act was unconstitutionally overbroad. Almost instantly, the legal literature began discussing this case as a leading precedent. See, e.g., Jonathan Zittrain, "Internet Points of Control," *Boston College Law Review* 44 (2003): 653; "3d Cir. Favors Web Publishers, Calls Child-porn Law 'Puritanical', *ACLU v. Ashcroft*," *Andrews Computer & Online Industry Litigation Reporter* 20 (2003): 8; Steven J. Heyman, "Ideological Conflict and the First Amendment," *Chicago-Kent Law Review* 78 (2003): 618.

[80] S. 792 § 101(a).

[81] S. 792 §§ 101(a), 2(8).

it clear, in the first prong of its four-part test, that the government could regulate commercial speech that is misleading.[82] The proposed law, S. 792, states that it is "deceptive" to "target" advertising to minors, and that it is necessary to protect children because media violence "can be harmful to children."[83]

Let us examine each of these three principles. First, 'deception': Is the marketing of movies, music, and video games to children a deceptive act? Second, 'causation': Is media violence harmful to children? Third and finally, we shall examine the question of 'targeting' children.

A. Deception: The question of allegedly misleading speech

Bear in mind that the first prong of *Central Hudson*[84] allows the government to regulate commercial speech that is actually misleading. This principle offers another way that the government might regulate advertisements regarding entertainment. S.792 capitalized on this first prong when it found that targeting advertising of adult-rated movies, media, and electronic games to minors is a "false and deceptive trade practice" because many companies in the entertainment industry have "continued to market adult-rated products in venues popular with children."[85] Is it "false and deceptive" when the industry truthfully markets an R-rated movie to sixteen-year-olds in a context where it is perfectly legal for sixteen-year-olds (and even younger children) to view the movie?

Under the case law, something does not become "false" or "deceptive" merely because there is a finding to that effect. Instead, the Court must determine for itself if it really is misleading. In *In Re R. M .J.* (1982), the Court unanimously invalidated various restrictions on advertising by lawyers in Missouri.[86] Among other things, in an advertisement, lawyer R. M. J. had emphasized in large boldface type that he was a member of the U.S. Supreme Court bar. The state court found this statement misleading, but the Supreme Court reversed. The Court acknowledged that the claim that one is a member of the U.S. Supreme Court bar is "relatively uninformative." Admittedly, admission to the U.S. Supreme Court bar does not mean that one is a better lawyer, and the reader of the advertisement might mistakenly assume that one had to pass a rigorous examination to be admitted. Instead, one only has to fill out an application and pay a small fee. Yet, the Court invalidated Missouri's restrictions on advertising by lawyers because the record did not show that this "relatively uninformative fact" was misleading or deceptive; hence, the

[82] *Central Hudson Gas & Electric Corp. v. Public Service Commission of New York*, 447 U.S. 557, 566 (1980).

[83] S. 792 §2 (4).

[84] 447 U.S. at 566.

[85] S. 792 §§ 2(6) and 2(7).

[86] 455 U.S. 191 (1982).

state action was unconstitutional. R. M. J. had truthfully stated that he was a member of the Supreme Court bar.

Peel v. Attorney Registration and Disciplinary Commission of Illinois (1990) offers another example.[87] An Illinois rule did not permit an attorney to hold himself out as "certified" or a "specialist" unless he was a patent, trademark, or admiralty lawyer. The Illinois Supreme Court censured Peel, whose letterhead stated that he was "certified" as a civil trial specialist by the National Board of Trial Advocacy (NBTA), a bona fide private group that has developed a set of standards and procedures for periodic certification of lawyers with experience and competence in trial work. The Illinois court said that Peel's letterhead was misleading because the state did not certify trial lawyers.

The U.S. Supreme Court reversed. Justice Stevens explained that the issue was whether "a lawyer has a constitutional right, under the standards applicable to commercial speech, to advertise his or her certification as a trial specialist by NBTA."[88] The facts on Peel's letterhead were both true and verifiable. Illinois argued that Peel's letterhead implied a higher quality or ability than noncertified lawyers, but the Court rejected Illinois's argument that Peel's statement was therefore misleading. The Court reasoned that Peel's truthful claim of certification by a private group, the NBTA, has no more potential to mislead than an attorney advertising that he is admitted to practice before the U.S. Supreme Court, a statement that *In Re R. M. J.* had found was constitutionally protected. Thus, Peel's letterhead was neither actually, nor inherently, nor potentially deceptive.

In *Ibanez v. Florida Department of Business and Professional Regulation, Board of Accountancy* (1994), Justice Ruth Bader Ginsburg spoke for a unanimous Court in holding that the Florida Board of Accountancy violated free speech when it reprimanded Silvia Ibanez, an attorney, because she had truthfully stated in her legal advertising that she was also a Certified Public Accountant (CPA).[89] The Florida Board of Accountancy had licensed her as a CPA. "[W]e cannot imagine," wrote Ginsburg, "how consumers could be misled by her truthful representation" that she is a CPA.[90]

In the circumstances that would be governed by S. 792, one wonders how it could be "misleading" for the movie industry to advertise truthfully that an R-rated movie is R-rated. There is something Orwellian about claiming that it is "deceptive" to promote an R-rated movie as R-rated, even if a sixteen-year-old sees the advertisement. A problem of deception would exist if the R-rated movie were promoted as G-rated, but this, of course, is not the complaint.

[87] 496 U.S. 91 (1990).

[88] *Id.* at 100. Stevens's plurality opinion was joined by Justices Brennan, Blackmun, and Kennedy.

[89] 512 U.S. 136 (1994).

[90] *Id.* at 144.

B. Causation: The factual assumption that "media violence can be harmful to children"

The typical justification for a new government role in regulating G-rated advertising of mature-audience entertainment is that "[m]edia violence can be harmful to children."[91] A central factual premise of S. 792 and similar proposals is that exposure to media "violence"[92] will cause children to engage in violent acts. It is commonly postulated that watching violence causes people to become violent.

Experience should make us question the commonplace assumption that people simply follow the media. There is a limit to the power of advertising: extensive media advertising promoted the Edsel, and yet Ford could not sell that car to the American public. The contemporary media, including movies and other entertainment as well as advertising, pay constant tribute to men and women who are trim and fit, and yet medical reports routinely tell us that Americans do not exercise enough and tend to be ever more overweight. If the media were truly persuasive, there would be no need to market all the products that promote dieting.

One need not rely on anecdotal analysis for one's skepticism, since the Federal Trade Commission conducted its own review of the scientific literature following the Columbine tragedy and concluded that it could not substantiate a causal connection between the entertainment industry and violence in America:

> There does appear to be general agreement among researchers that whatever the impact of media violence, it likely explains a relatively small amount of the total variation in youthful violent behavior.[93]

Shortly before the release of the FTC report in 2000, the Australian Office of Film and Literature Classification published a four-year study called *Computer Games and Australians Today.*[94] It concluded that there "is little evidence to support fears that playing computer games contributes substantially to aggression in the community."[95] In the United States, one might even contend that there is a negative correlation between violent crime and minors' exposure to video games, adult movies, etc. The U.S.

[91] S. 792 § 2(4).

[92] The proposed law does not define this term. Violence is not self-defining. It is sometimes "cartoon violence"; at other times it is quite realistic and graphic. Sometimes it may be science-fiction fantasy; at other times it may be offstage and left to the imagination. The violence may be essential to the plot, or it may be gratuitous.

[93] Federal Trade Commission, *Marketing Violent Entertainment to Children, supra* note 1, Appendix A, at p. 9.

[94] The Web site of the Australian Office of Film and Literature Classification may be found at http://www.oflc.gov.au/splash.html [accessed October 22, 2003].

[95] The 1999 study is discussed at http://www.law.gov.au/www/attorneygeneralhome.nsf/Web+Pages/506AE4858540DA4FCA256B5F0015C7EB [accessed October 22, 2003].

Department of Justice Office of Juvenile Justice and Delinquency Prevention reported that the peak year for juvenile arrest rates was 1994. Between 1994 and 2000, violent crime arrest rates for juveniles as measured by the Violent Crime Index "dropped 44% for youth ages 15-17, compared with 24% for adults ages 18-24." The decline continued for older adults, but the rate of decrease was less. The arrest rate dropped 26% for those ages 25-29, and 19% for those ages 30-39.[96]

In other words, since 1994, while the "tech craze" was steamrolling across America, while the video game industry was expanding at exponential rates, while the ever-expanding economy gave minors easier access to entertainment not suitable for them, while all of this was happening, the crime rates for juveniles *decreased.* Moreover, the crime rate decreased the most for minors, precisely the group most smitten with video games. If we consider a longer period of time—1980 to 2000—we find that juvenile crime rates *decreased* while *adult* crime rates (even adults over sixty) *increased.*[97]

In contrast, S. 792 baldly asserts: "Most scholarly studies on the impact of media violence find a *high correlation* between exposure to violent content and aggressive or violent behavior."[98] This "finding" of S. 792—that watching media violence "can be harmful to children"[99]—is a finding that the FTC report simply does not support. The FTC and researchers in general can find no *cause and effect* relationship between watching a film (such as *Saving Private Ryan*) and engaging in violent behavior. Indeed, there are rigorous studies that show salutary efforts: that video games, even violent ones, aid in the cognitive development of children by challenging them to solve complex puzzles.[100]

The effort to assign to the entertainment industry responsibility for present-day violence by American youth is not new. Historically, government censorship has been justified by a need to protect children. This

[96] U.S. Department of Justice, *OJJDP Statistical Briefing Book,* available online at http://ojjdp.ncjrs.org/ojstatbb/html/qa276.html [accessed October 22, 2003].

[97] Ibid. "Between 1980 and 2000, the Violent Crime Index arrest rates for youth ages 15-17 *decreased* 10% and the rates for adults *increased.* More specifically, the rates increased 5% for adults ages 18-24, 12% for adults ages 25-29, 31% for those ages 30-34, 44% for those ages 35-39, and 38% for those ages 40-44. Even the arrest rates for adults ages 60-64 increased 8%" (emphasis added).

[98] S. 792 § 2(4) (emphasis added).

[99] *Id.*

[100] James Paul Gee, *What Video Games Have to Teach Us About Learning and Literacy* (New York: Palgrave Macmillan, 2003). Professor Gee is Tashia Morgridge Professor of Reading in the Department of Curriculum and Instruction in the School of Education at the University of Wisconsin, Madison. In his book, he argues that video games, even violent ones, are intricate learning experiences that help children learn. See also C. Shawn Green and Daphne Bavelier, "Action Video Game Modifies Visual Selective Attention," *Nature* 423, May 29, 2003, 534-37; available online at http://www.nature.com/cgi-taf/DynaPage.taf?file=/nature/journal/v423/n6939/full/nature01647_r.html&filetype=&dynoptions= (concluding that video-game playing increases the capacity of the visual attentional system). Article accessed October 28, 2003.

rationale goes back at least to the time of the ancient Greeks.[101] The common supposition is that certain images or speech cause children to become immoral or engage in bad behavior. Yet, the FTC and scholars have been unable to document this hypothesis.

The case law requires substantially more than the mere supposition of a causal relationship between watching a movie or listening to music and engaging in illegal and violent behavior. There must be virtually an unthinking, knee-jerk connection—an *incitement*—between what one views or hears and the subsequent illegal action. Justice William Brennan, writing for the majority of the Court, reached this conclusion in *Carey v. Population Services International* (1977).[102]

Carey invalidated a New York law that made it a crime for anyone to advertise or display contraceptives. The state tried to justify the law by arguing that advertising contraceptives would encourage illegal sexual activity by young people. The Court simply rejected this argument. The state could not rely on such a causal relationship because there was no incitement:

> As for the possible "legitimation" of illicit sexual behavior, whatever might be the case if the advertisements directly incited illicit sexual activity among the young, none of the advertisements in this record can even remotely be characterized as "directed to inciting or producing imminent *lawless* action and ... likely to *incite* or produce such action."[103]

While *Central Hudson* does allow the state to regulate an advertisement that proposes an illegal transaction (e.g., an advertisement for a "white-only employee"),[104] *Carey* does not allow the state to outlaw advertisements that depict or even advocate unlawful behavior. The state must show that the speech in question "incites" illegal conduct, that is, causes "imminent lawless action" in the same way that someone might incite a lynch mob to engage in lawless action. Neither the FTC nor any other

[101] *E.g.*, Marjorie Heins, *Not in Front of the Children: Indecency, Censorship, and the Innocence of Youth* (New York: Hill and Wang, 2001).

[102] 431 U.S. 678 (1977).

[103] *Id.* at 701, citing *Brandenburg v. Ohio*, 395 U.S. 444, 447 (1969) (emphasis in original). Thus, a Louisiana state court dismissed a suit seeking damages when an Oklahoma couple shot and paralyzed a store clerk after watching a violent film, *Natural Born Killers*. The appellate court upheld the unpublished trial court ruling in *Byers v. Edmondson*, 826 So. 2d 551 (La. App. 1 Cir. 2002). See also Bruce Orwall, "Court Dismisses Suit on Movie Violence," *Wall Street Journal*, March 13, 2001, B10. The court ruled, as a matter of law, that Warner Brothers Studios and Oliver Stone did not intend to "incite" violence. By the way, if S. 792 had been the law, it would not have affected this situation: S. 792 would have been inapplicable because the two Oklahomans were not seventeen-years-old or younger.

[104] *Central Hudson Gas & Electric Corp. v. Public Service Commission of New York*, 447 U.S. 557, 566 (1980).

reputable authority argues that movies, or music lyrics, or video games have that exceedingly tight relationship of cause followed by immediate effect. Advertisements for movies, or music lyrics, or video games do not "incite" violence as Justice Brennan used that term in the *Carey* decision.

C. *Targeting advertising: Restricting truthful advertisements because children are in the audience*

What does it mean to "target" advertising to minors? S. 792 defines advertising to minors as advertising to an audience if a "substantial percentage" of that audience includes children under seventeen.[105] The bill would authorize the FTC to determine the meaning of "substantial" portion. For example, if the FTC decided that a "substantial percentage" of the audience meant that children under seventeen constituted 33 percent of an audience, then it would be illegal for a company to advertise certain products to an audience in which two-thirds of the members were adults.

The bill would also create what it calls a "safe harbor" for those who adhere to a "voluntary self-regulatory system." The bill then establishes government criteria for these "voluntary" systems, that the FTC would enforce. The bill would allow the FTC to impose a fine of $11,000 a day on a company that truthfully advertised an R-rated movie as R-rated if the FTC determined that children were in the target audience.[106] A bill that would impose a fine for not following a "voluntary" system does not appear to be truly voluntary, any more than the federal income tax is "voluntary."[107]

The voluntary movie, television, and music ratings system now in effect does not raise similar constitutional problems because the system is truly voluntary. Movies, television shows, and music lyrics are not required to be rated. If the distributors decide to rate a film, a movie theater that shows the film has no legal obligation to enforce the rating, by fines

[105] S. 792 § 2(5)(B).

[106] Dreazen, "Democrats May Be Goring Their Own Ox As Lieberman, Hollings Target Hollywood," *supra* note 3, at A20.

[107] One could read the proposal differently. Section 101(a) declares illegal the targeted marketing to minors of adult-rated media. Section 106(1), however, defines "adult-rated" as "a rating or label voluntarily assigned by the producer or distributor of such product, including a rating or label assigned pursuant to an industry-wide rating or labeling system." This language appears to allow producers or distributors to exempt themselves from the coverage of the proposed law simply by not rating the product. In that case, the bill's incentives would be perverse because they would encourage the publication of less, rather than more, information.

One might think that this incongruous outcome could be averted simply by more careful drafting, but if Congress were to require that the ratings system be mandatory—meaning everything must be rated—instead of voluntary, that would raise a host of other, more difficult issues, including prior restraint. If the ratings system were compulsory, how would one define the relevant terms, and who would enforce it? Would the tens of thousands of MP3 music files released on the Internet have to be labeled prior to publication? If a distributor objected to a rating, what would be the appeal process?

or any other mechanism. The first prong of *Central Hudson* allows the government to regulate commercial speech if it proposes an illegal transaction, but it is not illegal for a twelve-year-old to watch a PG-13-rated movie. Even an advertisement that explicitly urged sixteen-year-olds to watch an R-rated movie does not propose an illegal transaction.

"Accountability" of the entertainment industry is the latest buzz word. When parents decide not to give money to their thirteen-year-olds to view an R-rated movie, or when parents decide that their children should not see a particular R-rated movie, these actions make the industry accountable, but only to the extent that parents decide to use the information given to them. When the movie industry voluntarily provides ratings information, it does not act pursuant to any government mandate and does not restrict or ban speech, but, rather, it gives the general public more information, to use (or not use) as it sees fit. Neither the state nor any state agency has any role to play under the voluntary ratings system.[108]

It is interesting that the American Library Association (ALA) objects to any federal law that merely restricts access to information. Consider what the ALA has said about any government efforts to restrict children's access to entertainment. The ALA's "Library Bill of Rights" provides that libraries should lend videotapes and movies, regardless of the voluntary ratings system of the Motion Picture Association of America (MPAA) and regardless of the age of the minor seeking to borrow the material: "A person's right to use a library should not be denied or abridged because of origin, *age*, background, or views."[109] The ALA concludes that, as a

[108] In 1989, the Council of the American Library Association made it clear that libraries support access to all materials, including videotapes, regardless of the user's age or the content of the materials. ALA's "Free Access to Libraries for Minors: An Interpretation of the Library Bill of Rights" states:

> The "right to use a library" includes free access to, and unrestricted use of, all the services, materials, and facilities the library has to offer. Every restriction on access to, and use of, library resources, *based solely on the chronological age*, educational level, or legal emancipation of users violates Article V.
>
> ... [P]arents—and only parents—have the right and the responsibility to restrict the access of their children—and only their children—to library resources. Parents or legal guardians who do not want their children to have access to certain library services, materials or facilities, should so advise their children. Librarians and governing bodies cannot assume the role of parents or the functions of parental authority in the private relationship between parent and child. *Librarians and governing bodies have a public and professional obligation to provide equal access to all library resources for all library users.*
>
> Policies which set *minimum age limits for access to videotapes* and/or other audiovisual materials and equipment, *with or without parental permission, abridge library use for minors.* (emphasis added)

Document available online at http://www.ala.org/alaorg/oif/acc_chil.html [accessed October 24, 2003].

[109] American Library Association, "Library Bill of Rights," adopted June 18, 1948 (emphasis added).

matter of free speech, the MPAA voluntary guidelines *should not* control children's access to library videotapes that are R-rated.[110] Public libraries, in the view of the librarians, should not act as the parents or guardians of the users of the facilities, regardless of age.[111]

While the government does not have a role in the voluntary ratings system, it would have a central role to play if it were given the power to forbid the industry from truthfully disclosing—in a G-rated preview or movie trailer—that a movie is R-rated when children are in the audience. Even then, it would still be perfectly legal for a sixteen-year-old or a ten-year-old to watch *The Patriot*—a movie about the Revolutionary War, accompanied by some very graphic violence depicting the horrors of war—whether or not the child was accompanied by an adult.

The Supreme Court, in a series of cases, has held that the First Amendment protects marketing of "entertainment" or activities that are not suitable for children but permissible for adults, even though children may be in the audience. For example, in *Sable Communications of California, Inc. v. FCC* (1989), the Court concluded that Congress could not impose a ban on *"indecent"* interstate, prerecorded, commercial telephone messages because that speech is not "obscene" in the constitutional sense, even though the law's purpose was to protect children.[112] The Court found unpersuasive the government's argument that an outright ban was appropriate although the Court acknowledged that enterprising youngsters could evade the rules governing credit card access, scrambling rules, and so forth.

Later, in *Reno v. American Civil Liberties Union* (1997),[113] the Court turned its attention to the constitutionality of two statutory provisions enacted to protect minors from "indecent" and "patently offensive" communications on the Internet. The Court repeatedly rejected the argument that the

[110] The ALA has taken the position and advised its members that

> MPAA and other rating services are private advisory codes and have no legal standing. For the library to add such ratings to the materials if they are not already there, to post a list of such ratings with a collection, or *to attempt to enforce such ratings through circulation policies or other procedures* constitutes labeling, "an attempt to prejudice attitudes" about the material, and *is unacceptable*. The application of locally generated ratings schemes intended to provide content warnings to library users is also inconsistent with the Library Bill of Rights. (emphasis added)

See http://www.ala.org/alaorg/oif/acc_chil.html [accessed October 24, 2003].

In the fall of 2001, the San Francisco Board of Supervisors unanimously voted to ban Internet filters designed to keep pornography away from children at city libraries. Associated Press, "San Francisco Bans Use of Web Filters at Libraries," *Wall Street Journal*, October 3, 2001.

[111] The Council of the ALA *reaffirmed* the inclusion of "age" on January 23, 1996.

[112] 492 U.S. 115 (1989). The Court did allow Congress to impose a ban on *"obscene"* interstate, prerecorded, commercial telephone messages ("dial-a-porn") because "the protection of the First Amendment does not extend to obscene speech."

[113] 521 U.S. 844 (1997).

laudable goal of protecting children justified federal regulation. "Notwithstanding the legitimacy and *importance of the congressional goal of protecting children from harmful materials*, we agree with the three-judge District Court that the statute abridges 'the freedom of speech' protected by the First Amendment."[114]

Shortly after this declaration, Justice John Paul Stevens, for the Court, again dismissed the argument that the Court should defer to congressional judgment when it decides that only a total ban will be effective in preventing enterprising youngsters from gaining access to indecent communications:

> [The] *mere fact that a statutory regulation of speech was enacted for the important purpose of protecting children from exposure to sexually explicit material* does not foreclose inquiry into its validity. . . . that inquiry embodies an "overarching commitment" to make sure that Congress has designed its statute to accomplish its purpose "without imposing an unnecessarily great restriction on speech."[115]

The goal of proposals such as S. 792 is to protect children, which is commendable, but it is not enough to remove First Amendment protections. The Court will still engage in a searching inquiry and, based on the case law, proposals similar to S. 792 are unlikely to survive constitutional challenge. This conclusion becomes even more unavoidable given the decision in *Lorillard Tobacco Co. v. Reilly* (2001).[116]

Lorillard Tobacco acknowledged that tobacco is a heavily regulated industry and that there are important restrictions on selling tobacco to children. The arguments for regulating tobacco are much stronger than the arguments for regulating movies. In the case of tobacco, the Surgeon General has determined that smoking causes cancer and is a significant health risk. In contrast, the FTC has not determined that watching violent movies causes crime or is otherwise hazardous to children's welfare.[117] Moreover, watching movies, listening to CDs, and playing video games are, unlike smoking, a matter of free speech. While it is against the law for minors to purchase or smoke tobacco, it is not illegal for twelve-year-olds to view PG-13 movies. Hence, one would think that the government would have a stronger case for restricting advertising of tobacco products than movies, CDs, or videos when tobacco advertisements might be seen by children and cause them to engage in illegal acts (buying cigarettes).[118]

[114] 521 U.S. at 849 (emphasis added).

[115] 521 U.S. 844, 875–76 (emphasis added).

[116] 533 U.S. 525 (2001).

[117] Federal Trade Commission, *Marketing Violent Entertainment to Children*, *supra* note 1, at Appendix A, "A Review of Research on the Impact of Violence in Entertainment Media."

[118] Obviously, the cigarette advertisements did not "incite" the children to engage in illegal acts.

Yet, *Lorillard Tobacco* has held that tobacco companies have a constitutional right to engage in such advertising activities, even if it reaches children. If tobacco marketing activities that reach children are protected, then, a fortiori, one would think that marketing of movies, CDs, and video games is protected under the First Amendment. This, at least, is what the case law appears to say.

Lorillard Tobacco arose when the attorney general of Massachusetts promulgated comprehensive regulations governing the advertising and sale of cigarettes, smokeless tobacco, and cigars. Justice Sandra Day O'Connor wrote a lengthy and complex opinion for the Court.[119] The Court upheld free speech rights for advertising of tobacco—a product where the connection between use and ill health is very strong. How would the Court, then, look upon banning the advertising of mature-rated entertainment to children where the connection between exposure and violent and unlawful behavior is tenuous at best? The *Lorillard Tobacco* holding appears to doom proposals that seek to ban advertising when children are in the audience.

After deciding other issues, *Lorillard Tobacco* turned to the First Amendment claims of the smokeless tobacco and cigar manufacturers and retailers. Massachusetts imposed restrictions on advertising of tobacco in order to prevent or, at least, lessen the amount of smoking by children. Nonetheless, the Court invalidated the restrictions on advertising of tobacco products *even in areas where children are likely to be in the target audience,* such as on billboards near schools. The Court held that the state's regulations on outdoor advertising of smokeless tobacco and cigars violated free speech. The "broad sweep" of the state's prohibition of smokeless tobacco or cigar outdoor advertising within one thousand feet of a school or playground violated the First Amendment because it did not satisfy the fourth prong of *Central Hudson:* whether a regulation is not "more extensive than is necessary" to serve the government's interest in protecting children.[120] In practice, the restrictions at issue in *Lorillard Tobacco* prohibited advertising "in a substantial portion of the major metropolitan areas of Massachusetts."[121]

The Court acknowledged that the state has a "compelling" interest in preventing underage tobacco use, "but it is no less true that the sale and use of tobacco products by adults is a legal activity. We must consider that tobacco retailers and manufacturers have an interest in conveying truth-

[119] Other justices filed various opinions concurring in part and in the judgment and dissenting in part. First, Justice O'Connor held that the Federal Cigarette Labeling and Advertising Act (FCLAA) preempts Massachusetts' regulations targeting outdoor and point-of-sale cigarette advertising. Because the FCLAA, by its terms, only applies to cigarettes, the Court was required to address the First Amendment claims of the smokeless tobacco and cigar manufacturers and retailers.

[120] *Central Hudson*, 447 U.S. at 566.

[121] *Lorillard Tobacco*, 553 U.S. at 562.

ful information about their products to adults, and adults have a corresponding interest in receiving truthful information about tobacco products."[122]

The state regulations at issue in *Lorillard Tobacco* also limited indoor, point-of-sale advertising for smokeless tobacco and cigars: "Advertising cannot be 'placed lower than five feet from the floor of any retail establishment which is located within a one thousand foot radius of' any school or playground." *Lorillard Tobacco* invalidated this restriction as well. It failed both *Central Hudson*'s third prong (by not directly advancing the government's interest) and its fourth prong (by being more extensive than necessary). The state's purpose was to discourage minors from using tobacco by limiting their exposure to advertising. The five-foot rule did not advance this goal. "Not all children are less than 5 feet tall, and those who are certainly have the ability to look up and take in their surroundings."[123]

Nor is the height restriction a mere regulation of conduct, because the whole purpose of this restriction was "an attempt to regulate directly the communicative impact of indoor advertising." The lower court had justified this restriction on the theory that it "is very limited," but there "is no *de minimis* exception for a speech restriction that lacks sufficient tailoring or justification."[124]

From these cases, one would naturally conclude that movie theater owners and others have a First Amendment right, for example, to show G-rated previews of R-rated films. Children and adults will see these G-rated previews and the parents can determine if they want their children to attend the advertised films. Like *Lorillard Tobacco, Reno v. American Civil Liberties Union* cautioned

> It is true that we have repeatedly recognized the governmental interest in protecting children from harmful materials. But that interest does not justify an unnecessarily broad suppression of speech addressed to adults. As we have explained, the Government may not "reduce the adult population . . . to . . . only what is fit for children.[125]

Note that a state does have the power to ban children from seeing certain types of materials that an adult has a constitutional right to see.

[122] *Id.* at 564. The Court found no free speech problem with regulations requiring retailers to place tobacco products behind counters and requiring customers to have contact with a salesperson prior to the time that they can handle the product. These restrictions were on conduct, not speech. The retailers have "other means of exercising any cognizable speech interest in the presentation of their products. We presume that vendors may place empty tobacco packaging on open display, and display actual tobacco products so long as that display is only accessible to sales personnel." *Id.* at 569–70.

[123] *Id.* at 566.

[124] *Id.* at 567.

[125] 521 U.S. 844, 899–900 (1997) (internal citations omitted).

The state cannot ban *Playboy* because this magazine is not "obscene" in a constitutional sense for adults, but the state can prohibit a young child from buying *Playboy*. This was the holding of Justice Brennan, speaking for the Court in *Ginsberg v. New York* (1968).[126] New York had prohibited the sale to minors under seventeen years of age of material ("girlie" picture magazines) defined to be obscene on the basis of its appeal to them, even if the magazines would not be obscene to adults.

Justice Brennan explained that this case presented "the question of the constitutionality on its face of a New York criminal obscenity statute which prohibits the sale to minors under 17 years of age of material defined to be obscene on the basis of its appeal to them whether or not it would be obscene to adults."[127] The Court upheld the law even though the "'girlie' picture magazines involved in the sales are not obscene for adults."[128] The Court held that this "variable obscenity" (different rules for different people depending on their ages) is within the power of the state, for the state's power over children is broader than its power over adults.[129]

Ginsberg does not support a rule that would allow the state to ban *advertising* for *Playboy* simply because children may see the advertisements and want to read (or look at) the magazine. Hence, for the following reasons, proposals like S. 792 find little solace or support in the holding of *Ginsberg*.

First, these new proposals do not prohibit minors from seeing certain movies judged "obscene" as to them. Instead, the proposals relate to marketing: *Ginsberg* did not authorize any restrictions on marketing of "girlie" magazines. Just look around: corner newsstands freely display and advertise *Playboy* even though children might be in the vicinity. Besides, with reality shows on television that feature *Playboy* models, one would be hard pressed to keep knowledge of their existence from children.[130] Ask any ten-year-old what it means to be a *Playboy* bunny, and the child knows.

Second, the Court emphasized that the law did not ban youngsters from seeing the magazines. Instead, the law supported the parents' claim of authority to direct the rearing of their children because the law did not ban advertising the magazine and did not ban children from access to the magazines: if the parents wanted their children to see such materials, nothing in the law prohibited them from purchasing the magazines for their children. The state's "prohibition against sales to minors does not bar parents who so desire from purchasing the magazines for their chil-

[126] 390 U.S. 629 (1968).
[127] *Id.* at 631.
[128] *Id.* at 634.
[129] *Id.* at 636.
[130] *E.g.*, Reuters, "Playboy looking for 'Women of Starbucks'," February 28, 2003, posted online at 10:53 a.m., EST, "Lattes aren't the only steamy things at Starbucks these days," http://www.cnn.com/2003/US/West/02/28/offbeat.playboy.starbucks.reut/index.html [accessed February 28, 2003].

dren."[131] In contrast, proposals like S. 792 prohibit certain types of *marketing* without regard to what parents would prefer. These proposals, unlike the statute in *Ginsberg*, do not support parental choice but rather supplant it because these proposals, unlike *Ginsberg*, would ban *advertising* when children are in the audience.

Third, *Ginsberg* said nothing that even suggested it was undercutting the general principle that the state may not prohibit information from reaching adults because children might be in the audience. *Butler v. Michigan*, decided more than forty years ago, held that the state cannot ban sales of materials to adults on the grounds that the materials would be harmful to children: "Surely, this is to burn the house to roast the pig."[132] When matters of free speech are concerned, the government must draw with the precision of a surgeon's scalpel, not the rough hew of a butcher's axe.[133]

In its more recent decisions, the Court has reaffirmed the general principle. Thus, in a child pornography case the Court rejected the argument that a ban on "virtual pornography" (computer-generated images of child pornography that did not depict any real person) was necessary because the capacity to produce realistic images by using computer technology makes it very difficult to prosecute those who produce pornography by using real children. Although the government may punish adults who provide unsuitable materials to children, and it may punish those who use real children for purposes of child pornography, the precedents establish "that speech within the rights of adults to hear may not be silenced completely in an attempt to shield children from it."[134] The Court also invalidated a ban on "dial-a-porn" messages because they had "the invalid effect of limiting the content of adult telephone conversations to that which is suitable for children to hear."[135]

[131] 390 U.S. at 639.

[132] 352 U.S. 380, 383 (1957).

> It is clear on the record that appellant was convicted because Michigan, by § 343, made it an offense for him to make available for the general reading public (and he in fact sold to a police officer) a book that the trial judge found to have a potentially deleterious influence upon youth. The State insists that, by thus quarantining the general reading public against books not too rugged for grown men and women in order to shield juvenile innocence, it is exercising its power to promote the general welfare. Surely, this is to burn the house to roast the pig.

[133] *See, e.g., Bad Frog Brewery, Inc. v. New York State Liquor Authority*, 134 F.3d 87 (2d Cir. 1998) (holding that it was a violation of commercial speech for the New York State Liquor Authority to ban a particular label for *Bad Frog Beer.* The label displayed a frog giving a well-known insulting gesture: the frog had its middle finger extended. Various versions of the label featured slogans such as: "He just don't care," "An amphibian with an attitude," "Turning bad into good," and "The beer so good . . . it's bad." Another slogan, originally used but later abandoned, was "He's mean, green and obscene."

Although the Liquor Authority said that "it considered that approval of this label means that the label could appear in grocery and convenience stores, with obvious exposure on the shelf to *children of tender age*," the court rejected that rationale. 134 F.3d at 91 (emphasis added).

[134] *Ashcroft v. Free Speech Coalition*, 122 S.Ct. 1389, 1402 (2002).

[135] *Sable Communications of California, Inc. v. FCC*, 492 U.S. 115, 130–31 (1989).

The general principle is particularly apt when one appreciates the fact that children are ubiquitous. Under proposals like S. 792, it would be permissible to market an R-rated movie to seventeen-year-olds, but not to sixteen-year-olds. Yet, it is impossible to market to seventeen-year-olds without also reaching sixteen-year-olds. Teenagers, like adults, turn to the same entertainment section of the newspaper to read the movie advertisements and show times. There, they all see an advertisement for an R-rated movie, which is truthfully labeled as "R-rated," but—according to S. 792—such an advertisement is "deceptive" because a "substantial proportion of minors" are in the target audience.[136] They are also exposed to television shows (such as NBC's *Today Show* or movie reviews on PBS) that discuss and review recent movies, including some that are rated R or PG-13.

May an R-rated or PG-13 movie be advertised on *Who Wants to Be a Millionaire*? This game show did not target children, but in its heyday it reached about 3.2 million children under age seventeen, or about 12 percent of its audience. Any advertisement on *Who Wants to Be a Millionaire?* would have affected a large number of minors. May an R-rated or PG-13 movie be advertised on *The Wonderful World of Disney?* We may think that this show targets children, but less than 35 percent of its audience is comprised of teenagers and younger children. Can MTV accept any advertising for R-rated movies, even though two-thirds of its audience is over eighteen?[137]

In each of these cases, there is either an adult show with a substantial number of child-viewers or a children's show with a substantial number of adult viewers. If a proposal like S. 792 becomes law, it might be the case that the only way adults could see G-rated trailers of R-rated movies would be to buy a ticket to see an R-rated movie. Yet even that might not work, because children would still be in the audience of R-rated movies, inasmuch as children may lawfully view R-rated movies, and if the number of children who did so was not *de minimis,* then adults viewing an R-rated movie would still be unable to view G-rated trailers of R-rated movies because a "substantial percentage" of children would be in the target audience.

Moreover, what it means to "target" children or "market" to them is not a self-defining concept. S. 792 would authorize the FTC to determine if the entertainment industry uses "marketing practices designed to attract minors to such materials."[138] In the past, the entertainment industry has been accused of marketing "designed to attract minors" when it used cartoon characters to advertise its products. Yet, an insurance company, MetLife, markets its products by using Snoopy, the dog from the *Peanuts* comic strip series. On billboards, commercials, and its Internet homepage, MetLife prominently displays the cartoon dog. As one browses "related

[136] S. 792 § 103 (b)(1).

[137] Bruce Orwall, "Can Hollywood Shelter Kids from Its Ads?" *Wall Street Journal,* September 29, 2000, B1.

[138] S. 792, § 201(b)(1)(B).

links" on the Web site, one sees Snoopy, Lucy, and other *Peanuts* characters selling life insurance, advising about a will, and so forth. There is Snoopy pointing to a chart and explaining the need for long-term care insurance.[139] Is MetLife "targeting" children?

Owens Corning, on its billboards, commercials, and Web site, prominently features another cartoon character, the Pink Panther, touting, of all things, insulation, roofing systems, and Trumbull Asphalt.[140] Is Owens Corning "marketing to children"?

Pillsbury markets its bakery goods by using a cartoon character, the Pillsbury Dough Boy. Does this mean that Pillsbury thinks that little boys bake hot biscuits and are the real masters of the kitchen? Is Pillsbury marketing its bakery goods to nine-year-old boys?

VI. The Constitutional Significance of Inherent Inconsistencies in Proposed Legislation to Regulate Media Advertising

Proposed laws like S. 792 mark out various boundaries and create certain distinctions because of the need to take into account different interest groups and competing considerations. The problem is that, when a law seeks to navigate between Scylla and Charybdis, it invites internal inconsistencies; the exceptions and distinctions in the law tend to undercut its purported rationale. S. 792 is a good example of this principle. Under the case law, laws affecting speech that allow for exceptions that are inconsistent with their purported rationale are defective. S. 792 in this sense is no different than similar laws that the Court has invalidated in the past. S. 792, like its predecessors, makes findings of fact that appear to be inconsistent with the alleged evil that the proposed statute seeks to regulate.

For instance, S. 792 declares that nearly two-thirds of children between the ages of nine and seventeen watch videotapes for nearly one hour a day.[141] However, their video viewing pales in comparison to their broadcast television viewing. In fact, the average teenager will see forty thousand murders on television by the time he or she graduates from high school.[142] If it is important to regulate children's viewing habits, one would think that it is much more important to regulate broadcast or cable television rather than video rentals. Yet the proposed law specifically exempts any movie, no matter how violent, shown on broadcast television or cable television.[143]

[139] http://www.metlife.com/cgi-bin/frameit.cgi?topurl=/Lifeadvice/Family/Docs/getmarriedintro.html [accessed October 27, 2003].

[140] http://www.owenscorning.com/foryourhome/ [accessed October 27, 2003].

[141] S. 792 §2 (2)(A).

[142] Dreazen, "Democrats May Be Goring Their Own Ox As Lieberman, Hollings Target Hollywood," *supra* note 3, at A20.

[143] S. 792 § 106(5).

Under the proposed statutory scheme, S. 792 imposes various significant restrictions on a movie *if* parents decide to rent it at the video store in order to play it for their children, but it imposes no restrictions when children view the same movie (or a more violent one) on cable television when parents are not around to exercise any supervision. Similarly, the proposed statute governs the rental of a war documentary on videotape that shows accurate footage of violence, but exempts the same documentary entirely when it is aired on broadcast or cable television. The proposed law regulates video games but exempts any cable broadcast of a movie based on the same video game. S. 792 covers a rented movie (a situation where one would expect that a seven-year-old child could not, by herself, drive to Blockbusters and rent it without parental knowledge), but S. 792 exempts from its coverage the very same movie broadcast on cable during the afternoon when latch-key children are home from school and parents are at work. S. 792 would not govern the broadcast of a recent television miniseries, *Dune,* for example, but it would govern when that same series is sold or rented as a DVD.[144]

Such inconsistencies are of constitutional dimension in the context of a statute that regulates free speech. Consider, for example, *Greater New Orleans Broadcasting Association, Inc. v. United States* (1999).[145] In this case, the Court held that a federal law[146] may not constitutionally forbid radio and television stations located in Louisiana (where gambling is legal) from broadcasting advertisements of private casino gambling, *even though* broadcast signals are also heard or seen in neighboring Texas and Arkansas, where private casino gambling is unlawful. Justice Stevens, for the Court, said that because of its inconsistencies, this federal law could not satisfy the third and fourth prongs of *Central Hudson.* The government argued that limiting advertising will lessen gambling's social costs by curtailing demand, but the Court found this argument specious because section 1304 of the law at issue and its regulations were riddled by exemptions and inconsistencies.[147]

[144] The *Dune* science-fiction miniseries is available on videotape but it is not rated. See http://www.amazon.com/exec/obidos/tg/browse/-/286745/002-7282200-1708051 [accessed October 27, 2003].

[145] 527 U.S.173 (1999).

[146] 18 U.S.C. § 1304.

[147] 527 U.S. at 173.

> Congress' choice here was neither a rough approximation of efficacy, nor a reasonable accommodation of competing State and private interests. Rather, the regulation distinguishes among the indistinct, permitting a variety of speech that poses the same risks the Government purports to fear, while banning messages unlikely to cause any harm at all. Considering the manner in which § 1304 and its exceptions operate and the scope of the speech it proscribes, the Government's second asserted interest provides no more convincing basis for upholding the regulation than the first. (*Id.* at 195–96)

See discussion in Ronald D. Rotunda, "The Constitutional Future of the Bill of Rights: A Closer Look at Commercial Speech and State Aid to Religiously Affiliated Schools," *North Carolina Law Review* 65 (1987): 917.

Earlier, the Court made the same point in *Rubin v. Coors Brewing Co.*,[148] a 1995 case that Justice Stevens cited with approval. *Rubin* invalidated a federal law that prohibited beer labels from displaying alcohol content unless state law required disclosure of alcohol content. The Court found that the exceptions in the law doomed its constitutionality. The federal law did not "directly and materially advance" the purported interest in preventing "strength wars" among brewers. For example, the federal law allowed disclosure of alcohol content on the labels of wine and hard liquor, and even compelled disclosure for wines consisting of more than 14 percent alcohol. The law also allowed beer brewers to signal high alcohol content by using the term "malt liquor." In short, the federal labeling ban was not narrowly tailored to its goal and, hence, was unconstitutional.[149]

There is another important problem with the decision of the drafters of S. 792 to regulate almost all forms of movies, including movies downloaded from the Internet, *except* those broadcast on cable or network television.[150] One has to make an effort to download a movie or to go to a theater to see a movie. In *Reno v. American Civil Liberties Union*, the Court focused on this distinction between the Internet and television in one's home as a reason to invalidate a Pennsylvania statute because it regulated the former, less "invasive" medium, where the rationale for government intrusion is far less, but not the latter.[151] S. 792 shares the same flaw.

Justice Stevens explained that many steps must be taken to view a Web site on the Internet and then to download a document that is admittedly inappropriate for children. While computers are common today, they still are not as universal or as inexpensive as televisions. Then,

> Though such material [indecent material] is widely available [on the Internet], users seldom encounter such content accidentally. "A document's title or a description of the document will usually appear before the document itself . . . and in many cases the user will receive detailed information about a site's content before he or she need take the step to access the document. Almost all sexually explicit images are preceded by warnings as to the content." For that reason, the "odds are slim" that a user would enter a sexually explicit site by accident. *Unlike communications received by radio or television*, "the re-

[148] 514 U.S. 476 (1995).

[149] *Id.* at 488–91. Consider a movie popular in the fall of 2000, *Gone in 60 Seconds*. The movie glamorized car theft, linking it with sex and excitement. The film is PG-13, not R-rated. It would not appear to be covered by S. 792. But the proposed law would heavily regulate *Saving Private Ryan*, a film based on World War II, or *The Patriot*, a movie about the Revolutionary War, both of which were violent because they were based on violent events. However, neither of these movies glamorized war.

[150] S. 792 § 106(5), defining "motion picture" to include any electronic or online medium, "except" the term does not include "anything shown on broadcast television or cable television."

[151] 521 U.S. 844 (1997).

> ceipt of information on the Internet requires *a series of affirmative steps more deliberate and directed than merely turning a dial.* A child requires some sophistication and some ability to read to retrieve material and thereby to use the Internet unattended."[152]

The Court held that Pennsylvania's effort to regulate the Internet violated the First Amendment.

Under Justice Stevens's reasoning, proposals like S. 792 are less likely to be upheld than the law that *Reno v. ACLU* invalidated. Just as one must take some actions in order to see material on the Internet, one must take a series of deliberate actions to see an R-rated movie. One must first collect some money, then travel to the movie theater, pick out the movie among those that are rated G, PG-13, or R, and finally buy the ticket. One will have to engage in "a series of affirmative steps more deliberate and directed than merely turning a dial."[153]

The theory behind S. 792 is that it would discourage minors from attending, for example, an R-rated violent movie, by prohibiting advertising of that movie when children are likely to be in the audience that sees or hears the advertising. S. 792 turns upside down the rationale and reasoning of *Reno v. ACLU* because the proposal's marketing and advertising restrictions seek to regulate the area where the sixteen-year-old will have to engage in "a series of affirmative steps more deliberate and directed than merely turning a dial." Yet this proposed law would entirely exempt from marketing restrictions the area where the 16-year old can view violence by "merely turning a dial." After *Reno v. ACLU,* one would think that it is likely that the same Court would invalidate a law like S. 792, if enacted, because it would regulate the situation where one must engage in several steps (where the Court says regulation is not needed) and exempt the situation where one just turns the dial (where the Court suggests that some type of regulation may be permissible).

VII. Conclusion

Given the development of the relevant case law in the last half-century, culminating in *Lorillard Tobacco Co. v. Reilly* (2001), it is extremely likely that the Supreme Court would invalidate statutes that seek to ban advertising of R-rated movies, explicit music videos, or video games on the grounds that children may be in the audience. However, the fact that the First Amendment restricts government does not mean that government can do nothing. Government officials can lead by example. Public office provides a bully pulpit, and if officials believe that marketing is so effective, they can urge people not to attend R-rated movies, purchase explicit music, or buy M-rated video games.

[152] *Id.* at 854 (footnotes omitted) (emphasis added).
[153] *Id.*

If advertising is so effective, counteradvertising should be equally effective. Those opposed to children attending adult movies could sponsor advertising urging parents not to allow their young children to see movies rated PG-13. Still, one must take with a grain of salt those who argue that advertising is the hidden persuader that manipulates us. The Soviet Union had three-quarters of a century and a monopoly on the communications media to advertise its views of the proper role of government, and it utterly failed to persuade its people. If marketing and advertising were as effective as some suggest, there might still be a Soviet Union.

Granted, some people argue that we live in a vulgar age, and so we should be concerned that free speech protects liquor advertisements, tobacco advertisements, and movie trailers.[154] However, we must realize that free speech is one of the important rights that a free nation possesses. When the courts conclude that Nazis have a constitutional right to march in Skokie, Illinois,[155] the courts reach that conclusion to preserve the same hard-won right that was exercised by protestors against segregation in Birmingham, Alabama.[156] When the courts hold that liquor companies can advertise their products, they apply the basic principle that the government should not be able to manipulate what people do by denying them truthful information about lawful products or services. And when the courts hold that the government cannot restrict truthful advertising about lawful entertainment activities in order to discourage people from partaking of those activities, the courts follow a long series of precedents that extend the free speech guarantee to speech denominated as entertainment.

It is no accident that wherever they seized power Communists suppressed art as well as politics and religion. And when in 1989 the people overturned the Communist dictators of Eastern Europe, they

[154] Note that NBC has recently ended its self-imposed ban on hard liquor advertisements on television. The president of the NBC Television Network explained the new policy:

> The advertiser who wishes to run distilled spirits advertising on NBC must commit to a minimum of four months of 100 percent paid branded social responsibility messages prior to beginning product advertising. After that time has elapsed, the advertiser must agree that a minimum of 20 percent of its total advertising—one dollar in every five—be devoted to such social responsibility themes as designated drivers, moderation, the tragedy of impaired driving and the health consequences that can be associated with drinking, among others.

Randy Falco, "The Facts on NBC and Alcohol," *Washington Post*, December 19, 2001, A39. Local television and cable television began airing distilled liquor advertisements in 1996.

[155] *Collin and National Socialist Party v. Smith*, 578 F.2d 1197 (7th Cir. 1978), *certiorari denied*, 439 U.S. 916 (1978) (holding that a local ordinance designed to prevent a march of a Nazi organization, with its message of racial hatred, in Skokie, Illinois, is unconstitutional and violates freedom of speech). *See also: National Socialist Party v. Village of Skokie*, 432 U.S. 43 (1977) (per curiam); and Harry Kalven, Jr., *A Worthy Tradition: Freedom of Speech in America*, ed. Jamie Kalvern (New York: Harper and Row, 1988), 60–73.

[156] *Shuttlesworth v. City of Birmingham*, 394 U.S. 147 (1969).

regarded freedom of expression in entertainment as a premier right. The Czechs' "Velvet Revolution" began in the theaters, and the Czechs' first freely elected president since World War II, Vaclav Havel, was a writer and playwright. "[P]eople's spiritual needs, more than their material needs, [drove] the commissars from power."[157]

Law, George Mason University

[157] Salman Rushdie, "Is Nothing Sacred?" The Herbert Read Memorial Lecture, February 6, 1990 (New York: Granta, 1990), 8–9. Mr. Rushdie was the author of *The Satanic Verses*, published in 1989. In early 1989, Ayatollah Khomeini, the spiritual head of Iran, announced to the world that Mr. Rushdie must die because his book was offensive to Muslim beliefs. Mr. Rushdie, a British subject, went into hiding, protected by the British government that he often criticized.

FREE SPEECH IN THE AMERICAN FOUNDING AND IN MODERN LIBERALISM

By Thomas G. West

I. Introduction

It is widely believed that there is more freedom of speech in America today than there was at the time of the founding.[1] Indeed, this view is shared by liberal commentators, as one would expect, as well as by leading conservatives, which is more surprising. "The body of law presently defining First Amendment liberties," writes liberal law professor Archibald Cox, grew out of a "continual expansion of individual freedom of expression."[2] Conservative constitutional scholar Walter Berns agrees: "Legally we enjoy a greater liberty [of speech] than ever before in our history."[3] This shared assessment is correct—from the point of view of the political theory of today's liberalism—but it is incorrect from the point of view of the political theory of the American founding.

This paper will explore this paradox by laying out the two points of view, of the founders and of modern liberalism, from which these two

[1] In this paper, the phrase 'freedom of speech' includes freedom of the press. According to the First Amendment, Congress may not abridge "the freedom of speech, or of the press." I take 'freedom of the press' to mean the right, with the consent of the owner, to make use of any device that produces multiple copies of words or pictures, and to sell or distribute those copies to anyone who consents to accept or buy them (within the limits to be described below). The "press" would therefore include not just printing presses but also radio and television broadcasting facilities, cable television stations and the lines that carry them, movies, copying machines, computer printers, and the Internet. In James Madison's original proposed wording, the Amendment would have guaranteed the right of the people "to speak, to write, or to publish their sentiments." That is, what is protected is not just the right to use a printing press or to go into the newspaper business, but a right of every citizen to *publish*, to make and distribute copies of words and/or pictures communicating his or her sentiments to the public. The founders would never have accepted the view that the freedom of the press is limited to members of a particular industry called "the press" or "the media." *Annals of Congress*, June 8, 1789, in Philip B. Kurland and Ralph Lerner, eds., *The Founders' Constitution* (1987; reprint, Indianapolis, IN: Liberty Fund, 2000), 5:128 (quoting Madison).

[2] Archibald Cox, "First Amendment," in Kenneth L. Karst, ed., *The First Amendment: Selections from the Encyclopedia of the American Constitution* (New York: Macmillan, 1990), 3. See also Cass R. Sunstein, *Democracy and the Problem of Free Speech* (New York: Free Press, 1993), 17.

[3] Walter Berns, *The First Amendment and the Future of American Democracy* (1976; reprint, Chicago, IL: Gateway Editions, 1985), x. See also John O. McGinnis, "The Once and Future Property-Based Vision of the First Amendment," *University of Chicago Law Review* 63 (1996): 49: "For about the last fifty years, free speech has been the preeminent constitutional right, continually expanded by Supreme Court justices of varying jurisprudential views to protect ever more varied and vigorous expression."

opposite conclusions are drawn. First, I will explain the theory of free speech of the American founders. I will then examine the opposing theory developed by today's liberalism.

I use the term 'founders' to refer to the leading government officials of the period when America's political institutions were created and shaped, between about 1765 and 1820. Although these men had many disagreements, some of them intense, almost all agreed on the basic principles of government. Most of their disagreements arose from different judgments about the application of those principles, such as (in the dispute over the ratification of the Constitution of 1787) how much power the federal government should have, or (in the 1790s) what America's stance should be toward the French Revolution. At the time, these disputes seemed immensely important, as they were, to be sure, in the day-to-day politics of the period. But looking back on that era from today, one cannot help being struck by the broad consensus, transcending partisan differences, about the basic principles of government. This consensus united all the leading founders, from George Washington, Alexander Hamilton, and John Adams on the "right," to James Madison, Thomas Jefferson, and Thomas Paine on the "left."

As for the term 'liberalism', I am aware of the great variety of opinion that can be found under this label. Nevertheless, the word 'liberal' has a distinct meaning in everyday discourse in the United States. Hillary Clinton and Ted Kennedy are liberals; Ronald Reagan is a conservative. Academics, however, often use the term 'liberal' very differently. Michael Sandel, for example, writes:

> In the history of political theory, . . . liberalism describes a tradition of thought that emphasizes toleration and respect for individual rights and that runs from John Locke, Immanuel Kant, and John Stuart Mill to John Rawls. The public philosophy of contemporary American politics is a version of this liberal tradition of thought, and most of our debates proceed within its terms.[4]

For my purposes, this scholarly use of the term 'liberal' is misleading. John Rawls's views on the nature of human rights and of the purpose of government are almost entirely opposed to the views of Locke and the American founders. The most obvious difference is in regard to property. The founders strongly defended the individual right to acquire and hold private property. Modern liberals deny this right, or at least greatly qualify it for the sake of social utility. Rawls in particular favors expansive inroads on property rights for the sake of redistribution of income and

[4] Michael J. Sandel, *Democracy's Discontent: America in Search of a Public Philosophy* (Cambridge, MA: Harvard University Press, 1996), 4-5.

resources from those who have more to those who have less.[5] I propose, therefore, to use the term 'liberal' in the same commonsense manner as did the late Democratic Senator Paul Wellstone in his book, *The Conscience of a Liberal*.[6] In Wellstone's sense, a liberal is someone who favors what Wellstone calls "the compassionate agenda." Liberals want to use the power of government to compel the more affluent to provide money or services to those who have less, through policies like government-provided health care and requiring that businesses pay a "decent wage" to their employees.

In this essay, liberals are those whom Richard Rorty calls "the reformist left."[7] Liberalism in this contemporary sense was born in the late nineteenth century under the name of Progressivism. It did not fully acquire the label 'liberalism' until the 1930s. The liberal movement has grown in importance to the point where almost all American politicians embrace at least some of its doctrines. For example, hardly any Republican would defend the idea that major corporations should have a right to hire only those employees they happen to feel comfortable with. However, the right to freedom of association and to the noninjurious use of one's own property—including the right to hire and fire at will—was affirmed as a fundamental civil right in the American founding and long afterward.[8] Although liberals over the past century have fought bitterly among themselves over a great many policy matters, their overall approach to government has been quite consistent, as I will try to show later in this paper.

From the point of view of the founders, I will argue, speech in America today is much less free than it was in the early republic. For example, the United States now mandates limits on political speech by certain classes of citizens through campaign finance regulation and other laws, limits that the founders would have thought inconsistent with the right to free speech. They would also have disapproved of the imposition of a licensing scheme on electronic broadcasters. They would have condemned this scheme as an instance of the kind of hateful 'prior restraint' of the press by government that even the British government had abandoned almost a century before the American Revolution.

[5] John Rawls, *A Theory of Justice* (Cambridge, MA: Harvard University Press, 1971), 276 (arguing that a "competitive price system gives no consideration to needs and therefore it cannot be the sole device of distribution," against the founders' view that everyone should be permitted to keep the fruits of his own labor).

[6] Paul Wellstone, *The Conscience of a Liberal: Reclaiming the Compassionate Agenda* (Minneapolis: University of Minnesota Press, 2002).

[7] Richard Rorty, *Achieving Our Country: Leftist Thought in Twentieth-Century America* (Cambridge, MA: Harvard University Press, 1998), 39.

[8] Richard A. Epstein shows that the Jim Crow system in the post–Civil War South was a radical departure from the presumption in favor of the at-will employment contract, grounded in the natural law tradition of Locke and the founders, that prevailed elsewhere in America. Richard A. Epstein, *Forbidden Grounds: The Case against Employment Discrimination Laws* (Cambridge, MA: Harvard University Press, 1992), 98–99, 127, 134.

Further, although the United States has come close to abolishing limits on libel of public figures, on indecency, on obscenity, and on advocacy of violence as a means of political reform, the founders would not have regarded these changes as an expansion of free speech. They would have said that these reforms protect not freedom but *license*, the abuse of free speech. By permitting licentious speech, government, in the founders' view, is failing at one of its core tasks, namely, to secure the natural rights of person and property—rights that are threatened when the laws permit no redress for injury to reputation or to the moral conditions of free government.

Contrarily, from the point of view of the theory of free speech accepted by most contemporary liberals, the founders were wrong on both of the positions just sketched. First, limits on political speech actually serve the cause of free speech by preventing the wealthy from dominating public debate on candidates and elections. Liberals also believe that government regulation of broadcasters promotes, or should promote, a healthy diversity on the airwaves (which in practice often means exclusion of nonliberal viewpoints). Second, liberals condemn the founders' limits on obscenity and pornography as irrational and puritanical, for the same reason that liberals have little sympathy for the founders' belief that government should promote the heterosexual, monogamous family and discourage nonmarital sex.

From the point of view of today's liberalism, the founders restricted speech where it ought to be free (by banning obscenity and speech promoting the overthrow of government), while they allowed speech where it ought to be restricted (by permitting racial and sexual harassment in the workplace, allowing employers to impose their religious views on unwilling employees, and granting the wealthy an unlimited right to dominate elections by spending as much of their own money as they like).

From the founders' point of view, liberals restrict speech where it ought to be free. They ban some citizens from spending "too much" money publishing their opinions on candidates for election. Liberals lay down rules forbidding certain kinds of speech in private schools and workplaces. They impose prior restraint on speech by licensing electronic broadcasting and thereby manipulating the content of broadcasting. From the founders' perspective, liberals have reversed the earlier understanding. Liberals protect licentiousness but not liberty. The founders protected liberty but not licentiousness.

Thousands of books and articles have been written on the topic of free speech. Many of them are accurate and informative, but the tendency among scholars is to look at particular aspects of the question without seeing the matter as a whole. This means that the overall coherence of the earlier approach and today's liberal approach are rarely discussed thematically. For example, some students of free speech in the founding era have much to say about the debate over the Sedition Act of 1798, but not much about government regulation of obscenity, or the restrictions on speech imposed by government on its own property, or the absence of government regulation of publications during election campaigns. These latter issues are major topics today, and it is important to see why the founders would have disagreed with the more recent approach. My purpose is to look at the big picture. I intend to show all the major elements, and the coherence and intelligibility, of the consensus view shared by most of the founders, and then to do the same with the liberal approach.

I choose to discuss the founders' approach and the modern liberals' approach because these are the two main ways in which the question of free speech has been understood in American history. The founders' conception of politics prevailed—with the major exception of the Southern rejection of the founding principles after 1830—until about 1900. From then on, the political theory of liberalism has grown in importance, at first in intellectual circles and in some major but limited political reforms, but later, after 1965, increasingly in the major institutions of state and national government. America today, I argue, is a nation still governed in many ways by the founding principles, but governed in other ways by the principles of modern liberalism. It is likely that the nation will move in one direction or the other in the coming years. It is useful to know what the alternatives are, and on what principles they are grounded.

Speaking for myself, I find the founders' position superior not only to the liberal approach, but also to any other approach that I have read or heard of. It is worth clarifying the founders' approach to free speech, in my opinion, because their views on government produced what is arguably the best political order known to history. If they got that much right, then their views on free speech deserve our careful study and respect.

The first half of this paper begins with an overview of the founders' principles, then discusses the six leading elements of the founders' approach to free speech. The second half presents the liberal alternative, setting out the liberal redefinition of, or rejection of, these six elements.

II. Free Speech in the Founding: Basic Principles

To understand the founders' view of free speech, we begin with their understanding of the general principles of freedom. In their scheme, freedom of speech is only one aspect—certainly an important aspect—of the freedom that government is supposed to secure.

But what is that freedom? The principles of the American founding are not difficult to understand, yet they are widely misunderstood today. On the right, many conservatives believe (e.g., Robert Bork) that the political theory of the founding elevates liberty and equality above all other concerns. In principle, according to this view of the founding, liberty for the founders meant a complete lack of restraint, the right to do whatever one pleases. So according to these conservatives, the excesses of today's liberalism follow inexorably from the defective principles of the founding.[9] On the left, it is widely believed that although the founders spoke of liberty and equality, they really only meant liberty for white males, and equality was defined so narrowly that the poor had virtually no rights. So in this view, American history has been a long struggle, still incomplete, for the achievement of genuine liberty and equality for all. President Bill Clinton summed up this view in a 1997 speech:

> Keep in mind, when we started out with Thomas Jefferson's credo that all of us are created equal by God, what that really meant in civic political terms was that you had to be white, you had to be male, and that wasn't enough—you had to own property. . . . [T]he story of how we kept going higher and higher and higher to new and higher definitions—and more meaningful definitions—of equality and dignity and freedom is in its essence the fundamental story of our country.[10]

Both of these positions are demonstrably wrong.[11]

According to the Declaration of Independence, all human beings are created equal with regard to their inalienable rights, including life, liberty, and the pursuit of happiness. Five of the early state Declarations of Rights add to this list the acquisition and possession of property and the free

[9] Robert H. Bork, *Slouching toward Gomorrah: Modern Liberalism and American Decline* (New York: HarperCollins, Regan Books, 1996), 56–65. A variant on this view is held by some "paleoconservatives." They argue that the founding is based on British tradition and common law, not on the principles of natural rights that they fear lead to the excesses of today's liberalism and modern radicalism. Those holding this view include Russell Kirk, *The Conservative Constitution* (Washington, DC: Regnery Gateway, 1990); and M.E. Bradford, *A Better Guide than Reason: Studies in the American Revolution* (La Salle, IL: Sherwood Sugden, 1979). One view that I reject entirely is that of Justice Antonin Scalia, who writes, "what constitutes a 'law abridging the freedom of speech' is either a matter of history or else it is a matter of opinion. Why are not libel laws such an 'abridgment'? The only satisfactory answer is that they never were" (dissenting opinion, *O'Hare Truck Service v. City of Northlake*, 518 U.S. 712 [1996]. Justice Scalia's dissent, in which he was joined by Justice Clarence Thomas, may be found at *Board of County Commissioners, Wabaunsee County v. Umbehr*, 518 U.S. 668, 686 [1996]). For the founders, freedom of speech is neither a matter of history nor of opinion, but is a constitutionalized natural right that can be understood only in light of political philosophy. They wrestled with questions like whether seditious libel laws are compatible with the First Amendment precisely because they rejected the view that history or opinion could decide the question of what is right.

[10] President William Jefferson Clinton, remarks at the Human Rights Campaign Dinner, November 8, 1997 (pending completion of the Clinton presidential archives, information can be found online at www.clinton.archives.gov [accessed November 10, 2003]). On the poor, see John M. Blum, *Liberty, Justice, Order: Essays on Past Politics* (New York: Norton, 1993), 25: the poor were "defined . . . in a sense as an alien race that had to be held to close discipline."

[11] For a response to the critique from the Left, see Thomas G. West, *Vindicating the Founders: Race, Sex, Class, and Justice in the Origins of America* (Lanham, MD: Rowman & Littlefield, 1997).

exercise of religion. Article 1 of Virginia's Declaration of Rights, adopted in 1776, is typical: "That all men are by nature equally free and independent, and have certain inherent rights, of which, when they enter into a state of society, they cannot, by any compact, deprive or divest their posterity; namely, the enjoyment of life and liberty, with the means of acquiring and possessing property, and pursuing and obtaining happiness and safety." Article 16 reads: "That religion, or the duty which we owe to our Creator, and the manner of discharging it, can be directed only by reason and conviction, not by force or violence; and, therefore, all men are equally entitled to the free exercise of religion, according to the dictates of conscience."[12]

Equal natural rights also imply equal natural duties. Your right to life and liberty means that I have a duty not to harm or enslave you. The founders sometimes used the expressions "law" or "laws of nature" to make this point: reason discovers what the Declaration of Independence calls "the laws of nature and of nature's God." These are laws or rules that nature imposes on us, requiring everyone to respect the fundamental right to liberty of all, including the right to a "separate and equal station" (as stated in the Declaration of Independence) that all peoples or nations are entitled to, as well as the liberty and property of the individual.

Why, one might ask, did the founders believe in human equality in this sense: that no one has the right to rule another without that other's consent? Although the Declaration of Independence and the state Declarations of Rights do not offer an explanation, there are other official documents in the founding that do. And when they do, they tend to make the same argument. The reason that no one has a natural right to rule is because men are neither gods nor angels. Human beings, even the best among them, lack the wisdom and virtue that it would take to justify rule without consent. To put it in nontheological terms: the founders agreed wholeheartedly with Plato and Aristotle that perfect virtue is a just title to rule, but they denied that any human being has perfect virtue. Therefore, no one has the right to rule without consent. This means that all have an equal right to liberty. In a 1773 document published by the Massachusetts Council, James Bowdoin wrote:

> Supreme or unlimited authority can with fitness belong only to the sovereign of the universe: And that fitness is derived from the perfection of his nature.——To such authority, directed by infinite wisdom and infinite goodness, is due both active and passive obedience:

[12] Bernard Schwartz, ed., *The Roots of the Bill of Rights* (New York: Chelsea House, 1980), 2:234. Similar language appears in the Declarations of Rights of Pennsylvania (1776); Vermont (1777); Massachusetts (1780); and New Hampshire (1784) (all are reprinted in Schwartz). All five Declarations affirm a right to free exercise of religion or the equivalent; New Hampshire's, Art. 5, calls it a "natural and unalienable right." (In this paper, spelling and punctuation in quotations from older documents are occasionally modernized.)

> Which, as it constitutes the happiness of rational creatures, should with cheerfulness and from choice be unlimitedly paid by them.—— But with truth this can be said of no other authority whatever.[13]

Human nature is a combination of reason and passions, as was frequently observed in the founding era. God, in contrast, may be said to be pure mind without passion, while the "irrational creation" (as Madison calls them in *Federalist No. 54*), such as dogs and cattle, are purely passionate without reason. Thus, God has a right to rule men, and men have a right to rule dogs and cattle, and in neither case is consent necessary. But no human being is so far superior to any other human being that he or she may rationally be trusted to govern without that other's consent (except for children and those with severe mental defects). This truth is an inference from the fact that men are neither altogether rational nor altogether passionate, but a mixture of both. Therefore, they can be counted on to be both prone to error and not fully devoted to the common good. As Madison sums up the point in *Federalist No. 51*, "If men were angels, no government would be necessary. If angels were to govern men, neither external nor internal controls on government would be necessary."

These preliminaries lead to two conclusions about the purpose and foundation of good government. First, its purpose: "To secure these rights, governments are instituted among men," says the Declaration of Independence. Our rights are insecure when there is no government, because, as Jefferson later wrote, "it frequently happens that wicked and dissolute men, resigning themselves to the dominion of inordinate passions, commit violations on the lives, liberties, and property of others, and the secure enjoyment of these" is what "principally induced men to enter into society."[14]

The founders' equality principle—that all are equal with respect to their natural rights—leads to a second conclusion about good government, this one concerning its proper foundation. The Declaration of Independence says that governments derive "their just powers from the consent of the governed." If we are born equal with respect to the right to liberty, the only way that the rule of some human beings over others can be justified is if that rule is based on the consent of those who are ruled. Consent must be given in two ways. First, we consent when we become members of a political community. Second, we consent collectively to the laws we live under through periodic elections of those who make the laws. Accordingly, as part of its proof that the consent principle has been

[13] Answer of the Massachusetts Council, in *The Briefs of the American Revolution: Constitutional Arguments between Thomas Hutchinson, Governor of Massachusetts Bay, and James Bowdoin for the Council, and John Adams for the House of Representatives*, ed. John P. Reid (New York: New York University Press, 1981), 35.

[14] Jefferson, "A Bill for Proportioning Crimes and Punishments," 1778, in Kurland, *The Founders' Constitution*, 5:374.

violated, the Declaration gives numerous examples of the British denial of the right of Americans to be ruled by their elected representatives.

Before we turn to the particular question of free speech, we have to consider in the broadest terms how government secures our natural rights. To deal with threats to our rights from abroad, government must provide a common defense by means of diplomacy and, in the extreme case, of arms. For threats to our rights from our fellow citizens, government must establish criminal and civil law.

The rule of law—especially criminal law—is the most obvious remedy for the insecurity of the state of nature, which is the state of human beings living together without a common government. In the state of nature, as John Locke rightly notes, there are three major defects that make life, liberty, and possessions insecure. First, there is no clearly known law (for the law of nature, mandating that no one is to be injured except for just punishment, is not obvious to everyone). Second, there is no impartial judge (for each is judge in his own cause, which often leads to bias and error in judgment). Third, there is no effective punishment for those who violate the law of nature. A well-constructed government provides clear laws (defining injuries and the appropriate punishments), impartial judgment (through jury trials), and reliable punishment (by fines, imprisonment, or execution).[15] Here is the rationale for dividing state and federal governments in the United States into three branches: legislative, judicial, and executive.

The primary protection of free speech, therefore, is not normally discussed in the literature on the right of free speech. It is not constitutional limitations on government; rather, it is government's willingness and capacity to punish anyone who injures any person or group because of something published or said by that person or group. When a violent mob threw abolitionist Elijah Lovejoy's printing press into the Mississippi River in 1837, the city government, writes Michael Kent Curtis, "refused to act, except to advise Lovejoy and his friends not to reestablish a press in Alton."[16] Not long afterward, another mob attacked and killed Lovejoy when he acquired a new press. After the Civil War, when the Ku Klux Klan operated with impunity in the South, Senator Adelbert Ames (R-MS) noted that "[i]n some counties it was impossible to advocate Republican principles, those attempting it being hunted like wild beasts." Representative William L. Stoughton (R-MI) exclaimed: "If political opponents can be marked for slaughter by secret bands of cowardly assassins who ride forth with impunity to execute the decrees upon the unarmed and de-

[15] John Locke, *Two Treatises of Government* (1690), ed. Peter Laslett (Cambridge: Cambridge University Press, 1960), *Second Treatise*, sec. 123–31, pp. 350–53. On Locke's decisive influence on the founders' understanding of political principles, see Thomas G. West, "The Political Theory of the Declaration of Independence," in Ronald J. Pestritto and Thomas G. West, eds., *The American Founding and the Social Compact* (Lanham, MD: Lexington Books, 2003).

[16] Michael Kent Curtis, *Free Speech, 'The People's Darling Privilege': Struggles for Freedom of Expression in American History* (Durham, NC: Duke University Press, 2000), 216.

fenseless, it will be fatal alike to the Republican party and civil liberty."[17] More recently, government has failed to prosecute students who seized and destroyed copies of newspapers whose conservative editorial content they disliked. In each of these instances, government's failure to act constituted a denial of the right of free speech.

Liberals sometimes fail to notice that in the founders' view, although government can be the enemy of liberty, a good government is indispensable for securing liberty. Law professor Owen Fiss, for example, makes this error when he writes that "classical liberalism . . . puts the state at war with liberty."[18] This canard was invented long ago. It appears frequently in the work of John Dewey, who wrote that "the great enemy of individual liberty was thought to be the government."[19]

Of course, free speech can also be curtailed by government's own action against noninjurious speech that it does not like. This kind of failure to protect free speech is the focus of most scholars who write on this topic. The various state and federal constitutional provisions affirming the right of free speech are directed against this kind of government mischief.

In sum, government protects free speech in two ways: first, by protecting controversial speakers and publishers from private violence; and second, by controlling its own temptation to limit speech that it does not like.

This is the theoretical framework within which the founders understood freedom of speech and of the press. The first kind of protection of free speech—protecting individual speakers from private violence—is provided by the normal course of the criminal law, condemning robbery, trespass, destruction of property, assault, murder, and so on, and by the civil law, defining and protecting property and contract. The second kind of protection is more complicated, and I will discuss six topics that, taken together, collect the main elements of the founders' approach to setting limits on government's desire to curtail the speech of citizens:

1. There is a fundamental right of noninjurious speech.
2. Government is obliged to discourage or limit injurious speech.
3. Punishment of injurious speech must be by due process of law.
4. Government may not impose 'prior restraint' on speech (e.g., through licensing the right to publish).

[17] Stephen P. Halbrook, "The Fourteenth Amendment and the Right To Keep and Bear Arms: The Intent of the Framers," originally published as Report of the Subcommittee on the Constitution of the Committee on the Judiciary, United States Senate, 97th Congress, 2d Sess., *The Right to Keep and Bear Arms* (1982), 73–74; available online at http://www.constitution.org/2ll/2ndschol/42senh.pdf [accessed November 10, 2003].

[18] Owen M. Fiss, *The Irony of Free Speech* (Cambridge, MA: Harvard University Press, 1996), 49.

[19] John Dewey, *Liberalism and Social Action* (1935; reprint, Amherst, NY: Prometheus Books, 2000), 17. See also Dewey, "The Future of Liberalism" (1935), in Howard Zinn, ed., *New Deal Thought* (Indianapolis, IN: Bobbs-Merrill, 1966), 29: In the eighteenth-century approach, "governmental action and the desired freedom were placed in antithesis to each other."

5. Private associations may limit or dictate speech of guests, employees, and students.
6. Government as property owner (speaker, employer, and schoolmaster) has the same speech rights as private associations.

III. First Element of Free Speech: The Fundamental Right of Freedom of Noninjurious Speech

James Wilson and James Madison are the two founders who gave the most attention to freedom of speech. Wilson was a signer of the Declaration of Independence, a leading member of the Constitutional Convention of 1787, principal draftsman of the Pennsylvania Constitution of 1790, and later a justice of the U.S. Supreme Court. The more famous Madison was an even more influential member of the Constitutional Convention than Wilson. Madison became the principal author of the Bill of Rights in the first Congress and was later twice elected president of the United States.

In his *Lectures on Law* (1790–91), in which Wilson showed himself to be the foremost legal scholar of the founding generation, he explained the general principle that government must permit all noninjurious activity, whether in speech or deed: "Every wanton, or causeless, or unnecessary act of authority, exerted or authorized, or encouraged by the legislature over the citizens, is wrong, and unjustifiable, and tyrannical: for every citizen is, of right, entitled to liberty, personal as well as mental, in the highest possible degree which can consist with the safety and welfare of the state."[20] Wilson did not mean that in the name of safety and welfare, government may indefinitely expand. On the contrary, Wilson's view was similar to Jefferson's, as stated in the 1818 Report on the University of Virginia. A primary goal of university education, wrote Jefferson, is "to expound . . . a sound spirit of legislation, which, banishing all arbitrary and unnecessary restraint on individual action, shall leave us free to do whatever does not violate the equal rights of another."[21]

This liberty to which citizens are entitled includes, as a matter of course, the right to communicate opinions through speech and publishing. While Madison was preparing his speech introducing the Bill of Rights to the first Congress, he wrote that speech was one of the "*natural rights*, retained," in contrast with government-created rights such as trial by jury.[22] Thomas Paine similarly distinguished between natural rights, which may or may not be alienated to government, and civil rights, which are cre-

[20] James Wilson, *Lectures on Law* (1790–91), in Robert G. McCloskey, ed., *Works of James Wilson* (Cambridge, MA: Harvard University Press, 1967), 2:649.

[21] Thomas Jefferson, Report of the Commissioners for the University of Virginia, 1818, in Thomas Jefferson, *Writings*, ed. Merrill D. Peterson (New York: Library of America, 1984), 460.

[22] Madison, "Notes for Speech in Congress," June 8, 1789, in *Papers of James Madison*, vol. 12, ed. Charles F. Hobson et al. (Charlottesville: University Press of Virginia, 1979), 194.

ations of government.[23] In an early defense of free speech (1744), Elisha Williams, a prominent Connecticut politician and preacher, wrote, "In a state of nature men had a right to read Milton or Locke for their instruction or amusement: and why they do not retain this liberty under a government that is instituted for the preservation of their persons and properties, is inconceivable."[24] In this sense, there is an absolute right to freedom of speech, just as there is an absolute or inalienable right to liberty in general.

The founders did not hold a "self-expression" or a "democratic governance" theory of free speech. Such theories, which became fashionable in the twentieth century, leave unprotected many forms of noninjurious speech. For the founders, speech is simply a part of the overall natural right to liberty, which it is the main job of government to secure. As legal scholar John McGinnis notes,

> Thus, according to the first principles of the father of the Bill of Rights, free speech is not simply or even principally a means for sustaining a particular form of government; to the contrary, protecting free speech and other property rights is the end for which government is constituted. See *Federalist* 10 (Madison), . . . "The protection of these faculties [the different and unequal faculties for acquiring property] is the first object of government."

McGinnis correctly calls free speech a "property right" because in Madison's 1792 essay on property, speech is a form of property: "a man has a property in his opinions and the free communication of them."[25]

Besides being defended as a fundamental natural right, freedom of speech was also appreciated by the founders for its usefulness. Its social benefit is often mentioned in founding documents. For example, the Massachusetts Declaration of Rights of 1780 says, "The liberty of the press is essential to the security of freedom in a state: it ought not, therefore to be restrained in this commonwealth."[26] Because of the stated purpose of the

[23] Thomas Paine, "Candid and Critical Remarks on a Letter Signed Ludlow," June 4, 1777, in Schwartz, *The Roots of the Bill of Rights*, 2:315–16.

[24] Elisha Williams, *The Essential Rights and Liberties of Protestants* (1744), in Ellis Sandoz, ed., *Political Sermons of the American Founding Era, 1730–1805* (Indianapolis, IN: LibertyPress, 1991), 61.

[25] McGinnis, "The Once and Future Property-Based Vision of the First Amendment," 68, citing James Madison, *Federalist No. 10*, in Clinton Rossiter, ed., *The Federalist Papers*, with a new introduction and notes by Charles R. Kesler (New York: Penguin Putnam, 1999), 46. See also James Madison, "Property," March 29, 1792, in Kurland, *The Founders' Constitution*, 1:598. More than a half-century later, this view of speech was still the view of Thomas Cooley, *A Treatise on the Constitutional Limitations Which Rest upon the Legislative Power of the States* (1868), as noted by James W. Ely, Jr., in his introduction to "Property Rights and Free Speech: Allies or Enemies?" in this volume. Cooley's work, writes Ely, was "the most important analysis of constitutional law in the late nineteenth century."

[26] Declaration of Rights, Art. 16, Massachusetts Constitution of 1780, in Schwartz, *The Roots of the Bill of Rights*, 2:342.

clause ("security of freedom"), one might be tempted to take this to mean that, according to the founders, political speech was the only kind of free speech that government was strictly required to permit. However, another well-known founding document, the 1774 letter from the Continental Congress to Quebec, praises the usefulness of freedom of the press for additional reasons:

> The importance of this consists, besides the advancement of truth, science, morality, and arts in general, in its diffusion of liberal sentiments on the administration of Government, its ready communication of thoughts between subjects, and its consequential promotion of union among them, whereby oppressive officers are shamed or intimidated, into more honourable and just modes of conducting affairs.[27]

For these reasons—speech being both a natural right and highly useful to society—ten of the fourteen early state constitutions or Declarations of Rights, and the Bill of Rights in the U. S. Constitution, name freedom of speech or of the press as a fundamental right, but never a right that is limited to speech about political matters only.[28]

In the founders' approach, all citizens enjoy the right of free speech and the right to publish. Today, the organized news media often claim that they should enjoy heightened privileges that are not available to other citizens. For the founders, the "press" is not a "Fourth Estate." It is a

[27] Continental Congress, To the Inhabitants of the Province of Quebec, October 26, 1774, in Kurland, *The Founders' Constitution*, 1:442.

[28] Virginia Declaration of Rights, 1776, art. 12: "the freedom of the press is one of the greatest bulwarks of liberty, and can never be restrained but by despotic governments." Schwartz, *The Roots of the Bill of Rights*, 2:234.

Pennsylvania Declaration of Rights, 1776, art. 12: "the people have a right to freedom of speech, and of writing and publishing their sentiments: therefore the freedom of the press ought not to be restrained" (Schwartz, 266).

Delaware Declaration of Rights, 1776, sec. 23: "the liberty of the press ought to be inviolably preserved" (Schwartz, 278).

Maryland Declaration of Rights, 1776, art. 38: "the liberty of the press ought to be inviolably preserved" (Schwartz, 284).

North Carolina Declaration of Rights, 1776, art. 15: "the freedom of the press is one of the greatest bulwarks of liberty, and therefore ought never to be restrained" (Schwartz, 287).

Georgia Constitution, 1777, art. 61: "Freedom of the press and trial by jury to remain inviolate forever" (Schwartz, 300).

Vermont Declaration of Rights, 1777, art. 14: "the people have a right to freedom of speech, and of writing and publishing their sentiments; therefore, the freedom of the press ought not be restrained" (Schwartz, 324).

South Carolina Constitution, 1778, art. 43: "That the liberty of the press be inviolably preserved" (Schwartz, 335).

Massachusetts Declaration of Rights, 1780, art. 41: "the liberty of the press is essential to the security of freedom in a state; it ought not, therefore, to be restrained in this Commonwealth" (Schwartz, 342).

New Hampshire Declaration of Rights, 1783, art. 22: "the liberty of the press is essential to the security of freedom in a state; it ought, therefore, to be inviolably preserved" (Schwartz, 378).

means of communication. When Pennsylvania's 1790 Constitution says that "the printing presses shall be free to every person who undertakes to examine the proceedings of the legislature, or any branch of government," it means that government may not stand in the way of any person or organization that has the resources to purchase a printing press or any other means of duplicating written material. (Today, these would include movies, television, and the Internet.) Pennsylvania's phrase "every person" means that there are no special privileges for corporations or bodies that make money by selling newspapers.

IV. Second Element of Free Speech: Government Must Punish or Limit Injurious Speech

The speech that we have been discussing so far is noninjurious speech. As for injurious speech, government not only *may* punish it, but is *obliged* to do so (or at least to provide legal recourse for those injured), for the same reason that government is obliged to punish murder and rape. Speech, no less than assault or theft, is capable of harming others.

Government accomplishes its main purpose, namely, to secure the natural right to one's own person and the fruits of one's labor, primarily through the penalties of the criminal law and the compensations of the civil law. Jefferson explained the connection between the criminal law and the purpose of government in his preface, part of which I quoted earlier, to a proposed 1778 bill on crimes and punishments in Virginia:

> Whereas it frequently happens that wicked and dissolute men, resigning themselves to the dominion of inordinate passions, commit violations on the lives, liberties, and property of others, and the secure enjoyment of these having principally induced men to enter into society, government would be defective in its principal purpose, were it not to restrain such criminal acts by inflicting due punishments on those who perpetrate them.[29]

The Massachusetts Declaration of Rights, Article 11, affirms the same point:

> Every subject of the Commonwealth ought to find a certain remedy, by having recourse to the laws, for all injuries or wrongs which he may receive in his person, property, or character. He ought to obtain right and justice freely, and without being obliged to purchase it; completely, and without any denial; promptly, and without delay; conformably to the laws.

[29] Jefferson, "A Bill for Proportioning Crimes and Punishments," 1778, in Kurland, *The Founders' Constitution*, 5:374.

Jefferson and Massachusetts are both stating an implication of the basic purpose of government, which, as stated in the preamble to the Massachusetts Constitution, is "to furnish the individuals who compose it [that is, the body politic], with the power of enjoying, in safety and tranquillity, their natural rights."

Article 11 of the Massachusetts Constitution speaks of injury not only to person and property but also to character. An example would be libel that injures a person's reputation, such as a false rumor, deliberately spread, to the effect that a certain doctor's patients frequently die because of the doctor's incompetence. In this case, as in others, reputation would be a condition for the exercise of one's natural rights.

When limits on speech are discussed today, it is often said that the right of free speech must be balanced against the needs or interests of society. This approach implies that there really is no fundamental right of free speech that government is obliged to respect and protect. This "balancing" approach to rights was first developed during the Progressive Era.[30] It is not how the founders thought about this or like questions concerning natural rights. Instead, the question as they saw it was to discern where exercise of the right becomes abuse of the right or a danger to society—that is, where liberty under the law of nature becomes license, or a violation of the law of nature. The Town of Boston's 1772 Rights of the Colonists stated that "the first fundamental natural law" of all commonwealths or states, "which is to govern even the legislative power itself, is the preservation of the society."[31] Applied to free speech, this means that the question is where the proper liberty of speech ends and where speech becomes harmful to the personal rights of others or to the preservation of the society. Before reaching that limit, the right of free speech may never be rightfully abridged. In the contemporary approach, what is permissible today may be banned tomorrow, if some new social need comes to light against which speech is to be balanced. In its opinion upholding Congress's 1974 campaign finance act, the Supreme Court ruled that the right of free speech had to be balanced against the need "to deal with the reality or appearance of corruption."[32] The law in question abolished the right—which had existed uninterrupted from 1776 to 1976—to publish as often as one pleases one's

[30] For example, by Roscoe Pound, in "Equitable Relief against Defamation and Injuries to Personality, *Harvard Law Review* 29 (1916): 640 (promoting an approach to free speech balancing the right of free speech against social interests); discussed by David M. Rabban, *Free Speech in Its Forgotten Years* (Cambridge, MA: Cambridge University Press, 1997), 188–89. Also at 212: "The progressive position that individual rights should be recognized only to the extent that they contribute to social interests applied in principle to speech as well as liberty of contract. Pound explicitly acknowledged this point when he justified balancing social interests in free speech against competing social interests in the security of state institutions." Pound was "the leading legal figure" among "political progressives ... in the early twentieth century," according to Rabban (179).

[31] Town of Boston, Rights of the Colonists, 1772, in Samuel Adams, *Writings*, ed. Harry Alonzo Cushing (New York: Putnam's, 1906), 2:356–57.

[32] *Buckley v. Valeo*, 424 U.S. 1, 28 (1976). The Supreme Court reaffirmed this basic "balancing" approach to free speech in *McConnell v. Federal Election Commission* (2003), in which

opinions about all candidates in an election, including candidates with whom one happens to cooperate or coordinate.

In the U.S. Constitution, as in most of the early state constitutions, the right of free speech is not explicitly limited. The limit was implicit in the very concept of freedom. Freedom of speech is not freedom for licentious speech. However, later state constitutions, starting with Pennsylvania's 1790 revision, made the limit explicit: "The free communication of thoughts and opinions is one of the invaluable rights of man; and every citizen may freely speak, write, and print on any subject, being responsible for the abuse of that liberty."[33]

There was only one exception to the general rule that injurious speech should be punished, and it was stated explicitly in both the Massachusetts and the United States Constitutions: anything at all, however harmful, may be said in the legislative body.[34] This exception was meant to preserve the utmost freedom of deliberation for lawmakers on matters of public policy. The fact that the framers of both constitutions saw fit to include this provision, makes clear that it was an exception to the general rule of holding individuals accountable for injurious speech. Legislators, as all others, may be held legally accountable for anything said *outside* of the legislative body: they can be sued or prosecuted for injurious speech.

The founders recognized four principal kinds of injurious speech:

1. Personal libel: speech that injures an individual.
2. Seditious libel: speech that injures the government.
3. Speech that injures public health or the moral foundations of society.
4. Speech used in the course of, or promoting, other injurious conduct. This would include planning a bank robbery or encouraging others to commit a crime.

One important corollary of the idea of authorial responsibility is that there is no right to publish where an author or publisher cannot be determined, because otherwise no one can be held legally accountable in case of abuse. *The Federalist* and many other writings in the founding era were published anonymously, but always in a newspaper or book whose publisher was known. Nevertheless, it was thought that government should

---

the Court upheld extensive Congressional restrictions on independent expenditures by organizations wishing to publicize their views on candidates and public policy issues.

[33] Pennsylvania Constitution, 1790, art. 9, § 7; available online at the Pennsylvania Constitution Web Page of the Duquesne University Law School, http://www.paconstitution.duq.edu/con90.html [accessed November 10, 2003]. Cf. John Jay's view: "Under governments which have just and equal liberty for their foundation, every subject has a right to give his sentiments on all matters of public concern; provided it be done with modesty and decency." John Jay, "A Hint to the Legislature of the State of New York," 1778, in Richard B. Morris, ed., *John Jay, The Making of a Revolutionary: Unpublished Papers, 1745–1780* (New York: Harper & Row, 1975), 461.

[34] Massachusetts Constitution, 1780, Declaration of Rights, art. 21; U.S. Constitution, art. 1, § 6.

not require the actual writer of an article to be named. During the debate over ratification of the U.S. Constitution, "Philadelphiensis," an Antifederalist writer, noted that a suggestion had been made in a Massachusetts newspaper "that every writer, for or against the constitution, should leave his name with the printer, to be published if required." "Philadelphiensis" responded:

> When a political writer gives his name with his piece, he then shows where the opposite party may aim their shafts of malice, falsehood, and scurrility, with certainty and success. Will a man . . . expose his interest, his property, and perhaps his life, to the mercy of a revengeful and probably a powerful party? He certainly will not, if he has common sense.[35]

Today, because of rules limiting anonymous donations to nonprofit organizations, to ballot initiatives, and to candidates, government officials are easily able to target businesses and individuals who support candidates or political positions that they do not like. For example, when the owner of a major computer company publicly supported the 1993 school choice initiative in California, his company lost important state government contracts in retaliation.[36]

According to the founders' theory, it would follow that government may not limit the amount of money that a person spends publishing his own opinions about candidates for election, even (or rather above all) if he happens to coordinate his activities with one of the candidates. Yet precisely such limitations are currently the law of the land in the United States. In 1976, when the Supreme Court considered whether restrictive legislation was constitutional, it reasoned that government may ban expenditures on publishing one's views of candidates for election if the expenditures are coordinated with the candidate. The Court wrote: "It is unnecessary to look beyond the [1974 amendments to the Federal Election Campaign] Act's primary purpose—to limit the actuality and appearance of corruption resulting from large individual financial contributions—in order to find a constitutionally sufficient justification for the $1,000 contribution limitation."[37] The founders would have been shocked by the idea that government may forbid citizens to spend their own money publishing noninjurious political speech during election campaigns because of a mere "appearance of corruption"—that is, the suspicion that bribery *might* take place.

[35] Philadelphiensis VIII, *Philadelphia Freeman's Journal*, January 23, 1788, in John P. Kaminski and Gaspare J. Saladino, eds., *The Documentary History of the Ratification of the Constitution*, vol. 15: *Commentaries on the Constitution, Public and Private*, vol. 3 (Madison: State Historical Society of Wisconsin, 1984), 459–60. The editors give the background of this quarrel in 13:573.

[36] His company was AST Research, at that time a major manufacturer of personal computers. Facts from Larry P. Arnn, e-mail to the author, October 16, 1995.

[37] *Buckley v. Valeo*, 424 U.S. at 26.

It would also follow from the founders' principles that government may not ban the presentation of factual truth in the marketing of non-harmful commercial products. Further, government may not require employers to punish speech that the government disapproves of (e.g., telling jokes that some women or minorities find "harassing"), for government may never compel a private party to do something that government itself is not permitted to do.

A. Personal libel

In his *Lectures on Law,* James Wilson defined libel as "a malicious defamation of any person, published by writing, or printing, or signs, or pictures, and tending to expose him to public hatred, contempt, or ridicule." A fuller definition was given by Chancellor James Kent in his widely read *Commentaries on American Law* (1826): "a malicious publication, expressed either in printing or writing, or by signs or pictures, tending either to blacken the memory of one dead, or the reputation of one alive, and expose him to public hatred, contempt, or ridicule. A malicious intent towards government, magistrates, or individuals, and an injurious or offensive tendency, must concur to constitute the libel."[38]

In the founding era there were two views of why libel was regarded as an injury that government should view either as a crime or as something to be compensated. One was that libel is a personal injury, no different from assault or rape. In this view, there is a precise parallel to the analysis of gun rights. My right to bear arms has not been infringed if I am jailed for shooting my neighbor. Nor is my right to freedom of speech infringed if I am punished for maliciously harming the reputation of my neighbor. One member of the founders' generation made the comparison explicit: "Every free man has a right to the use of the press, so he has to the use of his arms." But if he commits libel, "he abuses his privilege, as unquestionably as if he were to plunge his sword into the bosom of a fellow citizen."[39] The remedy for abuse in both cases was not prior restraint, as in requiring a license to carry a gun or a censor's approval to publish a magazine, but punishment of an abuse of the right after a trial in a court of law.

In an important Pennsylvania Supreme Court case in 1788, Chief Justice Thomas McKean wrote,

[38] Wilson, *Lectures on Law,* in McCloskey, ed., *Works of James Wilson,* 2:647, 649–51. James Kent, *Commentaries on American Law,* 1826, in Kurland, *The Founders' Constitution,* 5:179–80.

[39] "Philodemos," *Pennsylvania Gazette,* May 7, 1788, reprinted in Merrill Jensen, ed., *The Documentary History of the Ratification of the Constitution: Ratification of the Constitution by the States,* vol. 2 suppl (Madison: State Historical Society of Wisconsin, 1976); quoted in Stephen P. Halbrook, *That Every Man Be Armed: The Evolution of a Constitutional Right* (Oakland, CA: The Independent Institute, 1990), 69. Cf. *Commonwealth v. Blanding,* 20 Mass. 304, 314 (Mass. 1825) (no number in the original), opinion of Chief Justice Isaac Parker (stating that in the Massachusetts Constitution, "The liberty of the press was to be unrestrained, but he who used it was to be responsible in case of its abuse; like the right to keep firearms, which does not protect him who uses them for annoyance or destruction"). Cited in Kurland, *The Founders' Constitution,* 5:177.

> With respect to the heart of the libeler, it is more dark and base than that of the assassin, or than his who commits a midnight arson. It is true, that I may never discover the wretch who has burned my house, or set fire to my barn; but these losses are easily repaired, and bring with them no portion of ignominy or reproach. But the attacks of the libeler admit not of this consolation: the injuries which are done to character and reputation seldom can be cured, and the most innocent man may, in a moment, be deprived of his good name, upon which, perhaps, he depends for all the prosperity, and all the happiness of his life.[40]

Clearly Justice McKean saw libel as a form of personal injury, even more destructive than the notorious criminal acts of the assassin or the arsonist.

The second founding-era view of libel was to look at instances of it "as breaches of the peace, and as much resembling challenges to fight," as Wilson writes in his *Lectures on Law.* As "a violation of the right of character," or of "the right of reputation," a libel tends to destroy the public safety by provoking citizens to anger that might break out into violent acts.[41]

Benjamin Franklin presents this view in a sarcastic essay published in 1789, in which he complains of the unrestraint of the press in attacking men's reputations. Franklin proposes that if the law will not permit libel lawsuits for damages, then "if an impudent writer attacks your reputation, dearer to you perhaps than your life, and puts his name to the charge, you may go to him as openly and break his head. If he conceals himself behind the printer, and you can nevertheless discover who he is, you may in like manner way-lay him in the night, attack him behind, and give him a good drubbing."[42]

Today, more often than in the past, government views libel as a matter of indifference or even as a right contained in the "liberty of the press." It is very difficult to win a lawsuit for libel, and such hard won victories are often overturned on appeal.[43] From the founders' viewpoint, this is

[40] *Respublica v. Oswald,* 1 U.S. 319, 324 (Pa. 1788). Cited in Kurland, *The Founders' Constitution,* 5:126.

[41] Wilson, *Lectures on Law,* in McCloskey, ed. *Works of James Wilson,* 2:647, 649–51.

[42] Benjamin Franklin, "An Account of the Supremest Court of Judicature in Pennsylvania, viz., The Court of the Press," September 12, 1789, in Kurland, *The Founders' Constitution,* 5:130.

[43] Libel Defense Resource Center, Report on Trials and Damages, 2002 (media defendants in libel trials win the great majority of cases, and at higher rates than in the past, not even counting those that never go to trial). Summary available online at http://www.ldrc.com/Press_Releases/bull2002-1.html [accessed November 10, 2003]. Richard Labunski, in his *Libel and the First Amendment: Legal History and Practice in Print and Broadcasting* (New Brunswick, NJ: Transaction, 1987), shows that the Supreme Court's libel rulings have made it harder for both "public figures" and private persons to win lawsuits for libel. However, Norman L. Rosenberg paints a more ambiguous picture in his *Protecting the Best Men: An Interpretive History of the Law of Libel* (Chapel Hill: University of North Carolina Press, 1986), 248–57.

either a likely occasion for personal injury through retaliation or a serious failure to protect citizens against a significant form of personal injury.

B. Seditious libel

The area of the founders' understanding of free speech where we have the least sympathy today is seditious libel. I will start with a general but still helpful definition: 'seditious libel' is speech that is intended to stir up sedition, that is, insurrection or rebellion against the government. The historian Leonard Levy's 1960 book on this subject was entitled *Legacy of Suppression*. Elsewhere, he insists that the founders' theory of free speech was "stunted."[44] But the prohibition of seditious libel follows logically from the founders' general theory of liberty, and from their theory of free speech in particular.

Reflecting the consensus of the founders, Supreme Court Justice Joseph Story authored a sensible discussion of the proper limits on free speech, including a brief discussion of seditious libel, in his *Commentaries on the Constitution* (1833). Story began with the liberty of the press clause in the Massachusetts Constitution:

> What is the true interpretation of this clause? Does it prohibit the legislature from passing any laws, which shall control the licentiousness of the press, or afford adequate protection to individuals, whose private comfort, or good reputations are assailed, and violated by the press? Does it stop the legislature from passing any laws to punish libels and inflammatory publications, the object of which is to excite sedition against the government, to stir up resistance to its laws, to urge on conspiracies to destroy it, to create odium and indignation against virtuous citizens, to compel them to yield up their rights, or to make them the objects of popular vengeance? . . . In short, is it contended, that the liberty of the press is so much more valuable, than all other rights in society, that the public safety, nay the existence of the government itself is to yield to it? . . . It would be difficult to answer these questions in favor of the liberty of the press, without at the same time declaring, that such a licentiousness belonged, and could belong only to a despotism; and was utterly incompatible with the principles of a free government.[45]

[44] Leonard W. Levy, *Legacy of Suppression: Freedom of Speech and Press in Early American History* (Cambridge, MA: Harvard University Press, 1960). The book was revised and republished later with the less provocative title *Emergence of a Free Press* (New York: Oxford University Press, 1985). The "stunted" remark is in Leonard W. Levy, *Freedom of the Press from Zenger to Jefferson* (1966; reprint Durham, NC: Carolina Academic Press, 1996), vii.

[45] Joseph Story, *Commentaries on the Constitution* (1833), sec. 1881, in Kurland, *The Founders' Constitution*, 5:184. Harry V. Jaffa, in his *Equality and Liberty: Theory and Practice in American Politics* (New York: Oxford University Press, 1965), 179, states the founders' view: free speech is "a necessary means for deliberating upon public policy. But this deliberation does not extend to everything: above all, it does not extend to the question of whether the

Story's point is that government exists to secure the equal rights of all. If a free government is overthrown, security for liberty will be gone. So there can be no fundamental right to turn the people against the government that secures their rights.

In contrast to the founders' position, Justice Oliver Wendell Holmes, Jr., wrote in *Gitlow v. New York* (1925): "If in the long run the beliefs expressed in proletarian dictatorship are destined to be accepted by the dominant forces of the community, the only meaning of free speech is that they should be given their chance and have their way."[46] Holmes no longer believed, with the founders, that the purpose of government is to secure the natural rights of the people on the basis of consent. Holmes was a legal positivist. For him, any purpose of government chosen by "the dominant forces of the community" is equally legitimate, whether it be a dictatorship that denies the consent principle and does not acknowledge the equal rights of the bourgeois, or the founders' democracy, which requires consent of the governed and the equal protection of the laws.

The founders denied that the right of free speech includes the right to persuade people to overthrow liberty and turn instead to despotic government. From this point of view, the propriety of laws against seditious libel was perhaps never more clearly seen than in 1940, when the Alien Registration, or Smith Act, was passed. This law made it a federal crime "to knowingly or willfully advocate . . . the . . . desirability . . . of overthrowing or destroying any government in the United States by force or violence."[47] At the time, Soviet and Nazi agents and their sympathizers were actively promoting this very thing in America, although the main target of the legislation at its inception was Nazi subversion. The Amer-

---

community shall exchange its freedom for slavery. Certain ends are fixed, and their fixity is the condition of mutability in other respects."

The founders' view was rejected by the Supreme Court after the liberal approach became predominant during the New Deal:

> But freedom to differ is not limited to things that do not matter much. That would be a mere shadow of freedom. The test of its substance is the right to differ as to things that touch the heart of the existing order.
>
> If there is any fixed star in our constitutional constellation, it is that no official, high or petty, can prescribe what shall be orthodox in politics, nationalism, religion, or other matters of opinion or force citizens to confess by word or act their faith therein.

West Virginia v. Barnette, 319 U.S. 624, 642 (1943). On the founders' understanding of seditious libel, see also Edward J. Erler, "The First Amendment and the Theology of Republican Government," *Interpretation* 27, no. 3 (2000): 231–57 (subversive speech may be banned consistently with natural right); 245 ("debates about whether natural rights are to be secured is not properly protected by the First Amendment"); 242–44 (the First Amendment cannot be grounded in the old British common law of libel because the Declaration of Independence is "the greatest example of seditious libel in history"). See also David Lowenthal, *No Liberty for License: The Forgotten Logic of the First Amendment* (Dallas, TX: Spence Publishing, 1977), 17: "The logic of the case [i.e., in the debate over the Sedition Act] is with the Federalists."

[46] 268 U.S. 652, 673 (1925) (Holmes, J., dissenting).

[47] Originally at 54 *Statutes at Large* (1940) 670–71. Now, 18 U.S.C. § 2385 (2000). Quoted in *Dennis v. United States,* 341 U.S. 494, 496 (1951).

ican Communist Party was publicly praising Hitler and denouncing Britain. This was the result of the 1939 alliance between Hitler and Stalin. Poland and France had been defeated; England was besieged. The two most powerful tyrants in world history stood on the brink of world conquest, while the United States was the only power that could possibly stop them. From the point of view of the founders, it was not the duty of the government to stand passively aside while the agents of the two murderous tyrannies were actively laboring to turn American public opinion against constitutional democracy.[48]

The question may be raised as to whether the kind of advocacy of the overthrow of the government criminalized in the Smith Act is really seditious libel in the founders' sense. In *Dennis v. United States* (1951), Justice Robert Jackson in a concurring opinion argued, quite plausibly, that "[w]hat really is under review here is a conviction of conspiracy,"[49] that is, something no different in principle from a conspiracy to commit murder or robbery. The seditious libel that caused such controversy in the founding era was much less obviously connected to the violent overthrow of the government. As we will see, there are reasons to doubt that the expansive idea of seditious libel that was widely accepted at the time of the founding was really compatible with the founders' own principles.

The Sedition Act of 1798 was passed by Federalists at a time when the nation was bitterly divided and on the brink of war with France. The Republican Party of Jefferson and Madison favored France, while President Adams and the Federalist Party, horrified by the excesses of the French Revolution, favored neutrality. Both America and France exacerbated these tensions by attacking each other's shipping, creating an undeclared quasi war. With Republican political meetings and newspapers stirring up hatred against the Adams Administration, the Federalists passed the Sedition Act. It became a federal criminal offense to publish:

> any false, scandalous, and malicious writing or writings against the government of the United States, . . . with intent . . . to stir up sedition within the United States, or to excite any unlawful combinations therein, for opposing or resisting any law of the United States, . . . or to resist, oppose, or defeat any such law or act, or to aid, encourage, or abet any hostile designs of any foreign nation against [the] United States.

This part of the Sedition Act is similar to the Smith Act: it outlaws what is, in effect, the crime of incitement to lawbreaking or aiding a foreign

[48] For a persuasive account of the danger in which the United States found itself at that time, see Harry V. Jaffa et al., *Original Intent and the Framers of the Constitution: A Disputed Question* (Washington, DC: Regnery, 1994), 331–39. See also Herbert Romerstein and Eric Breindel, *The Venona Secrets: Exposing Soviet Espionage and America's Traitors* (Washington, DC: Regnery, 2000).

[49] *Dennis*, 341 U.S. at 572.

enemy. More questionable was that part of the Sedition Act that outlawed "any false, scandalous, and malicious writing or writings . . . with intent to defame the said government, or either house of the said Congress, or the said President, or to bring them . . . into contempt or disrepute; or to excite against them . . . the hatred of the good people of the United States." Here the Sedition Act prohibits speech that may not be intended to create rebellion or insurrection, but merely undermines public regard for the government. Historian Gordon Wood writes that this law and the contemporaneous Alien Act "more than anything else have tarnished the historical reputation of the Federalists." Wood calls the Sedition Act a "desperate repressive measure."[50]

Was this measure really repressive? Not in the minds of the great majority of Americans at that time. It is often assumed today that the passionate debate in 1798 over the Sedition Act was about whether the punishment of defamatory speech against government officials was compatible with the principle of freedom of speech. Yet most members of Congress in 1798 believed that it *was* compatible, whether they voted for the act or not. It is true that Republican opponents of the act did sometimes deny any government power over seditious libel in a republican form of government. However, their main argument against the act was not over whether government should punish those who would maliciously "defame the said government," but only over whether the *national* government had that power under the Constitution. Hardly anyone doubted that the *state* governments could punish malicious defamation of government. As Michael Kent Curtis notes, "Republicans often noted that a remedy for libel existed at state law." In other words, the quarrel was, mostly, not over the meaning of free speech but over federalism.[51]

Federalists argued, correctly, that the federal Sedition Act was an improvement over state laws on the subject, for the Sedition Act stated that

> it shall be lawful for the defendant, upon the trial of the cause, to give in evidence in his defense, the truth of the matter contained in the publication charged as a libel. And the jury who shall try the cause, shall have a right to determine the law and the fact, under the direction of the court, as in other cases.

The common law of libel, which was followed at that time in the law of the several states, did not permit truth to be a factor in evidence, nor did it permit the jury to determine the law (that is, whether the publication

[50] The language of the Sedition Act is from the Avalon Project of Yale Law School, available online at http://www.yale.edu/lawweb/avalon/statutes/sedact.htm [accessed November 10, 2003]. The Act was scheduled to expire on March 3, 1801. Bernard Bailyn et al., *The Great Republic: A History of the American People*, 4th ed. (Lexington, MA: D.C. Heath, 1992), 329 (Wood was the author of this part).

[51] Levy, *Emergence of a Free Press*, 304–8. Curtis, *Free Speech*, 69.

was, in fact, injurious). The jury decided only the fact (whether the defendant actually published it). The Federalists were right when they claimed that the Sedition Act was more protective of published criticism of government than were state laws.

Not only was there no serious Republican opposition to the idea of seditious libel, but after Jefferson became president in 1801, he became a cheerleader for prosecutions (by state governments) of his Federalist critics. He even mentioned the subject in 1805 in his Second Inaugural Address:

> During this course of administration, and in order to disturb it, the artillery of the press has been leveled against us, charged with whatsoever its licentiousness could devise or dare. These abuses of an institution so important to freedom and science are deeply to be regretted. . . . [T]hey might, indeed, have been corrected by the wholesome punishments reserved and provided by the laws of the several States against falsehood and defamation; but public duties more urgent press on the time of public servants, and the offenders have therefore been left to find their punishment in the public indignation. . . .
>
> No inference is here intended that the laws, provided by the State against false and defamatory publications, should not be enforced; he who has time, renders a service to public morals and public tranquillity, in reforming these abuses by the salutary coercions of the law. . . .[52]

No participant on either side of the debate over the Sedition Act went so far as to propose the repeal of state laws limiting defamatory speech against government. Nevertheless, Republicans made some arguments that pointed in this direction. Everyone agreed that there ought to be a legal remedy for those harmed by injurious speech, but there were many on both sides who understood that speech against government was a special case that deserved different treatment from other forms of libel. America's government was elective, and elections cannot effectively control government misconduct unless criticism of elected officials is permitted.

The consensus on seditious libel that was reached during the founding era was most famously stated by Alexander Hamilton in the case of *People v. Croswell* (1804). His position was essentially the same as that of the Sedition Act, although one might be surprised to learn this in light of the hostile treatment given to this act in most American history and civil liberties textbooks. As Leonard Levy writes, Hamilton's argument in *Croswell* "was adopted by the state legislature [of New York] in the following year. That position spread rapidly throughout the nation."

Harry Croswell was a Federalist editor who had attacked President Jefferson for allegedly funding a newspaper attack on Washington and

[52] Jefferson, *Writings*, ed. Peterson, 521–22.

Adams. New York Republican politicians prosecuted Croswell for seditious libel. At his trial, Croswell tried to defend himself by presenting evidence that the things he said about Jefferson were true. The trial judge ruled, first, that truth was not admissible in evidence, and second, that the only question for the jury was whether Croswell had actually published the offending article, not whether the publication was libelous.[53]

Hamilton became Croswell's counsel when the case was appealed to the New York Supreme Court in 1804. He argued that

> The liberty of the press consists, in my idea, in publishing the truth, from good motives and for justifiable ends, though it reflect on government, on magistrates, or individuals. . . . It is essential to [be able to] say, not only that the measure is bad and deleterious, but to hold up to the people who is the author, [so] that, in this our free and elective government, he may be removed from the seat of power. If this be not to be done, then in vain will the voice of the people be raised against the inroads of tyranny. . . . In speaking thus for the freedom of the press, I do not say there ought to be an unbridled license. . . . I do not stand here to say that no shackles are to be laid on this license. I consider this spirit of abuse and calumny as the pest of society.[54]

Hamilton's argument—that a nation whose government is chosen by free elections has to allow considerable leeway for public criticism of government officials—had been anticipated by Adams in a 1789 letter:

> Our chief magistrates and senators etc. are annually eligible [i.e., elected] by the people. How are their characters and conduct to be known to their constituents but by the press? If the press is to be stopped and the people kept in ignorance, we had much better have the first magistrate and senators hereditary.[55]

Adams therefore recommended that "it would be safest to admit evidence to the jury of the truth of accusations, and if the jury found them true and that they were published for the public good, they would readily acquit." This is the standard that Hamilton recommended in *Croswell*. As

[53] *People v. Croswell*, 3 Johns. Cas. 337 (N.Y. Sup. Ct. 1804). My account is based on the excellent treatment of *People v. Croswell* in Julius Goebel, Jr., ed., *The Law Practice of Alexander Hamilton: Documents and Commentary* (New York: Columbia University Press, 1964), 1:775–806.

[54] Goebel, *Law Practice of Alexander Hamilton*, 1:809–10. Croswell lost his appeal for a new trial on a tie vote of the New York Supreme Court, but for some unknown reason he escaped being sentenced (804).

[55] John Adams to William Cushing, March 7, 1789, in Levy, *Freedom of the Press from Zenger to Jefferson*, 153.

mentioned earlier, it quickly became and remained the standard for most states until the 1960s.[56]

All sides in the debate over seditious libel in the founding era recognized that government must guarantee a right to criticize its errors and injustices. In his opinion in the *Croswell* case, then-Judge James Kent agreed with the Hamilton standard, while he criticized the much stricter English law of seditious libel:

> And if the theory of the prevailing doctrine in England . . . had been strictly put in practice with us, where would have been all those enlightened and manly discussions which prepared and matured the great events of our Revolution, or which, in a more recent period, pointed out the weakness and folly of the confederation, and roused the nation to throw it aside, and to erect a better government upon its ruins? They were, no doubt, libels on the existing establishments, because they tended to defame them, and to expose them to the contempt and hatred of the people. They were, however, libels founded in truth, and dictated by worthy motives.[57]

Whether the Hamilton-*Croswell* standard is sufficient to secure the proper freedom of public discussion may be doubted, however. In this respect Madison and the other critics of the Sedition Act had a strong argument. One can see the problem in Judge Samuel Chase's instruction to the jury in *United States v. Cooper* (1800). Chase, a Federalist, instructed the jury to punish criticism of the Adams Administration—criticism that, by today's standards, would be regarded as mild. For example, the newspaper at

[56] Ibid., 378. See *Beauharnais v. Illinois,* 343 U.S. 250, 296–97 (1952); Justice Jackson in dissent wrote that Hamilton's argument in *Croswell*

> led to a provision included in the [New York] Constitution of 1821 . . . and has remained in the several Constitutions of that State since: 'Every citizen may freely speak, write and publish his sentiments on all subjects, being responsible for the abuse of that right; and no law shall be passed to restrain or abridge the liberty of speech or of the press. In all criminal prosecutions or indictments for libels, the truth may be given in evidence to the jury; and if it shall appear to the jury that the matter charged as libelous is true, and was published with good motives and for justifiable ends, the party shall be acquitted; and the jury shall have the right to determine the law and the fact.' It would not be an exaggeration to say that, basically, this provision of the New York Constitution states the common sense of American criminal libel law.

[57] Opinion of Judge James Kent in *Croswell,* 3 Johns. Cas at 392–93. Cited in Kurland, *The Founders' Constitution,* 5:169. Kent continues

> [If the doctrine of the critics of the Sedition Act] was to prevail, the press would become a pest, and destroy the public morals. . . . The founders of our governments were too wise and too just, ever to have intended, by the freedom of the press, a right to circulate falsehood as well as truth, or that the press should be the lawful vehicle of malicious defamation, or an engine for evil and designing men, to cherish, for mischievous purposes, sedition, irreligion, and impurity. Such an abuse of the press would be incompatible with the existence and good order of civil society. (393)

issue in the case had said (as Chase summarized it) that Adams "has brought forward measures for raising a standing army." Chase told the jury:

> In fact, we cannot have a standing army in this country, the constitution having expressly declared that no appropriation shall be made for the support of an army longer than two years. . . . There is no subject on which the people of America feel more alarm, than the establishment of a standing army. Once persuade them that the government is attempting to promote such a measure, and you destroy their confidence in the government. Therefore, to say, that under the auspices of the president, we were saddled with a standing army, was directly calculated to bring him into contempt with the people, and excite their hatred against him.

Thomas Cooper's right to give truth as a defense (which was permitted under the Sedition Act) did not help him here. Certainly Cooper could have plausibly argued that Adams's measures for raising an army did look like a plan to establish a "standing army," given that the army was being established in time of peace. Nevertheless, the judge persuaded the jury that Cooper's words were false. He was fined four hundred dollars and imprisoned for six months.[58]

Among the leading founders, Madison alone, in his *Report on the Virginia Resolutions* (1800), confronted the difficult question of whether the Hamilton-*Croswell* standard was sufficient to secure the proper freedom of public discourse. He concluded that the "truth as a defense" standard, although it was superior to the old British common law (which punished even truthful libel against government), did not go far enough. Everyone agreed with Madison's statement that "[t]he nature of governments elective, limited, and responsible, in all their branches, may well be supposed to require a greater freedom of animadversion than might be tolerated by . . . Great Britain." But Madison argued that seditious libel should never be punishable. His strongest argument was that allowing truth as a defense is not sufficient, because most political writing is only opinion:

> [O]pinions, and inferences, and conjectural observations cannot be subjects of that kind of proof which appertains to facts before a court of law. . . .
>
> [I]t is manifestly impossible to punish the intent to bring those who administer the Government into disrepute or contempt, without striking at the right of freely discussing public characters and mea-

[58] *United States v. Cooper,* 25 F. Cas. 631 (Cir. Ct., District of Pa. 1800) (No. 14,865). Cited in Kurland, *The Founders' Constitution,* 5:147–51. The case is discussed in Curtis, *Free Speech,* 89–92.

sures; because those who engage in such discussions must expect and intend to excite these unfavorable sentiments, so far as they may be thought to be deserved.[59]

That is, allowing a libeler to claim truth as a defense is not sufficient to permit the necessary latitude for speech about government officials and measures. The case that I just discussed, *United States v. Cooper*, illustrates Madison's point well.

Madison did not deny that there is such a thing as the abuse of press freedom. ("The committee are not unaware of the difficulty of all general questions which may turn on the proper boundary between the liberty and licentiousness of the press.") He did not deny the right of a public official to sue his slanderer for damages. (The modern doctrine, which very nearly prevents public officials from recovering damages, was not established until 1964 in *New York Times v. Sullivan*.)[60] Like all the founders, Madison thought that laws providing legal recourse against injurious speech were necessary. What distinguished Madison from the rest of the founding generation was that he saw more clearly than others that the right of government to protect itself against injurious speech was in tension with the right of the people freely to discuss public officials and their policies. In this conflict of rights, Madison thought that the presumption should be in favor of greater freedom of discussion.[61]

[59] Madison, *Report on the Virginia Resolutions*, January 1800, written on behalf of the Virginia State Legislature; cited in Kurland, *The Founders' Constitution*, 5:145. A Massachusetts town, commenting on the state Constitution of 1780, discussed the question in terms similar to those that Madison would later use:

> Liberty of speech, as it respected public men in their public conduct, was an essential and darling right of every member of a free state upon which in a very eminent degree the preservation of their other rights depends; that nothing spoken with design to give information of the state of the public should be ever subject to the smallest restraint; and that any attempt to oppose such restraint ought to excite an alarm in the people as it inferred a consciousness of demerit on the part of those attempting; That such restraint was more degrading and more strongly marked them slaves than ever the privation of liberty of the press; and that the latter, so absolutely necessary, and therefore so justly dear to every free state, could not be maintained in its full force and vigor without the former. But while we hold up the liberty of the press, as essentially necessary to general freedom, as it respects public men and measures, we reject with abhorrence the idea of its abuse to the injury of private characters.

"Return of Boston," May 12, 1780, in Robert J. Taylor, ed., *Massachusetts, Colony to Commonwealth: Documents on the Formation of Its Constitution, 1775–1780* (Chapel Hill: University of North Carolina Press, 1961), 148.

[60] 376 U.S. 254 (1964).

[61] Jefferson seems to have struggled with this problem in his several attempts to propose adequate language for the Virginia state constitution. In his 1776 draft of a constitution, he could not decide whether to allow punishment of seditious libel or not. The first draft included the phrase, "but seditious behavior to be punishable by civil magistrate according to the laws." Jefferson put the phrase in brackets, perhaps indicating that he regarded it as questionable. In a second draft, he wrote, then crossed out, "but this shall not be held to justify any seditious preaching or conversations against the authority of the civil government." His hesitation suggests that he sensed the tension we have been discussing, namely,

The fact that legislators were exempted from the laws against libel in whatever they might say in Congress or in some state legislatures[62] shows that, in an inchoate way, Madison's point was understood in principle by everyone. What the founders on the whole did not see was that in a nation that governs itself through elected officials, the entire nation is, in a sense, in the same position as the legislative body. (During the debate over the Sedition Act, Congressman Nathaniel Macon argued that "[t]he people might be as safely trusted with free discussion, as they whom they have chosen to do their business.")[63] The people must be free to exchange opinions about men and measures if elections are to be an effective check on government. Recovery of civil damages for personal libel of public officials should probably be permitted, but there should be careful safeguards to allow a wide scope for expression of critical opinions of government policy.

Although the Hamilton-*Croswell* standard became the law of the land in most states, law professor George Anastaplo notes that even before the First Amendment was passed, "the popular meaning of 'freedom of the press' was far more liberal than the meaning lawyers had had occasion before 1791 to make explicit in judicial proceedings."[64] After 1800, writes Michael Kent Curtis, "State seditious libel prosecutions became less and less frequent, and eventually essentially ceased."[65] Leonard Levy makes a similar point, noting the wide disparity between the official limits imposed in the law of sedition and the actual practice of the press of the 1790s and later. To this extent, Madison's view became the de facto legal standard long before today's view, that laws against seditious libel violate freedom of speech, prevailed.

The West Virginia Constitution of 1862, written in the heat of the Civil War, provides a competent statement of the founders' understanding of free speech, as this understanding was modified and perfected by the

---

that it is necessary but hard to reconcile the need to permit honest criticism of government errors and the need to maintain public respect for government that secures our rights. Julian P. Boyd, ed., *Papers of Thomas Jefferson*, vol. 1 (Princeton, NJ: Princeton University Press, 1950), 344, 347n10, 353. However, in 1788, Jefferson would take the position that would later be enshrined in the Sedition Act. In a letter to Madison recommending a federal bill of rights, Jefferson wrote, "A declaration that the federal government will never restrain the presses from printing anything they please, will not take away the liability of the printers for false facts printed." Jefferson to Madison, July 31, 1788, in James Morton Smith, ed., *The Republic of Letters: The Correspondence between Thomas Jefferson and James Madison, 1776–1826* (New York: W. W. Norton, 1995), 1:545.

[62] U.S. Constitution, art. 1, § 6; Massachusetts Constitution, 1780, Declaration of Rights, art. 21.

[63] *Annals of Congress*, 5:2105 (1798), quoted by Curtis, *Free Speech*, 70.

[64] George Anastaplo, *The Constitutionalist: Notes on the First Amendment* (Dallas, TX: Southern Methodist University Press, 1971), 144.

[65] Curtis, *Free Speech*, 115. Curtis's informative discussion of limits on free speech in the pre-Civil War South (117–299) shows convincingly how laws against seditious libel can be the enemy of liberty in a political order that is based on the rejection of the principles of the Declaration of Independence. The Southern states outlawed almost all criticism of slavery, on the ground that such criticism threatened the public safety.

reasoning of Madison in his *Report on the Virginia Resolutions*. The traditional crime of seditious libel is omitted; its place is taken by the right of every person (including government officials) to sue for civil damages, and by the criminalization of any public defense of revolutionary violence:

> No law abridging freedom of speech or of the press shall be passed; but the legislature may provide for the restraint and punishment of the publishing and vending of obscene books, papers and pictures, and of libel and defamation of character, and for the recovery, in civil actions, by the aggrieved party, of suitable damages for such libel or defamation. Attempts to justify and uphold an armed invasion of the state, or an organized insurrection therein, during the continuance of such invasion or insurrection, by publicly speaking, writing or printing, or by publishing or circulating such writing or printing, may be, by law, declared a misdemeanor, and punished accordingly.[66]

C. *Speech injuring public health, safety, or the moral foundations of society*

The founders had no objection to government prohibiting or discouraging products or activities that are unsafe or unhealthy. For the same reason, government might decide to ban the advertising or the promotion of things that are unhealthy or dangerous, such as tobacco or liquor. Liberals today have no difficulty with this governmental power. They defend it, however, not as an exercise of government's legitimate power to regulate dangerous products, but as governmental control of "commercial speech," which they believe deserves little or no free speech protection. McGinnis notes that the earlier American approach did not distinguish between commercial speech and other speech: "as a historical matter, the development of a free press and a commercial press were inextricably linked at the time of the Framing." He cites historian Verner W. Crane, who writes, "It was a commercial age, and produced a commercial press."[67]

Regarding government's view of morality, Washington's Farewell Address in 1796 stated the consensus: "It is substantially true that virtue or morality is a necessary spring of popular government." For this reason, speech or conduct that tends to injure the public morals was subject to

[66] Constitution of West Virginia, 1862, Art. 2, sec. 4; Special Collections Department, University of Virginia; available online at http://www.vcdh.virginia.edu/vahistory/reconfiguring/constitution.html [accessed November 5, 2003].

[67] McGinnis, "Once and Future Property-Based Vision," 76, quoting Verner W. Crane's introduction to *Benjamin Franklin's Letters to the Press, 1758–1775* (Chapel Hill: University of North Carolina Press, 1950), xvi. The liberal Cass Sunstein disapproves of the view that commercial speech should be protected by the constitutional guarantee of free speech, stating (incorrectly) that "for most of the nation's history, no serious person thought that commercial speech enjoyed constitutional protection" (*Democracy and the Problem of Free Speech*, 3).

governmental control. This point was not controversial, but for that very reason, it was not much discussed during the founding era.

Profanity, obscenity, indecency, pornography, and even blasphemy were treated no differently than public nudity. In a famous 1824 case, *Updegraph v. Commonwealth*, Judge Thomas Duncan wrote for the Pennsylvania Supreme Court:

> [L]icentiousness endangering the public peace, when tending to corrupt society, is considered as a breach of the peace, and punishable by indictment. Every immoral act is not indictable, but when it is destructive of morality generally, it is, because it weakens the bonds by which society is held together. . . . If from a regard to decency and the good order of society, profane swearing, breach of the Sabbath, and blasphemy, are punishable by civil magistrates, these are not punished as sins or offenses against God, but crimes *injurious* to, and having a malignant influence on society; for it is certain, that by these practices, no one pretends to prove any supposed truths, detect any supposed error, or advance any sentiment whatever."[68]

In *People v. Ruggles* (1811), another well-known blasphemy case, the opinion authored by Chief Justice James Kent for the New York Supreme Court held that government should ban or at least limit "[t]hings which corrupt moral sentiment, as obscene actions, prints, and writings." These and similar "offences against religion and morality . . . are punishable because they strike at the root of moral obligation, and weaken the security of the social ties."[69]

One might wonder whether laws against blasphemy are consistent with the founders' principles. The purpose of government is to secure the natural rights of the citizens, not to save their souls. Duncan and Kent were aware of this. For that reason, their blasphemy opinions were careful to justify those laws with reasons that are entirely secular.

In *Updegraph*, Judge Duncan explained:

> It is open, public vilification of the religion of the country that is punished, not to force conscience by punishment, but to preserve the peace of the country by an outward respect to the religion of the country, and not as a restraint upon the liberty of conscience; but licentiousness endangering the public peace, when tending to corrupt society, is considered as a breach of the peace.

Duncan distinguished between the "inestimable freedom of conscience, one of the highest privileges and greatest interests of the human race,"

[68] *Updegraph v. Commonwealth*, 11 Serg. & Rawle 394, 408–9 (Pa. 1824); cited in Kurland, *The Founders' Constitution*, 5:174–75 (emphasis added).

[69] *People v. Ruggles*, 8 Johns. 290, 292 (N.Y. Sup. Ct. 1811) (Kent, Ch. J.); cited in Kurland, *The Founders' Constitution*, 5:101–2.

and "the right publicly to vilify the religion of his neighbors and of the country." Atheism as such, therefore, is not blasphemy.

Religion was thought to be necessary for morality, and morality was thought to be necessary for the preservation of a good society. ("Religion, morality, and knowledge, being necessary to good government and the happiness of mankind" were the famous words of the Northwest Ordinance, passed by Congress in 1787.)[70] Duncan put blasphemy into the category of an act like "profane swearing," which "weaken[s] those religious and moral restraints, without the aid of which mere legislative provisions would prove ineffectual."[71]

The idea that government may impose limits on speech that injures the public morals was anticipated by the founders' favorite philosopher, John Locke, in his *Letter on Toleration* (1689):

> Rectitude of morals, in which consists not the least part of religion and sincere piety, concerns civil life also, and in it lies the salvation both of men's souls and of the commonwealth; moral actions belong, therefore, to both courts; the external as well as the internal; they are subject to the government of both, of the civil as well as the domestic governor, that is, of the magistrate and conscience. . . .
>
> [Therefore] no doctrines adverse and contrary to human society, or to the good morals that are necessary for the preservation of civil society, are to be tolerated by the magistrate.[72]

In his *Lectures on Law*, James Wilson treats public indecency as one of the public nuisances "which attack several of those natural rights" of individuals: "Common nuisances are a collection of personal injuries which annoy the citizens generally and indiscriminately," such that "public peace, and order, and tranquility, and safety require them to be punished or abated." Therefore, "[t]o keep hogs in any city or market town is a common nuisance. Disorderly houses are public nuisances. . . . Indecency, pub-

[70] These words are chiseled into the stone over the entrance to the main administration building at Bowling Green State University, Ohio (visited 2003). The founders did not believe that such language, approved by government, violated anyone's religious liberty.

[71] *Updegraph*, 11 Serg. & Rawle at 408, 403, and 406; cited in Kurland, *The Founders' Constitution*, 5:172–75. The rarity of blasphemy prosecutions is alluded to on 172. Another important blasphemy case, in which the same argumentation is found, is *People v. Ruggles* (N.Y. Sup. Ct., 1811), opinion of Chief Justice James Kent; cited in Kurland, *The Founders' Constitution*, 5:101–2.

[72] John Locke, *Epistola de Tolerantia: A Letter on Toleration* (1689), ed. Raymond Klibansky (Oxford: Clarendon Press, 1968), 123, 131 (my translation). Scholars who write on Locke often miss this strongly antilibertarian strain in the *Letter*. For example, Robert Goldwin appears to think that Locke has no interest in government support of morality: Robert Goldwin, "John Locke," in Leo Strauss and Joseph Cropsey, eds., *History of Political Philosophy*, 3rd ed. (Chicago, IL: University of Chicago Press, 1987), 484. Similarly, Francis Canavan seems unaware that Locke advocated government supervision of "doctrines adverse . . . to the good morals that are necessary to the preservation of civil society": Francis Canavan, *Freedom of Expression: Purpose as Limit* (Durham, NC: Carolina Academic Press, 1984), 71.

lic and grossly scandalous, may well be considered as a species of common nuisance. . . . Profaneness and blasphemy are offenses, punishable by fine and by imprisonment."[73] Wilson in effect equates here the physical stench of a pigsty with the moral stench of public indecency and whorehouses.

As usual, the founders, in agreement with Locke, did not sharply distinguish between speech (indecency of speech) and deed (keeping hogs in the city or operating a whorehouse). Gross actions and expression that tended to undermine the moral basis of the community, especially of the family and the moral formation of the young, were subject to legal limitation.

For a full explanation of the ground of government prohibitions on obscenity and pornography, one would have to reflect on the founders' overall policy on sex and the family. There is no need to do that here.[74] But the gist of the problem can be easily stated. If sex is a matter of mere pleasure and entertainment with no further consequence, then such prohibitions as existed then were nothing more than puritanical prejudice. But if sex is viewed as an activity whose uniqueness lies in its potential to generate new life—life that is needy and vulnerable for many years—then government has an urgent interest in the terms on which sex is practiced. Government regulation of sex (and therefore of words and pictures promoting nonmarital sex) has two purposes. First, it aims to encourage the limitation of sex to marriage, so that most children will be born to married parents who have an interest, the resources, and a legal obligation to take care of them. Second, government seeks to encourage heterosexual sex and to discourage other forms, so that sex will lead to the birth of enough children, the next generation of citizens, without which the society cannot survive.[75]

D. Speech promoting ordinary crimes

The last kind of injurious speech that the founders thought could be rightly limited by government is relatively uncontroversial, so I will not say much about it. Government may ban speech by those planning or inciting an act that is otherwise criminal, such as a conspiracy to commit a crime. Speech used in planning a murder or bank robbery, or inciting a crowd to violence against an innocent person, is punishable.

[73] McCloskey, ed., *Works of James Wilson*, 2:670–71.

[74] See West, *Vindicating the Founders*, chap. 4, "Women and the Family." See also the opinion of Judge John Finis Philips in *United States v. Harmon*, 45 F. 414 (U.S. Dist. Ct. Kan., 1891). I know of no better defense by an American jurist of the founders' policy of suppressing obscenity, pornography, etc. Philips uses the language of the founders, concerning the security of natural rights and the social compact as the foundation of government, as the ground of government's right to ban obscene material from the U.S. mail.

[75] In addition to the materials mentioned in the previous note, see Wilson, *Lectures on Law*, in McCloskey, ed., *Works of James Wilson*, 2:598–603 (on the importance of the monogamous, heterosexual family).

V. Third Element of Free Speech: Restraint of Injurious Speech Must Be by Due Process of Law

It is not enough to say (for example, in a Bill of Rights) that noninjurious speech should be free and that only injurious speech is punishable. "Will it be sufficient," Madison famously asks in *Federalist No. 48*, ". . . to trust to these parchment barriers against the encroaching spirit of power?" How is government to be prevented from abusing its duty to protect people against injury? The founders' answer here, as in domestic politics generally, was to require government to operate through laws or general rules passed by elected representative bodies, applied and enforced through an independent executive and judiciary.

The rule of law is meant to enable government to secure our natural rights (protecting against injuries to individuals or to the society at large), while discouraging government from misusing its great power to oppress those with whom government officials happen to disagree. If government censors are in a position to decide behind closed doors which persons or companies will be denied a right to a broadcast or printing license, without having to answer in open court before a jury of ordinary citizens, the likely result is that broadcasting or printing will tend to be limited to friends of the views of government. This was, in fact, the case through most of the history of broadcast regulation, until the late 1980s.[76]

What the rule of law requires is 'due process'. Before government may take away anyone's liberty (including liberty of speech, press, or broadcast), it has to make a general rule that defines the kinds of injurious speech for which people will be held accountable. If government believes that an injury has taken place, it must proceed with a jury trial should the defendant request one.[77] Hamilton, in his argument in the *Croswell* case, made some savvy remarks indicating why impartial judgment requires that government officials not be permitted to judge cases of libel without the concurrence of a jury:

> [L]et me ask whether it is right that a permanent body of men, appointed by the executive, and, in some degree, always connected with it, should exclusively have the power of deciding on what shall constitute a libel on our rulers; or that they shall share it, united with a changeable body of men, chosen by the people. Let our juries still be selected, as they are now are, by lot. But it cannot be denied, that every permanent body of men, is, more or less, liable to be influenced by the spirit of the existing administration: that such a body may be

[76] Lucas A. (Scot) Powe, Jr., *American Broadcasting and the First Amendment* (Berkeley: University of California Press, 1987).

[77] Story, *Commentaries on the Constitution*, sec. 1879, paraphrasing an English author, writes with respect to publications, "if their character is questioned, whether they are lawful, or libelous, is to be tried by a jury, according to due proceedings at law."

> inclined to corruption, and that they may be inclined to lean over towards party modes. No man can think more highly of our judges, and I may say personally so, of those who now preside, than myself; but I must forget what human nature is, and what her history has taught us, that permanent bodies may be so corrupted, before I can venture to assert that it cannot be.... For though, as individuals, they may be interested in the general welfare, yet, if once they enter into the views of government, their power may be converted into an engine of oppression.[78]

VI. Fourth Element of Free Speech: No Prior Restraint

At the Pennsylvania Ratification Convention of 1787, James Wilson said: "what is meant by the liberty of the press is, that there should be no antecedent restraint upon it; but that every author is responsible when he attacks the security or welfare of the government or the safety, character, and property of the individual."[79]

This principle of 'no prior restraint' is a fundamental requirement not only of free speech, but of the rule of law altogether. John McGinnis explains: "Like a licensing law, a prior restraint can be understood as a deviation from the common law's treatment of business enterprises; under the common law, other enterprises were not normally subject to licenses or prior restraints, but rather only to after-the-fact liability for damages they caused."[80] Law, as understood in the founding, should not require citizens to ask for the permission of government officials before they are allowed to use their property. (There are some exceptions,[81] but the presumption was that the exceptions would serve the overall cause of securing the greatest liberty for all.) A person may not be incarcerated because the government believes he might harm or plan to harm someone. Government should not be permitted to infringe the citizens' right to keep and bear arms, for example (as is often done today) by granting licenses to carry firearms only to certain classes of citizens. Government is similarly forbidden to license the right to speak or publish. 'No prior restraint' means that government may not condition the right to publish

[78] *People v. Croswell*, in Goebel, ed., *Law Practice of Hamilton*, 1:810.

[79] Wilson, speech at Pennsylvania Ratifying Convention, December 1, 1787, in Merrill Jensen, ed., *The Documentary History of the Ratification of the Constitution*, vol. 2 (Madison: State Historical Society of Wisconsin, 1976), 455.

[80] McGinnis, "The Once and Future Property-Based Vision of the First Amendment," 92.

[81] William J. Novak, *The People's Welfare: Law and Regulation in Nineteenth-Century America* (Chapel Hill: University of North Carolina Press, 1996) (showing that nineteenth-century regulation was more extensive than one might expect from the myth of laissez faire; his examples, however, confirm the view that the scope and intrusiveness of regulation was far less than in the twentieth century). Andrew Rutten has a sensible assessment of Novak in "The Neglected Politics of the American Founding," *Independent Review* 2, no. 4 (1998), available online at http://www.independent.org/review.html [accessed November 13, 2003].

on prior permission from government officials. That is, government is not permitted to get into the business of granting licenses as a condition of publishing a newspaper or magazine, or (in the present time) operating an electronic broadcasting station. From the point of view of the founding, therefore, the entire licensing scheme for electronic broadcasting in the United States would be both unconstitutional and in violation of natural right.

One might respond by pointing out that the government owns the airwaves and, like any other property owner, is therefore legally entitled to dictate the terms of their use. This objection is correct, but its premise is that it is proper for government to ban private ownership of the most important medium of communication in existence. A parallel would be if government insisted that it should own all land because it is a scarce resource that government alone can allocate justly. Government would grant licenses to use this public land on whatever terms government happened to impose. (This arrangement, by the way, already exists on the 54.2 percent of land in the Western states that is owned by the federal government). From the founders' standpoint, a government's refusal to allow any private ownership of the right to broadcast is the equivalent of government ownership of all the land in the country. A society in which government owned the preponderance of the land would not be a free society.

VII. Fifth Element of Free Speech: Property Owners May Limit or Dictate Speech of Guests, Employees, and Students

How do these principles affect the private workplace or other private associations? The general rule is that private associations are permitted to do the same things as a private individual. Everyone is permitted to use his own property and money to promote and publish the views that he believes to be right, assuming that these views are noninjurious, as stated above. Everyone has the right to spend his own money to publish his own sentiments. No one is required to spend his own money or to allow the use of his own property in order to promote views that he disagrees with. Every homeowner may exclude from his property anyone who speaks or acts in a way that the homeowner does not approve. He may exclude atheists, Christians, white people or black, women or men, the disabled, the intelligent, or anyone else for any reason, however arbitrary. But he is not permitted to injure them in their persons or property. The same rule goes for every business, church, private school, club, or any other private association. The owner may set rules on what is permitted or required to be said and done on his property by those who visit or work there. If the visitor or worker does not approve of the rules, he or she may leave or quit. Likewise, if a visitor, worker, or student does not conform to the owner's rules, the owner is free to send him or her away.

In the founders' view, a private school or college may expel a student for insisting that 2 + 2 = 5, or for stating in or out of class that the teacher is a fool (even if this happens to be true). Unless a contract dictates otherwise, an employer may fire all workers who argue that Hitler was a good man (or a bad man). For the same reason—namely, the right to the noninjurious enjoyment of one's liberty and property—a worker may quit if he dislikes the conservative or liberal opinions of his boss.

Today, civil rights law has significantly curtailed these freedoms. In the same era when American governments turned the marriage contract into an at-will arrangement by creating no-fault divorce, they greatly limited traditional at-will employment.[82] Disabilities law, racial and sexual harassment law, and (already in the 1930s) labor law require employers to say or not say certain things in the workplace. The same laws hold employers liable for noninjurious remarks made by employees (that is, remarks that would be held noninjurious in a court of law if those remarks had been made outside the workplace), if those remarks create a hostile work environment on the basis of sex or race.

These laws would have been thought by the founders to violate the employer's or employee's fundamental civil right of free speech and freedom to use one's property in a noninjurious way. This long-standing legal doctrine was not questioned until the twentieth century, when liberal Supreme Court justices promoted a right of access to private property for First Amendment free exercise of religion and free speech purposes. In one of the early cases creating this right, *Marsh v. Alabama* (1946), Justice Stanley Reed's dissent hewed to the older view:

> This is the first case to extend by law the privilege of religious exercises beyond public places or to private places without the assent of the owner. . . .
>
> As the rule now announced permits this intrusion, without possibility of protection of the property by law, and apparently is equally applicable to the freedom of speech and the press, it seems appropriate to express a dissent to this, to us, novel Constitutional doctrine. . . .
>
> . . . The rights of the owner, which the Constitution protects as well as the right of free speech, are not outweighed by the interests of the

[82] Mary Ann Glendon, *The New Family and the New Property* (Toronto: Butterworths, 1981), 4: "In 1973, Sweden and the American state of Washington changed their laws to permit one spouse unilaterally to terminate a marriage for any reason, or no reason. In 1974, Sweden extended protection against dismissal without cause to all employees in the labor force, and the Supreme Court of New Hampshire became the first in the nation to repudiate the time-honored common-law rule that an employer may terminate an at-will employment contract for any reason, or no reason."

> trespasser, even though he trespasses in behalf of religion or free speech.[83]

In other words, the traditional doctrine was that the owner of private property has complete control over what is permitted to be said on his property. In a 1964 case in which the Court created a constitutional right to picket inside a privately owned restaurant, Justice Hugo Black defended the older view in his dissent: "The right to freedom of expression is a right to express views—not a right to force other people to supply a platform or a pulpit."[84]

Today, conservatives and libertarians have attempted to carve out an "expressive association" exception to civil rights laws. For example, in *Boy Scouts of America v. Dale*, the Boy Scouts were vindicated when the Supreme Court declared them to be an "expressive association" whose "speech" would be coerced if they were compelled to retain Dale, a homosexual assistant scoutmaster.[85] Dale had sued the Scouts for dismissing him, claiming that the Scouts had violated a New Jersey statute barring discrimination on the basis of sexual orientation in places of public accommodation. From the point of view of the founders, all associations are "expressive associations." Whether or not a private association announces a public code of belief (as the Boy Scouts do with their famous oath), every individual, alone or in association with others, has a right to say what he wants and to exclude those who say what he does not approve.

VIII. Sixth Element of Free Speech: Government as Property Owner (Speaker, Employer, and Schoolmaster) has the Same Speech Rights as Private Owners

The founders applied the rules outlined above to government officials no less than to private citizens. Within some minimal limits—such as the Establishment Clause and the provision in the U.S. Constitution against religious tests for public office—government schools, workplaces, military bases, and libraries were originally understood to be free to decide what would be allowed or required to be said, or not said, as a condition of being on the property or being admitted to the agency or institution. If government wanted to require all state university students to live in coed dorms, or to admit only those who believed in racial equality, these requirements would violate no one's right of free speech. (Of course, gov-

[83] *Marsh v. Alabama*, 326 U.S. 501, 512, 516 (1946). See also Ely, "Property Rights and Free Speech," in this volume.

[84] *Bell v. Maryland*, 378 U.S. 226, 345 (1964). See also *PruneYard Shopping Center v. Robins*, 447 U.S. 74 (1980) (upholding a state law compelling a shopping center owner to allow entry to solicitors of signatures for a political petition).

[85] *Boy Scouts of America v. Dale*, 530 U.S. 640 (2000). See the discussion of David E. Bernstein, "Expressive Association after *Dale*," in this volume.

ernment officials must operate within the limits of the civil and criminal law that applies to everyone in society.) The homeowner owns his property and may legally expel or admit on the basis of what is or is not said by those who enter his property. For the same reason, government's freedom to set admissions standards, hiring standards, and the content of school curricula and libraries was thought to be a normal and necessary implication of the fact that government owns the property in question. Therefore, government was free to choose to buy or remove library books from its own public or school libraries. It could admit students to or expel them from government-operated high schools and universities because of what they said. It could hire and fire workers on whatever criteria it wished, including political party affiliation or preferential treatment by race.

The older view was affirmed in 1892, when Justice Oliver Wendell Holmes, speaking for the Massachusetts Supreme Judicial Court, rejected the petition of a policeman who had been fired for violating a regulation restricting his political activities: "The petitioner may have a constitutional right to talk politics, but he has no constitutional right to be a policeman. . . . There are few employments for hire in which the servant does not agree to suspend his constitutional right of free speech, as well as of idleness, by the implied terms of his contract. The servant cannot complain, as he takes the employment on the terms which are offered him." A few years later, Holmes upheld the right of the City of Boston to require that speakers on the Boston Common first obtain a permit from the mayor: "For the Legislature absolutely or conditionally to forbid public speaking in a highway or public park is no more an infringement of the rights of a member of the public than for the owner of a private house to forbid it in his house. When no proprietary right interferes, the Legislature may end the right of the public enter upon the public place by putting an end to the dedication to public uses. So it may take the lesser step of limiting the public use to certain purposes."[86] Similarly, in *Ex Parte Curtis*, an 1882 Supreme Court case, the majority held that a law forbidding government employees from contributing for political purposes to other government employees is constitutional.[87]

The same right of free speech for government as for private owners also means that when government speaks, it can say whatever it wants. Gov-

[86] *McAuliffe v. Mayor of New Bedford*, 155 Mass. 216, 220 (1892). *Commonwealth v. Davis*, 162 Mass. 510 (1895), 511, *aff'd* 167 U.S. 43 (1897). Quoted in William W. Van Alstyne, "The Demise of the Right-Privilege Distinction in Constitutional Law," *Harvard Law Review*, 81 (1968): 1439.

[87] *Ex Parte Curtis*, 106 U.S. 371 (1882). Also *United States v. Wurzbach*, 280 U.S. 396 (1930), in which Holmes, for a unanimous court, citing *Curtis*, affirmed the right of the government to forbid public employees from soliciting or receiving money from another government employee for political purposes. Also *United Public Workers v. Mitchell*, 330 U.S. 75 (1947) (upholding the Hatch Act, which prohibited most federal employees from taking part in political campaigns).

ernment "speaks" by funding certain activities, such as book publishing or art, or by teaching in public schools and universities.

Under the founders' approach, many issues that are hotly debated today would be solved easily. Government would be free to refuse to fund "art" for reasons of indecency alone, such as public nudity displayed in "performance art." Government could hire chaplains for the armed forces or to give prayers in Congress or state legislatures with no concern for "diversity." The university press of a public university could reject a manuscript for any reason whatever, even for "discriminatory" reasons. To the founders, a government agency or school was not a public forum.

IX. Modern Liberalism: Basic Principles

We now turn to a comparison of the founders' approach with that of modern liberalism. The founders aspired to establish a society in which each person's right to liberty, including his right to acquire and use property, would be protected by government. Except for injury to person or property, and matters regarding sex, marriage, and other things connected with the propagation of children, government would mostly leave people alone to live their private lives as they pleased. Government coercion would generally be used only *after* actual injury had occurred, and it could only be applied through due process of law, with clear rules, prosecutions in open court with jury trials, and punishments established and limited by law. Liberals reject the founders' approach as unjust and unhistorical. I will explain what I mean by this in what follows.

Before I do, however, I should note that the typical liberal probably would not agree with all the elements that I will attribute to liberalism. It is equally true that the typical conservative would not agree with all the elements of the founders' position on free speech. One reason for this is that government, public opinion, and elite opinion in America today are neither fully liberal nor fully conservative, but an inconsistent blend of both. From the point of view of the founders, America today has become very liberal. But from the point of view of the most consistent and radical proponents of liberalism, America today remains a very old-fashioned nation, regrettably still living in many ways under the principles and constitutional order established by the founders.[88] The most clear-headed proponents of liberalism—men such as John Dewey in the late nineteenth and early twentiety centuries, and Ronald Dworkin, Cass Sunstein, Richard Rorty, and John Rawls in more recent times—articulate the liberal position with greater consistency than most.

Rorty, a lively and intelligent liberal, provides a useful summary of the main elements of modern liberalism in his book, *Achieving Our Country:*

[88] See Mark A. Graber's lament in "Constitutional Theory for People Out of Power," *Good Society* 11, no. 1 (2002): 89–93.

Leftist Thought in Twentieth-Century America. I will condense his argument into three points:

First, liberals believe that the "moral and social order" bequeathed to Americans by the founders became, by the late nineteenth century, "an economic system which starves and mutilates the great majority of the population." For this reason, liberals believe that there is "a constant need for new laws and new bureaucratic initiatives which would redistribute the wealth produced by the capitalist system." Before the 1960s, liberals "tried to help people who were humiliated by poverty and unemployment, or by ... the 'hidden injuries of class.'" After the 1960s, liberals turned increasingly to helping "people who are humiliated for reasons other than economic status," such as women, blacks, Hispanics, and homosexuals. Liberals' goal is "a classless and casteless society."[89]

Second, the liberal conception of liberty is an ideal that Rorty calls "self-creation" or "self-individualization,"[90] a cultivation of "a greater diversity of individuals," to the point where "[i]ndividual life will become unthinkably diverse and social life unthinkably free." As an example of what this means in practice, Rorty celebrates the "youth culture of the 1960s," with its "rock-and-roll, drugs, and the kind of casual, friendly copulation which is insouciant about the homosexual-heterosexual distinction." In the ideal of self-expression, "the only sin is limitation."[91]

These first two liberal principles rest on a third and more fundamental claim: according to Rorty, liberals deny that there is any fixed meaning in the world. Neither God nor nature set any significant limits on the human will. Human beings should be free, not just from oppression by other human beings, but above all free from any "higher" authority either in religion or in a transcendent moral law that binds everyone and limits their wills. (Therefore, liberals tend to be strongly opposed to the moral teachings of traditionalist Christianity and Judaism.) For liberals, the meaning of human life is something that is a product of human making, not divine will or natural law. "The subject is a social construction," writes Rorty. Life must not be "subjected ... to some 'authority' alleged to exist outside the process of experience." To state the same point in religious language, "we put ourselves in the place of God.... We redefine God as our future selves."[92]

In contrast to liberals, the founders believed in what Rorty disparagingly calls "Platonic and theocentric metaphysics"—that is, standards that are "built into human nature."[93] In the Declaration of Independence,

[89] Richard Rorty, *Achieving Our Country* (Cambridge, MA: Harvard University Press, 1998), 47 (quoting Herbert Croly); 60, 80 (quoting Richard Sennett); and 80–82, 30 (paraphrasing Walt Whitman and John Dewey).

[90] Richard Rorty, *Philosophy and Social Hope* (New York: Penguin, 1999), 118.

[91] Rorty, *Achieving Our Country*, 28, 30, 24, 26, and 34 (quoting Ralph Waldo Emerson).

[92] Ibid., 27–29; quotations are from 31 (paraphrasing Dewey and Foucault), 29 (quoting Dewey), and 22 (paraphrasing Whitman).

[93] Ibid., 29, 35.

the standards of political justice are the unchanging "laws of nature and of nature's God." That is, human nature and/or divine will limit and guide the human will. Accordingly, Jefferson wrote that "the people . . . are inherently independent of all but moral law." [94] One example of such a moral law is that no human being should harm or enslave another except to preserve his own life. Another is that sex ought to be confined as much as possible to marriage, so that most children will be brought up by their married biological mothers and fathers.[95]

Rorty refuses to give any theoretical justification for the three liberal principles described above, choosing instead to advise the Left to "put a moratorium on theory" and "try to kick its philosophy habit." [96] Yet it is a fact that modern liberalism came into existence as an outgrowth of nineteenth-century German philosophy, which was heavily influenced by the Frenchman, Rousseau. Rousseau had famously declared in 1755 that what human beings are by nature—hardly more than stupid beasts—has almost nothing to do with what human beings are in civilization.[97] Building on Rousseau's claim, Hegel and his successors elaborated a theory of history that explains man's transformation from beast to rational creature. The key point is that human beings largely make themselves what they are through the course of their own historical development. The human mind exists by nature only in embryo. Nature and the rational mind are opposed. Therefore, history replaces God and nature as the explanation of what we most deeply are.[98]

St. Paul, quoting a Greek poet, said that in God "we live and move and have our being." [99] In the Greek as well as the Christian perspective, human life is fundamentally dependent on something outside the will of man. For the Greek philosophers, it was nature; for Christians, God. John Dewey, in a provocative correction of the Bible no less than of Greek philosophy, wrote that it is "social conditions in which he [the human being] lives, moves, and has his being." [100] The *individual* human being on his own is nothing. "Social conditions"—that is, human beings collectively and over time—make us what we are. Human beings, in this light, are victims, mere playthings of historical contingency, because they are formed by forces outside their own wills. But at the same time, human beings are also creator-gods, for social conditions (in which man "lives,

[94] Jefferson, letter to Spencer Roane, September 6, 1819, in Peterson, ed., *Writings*, 1426.
[95] West, *Vindicating the Founders*, chap. 4.
[96] Rorty, *Achieving Our Country*, 91.
[97] Jean-Jacques Rousseau, *Discourse on the Origins and Foundations of Inequality among Men* (1755), in *The First and Second Discourses*, trans. Roger D. and Judith R. Masters (New York: St. Martin's Press, 1964).
[98] Georg W. F. Hegel, *Lectures on the Philosophy of World History: Introduction: Reason in History*, trans. H. B. Nisbet (New York: Cambridge University Press, 1975). On Hegel's influence on Dewey and Whitman (and therefore on the fundamental direction of later American liberalism), see Rorty, *Achieving Our Country*, 20.
[99] Acts 17:28.
[100] Dewey, *Liberalism and Social Action*, 58.

moves, and has his being") are made by the joint efforts of human beings over the course of their history. The human race is all powerful; the human individual is a powerless victim dominated by forces outside of his control.

If there are no permanent limits or standards, human life can become whatever we collectively want it to be. For liberalism, then, the question becomes how human beings can use their collective power to liberate every individual from whatever restrains his or her will. Freedom, in the view of modern liberals, is something radical. It is not freedom from the will of other human beings under the law of nature, as it was for the founders. It is freedom from all permanent limitations—from every constraint that human beings have traditionally believed was imposed on them by God or nature. Government, therefore, becomes an ongoing project of liberating human nature not only from political oppression, but above all from such limits as poverty and traditional morality.[101]

Man's natural vacuity or openness means that there is no such thing as *the* right or wrong way of life. Compared to Rorty, Dewey was practically the incarnation of old-fashioned decency. Dewey strongly opposed the notion that random or merely self-indulgent activity constitutes genuine freedom. He once wrote that "[i]t is equally fatal to an aim to permit capricious or discontinuous action in the name of spontaneous self-expression." But the terms of Dewey's argument anticipate the "rock-and-roll, drugs, and the kind of casual, friendly copulation" celebrated by Rorty. In his chapter on "Moral Reconstruction" in *Reconstruction in Philosophy,* Dewey calls for greater diversity in life choices. We must "advance to a belief in a plurality of changing, moving, individualized goods and ends." "Growth itself is the only moral 'end.'" In an earlier statement, anticipating the way we talk now, Dewey called the human task "self-realization."[102]

Dewey was the greatest liberal theorist of the twentieth century. During that century, liberalism gradually took over American intellectual life.

[101] One might object that once liberalism abandons any claim to be grounded in God or nature, there is no reason to choose liberalism over any other position, even fascism. Most liberals do not confront this objection. But Rorty admits it gleefully; he says that is why he is a *liberal ironist.* That is, he likes liberalism, but he knows that he can provide no reason for his groundless preference. If Rorty is correct that the premises of liberalism lead to this conclusion, then there is a profound instability built into liberalism, an instability that might lead some to return to God or nature in order to defend liberty, but might encourage others to descend into the abyss of tyranny and what Leo Strauss called "fanatical obscurantism." Richard Rorty, *Contingency, Irony, and Solidarity* (New York: Cambridge University Press, 1989), xv; Leo Strauss, *Natural Right and History* (Chicago, IL: University of Chicago Press, 1953), 6.

[102] John Dewey, *Reconstruction in Philosophy* (1920; enlarged ed., Boston, MA: Beacon Press, 1948), 161–86 (quotations on 162, 177). Dewey published an essay in 1893 entitled "Self-Realization as the Moral Ideal," in Jo Ann Boydston, ed., *The Early Works of John Dewey,* vol. 4 (Carbondale: Southern Illinois University Press, 1967), 42–53. John Dewey, *Democracy and Education* (New York: Macmillan, 1916), chap. 8, "Aims in Education," available online at http://www.ilt.Columbia.edu/publications/dewey.html [accessed December 17, 2003].

Now liberalism dominates the universities, the movie industry, journalism, and the world of writing and publishing. Liberalism has also made significant inroads into American political institutions, but its victory in politics is very incomplete compared with its academic and literary successes.

In 1992, four members of the Supreme Court gave voice to the relativistic side of liberalism celebrated by Dewey in this way: "At the heart of liberty is the right to define one's own concept of existence, of meaning, of the universe, and of the mystery of human life." [103] Jefferson would have replied that we are not free to define our own concept of existence and meaning. God and nature have already defined it for us.

X. First Element of Liberal Free Speech: "Complete Freedom for Noninjurious Speech" Redefined

I will now discuss the liberal alternative to the six elements of the founders' approach to free speech. We will see that liberalism does not reject the first two elements (freedom for noninjurious speech and government punishment of injurious speech), but it does redefine injury in a way that the founders would not have recognized. Liberalism rejects the other four elements (due process, no prior restraint, free use of private property, and similar freedom for government to control speech on its property).

It might seem surprising to say that liberals do not favor unlimited freedom of expression, but Stanley Fish is right when he writes that politics is always "the attempt to implement some partisan vision." Therefore, he says, it is inevitable that "a line must be drawn between protected speech and speech that might in some circumstances be regulated, and that line will always reflect a *political* decision to indemnify some kinds of verbal behavior and devalue others." [104] One such "partisan vision" is the founders' ideal of constitutional democracy that secures the natural rights of citizens. Another is a liberal welfare state that limits the individual rights of citizens in order to redistribute resources from the more privileged to the less. Every political standpoint therefore proposes to ban or at least discourage some speech. Liberals agree with the founders in this respect: some speech is injurious and ought to be made illegal. Fish's work is valuable because it clarifies a point that many liberals are reluctant to face, although all liberals believe in government-imposed limits on some speech, as we will see below.

Liberals agree with the founders' view that there should be complete freedom for noninjurious speech, but they understand it differently. For

[103] *Planned Parenthood v. Casey*, 505 U.S. 833, 980 (1992) (joint several opinion).

[104] Stanley Fish, *There's No Such Thing As Free Speech, and It's a Good Thing, Too* (New York: Oxford University Press, 1994), 116, 15.

liberalism, the purpose of government is, first, to make sure that the resources of society are made sufficiently available to the disadvantaged and underprivileged, and second, to foster the limitless diversity that will allow every person to achieve the ideal of moral autonomy and self-realization. What follows is that two kinds of speech that the founders disfavored now become favored: speech criticizing government in the name of radical reform, and speech that is obscene, pornographic, or otherwise immoral from the earlier standpoint.

In the first half of the twentieth century, when socialists and communists were sometimes prosecuted for advocating disobedience to the law or revolutionary overthrow of the government, liberals wanted to get rid of laws prohibiting such advocacy. In *Brandenburg v. Ohio* (1969), the Supreme Court accepted the liberal view that such laws are unconstitutional.[105]

Liberals believe people should be free to be morally autonomous, to express themselves as they please. Liberals, therefore, deny the founders' position that there is an unchanging moral code (e.g., sex confined to marriage and oriented toward the procreation of children) that government should promote to secure the liberty of all. Thus, liberals view with suspicion all government limitations on pictures or descriptions of sexual conduct. Law professor Cass Sunstein writes, "Sexually explicit works can be highly relevant to the development of individual capacities. For many, it is an important vehicle for self-discovery and self-definition."[106] The beneficent message of pornography, writes legal scholar David Richards, is "easy freedom without consequences, a fantasy of timelessly repetitive indulgence."[107] Government should not stand in the way of such self-indulgence, but facilitate it.

The liberal view of pornography received an unusually frank defense by the late Supreme Court Justice William O. Douglas. In his concurring opinion in *A Book Named "John Cleland's Memoirs of a Woman of Pleasure" v. Attorney General of Massachusetts* (1966), Douglas included, as an appendix, a speech defending Fanny Hill by Reverend John R. Graham of the First Universalist Church of Denver. Fanny is the whore who is the leading character of the pornographic novel that was the subject of the *Memoirs* case. (In his dissent, Justice Tom Clark described the novel in these terms: "Though I am not known to be a purist—or a shrinking violet—this book is too much even for me. . . . *Memoirs* is nothing more than a series of minutely and vividly described sexual episodes.") Graham argued against the view that sexual desire is something that we should try to control. He proposed to replace the old ideal of self-control with the new ideal of self-expression.

[105] *Brandenburg v. Ohio*, 395 U.S. 444 (1969).

[106] Sunstein, *Democracy and the Problem of Free Speech*, 215.

[107] Richards is quoted in Steven Shiffrin, "Obscenity," in Karst, *The First Amendment*, 208.

According to Graham, the old ideal is of "a closed world, where life is predetermined and animal-like." The Fanny Hill view is "an open encounter of the total person in the world. Growth and spontaneity and expression are the goals." It means people are free "to choose themselves." The older view offers "warm blankets and cocoons for those who want to lose their humanity." In other words, from the point of view of Justice Douglas and Reverend Graham, those who follow the founders' view of sex and marriage "lose their humanity," while those who follow the free and easy ways of Fanny Hill gain their humanity.[108]

Here is a manifesto for the sexual revolution, which was just getting under way in 1965, when Graham gave the speech published by Douglas. Far from injuring society, obscenity and pornography are, according to this version of liberalism, important vehicles for liberating society from its puritanical, constricted past.

The Douglas view was the culmination of a line of thought that was long marginal to the development of liberalism, but which became part of its mainstream by the 1960s. One of the early opponents of the founders' approach to obscenity was Theodore Schroeder, author of *"Obscene" Literature and Constitutional Law* (1911). Schroeder, trained in the law, was the leading activist in the early twentieth century for the abolition of all limits on freedom of expression. At the time, few took Schroeder's book seriously, but it articulated many of the themes that came to be widely accepted later in the century. Schroeder especially emphasized the argument, later taken up by Douglas, that opponents of obscenity are themselves corrupt, repressive, perverse, and monomaniacal. Morality is "relative and progressive." For Schroeder, only hysteria and superstition make people believe that there is anything wrong with obscenity.[109]

Political scientist Stanley Brubaker correctly explains why the founders held the opposite view. For them, "freedom of speech is meaningless unless tied to self-government, using that term in both its public and personal sense. . . . [F]reedom presupposes character, and character presupposes self-discipline or self-government. But self-discipline is not self-acquired. It is virtually impossible without cultivation by family, society, and, at least indirectly, by government."[110]

[108] "Dr. Peale and Fanny Hill," Appendix to the concurring opinion of Justice Douglas, *A Book Named "John Cleland's Memoirs of a Woman of Pleasure" v. Attorney General of Massachusetts*, 383 U.S. 413, 433–41 (1966).

[109] Quoted and paraphrased in Rochelle Gurstein, *The Repeal of Reticence: A History of America's Cultural and Legal Struggles over Free Speech, Obscenity, Sexual Liberation, and Modern Art* (New York: Hill and Wang, 1996), 101–6. Gurstein notes that in our time, "to raise objections to so-called free expression—no matter how graphically violent, sexually explicit, perverse, or morbid—is to invite the epithet 'puritan'" (5). See also Graber, *Transforming Free Speech*, 54–62 (discussing Schroeder).

[110] Stanley Brubaker, "Original Intent and Freedom of Speech and Press," in Eugene W. Hickok, ed., *The Bill of Rights: Original Meaning and Current Understanding* (Charlottesville: University Press of Virginia, 1991), 89.

XI. Second Element of Liberal Free Speech: Government Must Punish or Limit Injurious Speech

For the founders, as we saw earlier, injury is harm to the person or property of another, including his reputation; harm to the government that secures his natural rights; or harm to the morals necessary for the preservation of society. All speech that is injurious in any of these ways may be limited or banned by government. This includes speech injuring reputation; speech injuring the government that secures individual rights; speech injuring the public health, safety, or morals; and speech used in the course of committing ordinary crimes. All other speech is to be permitted.

For liberals, injury is thought to be endemic in a system of free markets, where human beings exchange goods and services on the basis of voluntary contracts. For the founders, free markets are an indispensable element of a free society, in which individuals are expected to take care of most of their daily needs through voluntary private associations freely interacting with other associations. It is a basic tenet of modern liberalism that the freedom achieved by such a system is largely illusory, because it leaves the weak and marginalized at the mercy of the strong and dominant classes. Early in the twentieth century, liberal Progressives emphasized that such a system leaves the underprivileged at the mercy of corporate capitalism. More recently, liberals have focused on the ways that a system securing the individual rights of life, liberty, and property putatively promotes heterosexual bigotry, male dominance of women, and discrimination by whites against people of color. When government fails to provide these victimized groups with the support they need, they are doubly injured by the system.

Woodrow Wilson, a Progressive, illustrates the early liberal position in his 1913 book, *The New Freedom*:

> We used to think in the old-fashioned days when life was very simple that all that government had to do was put on a policeman's uniform and say, "Now don't anybody hurt anybody else." We used to say that the ideal of government was for every man to be left alone and not interfered with, except when he interfered with somebody else; and that the best government was the government that did as little governing as possible. That was the idea that obtained in Jefferson's time. But we are coming now to realize that life is so complicated that we are not dealing with the old conditions, and that the law has to step in and create new conditions under which we may live, the conditions which will make it tolerable for us to live.[111]

C. Edwin Baker makes a similar argument in his contribution in this volume. Government, he writes, must "create the conditions that enhance

[111] Woodrow Wilson, *The New Freedom* (New York: Doubleday, 1913), 19–20.

meaningful autonomy. . . . [T]he concern is not with having the maximum abstract freedom of choice but with having opportunities to make those choices one actually wants to make."[112] It is not enough for government to stand aside while individuals make their choices. Government must actively change the conditions of society to make the full range of choices available to all.

The late Supreme Court Justice Thurgood Marshall gave a clear statement of the same point in his 1980 dissent in *Harris v. McRae*. Congress had passed a law excluding the funding of abortions through Medicaid. As Marshall saw it, the question was whether the Constitution requires government to pay for poor women's abortions. The Court said no. Marshall thought otherwise. He complained about the Court's decision:

> In today's decision ... the Court suggests that a withholding of funding imposes no real obstacle to a woman deciding whether to exercise her constitutionally protected procreative choice. . . . The Court perceives this result as simply a distinction between a "limitation on governmental power" and "an affirmative funding obligation." For a poor person attempting to exercise her "right" to freedom of choice, the difference is imperceptible.[113]

Here is Marshall's argument in the form of a syllogism:

> Every woman has a constitutional right to abortion.
> If government fails to fund a poor woman's right to abortion, she is being denied her constitutional right.
> Therefore, government has a constitutional obligation to pay for her abortion.

Marshall's argument, like Baker's, implies that government has an "affirmative funding obligation" to pay, not only for abortion, but also for *anything* a poor woman has a constitutional right to do. Otherwise, she has (in Baker's words) "abstract freedom of choice," but not "the opportunity to make those choices."

The liberal understanding of injury has a direct application to the question of what kind of speech is injurious. For liberals, speech that undermines the task of helping the poor and other disadvantaged groups is injurious. So also is speech that advances the interests of the dominant

[112] C. Edwin Baker, "Autonomy and Informational Privacy," in this volume. See sec. III A of Baker's article.

[113] *Harris v. McRae*, 448 U.S. 297 (1980), 347. See also the remarks of Jennifer Nedelsky, *Private Property and the Limits of American Constitutionalism* (Chicago, IL: University of Chicago Press, 1990), 263: The Court correctly "saw that once we acknowledge that some basic rights can only be enjoyed with state economic support, we have left the boundary of negative liberty behind (and, of course, further redistributive incursions on property are likely to follow)."

classes at the expense of those who are excluded. Here, then, is the ground of two kinds of liberal limitations on speech.

The first kind of limit is on what may be said to or about the underprivileged or marginalized classes of society. For liberals, whatever expression perpetuates the existing system of dominance by groups such as whites, males, heterosexuals, the rich, and the nondisabled is injurious speech. Examples would include speech defending the traditional male-headed family, criticizing working women who leave their children in day care, denouncing homosexuality and single motherhood as immoral, pointing out the fact of high crime rates among people of color, defending the right of employers to discriminate on the basis of the employer's view of merit, and making disparaging remarks or jokes at the expense of people of color, women, the poor, the disabled, and homosexuals.

Few liberals would go as far as Catharine MacKinnon, who argues that legal action should be permitted against schools that assign "academic books purporting to document women's biological inferiority to men, or arguing . . . that Fourteenth Amendment equality should be repealed."[114] But most liberals favor campus "hate speech" codes and harassment laws, which require that schools and businesses discipline those whose words create a "hostile environment" on the basis of sex, race, or religion. As we will see, such policies lead directly to the punishment of a wide range of speech on the ground that it is "offensive" to some students or workers. MacKinnon's position is more commonly accepted by liberals than one might think.

The second kind of liberal limit on speech is that privileged speakers from the dominant class must not be permitted to speak too much. As Owen Fiss writes, the state "may even have to silence the voices of some in order to hear the voices of the others. Sometimes there is simply no other way."[115] Fiss means that freedom of speech in the founders' sense is the right of the wealthy to spend vast quantities of money publishing and broadcasting their views, drowning out the views of the poor and disadvantaged. Fellow legal scholar Robert Post agrees with Fiss: "Liberated from traditional inhibitions against official suppression of speech, the left has mobilized to pursue a rich variety of political agendas."[116]

Many liberals would still be reluctant to make such a blunt declaration that they favor "official suppression of speech." This does not affect my argument. Within the broad framework just sketched, there is plenty of room for dispute over particular applications of the two liberal limitations on speech. As we will see, there is, in fact, a broad liberal consensus

[114] Catharine MacKinnon, *Only Words* (Cambridge, MA: Harvard University Press, 1993), 107.

[115] Fiss, *The Irony of Free Speech*, 4.

[116] Robert C. Post, "Censorship and Silencing," in Robert C. Post, ed., *Censorship and Silencing* (Los Angeles, CA: Getty Research Institute for the History of Art and the Humanities, 1998), 2; quoted in Daniel Jacobson, "The Academic Betrayal of Free Speech," in this volume. See the introduction of this article.

on quite a few policies that lead to "official suppression of speech." Even those liberals who regard themselves as civil libertarians often endorse the liberal approach to at least some of the policies discussed below.[117]

My argument goes further than this, emphasizing the continuity between the earlier, civil-libertarian position once preferred by most liberals, and today's growing embrace by liberals of "official suppression of speech" in the name of "democracy." That is, my view is that liberals have always favored, in some degree, government regulation of the content of speech. The most obvious example is broadcast regulation, which began with the Radio Act of 1927. Another is campaign finance regulation, which began in the Progressive Era. This is not to say that no difference exists at all between the earlier liberalism and today's. John McGinnis, noting today's liberal preference for suppression of speech, offers this explanation:

> While [Cass] Sunstein's redeployment of the self-governance theory in the service of increased regulation may seem curious at first, it is in fact a logical outcome of that theory's underlying structure. Because the self-governance theory views free speech as an instrument of a collective good—social democracy—rather than as an end in itself, the deregulation that it previously promoted was always contingent on the usefulness of free speech toward that good. Regulation becomes appropriate when a new understanding of the effects of speech makes regulation necessary for advancing the cause of social reform.[118]

A. Expression excluding or demeaning the underprivileged must be discouraged or punished

Herbert Marcuse's "Repressive Tolerance" (1965) frankly supported "the withdrawal of toleration of speech and assembly from groups and movements which promote ... discrimination on grounds of race and religion, or which oppose the extension of public services, social security, medical care, etc." Marcuse also advocated "new and rigid restrictions on teachings and practices in ... educational institutions" to silence defend-

[117] Thomas C. Grey believes he can reconcile the "civil-rights approach" with the "civil-liberties approach" by calling the latter a framework within which the civil-rights approach (leading to official suppression of speech) will occur: Thomas C. Grey, "Civil Rights vs. Civil Liberties: The Case of Discriminatory Verbal Harassment," in Ellen Frankel Paul, Fred D. Miller, Jr., and Jeffrey Paul, *Reassessing Civil Rights* (Cambridge, MA: Blackwell Publishers, 1991), 100. I believe that this reconciliation is impossible, for reasons made clear in my overview of the liberal approach, in the text that follows. The liberal approach is *essentially* a "civil-rights approach," because of the basic premises of liberalism. In case of conflict, civil liberties must go, as Fiss understands very well. As he notes, the real liberal view is not that there is "a conflict between liberty and equality but also, and perhaps more fundamental, a conflict between liberty and liberty.... What is at issue is two different ways of understanding liberty." Owen M. Fiss, *Liberalism Divided: Freedom of Speech and the Many Uses of State Power* (Boulder, CO: Westview, 1996), 5.

[118] McGinnis, "The Once and Future Property-Based Vision of the First Amendment," 56.

ers of the "established universe of discourse and behavior" and to promote progressive reforms. In sum, true tolerance "would mean intolerance against movements from the Right, and tolerance against movements from the Left."[119] Few liberals would put their argument in such blunt terms, but the policies they favor are, in fact, animated by a similar understanding.

There are many government policies initiated by liberals that punish or discourage expression that excludes or demeans those whom liberals regard as underprivileged. I will briefly discuss three of them: harassment law, broadcast regulation, and labor law.

Federal civil rights law forbids discrimination on the basis of race, sex, religion, and national origin in employment and education. For over twenty-five years, federal agencies have declared and courts have ruled that one impermissible form of discrimination is "hostile environment" harassment. The standard is so vague that the question of what constitutes a "hostile environment" is endlessly litigated. There are many cases in which ordinary political argumentation has been found punishable. One court ordered employees to "refrain from any racial, religious, ethnic, or other remarks or slurs contrary to their fellow employees' religious beliefs." Another court banned "all offensive conduct and speech implicating considerations of race."[120] There are some people who find any criticism of affirmative action "offensive," even racist. Others are offended when someone alludes to his own religious convictions. So the "hostile environment" rubric in effect makes it potentially illegal for employees to say anything about their own religious beliefs, or to defend the "wrong" kind of political opinions.

Although harassment law is defined neutrally, in the actual enforcement it is almost always women and minorities who are given its protection. The prohibition of speech that harasses women and minorities presupposes that these groups are victims, that is, inherently weak and vulnerable in the workplace, in schools, and in universities. Liberals argue that employers are in a privileged position of power over women and minorities. Government must ban some speech in the workplace in order to protect the victim groups. A woman is presumed to be exploited if she must endure insensitive opinions about women in the place where she

[119] Herbert Marcuse, "Repressive Tolerance," in Robert Paul Wolff, Barrington Moore, Jr., and Herbert Marcuse, *A Critique of Pure Tolerance* (1965; 2d printing, Boston, MA: Beacon Press, 1969), 100–101, 109. See the helpful discussion of Marcuse in Andrew Altman, "Equality and Expression: The Radical Paradox," in this volume (sec. IV of Altman's paper). Marcuse's line of argument is a venerable one; a famous early example is Karl Marx, "On the Jewish Question" (1843), in *The Marx-Engels Reader,* ed. Robert C. Tucker, 2d ed. (New York: W. W. Norton, 1978), 26–52 (calling for the abolition of individual religious and property rights because they exalt egoism).

[120] Eugene Volokh, "What Speech Does 'Hostile Work Environment' Harassment Law Restrict?" *Georgetown Law Journal* 85 (1997): 627; available online at http://www1.law.ucla.edu/~volokh/harass/breadth.htm [accessed November 5, 2003].

chooses to work. (The same presumption can be found in campaign finance regulation. The voices of the "privileged"—whites, males, heterosexuals, the rich—must be confined in order to protect the underprivileged.)

The public often confuses racial and sexual "hostile environment" rulings with the kinds of laws that the founders would have approved, such as laws against the solicitation of prostitution, laws against personal libel, and laws against obscenity. But sexual harassment is not the equivalent of solicitation of sex, nor is a racial insult tantamount to libel, nor is an off-color joke at work obscene. Yet the liberal theory of harassment law touches words or deeds that merely make a member of a victim class feel uncomfortable. In effect, government requires employers to censor their employees and to punish religious believers and conservatives who express their opinions "in a way that abuses or offends their co-workers." I do not say that it has never happened, but I know of no instance where a court has punished or enjoined as racial or sexual harassment disparaging remarks against whites or heterosexual males in the workplace.[121]

For example, according to a federal court in 1989, the University of Michigan's harassment policy guide

> explicitly stated that an example of sanctionable conduct would include: "A male student makes remarks in class like 'Women just aren't as good in this field as men,' thus creating a hostile learning atmosphere for female classmates." Doe [who was suing the University because of this policy] said in an affidavit that he would like to discuss questions relating to sex and race differences in his capacity as a teaching assistant in Psychology 430, Comparative Animal Behavior. He went on to say: "An appropriate topic for discussion in the discussion groups is sexual differences between male and female mammals, including humans. [One] ... hypothesis regarding sex differences in mental abilities is that men as a group do better than women in some spatially related mental tasks partly because of a biological difference. This may partly explain, for example, why many more men than women chose to enter the engineering profession." Doe also said that some students and teachers regarded such theories as "sexist" and he feared that he might be charged with a violation of the Policy if he were to discuss them. In light of the statements in the Guide, such fears could not be dismissed as speculative and conjectural. The ideas discussed in Doe's field of study bear sufficient similarity to ideas denounced as "harassing" in the Guide to constitute a realistic and specific threat of prosecution.[122]

[121] Eugene Volokh, "Freedom of Speech and Workplace Harassment," *UCLA Law Review*, 39 (1992): 1793-66, 1804-5. See also Kingsley R. Browne, "Title VII As Censorship: Hostile-Environment Harassment and the First Amendment," *Ohio State Law Journal*, 52 (1991): 481-550.

[122] *Doe v. University of Michigan*, 721 F. Supp. 852, 860 (E.D. Mich 1989).

The court declared the Michigan harassment policy unconstitutional, lamenting that "It is an unfortunate fact of our constitutional system that the ideals of freedom and equality are often in conflict. The difficult and sometimes painful task of our political and legal institutions is to mediate the appropriate balance between these two competing values." The founders would have said that the ideals of freedom and equality are one and the same: "all men are created equal" means that all human beings have the same right to be secure in their person and property against injuries committed by others. It does not mean that the liberty of some citizens may be curtailed because other citizens take offense at academic discussions of scientific questions. (In the case just mentioned, "[t]he record before the Court thus indicated that the drafters of the policy intended that speech need only be offensive to be sanctionable.")[123]

The history of broadcast regulation gives us a second example of government suppression of speech that allegedly demeans the underprivileged. Not surprisingly, the target has most often been conservative speech. From the 1930s to 1987, the Federal Communications Commission (FCC) required broadcasters to adhere to a policy of nonpartisanship or "fairness" in their treatment of controversial ideas. This doctrine was frequently used by the administrations of Franklin Roosevelt and John Kennedy to silence conservative broadcasters. In the 1930s, the FCC threatened not to renew the broadcast license of the Yankee Radio Network of New England. The network had made the mistake of broadcasting editorials critical of Roosevelt and the New Deal. In its ruling, the FCC said, "Radio can serve as an instrument of democracy only when devoted to the communication of information and exchange of ideas fairly and objectively presented. . . . It cannot be devoted to the support of principles he [the broadcaster] happens to regard most favorably. . . . These requirements are inherent in the conception of the public interest." No station that praised Roosevelt was threatened with nonrenewal. In fact, all stations were expected to broadcast Roosevelt's speeches and "fireside chats," many of which were intensely partisan.

From the founders' point of view, the Yankee Radio Network incident was a blatant example of the danger of government control over the content of what gets published. But from the Roosevelt Administration's point of view, government was merely requiring that broadcasters be responsible. The Yankee Radio Network was opposed to the New Deal, but the New Deal was, in Roosevelt's mind, a program that would rescue the average American from the clutches of "economic royalists"—the big

[123] *Id.* at 853, 860. The founders also would have said that Michigan may run its university in any way it pleases. If it chooses to impose an antiscientific policy on its students that makes it difficult to discuss important truths about the differences between men and women, there are no natural or constitutional rights of free speech to stand in the way. But the founders also would have said that such policies may not be imposed by government on *private* institutions.

corporations and other conservatives—who had no legitimate place in the system.[124]

Roosevelt's idea of freedom was made perfectly clear in his 1944 State of the Union address to Congress, a message that the Yankee Radio Network was presumably expected to carry without commentary. After Roosevelt outlined the liberal goals of his domestic policy, he said:

> [There are] grave dangers of "rightist reaction" in this Nation. . . . Indeed, if such reaction should develop—if history were to repeat itself and we were to return to the so-called "normalcy" of the 1920's—then it is certain that even though we shall have conquered our enemies on the battlefields abroad, we shall have yielded to the spirit of Fascism here at home.

In the midst of World War II, in which Americans of all political persuasions were fighting and dying for their country, Roosevelt equated the Republican Party—the party of the "normalcy" of the 1920s—to the Nazis. He meant this quite sincerely. For the Republicans were the party of the founders' idea of an individual right to property, one of those original inalienable "political rights" that, as Roosevelt explained earlier in the same speech, had "proved inadequate to assure us equality in the pursuit of happiness."[125] As the party of "economic royalism," the Republican Party of the 1920s had no legitimate place in a free America. We can see why Roosevelt would not be troubled by an FCC devoted to minimizing conservative broadcasting content. In his view, free speech for those who would overthrow the New Deal would be like the founders legitimizing seditious libel: it would be like the founders giving freedom of speech to those who would overthrow free government and replace it with monarchy.

In the 1960s, the Kennedy administration's FCC used the so-called Fairness Doctrine to threaten, intimidate, and occasionally take away the broadcast licenses of conservative radio stations. Kennedy's Assistant Secretary of Commerce, Bill Ruder, later admitted, "Our massive strategy was to use the Fairness Doctrine to challenge and harass right-wing broadcasters and hope that the challenges would be so costly to them that they would be inhibited and decide it was too expensive to continue." One of these cases went to the Supreme Court, which, in its unanimous decision in *Red Lion Broadcasting Co. v. Federal Communications Commission* (1969), saw no free speech concerns in an FCC threat to deny a broadcast license renewal to a station that refused to air a liberal attack on its own broad-

[124] Speech before the Democratic National Convention, June 27, 1936, in John Gabriel Hunt, ed., *The Essential Franklin Delano Roosevelt* (New York: Gramercy Books, 1995), 115.

[125] Message to the Congress on the State of the Union, January 11, 1944, in B.D. Zevin, ed., *Nothing to Fear: The Selected Addresses of Franklin Delano Roosevelt, 1932–1945* (New York: Houghton Mifflin, 1946), 397, 396.

cast.[126] In another 1969 case, the D.C. Circuit Court of Appeals ordered the FCC to revoke the broadcast license of WLBT television in Jackson, Mississippi, a station that had defended segregation, opposed the civil rights legislation of the 1960s, and failed to include blacks in its programming. Then-Judge Warren Burger, when this case was first heard by the court in 1966, thundered: "After nearly five decades of operation the broadcast industry does not seem to have grasped the simple fact that a broadcast license is a public trust subject to termination for breach of duty."[127]

Liberal law professor Lucas A. (Scot) Powe is a critic of broadcast licensing because he sees that government officials, including those in the Nixon Administration, have successfully and often cynically used licensing to manipulate broadcast content and ownership. Powe writes, "The laws of broadcasting have not changed in the years since Nixon's exile. Are we thus in any better position to fight off another president with an inclination to threaten his foes with financial devastation?" But most liberals (as well as many conservatives) support broadcast regulation as uncontroversial and desirable.

In 1967, while the FCC was requiring Red Lion to broadcast a liberal reply to its conservative criticisms, the Commission changed its regulations to make it clear that the Fairness Doctrine would not impose similar requirements on liberal broadcasters. Scot Powe writes:

> The FCC . . . exempted from its new rules bona fide news interviews and commentary or analysis in the course of bona fide newscasts. Eric Sevareid [a prominent liberal commentator on CBS News] was now in the clear; the Reverend Billy James Hargis [the conservative whose commentary was broadcast by Red Lion] was not.[128]

[126] *Red Lion Broadcasting Co. v. Federal Communications Commission*, 395 U.S. 367 (1969). Although the Fairness Doctrine has been repealed—by President Reagan's libertarian FCC, not by the courts—*Red Lion* is still considered good law in the federal judiciary.

[127] *Office of Communication of United Church of Christ v. Federal Communications Commission*, 359 F.2d. 994 (D.C. Cir. 1966). The case returned to the court three years later: 425 F.2d. 543 (D.C. Cir. 1969). Burger became Chief Justice of the Supreme Court shortly after the June 1969 decision.

[128] For detailed discussions of these and other examples of official suppression of speech on the airwaves, see Powe, *American Broadcasting and the First Amendment* (the quotation two paragraphs above is on 106 and this quotation is on 88–89); Thomas G. Krattenmaker and Lucas A. (Scot) Powe, Jr., *Regulating Broadcast Programming* (Cambridge, MA: MIT Press, 1994); Jonathan W. Emord, *Freedom, Technology, and the First Amendment* (San Francisco, CA: Pacific Research Institute, 1991); and Fred W. Friendly, *The Good Guys, the Bad Guys, and the First Amendment: Free Speech vs. Fairness in Broadcasting* (New York: Random House, 1976). On the WLBT case, see also Taylor Branch, *Pillar of Fire: America in the King Years, 1963–65* (New York: Simon & Schuster, 1998), 263–65, 271, 413, 504. For a fuller but still brief overview of the history of broadcast regulation in America, see Thomas G. West, "The Decline of Free Speech in Twentieth-Century America: The View from the Founding," in Kenneth L. Grasso and Cecilia Rodriguez Castillo, eds., *Liberty under Law: American Constitutionalism Yesterday, Today, and Tomorrow*, 2d ed. (Lanham, MD: University Press of America, 1998), 157–80.

The new rules, as former CBS News president, Fred Friendly, characterized them, "clearly defined protections for the broadcast journalist as opposed to the religious or political crusader": note the "crusader" imagery, used to demonize conservatives as warlike and aggressive. In other words, the FCC interpreted the Fairness Doctrine in such a way as to harass conservatives (Friendly's "religious or political crusaders"), but it gave liberals ("broadcast journalists") the freedom to say whatever they wished. Conservatives challenged liberal broadcasters on several occasions before and after the *Red Lion* case and lost every time. Friendly wrote:

> After virtually every controversial program—"Harvest of Shame," ... "Hunger in America" [1960s programs advocating liberal political reforms]—fairness complaints were filed, and the FCC rejected them all. As FCC general counsel Henry Geller put it, "We just weren't going to get trapped into determining journalistic judgments. ..."[129]

The contrast with the founders' approach could not be greater. The presumption of the FCC in the 1960s and 70s was that the Constitution's guarantee of freedom of speech and of the press applied only to "broadcast journalists" and not to "religious or political crusaders," as if the First Amendment was written to protect professionals who work for large news media organizations, but not ordinary citizens who might want to publish their right-wing and, therefore, presumably amateurish and ill-informed opinions.

The WLBT case provides an excellent illustration of what the liberal devotion to fairness, balance, and diversity means in practice. As Lee Bollinger summarizes the case, WLBT's "license was stripped after years of presenting only a prosegregationist point of view and refusing to permit blacks, who constituted over half of its community, an opportunity to respond."[130] In 1969, when this action occurred, very few television stations were promoting a "segregationist point of view." WLBT may have been the only television station in America that did so. Hundreds of other stations were promoting an antisegregationist point of view, with no attempt to provide balance and no right of reply for segregationists. Not one of those stations lost its license for failing to provide a proper forum for the prosegregationist viewpoint. No one would have dreamed of challenging a broadcast license for such a failure. If any station had lost its license on such grounds, there would have been a public uproar, because hardly anyone outside the deep South was willing to defend

[129] Friendly, *The Good Guys*, 28, 55. See also S. Robert Lichter et al., *The Media Elite* (Bethesda, MD: Adler & Adler, 1986), 15, 17, 55.

[130] Lee C. Bollinger, *Images of a Free Press* (Chicago, IL: University of Chicago Press, 1991), 131.

segregation publicly. (I am not defending segregation as a policy; rather, I am pointing out that the government's censorship of broadcasters had nothing whatever to do with "fairness" in the sense that all points of view should be properly represented in broadcasting. The government permitted only one point of view on civil rights and racial diversity.)

Similarly, the FCC stripped WXUR, a tiny Christian conservative radio station, of its license because of its failure to provide the balance mandated by the Fairness Doctrine. Judge David Bazelon of the D.C. Circuit Court of Appeals, dissenting from the opinion that endorsed the FCC's action, noted that by driving WXUR off the air, there was less diversity of viewpoint on the radio, not more: "WXUR was no doubt devoted to a particular religious and political philosophy; but it was also a radio station devoted to speaking out and stirring debate on controversial issues. The station was purchased by Faith Theological Seminary to propagate a viewpoint which was not being heard in the greater Philadelphia area. . . . The Commission's strict rendering of fairness requirements, as developed in its decision, has removed WXUR from the air. . . . It is beyond dispute that the public has lost access to information and ideas."[131] No liberal station has ever lost its broadcast license for failing to provide sufficient air time for conservative viewpoints. Apparently, for liberalism, "diversity" means inclusion of liberal viewpoints and exclusion of antiliberal viewpoints to the extent that the public and the politicians are willing to tolerate that exclusion.

Before we leave the subject of broadcast regulation, I should note that government ownership and regulation of the airwaves has not only curtailed conservative expression, but liberals have been targeted as well. President Nixon took advantage of the regulatory apparatus erected by liberals, but unlike the Kennedy Administration, Nixon's limited itself to threats rather than legal actions against broadcasters that it disliked. However, there were definite plans to go well beyond threats. If Nixon had not been driven from office as a result of the Watergate scandal, he probably would have attempted to punish the *Washington Post*, for its opposition to his policies, by creating license renewal problems for its television affiliate. Charles Colson, one of Nixon's top aides, had phoned the owner of CBS, another activist media critic of his administration, and threatened to "break the network." But what happened was the exact opposite. The *Washington Post* and the major networks brought Nixon to his knees and helped to break him by their determined investigations of Watergate.

The lesson of the Nixon episode is that liberals' trust in government regulation is a potential danger to liberalism itself. Once government is given the authority to dictate the content of broadcasting, then everything

[131] Powe, *American Broadcasting and the First Amendment*, 93–96 (describing the demise of WXUR). Judge Bazelon, dissenting in *Brandywine-Main Line Radio, Inc. v. FCC*, 473 F.2d 16 (D.C. Cir., 1972), 69–70; quoted in the concurring opinion of William O. Douglas, *Columbia Broadcasting System v. Democratic National Committee*, 412 U.S. 94 (1973), 160n11. The Supreme Court refused to review the *Brandywine* case on appeal: 412 U.S. 922 (1973).

depends on who happens to control the levers of political power. One purpose of political liberty, including freedom of speech and the press, is to enable those who are not in power to criticize those who are in power, to make the case to the public for a change of "men and measures." The liberal view of free speech curtails that liberty.

After President Ronald Reagan's appointees became a majority on the FCC, the Commission abolished the Fairness Doctrine in 1987. In the wake of this deregulation, airing of political views in the broadcast media dramatically increased, particularly in radio, where conservative viewpoints began to flourish. However, the end of the Fairness Doctrine does not mean that broadcast media are free. In fact, the growing presence of conservative views in the media was a result of the fact that the FCC itself became more conservative in the 1980s. The authority of the FCC over broadcasters remains in place. Since 1987, Democrats in Congress have made several unsuccessful efforts to reinstate the Fairness Doctrine. At some point they are likely to succeed, and the old policy of censorship could return in full force.

A third example of liberal limitations on speech that is supposedly hostile to the disadvantaged is in the area of labor law. In the 1960s, when the workers of the Gissel Packing Company were considering whether or not to join a labor union, the company argued that its "financial condition was precarious; that a possible strike would jeopardize the continued operation of the plant; and that age and lack of education [of the employees] would make re-employment difficult." When the union lost the election, it appealed to the National Labor Relations Board (NLRB). The NLRB reversed the election result, ruling that the company had unlawfully "interfered with the exercise of a free and untrammeled choice in the election." The Supreme Court upheld the NLRB's action: "[c]onveyance of the employer's belief, even though sincere, that unionization will or may result in the closing of the plant is not a statement of fact unless, which is most improbable, the eventuality of closing is capable of proof." By stating its opinion without proof, the company violated the NLRB rule against a "threat of retaliation based on misrepresentation and coercion."[132]

How, one might wonder, could the Court equate an expression of a sincere belief with "misrepresentation and coercion," or the suggestion by a company that unionization might lead to a plant closing with "a threat of force"? Unions, of course, are permitted to say whatever they wish against employers. The logic here is the same as in campaign finance regulation: "liberty" requires the silencing of one class of citizens in order to protect the victim class. Workers are supposedly systemically weaker than employers, so the government has to balance the scale by putting limits on the rights of employers to convey their honest opinions to workers.

Going beyond current policy, some liberals (for example, Catharine MacKinnon and Catherine Itzin) would like government to ban pornog-

[132] *NLRB v. Gissel Packing Co.*, 395 U.S. 575, 617–18 (1969).

raphy, not because it is immoral, but because it contributes to the subordination of women. Other liberals, such as Nadine Strossen, defend pornography because of its contribution to women's "freedom and autonomy": it conveys the message "that none of my thoughts are bad, that anything goes."[133] Here is a clash of one liberal principle with another liberal principle: expression serving personal self-realization and expression contributing to the continuing subordination of a victim class. That is why liberals can be found on both sides of the pornography debate.

B. Too much speech by the privileged must be discouraged or punished

In addition to the liberal restrictions on things said to or about groups that liberals designate as underprivileged or historically oppressed, there is another impetus to regulation that seeks to limit the speech of certain categories of speakers. This idea arises from the same liberal view that government must make sure that the disadvantaged are treated fairly. The problem, as liberals see it, is that those who are less privileged have less money to purchase broadcast companies, magazines, and publishing houses. Owen Fiss writes that "the concern is with the claims of those groups to a full and equal opportunity to participate in the public debate." To that end, "[s]ometimes we must lower the voices of some in order to hear the voices of others." After all, writes Fiss, the First Amendment "emphasizes social, rather than individualistic, values." In other words, freedom of speech is not an individual right.[134] Political scientist Mark Graber holds a similar view, as can be seen in this blunt remark: "Affluent Americans have no First Amendment right that permits them to achieve political success through constant repetition of relatively unwanted ideas."[135]

Fiss and Graber do not openly advocate the banning of conservative speech, as Herbert Marcuse did. They prefer to speak more vaguely of fairness, diversity of viewpoints, and "unwanted" speech. Fiss and Graber present a less aggressive version of Marcuse's argument, but the principle is the same. Those nonliberals who have the loudest voices under the current system must be silenced, and those liberals whose voices are excluded must be given a megaphone.

This may sound like a brand of radicalism that few liberals would adopt. However, the same kind of reasoning lay behind the Federal Election Campaign Act of 1971, as amended in 1974. The law limited not only

[133] MacKinnon, *Only Words*; Catherine Itzin, ed., *Pornography: Women, Violence, and Civil Liberties* (New York: Oxford University Press, 1992); and Nadine Strossen, *Defending Pornography: Free Speech, Sex, and the Fight for Women's Rights* (New York: Scribner, 1995), 14, 161 (quoting Sallie Tisdale). In support of Strossen's view, see also James Weinstein, *Hate Speech, Pornography, and the Radical Attack on Free Speech Doctrine* (Boulder, CO: Westview, 1999).

[134] Fiss, *The Irony of Free Speech*, 18, 2.

[135] Mark A. Graber, *Transforming Free Speech: The Ambiguous Legacy of Civil Libertarianism* (Berkeley, CA: University of California Press, 1991), 233.

donations to candidates but also spending on publications or broadcasting by candidates and even by private citizens and organizations acting independently but in support of an identifiable candidate. The purpose of this law, according to its supporters (as summarized by the Supreme Court), was "to mute the voices of affluent persons ... and thereby to equalize the relative ability of all citizens to affect the outcome of elections," or, in another formulation, to restrict "the voices of people and interest groups who have money to spend ..., equalizing the relative ability of all voters to affect electoral outcomes."[136] This is the view, as we have seen, that in a society that allows rich and poor to speak freely, the voice of the poor will be drowned out by loudspeakers paid for by the rich, and instead of freedom, the outcome will be domination by the privileged classes over the underprivileged.

Statements by supporters of the Campaign Reform Act of 2002, which was voted for by almost every House and Senate Democrat, and opposed by a large majority of Republicans,[137] reveal with perfect clarity that these laws are not really about corruption at all. Although all incumbents benefit from such laws, they are especially designed to limit the speech of conservatives. The following are quotations from the congressional debate. Senator Paul Wellstone (D-MN): "I think these issue advocacy ads are a nightmare." Senator Maria Cantwell (D-WA): The act "is about slowing political advertising and making sure the flow of negative ads by outside interest groups does not continue to permeate the airwaves." Senator Tom Daschle (D-SD): "I believe that negative advertising is the crack cocaine of politics." Representative Jan Schakowsky (D-IL), explaining which "issue ads" and "negative ads" these Democrats were worried about: "If my colleagues care about gun control, then campaign finance is their issue so that the NRA does not call the shots." Democratic Representatives Marty Meehan (D-MA), Rosa DeLauro (D-CT), and Christopher Shays (R-CT), and Democratic Senators Harry Reid (D-NV) and Dick Durbin (D-IL) said that the National Rifle Association's campaign statements were a problem that the act would solve. Several liberal Republicans echoed these sentiments.[138]

[136] *Buckley v. Valeo*, 424 U.S. 1, 25–26, 17 (1976). Liberal Senator Eugene McCarthy (D-MN) made the following comment on the 1974 act: "[T]here is no question that this new law gives special preference to the Democratic Party. I am surprised that the Republicans did not recognize that, though they did halfway sense it, all except the liberal Republicans, whose principal function is to shoot the wounded after the battle is over." Quoted in John Marini, "Money in Politics," in Peter W. Schramm and Dennis J. Mahoney, eds., *The 1984 Election and the Future of American Politics* (Durham, NC: Carolina Academic Press, 1987), 201. This article is one of the best analyses of the logic of campaign finance reform that I have seen.

[137] Bipartisan Campaign Reform Act of 2002, roll call votes, available online at http://thomas.loc.gov/bss/d107/d107laws.html [accessed November 6, 2003. See P.L. 107–151].

[138] Brief of the National Rifle Association, *McConnell v. Federal Election Commission* (251 F. Supp 2d 176 [D.D.C., 2003]), November 6, 2002, available online at http://www.cooperkirk.com/nra.doc [accessed December 19, 2003], 3–4, 19. Several of these remarks were quoted by Justice Antonin Scalia in his dissent in *McConnell v. Federal Elections Commission*, 540 U.S. ___ (2003).

The architects of the New Deal argued that the wealthy have to be restricted in how they may use their property in order to protect the interests of the poor. In campaign finance regulation, the wealthy have to be restricted in how they use their speech if liberal members of Congress—the self-styled defenders of the poor—are to avoid being criticized ("negative advertising"). Senator Jim Jeffords (I-VT) summed up the liberal view with perfect frankness: issue ads "are obviously pointed at positions that are taken by you saying how horrible they are."[139] In other words, an excellent method of preventing conservatives from "saying how horrible" liberals' views are is to use the power of government to punish those who have the gall to make such criticisms.

Ronald Dworkin argues, in an essay defending campaign finance regulation, that "money is the biggest threat to the democratic process." But Dworkin is not much concerned about the alleged buying of access to government by wealthy businessmen and lobbyists. More important, money distorts politics because television campaign ads are "aggressive, simple-minded." Dworkin argues that if reporters and nonpartisan groups provided more of the information on election campaigns to the public, "political argument might become less negative and more constructive." It would not really "violate free speech for Congress to deprive the public of everything a rich candidate might wish to tell it in repeated television commercials." For it is a "premise of democracy that citizens must be able, as individuals, to participate on equal terms." This means, says Dworkin, that "each citizen must have a fair . . . opportunity . . . to command attention for his own views." This cannot happen if the wealthy are permitted to publish their views freely on candidates and issues in an election campaign. An unlimited right of free speech merely permits "rich candidates to drown out poor ones."[140]

Similarly, arguing for a ban on the amount of money that may be spent publicizing one's views on candidates and elections, John Rawls wrote that government needs to maintain the "fair values of political liberties" by restricting the right of the wealthy to speak freely. "[T]he aim of achieving a fair scheme of representation can justify limits on and regulations of political speech in elections."[141]

The same arguments that are used to justify criminalization of campaign speech by the wealthy also justify government limits on media corporations. C. Edwin Baker writes, "a person does not have a first amendment right to use wealth to suppress the speech of others. . . .

[139] Brief of the National Rifle Association, 3.

[140] Ronald Dworkin, "The Curse of American Politics," *New York Review of Books*, October 17, 1996, 19–24.

[141] John Rawls, *Political Liberalism* (New York: Columbia University Press, 1996), 356–63 (quotation on 362). For a fine discussion, see Tiffany R. Jones, "Campaign Finance Reform: The Progressive Redefinition of Free Speech," paper presented at the annual meeting of the American Political Science Association, August 2003.

[Therefore,] a restriction on owning more than one media outlet would also be valid."[142] That is, government may decide at what point a person speaks "too much" and ban further speech by that individual or corporation. Jonathan Emord has shown, in his analysis of *Associated Press v. United States* (1945), how antitrust enforcement puts government in the position of dictating news content.[143] President Richard Nixon attempted to use threats of antitrust litigation against the *Washington Post* to influence its news coverage of his administration.[144] This was a rare instance in which regulation supported by liberals was used against liberals. In the end, Nixon did not succeed, while liberals did succeed for many years in postponing the emergence of a conservative electronic media.

Legal scholar Lino Graglia shows how liberals use codes of judicial conduct to discourage or ban campaign speech by conservative candidates for judgeships. These codes typically limit speech of judicial candidates to "nonpartisan" content. Just as was the case with the FCC's enforcement of the Fairness Doctrine, in *Republican Party of Minnesota v. White* (2002), acceptable nonpartisan topics for a judicial candidate were said to be "how he proposes to ensure that minorities and women are treated more fairly by the court system" and "remedies for race and gender bias."[145] In other words, liberal arguments are nonpartisan and therefore permitted; conservative arguments are partisan and therefore forbidden.

C. *Speech promoting ordinary crimes*

Liberals accept the founders' view that speech involved in planning or inciting an act that is otherwise criminal may rightly be limited by government. However, liberals want to exempt what Kent Greenawalt calls "public ideological encouragement," which includes advocacy of revolution or violence against government.[146] This difference from the founders can perhaps be explained by the fact that the most frequent and influential public ideological advocacy over the past century has come from the Left.

[142] C. Edwin Baker, *Human Liberty and Freedom of Speech* (New York: Oxford University Press, 1989), 268–69.

[143] Emord, *Freedom, Technology, and the First Amendment*, 222–24 (discussing *Associated Press v. United* States, 326 U.S. 1 [1945]).

[144] Powe, *American Broadcasting and the First Amendment*, 121–41 (on Nixon's use of broadcast regulation, including antitrust, to intimidate the networks).

[145] Lino A. Graglia, "Restrictions on Judicial Election Campaign Speech: Silencing Criticism of Liberal Activism," in this volume (citing *Republican Party of Minnesota v. White*, 122 S. Ct. 2528, 2553 [2002]).

[146] Kent Greenawalt, *Speech, Crime, and the Uses of Language* (New York: Oxford University Press, 1989), 266–69, 339–40. See also Steven H. Shiffren's defense of dissent in *Dissent, Injustice, and the Meanings of America* (Princeton, NJ: Princeton University Press, 1999).

XII. Third Element of Liberal Free Speech: Rejection of "Due Process of Law"

In the founders' view, if government wanted to punish or restrict speech, it was supposed to do it through due process of law. What this meant in most cases was the right to be accused only under a law that had a clear meaning, the right to a jury trial, the right to confront one's accusers and cross-examine them, the right to a lawyer, and the right to require government to make its case in public. Hamilton's remarks in the *Croswell* case emphasized the importance of juries to guard against government misconduct.[147]

In the liberal policy areas that we have discussed so far, and in some to be discussed later, due process in this sense is not available to those who are accused of injurious speech. It is difficult for there to be personal accountability if one's membership in a class (i.e., "the wealthy"), instead of one's unlawful conduct, determines one's right to speak. The "privileged" whose voices are determined by government to be too loud have no opportunity to defend the noninjuriousness of their speech. They are never accused of anything; they are simply silenced. The law treats all speech emanating from certain classes of people as ipso facto injurious, and there is nothing that the accused can do about it. For example, it is a criminal offense for a person to spend his own money publishing and mailing a book explaining and defending the views of a friend who is running for public office, if he spends more than the amount permitted by campaign finance law. The crime is in the amount spent, not the words spoken.

Similarly, enforcement of harassment law against accused employees or students rarely reaches a court of law. Typically, an internal investigation conducted behind closed doors in the business or educational institution (and sometimes no investigation at all, as I have observed at my own university) resolves the question, and the accused may find himself without a job as well as without an explanation. For it is often the case that employers deliberately conceal from an employee what the charges against him are, citing "privacy" concerns of the accuser. The employee is also often deprived of an opportunity to defend himself, to hire a lawyer, to cross-examine his accusers, or even to know who his accusers are. These "private trials" are not exactly mandated in the law, but the government puts employers and schools on notice that if they do not respond vigorously to claims of sexual and racial harassment, they will be liable for damages in lawsuits filed by the victims.

Finally, through all the years of regulation of broadcast content by the FCC, government has never had to prove that the speech it disapproved of was injurious. The only question was whether the broadcaster fol-

[147] See above, section IV B, *Seditious libel*.

lowed FCC guidelines. As discussed in the previous section, when the Fairness Doctrine was applied only against conservatives, silenced broadcasters had no effective legal remedy. That is, the real matter at issue—whether the broadcast content was improper or injurious—never came before a jury. As long as license renewal is based on a vague standard like "the public interest, convenience, or necessity," in the words of the 1934 Communications Act, a broadcaster has no opportunity to defend his broadcast content in a trial proceeding on the basis of clear legal definitions of injurious speech.

XIII. Fourth Element of Liberal Free Speech: Prior Restraint through Licensing is Permitted and Sometimes Preferred

Licensing is a hallmark of liberalism, but if owners must ask permission of government to use their property, they do not really own it in the founders' sense of ownership. A basic tenet of liberalism is suspicion of private owners and trust in government. As Owen Fiss writes, instead of viewing government with suspicion, as Americans used to, "we must contemplate the possibility that the state will use its considerable powers to promote goals that lie at the core of a democratic society."[148]

The liberal preference for licensing over private ownership may be seen most dramatically in the fact that the federal government owns over fifty percent of the Western land in the United States, but only four percent of land east of the Mississippi.[149] The reason is that the East was settled at a time when the founders' principles prevailed in government. Private ownership of land was thought to be desirable. Government did everything it could to get land into the hands of private owners as quickly as possible. But the government-owned parts of the West were settled mostly after 1900, when the liberal view came to predominate. In this view, private ownership was disfavored. Many farmers, ranchers, loggers, miners, and oil drillers throughout the West are not permitted to buy their land, but instead must ask the government for a permit (license) to use the land that the government refuses to sell.

Most liberals and conservatives seem unaware that the government today operates a vast system of prior restraint on electronic broadcasting through its licensing system. Yet all scholars know that the founders' concept of free speech precluded the use of prior restraint through licensing. Benno Schmidt, the former president of Yale University, writes, "the First Amendment tolerates virtually no prior restraints [on speech or the press]. This doctrine is one of the central principles of our law of freedom

[148] Fiss, *The Irony of Free Speech*, 26.

[149] U.S. Census Bureau, *Statistical Abstract of the United States* (Washington, DC: Government Printing Office, 1997), sec. 6, p. 228, table 369, "Total and Federally Owned Land, 1960 to 1994, and by State, 1994."

of the press. . . . the doctrine is presumably an absolute bar to any wholesale system of administrative licensing or censorship of the press, which is the most repellent form of government suppression of expression. . . ."[150] Yet we have had such a system in place since the Radio Act of 1927, and Schmidt does not notice it.

Parenthetically, we should note the weakness of a much belabored canard that broadcast regulation is necessary because of a scarcity of broadcast frequencies.[151] The absurdity of this claim can be seen by a comparison with land, which is also scarce. If broadcasting rights must be owned and allocated by government because of scarcity, why is all land not owned and allocated by government for the same reason? Even liberals such as Lee Bollinger now admit that the scarcity rationale makes no sense. Bollinger writes:

> These facts that more people would like to broadcast than there is space in the electronic spectrum . . . may be true, but it does not follow that the only possible method of allocation is through government licensing and regulation. There are alternatives, the most important being the system of private property rights and a market. Developing a system of private property rights in the spectrum, just as has been done with land, would permit the sale, or gift, of spectrum space.[152]

For liberals, the real justification for licensing is to make sure that what gets broadcasted actually serves the "public interest" as they conceive it.

We saw earlier the effect of licensing on broadcast content. If government can pull the plug on a business at will, it can dictate how that business conducts itself. It can regulate, as FCC critics have long noted, "by raised eyebrow."[153] Until the abolition of the Fairness Doctrine in 1987, the federal government often used the threat of nonrenewal to promote liberal (or, in Nixon's case, conservative) broadcast content. The founders saw the ban on licensing as the most important protection of free speech, yet the fact that broadcast licensing constitutes a massive

[150] Benno C. Schmidt, Jr., "Prior Restraint and Censorship," in Leonard W. Levy et al., ed., *The First Amendment: Selections from the Encyclopedia of the American Constitution* (New York: Macmillan, 1986), 246. McGinnis, "The Once and Future Property-Based Vision of the First Amendment," 92 n178: "There is substantial agreement that the [founders'] concept of the freedom of the press precluded federal licensing laws or government-enforced monopolies." For many years, broadcast regulation did both. Market entry was intentionally limited by the FCC, which restricted the number of television channels and held back the development of cable for many years: Powe, *American Broadcasting and the First Amendment*, 216–47.

[151] For example, in *Red Lion Broadcasting Co. v. Federal Communications Commission*, 395 U.S. at 390.

[152] Bollinger, *Images of a Free Press*, 89.

[153] Emord, *Freedom, Technology, and the First Amendment*, 186, quoting Erik Barnouw, *The Golden Web*, vol. 3, of *A History of Broadcasting in the United States* (New York: Oxford University Press, 1968).

instance of prior restraint has been routinely ignored by scholars as well as politicians ever since its inception in 1927.

Cass Sunstein is an enthusiastic proponent of government licensing of broadcasting. In *Democracy and the Problem of Free Speech,* Sunstein calls for a "New Deal for speech."[154] Sunstein has done scholars the service of making explicit what is often left implicit in liberal discussions of free speech. He begins from the fact that the New Deal essentially abolished property rights, which he takes to be a good thing. It means that we can get rid of the old habit of believing that human beings have natural rights. For Sunstein, all rights come from the government. "'Naturalness' is generally irrelevant from the point of view of law, politics, and morality." "Simply as a matter of fact, property rights are creations of law." The *New York Times* has a legal right to decide which writers to publish and which to exclude. Sunstein says that the *Times* has this right to exclude because government makes and enforces laws against trespassing. Since government in this sense "creates" property by defining it, Sunstein argues, it can and should rearrange the existing distribution of property in the public interest. It does so every time it tells a property owner that he must build wheelchair ramps for the disabled. Sunstein sees no difference between a broadcast license and "private" property micromanaged by government. Both are, in effect, conditional grants from government to private persons. His conclusion: government should treat "privately" owned newspapers and magazines the same way it treats broadcasters. From the point of view of the founders, this would mean the end of a free press.[155]

Sunstein himself is rather moderate in the practical inferences he draws from his radical premises. These premises would easily justify measures that most Americans (and Sunstein himself) would regard as extreme. For example, why not establish a Federal Publishing Commission (FPC), on the model of the FCC or the Equal Employment Opportunity Commission? Rejected authors could be given the right to sue publishers on the ground of discrimination against diverse viewpoints. If editorial policies had a disparate impact on points of view that have traditionally been underrepresented in print, the new FPC and the courts could order remedies, with appropriate goals and timetables. Book publishers whose lists were insufficiently inclusive might be required to publish a certain percentage of "diverse" manuscripts. Magazines and newspapers could be ordered to set aside a certain portion of each issue for groups representing "discreet and insular" minority viewpoints.

Using the FCC model, publishers would have to send a copy of everything they publish to the Federal Publishing Commission. Every few years the FPC would consider whether to renew the publisher's license. Renewal would be granted only if the publisher's product included suf-

[154] Sunstein, *Democracy and the Problem of Free Speech,* 17.

[155] Ibid., 28–34, 109. Sunstein's argument was anticipated by Jerome A. Barron, "Access to the Media—A New First Amendment Right," *Harvard Law Review* 80 (1967): 1641–78.

ficient diversity, access to those "whose views should be expressed," and "balance" in presentation of controversial topics.

These inferences, which follow from Sunstein's premise, are not as far outside the mainstream as one might hope. As we saw earlier, in the 1969 *Red Lion* decision, the Supreme Court strongly affirmed government's right to dictate the content of electronic broadcasting. Far from being forbidden by the First Amendment, the Court wrote, "Because of the scarcity of radio frequencies, the government is permitted to put restraints on licensees in favor of others whose views should be expressed.... It is the right of the viewers and listeners, not the right of the broadcasters, which is paramount." Otherwise, said the Court, the public would not hear from "those unable without government assistance to gain access to those frequencies for expression of their views."[156] By the same reasoning, the Court could have legitimized government control over the print media as well. After all, there is far greater scarcity in the number of commercially viable daily newspapers than there is in radio or television stations. The Court could have logically argued that "it is the right of the readers, not the right of the publishers, which is paramount," because otherwise the public would not hear from "those unable without government assistance to gain access to the print media for expression of their views." To quote another Supreme Court decision, "it would be strange indeed ... if the ... First Amendment should be read as a command that the government was without power to protect the freedom" of the press by regulating the print media so that they will provide the public with "information from diverse and antagonistic sources."[157]

In sum, according to Sunstein's version of the liberal understanding of free speech, in principle government is required to supervise the content of what gets published and broadcast, in order to promote an appropriate diversity of viewpoints in the marketplace of ideas. Sunstein's "New Deal for speech"—along with the radical policy implications already noted—is the logical culmination of this understanding.

Sunstein's position is widely shared by academic liberals. His *Democracy and the Problem of Free Speech* won a book prize from Harvard in 1994.[158] Legal scholar Stephen Carter writes: "Left unregulated, the modern media could present serious threats to democracy."[159] Bollinger in-

[156] *Red Lion*, 395 U.S. at 390, 400.

[157] *Associated Press v. United States*, 326 U.S. 1, 20 (1945). In later cases, the Supreme Court has backed away from the position that government may interfere with the content of the print media for the sake of diversity or fairness: *Miami Herald Publishing Co. v. Tornillo*, 418 U.S. 241 (1974). But libertarians like Emord and liberals like Sunstein agree: there is no significant difference in principle between print and broadcasting; therefore, either there is no reason for government to have any right to regulate content (Emord, *Freedom, Technology and the First Amendment*, 281–85) or there is every reason (Sunstein).

[158] Sunstein won the 1994 Goldsmith Book Prize from the Joan Shorenstein Barone Center on the Press, Politics and Public Policy at the John F. Kennedy School of Government at Harvard. McGinnis, "The Once and Future Property-Based Vision of the First Amendment," 56.

[159] Carter is quoted in Powe, *American Broadcasting and the First Amendment*, 252.

vites us to take note of "the risks to democracy of a more or less completely free press." He argues that "press freedom might, instead of enhancing public discussion and decision making, actually prove to be a threat to it. . . . The press can exclude important points of view." Like Sunstein, Bollinger approves of the tradition of government regulation of the content of electronic broadcasting through licensing.[160]

XIV. Fifth Element of Liberal Free Speech: Speech Rights Must Be Redistributed from Privileged to Oppressed by Limiting the Right of Private Owners to Use Their Property to Say What They Want or to Exclude Those with Whom They Disagree

For the founders, it was a fundamental natural right that property owners have an almost unlimited right to do whatever they wish with their property. The only limit was the principle that one must not harm others. This limit was to be defined in the civil law. The courts in the first century of American history often quoted the phrase *sic utere tuo ut alienum non laedas*: "use your own in such a way that you do not harm another's." Generally, if government believed that your use of your own property was injurious, it had to prove so in a court of law.

For the founders, it was also a gross violation of a fundamental natural right for government to take the property of one person and transfer ownership to another. Justice William Paterson wrote in the 1795 Supreme Court case of *Vanhorne's Lessee v. Dorrance*:

> The legislature, therefore, had no authority to make an act divesting one citizen of his freehold, and vesting it in another, without a just compensation. It is inconsistent with the principles of reason, justice, and moral rectitude; it is incompatible with the comfort, peace, and happiness of mankind; it is contrary to the principles of social alliance in every free government; and lastly, it is contrary both to the letter and spirit of the Constitution.[161]

For the founders, the private workplace or school was the equivalent of the private home or club. It was a place where the owner enjoyed complete freedom to dictate the terms on which guests, workers, or students would be invited to join or remain.

John Dewey regarded the distinction between the public and the private spheres as disastrous to the cause of liberty in the modern world. He believed that if government is required to leave the private sphere alone except for the punishment of overt injuries, the weak and underpriv-

[160] Bollinger, *Images of a Free Press*, 38, 26.
[161] *Vanhorne's Lessee v. Dorrance*, 2 U.S. 304 (1795).

ileged members of society will remain oppressed. Therefore, businesses and private schools are not viewed as private, but rather as quasi-public, or at least affected with a public interest. The employer is no longer free to operate a workplace as he wishes. Instead, he must conform to government rules on what may or may not be said. The purpose of this government intrusion is to protect the vulnerable groups in society: workers, racial minorities, women, the disabled, homosexuals, and any other categories that seem to be disadvantaged. For liberalism, the purpose of government is not to secure the natural rights of the governed, but, rather, to make sure that everyone has appropriate access to the resources that are needed to live as one wishes. This means that government has to micromanage relations between all persons in society who are unequal in power. It has to break down the integrity of the private sphere.

Therefore, liberals reject the founders' view that it is a fundamental right, both natural and civil, for private property owners and associations to do or say whatever they want, and to exclude or invite whomever they want, as long as they do not injure anyone. Liberals view the private sphere as inherently suspect, that is, as potentially oppressive of liberty or self-expression. Civil rights law in modern times has come to mean especially laws that limit the freedom of private employers and schools to conduct themselves as they wish. It is widely believed that if it were not for government coercion of private property owners, workers would have low wages, and women and racial minorities would not have access to decent jobs or schools. Part of the agenda of government oversight of the internal management of private associations is the regulation of what employers may or may not say; this limitation has been extended to employees as well. This follows naturally from the liberal view that owners of businesses and schools cannot be trusted to act responsibly unless their rights of free association are limited by government. How can the workplace be made comfortable for women and minorities unless government punishes employers for their employees who make jokes or unpleasant remarks about these groups?

Liberalism begins with the premise that private property is at the disposal of the public for the sake of the public welfare. If one citizen has more, and another less, government is authorized to transfer property without compensation. This kind of transfer is viewed as necessary because, as Mark Graber writes, "Many Americans are still financially unable to participate effectively in the marketplace of ideas. Hence, some policy must address whether, under contemporary conditions of material inequalities, persons should have unlimited power to convert their economic advantages into political resources."[162]

One liberal solution to this problem, as we saw earlier, is to "mute" or "silence" those who spend "too much" publishing or broadcasting

[162] Graber, *Transforming Free Speech*, 205.

their views. Another approach is to take speech rights (in the form of the use of a printing press or broadcast facilities) away from those who have "too much" and reallocate them to those who "need" them more. As Fiss writes, government "may have to allocate public resources—hand out megaphones—to those whose voices would not otherwise be heard in the public square."[163] The government will take the megaphones away from those who have them and give them to those who do not.

This mandatory reallocation of private resources was what the FCC's Fairness Doctrine did. A station would broadcast something that the FCC viewed as biased or partisan (usually, that meant nonliberal); it would then have to provide free air time to someone to respond. Liberals continue to favor "access regulation," that is, compelling owners of electronic media to turn some of their broadcast time over to people whose views they disagree with. The "need" for access is to be decided by government agencies, such as the Federal Communications Commission, staffed by supposedly nonpartisan experts. As Jeffrey Abramson and Elizabeth Bussiere write, "the public interest also requires that the crucial channels of mass communication be open to the citizenry at large, that political debate over the media be open to as wide an array of views and voices as is practically possible. If it takes legal regulations to achieve these access goals, then so be it."[164]

A similar liberal policy compelled private owners of shopping malls or airports to allow the uncompensated use of their property by demonstrators. The Supreme Court has upheld the right of state legislatures to compel private use of private property belonging to someone else.[165] But the Court has rejected the liberal idea that there is a constitutional right of access to a newspaper owned by another. Sunstein and some other liberals disagree. Steven Shiffrin, for example, writes, "Unless one thinks that the gatekeepers of the print and broadcast media afford meaningful access to dissenters, a strong commitment to the value of dissent should tilt one toward upholding schemes of regulation designed to afford mean-

[163] Fiss, *The Irony of Free Speech*, 4.

[164] Jeffrey Abramson and Elizabeth Bussiere, "Free Speech and Free Press: A Communitarian Perspective," in David M. O'Brien, ed., *The Lanahan Readings in Civil Rights and Civil Liberties*, 2d ed. (Baltimore, MD: Lanahan Publishers, 2003), 90. See also Bollinger, *Images of a Free Press*, 111, 114–15 (although "[a]ccess regulation carries the greatest potential for altering the press as we have known it and for exposing us to grave risks," it is desirable in electronic broadcasting); Sunstein, *Democracy and the Problem of Free Speech*, 55, 58, 88 (government should mandate access for excluded viewpoints because "access is the practical equivalent of the right to speak, and it is [currently] allocated very much on the basis of private willingness to pay"); Fiss, *Irony of Free Speech*, 69 (access regulations are desirable because they "limit the autonomy of the press in the name of freedom"); and Graber, *Transforming Free Speech*, 2 (access rights are needed because expression rights are "enfeebled in a world where their exercise increasingly depends on the economic power to have one's voice heard").

[165] *PruneYard Shopping Center v. Robins*, 447 U. S. 74 (1980).

ingful access."[166] In other words, government should compel private property owners to let nonowners use the property to publish or broadcast their own views.

XV. Sixth Element of Liberal Free Speech: Government Has Little Right to Control Expression in Public Funding of the Arts, Public Education, and Government Workplaces

For the founders, property owned by government could be used on the same terms as private property. Government could set the terms of use in any way it pleased. The only limit would be general principles such as "No man, nor corporation, or association of men, have any other title to obtain advantages, or particular and exclusive privileges, distinct from those of the community, than what arises from the consideration of services rendered to the public" (Massachusetts Declaration of Rights, 1780, Article 6). In other words, government ownership of property, and allocation of its use, is limited by the principle that government exists for the common good, not for the private advantage of particular persons or groups. Other than the citizen's privilege of access to public sidewalks and highways for the purpose of travel, this gave government a lot of leeway in its use of its property.

Today, liberals and most conservatives reject this view. Now there is constant litigation over what opinions government is allowed to favor or disfavor in its use of its own property. For example, as I stated previously, in the older view, a public school would be permitted to buy any books it wanted for a school library, and it would also have full discretion to get rid of any books from that library. Liberals argue, however, that once a public school buys a book for a school library, it is not permitted to remove that book, if its motive is objection to the book's ideological content. This view was upheld by the Supreme Court in 1982.[167] It was probably no coincidence that the Court affirmed this liberal view when a conservative group of parents objected to library books that were obscene and/or politically liberal or radical.

In the founders' view, public schools, acting in the place of parents, could treat students as they wished, short of injuring them in the legal sense. School authorities could spank students, expel them, or honor them on any basis the authorities pleased. Now, liberals argue that the right of free speech means that students must be allowed to express their political views in public school. In *Tinker v. DesMoines Independent Community School District* (1969), when a student was disciplined for wearing

[166] Steven H. Shiffrin, *The First Amendment, Democracy, and Romance* (Princeton, NJ: Princeton University Press, 1993), 99.

[167] *Board of Education v. Pico*, 457 U.S. 853 (1982).

a black armband in protest of the Vietnam War, the Supreme Court took the side of the student, saying that students do not "shed their constitutional rights to freedom of speech or expression at the schoolhouse gate."[168] The founders would have agreed that citizens never give up their constitutional rights, but if they exercise their rights on the job or in public school in a way that their employer or schoolmaster disapproves, they may not complain about the consequences. There is no free speech right in public school to give a frank opinion of one's teachers. There is also no right to display antiwar symbols if the school decides that such displays distract from its educational mission. In other words, students must conform to the school rules.

Similarly, in government employment, as I noted earlier, government was permitted to set any terms it wished. By 1983, this position had long been abandoned, as Justice Byron White wrote in *Connick v. Myers*:

> For most of this century, the unchallenged dogma was that a public employee had no right to object to conditions placed upon the terms of employment—including those which restricted the exercise of constitutional rights. The classic formulation of this position was that of Justice Holmes, who, when sitting on the Supreme Judicial Court of Massachusetts, observed: "[A policeman] may have a constitutional right to talk politics, but he has no constitutional right to be a policeman."[169]

Liberals also argue that when government gives grants to artists, it must not exclude some art on the grounds of indecency, because indecency is protected by the right of free speech. Owen Fiss writes that government's refusal to fund indecent art has a "silencing effect" that "arises from the scarcity of resources."[170] Failure to fund indecent "art" might mean that the Mapplethorpe exhibit launched in 1989—which included sexually explicit homosexual photographs, including one in which a man was urinating into the mouth of another—would not be shown in art museums that rely on taxpayer funding. In response to Fiss, the founders would have said that government not only has the right not to fund such material, but government should probably outlaw it on grounds of indecency.

It might seem, by Fiss's reasoning, that any art not funded, whether indecent or not, is silenced. If this is the argument, then every artist in America who is not funded has suffered from government censorship. Here the logic of the liberal position returns us to Thurgood Marshall's

[168] *Tinker v. DesMoines Independent Community School of District*, 393 U.S. 503, 506 (1969).
[169] *Connick v. Myers*, 461 U.S. 138, 143–44 (1983); citing *McAuliffe v. Mayor of New Bedford*, 155 Mass. at 220.
[170] Fiss, *The Irony of Free Speech*, 30, 35.

extravagant claim that any constitutional right that government fails to fund is, in effect, being denied by government. Fiss avoids this absurd conclusion by adding that since government must silence some artists by failing to fund them, the ones silenced should be those whose point of view is already available to the public; that is, the First Amendment "can be viewed as a mechanism for protecting the robustness of public debate, for exposing the public to diverse and conflicting viewpoints on issues of public importance." Since the late Robert Mapplethorpe's homosexual photographs "challenge orthodox views about sexuality," the First Amendment requires that such art be funded, while pro-heterosexual art is not required to be funded.[171]

Liberals argue that the older view was based on a distinction between rights (which government must protect) and privileges (which government may give to some but not others). Legal scholar Rodney Smolla correctly notes that this distinction is based on the Lockean approach of the founders. But he objects on the ground that the rights-privilege distinction "is intolerable in a modern society that aspires to make itself genuinely open and free. Government is now so large . . . that freedom of speech would be rendered an empty guarantee if government retained carte blanche to attach to the receipt of government benefits any restrictions on speech that it pleased."[172]

The obvious problem with this liberal view is that government often attaches to the receipt of benefits all kinds of restrictions on speech. It cannot help doing so. Approval of a grant from the National Endowment for the Humanities is contingent on saying and writing certain things that please the reviewers—things that, if left unsaid, would lead to the disapproval of the proposal. Grants approved generally must fall within the bounds of orthodox academic scholarship. The winning scholars have the *privilege* of a government grant, while the losers get no grant, because of what they said in their applications. From the founders' standpoint, the most serious objection to the liberal approach is that when government dispenses grants, it *should* discriminate on the basis of the public benefit that the grants are intended to secure. This is what justifies taxation in the first place: the public good. If government chooses to hire a teacher, it not only may but should refuse to hire those who believe that Nazism is the best form of government, or that sexual liaisons between teachers and students are desirable. (I am assuming that speech defending these beliefs is not against the law.) As Holmes said, there are a great many things a person has a constitutional right to say and do that might disqualify one for a government job or grant. This is as it should be.

[171] Ibid., 37–38. On Marshall, see the text accompanying note 113 in Section XI.

[172] Rodney A. Smolla, *Free Speech in an Open Society* (New York: Vintage, 1993), 182. See also Van Alstyne, "The Demise of the Right-Privilege Distinction in Constitutional Law," *supra* note 86.

XVI. Conclusion

Liberals and conservatives today often misunderstand each other when they discuss freedom of speech. They often accuse each other of failing to protect freedom of speech, not noticing that each has a different and opposing definition of this concept. This paper is meant to clarify the dramatic gulf dividing the founders' conception from the liberal conception. One common error made all too often by both liberals and conservatives—that the founders' view is simply that of today's liberalism in embryo, or in an incomplete or incoherent version[173]—is perhaps the greatest obstacle to an accurate analysis of American politics today.

A second common error that I have refuted is the view that liberals favor expansion of speech rights, while conservatives want to restrict them. What I have shown is that both liberals and those who follow the founders' view agree that some speech is harmful and should be restricted, while other speech is harmless and should be permitted. However, since the liberal view of harm is so distant from the founders' view, it is usually the case that where one side wants to restrict, the other wants to permit, and vice versa. As I said at the beginning, from the perspective of the founders, liberals want to restrict noninjurious speech while unleashing licentiousness, and from the perspective of liberals, the founders did the same. But what the two sides mean by "noninjurious" and "licentious" is almost diametrically opposed.

Finally, government policy on free speech in America today is neither what the founders wanted nor what liberals want. It is an incoherent blend of both positions. On the one hand, liberals have succeeded in getting most limits removed on obscenity and pornography. Liberal inroads on property rights are extensive, with far-reaching restrictions on the speech rights of business owners and others. As long as the Communications Act of 1934 remains unrepealed, government continues to have the legal right to dictate the content of electronic broadcasting. Perhaps most dangerously, liberal efforts to limit speech in elections through campaign finance laws have had considerable success.

On the other hand, in many ways the founders' view continues to hold sway. Government control over the content of print media continues to be mild. So far, the Internet is mostly unregulated. The FCC's abolition of the Fairness Doctrine during the Reagan Administration enabled the robust growth of conservative talk radio and television. As a consequence, the freedom of electronic broadcasting in the twenty-first century is closer to what the founders would have wanted than it was through most of the twentieth. While not without danger, American campaign finance law is far more tolerant of campaign speech than is the case in many European

[173] See the quotations from Robert Bork and Bill Clinton at the beginning of Section II.

countries. The Supreme Court still more or less agrees with the spirit of the founders that a ban on spending by candidates (at least of their own money) or by independent citizens to publicize their views (on particular issues if not candidates) violates the right of free speech: "the concept that government may restrict the speech of some elements of our society in order to enhance the relative voice of others is wholly foreign to the First Amendment."[174]

In the near future, America will probably continue to waver between the liberal and the founders' approaches to free speech. But because the understandings of justice behind each approach are so profoundly opposed, this mishmash of incompatibles is not likely to last indefinitely. This essay is meant to help Americans think more sensibly about the choice that they will eventually have to make in favor of liberty or despotism.

Politics, University of Dallas

[174] *Buckley v. Valeo,* 424 U.S. 1, 48–49 (1976).

DEMOCRATIC IDEALS AND MEDIA REALITIES: A PUZZLING FREE PRESS PARADOX

By Michael Kent Curtis*

I. Introduction

Freedom of speech, press, assembly, and petition have long been celebrated as crucial to democratic government. (I will often refer to these rights collectively as 'freedom of expression' or as 'freedom of speech'.) United States Supreme Court decisions have, quite rightly, justified strong protection of these freedoms because of their crucial role in the functioning of American democracy. (Of course, there are other justifications as well, but I will not discuss them in this paper.)

The Supreme Court has often noted the crucial function of free speech and press for democratic government. In *Stromberg v. California* (1931), Chief Justice Charles Evans Hughes' opinion for the Court said "a fundamental principle of our constitutional system" is "the maintenance of the opportunity for free discussion *to the end that government may be responsive to the will of the people*."[1] In *Roth v. United States* (1957), the Court said that "[t]he protection given speech and press was fashioned to assure unfettered interchange of ideas for the bringing about of political and social changes desired by the people."[2] Seven years later, the Supreme Court decided *New York Times v. Sullivan*, a case involving an Alabama public official who sued the *Times* for libel based on an advertisement. The ad had criticized the way state government officials responded to civil rights demonstrations. The Court said, "the First Amendment . . . 'presupposes that right conclusions are more likely to be gathered out of a multitude of tongues, than through any kind of authoritative selection. . . .' "[3] The modern Supreme Court has often quoted a famous concurring opinion by Justice Louis Brandeis in *Whitney v. California* (1927): the preferred remedy for "falsehood and fallacies" is "more speech, not

* Thanks to Ron Wright, Chris Coughlin, Malcolm Futhey III, Brian Charville, Alex Castle, Matthew Thomas, Joe Altman, Jim Hefferan, Mark Graber, and Ellen Frankel Paul for comments on an earlier draft of this article. The mistakes and misconceptions are, of course, my own. Thanks to Malcolm Futhey III, Alex Castle, and Matthew Thomas for assistance with research.

[1] 283 U.S. 359, 369 (1931) (emphasis added).

[2] 354 U.S. 476, 484 (1957) (Brennan, J.). The decision in *Roth*, however, seems inconsistent with this principle. See *City of Los Angeles v. Alameda Books, Inc.*, 535 U.S. 425, 453 (2002) (Souter, J., dissenting).

[3] *New York Times v. Sullivan*, 376 U.S. 254, 270 (1964) (quoting *United States v. Associated Press*, 52 F. Supp. 362, 372 [S.D.N.Y. 1943] [Judge Learned Hand]).

enforced silence."[4] In the United States, freedom of the press, in particular, has been celebrated for its role in checking government misconduct and informing the electorate.

Curiously, however, in the United States, freedom of expression sometimes thrived well before the rights were shielded by protective judicial doctrine. (Supreme Court decisions protecting freedom of expression date from the 1930s.) In spite of judicial rules, the social and political environment has either nurtured or inhibited freedom of expression.

At the moment at least, Supreme Court decisions provide fairly strong protection for speech that expresses ideas on matters of public concern. But history is rarely a story of simple progress. Today, changes in the mass media environment raise troubling questions about America's system of freedom of expression. The concerns are not "new,"[5] and they are hard to assess. They *are* a central free expression problem for the future. Government policy and "the market" are producing an ever more concentrated mass media, one that does an increasingly inadequate job of fulfilling its role as a facilitator of democracy. (By referring to "the market," I do not mean to suggest an impersonal force, like "the weather." While markets are a fact of life, the nature and performance of "the market" always depend on myriad government regulations.) The thesis of this paper is that changes in the media can undermine democratic self-government.

Section II will briefly explore free speech history from the end of the American Revolution to the ratification of the Fourteenth Amendment in 1868. During this period a fairly robust system of freedom of expression coexisted with a rather repressive legal doctrine. The repressive legal doctrine made criticism of government and public officials a crime—seditious libel—and it punished speech that judges thought had a tendency to cause bad effects. The quick historical tour provided in Section II demonstrates that a vibrant system of freedom of expression depends crucially on the larger environment. Free speech and press can thrive even as judges embrace repressive doctrines. The converse is also true. Judicial protection for free speech, important as it is, does not alone ensure a vibrant system of freedom of expression.

Section III will show that Supreme Court declarations about free speech and democracy made since the 1930s are in fact part of a long historic tradition that sees freedom of expression, and especially freedom of speech and press, as essential to democratic government. First, Section III will review historic defenses of freedom of expression. Second, it will look at assumptions about the environment of freedom of expression made by some leading writers in the period from 1830 to 1868. These writers often

[4] *Brown v. Hartlage*, 456 U.S. 45, 61 (1982) (quoting *Whitney v. California*, 274 U.S. 357, 377 [1927] [Brandeis, J., concurring]).

[5] See, e.g., *Miami Herald Publishing Co. v. Tornillo*, 418 U.S. 241 (1974).

assumed that promoting a vibrant outlet for debate was a crucial part of the democratic function of a free press.

Section IV will explore a basic free speech paradox. A strong public commitment to free speech values can itself protect free speech, though judicial doctrine would allow (but not require) suppression. At least this is so where diversity of media ownership and opinion foster free speech. Strong judicial rules protecting the right to express unpopular ideas are not sufficient.

In Section V, I will turn from early ideas about the press and past press practices to the current mass media, especially broadcasting. My contention is that many practices today and much of our environment is inconsistent with historic justifications for press freedom. There are losses as well as some gains in the transition from the press of the late eighteenth and nineteenth centuries to the mass broadcast media of the twenty-first.

In Section VI, I will explore a distinction between formal and functional freedom of expression, while in Section VIII, I will briefly consider a few reforms that might mitigate the antidemocratic tendencies of the present system. My main conclusion in Section VIII, however, is simply to argue that the problem of crafting a media to support democracy is a central free speech problem of our time and deserves careful study as a prelude to much-needed reform.

II. Freedom of Expression from 1783 to 1868: A Brief Overview

From the end of the American Revolution (1783) through the Civil War (1861–65), free speech history is paradoxical. In the years after the American Revolution and before the adoption of the First Amendment in 1791, a very broad free press practice coexisted with a repressive legal doctrine. The repressive legal doctrine—based on English law—held that expression that had a tendency to cause bad effects in the long run could be suppressed and that criticism of the government and its officials could be punished as the crime of sedition. Many insisted that the repressive doctrine survived the adoption of the First Amendment. In 1798, the Sedition Act prohibited "false" statements about Congress and the president, Federalist John Adams, but not about his likely opponent, Vice President Thomas Jefferson. Although Federalist judges upheld the Sedition Act, lectured grand juries on its necessity and wisdom, functioned as chief prosecutors during some of the trials, and jailed Jeffersonians, the act was repudiated. Federalists lost the election of 1800, and the new president, Jefferson, pardoned those convicted under the act. Set to expire with the inauguration of the new president in 1801, the act was not renewed, and, in the 1830s, Congress voted to repay the fines of at least one victim of the act on the ground that it violated the First Amendment. The law laid down by the Sedition Act judges and the popular system of freedom of expression had moved in markedly different directions.[6]

In the 1830s, abolitionists in the North were besieged by mobs, whose exploits were celebrated by some United States senators and other commentators. In addition, critics of the abolitionists demanded that Northern legislatures pass laws to silence the abolitionists. Although abolitionists were quite unpopular, many people who opposed the abolitionists defended their right to free speech. Northern legislatures generally rejected Southern demands for laws to silence the "incendiary" abolitionists and ban their organizations. In 1837, anti-slavery minister and journalist Elijah Lovejoy was killed defending his printing press from an anti-abolitionist mob. It was the fourth of his presses to be destroyed by such attacks. In the North the attacks on free speech did not succeed, but instead produced a vigorous free speech defense.[7]

In contrast, from the end of the Revolutionary War to 1868 (and beyond), judges (as in the case of the Sedition Act) and commentators often embraced a repressive vision of freedom of expression. For them, the First Amendment's protection of a free press was merely a protection against prior restraint. Speech with a bad tendency could be suppressed, repression could be justified by labeling the speech as "license," and "false" opinions about the government and those in power could be punished.[8] According to the Supreme Court, whatever protections the First Amendment afforded merely limited the national government and did not touch actions by the states.[9]

In the debate on whether to amend the Constitution by adding a bill of rights, James Madison presciently noted that states were as liable as the federal government to suppress the "invaluable privileges" of a free press and freedom of conscience. One of Madison's proposed amendments provided that "no state shall" abridge these rights. The House of Representatives accepted Madison's proposal, and it expanded his list of rights protected from state abridgement to include free speech and jury trial in criminal cases. The House sent this revised amendment to the Senate, where the proposed limit on the states was defeated. In 1833 in *Barron v. Baltimore*, the Supreme Court held that the U.S. Constitution did not protect the freedoms in the Bill of Rights from suppression by the states.[10] Most, but not all, state courts agreed.[11]

[6] See generally, Michael Kent Curtis, *Free Speech, "The People's Darling Privilege": Struggles for Freedom of Expression in American History* (Durham, NC: Duke University Press, 2000), 34–104 (hereafter, Curtis, *Free Speech*).

[7] *Id.* at 131–93, 215–70.

[8] E.g., *id.* at 246, 271–76.

[9] *Barron v. Mayor and City of Baltimore*, 32 U.S. 243 (1833).

[10] *Id.*

[11] Michael Kent Curtis, *No State Shall Abridge: The Fourteenth Amendment and the Bill of Rights* (Durham, NC: Duke University Press, 1986), 22–25; Michael Kent Curtis, "Historical

At the same time, however, there was a strong and protective view of freedom of expression in much of the nation. It came from editors, ministers, social activists, politicians, and ordinary citizens. By this view, freedom of speech, press, petition, and assembly were privileges or immunities of all Americans—recognized by the federal Constitution as well as by state constitutions—that no state or national government could rightfully deny. These guarantees protected Americans against both prior restraint and subsequent punishment.[12] They forbade government from enforcing an orthodox opinion, and so ensured a broad right to discuss public men and public measures and all questions that concerned the human race. No government—indeed no person—had a right to suppress such discussion. Neither a perceived bad tendency, nor a charge that the speech in question was "license" rather than "liberty," justified suppression. Though they did not use the modern terms, free speech defenders pointed to problems of 'vagueness' and the 'chilling effect' in legislation criminalizing speech on matters of public concern. A 'vague' statute would fail to make clear what sort of expression is permitted and what sort is prohibited. The result would be to vest government officials with broad power to pick and choose targets for suppression, allowing them to apply the law to their critics but not to their friends. The 'chilling effect' is the tendency of statutes suppressing speech to silence critics who fear that their legitimate speech might be within the scope of a statute punishing speech or press.

Free speech defenders also rejected the bad tendency approach (the view that speech with a "tendency" to cause harm in the future could be suppressed for that reason), noting that it is easy to predict horrific tendencies even from peaceful advocacy of fundamental change. Advocates of free speech insisted that majorities have no right to silence minorities and that citizens have a duty to protect the rights of those with whom they disagree.[13]

In the North, after a struggle, many embraced broad protection for freedom of expression on the issue of slavery—and on all other issues of human concern. For a time at least, free speech triumphed over demands for suppression. Since no repressive laws were passed to silence aboli-

---

Linguistics, Inkblots, and Life After Death: The Privileges or Immunities of Citizens of the United States," *North Carolina Law Review* 78 (2000): 1118–21. W. W. Crosskey and Charles Fairman, " 'Legislative History' and the Constitutional Limitations on State Authority," *University of Chicago Law Review* 22 (1954): 141–43. (Crosskey was a trailblazer on the question of the Bill of Rights, the Fourteenth Amendment, and the states, and my debt to his work is substantial.)

[12] A 'prior restraint' is a requirement that a person who wishes to publish a book, newspaper, or other item must first get the publication approved and licensed by the government. Under a prior restraint doctrine, printing without a license is a crime. Punishment after publication for what is said (as opposed to for failure to get a license) is referred to as 'subsequent punishment'.

[13] Curtis, *Free Speech*, *supra* note 6, e.g., at 66–77, 94–101, 166–81, 205–15, 227–40, 244–45, 250–56, 259, 266–70, 281–88, 296–99.

tionists, courts were mostly on the sidelines. Still, there were some repressive decisions. For example, William Lloyd Garrison was convicted of criminal libel for a somewhat inaccurate story about a Northern ship owner involved in the slave trade.[14]

The South, however, was a very different story. It became a closed society on the issues of slavery and race. The slaveholding elite used vigilance committees and repressive laws to suppress anti-slavery speech by abolitionists, and it later suppressed the speech of members of Abraham Lincoln's Republican Party. Still, even in the South there were crosscurrents. The reaction of the Southern courts to laws suppressing antislavery speech was mixed. None proclaimed broad principles of freedom of expression that protected critics of slavery, but several found somewhat technical ways to free the accused. One Southern court insisted on strict construction of laws that impinged on free speech.[15] Others did not.

Perhaps, the high tide of judicial repression came in 1860 when the North Carolina Supreme Court upheld the conviction of Daniel Worth, an anti-slavery Wesleyan minister and Republican Party activist.[16] (There were two parties that used the name "Republican" in American history: that of the Jeffersonians, which eventually adopted the name Democratic, and the party of Lincoln, founded in 1854. Worth belonged to the latter.) Worth's "crime" was giving Hinton Helper's book, *The Impending Crisis of the South: How to Meet It,* to other whites. Helper was a white North Carolinian. His book presented a harsh criticism of slavery and a call for democratic action in the Southern states to abolish it. The book was republished in an abridged version by Republicans for use in the 1860 election campaign. In the South distributors were treated as felons.

Worth was accused of violating a North Carolina statute that banned distribution of printed matter with a "tendency" to make slaves or free blacks discontented. The North Carolina Supreme Court held that it was no defense that Worth had given the book only to whites. Once Helper's ideas began to circulate, the court said, there was the danger that they would reach blacks. As the court saw it, the essence of the crime was to distribute the book with the intent of propagating its ideas. Curiously, the court said it would not necessarily be an offense for opponents of the book's ideas to circulate it. (Southern secessionist papers published excerpts from the Helper book and accounts of Republican endorsements to emphasize the danger posed by the Republican Party and the need for secession.)[17]

Republicans roundly criticized Southern repression, embraced broad protection for freedom of speech on all matters of public concern, and ran

[14] *Id.* at 199–201.

[15] *Id.* at 261–62. E.g., *Commonwealth v. Barrett,* 9 Leigh 665 (Va. 1839); *Bacon v. Commonwealth,* 48 Va. 602 (Va. 1850).

[16] *State v. Worth,* 52 N.C. 488 (1860).

[17] Curtis, *Free Speech, supra* note 6, at chap. 13.

for office proclaiming their devotion to free soil, free speech, free press, free territory, and free men.[18] Meanwhile, a North Carolina grand jury treated Republican endorsers of the Helper book as felons, indicted them, and the state demanded extradition.

Typically, studies of freedom of speech in the United States have been based almost exclusively on Supreme Court decisions. As a result, many people think that ideas protective of free speech were invented by the Supreme Court beginning in the 1930s.[19] Indeed, in the 1930s, the Court began making protective free speech principles the law.[20] But, as the history of freedom of expression shows, key free speech concepts and practices are far older. Opposition to government-imposed orthodoxy, equal protection for ideas on all sides of public issues, rejection of the bad tendency test, sensitivity to problems of vagueness and the chilling effect, and many other modern doctrines have a far older historic lineage.

The struggles for free speech for critics of slavery are crucial to understanding the second great safeguard for free speech, press, petition, and assembly that was added to the United States Constitution after the Civil War: the Fourteenth Amendment. In 1866 Congress proposed this amendment. Its first section provides that all persons born in the nation or naturalized are citizens, that no state shall abridge the privileges and immunities of citizens of the United States, and that no state shall deprive "any person of life, liberty, or property without due process of law; nor deny to any person . . . the equal protection of the laws." As understood by its two leading framers, Congressman John A. Bingham and Senator Jacob Howard, the Amendment was designed in part to nationalize protection of the privileges and immunities contained in the First Amendment by forbidding states from abridging these fundamental guarantees. The amendment was ratified in 1868.

There are lessons that can be learned from the struggles for free speech in early American history.[21] First is a point that free speech defenders emphasized again and again: free speech and a free press are central to American democracy, to the ideal that the people are sovereign. Advocates of free speech and press used the *functional role* of free speech in preserving representative government to elucidate the meaning of the constitutional guarantees.

[18] E.g., *id.* at chaps. 12 and 13.

[19] For a discussion of this approach and what has been omitted, see Michael Kent Curtis, "Teaching Free Speech from an Incomplete Fossil Record," *Akron Law Review* 34 (2000): 231.

[20] E.g., *Near v. Minnesota*, 283 U.S. 697 (1931); *Stromberg v. California*, 283 U.S. 359 (1931); *Herndon v. Lowry*, 301 U.S. 242 (1937); *De Jonge v. Oregon*, 299 U.S. 353 (1937); *Schneider v. State*, 308 U.S. 147 (1939).

[21] See generally, Curtis, *Free Speech*, *supra* note 6, at 428–34. See also Wilson Huhn, book review, "Compelling Lessons in the First Amendment," *Constitutional Commentary* 19 (2002): 795.

Jeffersonian Republicans responded to the Sedition Act by invoking the nature of the American government. They insisted that to be representative of the people, government must allow the people to have broad access to criticism of public men and public measures. Otherwise, the people could not perform their electoral function. Since public officials were agents of the people, the agents should not be permitted to restrict the people's information about how the officials performed their public trust. Restrictions that allowed praise, but punished blame, were even more impermissible. Representative government required equal opportunity for both sides of the debate.[22]

Similarly, in later years, critics of the suppression of anti-slavery speech noted that democracy entailed the right of the people to alter or reform any social or political institution. Popular sovereignty meant that no constitutional commitment—to tolerate slavery, for example—could preclude arguments for peaceful change and reform.

A second lesson can be learned from the early struggles for free speech. Justifications for suppression that *seem* attractive and plausible in theory have worked out quite differently in practice. It is plausible that people should not be permitted to incite others to commit crimes or to advocate ideas that have a "bad tendency" to cause crime and violence. In practice, however, these plausible justifications for repression of speech were often invoked against speech advocating peaceful change and democratic action. For example, Federalists treated Jeffersonian critiques of Adams as inciting revolution. Abolitionists called on slaveholders to repent and free their slaves at once, but, initially at least, rejected violence. Hinton Helper advocated political action in the Southern states to abolish slavery. He also called for peaceful political resolution of the slavery issue. Southerners treated each call for reform as an incitement to a slave revolt, or at least as having that bad tendency. In the 1850s and in 1860, mobs routed Southern supporters of Republican presidential candidates because of the supposed pernicious tendencies of their ideas.

The third lesson from early American history is that suppression theories are not administered with philosophical detachment. They are weapons employed by dominant groups to silence their critics. Federalist prosecutors, Federalist marshals, and Federalist judges administered the Sedition Acts, and they prosecuted criticism of the Adams Administration as sedition. Later, the slaveholding elite interpreted laws against speech tending to cause slave discontent in a manner that prevented Republicans from speaking to white voters in the South.

The fourth lesson to be learned from past struggles over free speech, and related to the third, suggests the need for clear and narrow rules. The vagueness of distinctions like 'license versus liberty' or terms like 'bad tendency' allowed the doctrines to be used for illicit political purposes.

[22] Curtis, *Free Speech*, *supra* note 6, at 68–77, 94–101.

The fifth lesson is that the function of free speech in a democracy helps to explain the very broad repudiation (in popular constitutional discussions) of the claim that free speech is merely a protection against prior restraint. Prior restraint theory prevented Federalists from requiring that Jeffersonians submit their newspapers to censors, but the editors still were jailed after publication for "false" opinions about President Adams. This result chilled and suppressed the very speech that lies at the heart of democratic choice. The Jeffersonian Republican newspaper, *Aurora*, denounced the prior restraint argument as "comical."[23] The democratic right to advocate reform of social institutions meant that protection of anti-slavery speech had to be more than a protection against prior restraint. This, indeed, was the position of Lincoln's Republican Party in the years immediately before the Civil War.

The sixth lesson is that private suppression of speech matters. Most guarantees of liberty in the United States Constitution are interpreted to limit only government action, not private action. Still, private suppression of free speech on matters of public concern by mobs and vigilantes is an attack on the liberties of free expression enshrined in the Bill of Rights. Though the issue is tricky, the lesson is clear: "censorship" by "private" actors can be a grave threat to freedom of expression. In early free speech history, discussion was most often aimed at protecting speech and press from government suppression. From the 1830s to the Civil War, however, at least as much energy was expended defending freedom of expression against threats from mobs and vigilantes. In either case, if you listen with care to these voices from long ago, they convey another message as well: the importance of multiple perspectives.

In free speech struggles from the Sedition Act through the Civil War, advocates of broad protection for freedom of expression looked not to the musty precedents of the English common law, but instead to how free speech rules needed to function in order to support democracy. Recognition of the relation of free expression to representative government has a long and rich history. A review of the historic commitment to freedom of expression as essential to democracy shows the close relation between the two. It also reveals why freedom of expression was considered so crucial to democracy. A review of the historic understanding of the function of freedom of expression may help us as we seek to translate eighteenth and nineteenth century guarantees into our twenty-first century world.[24]

[23] *Id.* at 75.

[24] *West Virginia State Board of Education v. Barnette*, 319 U.S. 624, 639 (1943): "True, the task of translating the majestic generalities of the Bill of Rights, conceived as part of the pattern of liberal government in the eighteenth century, into concrete restraints on officials dealing with the problems of the twentieth century, is one to disturb self-confidence." Lawrence Lessig, *Code and Other Laws of Cyberspace* (New York: Basic Books, 1999), 109–21 (hereafter, Lessig, *Code*).

III. The Historic Commitment to Free Speech, Free Press, and Representative Government: A Quick Overview

A. Historical defense of freedom of expression

The Levellers were the first mass-based, pro-democracy movement in English history. They were a group of seventeenth century English people who favored a written constitution with limits on governmental power, broad religious toleration, and Parliament elected by substantially broadened male suffrage from districts of roughly equal population. In one of their many pamphlets, the Levellers said censorship was an instrument of tyranny, for people "kept ignorant" were "fitted only to serve the unjust ends of Tyrants and Oppressers."[25] Freedom of the press was necessary to preserve "any nation from the worst . . . bondage." As a result, both for the government and the people, "it will be good, if not absolutely necessary . . . to hear all voices and judgments, which they can never do, but by giving freedom to the Press." Scandalous pamphlets about the government could be answered by counterspeech.[26] Though the Levellers were suppressed, similar and more elaborate ideas about freedom of expression continued to emerge. *Cato's Letters* are a prime example.

The *Letters* were a series of essays on civil and religious liberty first printed in England in the eighteenth century. The *Letters*, which were widely reprinted in America before and after the Revolution, also emphasized the connection between free speech and press and representative government. Since those who administered government were "but . . . trustees" doing the business of the people, it was in the interest of the people to see whether "public Matters" were "well or ill transacted." For this, free speech was essential.[27] In its "Address to the Inhabitants of Quebec" during the American Revolution, the Continental Congress expressed similar sentiments.

Critics of the Sedition Act of 1798 produced a strong defense of freedom of expression as central to democracy. As we have seen, the act was written and deployed to punish "false" opinions about President John Adams and the Federalist-controlled Congress. But it did not punish "false" statements about Republican Vice President Thomas Jefferson. Republican critics of the Sedition Act emphasized the relation of free speech and press to elective government. People had no means of examining the conduct of their elected officials except through the press and free speech. The "unrestrained investigation" by the press of the "conduct of the government" was essential; it was "the heart and soul of a free

[25] Richard Overton, *To . . . The Commons of England* (1649), in Don M. Wolfe, ed., *Leveller Manifestoes of the Puritan Revolution* (New York: T. Nelson and Sons, 1944; New York: Humanities Press, 1967), 327–28.

[26] *Id.* at 328.

[27] John Trenchard and Thomas Gordon, *Cato's Letters: Essays on Liberty, Civil and Religious*, No. 15 (New York: Da Capo Press, 1971) 1:96–98. See also No. 32, 1:246–54, and 2:42–43.

government." Restrictions on press freedom of the sort imposed by the Sedition Act would "destroy the elective principle" because the chilling effect of the Act would suppress all criticism.[28] For Republicans, one of the vices of the Sedition Act was that it silenced only one point of view in the political debate. Praise of President Adams was allowed. Criticism was silenced.

Strong defenses of freedom of expression as crucial to democracy also emerged, as we have seen, in the 1830s during controversies over slavery and anti-slavery expression. In 1836, Whig Senator John Davis of Massachusetts described the function of the press. Davis spoke in opposition to a bill sponsored by Senator John C. Calhoun that would have required the Post Office to censor publications touching on the subject of slavery when mailed to a slave state that forbade the expression. Davis declared:

> The press is the great organ of a free people. It is the medium through which their thoughts are communicated, through which they act upon one another, and by which they reason with, instruct, and move each other. It rouses us to vigilance, warns us of danger, rebukes the aspiring, encourages the modest, and, like the sun in the heavens, radiates its influence over the whole country. The people viewed it as vital to a republic, and gave it the mail as an auxiliary; and you might as well expect the blood to flow through the system without the heart, as to have the press exert its influence in a salutary manner through the country without the aid of the mail.[29]

Davis said that the reasons supporting this incendiary publication bill were the same ones always given for abridging the liberty of the press, that is, because the press

> sends forth incendiary, inflammable publications, disturbing the public peace, and corrupting the public mind. All censorships are established under the plausible pretense of arresting evils. . . . Great principles fundamental in their character, are thus assailed on proof of abuses which no doubt at all times exist; and when once, through such pretenses, a breach is made, the citadel falls.[30]

For this reason the Constitution prohibited abridging the liberty of the press "come what might."[31]

[28] Curtis, *Free Speech, supra* note 6, at 68–69 (quoting Congressman Nicholas); 94–96 (quoting James Madison).
[29] *Register of Debates* (Washington, DC: Library of Congress, 1999), 24th Cong., 1st sess. (1835–36), Senate, at 1152; available online at http://memory.loc.gov/ammem/amlaw/lwrdlink.html#anchor24 [accessed November 20, 2003].
[30] *Id.* at 1153.
[31] *Id.*

The *Boston Daily Advocate* discussed the function of free speech in an 1838 editorial condemning the killing of Elijah Lovejoy by an anti-abolition mob:

> We are advocates of the freedom of discussion in the broadest sense. Were it otherwise we could not call ourselves democrats. Democracy is a principle which recognizes mind as superior to matter, and moral and mental power over wealth or physical force. . . . Democracy is also a principle of reform; consequently, it must examine, compare, and analyze, and how can it do this without freedom of inquiry and discussion. . . .
>
> To argue that there are subjects, which ought not to be discussed, in consequence of their unpopularity with a majority of the people, is in reality to argue that the people are not capable of self-government; and the power of deciding what shall not be discussed, ought to be invested in a censorship. . . .[32]

While freedom of discussion might not produce truth, "it is reasonable," the editorial continued, "to suppose that a nearer approach to it will be made" than under a system of suppression.[33] In popular understanding, as the controversy over anti-slavery speech shows, subjects protected by free speech included harsh criticism of powerful private interests—in this case the "slave power"—that shaped public policy.

There were also trans-Atlantic influences on the development of American free speech doctrine. In 1859, the English philosopher John Stuart Mill emphasized the need to protect minority opinion, because without considering a full range of views we are unlikely to come to wise decisions. Wise decisions, he suggested, require hearing all sides.[34] Though Mill wrote well after the ratification of the First Amendment in 1791, his and similar ideas are part of the background for the Fourteenth Amendment. (The First Amendment limited only the federal government. The Fourteenth Amendment extended the protections for freedom of expression to the states, a fact the Supreme Court belatedly "assume[d]" in the 1925 case *Gitlow v. New York*.)

These ideas about the relation of free speech to democratic government, announced long ago, were echoed in twentieth century Supreme Court opinions. As noted above, the Supreme Court has emphasized the importance of free speech and diverse perspectives for democratic decision-making.

[32] "Freedom of Discussion," *Boston Daily Advocate*, January 3, 1838, at 2.

[33] *Id.* A line has been dropped from the copy of the paper I have examined, but I think this is the intended meaning.

[34] See John Stuart Mill, *On Liberty and Other Essays* (1859), reprinted in John Stuart Mill, *On Liberty and Other Essays*, John Gray, ed. (Oxford: Oxford World's Classics, 1991), 19–49.

As both the historic tradition and more modern expressions of it show, government suppression is problematic because it interferes with the democratic function of freedom of expression. In defending free speech and press as essential to democratic choice, the Court has assumed that freedom of expression provides citizens with a better basis for informed choice than a regime of suppression or of authoritative selection *and* that informed choice requires access to different perspectives and alternatives. Thus, suppression of minority points of view or enforcement of an orthodoxy is antidemocratic. As the twentieth century philosopher Friedrich Hayek noted, one should not confuse what the law is and what the law ought to be:

> Majority decisions tell us what people want at the moment, but not what it would be in their interest to want if they were better informed; and unless [majority decisions] could be changed by persuasion, they would be of no value. The argument for democracy presupposes that any minority opinion may become a majority one.[35]

To be sure, the historic emphasis on the need for broad freedom of expression never went unchallenged. In England, Parliament suppressed the Levellers; in the United States, as we have seen, attempts at suppression ranged from the Sedition Act to the harassment and jailing of abolitionists. Additional examples of suppression are not difficult to find: One of Lincoln's generals jailed a Northern Democratic politician for making an antiwar speech. After the end of Reconstruction in the South, both democracy and free speech were effectively suppressed for a substantial part of the population. When, in the 1960s, blacks in the deep South began demanding the right to vote, civil rights activists were shot, bombed, burned out of their homes and churches, and beaten. They were also arrested for peaceful protests that should have been protected by the guarantees of the First and Fourteenth Amendments.[36] Other twentieth century examples of suppression include the jailing of Eugene Debs for an antiwar speech during World War I[37] and the barring of Julian Bond from the Georgia Legislature for endorsing an antiwar circular during the Vietnam War—an effort that the Supreme Court held violated the First and Fourteenth Amendments.[38]

Of course, commitment to democracy has not been uniform throughout American history either. From early times, some Americans worried about

[35] Friedrich A. von Hayek, *The Constitution of Liberty* (Chicago, IL: University of Chicago Press, 1960), 109. See also *American Booksellers Association v. Hudnut*, 771 F.2d 323, 332 (7th Cir. 1985) ("Free speech has been on balance an ally of those seeking change").

[36] The story is well told in Taylor Branch, *Pillar of Fire: America in the King Years, 1963–65* (New York: Simon and Schuster, 1999).

[37] *Debs v. United States*, 249 U.S. 211 (1919).

[38] *Bond v. Floyd*, 385 U.S. 116 (1966).

economic "levelling" and responded to the worry by favoring property qualifications to limit the right to vote. During Reconstruction (1865–77), Ku Klux Klan terrorism destroyed the Republican Party in the South as an effective force and contracted the electorate by preventing blacks from voting. Later, similar tactics were aimed at Populists. After Reconstruction, certain influential Northern intellectuals accepted Southern disfranchisement of blacks, rejected universal male suffrage, and considered restricting the vote for some white Northern men as well. During the Great Depression, the Republican chair of the Board of Elections in Lewiston, Maine, attempted to disfranchise relief recipients as ineligible paupers, a move that would have disfranchised one thousand people in that town alone.[39] When blacks sought to register and vote in the deep South in the 1960s, they were attacked by Klan terrorists and blocked by elected officials. While actual practice often has been inconsistent in American history, democracy and a functional view of free press and free speech have been vibrant American ideals, now accepted by most Americans.

B. The environment of freedom of expression: 1830–1868

To be more nearly complete, free speech history should examine the role of the larger environment in nurturing or hindering free speech and press. I will now look at the free speech environment, particularly in the years 1830–1868.[40] These were the years leading up to the Civil War, Reconstruction, and the ratification of the Fourteenth Amendment. My focus will be on the nature of the mass communication environment and how it interacted with the democratic goals of a system of freedom of expression.

The past is not a free speech golden age, as the killing of Elijah Lovejoy and the suppression of anti-slavery speech in the pre-Civil War South show. Adherence to the ideal of freedom of expression has often had its shortcomings, and no doubt always will. Yet, the free speech environment of the past embodied some positive values that are being lost in the modern world.

The era I have studied most closely runs from the 1830s through the Civil War, which ended in 1865, three years before the adoption of the Fourteenth Amendment. During that time the mass media consisted mainly of newspapers, books, pamphlets, and public meetings. There were numerous periodicals, mostly separately owned. Publishing for a mass mar-

[39] E.g., Alexander Keyssar, *The Right to Vote: The Contested History of Democracy in the United States* (New York: Basic Books, 2000), 105–16, 119–63, 238–39.

[40] For a brief discussion of the role of the press in American history, see Patrick M. Garry, *Scrambling for Protection: The New Media and the First Amendment* (Pittsburgh, PA: University of Pittsburgh Press 1994), 97–106, 128–32.

ket was decentralized, and the press carried on a lively dialogue on political issues and candidates.

William Seward, a Whig and later Republican politician, governor of New York, United States Senator, and Lincoln's Secretary of State, marveled at the development of the press. In his 1853 *Notes on New York*, Seward commented on the technological innovations of new labor-saving machinery and stereotype foundries that had made publishing so much more efficient.[41] Books and newspapers, fiction and nonfiction, proliferated. The political press was, he said, "divided between contending parties," and subdivided further based on the "tempers and the tastes, the passions and the prejudices of the community." It conducted "political warfare" with "energy, zeal, and . . . unsparing severity."[42] Still, Seward had a sanguine view of the press:

> The press studies carefully the condition of all classes, and yields its reports with such a nice adaptation of prices as to leave no portion of the community without information [on] all that can . . . concern their welfare. . . . It . . . not unfrequently forms the public opinion which controls everything. Yet the press is not despotic. Its divisions distract its conduct, and prevent a concentration of its powers upon any one object. [T]he newspaper press is capricious and often licentious. . . ; yet if it assails, it arms the party assaulted with equal weapons of defence and yields redress for the injuries it inflicts. . . . Every improvement of the public morals, and every advance of the people in knowledge, is marked by a corresponding elevation of the moral and intellectual standard of the press; and it is at once the chief agent of intellectual improvement and the palladium of civil and religious liberty.[43]

Another commentator on the press, Frederick Grimke, was born in Charleston, South Carolina and trained in the law. He was the brother of Sarah and Angelina Grimke, who became famous abolitionists and advocates of women's rights. After practicing law in South Carolina, Frederick Grimke migrated to Ohio where he served first as a trial judge and later on the Ohio Supreme Court. He wrote about the press in the 1856 edition of his book, *Considerations upon the Nature and Tendency of Free Institutions*. For Grimke, the press was "the organ of public opinion," and it distributed knowledge and a common sympathy among the great mass of the population.[44] "[F]reedom of the press was to knowledge what the abolition of primogeniture was to property: the one diffuses knowledge as the

[41] William Seward, *Notes on New York*, in vol. 2 of *The Works of William H. Seward*, George E. Baker, ed. (New York: Redfield, 1853), 37.

[42] *Id.* at 37.

[43] *Id.* at 38.

[44] Frederick Grimke, *The Nature and Tendency of Free Institutions* (1848), John William Ward, ed., (Cambridge, MA: Harvard University Press, 1968), 396.

other diffuses property."[45] "If the press were extinguished, the great principle on which representative government hinges, the responsibility of public agents to the people, would be lost. . . ."[46]

Grimke saw the crucial democratic function of the press in terms of political power. The power of opinions depended on their "intrinsic value" and on "the publicity which they acquire."[47] The principal political function performed by the press was to "equalize power throughout all parts of the community."[48] The press was "an extension or amplification of the principles of representation. It reflects the opinions of all classes as completely as do the deputies of the people."[49]

Grimke had faith in the ability of the great mass of mankind to acquire knowledge "when it is communicated in detail."[50] Indeed, as Grimke saw it, much improvement in society had come from "the sagacious and inquisitive spirit of very obscure men in the inferior walks of life."[51] "The freedom of religion, of suffrage, and of the press . . . was brought about by the very reasonable complaints of men who occupied an inferior position in society."[52] In the United States, the press was "emphatically the organ of popular opinion." But "the power of the press is broken up into small fragments. . . ."[53]

Grimke had a realistic view of the function of government censorship in human history. It was "applied to restrain one class of publications only. No one ever heard in a monarchical or aristocratical government of any attempt to forbid the circulation of writings which were calculated to increase the influence of the prince and nobility. The utmost indulgence is extended to them. . . ." Still, the licentiousness of the press was a problem, but not one to be solved by government regulation. Instead, abuse of press power was to be controlled by the structure of the press:

> There is but one way of remedying the defect and that is by causing the press itself to perform the office of censor; in other words, to grant such absolute freedom to all the political journals that each shall be active and interested in detecting the misrepresentations . . . of the others. There is real and formidable censorship of the press in America, but the institution is in and not out of the press. . . . [T]he efforts of all parties are most vehement and untiring, and yet more harmless and pacific than in any other country.[54]

[45] *Id.* at 396.
[46] *Id.* at 397.
[47] *Id.*
[48] *Id.*
[49] *Id.* at 399.
[50] *Id.* at 400.
[51] *Id.*
[52] *Id.* at 401.
[53] *Id.*
[54] *Id.* at 403.

Thomas M. Cooley, a Chief Justice of the Michigan Supreme Court, wrote a famous treatise on constitutional law. His appreciation for the importance of a free press in a democracy was as keen as Grimke's. In his 1868 book, *A Treatise on the Constitutional Limitations Which Rest upon the Legislative Power of the States,* he ranked the newspaper among the inventions of modern times that had powerfully influenced and advanced civilization. Newspapers brought the debates of leading legislative bodies, the events of war, the triumphs of peace, and many other subjects to "the knowledge of every reading person."[55]

The press made the actions and words of public men "public property."[56] Cooley noted the importance of the press in reporting matters of public and commercial concern. "The public demand and expect accounts of every important meeting, of every important trial, and of all the events which have a bearing upon trade ... or upon political affairs."[57] The power of the press was great, but its power was dispersed. "Every party has its newspaper organs; every shade of opinion on political, religious, literary, moral [and other] questions has its representative; every locality has its press to advocate its claims."[58] It was "one of the chief means for the education of the people" and on politics it was their "chief educator."[59] As he praised the press and remarked on its power and importance, Cooley also noted, paradoxically, that the law was not strongly protective.[60]

The decentralized nature of the press helped to defeat a censorship proposal made in the mid-1830s. As noted in subsection III A, in the 1830s, Congress debated a bill to censor abolitionist publications aimed at the South. Senator John C. Calhoun had proposed a bill to prohibit postmasters from mailing any publication touching on the subject of slavery to a state whose laws prohibited the expression. The bill would have required postmasters to examine each newspaper, magazine, and pamphlet and compare its contents to the laws of the Southern state to which it was directed.[61] Senator John Milton Niles of Connecticut noted that more than fifty periodicals were issued from New York City alone. Many were published daily and contained items taken from other papers. "[E]ach paper must be carefully examined in its entire contents, to see if it contains anything touching the subject of slavery. This would be utterly impracticable."[62]

[55] Thomas M. Cooley, *A Treatise on the Constitutional Limitations Which Rest upon the Legislative Power of the States of the American Union* (Boston, MA: Little, Brown and Co., 1868), 451.

[56] *Id.*

[57] *Id.* at 454.

[58] *Id.* at 452.

[59] *Id.*

[60] *Id.* at 455–56.

[61] Curtis, *Free Speech, supra* note 6, at 162–63.

[62] *Id.* at 173.

Seward, Grimke, and Cooley shared some common assumptions. For each, the press was crucial to the functioning of democracy. Each emphasized the connection between freedom of expression and representative government. "The people" needed detailed information about public questions in order to perform their democratic function, and these writers thought that the press supplied it. Crucially, the press as a whole provided a wide range of points of view, and ownership was decentralized and dispersed among various political and other factions. A "checking function" is essential to a free press, but the checking function envisioned by these thinkers went beyond merely checking abuses of government power. They also saw that the dispersed and decentralized nature of the press would check abuses of press power, a power which they recognized to be potentially great.

Past supporters of broad protection for free speech and press emphasized or assumed a press environment that fostered democratic ideals. The environment included dispersed ownership, politicians and political parties that had substantial access to the press, and a press that purveyed diverse points of view.

I have spent a good amount of time in the past twenty years or so reading old newspapers from the 1830s through the Civil War. In contrast to our times, there was a great profusion of newspapers, often quite a number in each major city. Ownership was dispersed. Many papers were overtly partisan. Partisanship had advantages as well as drawbacks for democracy. Major parties and their candidates had substantial direct access to the mass media because newspapers typically and strongly supported one party or the other.

Newspapers presented very detailed information on major public controversies, often extensively reprinting debates in Congress. Most reprinted stories and editorials from other papers, sometimes for purposes of criticism. A few gave both sides considerable space. Abolitionist papers often reprinted pro-slavery arguments, in part because their editors were convinced that these arguments would aid the anti-slavery cause. While partisan newspapers generally did not reprint campaign speeches from leaders of the opposing party, they did give detailed accounts of the speeches of members of their own parties. In exceptional cases, such as the Lincoln-Douglas debates, speeches of both sides were presented and reported with reasonable accuracy.[63]

Consider the following example: in the summer of 1866, a major issue was whether the Fourteenth Amendment should be ratified by the states. The amendment contained new limits on the states in order to protect civil liberties, and it did not allow Southern states to count disfranchised black males for purposes of representation in Congress or the electoral

[63] Paul M. Angle, ed., *Created Equal: The Complete Lincoln-Douglas Debates of 1858* (Chicago, IL: University of Chicago Press, 1985), xxv.

college. Page one of the *Cincinnati Commercial* for August 17, 1866, reported a speech by Congressman John A. Bingham of Ohio under the headline, "The Constitutional Amendment—Discussed by Its Author." The report covered virtually the entire front page.

Though newspapers typically had political allegiances, the dispersion of ownership produced diversity, even among papers affiliated with the same political party. In the mid-1830s, the Democratic *New York Post* strongly condemned efforts by government officials, legislators, or mobs to silence abolitionists, while the Democratic *Washington Globe* chortled gleefully at efforts to shut them up. Groups that at first had difficulty getting a hearing in the partisan press, such as the abolitionists, founded their own newspapers.

The major shortcoming of these nineteenth century papers was lack of balance within each paper, while the major virtue was that they provided an avenue through which politicians could directly and fully address their constituents. The newspapers also afforded a forum where citizens could express their views.

The press was one way to reach a mass audience. Another was public meetings. Speakers needed the ability to draw a crowd, but costs were minimal: the location could be a tree stump or a simple platform, and the largest cost might be advertisements for the meeting. With few other sources of entertainment, a speech on politics or the law could draw a crowd. Books and pamphlets offered another way to reach a large audience. Books such as the anti-slavery novel *Uncle Tom's Cabin* (1851) and Helper's *The Impending Crisis of the South: How to Meet It* (1857) became best sellers. Both helped to focus national attention on slavery in the South. Political leaders could and did get their messages out to the party faithful and the larger public through the mass media of newspapers, speeches, books, and pamphlets.

IV. The Paradox

Most of us think of speech-protective Supreme Court decisions as crucial. There is no doubt that protective decisions play a very important role in America's system of freedom of expression. The decision in *New York Times v. Sullivan* (1964)[64] stopped the effort to punish the national press for the way it reported the integration struggle in the South. More recently, the Supreme Court's decision in the "Pentagon papers" case (1971)[65] kept the government from banning publication of the "papers." (The federal government had sought an injunction to prevent the *New York*

[64] 376 U.S. 254 (1964). See generally, Anthony Lewis, *Make No Law: The Sullivan Case and the First Amendment* (New York: Random House, 1991), on the effort to silence press reports on the struggle of the Civil Rights movement in the South.
[65] *New York Times Co. v. United States*, 403 U.S. 713 (1971).

Times and *Washington Post* from publishing the contents of a classified study, entitled "History of U.S. Decision-Making Process on Viet Nam Policy.") As a result of the Court's decision, the public got to read a secret Defense Department discussion of the major public policy issue of the day: the war in Vietnam. In spite of the crucial role played by the Supreme Court in these and other landmark cases, the judiciary's role in the history of freedom of expression in America is somewhat paradoxical.

Briefly, here is the paradox I see. Free speech triumphed in the North before the Civil War without strong protection from the judiciary. At the same time, free speech was suppressed in the South even though some Southern courts seemed less than enthusiastic. Judicial doctrine is important, but it is only one factor shaping the system of freedom of expression. The experience from the end of the American Revolution to the end of Reconstruction after the Civil War suggests that whether freedom of expression thrives or withers depends on a number of factors in the social, political, and economic environment. Protective court decisions are only one factor.

There is an ecology of freedom of expression. The environment can protect and foster freedom of expression even in the face of judicial doctrines that support suppression and punish ideas with "bad tendencies." If this is so, then the converse is probably also true: changes in the environment can undermine effective freedom of expression, even if judicial doctrine broadly protects from punishment by government those who criticize dominant social, political, and economic orthodoxies. Today, judicial doctrine protects dissenters from being punished because of the content of their expression, but finding a place to speak in the incredible shrinking public forum is a different matter, as the cases show. For example, the Court has held that the interior sidewalk surrounding a post office building is not a public forum. Nor are advertising slots on city buses.[66] Structural changes beyond Court decisions have an impact on the free speech environment and can undermine effective freedom of expression.

V. From the Past to the Present

A. Characteristics of today's mass media

In the United States today, the mass media is, of course, far different from that of the nineteenth century. Although the differences are numer-

[66] E.g., *United States v. Kokinda*, 497 U.S. 720 (1990) (upheld arrests and jail time for sale of political literature on sidewalk outside a United States Post Office); *Lehman v. Shaker Heights*, 418 U.S. 298 (1974) (ban upheld on all political ads in the advertising slots provided in city buses); *Amalgamated Food Employees Union Local 590 v. Logan Valley Plaza*, 391 U.S. 308 (1968) (public forum recognized in common areas of shopping center), limited by *Lloyd Corp. v. Tanner*, 407 U.S. 551 (1972) and overruled in *Hudgens v. NLRB*, 424 U.S. 507 (1976). But see, e.g., *Watchtower Bible and Tract Society of New York v. Village of Stratton*, 536 U.S. 150 (2002) (striking down requirement of a permit for door-to-door citizen activity).

ous, I will discuss only the four most striking dissimilarities. First, there is so much more media today: movies, videos, DVDs, a dizzying array of television channels, radio, the Internet, etc. Few of us would be willing to return to the monochromatic media of the nineteenth century, whatever its virtues. Second, the mass media today is dominated by television. Americans spend a huge amount of time watching television. In 1999, the television set was in use for 7 hours and 24 minutes per day in the average household.[67] Women from age twenty-five to fifty-five spent over 30 hours per week viewing television; men in the same age group spent over 27 hours per week.[68] For women older than fifty-five the figure jumped to more than 41 hours per week, and for men older than fifty-five, to more than 36 hours per week.[69] A significant number of Americans get their political news only from television and even more get most of their news there.[70] Radio is the second major source of information.

Third, below the apparent diversity of the modern mass media is an ever growing corporate centralization. The media world of the first decade of the twenty-first century is consolidated and centralized to a degree unimaginable in the nineteenth century. Most Americans get the vast majority of their political information from a few mass media outlets owned by a few major corporations.[71] It is true, of course, that information is now much more widely disseminated than in the nineteenth century, and with television and radio, it is available even to the illiterate. Depending on the quality of the information, this could be positive or negative.

Concentrated media control can be used for deleterious purposes and is prone to manipulation. By his control of most of Yugoslavia's television, then-President Slobodan Milosevic was able to control public opinion by pervasive propaganda. By his control of a "private" television empire, Silvio Berlusconi, the Prime Minister of Italy, can be assured of favorable

[67] See Nielsen Media Research, *2000 Report on Television* (2000), 14, as cited in Michael Kent Curtis, "The Constitution and the Other Constitution," *William and Mary Bill of Rights Journal* 10 (2002): 359, 366 (hereafter, Curtis, "The Other Constitution").

[68] See *id.*

[69] See *id.*

[70] In 1992, 41 percent of Americans got their news exclusively from television and 80 percent got most of their news there. Reed Hundt, "The Public's Airwaves: What Does the Public Interest Require of Television Broadcasters?" *Duke Law Journal* 45 (1996): 1089, 1102 (citing Thomas B. Rosentiel, "Survey: Public Prefers Tyson to Politics," *Los Angeles Times*, March 5, 1992, A13). As of 2000, one in three Americans got some of their news online: "Internet Sapping Broadcast News Audience," http://people-press.org/reports/display.php3?PageID=202 [accessed July 11, 2003]. About 40 percent of the 33 percent who are online news consumers go to the Internet for political news: http://people-press.org/reports/display.php3?PageID=204 [accessed July 11, 2003]. Curtis, "The Other Constitution," *supra* note 67, at 366 n.34.

[71] Material in the preceding paragraph on television viewing and material that follows on conflicts of interest also appear in slightly earlier form in Curtis, "The Other Constitution," *supra* note 67, at 365–68. See also Michael Kent Curtis, "Judicial Review and Populism," *Wake Forest Law Review* (2003): 313, 330.

news coverage on at least half of Italy's television stations.[72] His influence over Italian public television has made his control nearly universal. Concentrated media power can be abused, and this is true even when the power is "private."

Consider the media world of 1999, as described by columnist Molly Ivins:

> At the end of World War II, 80 percent of American newspapers were independently owned. When Ben Haig Bagdikian published "Media Monopoly" (Beacon Press) in 1982, 50 corporations owned almost all of the major media outlets in the United States. That included 1,787 daily newspapers, 11,000 magazines, 9,000 radio stations, 1,000 television stations, 2,500 book publishers and seven major movie studios. By the time Bagdikian put out the revised edition in 1987, the number was down to 29 corporations. And now there are nine. They own it all.[73]

Since 1999 consolidation has proceeded apace. Ivins' description ignored university presses, but it is an accurate picture of the major mass media as of the time she wrote.

The Federal Communications Commission, the courts, and Congress have all done their part in recent years to contribute to the consolidated corporate media world and to undermine guaranteed access for diverse points of view, for example by removing barriers to media consolidation, repealing the Fairness Doctrine (which required some air time for opposing points of view), and imposing legal barriers on legislative efforts to protect or promote diversity. (As of this writing it seems as though Congress, for the first time in recent years, may overrule the FCC's decision to allow greater consolidation of media holdings.) Government actions removing barriers to consolidation, together with other factors, have pro-

[72] See generally, PBS, *Wide Angle*, "Media by Milosevic," at http://www.pbs.org/wnet/wideangle/shows/yugoslavia/index.html [accessed November 20, 2003]. Consider the following news story discussing Italian press coverage of Berlusconi's comparison of a German Social Democratic delegate to the European Parliament to a concentration camp guard:

> [T]he reaction of the Italian media to his comments was almost a test case of the extent of his unhealthy domination of that industry. *Il Foglio* headlined its leading article: "Premeditated Aggression: A Just Reply". It is owned by his wife. *Il Giornale* accused the Germans and French of a plot against Italy. It is owned by his brother. The main news on the state television channels played down the story—they are not directly controlled by Mr. Berlusconi but are part of a web of political patronage. The prime minister also owns the three main private television channels, one of which did not even report Mr Berlusconi's words.

"Mr. Berlusconi's 'Joke' Exposes the Democratic Flaw at the Heart of the EU," *The Independent*, July 4, 2003.

[73] Molly Ivins, "Three New Books Offer Suggestions for Fixing the Media Mess," *Charleston Gazette*, November 2, 1999, A-4. See Curtis, "The Other Constitution," *supra* note 67, at 365.

duced both a much more consolidated electronic media and one far freer from requirements for viewpoint diversity.

Fourth, compared to the press of the nineteenth century, commercial television devotes a tiny amount of news time to serious discussion of candidates' views and policy issues. As one observer noted, "two elections ago [in 1998], the three networks together gave you about 25 minutes a night of election news, or about eight minutes apiece. This [2000] election they gave you about 12 minutes, or four minutes apiece per night."[74] But even this reduced amount was news of a special type. The Annenberg Public Policy Center found that only an average of 64 seconds per night was quality, "candidate-centered" time during which the candidates themselves had an opportunity to discuss their views on issues. The rest was "heavily filtered reporting about the suspense of who might win the horse race. . . ."[75] Of course, C-SPAN and some other cable networks provide more candidate time, but even this time can be degraded by journalists. In a December 2003 televised "debate" among Democratic candidates in New Hampshire, an event moderated by ABC's Ted Koppel, during the first forty-five minutes the journalist did not ask a single question devoted to public policy issues. All questions focused on Al Gore's endorsement of a candidate, on polls, candidate fundraising, and so forth.

Journalists typically frame campaigns as strategic games of people struggling for power. Policy issues and debates become noteworthy not in themselves but at most as moves in a strategic game.[76] Of course, the "horse race" is a part, but only part, of what is going on.

In 1968, the average presidential campaign sound bite on network news was 43 seconds. In the 1996 election, it dropped to 8.2 seconds.[77] Journalists spoke six minutes for every minute George Bush or Al Gore spoke on the evening news in the 2000 campaign.[78] An Annenberg study found that only one in four campaign stories aired in the month before the election was issue-oriented; the rest focused on the bumps and dips of polls and campaign strategy.[79] Journalists talking about the election accounted for 74 percent of the news airtime. Candidates actually shown speaking accounted for 11 percent. Sixteen of nineteen top-rated TV stations in the top eleven markets broadcast, on average, only 39 seconds a night about political campaigns, while top stations in Philadelphia and Tampa averaged 6 seconds a night.[80]

[74] Steven Hill, *Fixing Elections: The Failure of America's Winner Take All Politics* (New York: Routledge, 2002), 189.

[75] *Id.* at 190.

[76] Thomas E. Patterson, *The Vanishing Voter: Public Involvement in an Age of Uncertainty* (New York: Knopf, 2002), 69

[77] Hill, *Fixing Elections,* 190. Compare, Patterson, *The Vanishing Voter,* 68.

[78] Patterson, *The Vanishing Voter,* 68.

[79] Hill, *Fixing Elections,* 190.

[80] See Charles Lewis, "Media Money: How Corporate Spending Blocked Political-Ad Reform, and Other Stories of Influence," *Columbia Journalism Review* (Sept./Oct. 2000): 20, 26;

However bad the situation is for candidates for president, coverage of other races is worse. There is very little day-to-day coverage, for example, of state politics and government. News reporting on state legislatures and almost all races for governor has virtually disappeared from much television news. The 2003 California recall, featuring a movie star as candidate for governor, was a rare exception. In the 1998 California gubernatorial race, local TV news on the subject was less than one third of one percent of possible news time—one tenth of what it had been in 1974.[81]

There are additional serious problems with today's mass media. First, broadcast and cable news coverage is often devoted to trivial issues. Trivial issues have always been aired, but based on my unscientific survey, the percentage of trivia in political discussion has grown dramatically compared to newspapers of the period from 1830 through the end of the Civil War. George W. Bush's arrest for drunk driving twenty-five years before the 2000 election got more election coverage than all foreign policy issues combined.[82] The problem has existed for some time. Examples of quite trivial news coverage include Gerald Ford's statement in a 1976 presidential debate suggesting that Poland was not a puppet state of the Soviet Union; Jimmy Carter's 1976 "lust in my heart" Playboy interview (in which he confessed to feelings for women other than his wife); and, of course, obsessive reporting of politicians' sexual adventures.[83]

After the first debate in the 2000 Presidential election, one network took footage from the debate and clipped out everything except Gore sighing or showing expressions of dismay. One after another, photos of Gore's expressions flashed across the screen. All context had been removed. The viewer did not hear or see the Bush statements that produced these reactions; the viewer did not hear or see what Gore had said, if anything, in response to statements that elicited these reactions. Then a group of journalists gravely discussed Gore's facial expressions in the debate. The episode is a metaphor for the current state of American television journalism, a journalism that drains substance from the discussion of politics and substitutes predictions about the horse race and critiques of style.

For the press at large, more than 50 percent of candidate gaffes got news coverage extended over at least two days compared with 15 percent of policy stories. Network news gave extended coverage to more than 65 percent of gaffes compared with 15 percent of policy issues.[84] News audiences took more notice of stories about gaffes and recalled them bet-

Robert W. McChesney, *Rich Media, Poor Democracy: Communication Politics in Dubious Times* (Urbana: University of Illinois Press, 1999), 263–64. Curtis, "The Other Constitution," *supra* note 67, at 370.

[81] McChesney, *Rich Media, Poor Democracy*, 263–64.

[82] Patterson, *The Vanishing Voter*, *supra* note 76, at 48.

[83] *Id.* at 55.

[84] *Id.* at 56.

ter,[85] but at least part of this effect can be attributed to the greater press attention that the gaffes received.

Gaffes (or alleged gaffes) and the evidence they supposedly provided that Gore was untrustworthy or Bush was ignorant and dumb were of major importance in the 2000 election.[86] Examples include Bush's "failure" of a pop quiz asking him to name leaders in various third world countries; Gore's statement that a schoolgirl "has" to stand for want of a desk and chair in her crowded science class when, in fact, she only "had" to stand for a time; and Gore's mistaken assertion that he had accompanied the Director of the Federal Emergency Management Agency to Texas in connection with forest fires. In fact, Gore had often accompanied the Director to scenes of disasters, but in this case he had been briefed by the Director's deputy.[87]

Obsessive and often inaccurate press accounts become received wisdom too rarely corrected by the press. The checking function that Grimke saw in the press of the nineteenth century seems not to be functioning well in the twenty-first.[88] As the number of outlets run by diverse owners shrinks, viewpoint diversity and critiques of press orthodoxies in the mass media also seem to shrink.

The second serious problem with today's mass media is that, because most candidates cannot hope to reach viewers and listeners through free news coverage, candidates must spend more and more money to buy television or radio time. As serious news coverage has declined, revenue spent on political advertising has increased. In 2000, television political ads produced an estimated $1 billion in revenue for broadcasters.[89] Revenue from political spots was up 40 percent from 1996 and, adjusted for inflation, amounted to a five-fold increase from the level of spending in 1980. Though they run only during a part of the year, political commercials were the third largest source of advertising revenue for broadcasters in 2000. Campaign coverage has decreased as ad revenue has increased.[90] (In the nineteenth century, in contrast, heavily partisan newspapers typically gave extensive, free coverage to the candidates of the party they supported.)

Critics charge that there is something amiss when stations, having received their broadcast licenses for free from government, turn around and sell access to their audiences to candidates for political office. Cable is a special case, but the dominance of existing cable companies was

[85] *Id.*

[86] For a detailed discussion of the effect of gaffes on each of these candidates, see Kathleen Hall Jamieson and Paul Waldman, *The Press Effect: Politicians, Journalists, and the Stories that Shape the Political World* (Oxford: Oxford University Press, 2003), 48–60.

[87] *Id.* at 55.

[88] See *id.* at 50–51; also Paul Waldman, "Gored by the Media Bull," *The American Prospect*, January 13, 2002, at 20.

[89] Hill, *Fixing Elections*, *supra* note 74, at 189.

[90] *Id.*

substantially advanced by monopolies granted to them by local governments. At any rate, the present system makes it ever more expensive for candidates to run for office, and it tends to undermine democracy, both by limiting who can run and the sort of appeal candidates can make, and by actually or apparently undermining the relationship of trust between public officials and voters. In three separate, recent polls, over three-fourths of the respondents agreed with the statement that "Congress is largely owned by the special interest groups," which "have too much influence," and "our present system of government is democratic in name only" because special interests run things.[91]

A third serious problem with the media is that coverage is even worse on issues of public policy that are not immediately connected with candidates for election. In 1998, when the tobacco industry decided to oppose the amended version of Senator John McCain's Universal Tobacco Settlement Act—which unlike an earlier version did not protect tobacco companies from tort suits—the industry spent $35 million on television ads attacking the bill.[92] Viewers were regaled with pictures of a cuckoo bird coming out of a clock, while an announcer solemnly intoned that it was cuckoo time in Washington—with the settlement likely to cause huge new taxes on working people and sixty new bureaucracies.[93]

Kathleen Hall Jamieson of the Annenberg School for Communication says that the ads lacked context and were misleading.[94] They did not explain, she points out, the purpose of the taxes or the use to which the money would be put. The charge of sixty new bureaucracies cited an apparently impartial source, yet in fact, the source was merely quoting from a speech made by a tobacco company executive.[95] By contrast, the American Cancer Society sponsored the only ad supporting the bill, which ran for a single week and reached a far smaller number of viewers. Both the *New York Times* and ABC News ran a single story pointing out inaccuracies in the tobacco industry ads. CNN, which aired most of the ads, did not run a single piece evaluating the accuracy of the tobacco companies' ads.[96] In spite of very strong early support, this version of the bill was defeated.

Citizens for Better Medicare spent $65 million in ads opposing an effort during the Clinton Administration to add a prescription drug benefit to

[91] E. Joshua Rosenkrantz, *Buckley Stops Here: Loosening the Judicial Stranglehold on Campaign Finance Reform* (New York: Century Foundation Press, 1998), 16; "What Americans Think," *Washington Post Weekly*, May 17, 1999, at 34. See also Daniel A. Farber and Phillip P. Frickey, *Law and Public Choice: A Critical Introduction* (Chicago, IL: University of Chicago Press, 1991), 12. Curtis, "The Other Constitution," *supra* note 67, at 359, 373.

[92] See *Bill Moyers: Free Speech for Sale*, PBS television broadcast, June 8, 1999, transcript by Burrelle's Information Service; Waldman, *The Press Effect*, *supra* note 86, at 9–12; and Curtis, "The Other Constitution," *supra* note 67, at 367–69.

[93] See all of the sources cited above in note 92.

[94] See *id.*

[95] See *id.*

[96] Waldman, *The Press Effect*, *supra* note 86, at 9.

Medicare.[97] In the ads, a woman named "Flo" warned viewers of the need to keep the government out of their medicine cabinets.[98] Under the law at that time, the ads did not need to tell viewers that Citizens for Better Medicare was created by the pharmaceutical industry.[99] The corporate owners of television did little or nothing to inform viewers on that score. The checking function of television journalism is hardly robust in such cases.

In initiative and referendum elections, poorly funded grassroots coalitions typically face well-financed, corporate-backed organizations. Often only one side gets a meaningful hearing in the electronic square, where advertising, especially on television, is expensive. The "debate" is closer to a monologue.

The fates of two recent Oregon ballot measures exemplify this disparity and the difficulty of overcoming the power of corporations to disseminate their preferred messages. Opponents of Oregon Measure 27, which would have required labeling of food containing genetically engineered material, spent $5.4 million to defeat the measure; its supporters spent barely $80,000. The measure failed in November 2002. The same year, insurance companies and their allies spent $1.3 million to defeat Oregon Measure 23, which would have extended health insurance coverage to all Oregonians and authorized tax increases to pay for the program. Supporters spent about $70,000.[100] This measure also failed.

In a 2002 California public power initiative, Pacific Gas and Electric (PG&E) spent $2.7 million in its successful effort to defeat the measure, compared to $50,000 spent by supporters. The initiative would have allowed the San Francisco Public Utilities Commission to provide power to all of San Francisco, rather than just its 30 percent share, and would have given it the prerogative to buy out PG&E's local distribution network. PG&E outspent the supporters of public power by a ratio of fifty to one. As a result, according to news reports, PG&E was able to "blanket the city in broadcast and print advertisements."[101]

A study of seventy-two ballot issues in California, Massachusetts, Michigan, and Oregon showed that the higher spending side won 76 percent

[97] See The Annenberg Public Policy Center of the University of Pennsylvania, Issue Ads @ APPC, http://appcpenn.org/issueads/citizens%20for%better%20medicare.htm [modified August 2000, accessed January 24, 2001]; as cited in Curtis, "The Other Constitution," *supra* note 67, at 368.

[98] See *id.*

[99] See *id.*

[100] Peter Wong, "Spending in Recent Election Broke Records," *Statesman Journal* (Salem, OR), December 6, 2002, 1C. See also Tim Christie, "Health Care Plan Gets Little Backing from Oregon Voters," *The Register Guard*, November 7, 2002; and James Mayer and Michelle Cole, "Oregon Voters Make Policy Choices at Polls," *The Oregonian*, November 6, 2002.

[101] Lance Williams, "Ethics Boss Raps Worker for Revealing PG&E Error," *San Francisco Chronicle*, January 10, 2002, A1; Chuck Finnie and Susan Sward, "PG&E Spends Big to Defeat Prop. D," *San Francisco Chronicle*, October 29, 2002, A1.

of the time. Lopsided spending is most effective in defeating proposals.[102] With the repeal of the Fairness Doctrine, which guaranteed some degree of balance, the disparity in the amount of television time each side can obtain has increased.

The fourth serious problem with today's media is conflicts of interest. The press has always had such conflicts, but media consolidation has aggravated the problem. The Walt Disney Corporation hopes to market its products in China's huge and lucrative market. The Chinese elite dislikes films and news stories critical of how China treats Tibet.[103] Will Chinese objections affect how Chinese rule in Tibet is portrayed in future films or in the news outlets owned by Disney? In some cases, Chinese market power has already distorted the news. Television and press baron Rupert Murdoch wants to expand his media products in the Chinese market, and he has been careful to avoid offending the Chinese government.[104] In 1994, his Star TV eliminated the BBC international news from its satellite service because Chinese authorities objected to some of its coverage on human rights issues, and in 1998 his publishing house broke a contract to publish a book by the last British governor of Hong Kong because he was critical of China's antidemocratic policies.[105] Fortunately, the author found another publisher.[106]

Many multinational corporations have substantial economic power that can affect press coverage. A number of magazines now allow advertisers to preview stories. In a 1977 article, the *Wall Street Journal* cited a letter from the Chrysler Corporation: "In an effort to avoid potential conflicts, it is required that Chrysler Corporation be alerted in advance of any and all editorial content that encompasses sexual, political, social issues or any editorial that might be construed as provocative or offensive." The *Journal* article suggested that business mergers have given advertisers far greater clout with publishers than they had in the past.[107]

[102] See Robyn R. Polashuk, "Protecting the Public Debate: The Validity of the Fairness Doctrine in Ballot Initiative Elections," *UCLA Law Review* 41 (1993): 391, 405 (citing Betty H. Zisk, *Money, Media, and the Grass Roots: State Ballot Issues and the Electoral Process* [Newbury Park, CA: Sage Publications, 1987], 93–95, 198–99).

[103] See Seth Faison, "Dalai Lama Movie Imperils Disney Future in China," *New York Times*, November 26, 1996, A1. Curtis, "The Other Constitution," *supra* note 67, at 366–68.

[104] See John Gittings, "Murdoch's Beijing Love-Fest," *The Guardian* (London), December 12, 1998, at 14. (Available online in LEXIS News Library, *The Guardian* [London file].) Cited in Curtis, "The Other Constitution," *supra* note 67, at 367.

[105] See *id.*

[106] See *id.* Murdoch denies that the decision was commercially motivated. C. Edwin Baker, *Media, Markets, and Democracy* (New York: Cambridge University Press, 2002), 195. In a world of ever-more concentrated media power in fewer and fewer hands, an admission that the decision was ideological would not be reassuring either.

[107] See G. Bruce Knecht, "Magazine Advertisers Demand Prior Notice of Offensive Articles," *Wall Street Journal*, April 30, 1997, at 1. Most of the specific issues reported in the article involve sexual matters. Magazines discussed in the article include *The New Yorker, Esquire,* and *People.* It seems likely that holders of such market power would be tempted to use it to

In a 2000 poll, some 26 percent of journalists admitted to engaging in self-censorship of news stories because of conflicts of interest involving their news organization, its parent company, advertisers, or friends of the boss.[108] Forty-one percent admitted to reshaping or softening stories.[109]

America's ever more consolidated media have other serious conflicts of interest. As we have seen, television and cable corporations reaped rich rewards from the tobacco company ads against the McCain Bill, while they did almost no critical (or other) reporting about this massive advertising campaign.[110] The problem is not that tobacco, insurance, utility, and drug companies can and do buy a lavish hearing for their preferred views. It is that the other side is often virtually absent from the televised "debate." The mass media is in the business of selling viewers to advertisers. An arrangement in which one side can afford to buy massive amounts of media time and viewer attention while the other cannot is, of course, not ideologically neutral. The United States has a regulatory system that favors the opulent over the poorly funded side of the debate.

Advertising is, of course, a major source of conflicts of interest between the fiduciary role of the press in a democracy and its role as a profit-seeking business. Advertisers can threaten to withdraw advertising from stations that carry stories critical of them. In addition, the pursuit of advertising revenue may tilt news coverage toward subjects and perspectives most likely to generate viewers in advertisers' target audiences.[111]

The fifth problem with the media, especially the broadcast media, is the failure to perform their checking function. A version of 'Gresham's law' may be at work, by which simple stories that are cheaper to produce and easier to state in a few seconds drive out more complex and expensive investigative stories. The Savings and Loan scandal of the 1980s is estimated to have cost U.S. taxpayers between $500 billion and $1 trillion. Professor C. Edwin Baker observes that, "The media . . . found that early reporting was simply too difficult or boring."[112] Welfare fraud, costing perhaps 1/500th as much, was better covered.[113] Similarly, even as crime was declining in the 1990s, reporting of crime stories increased.

B. *Censorship by the media*

The prohibitive cost of television time for the less well-funded side of public issues is a serious problem, as I noted above. Another related

protect themselves and their products from criticism. See also Curtis, "The Other Constitution," *supra* note 67, at 367.

[108] See Andrew Kohut, "Self Censorship: Counting the Ways," *Columbia Journalism Review* (May/June, 2000): 42–43; as cited in Curtis, "The Other Constitution," *supra* note 67, at 366.

[109] See *id.*

[110] See Curtis, "The Other Constitution," *supra* note 67, at 366.

[111] Baker, *Media, Markets and Democracy, supra* note 106, at 13–14.

[112] *Id.* at 196–97.

[113] *Id.*

problem is the power of media corporations simply to refuse to carry ads for dissenters, even when they are able to pay. For example, television executives would not permit the Media Foundation, a group opposed to the ethic of consumption, to purchase television time for its advertisements, a denial that is hardly surprising since the major purpose of television commercials is to promote precisely this ethic of consumption.[114]

Similarly, in 2003 a group called Win Without War, whose members include the National Council of Churches, attempted to place television ads opposing the war in Iraq. CNN, Fox, and NBC declined to sell airtime on their national networks. CNN explained that it did not accept "international advocacy ads on regions in conflict." An NBC spokesman, who confirmed the refusal of a local station to run the ad, said "[i]t pertained to a controversial issue which we prefer to handle in our news and public affairs programing." Officials at Fox did not respond to repeated calls from a journalist seeking their comment.[115]

Other antiwar groups experienced similar frustrations at the local level. The Princeton-based Coalition for Peace Action had planned to run six ads. Comcast had accepted $5,000 in payment for the ads and agreed to run them in the Washington, DC, area, where the peace activists hoped to get the attention of lawmakers. Before any of the ads were telecast, Comcast issued a statement saying that it rejected the ads because it could not substantiate some of the claims made in them. Reverend Robert Moore, a United Church of Christ minister who is executive director of the coalition, was surprised: "I was under the impression that we enjoy freedom of speech in this country."[116] Experts in constitutional law know, of course, that, with reference to the mass media, as journalist A. J. Liebling put it many years ago, "[F]reedom of the press is limited to those who own one." The Supreme Court, over only two dissenting votes in *Columbia Broadcasting System v. Democratic National Committee* (1973), found no free speech right to nondiscriminatory access to advertising on television.[117] The question is not simply whether the Court's decision, viewed in isolation, was correct. The question is the effect of the decision as part of a larger pattern of media practices.

Understandably, media corporations often do a poor job of reporting stories that involve claims that their own interests and lobbying activities conflict with the public interest. Examples include conflicts over the tele-

[114] *Affluenza*, PBS television broadcast, transcript (c) 1997, KCTS Assn. (*Affluenza* was a production of KCTS/Seattle and Oregon Public Broadcasting); cited in Curtis, "The Other Constitution," *supra* note 67, at 369.

[115] Alan Cooperman, "Bishop in Bush's Church in New Antiwar Ad," *Washington Post*, January 31, 2003, A18.

[116] Jeff Pillets, "Peace Ads Deemed Not Ready for Prime Time," *The Record* (Bergen County, NJ), January 29, 2003, A8.

[117] 412 U.S. 94 (1973); for dissents by Justices Brennan and Marshall, see *id*. at 118.

vision spectrum and high definition television, and demands for free time for political candidates.[118]

C. *The Internet*

Of course, the Internet has greatly democratized publishing. For the moment, anyone can be a publisher, just as anyone can be a speaker in the public forum. Reaching a mass audience or even a modest one, however, is a very different proposition. Most people still get most of their political information from television and, to a lesser degree, radio. Many of those who get political information from the Web get most of it from major media companies such as AOL–Time Warner, General Electric, News Corporation, Disney, and Viacom. Often the most heavily visited sites are ones that are publicized in the mass media. Still, the Internet has provided remarkable opportunities for outsiders to organize and to get their messages heard by others. For people today who share a commitment to a broad-based popular democracy, preservation of the democratic character of the Internet is a prime concern.

Corporate interests may be winning the battle to transform the Internet from a kind of public forum to something closer to a private shopping mall.[119] For those who champion some form of participatory democracy, who seek to come closer to the ideal of a government in which all have an equal voice, the prospect of effective corporate control of the "information superhighway" is distressing.

Initially, the Internet used telephone lines. The phone companies were obligated to operate their lines as common carriers. They had to open their lines to all and could not interfere with the message or decide who could send or receive it. Now the Internet is migrating to broadband, a much faster and more flexible system offered by local cable companies and by phone companies through digital subscriber lines (DSL). Eighty percent of U.S. households have access to these broadband systems, though so far only 10 percent of Internet users use these more expensive services. Led by Chairman Michael Powell, the FCC voted to classify cable modem service in a way that left it free of common carrier, open-access requirements. The FCC is also moving to deregulate DSL and free it from common carrier restrictions.[120] This is the most recent defeat for those who battle for more open access to the media.

We can hope that wide access to the Internet is preserved, and that access is not severely undermined by the FCC's ruling, as access has been lost to other media by regulatory changes. Preservation of democratic

[118] Dean Alger, *Megamedia: How Giant Corporations Dominate Mass Media, Distort Competition, and Endanger Democracy* (Lanham, MD: Rowman and Littlefield, 1998), 100–11.

[119] See Curtis, "Judicial Review and Populism," *supra* note 71, at 368–70.

[120] See Karen Charman, Recasting the Web, *Extra*, July/August 2002, at 22–24; available online at http://fair.org/extra0207/open-access.html [accessed November 20, 2003].

access would be served by regulation. As C. Edwin Baker notes, "prohibiting enterprises that own and operate transmission facilities from also owning and marketing media content . . . [was] a clean, structural solution" to the incentive that companies have to use their power to disadvantage creators of competitive content or, for that matter, to block disfavored ideas. This approach led to "sensible legal prohibitions on telephone companies owning and selling (as opposed to carrying) cable programming. By requiring phone companies only to carry content, the incentive for the phone companies was to . . . reduc[e] bottlenecks and increas[e] communications flows."[121]

D. The incredible shrinking forum

Public streets and sidewalks of the 1930s were a judicially protected public forum. People on downtown sidewalks weren't just shoppers; they were also citizens. They could go about their shopping, but their fellow citizens could also ask them to take political leaflets or listen to a street-corner speech. Then a change in architecture and ownership, combined with a change in the Court, transformed yesterday's citizen-shoppers into today's mall consumers. The change from public to private streets and sidewalks and malls set the stage for a greatly eroded public forum. The change was largely completed when the Burger Court reversed an earlier Supreme Court decision and held there was no free speech right in common areas of shopping malls.[122]

Recently, sixty-year-old attorney Steve Downs refused to remove his "Give Peace a Chance" T-shirt on orders from a mall security guard at Crossgates Mall in New York. When he refused, he was ordered to leave the mall, and when he refused to leave, he was arrested.[123] As a free speech matter before the courts, the prospects for Downs' vindication were bleak. New York's highest court had found no free speech rights in common areas of shopping malls under its state constitution.[124] As a matter of federal and state constitutional law, the mall could disallow all political statements or it could discriminate among them, permitting, say, "Give War a Chance" T-shirts while banning those advocating peace.

[121] Baker, *Media, Markets and Democracy, supra* note 106, at 295–96.

[122] See *Amalgamated Food Employees Union Local 590 v. Logan Valley Plaza,* 391 U.S. 308 (1968), limited by *Lloyd Corp. v. Tanner,* 407 U.S. 551 (1972), and overruled in *Hudgens v. NLRB,* 424 U.S. 507 (1976). But see, e.g., *Watchtower Bible and Tract Society of New York v. Village of Stratton,* 536 U.S. 150 (2002) (striking down requirement of a permit for door-to-door citizen activity). In recent years, the Court has usually constricted the public forum doctrine. E.g., *United States v. Kokinda,* 497 U.S. 720 (1990); *Lehman v. Shaker Heights,* 418 U.S. 298 (1974) (ban upheld on all political ads in the advertising slots provided in city buses).

[123] Carol Demare, "He Kept His Shirt on—and Got Arrested," *Times Union* (Albany, NY), March 5, 2003, B1.

[124] *SHAD Alliance v. Smith Haven Mall,* 66 N.Y.2d 496 (Ct. App. 1985).

Still, there is a happy ending to the New York shopping mall story. Hundreds of people—peace activists and civil libertarians—appeared at the mall to protest its policy. Though the mall had legal precedent on its side, the mall sought to drop the prosecution. The popular perception that the mall's censorship was a violation of free expression seemed to be a powerful force, even overcoming the "correct" legal view.

In *Tinker v. Des Moines Independent Community School District* (1969),[125] the Court, in an opinion by Justice Abe Fortas, upheld the right of public school children to wear black armbands to school to protest the war in Vietnam. Public schools, he wrote, are not enclaves of totalitarianism. In contrast, under Supreme Court precedent, "private" shopping malls, the successors to the downtown business districts of the 1930s and 1940s, can be enclaves of totalitarianism if they choose.

The danger is that corporations that own the cable or DSL lines that enter most of our homes will join the shopping malls. Thanks to the miracles of technology and a legal doctrine that treats the cable as purely private property, corporations might have the same control over expression that shopping malls now enjoy. Furthermore, corporate suppression of Internet speech might be harder to spot and might also get less publicity from the media.

The response to this concern, of course, is that the market would never tolerate such a transformation and that, in any case, regulation would violate the constitutional rights of the corporations. On this view, the cable or DSL lines that carry the speech that reaches mass audiences are treated as speakers, and the corporations that own them are treated as persons who may not be forced to carry ideas with which they disagree.[126] Thus, there is no public forum aspect to the information superhighway. Once corporations establish control over their "information private highway," how will megamedia companies respond to Web sites that criticize their power?

As the case of Steve Downs and the shopping mall shows, public protest can sometimes make a difference, at least to a degree. At a minimum, however, for effective public protest any private censorship needs to be visible and widely publicized. Some Internet codes and filters that limit free expression are invisible.

VI. Do the Multiple Media Problems Make a Difference? Formal and Functional Freedom of Expression in the Mass Media

Today, the American mass media is more consolidated, is dominated by a few major corporations, suffers from serious conflicts of interest that

[125] 393 U.S. 503 (1969).

[126] See *West Virginia State Board of Education v. Barnette*, 319 U.S. 624 (1943); *Wooley v. Maynard*, 430 U.S. 705 (1977); *Abood v. Detroit Board of Education*, 431 U.S. 209 (1977).

undermine the fiduciary nature of the press, censors points of view either directly or by pricing, and replaces serious discussion of issues with trivial matters. Do these things matter? Do these trends (assuming one agrees that they exist) make any difference to the sort of democracy Americans have? Does it matter, as Kathleen Hall Jamieson reports, that surveys show that the deceptive claims in the tobacco ads criticizing the 1998 McCain Bill were believed where the ads were widely aired and where there was little rebuttal? Many more people saw the deceptive claims than saw the isolated reports questioning the ads in the *New York Times* or on ABC News, and deception triumphed.[127] Of course it matters.

Where the government controls the media and provides a steady diet of propaganda we all agree that freedom of expression is seriously compromised. A pervasive private propaganda system is not much of an improvement. Is that the direction in which America is headed? At any rate, America's *mass* media environment is not conducive to vibrant democracy.

The Supreme Court once understood that freedom of expression requires more than a broad prohibition on government suppression based on the ideas expressed. The Court recognized this, for example, in 1939 when it announced the public forum doctrine: that the streets and parks are held by government as a public trust and that citizens have a right to assemble there to discuss public questions. In the 1940s, the Court said that the public forum was a place where the poorly financed causes of "little people" might have at least an opportunity to reach a larger audience.[128] In 1945, when upholding the application of antitrust laws to the Associated Press, Justice Hugo Black, one of the Court's strongest champions of a broad reading of First Amendment freedoms, wrote: "Surely a command that the government itself shall not impede the free flow of ideas does not afford non-governmental combinations a refuge if they impose restraints upon that constitutionally guaranteed freedom. . . . Freedom of the press from governmental interference . . . does not sanction repression of that freedom by private interests."[129] Similarly, in *Red Lion Broadcasting Co. v. Federal Communications Commission* (1969), a unanimous Court held: "There is nothing in the First Amendment which prevents Government from requiring a licensee to share his frequency with others and to conduct himself as a proxy or fiduciary with obligations to present those views and voices which are representative of his community and which would otherwise, by necessity, be barred from the airwaves."[130] Still, as C. Edwin Baker noted, the recent trend of lower court decisions

[127] Waldman, *The Press Effect*, *supra* note 86, at 11–12.

[128] The case stating the public forum doctrine is *Hague v. CIO*, 307 U.S. 496, 515 (1939). See also *Schneider v. State*, 308 U.S. 147, 163 (1939); *Martin v. City of Struthers*, 319 U.S. 141 (1943); *Jamison v. Texas*, 318 U.S. 413 (1943); and *Murdock v. Pennsylvania*, 319 U.S. 105 (1943).

[129] *Associated Press v. United States*, 326 U.S. 1, 20 (1945). C. Edwin Baker, "Media Concentration: Giving Up on Democracy," *Florida Law Review* 54 (2002): 839.

[130] 395 U.S. 367 (1969).

has been to treat broadcast media corporations as individuals, as holders of rights, substantially shielded from structural government regulation designed to ensure a more diverse and broadly accessible mass broadcast media.[131]

The *functional view* of freedom of expression looks at the practical operation of the system. This view has coexisted with a *formal*, legalistic view of speech and press freedom that emphasizes legal protections that in theory protect all. By the formal, legalistic view, the right to free speech and free press is simply and entirely a right against government suppression; indeed, by some interpretations, it is merely a right to protection against government suppression because of the content of the expression. The argument is a neat syllogism. The First Amendment begins, "*Congress* shall make no law." The Fourteenth Amendment forbids any *state* from making or enforcing any law abridging the privileges or immunities of citizens of the United States and from depriving any person of liberty without due process of law. Private persons (including corporate persons) are neither Congress nor states. So "private" suppression of speech does not violate the First or Fourteenth Amendments. This is the state action syllogism.

Justice Sandra Day O'Connor, joined by Justices Antonin Scalia, Clarence Thomas, and Ruth Bader Ginsburg, summarized the formal, legalistic view in *Turner Broadcasting System v. FCC* (1994): "[T]he First Amendment as we understand it today rests on the premise that it is government power, rather than private power, that is the main threat to free expression; and as a consequence, the Amendment imposes substantial limitations on the Government even when it is trying to serve concededly praiseworthy goals."[132] As applied to government actions that imperil the power of the press to check abuses of power, the approach taken by Justice O'Connor and her colleagues is wise. As applied to preventing structural regulation designed to protect the system of freedom of expression from the dangers of concentrated private power or to provide somewhat wider access for political campaigns to *broadcast* media, the approach is far more dubious. But even if one favors such structural regulation, the problem is complex. Without careful limits, government regulations in the name of access could so occupy broadcast time as to undermine the checking function of the media.

The common refrain of the formalists—that the only threat to a vibrant system of freedom of expression comes from the government passing laws aimed at the content of speech—is grossly misleading. People in the nineteenth century understood that freedom of expression required more than lack of government intrusion. Again and again they characterized mobs that attacked abolitionists, destroyed their presses, dispersed their

[131] See Baker, "Giving Up on Democracy," 842.

[132] *Turner Broadcasting System v. FCC*, 512 U.S. 622, 685 (1994).

meetings, and burned their literature, as assailing the freedom of expression protected by the "American Magna Carta," the Bill of Rights. The fact that the suppression came from private sources did not strike most people as reassuring or as evidence that the freedom of expression set out in the Bill of Rights was not imperiled. They read the guarantees in the First Amendment functionally, not formally or technically. The formalistic view is different: mobs are not Congress nor even the federal government, so, First Amendment rights are irrelevant.

As history shows, the formal, technical, legalistic understanding of the guarantees of freedom of expression has had costs as well as benefits. For example, the state action syllogism, together with the idea that First Amendment freedoms merely limited the national government—even after passage of the Fourteenth Amendment—combined to nullify congressional efforts to punish Klansmen and others who killed and terrorized people for supporting the Republican Party in the South during Reconstruction. As a result, the electorate was contracted, debate and democratic choice were stifled, and white supremacist "redeemers" regained control of the Southern states—control that lasted until the mid-1960s.[133] Again, during the struggle for voting rights in the deep South in the 1960s, private actors used bombs, guns, arson, and clubs in an effort to silence dissent. Obviously, these widely practiced tactics had a very chilling effect on political expression and dissent.

If the government produced all television programs, books, newspapers, and magazines, Americans would not believe that they had a functional system of freedom of expression. This would be so even if individuals retained an unfettered right of free speech. With only one official view permitted in the mass media, America would not produce effective "free discussion *to the end that government may be responsive to the will of the people,*"[134] or "unfettered interchange of ideas for the bringing about of political and social changes desired by the people,"[135] or a media environment where conclusions would "be gathered out of a multitude of tongues," rather than "through any kind of authoritative selection. . . .' "[136] This would be true even if the government media apparatus, in order to make itself seem more credible, occasionally devoted limited space to dissenting views.

This imaginary world of government monopoly over the mass media offends both the functional and the formal understandings of America's constitutional protections for speech and press. A government monopoly could only be maintained by suppressing rival outlets. This would violate the formal understanding of freedom of the press: that the guarantee

[133] See generally, Branch, *Pillar of Fire, supra* note 36.

[134] *Stromberg v. California*, 283 U.S. 359, 369 (1931) (emphasis added).

[135] *Roth v. United States*, 354 U.S. 476, 484 (1957).

[136] *New York Times v. Sullivan*, 376 U. S. 254, 270 (1964) (quoting *United States v. Associated Press*, 52 F. Supp. 362, 372 [S.D.N.Y.1943] [Judge Learned Hand]).

precludes governmental suppression. Of course, government monopolization of the mass media would violate the functional understanding of our constitutional guarantees as well.

Suppose that instead of a government monopoly on the mass media, the monopoly was privately owned. Suppose that a combination of legal rules and economic factors combined to extinguish competition from rival mass media outlets and that the private monopoly had a predominant political perspective, but not one that kept it from retaining a mass audience. Would the situation be greatly improved if there were several mass media corporations instead of one? Regardless of how eagerly consumers lapped up the latest episodes of *Survivor*, many would doubt that this sort of media is what is required for a robust popular democracy. Threats to the checking function can come from private consolidation as well as from government monopoly. Indeed, a prime purpose of government is to check abuses of private power.

Since the modern world is characterized by the growth of multinational corporations that exert a profound influence both on the life of ordinary citizens and on government policy, any free speech policy translated into the realities of the modern world also needs to protect criticism of concentrated private power—from both government and private suppression. As Chief Justice Earl Warren noted in 1967, there has been "a rapid fusion of economic and political power . . . and a high degree of interaction between the intellectual, governmental, and business worlds."[137] Because those with power seek to suppress criticism of themselves, media consolidation can itself produce an effective form of mass media censorship.

A functional approach to freedom of expression asks what sort of a mass media is required by democracy. As shown by the experiences of the abolitionists, the Southern Republicans during Reconstruction, and the advocates of black voting rights in the South—all of whom suffered suppression at the hands of fellow citizens—rights can be threatened by private action as well as by government suppression. Similarly, censorship of access to the debate by a wealth test or by decisions of a few media conglomerates could threaten the democratic function of freedom of speech and press.

VII. Imagining Constitutional Provisions to Provide a Media That Serves Democracy

If we set out to create a constitutional structure for mass media that would support robust democratic government, would we replicate the media world now being established by government policy and market

[137] *Curtis Publishing Co. v. Butts*, 388 U.S. 130, 164 (1967) (Warren, C.J., concurring); see also *Gertz v. Robert Welch, Inc.*, 418 U.S. 323, 345 (1974) (referring to private power and influence as factors making a person a public figure).

power? This is a central free speech question today. It is not resolved by the fact that the Court so far has done a reasonably good job of protecting speakers from government punishment for expressing unorthodox ideas. Yet, what a strong democracy requires and what the current United States Constitution will allow are quite different questions.

How one answers the question of what democracy requires depends both on what sort of democracy and electoral system one wants and on how well one thinks the current mass media and democratic system are functioning.

There is a vision of democracy embedded in most of the historic defenses of free speech and press that I have reproduced in this essay. This vision assumes that public understanding and political participation are important in order to protect individuals as well as the public interest, that is, that a well-functioning democracy requires a well-functioning system of free speech and press so that it can be an effective guardian of all other rights.[138] This vision is predicated on the assumption that people have the potential to perform their democratic role: it takes seriously the idea of popular sovereignty and assumes that the public needs substantial and reasonably diverse sources of information in order to perform its supervisory function. It rejects the idea that the people should hear only one side of public questions.

James Madison captured part of this vision in his 1822 letter to William T. Barry commending a generous appropriation the Kentucky legislature made for public education. "A popular Government," Madison wrote, "without popular information, or the means of acquiring it, is but a Prologue to a Farce or a Tragedy; or perhaps both. Knowledge will forever govern ignorance; And a people who mean to be their own Governors, must arm themselves with the power which knowledge gives."[139]

I know, of course, that this vision is contestable. At best, it describes an ideal to be pursued. The vision does not explain how it is to be implemented. In some circumstances, a broad prohibition of government censorship might be enough. In other conditions, achieving the same vision would require more.

If, in spite of its problems, the vision still appeals to us, and if, like me, one fears that the United States is moving away from the ideal rather than closer to it, then the real problem is what to do. Here I have only four suggestions for general guidelines.

First, we should recognize that the free speech and free press environment, including the structure of the media, is crucial.[140] As a result, public policy needs to shape the environment to produce a media that supports democracy.

[138] See the Virginia Resolution of 1798, quoted in Curtis, *Free Speech*, *supra* note 6, at 76.
[139] James Madison, *Writings* (New York: Library of America, 1999), 179.
[140] Curtis, "Judicial Review and Populism," *supra* note 71, at 325–28.

Second, the checking function of free speech and press is crucial, but it is a function that needs to check both governmental and private abuses of power. Thus, broad protection for both citizen and press criticism of government and private power are essential. Consolidation has the potential to curb criticism of the exercise of private and governmental power. Accordingly, one-sided television advertising campaigns on issues of public concern need to be checked by counterspeech.

The power of the few mass media corporations must be checked as well. One way to achieve such a check is to foster diversity of ownership and to seek to preserve what little diversity remains. The policies of the Reagan, Bush I, Clinton, and Bush II Administrations that promoted media consolidation are attacks on the environment required for a democratic media.

Third, the structure of the free speech environment is often the product of regulation. Should phone companies with DSL lines or owners of cables also be able to provide content with the inevitable conflicts of interest that consolidation of power provides? Should such lines be treated as common carriers or as speakers? The choice is simply between two forms of regulation. Should we insist on mandated free access to television time for candidates and ballot measures? Should we delegate to private broadcast companies the power to control access and censor ideas at their unfettered discretion and, even for permitted ideas, to ration access to viewers and voters based on wealth?[141] Either response is a form of regulation and either involves dangers to freedom of expression. We should pursue policies that foster rather than impede the environment needed for a mass media that supports meaningful democracy, but how to do so is more complex than the principle itself.

It is important to recognize the dangers that government poses to the watchdog role of the press. The Nixon Administration, for example, had plans to obstruct the renewal of the Washington Post Company's television and radio broadcast licenses in order to punish it for Watergate reporting. As Professor Baker notes, "If the political branches must be watched, wisdom counsels against granting them power to control the watchdog."[142] Of course, government can seduce or punish the press in a variety of ways, and many of these are quite difficult to control. Reporters are reluctant to be critical of sources that give them "inside access," for example.

The dangers to the watchdog role counsel caution. The public forum is a case where government is involved in the management of speech, but legal rules strictly limit government discretion. Public forum doctrine could provide a useful analogy. Fixed and generally applied limits on media consolidation seem not to have threatened the watchdog role of the

[141] See *id.* at 313.
[142] Baker, *Media, Markets, and Democracy, supra* note 106, at 198.

press in the past. Indeed, for reasons that Grimke and others suggested, media consolidation may pose an even greater threat than government to the watchdog role, particularly if the press is also an institution that should watch itself. Similarly, what if a suitable, though not perfect, formula could be arrived at for a limited, dedicated public forum? A fixed amount of free time for political candidates and ballot measures would limit the total control that broadcasters presently exercise, and this would not seem to pose much of a threat to the watchdog role, provided that the time involved was suitably limited. But if government went too far in reserving public forum space for candidates and issues, it could well imperil the checking function. In an ideal world, strict limits and criteria would be set by the constitution: it could constrain government discretion and also provide a statement of principle around which public opinion could coalesce.

My fourth and final suggestion for protecting the environment needed for a democratic system of freedom of expression is to encourage citizen activism. A recent example, as I noted earlier, is the citizen protest produced by a New York mall's censorship of a "Give Peace a Chance" T-shirt. Elsewhere I have suggested another form of protest to promote television time at no cost to candidates and advocates of ballot measures.[143] I noted:

> Some Americans have politely asked television networks to do their part to respond to the current crisis in representative government. A group called Alliance for Better Campaigns (led by former Presidents Ford and Carter and Walter Cronkite) has suggested a modest beginning. It has called on television stations and networks, in the thirty days before an election, to devote 5 minutes a night to broadcasting what candidates say—up they say from a total of 40 seconds typically provided to all candidates.
>
> The public has given television a license to use the public airways and has historically provided advantages for cable, and has not charged for the privilege. A contribution to democracy seems a small price to ask. . . .
>
> Rather than dumping their TV sets in the nearest harbor, people could simply turn off those stations and networks that refuse to provide substantial time for candidates. They could also let the holdouts know they have done so. People might also advertise the cause by picketing local television stations and network headquarters. It would be interesting to see if the protests make it onto the evening news. [144]

[143] Curtis, "The Other Constitution," *supra* note 67, at 391–93. (Some of the examples of problems with media consolidation that I list here are also set out in the article.)

[144] *Id.* at 391–92.

Some people may believe such a protest is a terrible idea. (If so, they should relax. So far at least, this protest is not catching on.) To be sure, there are dangers. Boycotts could be—and already are—used as weapons of censorship as well as in an effort to provide broader candidate and issue access.[145] I assume, however, that most people would agree that the idea behind such an "access boycott" is to protect speech,[146] and that diverse political views should have a reasonable opportunity to become part of the public dialogue. Consider, however, consolidated media companies that own cable or DSL lines, television stations, and newspapers. Could we expect broad reporting of a planned boycott? Might targeted companies be tempted to block Web sites that advocate such action against them and use other devices at their disposal to keep their critics out of the mass media's public square? Some seem to think the Internet is impervious to regulation, but this, of course, is a fallacy, as the Chinese government has demonstrated by blocking search engines and substituting carefully filtered information instead.[147] Indeed, the Chinese government is reported to have blocked some 50,000 Web sites. Of course, regulation of cyberspace is by no means limited to government. In *Code*, Lawrence Lessig shows how private corporate regulation of the Internet can and does work.[148]

Some structural decisions about the media are easier to evaluate than others. For many years, the United States has had limits on media concentration. Limits on concentration seem to be among the least problematic regulations. Reserving a portion of television or cable time for competing candidates, ballot measures, or discussion of pending legislation, however, is more complex. How would candidates or speakers for different sides of ballot measures qualify? A second conceptual problem is the claim that broadcasters would be denied editorial control over what is broadcast by candidates and that such a denial would violate their right to free speech.

The public airways might be analogized to a public park. Cities can lease public parks to private enterprises to put on plays, concerts, circuses, etc., much as the broadcast spectrum has been allocated to licensees. If a city chooses to reserve a portion of a park as a public forum, should we treat the decision as a violation of a private company's right to

[145] Louis B. Parks, "Chicks Face Landslide of Anger After Remarks," *Houston Chronicle*, March 15, 2003. (A number of country music stations banned music by the Dixie Chicks after the group criticized President Bush's plan for war in Iraq. Here, however, the *stations* initiated the ban and polls on whether to impose a ban. In the case of those that initiated polls, the results were that over 70 percent of listeners favored a ban.)

[146] *NAACP v. Claiborne Hardware*, 458 U.S. 886 (1982).

[147] Joseph Kahn, "China Toughens Obstacles to Internet Searches: Google Users Sent to Tamer Sites," *New York Times*, September 12, 2002, late edition-final, A3; Joseph Kahn, "China Has World's Tightest Internet Censorship, Study Finds," *New York Times*, December 4, 2002, late edition-final A13.

[148] See e.g., Lessig, *Code*, *supra* note 24, at 211-21.

free speech? Of course not. At least as an initial matter, government ownership implies power to reserve a part of the grant as a forum for public dialogue.

Cable companies and networks are a more complicated case. They exist because the cable companies have been granted easements by local governments. Should it be treated as a denial of a cable company's free speech rights to reserve a portion of its broadcast days during election seasons for discussion of candidates and ballot measures? Reforms such as allocation of a small portion of the broadcast franchise for free time for candidates and advocates of ballot measures could contribute to a media better suited to democracy, and such reforms could respond to some of the shortcomings of the present system. These reforms are hardly a panacea, however.

VIII. Conclusion

A media that supports democracy is a public good. As C. Edwin Baker has shown, the unregulated market alone (if there is such a thing) is unlikely to deliver such benefits.[149] Still, broad government supervision of broadcast content is too dangerous to undertake, so creative thought is necessary to consider how the free marketplace of ideas can be structured to promote democracy. Possibilities include subsidy, limited mandated access to the electronic media along the lines of a public forum, and limits on concentration with its attendant conflicts of interest.

Reforms might bring us more thoughtful discussion of public issues than that provided by opinion polls. We could encourage programs to bring together a cross section of citizens for weekend discussions with experts and advocates on issues of major public importance, such as tax policy, Social Security, foreign policy, etc. We could publicize both the evidence and the arguments they considered, as well as the conclusions they reached. This sort of deliberative jury held four or five times per year might produce more thoughtful, deliberative polling and also provide a basis for more trenchant reporting of public issues.[150]

The media environment is only one obstacle to implementing a more meaningful democracy. Democracy requires contested elections. The current winner-take-all electoral system combined with gerrymandering, raised to a fine art with the aid of computers, has helped to make contested elections an endangered species.[151]

The media environment should be a major concern for those who seek a more effective popular democracy. At a minimum, a healthy democracy and a vibrant system of freedom of expression require more than protec-

149 See generally, Baker, *Media, Markets, and Democracy*, *supra* note 106.

150 Lessig, *Code*, *supra* note 24, at 227–29.

151 See generally Hill, *Fixing Elections*, *supra* note 74; Robert Dahl, *How Democratic is the American Constitution?* (New Haven, CT: Yale University Press, 2001), 55–61.

tion against broad government power to punish speech on matters of public concern because that speech expresses the "wrong" ideas—as crucial as such protection is.[152] The problems with the present system are more obvious than the solutions. Because the problems are important and complex, the work of those legal and other scholars who have focused on the problem deserves our careful attention.[153] A media environment that fosters democracy is one of the central free press problems of the future.

Law, Wake Forest University School of Law

[152] Mark A. Graber, *Transforming Free Speech: The Ambiguous Legacy of Civil Libertarianism* (Berkeley: University of California Press, 1991), 225.

[153] See e.g., Alger, *Megamedia, supra* note 118; Baker, *Media, Markets, and Democracy, supra* note 106; C. Edwin Baker, "Giving Up on Democracy," *supra* note 129; Jack M. Balkin, "Populism and Progressivism As Constitutional Categories: Book Review of Cass R. Sunstein, *Democracy and the Problem of Free Speech*," *Yale Law Journal* 104 (1995): 1935; Herbert J. Gans, *Democracy and the News* (New York: Oxford University Press, 2003); McChesney, *Rich Media, Poor Democracy, supra* note 81; Lessig, *Code, supra* note 24; Robert Post, "Meiklejohn's Mistake: Individual Autonomy and the Reform of Public Discourse," *University of Colorado Law Review* 64 (1993): 1109. See also, Garry, *Scrambling for Protection, supra* note 40, chap. 10.

INDEX

Index of Cases

For EU product safety concerns, contact us at Calle de José Abascal, 56–1°, 28003 Madrid, Spain or eugpsr@cambridge.org.

www.ingramcontent.com/pod-product-compliance
Ingram Content Group UK Ltd.
Pitfield, Milton Keynes, MK11 3LW, UK
UKHW020807190625
459647UK00032B/2305

* 9 7 8 0 5 2 1 6 0 3 7 5 1 *